# Pro SQL Server 2012 Practices

Bradley Ball, TJay Belt, Glenn Berry,
Jes Borland, Carlos Bossy, Louis Davidson,
Ben DeBow, Grant Fritchey, Jonathan Gardner,
Jesper Johansen, Jeremy Lowell, Wendy Pastrick,
Kellyn Pot'vin, Mladen Prajdić, Herve Roggero,
Chris Shaw, Gail Shaw, Jason Strate

Apress®

## Pro SQL Server 2012 Practices

ISBN-13 (pbk): 978-1-4302-4770-8

ISBN-13 (electronic): 978-1-4302-4771-5

President and Publisher: Paul Manning
Lead Editor: Jonathan Gennick
Developmental Editor: Brian MacDonald
Technical Reviewer: Rudi Bruchez, Robin Dewson, David Dye, Edgar Lanting, Ken Simmons
Editorial Board: Steve Anglin, Ewan Buckingham, Gary Cornell, Louise Corrigan, Morgan Ertel, Jonathan Gennick, Jonathan Hassell, Robert Hutchinson, Michelle Lowman, James Markham, Matthew Moodie, Jeff Olson, Jeffrey Pepper, Douglas Pundick, Ben Renow-Clarke, Dominic Shakeshaft, Gwenan Spearing, Matt Wade, Tom Welsh
Coordinating Editor: Anamika Panchoo
Copy Editors: Roger LeBlanc, Vanessa Moore
Compositor: Bytheway Publishing Services
Indexer: SPi Global
Artist: SPi Global
Cover Designer: Anna Ishchenko

Distributed to the book trade worldwide by Springer Science+Business Media New York, 233 Spring Street, 6th Floor, New York, NY 10013. Phone 1-800-SPRINGER, fax (201) 348-4505, e-mail orders-ny@springer-sbm.com, or visit www.springeronline.com.

For information on translations, please e-mail rights@apress.com, or visit www.apress.com.

Apress and friends of ED books may be purchased in bulk for academic, corporate, or promotional use. eBook versions and licenses are also available for most titles. For more information, reference our Special Bulk Sales–eBook Licensing web page at www.apress.com/bulk-sales.

Any source code or other supplementary materials referenced by the author in this text is available to readers at www.apress.com. For detailed information about how to locate your book's source code, go to www.apress.com/source-code.

*To my wife, Silva, and my children, Zachary, William, Serenity, and Chesney: Thank you for putting up with my long hours on the computer. I love you all No Matter What!*
*–Bradley Ball*

*To Ali, Adam, and Gaby, for all they taught me about writing, computer science, and devotion.*
*–Carlos Bossy*

*I dedicate my chapter on database design to the poor programmers having to suffer with malformed databases.*
*–Louis Davidson*

*I type this on the date 9/11/2012. I've never dedicated one of my books before because I never saw the point. But this time, I'd like to dedicate my contribution to this book to all the first responders and those who serve in the military. Thanks for everything you do to protect our civilization.*
*–Grant Fritchey*

*To my lovely wife, Birgitte; my wonderful children, Alexander, Andreas, Jakob, Mathilde; my father, Ib; my best friend, Lars; and not least, Morten.*
*–Jesper Johansen*

*I'd like to dedicate my chapter to my children, Sam, Cait, and Josh. Everything I do, I do for them—as a Mom, a caregiver, and most of all, as an example for them to take into this world.*
*–Kellyn Pot'Vin*

*I'd like to dedicate this book to my mom, Desanka, and sister, Tajana, who are awesome supporters of my endeavors.*
*–Mladen Prajdić*

*How can I dedicate my work to all those who have influenced me over my lifetime in a few short words? Only one word is needed, family.*
*To my wife, Gigi; my son, Mike; my mom, Ruth; our best friend, Rock; and brother, Anthony. To my Italian by association family Dick, Linda, Grandma (Barbara), and Grandpa (Don).*
*For my Marine brothers and sisters, and those who stand or stood next to us.*
*For my #SQLFamily: we can do it together.*
*For my Dad, Herb: you may be gone but you will never be forgotten.*
*–Chris Shaw*

*To Nikolai, Aspen, and Dysin who missed out on a few rounds of Dungeon Defenders while I worked on this book.*
*–Jason Strate*

# Contents at a Glance

# Contents

# About the Authors

■ **Bradley Ball** is a husband and a father. During the work day, he is also a SQL DBA with over 10 years of IT experience. Bradley spent 8 years working as a defense contractor for clients such as the U.S. Army and The Executive Office of the President of the United States. He is currently a Senior Consultant with Pragmatic Works, specializing in DBA and BI solutions. He has presented at many SQL Saturdays, for the MAGICPASS & OPASS SSUGs, SQL Rally 2011 and 2012, DevConnections 2012, and at the PASS Summit in 2011 and 2012. Bradley can be found blogging on http://www.sqlballs.com.

■ **TJay Belt** is a professional database administrator and has been developing his expertise over the past eight years. He has been working in IT for over 18 years. He enjoys delivering technical presentations and has presented for Microsoft, Professional Association for SQL Server, SQL Server Worldwide User Group, PASS SQL Saturday events, and local SQL Server user groups. TJay has published technical articles for SQL Server Central, Simple Talk, and SQL-Server-Performance. He is the founder and was the leader of the PASS chapter of the SQL Server user group in Utah County. TJay has volunteered as a chapter leader for PASS, a regional mentor for PASS chapters, and the PASS Chapter Committee. He also was the founder of the Auditing & Compliance Special Interest Group with PASS. TJay currently volunteers as a regional mentor for PASS chapters.

■ **Glenn Berry** works as a database architect at Avalara in Parker, Colorado (USA). He has been a SQL Server MVP since 2007 and has a whole collection of Microsoft certifications, including MCITP, MCDBA, MCSE, MCSD, MCAD, and MCTS, which proves that he likes to take tests. His expertise includes DMVs, high availability, hardware selection, full text search, and SQL Azure. He is also an adjunct faculty member at University College at the University of Denver, where has been teaching since 2000. He has completed the Master Teacher Program at University College at the University of Denver. He is heavily involved in the SQL Server community and is a frequent speaker at user groups, SQL Saturdays, and the PASS Community Summit. He is the author of the book *SQL Server Hardware* (Red Gate Books, 2011), and he wrote chapters for *SQL Server MVP Deep Dives* (Manning Publications, 2009) and *SQL Server MVP Deep Dives Volume 2* (Manning Publications, 2011). Glenn blogs regularly at http://sqlserverperformance.wordpress.com. He is active on Twitter as @GlennAlanBerry.

■ **Jes Borland** is a consultant with Brent Ozar PLF and a Microsoft SQL Server MVP. She holds an AAS - Programmer/Analyst degree and loves SQL Server Reporting Services and day-to-day administration. She is an active member of PASS, a user-group founder, a Tech on Tap brewmaster, and a LessThanDot.com blogger. She's a frequent presenter at user groups, SQL Saturdays, and other community events. She is also an avid runner and novice chef.

■ **Carlos Bossy** (MCTS, MCP SQL Server 2008 BI, CBIP) is a consultant with 25 years of experience in software and database development. As the Principal of his company, Carlos focuses on the development of Business Intelligence solutions, including data warehouses, predictive analytics, integration, and reporting. He has worked with SQL Server for 12 years and is very enthusiastic about its powerful features. Carlos has developed data warehouses and BI solutions for a variety of industries and state agencies and is a frequent speaker at SQL Server events.

■ **Louis Davidson** has been in the IT industry for what is starting to seem like a really long time as a corporate database developer and architect. He has been a Microsoft MVP for 9 years and has written five books on database design for Apress, including *Pro SQL Server 2012 Relational Database Design and Implementation* (2012). Louis has been active speaking on the topic of of database design and implementation at many conferences over the past ten years, including SQL PASS, SQL Rally, SQL Saturday events, and CA World, as well as the Devlink developer conference. Louis has worked for the Christian Broadcasting Network as a developer, DBA, and Data Architect supporting offices in Virginia Beach, Virginia, and Nashville, Tennessee for over 14 years. Despite what his website at drsql.org implies, Louis has a bachelor's degree from the University of Tennessee at Chattanooga in computer science.

■ **Ben DeBow** is a consultant who works with customers of all sizes on their mission-critical applications and SQL Server deployments. His versatility allows him to assist with everything from virtualization and consolidation to schema design, performance tuning, and disk architectures. He has tuned and deployed some of the largest and most complex SQL Server solutions in the world. An active member of the SQL Server community, Ben is also an MCDBA, MCSE, and MCITP. He is also the co-founder of SQLHA with Allan Hirt, and can be reached at `http://www.sqlha.com`.

■ **Grant Fritchey** works for Red Gate Software—a market–leading, software-tools vendor—as its product evangelist. He has done development of large-scale applications in languages such as VB, C#, and Java; and he has worked in SQL Server since version 6.0. In addition, he has worked in insurance, finance, and consulting, as well as for three failed dot coms. He is the author of *SQL Server Execution Plans* (Simple Talk Publishing, 2008) and *SQL Server 2012 Query Performance Tuning* (Apress, 2012). Grant is a co-author of *Beginning SQL Server 2012 Administration* (Apress, 2012) and has one chapter in *SQL Server MVP Deep Dives Volume 2* (Manning Publications, 2011).

**Jonathan Gardner** is a senior systems architect, PMP, and MCITP working with Geocent, L.L.C. in New Orleans, Louisiana (USA). He has over 10 years of experience with a wide range of IT solutions, including database administration, virtualization, SAN administration, and Windows Server environments. He writes from his website http://jonathanagardner.com.

**Jesper Johansen** has been a SQL Server DBA for more than two decades. He is one of the heavy guys in the Danish SQL Server field.

Jesper joined Miracle Five years ago and has since developed efficient techniques for helping customers save time, money, and energy by consolidating their SQL Server installations.

Apart from consolidation, Jesper enjoys the occasional Backup/Restore game, helping customers realize that what they thought was lost can still can be dug out from the belly of SQL Server.

As if the above wasn't enough to keep Jesper busy, he is also known to take on DB2 tasks from time to time. He is a board member of the Danish SQL Server User Groupe.

**Jeremy Lowell** is the founder of Data Realized and has been helping DBAs and clients with SQL Server for over a decade. Jeremy has a track record of solving complex issues for small and large enterprises at any point in the life cycle of a business. From startups to Fortune 100 enterprises, Jeremy has been a leader in implementing best practices and helping business leaders realize their data.

**Wendy Pastrick** (@wendy_dance) is a self-taught database administrator in Chicago, Illinois (USA) since 2000, replicating data across environments using various SQL methods. You can find her at SQL PASS (Professional Association for SQL Server) events, such as SQL Saturday or the annual Summit, either volunteering or presenting, or perhaps singing at an after-event gathering. With a degree in Psychology and previous technical training experience, she has taken the podium across the country at events talking about SQL Server, personal networking, and support for Women In Technology.

**Kellyn Pot'vin** has more than 15 years of experience in information technology and more than 12 years of experience with Oracle and SQL Server. She specializes in database performance-tuning and the glories of simplifying database management. In recent years, she has been working with large SSD databases and Exadata, taking advantage of the newest technology and performance-tuning features. Kellyn is known for her technical blog, http://dbakevlar.com, and contributions to numerous technical sites. She is on the board of directors for RMOUG (Rocky Mountain Oracle User Group) as the group's Training Days Director, a yearly conference of almost 1000 attendees. She has performed numerous presentations in the US and abroad at both Oracle and SQLPass User Group conferences. Kellyn lives with her partner, Tim, and her three children in Broomfield, Colorado (USA). Currently, she is honing her technical skills at Enkitec (http://www.enkitec.com) and can be followed on twitter under the tweet handle @DBAKevlar.

▨ **Mladen Prajdić** is a SQL Server MVP from Slovenia. He started programming in 1999 in Visual C++. Since 2002, he has been actively developing different types of applications in .Net (C#) and SQL Server, ranging from standard line-of-business to image-processing applications.

He graduated from the College of Electrical Engineering at the University of Ljubljana, majoring in Medical Cybernetics. He's a regular speaker at various conferences and user-group meetings. He blogs at http://weblogs.sqlteam.com/mladenp and has authored various articles about SQL Server. He really likes to optimize slow SQL statements, analyze performance, and find unconventional solutions to difficult SQL Server problems.

In his free time, among other things, he also develops a very popular add-in for SQL Server Management Studio, called SSMS Tools Pack.

▨ **Herve Roggero**, Windows Azure MVP, is the founder of Blue Syntax Consulting, a company specializing in cloud-computing products and services. Herve's experience includes software development, architecture, database administration, and senior management, with both global corporations and startup companies. Herve holds multiple certifications, including an MCDBA, MCSE, and MCSD. He also holds a Master's degree in Business Administration from Indiana University. Herve is the co-author of *PRO SQL Azure* (Apress, 2010). For more information, visit http://www.bluesyntax.net.

▨ **Chris Shaw** started his database career in 1993. He began by working with Lotus during his time in the Marine Corps. Following his time with the Marines, Chris continued working with databases for companies such as Wells Fargo, Pulte Mortgage, and Yellow Pages Inc. He later consulted with insurance companies, including Anthem Blue Shield and Admini Quest. Chris has been writing and speaking about SQL Server for over 15 years at events such as SQL Connections, PASS, and SSWUG Ultimate conferences. Chris was the Conference Director for SSWUG in 2008. Chris received the Microsoft MVP award in 2009, 2010, and 2011, and he just received his fourth MVP award in April 2012. He is the founding member of the Colorado Springs SQL Server User Group and presently is the Co-President. Chris has many featured articles on the SSWUG website, and he was a contributing author for *SQL Server 2005 Bible* (Wiley, 2006) and *SQL Server MVP Deep Dives, Volume 2* (Manning Publications, 2011). Blogs, information, questions, quizzes, and interviews can be found at Chris' blog site at *http://chrisshaw.wordpress.com*. He can also be reached on twitter at @SQLShaw or by email at Chris@sqlshaw.com

■ **Gail Shaw** is a senior consultant with Xpertease, based in Johannesburg, South Africa. She specializes in database performance tuning and database recovery, with a particular focus on topics such as indexing strategies, execution plans, and writing T-SQL code that performs well and scales gracefully.

Gail is a Microsoft Certified Master for SQL Server 2008 and a SQL Server MVP. She is a frequent poster on the SQL Server Central forums, writes articles for both SQLServerCentral and Simple-Talk, and blogs on all things relating to database performance at `http://sqlinthewild.co.za`. She has spoken at TechEd Africa, at a number of the 24 Hours of PASS web events and, on multiple occasions, at the PASS Community Summit.

Gail is an Aikido Shodan (1st degree black belt) and a keen archer. In her copious spare time, she is pursuing a Master's degree in Computer Science at the University of South Africa.

■ **Jason Strate** is a database architect at Pragmatic Works, with more than 15 years of experience. He has been a recipient of Microsoft's "Most Valuable Professional" designation for SQL Server since July 2009. His experience includes the design and implementation of both OLTP and OLAP solutions, as well as the assessment and implementation of SQL Server environments for best practices, performance, and high-availability solutions.

Jason is an active member of the SQL Server community. He currently serves as regional mentor for the North Central PASS region, helping community members and chapters connect with each other. In the community, he presents on SQL Server and related topics at local, regional, and national events, including SQL Saturdays and the PASS Summit. He also blogs at `http://www.jasonstrate.com` and `http://www.sqlkaraoke.com`, and he can be contacted on twitter as @stratesql.

# About the Technical Reviewers

**Rudi Bruchez** is an independent consultant and trainer based in Paris, France. He has 15 years' experience with SQL Server. He worked as a DBA for CNET Channel, a subsidiary of CNET.com, at the MSC (Mediterranean Shipping Company) headquarters in Geneva, and at Promovacances, an online travel company in Paris. Since 2006, he has provided consulting and audits as well as SQL Server training sessions. As SQL Server is evolving into a more complex solution, he is trying to make sure that developers and administrators keep mastering the fundamentals of the relational database and the SQL language. He co-authored one of the best-selling books about the SQL language in French, and in 2008, he published the only book in French about SQL Server optimization. He can be contacted at http://www.babaluga.com/.

**Robin Dewson** has been hooked on programming ever since he bought his first computer in 1980, a Sinclair ZX80. His first major application of his own was a Visual FoxPro program that could be used to run a Fantasy League system. At this point, he met up with a great help in his PC development life, Jon Silver, at Step One Technologies. In return for training, he helped Jon with some other Visual FoxPro applications. From there, realizing that the marketplace for Visual FoxPro was limited, he decided to learn Visual Basic and SQL Server.

Starting out with SQL Server 6.5, Robin soon moved to SQL Server 7 and Visual Basic 5 and became involved in developing several applications for clients both in the UK and in the United States. From there, he has moved through each version to SQL Server 2012. Robin now specializes in C# and VB .NET. Robin can be contacted at robin@fat-belly.com or at http://www.fat-belly.com.

**David Dye** is a Microsoft SQL Server MVP, instructor, and author specializing in relational database management systems, business intelligence systems, reporting solutions, and Microsoft SharePoint. For the past nine years, David's expertise has been focused on Microsoft SQL Server development and administration. His work earned him recognition as a Microsoft MVP in 2009 and 2010. He has been a moderator for the Microsoft Developer Network for SQL Server forums and was the Innovator of the Year runner-up in 2009 by *SQL Server Magazine*. He was also featured in the Training Associates Technical Trainer Spotlight in April 2011. David currently serves as a technical reviewer and co-author with Apress Publishing in the SQL Server 2012 series, and as an author with Packt Publishing.

**Edgar Lanting** is a certified database specialist from the Netherlands with over 18 years of experience in IT. He is currently working as a database consultant for Ciber, where he assists various companies with the support and management of their database environments running on Microsoft SQL Server and Oracle software.

In his spare time, he enjoys hikes and walks with his wife and dog, is a big animal and nature photography enthusiast, and enjoys an occasional snowboarding trip when wintertime has arrived.

**Ken Simmons** is a database administrator and developer specializing in Microsoft SQL Server. He is an author for multiple SQL Server websites and books, including *Pro SQL Server 2008 Administration* (Apress, 2009), *Pro SQL Server 2008 Mirroring* (Apress, 2009), *Pro SQL Server 2008 Policy-Based Management* (Apress, 2010), and *Pro SQL Server 2012 Administration* (Apress, 2012). He currently holds certifications for MCP, MCAD, MCDBA, MCTS for SQL Server 2005, and MCITP for SQL Server 2008.

# Acknowledgments

At some point early in 2012, my friend Chris Shaw innocuously asked me if I would be interested in writing. Chris and I were preparing for a presentation for a SQL event. I really thought that the question was simple. I had some articles at various SQL Server websites under my belt and had even just finished a series of three articles. It turned into much, much more.

As I was struggling with my early versions of my chapter, Allen Hirt went above and beyond the call of duty, as he volunteered to edit my document in its early stages. As an established author, he was profoundly helpful. I learned so much from him.

As other authors were working on their chapters, several of them spurred me on as they tweeted about their tasks via Twitter, reminding me of my own tasks. Special thanks go to my fellow authors Gail, Mladen, Chris, Grant, Jes, and Jonathan for their examples and pushes.

For years, I have tried to be like my heroes in the #SQLFamily who have gone before me with writing books, articles, blogs, and more. Thanks to Steve, Tom, Grant, Tim, and Brad. Thanks to the editors of the various websites and other resources who kept telling me to write. Thanks to each website that has published an article of mine and allowed me to practice this craft.

Thanks to each coworker, DBA, developer, project manager, and so on who helped me perfect this process of Release Management to the point that I could put all these actions and lessons to paper to describe a process I have grown to love and hate.

Thanks to all the fine folks at Apress who helped me along the way of creating this chapter. It was an experience I appreciate, and I am grateful for their expertise and assistance.

Super special thanks go out to the one person who had no idea how much he was helping me by kick-starting all my extracurricular activities. He happened to say the right thing at the right time that got me going. I will forever be grateful to Pat Wright for pushing me out of my comfort zone.

–TJay Belt

Thanks to Jonathan Gennick for giving me yet another project to do right after I finished my book *Pro SQL Server 2012 Relational Database Design and Implementation.*

Thanks to all of my MVP friends, who provide me with a plethora of new ideas, excellent examples, and horror stories that remind me that reality is often worse than any example that you can think of.

Thanks to the PASS Community for all of the opportunities to speak and get better at my craft over the past few years. SQL Saturday events have increased the number of speaking opportunities by orders of magnitudes, and the more people I get to speak to, the more I learn what they want to hear about.

–Louis Davidson

First, thanks to my wife, Danielle, for continuing to support me on this journey and listening to all of my technical conversations. Thanks to Jeremy Lowell for thinking of me when this opportunity came up and to Allan Hirt for reviewing the content and being a great sounding board. Lastly, thanks to everyone at Apress for putting together a great group of authors to share their industry expertise with the community. The strength of the SQL Server community starts with people giving back and sharing.

–Ben DeBow

Several of the great people you see on the cover of this book were already committed to this project when I was asked to take part. Looking at that list of amazing people, realizing that I could be a small part of it, I jumped at the chance. Thanks, guys, for all the learning and motivation you supply to our extended SQL family. All the fine folks at Apress have done another excellent job. Special thanks to Jonathan Gennick of Apress. I really appreciate every chance he has given me. I work for a great company at Red Gate, and I appreciate all that it does for me. Thanks Gareth, Ben, Neil, and Simon for all you've done to make it a fantastic place to work for, learn, and grow. Finally, thanks to my long-suffering family to whom I said I'd never write another book until next time. Well, next time came rather quickly.

–Grant Fritchey

Thanks to Jonathan Gennick for giving me the opportunity to write a chapter in this book, and to Anamika—what a job :-)

Special thanks to Morten for giving good input and helping with translation. Thanks to my wife for keeping me on my toes, and to my best friend, who woke me up from being a dusty DBA.

And thank you to all the wonderful people at Miracle and the Danish SQL Server user group that makes life exciting.

–Jesper Johansen

My chapter was made possible by the best clients any consultant can hope for. They continually present me with unique and challenging opportunities. All of the folks at Apress who helped me in writing my first chapter, ever—their professionalism is outstanding. Feedback from Richard Rodriguez, Chris Shaw, and Ben DeBow were instrumental in making this chapter relevant. Of course, I'd be remiss to not include my wonderful wife, who endured proofreading this a few times, and my six-year-old daughter, who makes it her mission to put a smile on my face. Thank you!

–Jeremy Lowell

Special thanks to Chris Shaw (@SQLShaw) for inspiring me to write. I'm sure he doesn't realize it, but he has had a significant impact on my interest in writing and presenting. Thank you, Chris, for the opportunities you have opened up for me, my friend. I would also like to thank Allan Hirt (@SQLHA) for helping me pick up the pieces and for providing guidance on this path to authorship. He has been a friend, mentor, and teacher, and his time and experience has taught me many things. Finally, having the support of my family in my endeavors in the SQL community is a blessing I am honored to benefit from.

–Wendy Pastrick

I want to thank Tim Gorman for all his loving support as I embraced my first challenge as an author of published work. His emotional support, as someone who understands what I hope to accomplish and as my partner, is more than anyone could hope for in this life.

–Kellyn Pot'vin

I don't want to let this opportunity go without saying thank you to my #SQLFamily for sharing ideas and opinions.

–Chris Shaw

# Introduction

*Pro SQL Server 2012 Practices* is an anthology of writings on practices and techniques you should become familiar with on the way to becoming a top-notch database administrator (DBA) or database programmer. The authors have deep insight, and they want to share. The book covers a very wide array of topics, such as what makes for a well-performing design, how to choose database server hardware, indexing, tuning, tools to help you build your database, techniques for managing replication, compliance, backups, high availability, and more.

Working as a SQL Server professional is daunting and exhilarating at the same time. It's daunting due to the immense amount of "mechanics" that one must learn simply to run and program against a SQL Server database at a basic level. Exhilaration comes at first from mastering the mechanical aspects of creating a database, creating tables, adding users, storing data, retrieving data, and so forth. Then, in the long run, you get past the basic tasks and activities and begin to gain deep insight into SQL Server and how it operates. One day, you realize you actually do know a few things. You want to share. And that's how this book came about.

Could you come up with these practices on your own? Yes, given enough time and experience you would likely learn everything for yourself, from first principles. The authors' goal in this book, however, is to speed you on your way—not so that you can cheat the natural order of things, but so that you can continue from where they left off and go on to develop even greater insights, and then share what you have learned with those who come after.

## Audience

*Pro SQL Server 2012 Practices* is written for working SQL Server professionals. The book is primarily aimed at DBAs, but it is also of interest to developers who are serious about building their reputation and expertise around Microsoft SQL Server. The book targets intermediate users, presuming a baseline of experience with the underlying product. Its goal is to provide the sort of deep expertise and guidance that lets you stand on the shoulders of giants—so to speak—as you build your own career and reputation in the field.

# Authors

The author team on this book is a group of dedicated professionals who are passionate about using SQL Server, using it well, and sharing their expertise with those around them. Each of the authors has chosen a chapter in the belief that what you learn will make a significant and positive contribution to your growth as a SQL Server professional.

Topics covered in this book, listed by chapter, include the following:

1. Be Your Developer's Best Friend, by Jesper Johansen

2. Getting It Right: Designing for Database Performance, by Louis Davidson

3. Hidden Performance Gotchas, by Gail Shaw

4. Dynamic Management Views, by Kellyn Pot'vin

5. From SQL Trace to Extended Events, by Mladen Prajdić

6. The Utility Database, by Chris Shaw

7. Indexing Outside the Bubble, by Jason Strate

8. Release Management, by TJay Belt

9. Compliance and Auditing, by Jonathan Gardner

10. Automating Administration, by Jes Borland

11. The Fluid Dynamics of SQL Server Data Movement, by Wendy Pastrick

12. Windows Azure SQL Database for DBAs, by Herve Roggero

13. I/O: The Untold Story, by Jeremy Lowell

14. Page and Row Compression, by Bradley Ball

15. Selecting and Sizing the Server, by Glenn Berry

16. Backups and Restores Using Availability Groups, by Grant Fritchey

17. Big Data for the SQL Server DBA, by Carlos Bossy

18. Tuning for Peak Load, by Ben DeBow

# Example Code

Downloadable example code is available for some chapters in the book. You'll find the code from the book's catalog page on the Apress.com website:

http://www.apress.com/9781430247708

Click on the Source Code/Downloads tab. You will see a link from which to download the example code archive.

# CHAPTER 1

■ ■ ■

# Be Your Developer's Best Friend

## By Jesper Johansen

When asked to write a chapter for this book, I was in doubt about which subject to choose. Should I write about common problems I normally see? About how Microsoft SQL Server's easy installation is at the same time a strength and a weakness? About how to fix the 10 most general problems with SQL Server installation by querying a couple of dynamic management views (DMVs)? Or how about the *Yet Another Performance Profiling* (YAPP) method—a well-known performance method in the Oracle community that is just as usable in SQL Server with the implementation of Extended Events and DMVs that will show you what you are waiting for?

No. What really makes me tick is becoming friends with the developers by creating a good SQL Server environment and fostering an understanding of one another's differences. Just think what can be accomplished if both sides can live peacefully together instead of fighting every opposite opinion, digging the trenches even deeper and wider. Through fostering good relationships, I have seen environments move from decentralized development systems and standalone production databases to central solutions with easy access for developers, and calm uninterrupted nights for me. However, this does mean that you have to give up some sovereignty over your systems by relinquishing some of your admin power.

The main problem is focus. While the DBA thinks of space issues, data modeling, and the stability of everyday operations, the developers thinks of making things smarter, sexier, and shiny. To make the relationship work, we have to move through the entire palette of the system—standardization, accessibility, logging, information flow, performance information—all while ensuring that systems are stable and that developers know that they are not alone, and that DBAs still exist and decide things.

## My Experience Working with SQL Server and Developers

After finishing my engineering studies, I started as a developer. I worked on CRM systems in DataEase under DOS and OS/2, and that combination gave me plenty of insight into the issues developers have with the DBA function. DataEase was the Microsoft Access of that time, and it had connectors to all the major databases (Oracle, SQL Server, and DB2). But most of the time, DBAs would not allow dynamic access to production data. Their resistance led to friction with the developers.

By coincidence, I ended up as a Microsoft Visual Basic programmer in a company developing and running systems for all the Danish municipalities. I was placed among the DB2/MVS DBAs, and I was by far the youngest (and only) GUI person (OS/2 and Windows). While I coded Visual Basic 3 applications, those DBAs were taking care of decentralized connections, such as ODBC on DB/2 MVS. These were the days before having TCP/IP on the mainframe, so we're talking Systems Network Architecture (SNA) and IBM Communications Manager.

One day, my boss gave me responsibility for a new product called SQL Server. Why? Because I was the only one working with Windows.

My biggest problem was how to approach the current environment within the company. How many SQL Server databases did we already have? Which development groups were using it? Those were just some of the questions I had to grapple with.

I had to start from scratch. So I asked my DB/2 colleagues for help. After all, they had been working in these kind of environments for the last 15 years, handling systems with 15,000 concurrent users, 50,000 different programs, thousands of individual databases, and lots of data on every Danish citizen, such as taxes, pension funds, and other personal information. I wanted the benefit of their experience.

What I learned was that data modeling is a must. You need to have a naming standard for servers, for database objects, for procedures—for everything, actually. Starting the battle for naming standards and consistency took me on a six-year-long journey with developers, until most developers actually started to live safely. They came to understand that my requirements gave them more stable and consistent environments to develop on, made them more efficient, and got the job done faster for all.

# Reconciling Different Viewpoints Within an Organization

The everyday battles between DBAs and developers mostly concern routine administrative tasks. Limitations on space allocations and limits to changes in production are perceived by developers as inhibiting innovation and stopping them from making a difference. They often see the DBA as someone who purposely limits them from doing their job. On the other hand, the admin group thinks that developers rarely plan ahead longer than the next drop-down box or the next screen, and that they never think in terms of the time period over which the software they build must run, which is often five to ten years or even longer.

The consequences of these differences are that developers create their own secret systems, move budget money out of reach of the DBA team, and generally do everything in their power to limit the admins in setting up the imaginary borders they believe are being set up. For example, often I would hear the sentence, "If you take away that privilege from me, I can no longer boot the machine at will." The problem with that thinking is that well-configured SQL Server systems need no more restarts than any other type of systems.

So how do we get out of this evil spiral, and what are the benefits of doing so? Dialog is the way out, and the benefits are a controlled production environment, clearly defined ownership of databases, consistent environments patched correctly, lower cost of maintenance, possible license savings, and almost certainly fewer calls at 4:00 in the morning interrupting your sleep.

Remember, all change starts with one's self, and it is far easier to change yourself than to change others. So get a hold of a piece of paper, divide it into a plus and a minus side, and start listing the good and bad things in your environment. For instance, it could be a plus that some developers have sysadmin privileges because they fix some things for themselves, but it could also be a minus because they meddle with things they are not supposed to meddle with and create objects without the knowledge of the DBA.

What you'll get from this chapter is my experience and how I managed to foster a productive and good relationship with developers. I'll provide a couple of code examples to help you on the way to success, or to just inspire you. My approach is not the only way to achieve good developer relations, but it has proven effective in the environments in which I've worked.

# Preparing to Work with Developers to Implement Changes to a System

To make progress, you have to prepare for it. Implementing change will not work if you make demands of the developers without preparing. The battle will be hard, but it will be worth fighting for, because in the end you'll be eating cake with the developers while talking about the bad-old days with their unstable systems, anarchy, and crashes without backups.

Bring some good suggestions to the table. Do not approach developers without having anything to offer to make *their* lives easier. Think of yourself as a salesperson of stability and consistency—not even developers will disagree with those goals. As in any good marriage, however, the needs of both parties must be aired and acknowledged.

Put yourself in their place as well. Try to understand their work. You'll find that most of their requests are actually not that bad. For example, a common request is to be able to duplicate the production environment in the development environment on the weekend to test new ideas in their software. Would you rather spend your weekend doing that work for them? Isn't it preferable to facilitate having them do the work on their own so that you can be home with your family?

Listen to your developers. Ask them what they see as the biggest hurdles put in their way by the admin group. Your goal, ultimately, should be to create an environment that is good for the business. That means making everybody as happy as possible, easing the bureaucracy, and ensuring stable access for all.

A well-prepared environment can also lead to server consolidation, which in turn leads to saving power, simplifying patching, and ultimately less administrative effort. The money saved from having well-prepared environments can then be used for better things, such as buying Enterprise Edition or enabling Always On availability groups to provide an environment more resilient to failure.

By now, you are beginning to think that I am all talk. How can you get this process of working closely with developers started? The answer depends on how your business is structured. Following is a list of steps. Don't start by doing everything at once. Keep it simple. Build on each success as you go along. Remember that the goal is to create a stable environment for all:

1. Make a map of your existing environment.

2. Create a description of what your new environment should look like.

3. Document your description in written form so that it is clear and convenient to pass on to management and vendors.

4. Create system-management procedures for most changes.

5. Create system reports to report on all those changes.

These are a good series of steps to follow. Don't be too rigid, though. Sometimes you will need to divert from this sequence to make your business work. Adapt and do what is right for your business.

## Step 1: Map Your Environment

If you have never experienced discovering an instance or server that has existed without your knowledge and without your knowing who owns it or uses it, you are a member of the 0.1 percent of SQL Server DBA in the world that has it easy. Indeed, not only is it common to run across unknown servers and instances, sometimes you'll find one and not even know what applications, if any, are running on it. Thus, Step 1 is to begin mapping your infrastructure so that you can know what you currently have.

Start by finding all the servers in your domain. Several free tools are available on the Internet to help you do this. Or maybe you already have the information in your Configuration Management Database (CMD) but you have never created reports on that data.

Try executing the following in a command prompt window:

```
SQLCMD -L
```

This command will list all the available servers on your network that are visible. You can get much more detailed information using tools such as SQLPING, Microsoft Map, Quest Discovery Wizard, or other similar products. A benefit of these products is that they often provide information like version numbers or patch levels.

Once you find your servers, you need to find out whether they are actually still in use. Most likely, you will have servers that were used only during an upgrade, but no one thought to shut them down once the upgrade was complete. One place where I have seen this go horribly wrong was in an organization that forgot the old server was still running, so it no longer got patched. Along came the SLAMMER virus, and down went the internal network. Another project I was on, involved consolidating about 200 servers. We found we could actually just switch off 25 percent of them because they were not being used.

Following is a piece of code to help you capture information about logins so that you can begin to identify who or what applications are using a given instance. The code is simple, using the sysprocesses view available on most versions of SQL Server. Why not use audit trace? Because audit trace takes up a lot of space. You need only unique logins, and viewing logs of all login attempts from audit trace is not easy on the eyes.

First, create the following small table in the msdb database. I use msdb because it is available in all versions of SQL Server. The table will record unique logins.

```
CREATE TABLE msdb.dbo.user_access_log
( id            int IDENTITY(1,1) NOT NULL,
  dbname        nvarchar(128)     NULL,
  dbuser        nvarchar(128)     NULL,
  hostname      nchar(128)        NOT NULL,
  program_name  nchar(128)        NOT NULL,
  nt_domain     nchar(128)        NOT NULL,
  nt_username   nchar(128)        NOT NULL,
  net_address   nchar(12)         NOT NULL,
  logdate       datetime          NOT NULL
  CONSTRAINT DF_user_access_log_logdate DEFAULT (getdate()),
  CONSTRAINT PK_user_access_log PRIMARY KEY CLUSTERED (id ASC) )
```

Then run the following code to sample logins every 15 seconds. If you need smaller or larger granularity, you can easily just change the WAITFOR part of the code. You can even make the code into a job that automatically starts when the SQL Server Agent starts.

```
WHILE 1=1
BEGIN

  WAITFOR DELAY '00:00:15';

  INSERT INTO msdb.dbo.user_access_log
  ( dbname,
    dbuser,
    hostname,
    program_name,
    nt_domain,
```

```
  nt_username,
  net_address )
SELECT distinct
  DB_NAME(dbid) as dbname,
  SUSER_SNAME(sid) as dbuser,
  hostname,
  program_name,
  nt_domain,
  nt_username,
  net_address
FROM master.dbo.sysprocesses a
WHERE spid>50
  AND NOT EXISTS( SELECT 1
                  FROM msdb.dbo.user_access_log b
                  WHERE b.dbname = db_name(a.dbid)
                    AND NULLIF(b.dbuser,SUSER_SNAME(a.sid)) IS NULL
                    AND b.hostname = a.hostname
                    AND b.program_name = a.program_name
                    AND b.nt_domain = a.nt_domain
                    AND b.nt_username = a.nt_username
                    AND b.net_address = a.net_address )
END
```

When you begin this process of capturing and reviewing logins, you should create a small team consisting of a couple of DBAs and a couple of the more well-liked developers and system owners. The reason to include others, of course, is to create ambassadors who can explain the new setup to other developers and system owners. Being told something by your peers makes it that much harder to resist the changes or even refuse them. And these people also have a lot of knowledge about the business, how the different systems interact, and what requirements most developers have. They can tell you what would be a show-stopper, and catching those in the beginning of the process is important.

# Step 2: Describe the New Environment

The next step is to describe your new environment or the framework in which you plan to operate. What should this description contain? Make sure to address at least the following items:

- **Version of SQL Server**   The fewer SQL Server versions you have to support, the easier it is to keep systems up and running. You will have fewer requirements to run different versions of Windows Server, and the newer the version you keep, the easier it is to get support from Microsoft or the community at large. I have seen several shops running versions spanning the gamut from 7.0, 2000, 2005, 2008, 2008 R2 through to 2012. Why not just choose 2012? Having the latest version as the standard is also a good selling point to developers, because most of the exciting new features will then be available to them. You might not be able to get down to just one version, but work hard to minimize the number you are stuck with supporting.

- **Feature support**   Get started studying all the different features. Describe how your environment is implemented, how it is used, what features are accepted, and which features are not. Take into account whether features require privileges such as sysadmin, access to the command shell, and so forth. The important thing in this process is to understand the advantages and disadvantages of every feature, and to try to think through how to explain why a certain feature will not be enabled—or instance, the use of globally unique identifiers (GUIDs) as primary keys. Developers tend to want to able to create the parent keys on their own, because it is then easier to insert into parent and child tables in the same transaction. In this case, SQL Server 2012's new support for stored sequences can be an easy replacement for GUIDs created in an application.

- **Editions**  Editions can be thought of as an extension of the feature set. How does the company look at using, say, the Express Edition? Should you use only Standard Edition, or do you need to use Enterprise Edition? Do you use Developer Edition in development and test environments and then use Standard Edition in production, which leaves you with the risk that the usage features in development cannot be implemented in production? How do you help developers realize what they can do and cannot do, and what advanced features they can actually use? Do you use policy-based management to raise an alarm whenever Enterprise Edition features are used? Or do you just periodically query the view sys.dm_db_persisted_sku_ features, which tells you how many Enterprise Edition features are in use?

- **Naming standards**  Naming standards are a must. The lowest level should be on the server level, where you choose standard names for servers, ports, instances, and databases. Standardization helps to make your environment more manageable. Do you know which ports your instances use? Knowing this makes it a lot easier to move systems around and connect to different servers. Also, databases tend to move around, so remember that two different systems should not use the same database name. Prefix your databases with something application specific to make them more recognizable.

- **Patching**  Version change is important to remember, because it is easily overlooked. Overlook it, and you end up with a lot of old versions running in both production and development environments. Try and implement reasonable demands here. You could choose, for example, to say that development and test environments should be upgraded to the latest version every six months after release, and production environments get upgraded a maximum of three months after that upgrade. Also, you can require that service packs be implemented no later than three months after release.

- **Privileges**  Privileges are very important to control. Some privileges might be acceptable in development and test environments, but not in production, which is OK. Just remember to write down those differences so that everybody is aware of them and the reasons why they exist. Start out by allowing developers dbo access to their own databases in development. That way, you do not constrain their work. If they crash something, they only ruin it for themselves. In production, users should get nothing beyond read, write, and execute privileges. You can implement wrapped stored procedures for people truly in need of other types of access. For example, many developers believe they should have dbo privileges, but they rarely need all the rights that dbo confers. Here, explicit grants of privilege can be offered as a replacement. If people want the ability to trace in production, you can wrap trace templates in stored procedures and offer access to the procedures.

You might have other items to address than just the ones I've listed. That is OK and to be expected. Take my list as the base, and add other concerns as needed to support your business. Don't go overboard, but take care to cover what's truly important to your business.

# Step 3: Create a Clear Document

Write everything down clearly. Create a single document you can hand to vendors, management, and new personnel to help them get up to speed.

I've often experienced systems going into production that did not adhere to our standards. These were primarily purchased applications that were bought without asking the IT department about demands related to infrastructure. Most of the time this happened because the rest of the business did not know about the standards IT had in place, and sometimes it happened because of the erroneous belief that our business could not make demands of the vendors. Here is where a piece of paper comes into play. Create a quick checklist so that people who buy applications can ask the vendor about what is needed to fit applications into your environment. Some possible questions that you might want to put to a vendor include the following:

- Do you support the latest release?
- Do you require sysdamin rights?
- What collation do you use?

When all the questions have been asked and answered, you have an actual possibility to see whether the vendor's application is a realistic fit with your environment, or whether you should cancel the purchase and look for other possibilities. In most cases, when pressed on an issue, third-party vendors tend to have far fewer requirements than first stated, and most will make an effort to bend to your needs.

# Step 4: Create System-Management Procedures

You will get into a lot of battles with your developers about rights. You'll hear the argument that they cannot work independently without complete control. You can't always give them that freedom. But what you *can* do is give them access to a helper application.

What I often found is that, as the DBA, I can be a bottleneck. Developers would create change requests. I would carry out the changes, update the request status, close the request, and then inform the required people. Often, it would take days to create a database because of all the other things I had to do. Yet, even though creating a database requires extensive system privileges, it is an easy task to perform. Why not let developers do these kind of tasks? We just need a way to know that our standards are followed—such as with the naming and placement of files—and and to know what has been done.

Logging is the key here. Who does what and when and where? For one customer, we created an application that took care of all these basic, but privileged, tasks. The application was web-based, the web server had access to all servers, and the application ran with sysadmin rights. Developers had access to run the application, not access to the servers directly. This meant we could log everything they did, and those developers were allowed to create databases, run scripts, run traces, and a lot more. What's more, they could do those things in production. Granting them that freedom required trust, but we were convinced that 99.99 percent of the developers actually wanted to do good, and the last 0.01 percent were a calculated risk.

You don't need an entire application with a fancy interface. You can just start with stored procedures and use EXECUTE AS. I'll walk you through a simple example.

First create a user to access and create objects that the developers will not be allowed to create directly. The following code example does this, taking care to ensure the user cannot be used to log in to the database directly. The user gets the dbcreator role, but it is completely up to you to decide what privileges the user gets.

```
USE [master];

CREATE LOGIN [CreateDbUser]
WITH PASSWORD=N'Allw@ysSq1',
    DEFAULT_DATABASE=[master],
    CHECK_EXPIRATION=OFF,
    CHECK_POLICY=OFF;

DENY CONNECT SQL TO [CreateDbUser];

EXEC sp_addsrvrolemember
    @loginame = N'CreateDbUser',
    @rolename = N'dbcreator';

USE [msdb]

CREATE USER [miracleCreateDb] FOR LOGIN [miracleCreateDb];

EXEC sp_addrolemember N'db_datareader', N'miracleCreateDb';

EXEC sp_addrolemember N'db_datawriter', N'miracleCreateDb';
GO
```

Next, create a table to log what the developers do with their newfound ability to create databases independently. The table itself is pretty simple, and of course, you can expand it to accommodate your needs. The important thing is that all fields are filled in so that you can always find who is the owner and creator of any given database that is created.

```
CREATE TABLE DatabaseLog
( [databasename] sysname PRIMARY KEY NOT NULL,
  [application] nvarchar(200) NOT NULL,
  [contact] nvarchar(200) NOT NULL,
  [remarks] nvarchar(200) NOT NULL,
  [creator] nvarchar(200) NOT NULL,
  [databaselevel] int NOT NULL,
  [backuplevel] int NOT NULL )
```

Then create a stored procedure for developers to invoke whenever they need a new database. The following procedure is straightforward. The create database statement is built in a few steps, using your options, and then the statement is executed. The database options are fitted to the standard, and a record is saved in the DatabaseLog table. For the example, I decided to create all databases with four equal-sized data files, but you can choose instead to create a USERDATA file group that becomes the default file group. Do whatever makes sense in your environment.

```
CREATE PROCEDURE [CreateDatabase]
    @databasename  nvarchar(128),
    @datasize      int = 100,
    @logsize       int = 25,
    @application   nvarchar(100) = '',
    @contact       nvarchar(50)  = '',
    @remarks       nvarchar(max) = '',
    @databaselevel int = 1 ,
```

```
    @backuplevel    int = 1

AS
BEGIN
  SET NOCOUNT ON;

  EXECUTE AS Login = 'miracleCreateDb';

  DECLARE @datafiles nvarchar(200),
          @logfiles  nvarchar(200),
          @DatafilesPerFilegroup int,
          @sqlstr    varchar(max),
          @serverid int,
          @i int

  SET @dataFiles = 'C:\DATA'

  SET @logFiles  = 'C:\LOG'

  SET @DatafilesPerFilegroup = 4

  SET @datasize = @datasize / @DatafilesPerFilegroup

  SET @sqlstr  = 'CREATE DATABASE ' + @databasename + ' ON  PRIMARY '
  SET @sqlstr += '( NAME = N''' + @databasename + '_data_1'', FILENAME = N'''
                 + @datafiles + '\' + @databasename + '_data_1.mdf'' , SIZE = '
                 + CAST(@datasize as varchar(10)) + 'MB , MAXSIZE = UNLIMITED ,'
                 + ' FILEGROWTH = 100MB )'

  SET @i = 1

  WHILE @i < @DatafilesPerFilegroup
  BEGIN
    SET @i += 1
    SET @sqlstr += ',( NAME = N''' + @databasename + '_data_'
                   + cast(@i as varchar(2)) + ''', FILENAME = N''' + @datafiles + '\'
                   + @databasename + '_data_' + cast(@i as varchar(2)) + '.mdf'' , SIZE = '
                   + CAST(@datasize as varchar(10)) + 'MB , MAXSIZE = UNLIMITED ,'
                   + ' FILEGROWTH = 100MB )'
  END

  SET @sqlstr += ' LOG ON ( NAME = N''' + @databasename + '_log'', FILENAME = N'''
                 + @logfiles + '\' + @databasename + '_log.ldf'' , SIZE = '
                 + CAST(@logsize as varchar(10)) + 'MB , MAXSIZE = UNLIMITED ,'
                 + ' FILEGROWTH = 100MB );'

  EXEC (@sqlstr)

  SET @sqlstr = 'ALTER DATABASE [' + @databasename + ']
                 SET COMPATIBILITY_LEVEL = 100' + ';'+
                 'ALTER DATABASE [' + @databasename + ']
```

```
                SET AUTO_UPDATE_STATISTICS_ASYNC ON WITH NO_WAIT' + ';'+
                'ALTER DATABASE [' + @databasename + ']
                SET READ_COMMITTED_SNAPSHOT ON' + ';'

    EXEC (@sqlstr)

    INSERT INTO DatabaseLog
      ( [databasename],
        [application],
        [contact],
        [remarks],
        [creator],
        [databaselevel],
        [backuplevel] )
    VALUES
      ( @databasename,
        @application,
        @contact,
        @remarks,
        ORIGINAL_LOGIN(),
        @databaselevel,
        @backuplevel )

PRINT 'Connection String : ' +
        'Data Source=' + @@SERVERNAME +
        ';Initial Catalog=' + @databasename +
        ';User Id='+
        ';Password='+
        ';Application Name=' + @application

END
```

This small example can easily be expanded to include the creation of standard users, default privilege assignments, and so on. As a small bonus, I returned the connection string to the database just created. That helps developers use the real drivers, and it helps ensure they include the application name, because there is nothing worse than to do diagnostics on a SQL Server instance in which all users are named "Joe" and the application is "Microsoft .Net Provider".

As you can see, EXECUTE AS opens up a lot of options to create stored procedures that allow your developers to execute privileged code without having to grant the privileges to the developers directly.

# Step 5: Create Good Reporting

So what do I mean by "good reporting"? It is the option to draw information from a running system that can tell you how SQL Server is running at the moment. As with the system-management part, only your imagination sets the limit. You can start out using the tools already at hand from SQL Server, such as Data Collector, dynamic management views, and Reporting Services. With Data Collector, you have the opportunity to gather information about what happens in SQL Server over time, and then use Reporting Services to present that data in an easy-to-understand and read format.

Think both globally and locally.

Think globally by creating a general overview showing how a server is performing. What, for example, are the 35 most resource-consuming queries? List those in three different categories: most executions, most I/O, and most CPU usage. Combine that information with a list of significant events and the trends in disk usage.

But also think locally by creating the same type of overview for individual databases instead of for the server as a whole. Then developers and application owners can easily spot resource bottlenecks in their code directly and react to that. Such reports also give developers an easy way to continuously improve their queries without involving the DBA, which means less work for you.

In addition to including performance information, you can easily include information from log tables, so the different database creations and updates can be reported as well.

Finally, take care to clearly define who handles exceptions and how they are handled. Make sure nobody is in doubt about what to do when something goes wrong, and that everyone knows who decides what to do if you have code or applications that cannot support your framework.

# Ensuring Version Compatibility

If you choose to consolidate on SQL Server 2012, you will no doubt discover that one of your key applications requires SQL Server 2008 to be supported from the vendor. Or you might discover that the application user requires sysadmin rights, which makes it impossible to have that database running on any of your existing instances.

You might need to make exceptions for critical applications. Try to identify and list those possible exceptions as early in the process as possible, and handle them as soon as you possible also. Most applications will be able to run on SQL Server 2012, but there will inevitably be applications where the vendor no longer exists, code is written in Visual Basic 3 and cannot directly be moved to Visual Basic 2010, or where the source has disappeared and the people who wrote the applications are no longer with the company. Those are all potential exceptions that you must handle with care.

One way to handle those exceptions is to create an environment in which the needed older SQL Server versions are installed, and they're installed on the correct operating system version. Create such an environment, but do not document it to the outside world. Why not? Because then everyone will suddenly have exceptions and expect the same sort of preferential treatment. Support exceptions, but only as a last resort. Always try to fix those apparent incompatibilities.

Exceptions should be allowed only when all other options are tried and rejected. Vendors should not be allowed to just say, "We do not support that," without justifying the actual technical arguments as to why. Remember you are the customer. You pay for their software, not the other way around.

Back when 64-bit Windows was new, many application vendors didn't create their installation program well enough to be able to install it into a 64-bit environment. Sometimes they simply put a precheck on the version that did not account for the possibility of a 64-bit install. When 64-bit-compatible versions of applications finally arrived, it turned out that only the installation program was changed, not the actual application itself. I specifically remember one storage vendor that took more than a year to fix the issue, so that vendor was an exception in our environment. As soon as you create an exception, though, get the vendor to sign an end date for that exception. It is always good practice to revisit old requirements, because most of them change over time. If you do not have an end date, systems tend to be forgotten or other stuff becomes more important, and the exception lives on forever.

Remember finally, that you can use compatibility mode to enable applications to run on SQL Server 2012 when those applications would otherwise require some earlier version. Compatibility with SQL Server 2000 is no longer supported, but compatibility with the 2005 and 2008 versions is.

---

**Tip**   A very good reason to use compatibility mode instead of actually installing an instance on an older version is that compatibility mode still provides access to newer administrative features, such as backup compression. For example, SQL Server 2000 compatibility mode in SQL Server 2008 gave me the option to partition some really big tables, even though partitioning was not supported in 2000. In checking with Microsoft, I was told that if the feature works, it is supported.

---

# Setting Limits

All is not well yet, though. You still have to set limits and protect data.

I'm sure you have experienced that a login has been misused. Sometimes a developer just happens to know a user name and password and plugs it into an application. That practice gives rise to situations in which you do not know who has access to data, and you might find that you don't reliably know which applications access which databases. The latter problem can lead to production halts when passwords are changed or databases are moved, and applications suddenly stop working.

I have a background in hotel environments supporting multiple databases in the same instance, with each database owned by a different department or customer. (You can get the same effect in a consolidation environment.) SQL Server lacks the functionality to say that Customer A is not allowed to access Customer B's data. You can say that creating different database users solves the problem, but we all know that user names and passwords have a tendency to be known outside of the realm they belong in. So, at some point, Customer A will get access to Customer B's user name and password and be able to see that data from Customer A's location. Or if it's not outside customers, perhaps internal customers or departments will end up with undesired access to one another's data.

Before having TCP/IP on the mainframe, it was common to use System Network Architecture (SNA) and Distributed Data Facility (DDF) to access data in DB2. DDF allowed you to define user and Logical Unit (LU) correlations, and that made it possible to enforce that only one user-id could be used from a specific location. When TCP/IP was supported, IBM removed this functionality and wrote the following in the documentation about TCP/IP: "Do you trust your users?". So, when implementing newer technology on the old mainframe, IBM actually made it less secure.

## Logon Triggers

The solution to the problem of not being able to restrict TCP/IP access to specific locations was to use a logon user exit in DB2. That exit was called *Resource Access Control Facility (RACF)*. (It was the security implementation on the mainframe.) RACF was used to validate that the user and IP address matched and, if not, to reject the connection.

In 2000, at SQLPASS in London, I asked about the ability of SQL Server to do something similar to DB2's logon exit feature. Finally, the LOGON TRIGGER functionality arrived, and we now have the option to do something similar. In the following example, I will show a simple way to implement security so that a user can connect only from a given subnet. This solution, though, is only as secure and trustworthy as the data in the DMVs that the method is based upon.

---

**Caution** Be careful about LOGIN triggers. An error in such a trigger can result in you no longer being able to connect to your database server or in you needing to bypass the trigger using the Dedicated Administrator Connection (DAC).

---

Following is what you need to know:

- The logon trigger is executed after the user is validated, but before access is granted.

- It is in sys.dm_exec_connections that you find the IP address that the connection originates from.

- Local connections are called <local machine>. I don't like it, but such is the case. Dear Microsoft, why not use 127.0.0.1 or the server's own IP address?

- How to translate an IP address for use in calculations.

First, you need a function that can convert the IP address to an integer. For that, you can cheat a little and use PARSENAME(). The PARSENAME() function is designed to return part of an object name within the database. Because database objects have a four-part naming convention, with the four parts separated by periods, the function can easily be used to parse IP addresses as well.

Here's such a function:

```
CREATE FUNCTION [fn_ConvertIpToInt]( @ip varchar(15) )
RETURNS bigint
WITH SCHEMABINDING
BEGIN
  RETURN (CONVERT(bigint, PARSENAME(@ip,1)) +
          CONVERT(bigint, PARSENAME(@ip,2)) * 256 +
          CONVERT(bigint, PARSENAME(@ip,3)) * 65536 +
          CONVERT(bigint, PARSENAME(@ip,4)) * 16777216)
END
```

Next you need a table that can contain the names of users who need protection. The table will include Login Name and ip-ranges. The IP address is written in normal form (for example, 10.42.42.42), and at the same time in its integer value. It is the integer value that enables you to easily check whether an IP address falls within a given range. Following is a table that you might use:

```
CREATE TABLE [LoginsAllowed]
( [LoginName]    [sysname] NOT NULL,
  [IpFromString] [varchar](15) NOT NULL,
  [IpToString]   [varchar](15) NOT NULL,
  [IpFrom]    AS ([fn_ConvertIpToInt]([IpFromString])) PERSISTED,
  [IpTo]      AS ([fn_ConvertIpToInt]([IpToString]))   PERSISTED )

ALTER TABLE [LoginsAllowed]
  WITH CHECK
  ADD  CONSTRAINT [CK_LoginsAllowed_IpCheck]
  CHECK  (([IpFrom]<=[IpTo]))
GO

CREATE UNIQUE CLUSTERED INDEX [IX_LoginsAllowed] ON [LoginsAllowed]
( [LoginName] ASC,
```

```
[IpFrom] ASC,
[IpTo] ASC )
```

Then create a user to execute the trigger. Grant the user access to the table and SERVER STATE. If you do not do this, the trigger will not have access to the required DMV. Here's an example:

```
CREATE LOGIN [LogonTrigger] WITH PASSWORD = 'Pr@s1ensGedBag#' ;

DENY CONNECT SQL TO [LogonTrigger];

GRANT VIEW SERVER STATE TO [LogonTrigger];

CREATE USER [LogonTrigger] FOR LOGIN [LogonTrigger] WITH DEFAULT_SCHEMA=[dbo];

GRANT SELECT ON [LoginsAllowed] TO [LogonTrigger];

GRANT EXECUTE ON [fn_ConvertIpToInt] TO [LogonTrigger];
```

Now for the trigger itself. It will check whether the user logging on exists in the LOGIN table. If not, the login is allowed. If the user *does exist* in the table, the trigger goes on to check whether the connection comes from an IP address that is covered by that user's IP range. If not, the connection is refused. Here is the code for the trigger:

```
CREATE TRIGGER ConnectionLimitTrigger
ON ALL SERVER
WITH EXECUTE AS 'LogonTrigger'
FOR LOGON
AS
BEGIN
  DECLARE @LoginName sysname, @client_net_address varchar(48), @ip bigint

  SET @LoginName = ORIGINAL_LOGIN()

  IF EXISTS (SELECT 1 FROM LoginsAllowed WHERE LoginName = @LoginName)
  BEGIN
    SET @client_net_address=(SELECT TOP 1 client_net_address
                             FROM sys.dm_exec_connections
                             WHERE session_id = @@SPID)

    -- Fix the string, if the connection is from <local host>
    IF @client_net_address = '<local machine>'
      SET @client_net_address = '127.0.0.1'

    SET @ip = fn_ConvertIpToInt(@client_net_address)

    IF NOT EXISTS (SELECT 1 FROM LoginsAllowed
                   WHERE LoginName = @LoginName AND
                         @ip BETWEEN IpFrom AND IpTo)
      ROLLBACK;
  END
END
```

When you test this trigger, have more than one query editor open and connected to the server. Having a second query editor open might save you some pain. The trigger is executed only on new connections. If there is a logical flaw in your code that causes you to be locked out of your database, you can use that spare connection in the second query editor to drop the trigger and regain access to your database. Or you need to make a DAC connection to bypass the trigger.

## Policy-Based Management

Policy-based management (PBM) allows you to secure an installation or to monitor whether the installation adheres to the different standards you have defined. PBM can be used in different ways. One customer I worked for had the problem of databases with enterprise features making it into production. This was a problem because the customer wanted to move to Standard Edition in the production environment. So they set up an enterprise policy to alert them whenever those features were used. They chose to alert rather than to block usage entirely because they felt it important to explain their reasoning to the developer instead of just forcing the decision.

## Logging and Resource Control

If you need to log when objects are created, you probably also want to log whenever they are deleted. A procedure to drop a database, then, would perform the following steps:

1.   DROP DATABASE

2.   UPDATE DatabaseLog

When many resources are gathered in one place, as in consolidation environments, you need to control the usage of those resources to prevent one database from taking them all. There are two different levels to think about when you talk about resource control in SQL Server: resource usage across multiple instances, and by individual users in an instance.

One process (for example, a virus scan, backup agent, and so forth) could take all CPU resources on a machine and take away all CPU resources for all the other processes on that same server. SQL Server cannot guard itself against problems like that. But Windows can guard against that problem. Windows includes a feature called *Windows System Resource Manager (WSRM)*, which is a not-well-known feature available starting with Windows Server 2008. When WSRM is running, it will monitor CPU usage and activate when usage rises above the 70 percent mark. You can create policies in which, when the resource manager is activated, you will allocate an equal share of CPU to all instances.

# Next Steps

When all the details are in place, your target framework is taking shape, and your environment is slowly being created, you have to think about how to make your effort a success. Part of the solution is to choose the right developers to start with. Most would take the developers from the biggest or most important applications, but I think that would be a mistake. Start with the easy and simple and small systems, where you almost can guarantee yourself success before you begin. Then you will quietly build a good foundation. If problems arise, they will most likely be easier to fix than if you had chosen a big complex system to start from. Another reason for starting small is that you slowly build up positive stories and happy ambassadors in your organization. In the long run, those happy ambassadors will translate into more systems being moved to your environment.

# CHAPTER 2

■ ■ ■

# Getting It Right: Designing the Database for Performance

## By Louis Davidson

Most of the topics in the book are related to admin tasks: indexing, performance tuning, hardware, backup, compression, and so forth. Many times, database administrators (DBAs) don't have input into the design of the database they are responsible for. But even if you don't have control over the design, it's nice to know what a good design ought to look like—if for no other reason than you can be specific in your complaints when you are struggling with a piece of software.

In this chapter, I'll present an overview of the entire process of designing a database system, discussing the factors that make a database perform well. Good performance starts early in the process, well before code is written during the definition of the project. (Unfortunately, it really starts well above of the pay grade of anyone who is likely to read a book like this.) When projects are hatched in the board room, there's little understanding of how to create software and even less understanding of the unforgiving laws of time. Often the plan boils down to "We need software X, and we need it by a date that is completely pulled out of…well, somewhere unsavory." So the planning process is cut short of what it needs to be, and you get stuck with the seed of a mess. No matter what part you play in this process, there are steps required to end up with an acceptable design that works, and that is what you as a database professional need to do to make sure this occurs.

In this chapter, I'll give you a look at the process of database design and highlight many of the factors that make the goals of many of the other chapters of this book a whole lot easier to attain. Here are the main topics I'll talk about:

- **Requirements**   Before your new database comes to life, there are preparations to be made. Many database systems perform horribly because the system that was initially designed bore no resemblance to the system that was needed.

- **Table Structure**   The structure of the database is very important. Microsoft SQL Server works a certain way, and it is important that you build your tables in a way that maximizes the SQL Server engine.

- **Design Testing**   The process of testing should go beyond code and extend into the design process, with the primary goal of the process being to make sure the software that is created matches to needs of the user.

The process of database design is not an overly difficult one, yet it is so often done poorly. Throughout my years of writing, working, speaking, and answering questions in forums, easily 90 percent of the problems came from databases that were poorly planned, poorly built, and (perhaps most importantly) unchangeable because of the mounds of code accessing those structures. With just a little bit of planning and some knowledge of the SQL Server engine's base patterns, you'll be amazed at what you can achieve and that you can do it in a lot less time than initially expected.

# Requirements

The foundation of any implementation is an understanding of what the heck is supposed to be created. Your goal in writing software is to solve some problem. Often, this is a simple business problem like creating an accounting system, but sometimes it's a fun problem like shuffling riders on and off of a theme-park ride, creating a television schedule, creating a music library, or solving some other problem. As software creators, our goal ought to be to automate the brainless work that people have to do and let them use their brains to make decisions.

Requirements take a big slap in the face because they are the first step in the classic "waterfall" software-creation methodology. The biggest lie that is common in the programming community is that the waterfall method is completely wrong. The waterfall method states that a project should be run in the following steps:

- **Requirements Gathering**   Document what a system is to be, and identify the criteria that will make the project a success.

- **Design**   Translate the requirements into a plan for implementation.

- **Implementation**   Code the software.

- **Testing**   Verify that the software does what it is supposed to do.

- **Maintenance**   Make changes to address problems not caught in testing.

- **Repeat the process.**

The problem with the typical implementation of the waterfall method isn't the steps, nor is it the order of the steps, but rather it's the magnitude of the steps. Projects can spend months or even years gathering requirements, followed by still more months or years doing design. After this long span of time,  the programmers finally receive the design to start coding from. (Generally, it is slid under their door so that the people who devised it can avoid going into the dungeons where the programmers are located, shackled to their desks.) The problem with this approach is that, the needs of the users changed frequently in the years that passed before software was completed. Or (even worse) as programming begins, it is realized that the requirements are wrong, and the process has to start again.

As an example, on one of my first projects as a consultant, we were designing a system for a chemical company. A key requirement we were given stated something along the lines of: "Product is only sold when the quality rating is not below 100." So, being the hotshot consultant programmer who wanted to please his bosses and customers, I implemented the database to prevent shipping the product when the rating was 99.9999 or less, as did the UI programmer. About a week after the system is shipped, the true requirement was learned. "Product is only sold when the quality rating is not below 100…or the customer overrides the rating because they want to." D'oh! So after a crazy few days where sleep was something we only dreamt about, we corrected the issues. It was an excellent life lesson, however. Make sure requirements make sense before programming them (or at least get it down in writing that you made sure)!

As the years have passed and many projects have failed, the pendulum has swung away from the pure waterfall method of spending years planning to build software, but too often the opposite now occurs. As a reaction to the waterfall method, a movement known as Agile has arisen. The goal of Agile is to attempt to shorten the amount of time between requirements gathering and implementation by shortening the entire process from gathering requirements to shipping software from years to merely weeks. (If you want to know more about Agile, start with their "manifesto" http://agilemanifesto.org/.) The critisisms of Agile are very often the exact opposite of the waterfall method: very little time is spent truly understanding the problems of the users, and after the words "We need a program to do…" are spoken, the coding is underway. The results are almost always predictably (if somewhat quicker…) horrible.

---

■ **Note** In reality, Agile and Waterfall both can actually work well in their place, particularly when executed in the right manner by the right people. Agile methodologies in particular are very effective when used by professionals who really understand the needs of the software development process, but it does take considerable discipline to keep the process from devolving into chaos.

---

The ideal situation for software design and implementent lies somewhere between spending no time on requirements and spending years on them, but the fact is, the waterfall method at least has the order right, because each step I listed earlier needs to follow the one that comes before it. Without understanding the needs of the user (both now and in the future,) the output is very unlikely to come close to what is needed.

So in this chapter on performance, what do requirements have to do with anything? You might say they have everything to do with everything. (Or you might not—what do I know about what you would say?) The best way to optimize the use of software is to build correct software. The database is the foundation for the code in almost every business system, so once it gets built, changing the structure can be extremely challenging. So what happens is that as requirements are discovered late in the process, the database is morphed to meet new requirements. This can leave the database in a state that is hard to use and generally difficult to optimize because, most of the time, the requirements you miss will be the obscure kind that people don't think of immediately but that are super-important when they crop up in use. The SQL Server engine has patterns of use that work best, and well-designed databases fit the requirements of the user to the requirements of the engine.

As I mentioned in the opening section of this chapter, you might not be the person gathering requirements, but you will certainly be affected by them. Very often (even as a production DBA who does no programming), you might be called on to give opinions on a database. The problem almost always is that if you don't know the requirements, almost any database can appear to be correct. If the requirements are too loose, your code might have to optimize for a ridiculously wide array of situations that might not even be physically possible. If the requirements are too strict, the software might not even work.

Going back to the chemical plant example, suppose that my consulting firm had completed our part of the project, we had been paid, and the programmers had packed up to spend our bonuses at Disney World and the software could not be changed. What then? The user would then find some combination of data that is illogical to the system, but tricks the system into working. For example, they might enter a quality rating of 10,000 + the actual rating. This is greater than 100, so the product can ship. But now every usage of the data has to take into consideration that 10,000 and greater actually means that the value was the stored value minus 10,000 that the customer has accepted, and values under 100 are failed products that the user did not accept. In the next section, I'll discuss normalization, but for now take my word for it that designing a column that holds multiple values and/or multiple meanings is not a practice that you would call good, making it more and more difficult to achieve adequate performance.

As a final note about requirements, requirements should be written in such a way that they are implementation non-specific. Stating that "We need to have a table to store product names and product quality scores" can reduce the quality of the software because it is hard to discern actual requirements from poorly written prose. This statement could mean, "Products have names, and each batch of that product has a quality score" or "Each batch will have a different name and a quality score." As you build your tables, your goal will be to match your design to the version that is correct. Sure the first makes sense, but business doesn't always make sense.

---

░ **Note**　In this short chapter on design and the effect on performance, I am going to assume you are acclimated to the terminology of the relational database and understand the basics. I also will not spend too much time on the overall process of design, but you should spend time between getting requirements and writing code visualizing the output, likely with a data-modeling tool. For more information on the overall process of database design, might I shamelessly suggest *Pro SQL Server 2012 Relational Database Design and Implementation* (Apress, 2012)? My goal for the rest of this chapter will be to cover the important parts of design that can negatively affect your performance of (as well as your happiness when dealing with) your SQL Server databases.

---

# Table Structure

The engineers who work for Microsoft on the SQL Server team are amazing. They have built a product that, in each successive version, continues to improve and attempt to take whatever set of structures is thrown at them, any code that a person of any skill level throws at it, and make the code work well. Yet for all of their hard work, the fact remains that the heart of SQL Server is a relational database engine and you can get a lot more value by using the engine following good relational practices. In this section, I will discuss what goes into making a database "relational," and how you can improve your data quality and database performance by just following the relational pattern as closely as possible.

To this end, I will cover the following topics:

- **A Really Quick Taste of History**　Knowing why relational databases are what they are can help to make it clear why SQL Server is built the way it is and why you need to structuring your databases that way too.

- **Why a Normal Database Is Better Than an Extraordinary One**　Normalization is the process of making a database work well with the relational engine. I will describe normalization and how to achieve it in a practical manner.

- **Physical Model Choices**　There are variations on the physical structure of a database that can have distinct implications for your performance.

Getting the database structure to match the needs of the engine is the second most important part in the process of performance tuning your database code. (Matching your structure to the user's needs being the most important!)

## A Really Quick Taste of History

The concept of a relational database originated in the late 1970s. (The term *relation* is mostly analogous to a table in SQL and does not reference relationships.) In 1979, Edgar F. Codd, who worked for the IBM Research Laboratory at the time, wrote a paper titled "A Relational Model of Data for Large Shared Data Banks," which was printed in "Communications of the ACM." ("ACM" stands for the Association for Computing Machinery, which you can learn more about at www.acm.org.) In this 11-page paper, which really should be required reading, Codd introduced to the world outside of academia the fairly revolutionary idea for how to break the physical barriers of the types of databases in use at that time.

Following this paper, in the 1980s Codd presented 13 rules for what made a database "relational," and it is quite useful to see just how much of the original vision persists today. I won't regurgitate all of the rules, but the gist of them was that, in a relational database, all of the physical attributes of the database are to be encapsulated from the user. It shouldn't matter if the data is stored locally, on a storage area network (SAN), elsewhere on the local area network (LAN), or even in the cloud (though that concept wasn't quite the buzz worthy one it is today.) Data is stored in containers that have a consistent shape (same number of columns in every row), and the system works out the internal storage details for the user. The higher point is that the implementation details are hidden from the users such that data is interacted with only at a very high level.

Following these principles ensures that data is far more accessible using a high level language, accessing data by knowing the table where the data resided, the column name (or names), and some piece of unique data that could be used to identify a row of data (aka a "key"). This made the data far more accessible to the common user because to access data, you didn't need to know what sector on a disc the data was on, or a file name, or even the name of physical structures like indexes. All of those details were handled by software.

Changes to objects that are not directly referenced by other code should not cause the rest of the system to fail. So dropping a column that isn't referenced would not bring down the systems. Moreover, data should not only be treated row by row but in sets at a time. And if that isn't enough, these tables should be able to protect themselves with integrity constraints, including uniqueness constraints and referential integrity, and the user shouldn't know these constraints exist (unless they violate one, naturally). More criteria is included in Codd's rules, including the need for NULLs, but this is enough for a brief infomercial on the concept of the relational database.

The fact is, SQL Server—and really all relational database management systems (RDBMSs) —is just now getting to the point where some of these dreams are achievable. Computing power in the 1980s was nothing compared to what we have now. My first SQL Server (running the accounting for a midsized, nonprofit organization) had less than 100 MB of disk space and 16 MB of RAM. My phone five years ago had more power than that server. All of this power we have now can go to a developer's head and give him the impression that he doesn't need to spend the time doing design. The problem with this is that data is addictive to companies. They get their taste, and they realize the power of data and the data quantity explodes, leading us back to the need of understanding how the relational engine works. Do it right the first time…. That sounds familiar, right?

## Why a Normal Database Is Better Than an Extraordinary One

In the previous section, I mentioned that the only (desirable) method of directly accessing data in a relational database is by the table, row key, and column name. This pattern of access ought to permeate your thinking when you are assembling your databases. The goal is that users have exactly the right number of buckets to put their data into, and when you are writing code, you do not need to break down data any further for usage.

As the years passed, the most important structural desires for a relational database were formulated into a set of criteria known as the *normal forms*. A table is normalized when it cannot be rewritten in a simpler manner without changing the meaning. This meaning should be more concerned with actual utilization than academic exercises, and just because you can break a value into pieces doesn't mean that you have to. Your decision should be based mostly on how data is used. Much of what you will see in the normal forms will seem very obvious. As a matter of fact, database design is not terribly difficult to get right, but if you don't know what right is, it is a lot easier to get things wrong.

There are two distinct ways that normalization is approached. In a very formal manner, you have a progressive set of draconian "rules" that specify "forms" to adhere to. There is nothing wrong with that approach, and it's an essential exercise to do before building a "great" database, but progressing through the forms in a stepwise manner is not how any seasoned data architect is likely to approach the process of design. Instead, you design with the principles of normalization in mind, and use the normal forms as a way to test your design.

The problem with getting a great database design is compounded with how natural the process seems. The first database that "past, uneducated me" built had 10+ tables—all of the obvious ones, like customer, orders, and so forth that are set up so that the user interface could be produced to satisfy the client. However, addresses, order items, and other items were left as part of the main tables, making it a beast to work with for queries. As my employer wanted more and more out of the system, the design became more and more taxed (and the data became more and more polluted). The basics were there, but the internals were all wrong and the design could have used about 50 or so tables to flesh out the correct solution. Soon after (at my next company, sorry Terry), I gained a real education in the basics of database design, and the little 1000-lumen light bulb in my head went off.

That light bulb was there because what had looked like a more complicated database than a normal person would have created in my college database class was there to help designs fit the tools that I was using (SQL Server 1.0). And because the people who create relational database engines use the same concepts of normalization to help guide how the engine works, it was a win/win situation. So if the relational engine vendors are using a set of concepts to guide how they create the engine, it turns out to be actually quite helpful if you follow along.

In this section, I will cover the concept of normalization in two stages:

- **(Semi-)Formal Definition**   Using the normal-form definitions, I will establish what the normal forms are.

- **Practical Application**   Using a simple restatement of the goals of normalization, I will work through a few examples of normalization and demonstrate how violations of these principals will harm your performance as well as your data quality.

In the end, I will have established at least a basic version of what "right" is, helping you to guide your designs toward correctness. Here's a simple word of warning, though: all of these principles must be guided by the user's desires, or the best looking database will be a failure.

## (Semi-)Formal Definition

First, let's look at the "formal" rules in a semi-formal manner. Normalization is stated in terms of "forms," starting with the first normal form and including several others. Some forms are numbered, and others are named for the creators of the rule. (Note that in the strictest terms, to be in a greater form, you must also conform to the lesser form. So you can't be in the third strictest normal form and not give in to the definition of the first.) It's rare that a data architect actually refers to the normal forms in conversation specifically, unless they are trying to impress their manager at review time, but understanding the basics of normalization is essential to understanding why it is needed. What follows is a quick restatement of the normal forms:

- **First Normal Form/Definition of a Table**   Attribute and row *shape*:

  - All columns must be *atomic*—one individual value per column that needn't be broken down for use.

  - All rows of a table must contain the same number of values—no arrays or repeating groups (usually denoted by columns with numbers at the end of the name, such as the following: payment1, payment2, and so on).

  - Each row should be different from all other rows in the table. Rows should be unique.

- **Boyce-Codd Normal Form** Every possible key is identified, and all attributes are fully dependent on a key. All non-key columns must represent a fact about a key, a whole key, and nothing but a key. This form was an extension of the second and third normal forms, which are a subset of the Boyce-Codd normal forms because they were initially defined in terms of a single *primary* key:

    - **Second Normal Form** All attributes must be a fact about the entire primary key and not a subset of the primary key.

    - **Third Normal Form** All attributes must be a fact about the primary key and nothing but the primary key.

- **Fourth Normal Form** There must not be more than one multivalued dependency represented in the entity. This form deals specifically with the relationship of attributes within the key, making sure that the table represents a single entity.

- **Fifth Normal Form** A general rule that breaks out any data redundancy that has not specifically been culled out by additional rules. If a table has a key with more than two columns and you can break the table into tables with two column keys and be guaranteed to get the original table by joining them together, the table is not in Fifth Normal Form. The form of data redundancy covered by Fifth Normal Form is very rarely violated in typical designs.

▓ **Note** The Fourth and Fifth Normal Forms will become more obvious to you when you get to the practical applications in the next section. One of the main reasons why they are seldom covered isn't that they aren't interesting, but more because they are not terribly easy to describe. However, examples of both are very accessible.

There are other, more theoretical forms that I won't mention because it's rare that you would even encounter them. In the reality of the development cycle of life, the stated rules are not hard-and-fast rules, but merely guiding principles you can use to avoid certain pitfalls. In practice, you might end up with *denormalization* (meaning purposely violating a normalization principle for a stated, understood purpose, not ignoring the rules to get the job done faster, which should be referred to as *unnormalized*). Denormalization occurs mostly to satisfy some programming or performance need from the consumer of the data (programmers, queriers, and other users).

Once you deeply "get" the concepts of normalization, you'll that you build a database like a well-thought-out Lego creation. You'll design how each piece will fit into the creation before putting the pieces together because, just like disassembling 1000 Lego bricks to make a small change makes Lego building more like work than fun, database design is almost always work to start with and usually is accompanied by a manager who keeps looking at a watch while making accusatory faces at you. Some rebuilding based on keeping your process agile might be needed, but the more you plan ahead, the less data you will have to reshuffle.

## Practical Application

In actual practice, the formal definition of the rules aren't referenced at all. Instead, the guiding principles that they encompass are referenced. I keep the following four concepts in the back of my mind to guide the design of the database I am building, falling back to the more specific rules for the really annoying or complex problem I am trying to solve:

- **Columns** Make sure every column represents only one value.

- **Table/row uniqueness**  One row represents one independent thing, and that thing isn't represented anywhere else.

- **Columns depend only on an entire key**  Columns either are part of a key or describe something about the row identified by the key.

- **Keys always represent a single expression**  Make sure the dependencies between three or more key values are correct.

Throughout this section, I'll provide some examples to fortify these definitions, but it is a good point here to understand the term: *atomic*. Atomic is a common way to describe a value that cannot be broken down further without changing it into something else. For example, a water molecule is made up of hydrogen and oxygen. Inside of the molecule, you can see both types of atoms if you look really close. You can split them up and you still have hydrogen and oxygen. Try to split hydrogen, and it will turn into something else altogether (and your neighbors are not going to be pleased one little bit). In SQL, you want to break things down to a level that makes them easy to work with without changing the meaning beyond what is necessary.

Tables and columns split to their atomic level have one, and only one, meaning in their programming interface. If you never need to use part of a column using SQL, a single column is perfect. (A set of notes that the user uses on a screen is a good example.) You wouldn't want a paragraph, sentence, and character table to store this information, because the whole value should be useful only as a whole. If you are building a system to count the characters in that document, it could be a great idea to have one row per character.

If your tables are too coarsely designed, your rows will have multiple meanings that never share commonality. For example, if one row represents a baboon and the other represents a manager, even though the comedic value is worth its weight in gold, there is very likely never going to be a programming reason to combine the two in the same row. Too many people try to make objects extremely generic, and the result is that they lose all meaning. Still others make the table so specific that they spend extreme amounts of coding and programming time reassembling items for use.

As a column example, consider a column that holds the make, model, and color of a vehicle. Users will have to parse the data to pick out blue vehicles. So they will need to know the format of the data to get the data out, leading to the eventual realization of the database administrator that all this parsing of data is slowing down the system and just having three columns in the first place would make life much better.

At the same time, we can probably agree that the car model name should have a single column to store the data, right? But what if you made a column for the first character, the last character, and middle characters? Wouldn't that be more normalized? Possibly, but only if you actually needed to program with the first and last characters independently on a regular basis. You can see that the example here is quite silly, and most designers stop designing before things get weird. But like the doctor will tell you when looking at a wound you think is disgusting, "That is nothing, you should have seen the..." and a few words later you are glad to be a computer programmer. The real examples of poor design are horribly worse than any example you can put in a chapter.

## Columns

*Make sure every column represents only one value.*

Your goal for columns is to make sure every column represents only one value, and the primary purpose of this is performance. Indexes in SQL Server have key values that are complete column values, and they are sorted on complete column values. This leads to the desire that most (if not all, but certainly most) searches use the entire value. Indexes are best used for equality comparisons, and their next-best use is to make range comparisons. Partial values are generally unsavory, with the only decent partial-value usage is a string or binary value that uses the leftmost character or binary value, because that is how the data is sorted in the index. To be fair, indexes can be used to scan values to alleviate the need to touch the table's data (and possibly overflow) pages, but this is definitely not the ideal utilization.

To maximize index usage, you should never need to parse a column to get to a singular piece of data. A common scenario is a column that contains a comma-delimited list of values. For example, you have a table that holds books for sale. To make displaying the data more natural, the following table is built (the key of the table is BookISBN):

| BookISBN | BookTitle | BookPublisher | Authors |
| --- | --- | --- | --- |
| 111111111 | Normalization | Apress | Louis |
| 222222222 | T-SQL | Apress | Michael |
| 333333333 | Indexing | Microsoft | Kim |
| 444444444 | DB Design | Apress | Louis, Jessica |

On the face of things, this design makes it easy for the developer to create a screen for editing, for the user to enter the data, and so forth. However, although the initial development is not terribly difficult, using the data for any reason that requires differentiating between authors is. What are the books that Louis was an author of? Well, how about the following query? It's easy, right?

```
SELECT BookISBN, BookTitle
FROM   Book
WHERE  Authors LIKE '%Louis%'
```

Yes, this is exactly what most designers will do to start with. And with our data, it would actually work. But what happens when author "Louise" is added? And it is probably obvious to anyone that two people named Louis might write a book, so you need more than the author's first name. So the problem is whether you should have AuthorFirstName and AuthorLastName—that is, two columns, one with "Louis, Jessica" and another with "Davidson, Moss". And what about other bits of information about authors? What happens when a user uses an ampersand (&) instead of a comma (,)? And…well, these are the types of questions you should be thinking about when you are doing design, not after the code is written.

If you have multiple columns for the name, it might not seem logical to use the comma-delimited solution, so users often come up with other ingenious solutions. If you enter a book with the ISBN number of 444444444, the table looks like this (the key of this set is the BookISBN column):

| BookISBN | BookTitle | BookPublisher | AuthorFirstName | AuthorLastName |
| --- | --- | --- | --- | --- |
| 444444444 | DB Design | Apress | Jessica | Moss |

That's fine, but now the user needs to add another author, and *her* manager says to make it work. So, being the intelligent human being she is, the user must figure out some way to make it work. The comma-delimited solution feels weird and definitely not "right":

| BookISBN | BookTitle | BookPublisher | AuthorFirstName | AuthorLastName |
| --- | --- | --- | --- | --- |
| 444444444 | DB Design | Apress | Jessica, Louis | Moss, Davidson |

So the user decides to add another row and just duplicate the ISBN number. The uniqueness constraint won't let her do this, so voila! The user adds the row with the ISBN slightly modified:

| BookISBN | BookTitle | BookPublisher | Author |
| --- | --- | --- | --- |
| 444444444 | DB Design | Apress | Jessica |
| 444444444-1 | DB Design | Apress | Louis |

You might think is grounds to fire the user, but the fact is, she was just doing her job. Until the system can be changed to handle this situation, your code has to treat these two rows as one row when talking about books, and treat them as two rows when dealing with authors. This means grouping rows when dealing with substringed BookISBN values or with foreign key values that could include the first or second values. And the mess just grows from there. To the table structures, the data looks fine, so nothing you can do in this design can prevent this from occurring. (Perhaps the format of ISBNs could have been enforced, but it is possible the user's next alternative solution may have been worse).

Designing this book and author solution with the following two tables would be better. In a second table (named BookAuthor), the BookISBN is a foreign key to the first table (named Book), and the key to BookAuthor is BookISBN and AuthorName. Here's what this solution looks like:

| BookISBN | BookTitle | BookPublisher |
| --- | --- | --- |
| 111111111 | Normalization | Apress |
| 222222222 | T-SQL | Apress |
| 333333333 | Indexing | Microsoft |
| 444444444 | DB Design | Apress |

| BookISBN | AuthorName | ContributionType |
| --- | --- | --- |
| 111111111 | Louis | Primary Author |
| 222222222 | Michael | Primary Author |
| 333333333 | Kim | Primary Author |
| 444444444 | Louis | Primary Author |
| 444444444 | Jessica | Contributor |

Note too that adding more data about the author's contribution to the book was a very natural process of simply adding a column. In the single table solution, identifying the author's contribution would have been a nightmare. Furthermore, if you wanted to add royalty percentages or other information about book's author, it would be an equally simple process. You should also note that it would be easy to add a table for authors and expand the information about the author. In the example, you would not want to duplicate the data twice for Louis, even though he wrote two of the books in the example.

## Table/row uniqueness

*One row represents one independent thing, and that thing isn't represented anywhere else.*

The first normal form tells you that rows need to be unique. This is a very important point, but it needs to be more than a simple mechanical choice. Just having a uniqueness constraint with a meaningless value technically makes the data unique. As an example of how generated values lead to confusion, consider the following subset of a table that lists school mascots. (The primary key is on MascotId.)

| MascotId | Name |
| --- | --- |
| 1 | Smokey |
| 112 | Bear |
| 4567 | Bear |
| 9757 | Bear |

The rows are technically unique, because the ID values are different. If those ID numbers represent a number that the user uses to identify rows in all cases, this might be a fine table design. However, in the far more likely case where MascotId is just a number generated when the row is created and has no actual meaning, this data is a disaster waiting to occur. The first user will use MascotId 9757, the next user might use 4567, and the user after that might use 112. There is no real way to tell the rows apart. And although the Internet seems to tell me that the mascot name "Smokey" is used only by the University of Tennessee, the bear is a common mascot used not only by my high school but by many other schools as well.

Ideally, the table will contain a natural key (or a key based on columns that have a relationship to the meaning of the table of data being modeled instead of an artificial key that has no relationship to the same). In this case, the combination of SchoolName and the mascot Name probably will suffice:

| MascotId | Name | SchoolName |
| --- | --- | --- |
| 1 | Smokey | University of Tennessee |
| 112 | Bear | Bradley High School |
| 4567 | Bear | Baylor University |
| 979796 | Bear | Washington University |

You might also think that the SchoolName value is unique in and of itself, but many schools have more than one mascot. Because of this, you may need multiple rows for each SchoolName. It is important to understand what you are modeling and make sure it matches what your key is representing.

---

▓ **Note**   Key choice can be a contentious discussion, and it's also is a very important part of any design. The essential part of any design is that you can tell one row from another in a manner that makes sense to the users of the system. SQL Server physical considerations include what column is used to cluster the table (or physically order the internal structures), what columns are frequently used to fetch data based on user usage, and so forth. The physical considerations should be secondary to making sure the data is correct.

---

Why is uniqueness so important to performance? When users can do a search and know that they have the one unique item that meets their needs, their job will be much easier. When duplicated data goes unchecked in the database design and user interface, all additional usage has to deal with the fact that where the user expects one row, he might get back more than one.

One additional uniqueness consideration is that a row represents one unique thing. When you look at the columns in your tables, does this column represent something independent of what the table is named and means? In the following table that represents a customer, check each column:

| CustomerId | Name | Payment1 | Payment2 | Payment3 |
| --- | --- | --- | --- | --- |
| 0000002323 | Joe's Fish Market | 100.03 | 120.23 | NULL |
| 0000230003 | Fred's Cat Shop | 200.23 | NULL | NULL |

CustomerId and Name clearly are customer related, but the payment columns are completely different things than customers. So now two different sorts of objects are related to one another. This is important because it becomes difficult to add a new payment type object. How do you know what the difference is between Payment1, Payment2, and Payment3? And what if there turns out to be a fourth payment? To add the next payment for Fred's Cat Shop, you might use some SQL code along these lines:

```
UPDATE dbo.Customer
SET Payment1 = CASE WHEN Payment1 IS NULL THEN 1000.00 ELSE Payment1 END,
    Payment2 = CASE WHEN Payment1 IS NOT NULL AND Payment2 IS NULL
```

```
                            THEN 1000.00 ELSE Payment2 END,
        Payment3 = CASE WHEN Payment1 IS NOT NULL
                              AND Payment2 IS NOT NULL
                              AND Payment3 IS NULL
                            THEN 1000.00 ELSE Payment3 END
   WHERE CustomerId = '0000230003';
```

If payments were implemented as their own table, the table might look like this:

| CustomerId | PaymentNumber | Amount | Date |
| --- | --- | --- | --- |
| 0000002323 | 1 | 120.23 | 2012-10-15 |
| 0000002323 | 2 | 100.03 | 2012-11-12 |
| 0000230003 | 1 | 200.23 | 2012-08-13 |

Adding a new payment would be as simple as adding another row, and adding metadata about the payment is as easy as adding a single column. Although the payments example is probably a bit unrealistic and certainly a case where most anyone would see the need for multiple rows, there are many cases where designers think that just using columns is the best answer. A system I am working with right now has email addresses stored as emailAddress1, emailAddress2, and emailAddress3. The emailAddress1 value is used straightforwardly as the primary email address, but the values in emailAddress2 and emailAddress3 are used either as previous email addresses or alternate email addresses. And without adding 10 to 20 new columns of metadata (one set for each email address), it will be nearly impossible to reign in usage and know what all the values mean.

Keep in mind that even if all of the payment entries are done manually through the UI, even things like counting the number of payments tends to be a difficult task. How many payments has Fred made? You could do something like this:

```
SELECT  CASE WHEN Payment1 IS NOT NULL THEN 1 ELSE 0 END +
        CASE WHEN Payment2 IS NOT NULL THEN 1 ELSE 0 END +
        CASE WHEN Payment3 IS NOT NULL THEN 1 ELSE 0 END AS PaymentCount
FROM    dbo.Customer
WHERE   CustomerId = 0000230003;
```

When you do it that way and you have to start doing this work for multiple accounts simultaneously, it gets complicated. In many cases, the easiest way to deal with this condition is to normalize the set, probably through a view:

```
CREATE VIEW  dbo.CustomerPayment
AS
   SELECT  CustomerId, 1 AS PaymentNumber, Payment1 AS PaymentAmount
   FROM    dbo.Customer
   WHERE   Payment1 IS NOT NULL
   UNION ALL
   SELECT  CustomerId, 2 AS PaymentNumber, Payment2 AS PaymentAmount
   FROM    dbo.Customer
   WHERE   Payment2 IS NOT NULL
   UNION ALL
   SELECT  CustomerId, 3 AS PaymentNumber, Payment3 AS PaymentAmount
   FROM    dbo.Customer
   WHERE   Payment3 IS NOT NULL
```

Now you can do all of your queries just as if the table was properly structured, although it's not going to perform nearly as well as if the table was designed correctly:

```
SELECT CustomerId, COUNT(*)
FROM    dbo.CustomerPayment
GROUP   BY CustomerId
```

Now you just use the columns of the customer objects that are unique to the customer, and these rows are unique for each customer payment.

## Columns depend only on an entire key

*Columns either are part of a key or describe something about the row identified by the key.*

In the previous section, I focused on getting unique rows, based on the correct kind of data. In this section, I focus on finding keys that might have been missed earlier in the process. The keys I am describing are simply dependencies in the columns that aren't quite right. For example, consider the following table (where $X$ is the declared key of the table):

| X | Y | Z |
|---|---|---|
| 1 | 1 | 2 |
| 2 | 2 | 4 |
| 3 | 2 | 4 |

Values in the X column are unique, so that is fine. You can determine the corresponding Y and Z values from the value of X. Now look at the other, non-key columns. Given a value of Y, you can't determine a specific value of X, but you seemingly can determine the value of Z. For all cases where Y = 1, you know that Z = 2, and when Y = 2, you know that Z = 4. Before you pass judgment, consider that this could be a coincidence. It is very much up to the requirements to help you decide if Y and Z are related (and it could be that the Z value determines the Y value also).

When a table is designed properly, any update to a column requires updating one and only one value. In this case, if Z is defined as Y*2, updating the Y column would require updating the Z column as well. If Y could be a key of your table, this would be acceptable as well, but Y is not unique in the table. By discovering that Y is the determinant of Z, you have discovered that YZ should be its own independent table. So instead of the single table you had before, you have two tables that express the previous table with no invalid dependencies, like this (where X is the key of the first table and Y is the key of the second):

| X | Y |
|---|---|
| 1 | 1 |
| 2 | 2 |
| 3 | 2 |

| Y | Z |
|---|---|
| 1 | 2 |
| 2 | 4 |

For a somewhat less abstract example, consider the following set of data, representing book information (the key of the table is BookISBN):

| BookISBN | BookTitle | PublisherName | PublisherLocation |
| --- | --- | --- | --- |
| 111111111 | Normalization | Apress | California |
| 222222222 | T-SQL | Apress | California |
| 444444444 | DMV Book | Simple Talk | England |

BookISBN is the defined key, so every one of the columns should be completely dependent on this value. The title of the book is dependent on the book ISBN and the publisher, too. The concern in this table is the PublisherLocation value. A book doesn't have a publisher location, a publisher does. So if you needed to change the publisher, you would also need to change the publisher location.

To correct this situation, you need to create a separate table for the publisher. Following is one approach you can take (in which the key of the first table is BookISBN and the key of the second table is Publisher):

| BookISBN | BookTitle | PublisherName |
| --- | --- | --- |
| 111111111 | Normalization | Apress |
| 222222222 | T-SQL | Apress |
| 444444444 | DMV Book | Simple Talk |

| Publisher | PublisherLocation |
| --- | --- |
| Apress | California |
| Simple Talk | England |

Now a change of publisher for a book requires only changing the publisher value in the Book table, and a change to publisher location requires only a single update to the Publisher table. Note, however, that if PublisherLocation *actually* represented the location of the publisher at the time the book was printed, the design might have been just fine because you might have a new book with Apress and they could be in New York now:

| BookISBN | BookTitle | PublisherName | PublisherLocation |
| --- | --- | --- | --- |
| 111111111 | Normalization | Apress | California |
| 222222222 | T-SQL | Apress | California |
| 444444444 | DMV Book | Simple Talk | England |
| 555555555 | Expert Practices | Apress | New York |

| Publisher | PublisherLocation |
| --- | --- |
| Apress | New York |
| Simple Talk | England |

Now you can get the current location of Apress, and the location of Apress when the book was published. Is this important information? If you think you know, you missed the point of the first section of this chapter. What matters is the requirements, not what seems to be right when you are designing.

Of course, you should consider all sorts of dependencies, in the same table, like calculations (which ought to be done with a calculated column if it is necessary and cannot be overridden), summary data like the total on an invoice, or the count of employees who work for a department. Usually, the cost to store and maintain incorrect dependencies is far more than the cost of calculating the values as you need them. In our example, if updating the publisher table required updates to the book table, you probably would have issues (except in the case of fixing a mistake in the current location, perhaps).

Are there cases where calculating summary values at the time they are needed is more costly than the maintenance? Yes, but the best rule of thumb is to try the correct or easy way first. Usually, if your tables follow the normal patterns, optimization almost just happens.

## Keys always represent a single expression

*Make sure dependency relationships between three values or tables are correct.*

Once you have reached the point that your tables have only atomic values for columns and tables have a single meaning, unique rows, and seemingly no dependency issues, you are really close to being done. In fact, you're basically in Boyce–Codd normal form, which (as I stated earlier) is a better version of the third normal form that is so highly touted as the ultimate normal form. However, you aren't quite done, and the last test is still interesting and corresponds to the fourth and fifth normal forms.

You need to check out whether the keys that have been chosen represent only one thing. Consider the following example table that represents the types of vehicles a driver likes to drive (where the keys of the table are Driver and VehicleStyle):

```
Driver    VehicleStyle      DesiredModelLevel
--------  ----------------  ------------------
Louis     CUV               Premium
Louis     Sedan             Standard
Ted       Coupe             Performance
```

The relationship between Driver and VehicleStyle represents a multivalued dependency for the Driver and the VehicleStyle entities. The driver Louis will drive either CUV or Sedan vehicles, and Louis is the only driver who drives the CUV style. As you add more data, each vehicle style will have many drivers that choose the type as a preference. A table such as this one for Driver and VehicleStyle is used frequently to resolve a many-to-many relationship between two tables—in this case, the Driver and VehicleStyle tables, which define the characteristics that pertain specifically to the driver and the vehicle style. The DesiredModelLevel in this case is a characteristic that applies only to the intersection of Driver and VehicleStyle.

The modeling problem comes when you need to model a relationship between three entities, modeled as three columns in a key (usually) from three separate table types. As an example, consider the following table representing the assignment of a trainer to a class that is assigned to use a certain book (where all three columns make up the key currently):

```
Trainer     Class           Book
----------  --------------  ------------------------------
Louis       Normalization   DB Design & Implementation
Chuck       Normalization   DB Design & Implementation
Fred        Implementation  DB Design & Implementation
Fred        Golf            Topics for the Non-Technical
```

To decide if this table is acceptable, you need to look at each column and determine how they are related to the others. If any two columns are not directly related to one another, there will be an issue with the table design because the key actually represents more than one independent thing. Here are the possible combinations and their relationships:

- Class (in this case, the type of class) and Trainer are related, and a class might have multiple trainers.

- Book and Class are related, and a book might be used for multiple classes.

- Trainer and Book are not directly related, because the rule stated that the class uses a specific book.

Hence, regardless of how correct the table initially seemed, what you really have here are two independent types of information being represented in a single table. To deal with this, you will split the table on the column that is common to the two dependent relationships. Take this one table and make two tables that express the data that was in the first table:

```
Class           Trainer
--------------- ---------------
Normalization   Louis
Normalization   Chuck
Implementation  Fred
Golf            Fred


Class          Book
-------------- --------------------------
Normalization  DB Design & Implementation
Implementation DB Design & Implementation
Golf           Topics for the Non-Technical
```

Joining these two tables together on Class, you will find that you get the exact same table as before. However, if you change the book for the Normalization class, it will be changed immediately for both of the classes that are being taught by the different teachers. Note that initially it seems like you have more data because you have more rows and more tables. However, notice the redundancy in the following data from the original design:

```
Louis      Normalization  DB Design & Implementation
Chuck      Normalization  DB Design & Implementation
```

The redundancy comes from stating twice that the book *DB Design & Implementation* is used for the Normalization class. The new design conveys that same information with one less row of data. When the system grows to the point of having 50 Normalization classes being taught, you will have much less data, making the storage of data more efficient, possibly creating some performance benefits, and reducing the amount of redundant data that can get out of sync.

Note, too, that if the table was modeling an instance of the class, the key would be class, time, location, and the teacher and book would be simply columns. (This assumes a class can have only one teacher and classroom; otherwise, you end up with more multivalued dependencies.) Most of these conditions are caught during testing, but not always.

As an alternate situation, consider the following table of data, which might be part of the car rental system that I used in the initial example before. This table defines the brand of vehicles that the driver will drive:

```
Driver              VehicleStyle                 VehicleBrand
------------------- ---------------------------- -------------------------
Louis               Station Wagon                Ford
Louis               Sedan                        Hyundai
Ted                 Coupe                        Chevrolet
```

- Driver and VehicleStyle are related, representing the style the driver will drive.

- Driver and VehicleBrand are related, representing the brand of vehicle the driver will drive.

- `VehicleStyle` and `VehicleBrand` are related, defining the styles of vehicles the brand offers that can be rented.

This table defines the types of vehicles that the driver will take. Each of the columns has a relationship to the other, so it properly represents a single thing only. As our final multiple-key example, consider the following key that is meant to represent book `Authors` and `Editors`:

| Book | Author | Editor |
| --- | --- | --- |
| Design | Louis | Jonathan |
| Design | Jeff | Leroy |
| Golf | Louis | Steve |
| Golf | Fred | Tony |

There are two possible interpretations that might be made somewhat clear by the name of the table (and the documentation as well):

- This key does not represent a singular value if it represents the following independent relationships:

  - The book *Design* has authors Louis and Jeff, and it has editors Jonathan and Leroy.

  - The book *Golf* has authors Louis and Fred, and it has editors Steve and Tony.

- The key does represent a singular value if it represents the following:

  - For the book *Design*, editor Jonathan edits Louis' work and editor Leroy edits Jeff's work.

  - For the book *Golf*, editor Steve edits Louis' work and editor Tony edits Fred's work.

In the first case, the author and editor are independent of each other, meaning that, technically, you should have a table for the `Book-to-Author` relationship and another for the `Book-to-Editor` relationship. In the second case, the author and editor are directly related. Hence, all three of the values are required to express the single thought of "for book X, editor Y edits Z's work."

Like in many cases we have discussed so far, the goal of this rule is to get the design right so that you don't have to mess around with poorly formatted data. When the keys that you expect to represent a single value actually represent multiple values, your data gets messy and dealing with bad data is the single largest cause of poor performance on many levels. Of course, sometimes the performance issues arise only after you discover that your data is massively messed up and you have layered on tons of hacks to keep it in order.

## Physical Model Choices

In this section, I will discuss a few of the physical model choices that can greatly affect the performance of your database system. Normalization gets you to the point of having the data structured in the correct way, but next you have to fine-tune the implementation details. In this section, I will talk about the following topics:

- **Datatype** Datatypes are often implemented as an afterthought. This is actually one of the more important choices you make, both for data-integrity purposes and in terms of performance.

- **Constraints**   Protecting the integrity of the data might not have an immediate positive effect on the performance of your system, but not having to worry about the quality of the data pays tremendous benefits when the data is used.

- **Indexing**   A database without indexes is probably unusable. (For starters, uniqueness constraints are implemented with indexes.) Getting the indexing right during design (and testing) can limit the amount of tuning you need to do once the cranky users get their hands on your code.

One choice that I won't talk about any more than I have already is primary key choice. Choosing to use natural key values or surrogates is not likely to kill your system's performance as long as your choice is reasonable. Either approach has its own difficulties depending on how complex your natural key values are or what you choose for a surrogate value. I will touch on the indexing considerations in the indexing section, but as long as your indexes are optimum and your data is unique enough that the user doesn't have to randomly choose between rows, any reasonable primary key choice is going to be just fine.

## Datatype

Choosing proper datatypes to match the domain chosen during logical modeling is an important task. One datatype might be more efficient than another of a similar type. For example, you can store integer data in an integer datatype, a numeric datatype, a floating-point datatype, or even a varchar(10) type, but these datatypes are certainly not alike in implementation or performance. Matching the datatype to the need is a large step in getting the data quality that will make your users happy with their database.

Getting the datatype right is the first step in getting the implementation correct, so it can really help to spend a reasonable amount of time here making sure it is right. Too many databases end up with all datatypes the same size and nullable (except for primary keys, if they have them) and lose the integrity of having properly sized and constrained data storage.

It usually isn't that difficult a task, but all too often it is a choice that is ignored. Too many databases have no more than three datatype configurations (consider varchar(10) and varchar(20) as two configurations of varchar) in their database. Using int, varchar(200), and varchar(max), you *could* implement almost any database. Of course, there are two problems with only using very generic datatypes for every column.

First, although you could implement most numbers as integers, some numbers need decimal places. (Yes, you could store your monetary values in pennies instead of dollars, but that would confuse the heck out of most users and make using the data confusing.) And you can also put all other types of data in a varchar(200) and a varchar(max). Any data that you can store in SQL Server can be translated into a textual representation, but not necessarily in a manner that is conducive to use, either by the user or the computer system. The first goal of datatypes is to represent the data in the most natural manner so that the computer can work with it best and the user will be less likely to make a mistake. SQL Server provides a rich set of datatypes, including the following groups of types:

- **Precise numeric data**   Stores data with no loss of precision due to storage. This group includes integer types, which are implemented in hardware (bit, tinyint, smallint, int, bigint); decimal; money; and smallmoney. (The money types are based on integers, which leads to some mathematical limitations and should be rarely used. Use decimal instead.)

- **Approximate numeric data**   Stores approximations of numbers. This group provides for a large range of values. It includes the float and real floating point types, which are based on IEEE standards and are supported via hardware but have round-off issues that have to be understood. Use this group primarily for scientific applications that may need to store extremely small or extremely large values in the same column, and can handle a small amount of rounding error.

- **Date and time**    Stores date values, including the time of day. This group includes the types date, time, datetime2, datetimeoffset, smalldatetime, and datetime. (Note: You should phase out usage of this smalldatetime and datetime and use the more standards-oriented datetime2, though neither are technically deprecated.)

- **Character (or string) data**    Used to store textual data, such as names, descriptions, notes, and so on. This group includes Char, varchar, varchar(max), and their Unicode equivalents: nchar, nvarchar, and nvarchar(max). (Note that there also text/ntext datatypes that are deprecated (and fairly unpleasant) and that you should phase out for the varchar(max)/nvarchar(max) datatypes, immediately if not sooner.)

- **Binary data**    Data stored in bytes (rather than as human-readable values, for example), files, or images. This group includes Binary, Varbinary, and varbinary(max). (Note that there is also an image datatype that is deprecated and that you should phase out for the varbinary(max) datatype, immediately if not sooner.)

- **And the rest**    Datatypes that don't fit into any other groups nicely but are still interesting. This group includes rowversion (also known as timestamp), uniqueidentifier, sql_variant, XML, hierarchyId, and spatial types (such as geometry and geography).

Picking the right datatype from these types to match your need is an important step in establishing data integrity, and it's crucial for performance. (There is even the sql_variant type that you can use in the rare case that you can't actually predict the datatype.) SQL Server (believe it or not) is optimized to work with data in a certain way, and to do comparisons in each datatype in a natural way, not in the way that you may imagine it will in a given situation. For example, say you store numbers in a character string. Then you evaluate the following expression: '100' > '2'. Even when just looking at this, your mind really wants to say that it is true. CAST('100' AS int) > CAST('2' AS int) will evaluate to true, but '100' > '2' will evaluate to false because character strings are ordered from left to right in the way character strings are in the real world. This is obvious when you ask whether 'Apple' < 'Microsoft'. This evaluates to true because the 'A' is less than 'M' regardless of the size of the string (and for no other reason, no matter what humor I might be trying to derive from the names of those companies.)

If you don't get how a relational database uses indexes, the significance of this previous paragraph has probably not yet hit you. (You also really need to read the indexing chapter later in this book.) In procedural programming, executing CAST(value AS type) > CAST(value2 AS type) is no slower than executing value > value2. You'll see this if you frequently use SQL Server Integration Services (SSIS) to do comparisons, because you'll do a lot of type casts and uppercasing for comparisons since data is all case sensitive as you work on the data row by row.

But in a set-based and declarative language like SQL, your goal isn't to take complete control over the entire process, but rather to set up the scenario for the engine to get the right answer fast. There are two ways that indexes are used optimally in a query like the following one:

```
SELECT  <columnList>
FROM    <tableName>
WHERE   <column1> = <comparisonValue1>
```

The ideal case is that column1 and comparisonValue1 have the exact same datatype. The next best case is that the comparisonValue can be implicitly converted to the datatype of the column. Implicit conversion is generally possible when one datatype is less complex than the other. For example, you can implicitly convert an ASCII string to a Unicode string, but you cannot do it the other way around. For the complete chart, check the "Data Type Precedence" topic in SQL Server books online. As an example, consider a table such as this (which I will create in tempdb):

```
CREATE TABLE dbo.testType
(
    varcharType varchar(20),
    nvarcharType varchar(20)
)
```

Obviously, this is not the most useful table, but even a table this simple will show you how performance will be affected by a simple datatype choice. In the following query, the column is higher in datatype precedence. So the value that is lower in precedence will be converted to the higher one. In the following query:

```
SELECT  *
FROM    testType
WHERE   nvarcharType = 'Test'
```

This is okay, because the optimizer will convert the literal value to the more complex type. (The value that is implicitly converted will always be less complex, because implicit conversions are always non-lossy in nature.) In the query plan, you will find the following expression: [tempdb].[dbo].[testType]. [nvarcharType] = CONVERT_IMPLICIT( nvarchar(4000),[@1],0). However, consider the following query:

```
SELECT  *
FROM    testType
WHERE   varcharType = N'Test' --Note: A capital N before a string literal makes it UNICODE
```

You will see the following expression: CONVERT_IMPLICIT(nvarchar(20),[tempdb].[dbo].[testType]. [varcharType],0)=[@1]. This indicates that it has converted the column value, effectively rendering any indexes on the varcharType column useless for any seek operation. Note, too, that when it comes to character values, there is also a collation that controls how values are sorted and compared that can also cause type mismatches.

These are simple examples, but these issues crop up all of the time because there are plenty of places where you have to compare values, in joins, searches, and so on. Attention to the detail of getting the datatypes right can give you great dividends in terms of performance and data quality. In the next section, I'll expand the topic of data quality and limiting data beyond datatypes, but the datatype choice is quite often your first physical model choice that you will make.

## Constraints

Once you have designed the tables, and picked the datatype to match the need, you need to constrain the data to only what is "legal." The more correct you can keep the data, the less time you'll spend correcting mistakes. Any data that can be realistically constrained ought to be. For example, often someone will design a column to hold the country name in an address. There are fewer than two hundred countries in the world, but if you give users a simple text column to enter the country name, you might get over 200 different spellings of each country. With a little ingenuity, you can prevent misspellings by using one of SQL Server's declarative constraints. It might not be possible to validate all data—for example, in the US, it is pretty easy to validate states, but validation gets more difficult as you get more granular. Validating counties and cities gets costly, and making sure postal codes match the city and state is a bit more difficult because there are so many allowable exceptions. Validating complete addresses may only be worth the effort only when you are doing bulk mailing operations that will give you a mailing discount.

To aid in constraining and guiding data-integrity challenges, SQL Server has five kinds of declarative constraints:

- NULL   Determines if a column will accept NULL for its value. Though NULL constraints aren't objects like the other constraint types, they behave very much in the same manner.

- PRIMARY KEY and UNIQUE constraints   Used to make sure your rows contain only unique combinations of values over a given set of key columns. This type of constraint is used to protect the keys you design from duplicate data.

- FOREIGN KEY   Used to make sure that any foreign-key references have only valid values that match the key columns they reference.

- DEFAULT   Used to set an acceptable default value for a column when the user doesn't provide one. (Some people don't count defaults as constraints, because defaults don't constrain updates.)

- CHECK   Used to limit the values that can be entered into a single column or an entire row.

Constraints are part of the base implementation of a table that helps to ensure data quality. You should use constraints as extensively as possible to protect your data, because they're simple and, for the most part, have minimal overhead. Of course, they are not free, and they can slow down your data creation to some extent (definitely for CHECK, FOREIGN KEY, and PRIMARY KEY/UNIQUE constraints), but poorly formatted data is far worse for your performance over time.

---

▓ **Note**   SQL Server also provides triggers that can be used for complex data-integrity implementation. However, they should be used only as a last resort because they can be tricky to get correct and can be very harmful to data integrity if not used correctly.

---

One of the greatest aspects of all of SQL Server's constraints (other than defaults) is that the query optimizer can use them to optimize queries, because the constraints tell the optimizer about some additional quality aspect of the data. For example, say you place a constraint on a column that requires all values for that column to fall between 5 and 10. If a query is executed that asks for all rows with a value greater than 100 for that column, the optimizer will know without even looking at the data that no rows meet the criteria.

Regardless of whether constraints help query performance directly, their part in maintaining data quality is one of the biggest factors in overall system performance. Beyond the topics I covered on normalization and datatypes, consider a database that contains the calendar of speakers for an event. Suppose that the database is perfectly designed but a few speaker assignments are not right. So every user now has to qualify all usage for all rows by manually checking values for bad data (a significant waste of time) and dealing with the data values that are wrong.

Of course, while you can do a lot with constraints, you can only do so much. Users are humans (for the most part), so sometimes they hear things wrong. Sometimes they spell things wrong. (Trust me, the name Louis has always been a delight to see spelled; at least *some* of the spellings are masculine.). For example, say you have spent a large amount of time designing a customer database and your user has the following conversation with the customer:

*Computer operator: "Hi, what is your first name?"*

*Phone Voice: "Fred."*

*[Computer keys click; pan to computer screen.]*

*Input invalid: 23720823437 is not a valid person name*

*Computer operator: "Hmm, I think I misspelled that. Can you spell it again?"*

*Phone Voice (less happily): "F-r-e-d."*

*[Computer keys click; pan to computer screen.]*

*First Name (as shown on screen): Jerkface*

There is really nothing you can do about these types of "mistakes". First, the caller's name might have been Jerkface (but probably actually spelled Jearkfase!), so maybe it was entered correctly, but the software has no way of preventing the user's error. Second, it might have been a female voice and the name "Fred" could have been wrong as it is a very uncommon female name(though the name Frederica could be shortened to Fred). These sorts of data issues are just the start of how complicated it is to stop all of the sorts of data integrity issues. I have worked with databases of addresses (all adequately designed for their purpose) with many permutations of American state, country, city, and street names that just couldn't be correct. Yes, there is a country named Georgia, but it doesn't have a state of Atlanta most likely.

A useful implementation pattern is to take a column with a naturally fixed domain (such as the primary colors, or names of football teams in a league) and instead of trying to have a constraint that hard-codes a list of values (or perhaps hard-codes the list of values in the UI layer), create a table that implements a fixed domain. For example, suppose you have an address table like this:

```
CREATE TABLE Address
(
    ...
    CountryName varchar(30)
    ...
);
```

This table would allow users to enter anything for the country. Instead of leaving this open for users to enter fifteen different spellings of "United States," adding a table to implement the domain of countries such as the following forces users to always enter (or choose) an actual, correctly spelled value.

```
CREATE TABLE Country
(
    CountryName varchar(30) NOT NULL PRIMARY KEY
);
```

```
ALTER TABLE Address
   ADD FOREIGN KEY (CountryName) REFERENCES Country (CountryName);
```

Now the only values that can be contained in the `Address.CountryName` column must also exist in the `Country` table. Without changing the existing schema, you have constrained the values to a set of known values that cannot be violated. Using a domain table has several benefits:

- **The domain is known to users**  Because the values are in a table, users can use them to see what the possible values are without having foreknowledge of the system or looking in the metadata.

- **Associating additional information with the value is easy**  This domain might have information that is useful for users of the data. For example, in the country example mentioned earlier, you might associate an abbreviation with the country, population, geographic information, and so forth.

I nearly always include tables for all domains that are essentially lists of items because it's far easier to manage, even if it requires more tables. (This is particularly true when you want to allow users to make changes on their own.) The choice of key in this case is a bit different than for most tables. Sometimes I use an artificial key for the actual primary key, and other times I use a natural key. The general difference in key choice is whether or not using the integer or GUID key value has value for the client's implementation, usually based on whether their implementation tools care about tables' primary key structures. Either a natural or an artificial key for primary key will suffice for tables that are specifically built to implement a domain.

Of course, the key benefit of constraints of any sort is the improved performance users experience when using the data. This improvement occurs because you don't need to clean the data on every usage. When the data contains "USA," "U.S.A," and "United States," this looks to your code like three values, even though you know it's actually just one. And while known variants can be easily repaired, but a misspelling like "Urnited States," not so much.

## Indexing

Probably the most common area of overdesign and underdesign is indexes. The difficult part of indexing is that there are multiple places along the journey of implementation where you have to apply indexes. During the design phase, you specify indexes in the form of uniqueness constraints. Sometimes the indexes are useful only to protect uniqueness, but often columns that are required to be unique are also the same ones people use to do common searches. You also add indexes in some typically useful situations, like most foreign keys. During implementation, you apply indexes to places where it is obvious that there will be the need for performance improvements, often because these places are obvious even on small sets you are working with in development. Finally, during the testing and production phases of the database's lifecyle, you need to add indexes to tune queries that don't perform well enough.

Indexing is a pretty complex topic, but it is one that every DBA and database developer should understand deeply. Because there is an indexing chapter later in the book, I will simply point out a few concerns you should consider during the design phase. Typically, even before development, you specify the following types of indexes:

- **Uniqueness**  Indexes should be declared as unique whenever possible because the optimizer can use that information when determining how to optimize a query. Commonly, you try to enforce uniqueness with constraints and speed up queries with indexes. Indexes should typically not change the meaning of the system. (An exception is that sometimes you can use filtered indexes to implement uniqueness on a subset of rows, such as non-null values.)

- **Foreign Keys** Foreign key columns are a special case where you often need an index of some type. This is because you build foreign keys so that you can match up rows in one table to rows in another. For this, you have to take a value in one table and match it to another. Be careful to consider how many unique values will be in the rows of the index. Foreign keys used with domain tables are sometime not useful to index because of the low number of values in the domain compared to the base table. But even then, when you are deleting a domain value, it can be useful.

The biggest key to indexing is to manage how useful the indexes are that you apply. If indexes are never used in a query, they can be removed (unless they are implementing a uniqueness constraint). You can use the `sys.dm_db_index_usage_stats` dynamic management function to see how often SQL Server is using the index.

# Design Testing

Testing is a large topic, and one that I will not even attempt to do complete justice to. However, I do want to mention testing during the phases that happen even before the programming begins. The first section of this chapter was titled "Requirements," and it is essential that the requirements be very well done for the rest of any computer project to succeed in any organized fashion.

Throughout the design phase, you might think that you can't start doing any testing because there is no software created. However, every step in the process can be tested. From the requirements, the design team creates a design that will serve as the blueprint for the implementation. In many methodologies (and sometimes just because the design takes too long to actually create), the requirements are somewhat simultaneously created along with the design. (And yes, too often the requirement are barely even done, or are mixed in with implementation details. All I can do is advise you on what is the easiest path to well-built software. I won't lie to you and pretend I always do things perfectly either.) In any case, the goal of testing will always be to make sure the target you hit is the target you planned to hit.

After you have designed your tables, it is time to test your design. By working through scenarios of utilization, you will probably discover many holes in your initial designs. For example, most of the time, when a design is not that well thought out, the holes usually stem from a desire to keep designs reasonable. So the requirements-gathering team consider only the most typical cases but ignore the abnormal cases. For example, suppose your company has a maximum salary it will pay a new DBA, even if that person has lots of experience. Then the best DBA in the world (one of the other writers of this book would do as an example!) might want the job but needs 10 percent more than the maximum allowed. The system denies the request for an increased salary amount, so the company has to hire this DBA as a second Chief Information Officer (CIO). Writing software to handle only the reasonable case, as I just described, is not the kind of "reasonable" I am talking about. During the design testing process, look for obvious holes in your design (and in the requirements as well) and make sure that the final product does what the users realistically would desire (and make sure that they agree, naturally).

On the other end of the spectrum, you have the case where during the normalization phase, the designer went hog wild breaking tables down into more and more separate tables. In some cases, this is absolutely necessary, but the goal of design is to match the actual user's needs to the software created. In the previous example, the database had too simplistic of a system view. However, the opposite case, where the system takes an overly complex view of the problem solved, is equally difficult.

Suppose you were designing a database to store information about camp activities and manage signups for the activities. It might be tempting to have an individual table for archery classes, polka dances, tango dances, snorkeling, basket weaving, s'mores baking, aerobics, canoeing, swimming lessons, fishing and so on, because each of these activities is really nothing like the other. So you go off and model with great details of each camp activity that were described in some detail in the requirements. If there were 50 activities at the camp, you would design 50 tables, plus a bunch of other tables to tie these 50 together. All of these tables are massive enough to document the entire camp and track the movements of all the counselors and campers…if the users had the time and inclination to enter all of that data.

It's probably more likely that the client really wanted to automate the administrative processes of the camp, such as assigning an instructor, signing up attendees, and associating a description with each class. Rather than having the system meticulously model each activity, what you truly needed was to model was the abstraction of a camp activity that can then have people assigned to it. Camp activity description sheets are probably a Microsoft Word document that gets printed out for each new season (and could possibly be stored as a Word document in the database to make sure the documents don't get lost).

By taking the time to test your design and make sure that it matches the actual requirements and needs of the user/application, you can make changes to the design when all that is required is the eraser end of the pencil. That is always the value of testing: to catch errors before they compound themselves into bigger issues. As you move to implementation, use the requirements and design to get the implementation correct. If you have already coded and tested the system in your mind, that is a solid first step toward creating a great piece of software. Matching the needs of the data with the needs of the user will make sure that what the user needs is covered without the performance overhead of software running that is never even used.

# Conclusion

Performance is often mistaken as a purely technical topic. If you are great at SQL and know everything there is about the internals of SQL Server, you probably feel pretty confident that you are good at optimizing performance. It might be true, and without any knowledge of what is the right way to implement, sometimes one can squeeze out good performance from even the worst databases. But unless you are a consultant who makes money off of fixing poorly created software, actual performance considerations start way before the first line of code is written and even before anyone technical is involved with the process.

The first, most important step to great performance is actually understanding the problem you are trying to solve. It doesn't matter if you use the waterfall method or an Agile methodology with nearly religious reverence. It doesn't matter how fast you perform a task if you aren't headed in the right direction. The process for planning for a trip to DisneyWorld or an Alaskan cruise will be quite similar, but the outcome will be worlds apart. Without knowing where the final destination is, successfully arriving at your destination with the right clothes in your luggage is nearly impossible. If you end up in Alaska in February wearing Bermuda shorts and with summer tires on your car, your performance traveling from point A to point B is going to suffer.

Once you have gathered the requirements, and you know what you want to build, the process takes a turn towards how you will implement the solution. The table structure is formed, using patterns that were formed in the 1970s and are still valid today. Tables are normalized, making tables that are atomic, with each table having a single meaning, and each column in the table having a single value. A normalized table has little redundancy in information, leading not only to a high level of data integrity, but structures that are well suited to work with the relational engine that SQL Server is based upon. A very important part of normalization is to match the needs of the users to the needs of the relational engine, not as some form of academic one-upmanship to show that you understand the data better than your user. A database that is over engineered, with fifty tables where five meet the requirements frequently leads to poor performance.

After I discussed getting tables normalized in a practical manner, I discussed several choices for building your tables. Datatypes are chosen to closely match the shape and physical characteristics of the data to be stored to the engine's method of storage. Constraints are chosen to make sure that the data that is created matches the set of rules (requirements!) that govern the data. Indexes are applied as needed to make access to the data optimal. In particular, these three choices are most often made easier by the normalization process. Scalar values (as defined by the First Normal Form) make choosing a datatype straightforward because only one value needs to be stored. Indexes are straightforward because most common access to data can be done using entire data values.

The final topic was a process I referred to as design testing. This process is basically testing before actual implementation occurs, and throughout the process. It is not always possible to catch every issue before the user gets to the software, but spending time, mapping the expected and typical usage patterns to the design at every step, from your data structures that you have applied normalization to, as well as the final table structures that you plan to turn into physical tables in a database can help you see the issues before they are too late to be changed.

This chapter is titled as being about performance, but ideally, in the end, performance is not a thing that you achieve by accident, no more than you arrive at your perfectly restful vacation without planning ahead. Rather, database performance boils down to three things: solid requirements, good design, and defensive coding. Get the design right, and the performance will follow. The real cases you will deal with will be less simplistic than the ones shown in this chapter, and the politics that surround the requirements and eventual design and implementation often will eat up tiny parts of your soul that you will wish you could get back. Getting the design right the first time does matter, however, because databases last for a very long time.

# CHAPTER 3

■ ■ ■

# Hidden Performance Gotchas

## By Gail Shaw

Performance tuning is often considered to be one of those dark arts of Microsoft SQL Server, full of secrets and mysteries that few comprehend. Most of performance tuning, however, is about knowing how SQL Server works and working with it, not against it.

To that end, I want to look at some not-so-obvious causes of performance degradation: predicates, residuals, and spills. In this chapter, I'll show you how to identify them and how to resolve them.

## Predicates

The formal definition of a *predicate* (in the database sense) is "a term designating a property or relation," or in English, a comparison that returns true or false (or, in the database world, unknown).

While that's the formal term, and it is valid, it's not quite what I want to discuss. Rather, I want to discuss where, during the query execution process, SQL evaluates the predicates (the where clause mostly) and how that can influence a query's performance.

Let's start by looking at a specific query:

```
SELECT  FirstName ,
        Surname ,
        OrderNumber ,
        OrderDate
FROM    dbo.Orders AS o
        INNER JOIN dbo.Customers AS c ON o.CustomerID = c.CustomerID
WHERE   OrderStatus = 'O'
        AND OrderDate < '2010/02/01'
```

That's very simple: two tables, two predicates in the where clause, and one in the from (the join predicate). Figures 3-1 and 3-2 show two execution plans from that query's execution.

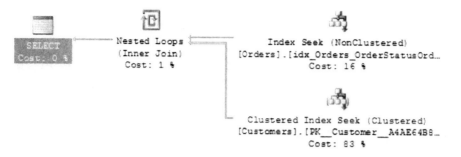

*Figure 3-1. Execution plan 1.*

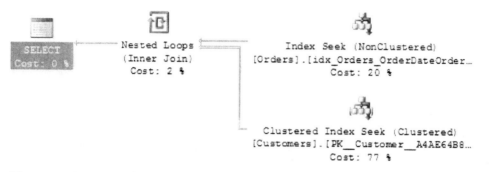

*Figure 3-2. Execution plan 2.*

At first glance, those two execution plans look pretty much the same, except for some slight differences in the relative cost percentages. They also look rather optimal (with two index seeks and a loop join). But what if I tell you that the execution statistics for the two executions were quite different?

Execution plan 1:

Table 'Worktable'. Scan count 0, logical reads 0.

Table 'Orders'. Scan count 1, logical reads 5.

Table 'Customers'. Scan count 1, logical reads 4.


SQL Server Execution Times:

   CPU time = 0 ms,  elapsed time = 1 ms.


Execution plan 2:

Table 'Worktable'. Scan count 0, logical reads 0.

Table 'Orders'. Scan count 1, logical reads 301.

Table 'Customers'. Scan count 1, logical reads 4.

SQL Server Execution Times:

CPU time = 0 ms, elapsed time = 4 ms.

You can see that there are 5 reads against the Orders table in execution plan 1, compared with 301 reads against the Orders table in execution plan 2, and both are index seek operations. What causes that difference?

Quite simply, it has to do with when, in the execution of the index seek, SQL Server evaluates the predicates. Let's take a closer look at the execution plans—specifically, at the properties of the index seek (as shown in Figure 3-3).

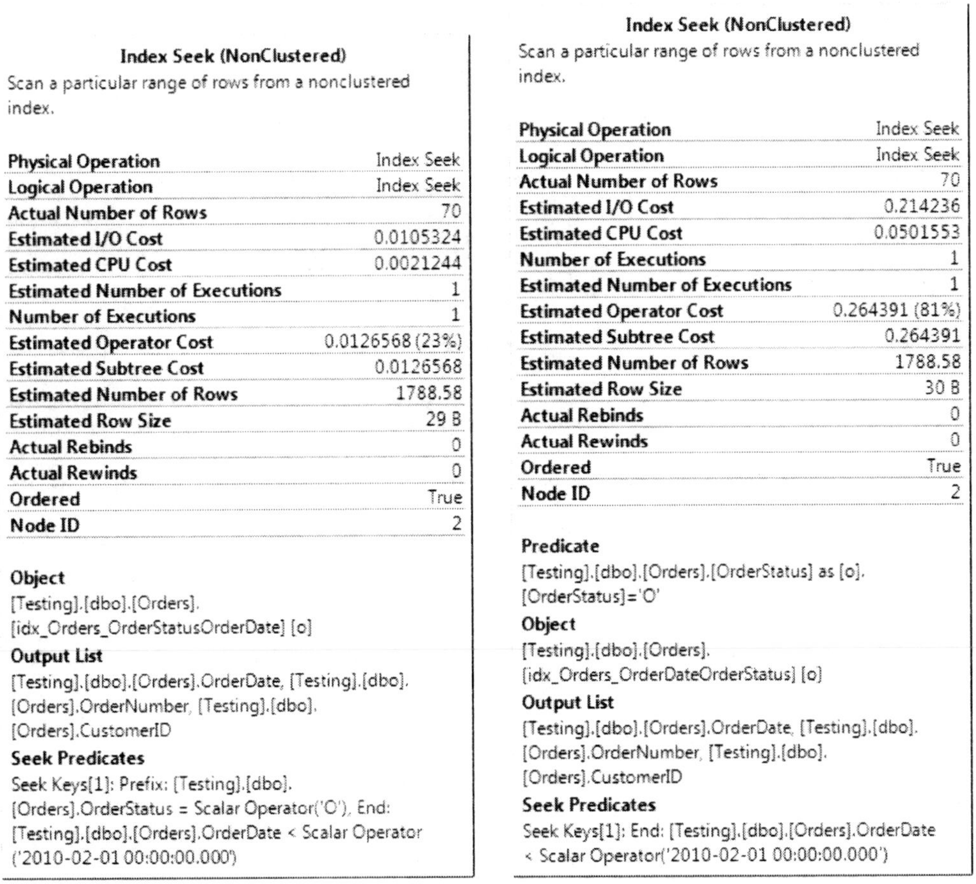

**Index Seek (NonClustered)**

Scan a particular range of rows from a nonclustered index.

| | |
|---|---|
| **Physical Operation** | Index Seek |
| **Logical Operation** | Index Seek |
| **Actual Number of Rows** | 70 |
| **Estimated I/O Cost** | 0.0105324 |
| **Estimated CPU Cost** | 0.0021244 |
| **Estimated Number of Executions** | 1 |
| **Number of Executions** | 1 |
| **Estimated Operator Cost** | 0.0126568 (23%) |
| **Estimated Subtree Cost** | 0.0126568 |
| **Estimated Number of Rows** | 1788.58 |
| **Estimated Row Size** | 29 B |
| **Actual Rebinds** | 0 |
| **Actual Rewinds** | 0 |
| **Ordered** | True |
| **Node ID** | 2 |

**Object**
[Testing].[dbo].[Orders].
[idx_Orders_OrderStatusOrderDate] [o]
**Output List**
[Testing].[dbo].[Orders].OrderDate, [Testing].[dbo].
[Orders].OrderNumber, [Testing].[dbo].
[Orders].CustomerID
**Seek Predicates**
Seek Keys[1]: Prefix: [Testing].[dbo].
[Orders].OrderStatus = Scalar Operator('O'), End:
[Testing].[dbo].[Orders].OrderDate < Scalar Operator
('2010-02-01 00:00:00.000')

**Index Seek (NonClustered)**

Scan a particular range of rows from a nonclustered index.

| | |
|---|---|
| **Physical Operation** | Index Seek |
| **Logical Operation** | Index Seek |
| **Actual Number of Rows** | 70 |
| **Estimated I/O Cost** | 0.214236 |
| **Estimated CPU Cost** | 0.0501553 |
| **Number of Executions** | 1 |
| **Estimated Number of Executions** | 1 |
| **Estimated Operator Cost** | 0.264391 (81%) |
| **Estimated Subtree Cost** | 0.264391 |
| **Estimated Number of Rows** | 1788.58 |
| **Estimated Row Size** | 30 B |
| **Actual Rebinds** | 0 |
| **Actual Rewinds** | 0 |
| **Ordered** | True |
| **Node ID** | 2 |

**Predicate**
[Testing].[dbo].[Orders].[OrderStatus] as [o].
[OrderStatus]='O'
**Object**
[Testing].[dbo].[Orders].
[idx_Orders_OrderDateOrderStatus] [o]
**Output List**
[Testing].[dbo].[Orders].OrderDate, [Testing].[dbo].
[Orders].OrderNumber, [Testing].[dbo].
[Orders].CustomerID
**Seek Predicates**
Seek Keys[1]: End: [Testing].[dbo].[Orders].OrderDate
< Scalar Operator('2010-02-01 00:00:00.000')

*Figure 3-3. Optimal Index Seek (left) and a less-optimal Index Seek (right).*

You might have noticed that the index names are different in the two displayed execution plans, and that is indeed the case. The indexes that SQL used for the two seeks were different (although the data returned was the same). That difference, although it did not result in a difference in execution plan operators that were used between the two queries, did result in a difference in performance. This difference is related to the properties shown in the Index Seek tooltips, the seek predicate (which both queries had), and the predicate (which only the not-so-optimal one had).

One thing to note, the actual row count shown in those tooltips is the number of rows that the operator output, not the number of rows that it processed. The total number of rows that the index seek actually read is not shown in the tooltip. The way to get a rough idea of that is to look at the Statistics IO and examine the logical reads (the number of pages read from memory) for the table that the index seek operates on. It's not a perfect way to do it, but it's usually adequate.

To understand the difference between the performance of those two queries, we need to make a brief diversion into index architecture and how index seeks work.

An index is a b-tree (balanced tree) structure with the data at the leaf level logically ordered by the index keys, as shown in Figure 3-4.

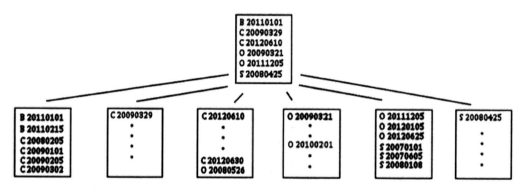

**Figure 3-4.** *Index architecture of an index on OrderStatus, OrderDate.*

An index seek operation works by navigating down the b-tree to the start (or sometimes end) of the required range and reading along the leaf level until the no more rows could possibly qualify. The seek predicate that is listed in the properties of the index seek is the condition used to locate the start (or end) of the range.

So let's look at the two scenarios that are shown in the example.

In the first case, the optimal index seek, the seek predicate consisted of both the where clause expressions for the table. Hence, SQL was able to navigate directly to the start—or, in this particular case, the end—of the range of rows, and it was then able to read along the index leaf level until it encountered a row that no longer matched the filter. Because both of the where clause expressions on this table were used as seek predicates, every row read could be returned without further calculations being done.

In the second case, only one of the where clause expressions was used as a seek predicate. SQL again could navigate to the end of the range and read along the index leaf level until it encountered a row that no longer matched the seek predicate. However, because there was an additional filter (the one listed in the predicate section of the index seek properties), every row that was read from the index leaf had to be compared to this secondary predicate and would be returned only if it qualified for that predicate as well. This means that far more work was done in this case than for the first case.

What caused the difference? In the example, it was because the index column orders were different for the two examples.

The where clause for the query was OrderStatus = '0' AND OrderDate < '2010/02/01'.

In the first example—the one with the optimal index seek—the index was defined on the columns OrderStatus, OrderDate. In the second example—the one with the not-so-optimal index seek—the column order was OrderDate, OrderStatus.

Let's have another look at index architecture and see how those differ. See Figure 3-5.

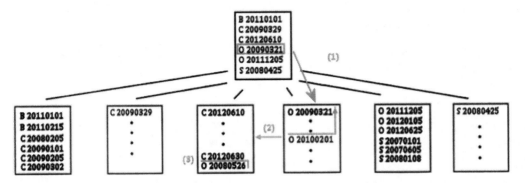

*Figure 3-5. Index seek execution with an index on OrderStatus, OrderDate.*

With the first index ordered by OrderStatus, OrderDate, SQL could execute the seek by navigating down the b-tree looking for the row that matched one end of that range, seeking on both columns (1). In this case, it searched for the row at the upper end, because that inequality is unbounded below. When it found that row, it could read along the leaf level of the index (2) until it encountered a row that did not match either (or both) predicates. In this case, because the inequality is unbounded below, it would be the first row that had an OrderStatus not 'O' (3). When that's done, there's no additional work required to get matching rows. That index seek read only the data that was actually required for that query.

Now, what about the other index—the one that had the columns in the other order? Take a look at Figure 3-6.

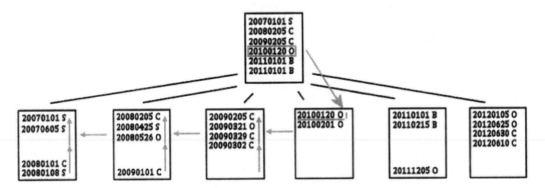

*Figure 3-6. Index seek execution with an index on OrderDate, OrderStatus.*

In the second case, SQL can still navigate down the b-tree looking for the row that matches one end (the upper end) of the range using both columns. This time, though, when it reads along the leaf level of the index, it can't just read the rows that match both predicates, because the index is ordered first by the date and only within that by the OrderStatus. So all rows that match the OrderDate predicate must be read, and then a secondary filter must be applied to each row to see if it matches the OrderStatus. This secondary filter is what is shown in the tooltip as the predicate.

The reduced efficiency comes from two things. First, more rows are read than is necessary. Second, the evaluation of the filter requires computational resources. It doesn't require a lot, but if the secondary filter has to be applied to millions of rows, that's going to add up.

A more dramatic form of the secondary filter is when there is no where clause predicate that can be used as a seek predicate and, hence, SQL performs an index scan and applies the predicate to all rows returned from the index scan. Say, for example, I amend the earlier example and remove the where clause predicate on OrderStatus, but the only index is one with OrderStatus as the leading column. The plan for this new query is shown in Figure 3-7, along with the results.

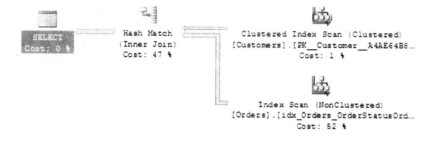

| **Index Scan (NonClustered)** | |
| --- | --- |
| Scan a nonclustered index, entirely or only a range. | |
| **Physical Operation** | Index Scan |
| **Logical Operation** | Index Scan |
| **Actual Number of Rows** | 45442 |
| **Estimated I/O Cost** | 0.260162 |
| **Estimated CPU Cost** | 0.066157 |
| **Estimated Number of Executions** | 1 |
| **Number of Executions** | 1 |
| **Estimated Operator Cost** | 0.326319 (52%) |
| **Estimated Subtree Cost** | 0.326319 |
| **Estimated Number of Rows** | 45453 |
| **Estimated Row Size** | 29 B |
| **Actual Rebinds** | 0 |
| **Actual Rewinds** | 0 |
| **Ordered** | False |
| **Node ID** | 2 |

**Predicate**
[Testing].[dbo].[Orders].[OrderDate] as [o].[OrderDate]
< '2010-02-01 00:00:00.000'
**Object**
[Testing].[dbo].[Orders].
[idx_Orders_OrderStatusOrderDate] [o]
**Output List**
[Testing].[dbo].[Orders].OrderDate, [Testing].[dbo].
[Orders].OrderNumber, [Testing].[dbo].
[Orders].CustomerID

***Figure 3-7.*** *Index scan with a predicate on the OrderDate column*

This results in an index scan with a predicate. (There's no seek predicate. If it had one, it would be a seek, not a scan.) This means that every row gets read from the table and then tested against the OrderDate predicate.

So what causes this? There are a number of things. The most common are the following:

- The order of the columns in the index are not perfect for this query or necessary columns are not in the index at all.

- Any functions applied to the columns.

- Any implicit conversations.

I showed the order of the columns in the previous example. I can't go into a full discussion of indexes here; that's a topic large enough to need a chapter of its own. In short, SQL can use a column or set of columns for an index seek operation only if those columns are a left-based subset of the index key, as explained in a moment.

Let's say you have a query that has a where clause of the following form:

```
WHERE Col1 = @Var1 and Col3 = @Var3
```

If there is an index (for example, Col1, Col2, Col3), SQL can use that index to seek on the Col1 predicate as it is the left-most (or first) column in the index key definition. However, Col3 is not the second column, it's the third. Hence, SQL cannot perform a seek on both Col1 and Col3. Instead, it has to seek on Col1 and execute a secondary filter on Col3. The properties of the index seek for that query would show a seek predicate on Col1 and a predicate on Col3.

Now consider if you have the same index (Col1, Col2, Col3) and a query with a where clause of the form:

```
WHERE Col1 = @Var1 and Col2 = @Var2
```

Now the two columns referenced in the where clause are the two left-most columns in the index key (first and second in the index key definition) and hence SQL can seek on both columns.

For further details on index column ordering, see these two blog posts:

- http://sqlinthewild.co.za/index.php/2009/01/19/index-columns-selectivity-and-equality-predicates/

- http://sqlinthewild.co.za/index.php/2009/02/06/index-columns-selectivity-and-inequality-predicates/

There's another form of the secondary, where one of the columns required is not even part of the index used. Let's take this example:

```
SELECT OrderID
FROM Orders
WHERE SubTotal < 0 AND OrderDate > '2012/01/01'
```

Assume you have an index on SubTotal only and that the column OrderDate is not part of that index at all. SQL knows from the statistics it has that very few rows satisfy the SubTotal < 0 predicate. (Actually, none do, but there's no constraint on the column preventing negative values. Hence, SQL cannot assume that there are no rows.) Figure 3-8 shows the execution plan for this query.

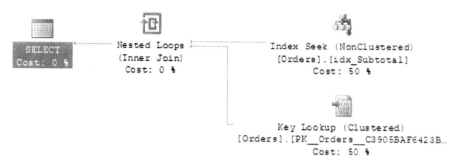

*Figure 3-8. Execution plan with a seek and key lookup.*

You get an index seek on the Subtotal index and a key lookup back to the clustered index, as shown in Figure 3-9.

### Index Seek (NonClustered)
Scan a particular range of rows from a nonclustered index.

| | |
|---|---|
| **Physical Operation** | Index Seek |
| **Logical Operation** | Index Seek |
| **Actual Number of Rows** | 0 |
| **Estimated I/O Cost** | 0.003125 |
| **Estimated CPU Cost** | 0.0001581 |
| **Estimated Number of Executions** | 1 |
| **Number of Executions** | 1 |
| **Estimated Operator Cost** | 0.0032831 (50%) |
| **Estimated Subtree Cost** | 0.0032831 |
| **Estimated Number of Rows** | 1 |
| **Estimated Row Size** | 11 B |
| **Actual Rebinds** | 0 |
| **Actual Rewinds** | 0 |
| Ordered | True |
| Node ID | 1 |

**Object**
[Testing].[dbo].[Orders].[idx_Subtotal]
**Output List**
[Testing].[dbo].[Orders].OrderID
**Seek Predicates**
Seek Keys[1]: End: [Testing].[dbo].[Orders].Subtotal <
Scalar Operator(($0.0000))

*Figure 3-9. Index seek on the Subtotal index with no mention of the OrderDate predicate*

The index seek has only a seek predicate. The key lookup, however, has something interesting in it. It has a predicate, as shown in Figure 3-10.

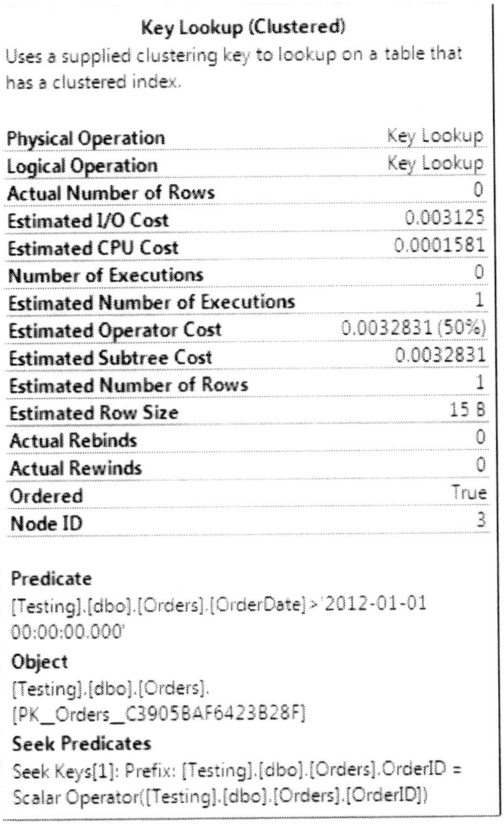

**Key Lookup (Clustered)**
Uses a supplied clustering key to lookup on a table that
has a clustered index.

| | |
|---|---|
| Physical Operation | Key Lookup |
| Logical Operation | Key Lookup |
| Actual Number of Rows | 0 |
| Estimated I/O Cost | 0.003125 |
| Estimated CPU Cost | 0.0001581 |
| Number of Executions | 0 |
| Estimated Number of Executions | 1 |
| Estimated Operator Cost | 0.0032831 (50%) |
| Estimated Subtree Cost | 0.0032831 |
| Estimated Number of Rows | 1 |
| Estimated Row Size | 15 B |
| Actual Rebinds | 0 |
| Actual Rewinds | 0 |
| Ordered | True |
| Node ID | 3 |

**Predicate**
[Testing].[dbo].[Orders].[OrderDate] > '2012-01-01
00:00:00.000'
**Object**
[Testing].[dbo].[Orders].
[PK_Orders_C3905BAF6423B28F]
**Seek Predicates**
Seek Keys[1]: Prefix: [Testing].[dbo].[Orders].OrderID =
Scalar Operator([Testing].[dbo].[Orders].[OrderID])

*Figure 3-10. Key lookup with a predicate.*

What's happening here is that the index seek could evaluate only the SubTotal < 0 predicate because the OrderDate column was nowhere within the index. To get that column, SQL had to do key lookups back to the clustered index to fetch it. However, that column isn't needed for output—because it's not in the select clause—it's needed only for the where clause predicate. Hence, each row fetched by the key lookup is filtered, within the key lookup operator, to discard any rows that don't match the OrderDate predicate, and only rows that do match get returned from the key lookup.

Another common cause of inefficient index usage and secondary filters is the use of functions on the column in the where clause of the query. Consider the case of the table used in the example earlier, with the index on OrderStatus, OrderDate. Suppose you have an index on OrderStatus, OrderDate and the following where clause:

```
WHERE OrderStatus = 'S' AND DATEADD(mm,1, OrderDate) > GETDATE()
```

In other words, get all orders with a status of S that have order dates in the last month. Figure 3-11 shows part of the execution plan for that.

**Index Seek (NonClustered)**

Scan a particular range of rows from a nonclustered index.

| | |
|---|---|
| **Physical Operation** | Index Seek |
| **Logical Operation** | Index Seek |
| **Actual Number of Rows** | 1829 |
| **Estimated I/O Cost** | 0.0451109 |
| **Estimated CPU Cost** | 0.0110965 |
| **Number of Executions** | 1 |
| **Estimated Number of Executions** | 1 |
| **Estimated Operator Cost** | 0.0562074 (100%) |
| **Estimated Subtree Cost** | 0.0562074 |
| **Estimated Number of Rows** | 397.651 |
| **Estimated Row Size** | 19 B |
| **Actual Rebinds** | 0 |
| **Actual Rewinds** | 0 |
| **Ordered** | True |
| **Node ID** | 0 |

**Predicate**
dateadd(month,(1),[Testing].[dbo].[Orders].[OrderDate])
>getdate()
**Object**
[Testing].[dbo].[Orders].
[idx_Orders_OrderStatusOrderDate]
**Output List**
[Testing].[dbo].[Orders].OrderID
**Seek Predicates**
Seek Keys[1]: Prefix: [Testing].[dbo].[Orders].OrderStatus
= Scalar Operator('S')

*Figure 3-11. Index seek with a function resulting in a predicate.*

The reason you have a predicate here and not just two seek predicates is that as soon as there is a function on the column, the where clause predicate that contains that function can no longer be used for an index seek. This is because the index is built on the column, not on function(column).

These kinds of predicates are often referred to as not being SARGable, (SARG standing for Search ARGument), a phrase that just means that the predicate cannot be used for index seek operations.

The third thing that can result in SQL having to apply secondary filters is the implicit conversion. Consider this common scenario:

```
WHERE VarcharColumn = @NVarcharParameter
```

The data types of the column and the parameter are different. SQL cannot compare two different data types, so one has to be converted to match the other. Which one is converted depends on the precedence rules of data types (http://msdn.microsoft.com/en-us/library/ms190309.aspx). In this case, the nvarchar data type has higher precedence than varchar, so the column must be converted to match the data type of the parameter. That query is essentially WHERE CAST(VarcharColumn AS NVARCHAR(<Column Length>) = @NVarcharParameter. That's a function on the column. As in the previous discussion, this means that the predicate cannot be used for an index seek operation (it's not SARGable) and can be applied only as a secondary predicate.

So, you've seen several causes. Now let's look at what you can do about these.

The first thing to note is that the predicates are not always a problem. It is not always important to remove them. What is important to investigate before spending time trying to change indexes or rewrite queries is the number of rows involved. Specifically, you should determine the number of rows returned by the seek predicate and what proportion of them are then removed by the predicate.

Consider the following two scenarios: one where the seek predicate returns 100,000 rows and the predicate then eliminates 5 rows, for a total of 99,995 rows returned; and one where the seek predicate returns 100,000 rows and the predicate then removes 99,500 rows, for a total of 500 rows returned. The second scenario is a bigger problem and a bigger concern than the first.

Why? Because one of the primary goals for an index is to eliminate unnecessary rows as early as possible in the query's execution. If a row is not needed, it is better not to read it at all rather than read it and then eliminate it with a filter. The first approach is efficient; the second approach is a waste of time and resources.

In the initial example in this chapter, the efficient option read 5 pages from the table and the inefficient option read over 300. That difference is sufficient to warrant investigation. However, if the efficient option had read 100 pages and the inefficient one had read 108, it wouldn't be particularly worthwhile spending the time resolving the problem. You could find bigger wins elsewhere.

The first step, of course, is finding queries that have these problems. Probably the easiest way to do this is as part of regular performance tuning. Capture a workload with SQL Profiler or an extended events session, analyze it for queries doing excessive reads, and as part of the analysis see if they have inefficient index seeks.

The resolution depends on what specifically is causing the inefficient seek.

If the problem is the column order within the index, the solution is to change the order of columns in the index or create another index to fully support the query. Which option is best (and, in fact, whether either is desirable) depends on other queries that run against the particular table, the amount of data modifications that take place, the importance of the query, and how inefficient it really is. Unfortunately, a complete discussion on indexing changes is beyond the scope of this chapter.

If the cause of the inefficient seek is a function applied to a column, it's a lot easier to resolve. Just remove the function.

Well, maybe it's not that simple. It depends on what the function is doing as to whether it can be removed or altered.

In some cases, you can apply a function to the variable, parameter, or literal instead of the column to get the same results. An example of this is the following:

```
WHERE Subtotal * 1.14 >= @MinimumDiscount
```

The execution plan is shown in Figure 3-12.

**Index Scan (NonClustered)**

Scan a nonclustered index, entirely or only a range.

| | |
|---|---|
| **Physical Operation** | Index Scan |
| **Logical Operation** | Index Scan |
| **Actual Number of Rows** | 0 |
| **Estimated I/O Cost** | 0.103125 |
| **Estimated CPU Cost** | 0.066157 |
| **Estimated Number of Executions** | 1 |
| **Number of Executions** | 1 |
| **Estimated Operator Cost** | 0.169282 (100%) |
| **Estimated Subtree Cost** | 0.169282 |
| **Estimated Number of Rows** | 1 |
| **Estimated Row Size** | 19 B |
| **Actual Rebinds** | 0 |
| **Actual Rewinds** | 0 |
| **Ordered** | False |
| **Node ID** | 0 |

**Predicate**
CONVERT_IMPLICIT(numeric(19,4),[Testing].[dbo].
[Orders].[Subtotal],0)*[@1]>=CONVERT_IMPLICIT
(numeric(23,6),[@2],0)
**Object**
[Testing].[dbo].[Orders].[idx_Subtotal]
**Output List**
[Testing].[dbo].[Orders].OrderID

*Figure 3-12. Scan caused by a function on the column in the where clause.*

The multiplication that is applied to the column means that any index on Subtotal cannot be used for an index seek. If there is another predicate in the where clause, SQL might be able to seek on that and apply a secondary filter on Subtotal. Otherwise, the query has to be executed as an index scan with a secondary filter.

Basic algebra tells you that the expression $x*y >= z$ is completely equivalent to $x >= z/y$ (unless $y$ is zero), so you can change that where clause to read as follows:

```
WHERE Subtotal  >= (@MinimumDiscount/1.14)
```

This example is not quite as intuitive as the first one, but it is more efficient, as Figure 3-13 shows.

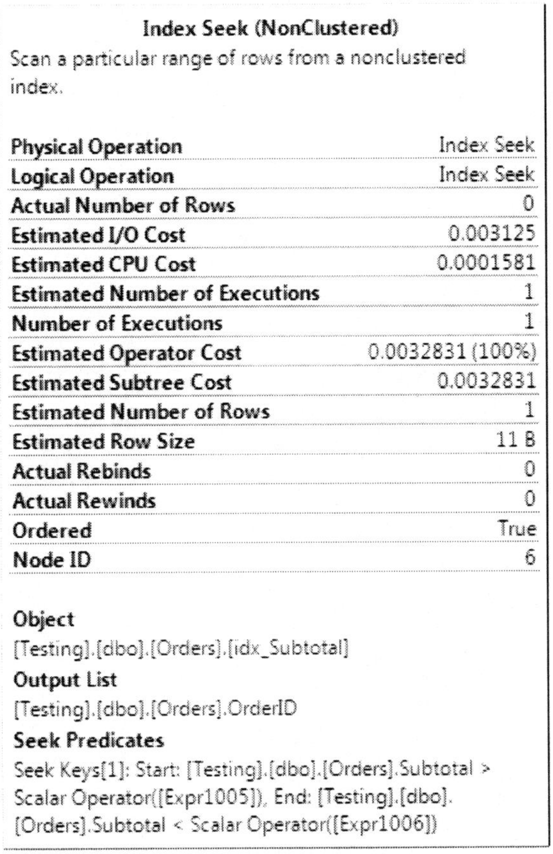

**Index Seek (NonClustered)**

Scan a particular range of rows from a nonclustered index.

| | |
|---|---|
| **Physical Operation** | Index Seek |
| **Logical Operation** | Index Seek |
| **Actual Number of Rows** | 0 |
| **Estimated I/O Cost** | 0.003125 |
| **Estimated CPU Cost** | 0.0001581 |
| **Estimated Number of Executions** | 1 |
| **Number of Executions** | 1 |
| **Estimated Operator Cost** | 0.0032831 (100%) |
| **Estimated Subtree Cost** | 0.0032831 |
| **Estimated Number of Rows** | 1 |
| **Estimated Row Size** | 11 B |
| **Actual Rebinds** | 0 |
| **Actual Rewinds** | 0 |
| **Ordered** | True |
| **Node ID** | 6 |

**Object**
[Testing].[dbo].[Orders].[idx_Subtotal]
**Output List**
[Testing].[dbo].[Orders].OrderID
**Seek Predicates**
Seek Keys[1]: Start: [Testing].[dbo].[Orders].Subtotal >
Scalar Operator([Expr1005]), End: [Testing].[dbo].
[Orders].Subtotal < Scalar Operator([Expr1006])

*Figure 3-13. Changing where the function is evaluated results in an index seek.*

Another common case is date functions, especially if a date is stored with its time in the database and the query needs to fetch all rows for a particular day. It's common to see queries like this:

```
WHERE CAST(OrderDate AS DATE) = @SpecificDate
```

The cast to date eliminates the time portion of the datetime, so the comparison to a date returns all rows for that day. However, this is not a particularly efficient way of doing things, as you can see in Figure 3-14.

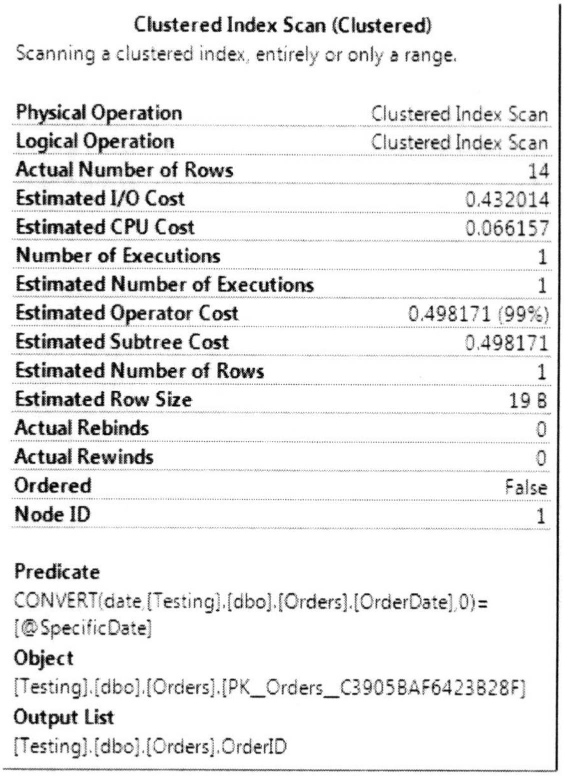

**Clustered Index Scan (Clustered)**

Scanning a clustered index, entirely or only a range.

| | |
|---|---|
| **Physical Operation** | Clustered Index Scan |
| **Logical Operation** | Clustered Index Scan |
| **Actual Number of Rows** | 14 |
| **Estimated I/O Cost** | 0.432014 |
| **Estimated CPU Cost** | 0.066157 |
| **Number of Executions** | 1 |
| **Estimated Number of Executions** | 1 |
| **Estimated Operator Cost** | 0.498171 (99%) |
| **Estimated Subtree Cost** | 0.498171 |
| **Estimated Number of Rows** | 1 |
| **Estimated Row Size** | 19 B |
| **Actual Rebinds** | 0 |
| **Actual Rewinds** | 0 |
| Ordered | False |
| Node ID | 1 |

**Predicate**
CONVERT(date,[Testing].[dbo].[Orders].[OrderDate],0)=
[@SpecificDate]
**Object**
[Testing].[dbo].[Orders].[PK_Orders__C3905BAF6423B28F]
**Output List**
[Testing].[dbo].[Orders].OrderID

*Figure 3-14. Conversion of the column to DATE results in a scan.*

Instead, the query can be rewritten to use an inequality predicate and search for a range of times for the particular day, like this:

```
WHERE OrderDate >= @SpecificDate and OrderDate < DATEADD(dd,1,@SpecificDate)
```

I don't use BETWEEN because BETWEEN is inclusive on both sides and requires slightly more complex date manipulation if the rows with an OrderDate of midnight the next day are not required.

This form of the where clause is more complex, but it is also more efficient, as Figure 3-15 shows.

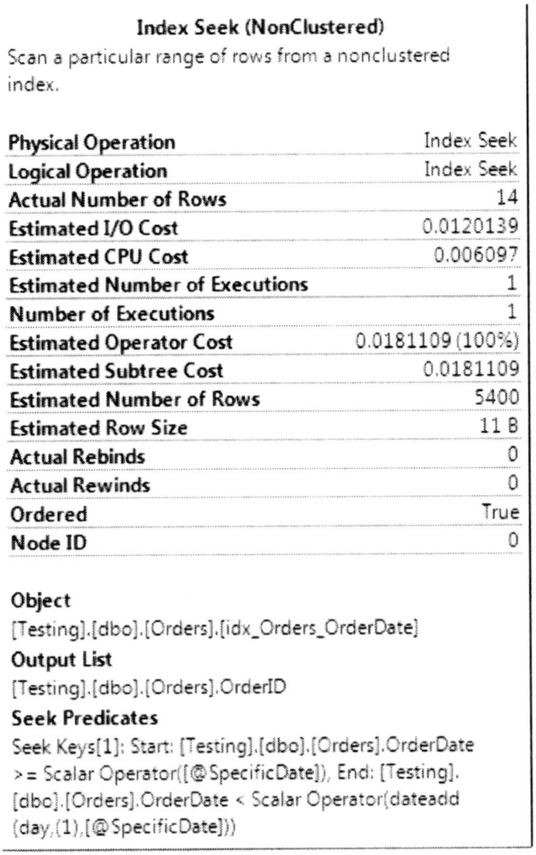

**Index Seek (NonClustered)**
Scan a particular range of rows from a nonclustered index.

| | |
|---|---|
| Physical Operation | Index Seek |
| Logical Operation | Index Seek |
| Actual Number of Rows | 14 |
| Estimated I/O Cost | 0.0120139 |
| Estimated CPU Cost | 0.006097 |
| Estimated Number of Executions | 1 |
| Number of Executions | 1 |
| Estimated Operator Cost | 0.0181109 (100%) |
| Estimated Subtree Cost | 0.0181109 |
| Estimated Number of Rows | 5400 |
| Estimated Row Size | 11 B |
| Actual Rebinds | 0 |
| Actual Rewinds | 0 |
| Ordered | True |
| Node ID | 0 |

**Object**
[Testing].[dbo].[Orders].[idx_Orders_OrderDate]
**Output List**
[Testing].[dbo].[Orders].OrderID
**Seek Predicates**
Seek Keys[1]: Start: [Testing].[dbo].[Orders].OrderDate
>= Scalar Operator([@SpecificDate]), End: [Testing].
[dbo].[Orders].OrderDate < Scalar Operator(dateadd
(day,(1),[@SpecificDate]))

*Figure 3-15. No function on the column; hence, a seek is used.*

A third case is unnecessary string functions. I keep seeing code like this:

```
WHERE UPPER(LTRIM(RTRIM(LastName))) = 'SMITH'
```

Unless the database is running a case-sensitive collation, UPPER is unnecessary (and I often see this in case-insensitive databases). RTRIM is unnecessary because SQL ignores trailing spaces when comparing strings. So 'abc' equals 'abc ' when SQL does string comparisons. Otherwise, how would it compare a CHAR(4) and a CHAR(10)? LTRIM potentially has a use if the database is known to have messy data in it. My preference here is to ensure that inserts and loads always remove any leading spaces that might creep in. Then the queries that retrieve the data don't need to worry about leading spaces and, hence, don't need to use LTRIM.

The implicit conversion is probably the easiest problem to fix (though it's often one of the harder ones to find). It's mostly a case of ensuring that parameters and variables match the column types; of explicitly casting literals, variables, or parameters if necessary; and ensuring that front-end apps are passing the correct types if they are using dynamic or parameterized SQL statements.

A common culprit here is JDBC (the Java data access library), which by default sends strings through as nvarchar no matter what they really are. In some cases when dealing with this, you might need to alter the column's data type to nvarchar just to avoid the implicit conversions if the application cannot be changed. Some ORM tools show the same default behavior.

One implication of this discussion that I need to draw particular attention to is that not all index seeks are equal, and just having an index seek in a query's execution plan is no guarantee that the query is efficient.

I recall a discussion on a SQL forum a while back where someone was asking how to get rid of the clustered index scan that he had in his query execution plan. The pertinent portion of the query was something like this:

```
WHERE CAST(OrderDate AS DATE) = @SpecificDate
```

As mentioned earlier, the way to optimize that query is to remove the function from the column, change the where clause to use either BETWEEN or >= and < operators, and ensure that there's a suitable index on the OrderDate column to support the query. The solution that someone posted was to add a second predicate to the where clause, specifically an inequality predicate on the primary key column (which was an integer and had the identity property with default seed and increment, and hence was always greater than 0) as such:

```
WHERE CAST(OrderDate AS DATE) = @SpecificDate AND OrderID > 0
```

Does that achieve the desired goal? Figure 3-16 has part of the answer.

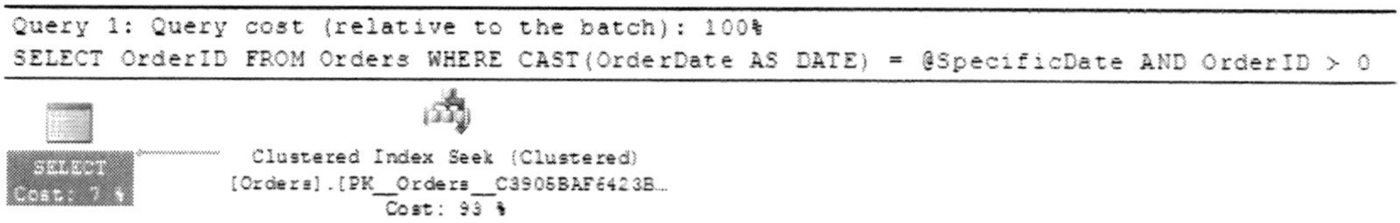

*Figure 3-16. Clustered index seek.*

It seems to achieve the desired goal because there's a clustered index seek now. But what's that seek actually doing? See Figure 3-17.

**Clustered Index Seek (Clustered)**

Scanning a particular range of rows from a clustered index.

| | |
|---|---|
| **Physical Operation** | Clustered Index Seek |
| **Logical Operation** | Clustered Index Seek |
| **Actual Number of Rows** | 14 |
| **Estimated I/O Cost** | 0.432014 |
| **Estimated CPU Cost** | 0.066157 |
| **Number of Executions** | 1 |
| **Estimated Number of Executions** | 1 |
| **Estimated Operator Cost** | 0.498171 (93%) |
| **Estimated Subtree Cost** | 0.498171 |
| **Estimated Number of Rows** | 1 |
| **Estimated Row Size** | 19 B |
| **Actual Rebinds** | 0 |
| **Actual Rewinds** | 0 |
| **Ordered** | True |
| **Node ID** | 1 |

**Predicate**
CONVERT(date.[Testing].[dbo].[Orders].[OrderDate],0)=
[@SpecificDate]
**Object**
[Testing].[dbo].[Orders].[PK__Orders__C3905BAF6423B28F]
**Output List**
[Testing].[dbo].[Orders].OrderID
**Seek Predicates**
Seek Keys[1]: Start: [Testing].[dbo].[Orders].OrderID > Scalar
Operator((0))

*Figure 3-17. Very inefficient clustered index seek.*

The seek predicate OrderID > 0 matches every single row of the table. It's not eliminating anything. (If it did, adding it would change the meaning of the query, which would be bad anyway.) The predicate is the same as it was before on the index scan. It's still being applied to every row returned from the seek (which is every row in the table), so it's just as inefficient as the query was before adding the OrderID > 0 predicate to the where clause. An examination of the output of statistics IO (which I will leave as an exercise to the reader) will show that adding that OrderID > 0 predicate made no improvements to the efficiency of the query.

Be aware, not all index seeks are created equal and adding predicates to a where clause just so that the execution plan shows a seek rather than a scan is unlikely to do anything but require extra typing.

# Residuals

Moving on to residuals, they are similar in concept to the predicates on index seeks, index scans, and key lookups, but they are found in a different place. They're found on joins, mainly on merge and hash joins. (Residuals on a loop join usually show up as predicates on the inner or outer table, or sometimes both.)

Let's start with an example:

```
SELECT   *
FROM     dbo.Shifts AS s
         INNER JOIN dbo.ShiftDetails AS sd
         ON s.EmployeeID = sd.EmployeeID
AND s.ShiftStartDate BETWEEN sd.ShiftStartDate AND DATEADD(ms,-3,DATEADD(dd,1,
sd.ShiftStartDate))
WHERE  CAST(sd.ShiftStartDate AS DATETIME) > '2012/06/01'
```

The plan for this query is shown in Figure 3-18.

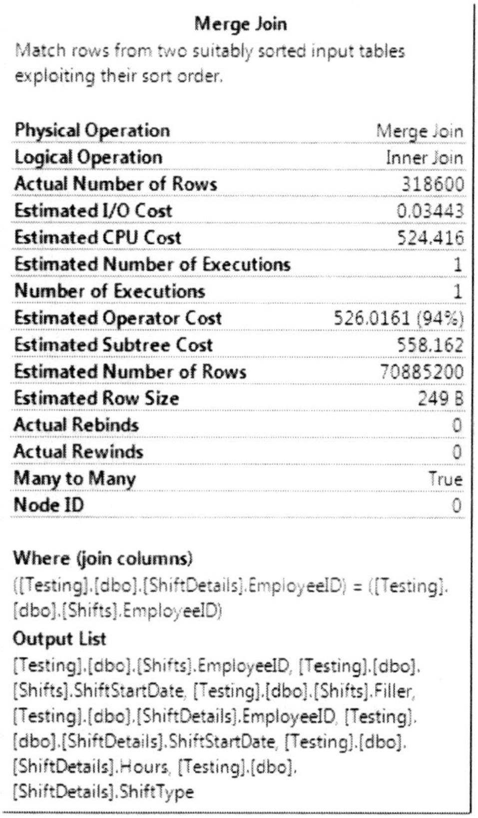

**Merge Join**

Match rows from two suitably sorted input tables
exploiting their sort order.

| | |
|---|---|
| **Physical Operation** | Merge Join |
| **Logical Operation** | Inner Join |
| **Actual Number of Rows** | 318600 |
| **Estimated I/O Cost** | 0.03443 |
| **Estimated CPU Cost** | 524.416 |
| **Estimated Number of Executions** | 1 |
| **Number of Executions** | 1 |
| **Estimated Operator Cost** | 526.0161 (94%) |
| **Estimated Subtree Cost** | 558.162 |
| **Estimated Number of Rows** | 70885200 |
| **Estimated Row Size** | 249 B |
| **Actual Rebinds** | 0 |
| **Actual Rewinds** | 0 |
| **Many to Many** | True |
| **Node ID** | 0 |

**Where (join columns)**
([Testing].[dbo].[ShiftDetails].EmployeeID) = ([Testing].
[dbo].[Shifts].EmployeeID)
**Output List**
[Testing].[dbo].[Shifts].EmployeeID, [Testing].[dbo].
[Shifts].ShiftStartDate, [Testing].[dbo].[Shifts].Filler,
[Testing].[dbo].[ShiftDetails].EmployeeID, [Testing].
[dbo].[ShiftDetails].ShiftStartDate, [Testing].[dbo].
[ShiftDetails].Hours, [Testing].[dbo].
[ShiftDetails].ShiftType

***Figure 3-18.*** *Partial join.*

The tooltip of the join operator shows that the Join columns was EmployeeID only. There's no mention of my date expression. Where did that go? See Figure 3-19 for the answer. It shows that it went into the residual section in the properties of the join operator.

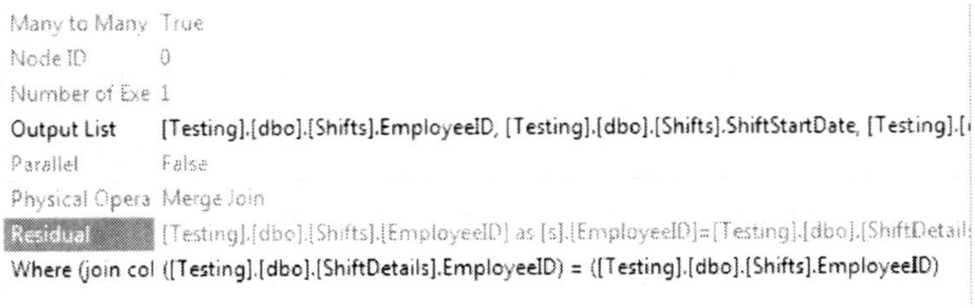

```
Many to Many  True
Node ID       0
Number of Exe 1
Output List   [Testing].[dbo].[Shifts].EmployeeID, [Testing].[dbo].[Shifts].ShiftStartDate, [Testing].[
Parallel      False
Physical Opera Merge Join
Residual      [Testing].[dbo].[Shifts].[EmployeeID] as [s].[EmployeeID]=[Testing].[dbo].[ShiftDetails
Where (join col ([Testing].[dbo].[ShiftDetails].EmployeeID) = ([Testing].[dbo].[Shifts].EmployeeID)
```

*Figure 3-19. Join residual as seen in the properties of the join operator.*

It's hard to see what's happening there, so I repeated it and cleaned it up here:

```
Shifts.EmployeeID =ShiftDetails.EmployeeID
AND Shifts.ShiftStartDate >= CONVERT_IMPLICIT(datetime, ShiftDetails.ShiftStartDate,0)
AND Shifts.ShiftStartDate <= dateadd(millisecond,(-3), dateadd(day,(1),
CONVERT_IMPLICIT(datetime,ShiftDetails.ShiftStartDate, 0)))
```

The join columns just contains the EmployeeID; it's the residual that has both. What's happening here is that SQL evaluates the join on the join columns (in this case, EmployeeID) and then applies the filter listed in the residual to every row that qualifies for the join. If the match on just the join columns isn't very restrictive, you can end up with a huge intermediate result set (a partial cross join, technically) that SQL has to find memory for and has to work through and apply the residual to. This can be seen in the properties of the join, as shown in Figure 3-20.

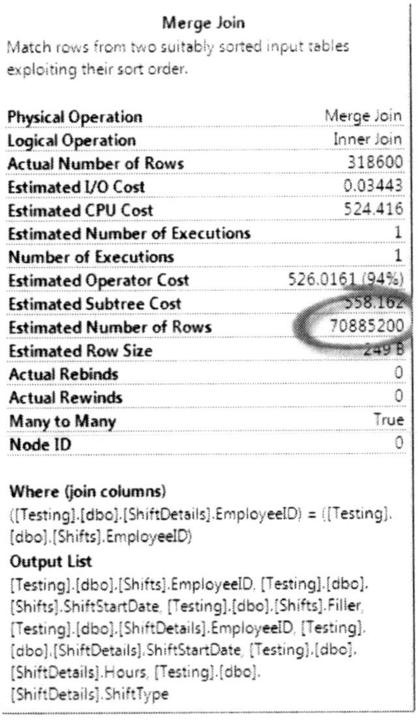

**Merge Join**
Match rows from two suitably sorted input tables exploiting their sort order.

| | |
|---|---|
| **Physical Operation** | Merge Join |
| **Logical Operation** | Inner Join |
| **Actual Number of Rows** | 318600 |
| **Estimated I/O Cost** | 0.03443 |
| **Estimated CPU Cost** | 524.416 |
| **Estimated Number of Executions** | 1 |
| **Number of Executions** | 1 |
| **Estimated Operator Cost** | 526.0161 (94%) |
| **Estimated Subtree Cost** | 558.162 |
| **Estimated Number of Rows** | 70885200 |
| **Estimated Row Size** | 249 B |
| **Actual Rebinds** | 0 |
| **Actual Rewinds** | 0 |
| **Many to Many** | True |
| **Node ID** | 0 |

**Where (join columns)**
([Testing].[dbo].[ShiftDetails].EmployeeID) = ([Testing].
[dbo].[Shifts].EmployeeID)
**Output List**
[Testing].[dbo].[Shifts].EmployeeID, [Testing].[dbo].
[Shifts].ShiftStartDate, [Testing].[dbo].[Shifts].Filler,
[Testing].[dbo].[ShiftDetails].EmployeeID, [Testing].[dbo].
[dbo].[ShiftDetails].ShiftStartDate, [Testing].[dbo].
[ShiftDetails].Hours, [Testing].[dbo].
[ShiftDetails].ShiftType

*Figure 3-20. Many-to-many join with a huge row count.*

There are 70 million rows estimated, and that's estimated based on what SQL knows of the uniqueness of the join columns on each side of the join (and in this case, the EmployeeID is not very unique in either table). The Actual Row Count (as mentioned earlier) is the total rows that the operator output, not the total rows that the join had to work over. In this case, the number of rows that the join operator had to process is a lot higher than the number that were output (probably close to the estimated rows).

Depending on how many rows match on just the join columns (vs. both the join and the residual), this can result in minor overhead or major overhead.

To put things in perspective, the prior example ran for 14 minutes. A fixed version that joined on a direct equality on both EmployeeID and ShiftStartDate and had both predicates listed in the join columns (and returned the same rows) ran in 20 seconds.

Hash joins can also have residuals. The properties of the hash join (shown in Figure 3-21) show the join and the residual slightly differently to the merge.

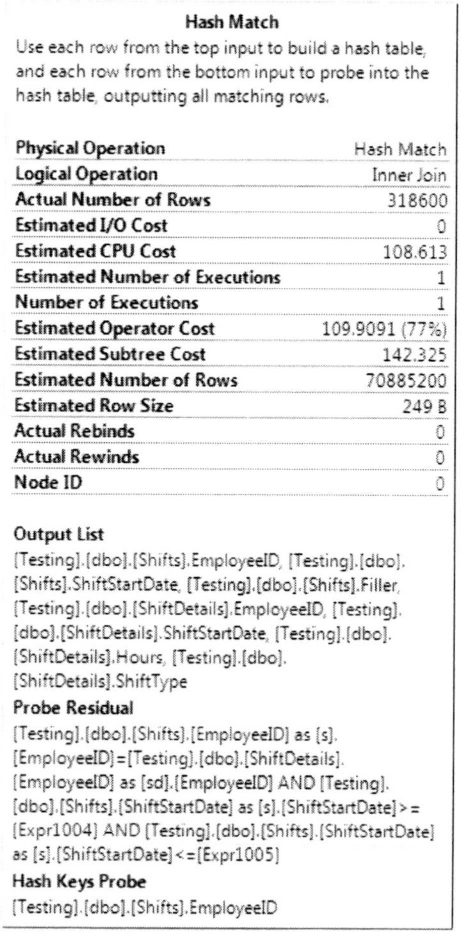

---

**Hash Match**

Use each row from the top input to build a hash table, and each row from the bottom input to probe into the hash table, outputting all matching rows.

| | |
|---|---|
| **Physical Operation** | Hash Match |
| **Logical Operation** | Inner Join |
| **Actual Number of Rows** | 318600 |
| **Estimated I/O Cost** | 0 |
| **Estimated CPU Cost** | 108.613 |
| **Estimated Number of Executions** | 1 |
| **Number of Executions** | 1 |
| **Estimated Operator Cost** | 109.9091 (77%) |
| **Estimated Subtree Cost** | 142.325 |
| **Estimated Number of Rows** | 70885200 |
| **Estimated Row Size** | 249 B |
| **Actual Rebinds** | 0 |
| **Actual Rewinds** | 0 |
| **Node ID** | 0 |

**Output List**
[Testing].[dbo].[Shifts].EmployeeID, [Testing].[dbo].
[Shifts].ShiftStartDate, [Testing].[dbo].[Shifts].Filler,
[Testing].[dbo].[ShiftDetails].EmployeeID, [Testing].
[dbo].[ShiftDetails].ShiftStartDate, [Testing].[dbo].
[ShiftDetails].Hours, [Testing].[dbo].
[ShiftDetails].ShiftType

**Probe Residual**
[Testing].[dbo].[Shifts].[EmployeeID] as [s].
[EmployeeID]=[Testing].[dbo].[ShiftDetails].
[EmployeeID] as [sd].[EmployeeID] AND [Testing].
[dbo].[Shifts].[ShiftStartDate] as [s].[ShiftStartDate]>=
[Expr1004] AND [Testing].[dbo].[Shifts].[ShiftStartDate]
as [s].[ShiftStartDate]<=[Expr1005]

**Hash Keys Probe**
[Testing].[dbo].[Shifts].EmployeeID

*Figure 3-21. Hash join properties.*

The columns that are used to join appear as Hash Keys Probe in the tooltip, and as Hash Keys Build and Hash Keys Probe in the properties of the join operator (as shown in Figure 3-22). The columns for the residual appear in the probe residual in both the tooltip and the properties.

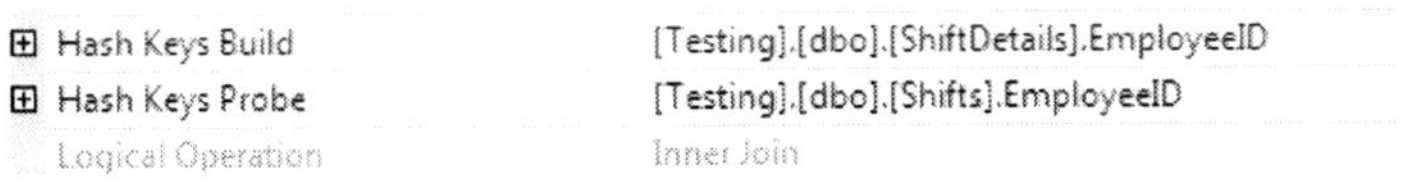

| ⊞ | Hash Keys Build | [Testing].[dbo].[ShiftDetails].EmployeeID |
|---|---|---|
| ⊞ | Hash Keys Probe | [Testing].[dbo].[Shifts].EmployeeID |
| | Logical Operation | Inner Join |

**Figure 3-22.** *Hash join build and probe columns.*

As with the merge join, the number of rows that the residual has to process affects just how bad it will be in terms of performance.

That's all well and good, but how do you fix them?

As with the predicates on index seeks and scans, multiple things can cause residuals.

Unlike predicates, the index column order is not a main cause. Hash joins don't mind the index column order much. Merge joins do because they need both sides of the join to be sorted on the join columns, and indexes do provide an order. However, if the order isn't as the merge wants it, the optimizer can put a sort into the plan or it can use a different join, such as a hash join.

Mismatched data types can result in joins that have residuals, as Figure 3-23 shows. By "mismatched data type," I mean joins where the two columns involved are of different data types. The most common ones I've seen in systems are varchar and nvarchar, varchar and date, and varchar and int.

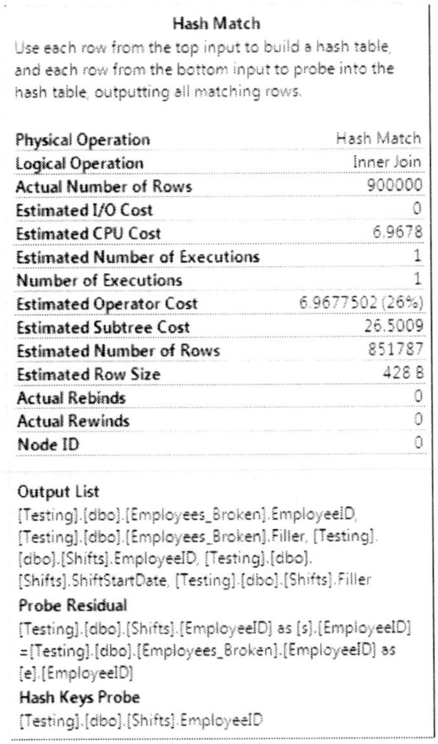

**Hash Match**

Use each row from the top input to build a hash table, and each row from the bottom input to probe into the hash table, outputting all matching rows.

| Physical Operation | Hash Match |
|---|---|
| Logical Operation | Inner Join |
| Actual Number of Rows | 900000 |
| Estimated I/O Cost | 0 |
| Estimated CPU Cost | 6.9678 |
| Estimated Number of Executions | 1 |
| Number of Executions | 1 |
| Estimated Operator Cost | 6.9677502 (26%) |
| Estimated Subtree Cost | 26.5009 |
| Estimated Number of Rows | 851787 |
| Estimated Row Size | 428 B |
| Actual Rebinds | 0 |
| Actual Rewinds | 0 |
| Node ID | 0 |

Output List
[Testing].[dbo].[Employees_Broken].EmployeeID, [Testing].[dbo].[Employees_Broken].Filler, [Testing]. [dbo].[Shifts].EmployeeID, [Testing].[dbo]. [Shifts].ShiftStartDate, [Testing].[dbo].[Shifts].Filler
Probe Residual
[Testing].[dbo].[Shifts].[EmployeeID] as [s].[EmployeeID] =[Testing].[dbo].[Employees_Broken].[EmployeeID] as [e].[EmployeeID]
Hash Keys Probe
[Testing].[dbo].[Shifts].EmployeeID

**Figure 3-23.** *Hash join with a residual caused by a data type mismatch.*

It's not clear from the tooltip shown in Figure 3-23 that any conversions are occurring; even the properties do not show anything wrong. In fact, the presence of the residual is the only hint that something's not right. If you compare that to a query where the data types do match (shown in Figure 3-24), you'll notice that there's no residual in that case.

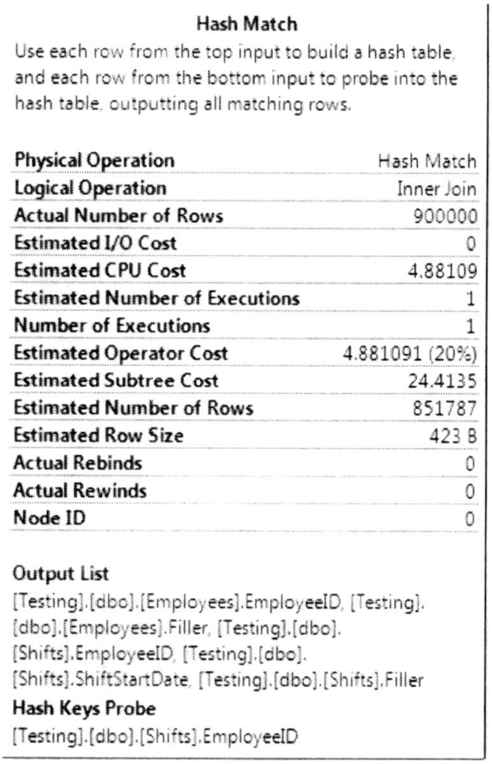

**Hash Match**

Use each row from the top input to build a hash table, and each row from the bottom input to probe into the hash table, outputting all matching rows.

| | |
|---|---|
| Physical Operation | Hash Match |
| Logical Operation | Inner Join |
| Actual Number of Rows | 900000 |
| Estimated I/O Cost | 0 |
| Estimated CPU Cost | 4.88109 |
| Estimated Number of Executions | 1 |
| Number of Executions | 1 |
| Estimated Operator Cost | 4.881091 (20%) |
| Estimated Subtree Cost | 24.4135 |
| Estimated Number of Rows | 851787 |
| Estimated Row Size | 423 B |
| Actual Rebinds | 0 |
| Actual Rewinds | 0 |
| Node ID | 0 |

**Output List**
[Testing].[dbo].[Employees].EmployeeID, [Testing].
[dbo].[Employees].Filler, [Testing].[dbo].
[Shifts].EmployeeID, [Testing].[dbo].
[Shifts].ShiftStartDate, [Testing].[dbo].[Shifts].Filler
**Hash Keys Probe**
[Testing].[dbo].[Shifts].EmployeeID

*Figure 3-24. Hash join without a residual.*

The last cause I'll look at is strange join predicates. By "strange," I mean something like an inequality in the join predicate.

Merge joins and hash joins are both limited to being able to use equality predicates only for the actual join. Anything other than an equality has to be processed as a residual. (Nested loop joins do not have such a limitation.) This was the example I used initially: a join with a between because the date in one table was a date with the time set to midnight, and the date in the other table had a date with a time other than midnight. Hence, the only way to join those was with a between, and that resulted in the inefficient join.

Mismatched data types and non-equality join predicates are often indications of underlying database design problems—not always, but often. Fixing them can be difficult and time consuming. In the case of the mismatched data types, fixing the problem might require altering the data type of one or more columns in a database, or possibly even adding additional columns (usually computed columns) that convert the join column to the matching data type for an efficient join.

Queries that join on inequalities are harder to fix. Although there are certainly legitimate reasons for such a join, they should not be common. The fixes for queries using inequality joins depend very much on the underlying database and how much (if at all) it can be modified.

The example I started the section with has a `Shifts` table with a `ShiftStartDate` that always contains a `datetime` where the date portion is midnight and a `ShiftDetails` table with a `ShiftStartDate` that has dates with time portions that are not midnight, and the join needs to be on the date. To optimize that query and to avoid the inequality join predicate you could add another column to the `ShiftDetails` table that stores the date only. This would likely be a persisted computed column. Of course, that assumes the application using those tables won't break if another column is added.

Fixing these kinds of problems in an existing system is very difficult and, in many cases, is not possible. It is far better to get a correct design up front with appropriate data type usage and properly normalized tables.

# Spills

The third form of hidden performance problem that I want to discuss is the spill. Before I can explain what a spill is, I need to briefly explain what memory grants are.

A *memory grant* is an amount of memory that the query processor will request before it starts executing the query. It's additional memory that the query needs for things like hashes and sorts. The memory grant amount is based on the number of memory-requiring operations, on whether or not the query will be executed in parallel, and on the cardinality estimates in the execution plan.

I don't want to go too deep into the process of requesting and granting that memory; it's not essential for the rest of this section. If you are interested in the topic, you can refer to the following blog entries for further detail: `http://blogs.msdn.com/b/sqlqueryprocessing/archive/2010/02/16/understanding-sql-server-memory-grant.aspx` and `http://www.sqlskills.com/blogs/joe/post/e2809cMemoryGrantInfoe2809d-Execution-Plan-Statistics.aspx`. Also, you can view the presentation that Adam Machanic did at the Pass Summit in 2011 (`http://www.youtube.com/watch?v=j5YGdIk3DXw`)

The use of memory grants is all well and good, but those memory grants are based on cardinality estimates and estimates can be wrong. So what happens when they are wrong?

Let's compare two examples, one with an accurate estimate and one with a badly inaccurate one. (I'll use some hints to force a bad estimate because it's both easier and more repeatable than creating actual stale statistics or simulating other conditions that result in poor estimates.)

The two plans look identical, so I'm not going to show them (two index seeks, a hash join, and a select). I'll just show the properties of the hash joins and of the selects for the two.

The first query, with accurate estimations, is shown in Figure 3-25.

The second query, with poor estimations, is shown in Figure 3-26.

Ignore "Estimated Number of Rows 1" on the tooltip of the select. That shows up because the outer select was a `COUNT (*)`.

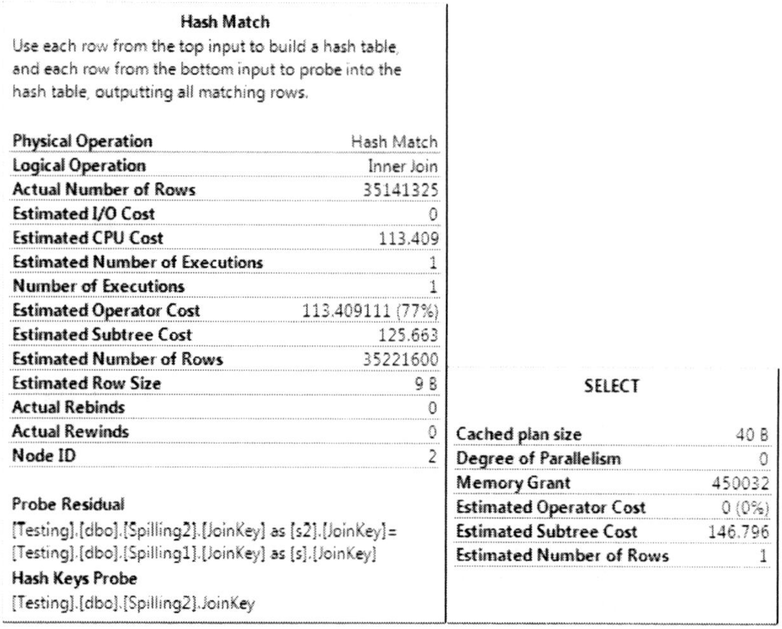

**Hash Match**

Use each row from the top input to build a hash table, and each row from the bottom input to probe into the hash table, outputting all matching rows.

| | |
|---|---|
| Physical Operation | Hash Match |
| Logical Operation | Inner Join |
| Actual Number of Rows | 35141325 |
| Estimated I/O Cost | 0 |
| Estimated CPU Cost | 113.409 |
| Estimated Number of Executions | 1 |
| Number of Executions | 1 |
| Estimated Operator Cost | 113.409111 (77%) |
| Estimated Subtree Cost | 125.663 |
| Estimated Number of Rows | 35221600 |
| Estimated Row Size | 9 B |
| Actual Rebinds | 0 |
| Actual Rewinds | 0 |
| Node ID | 2 |

Probe Residual

[Testing].[dbo].[Spilling2].[JoinKey] as [s2].[JoinKey] =
[Testing].[dbo].[Spilling1].[JoinKey] as [s].[JoinKey]

**Hash Keys Probe**

[Testing].[dbo].[Spilling2].JoinKey

**SELECT**

| | |
|---|---|
| Cached plan size | 40 B |
| Degree of Parallelism | 0 |
| Memory Grant | 450032 |
| Estimated Operator Cost | 0 (0%) |
| Estimated Subtree Cost | 146.796 |
| Estimated Number of Rows | 1 |

*Figure 3-25. Accurate estimations.*

If you take a look at those, the first hash join has an estimated row count of 35 million and an actual

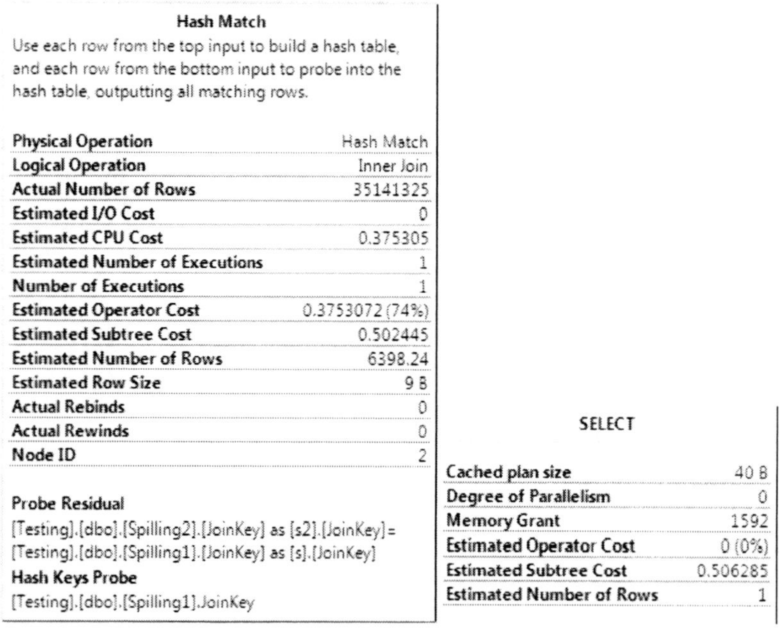

**Hash Match**

Use each row from the top input to build a hash table, and each row from the bottom input to probe into the hash table, outputting all matching rows.

| | |
|---|---|
| Physical Operation | Hash Match |
| Logical Operation | Inner Join |
| Actual Number of Rows | 35141325 |
| Estimated I/O Cost | 0 |
| Estimated CPU Cost | 0.375305 |
| Estimated Number of Executions | 1 |
| Number of Executions | 1 |
| Estimated Operator Cost | 0.3753072 (74%) |
| Estimated Subtree Cost | 0.502445 |
| Estimated Number of Rows | 6398.24 |
| Estimated Row Size | 9 B |
| Actual Rebinds | 0 |
| Actual Rewinds | 0 |
| Node ID | 2 |

Probe Residual

[Testing].[dbo].[Spilling2].[JoinKey] as [s2].[JoinKey] =
[Testing].[dbo].[Spilling1].[JoinKey] as [s].[JoinKey]

**Hash Keys Probe**

[Testing].[dbo].[Spilling1].JoinKey

**SELECT**

| | |
|---|---|
| Cached plan size | 40 B |
| Degree of Parallelism | 0 |
| Memory Grant | 1592 |
| Estimated Operator Cost | 0 (0%) |
| Estimated Subtree Cost | 0.506285 |
| Estimated Number of Rows | 1 |

*Figure 3-26. Inaccurate estimates.*

row count of 35 million. To do the hash join (which was a many-to-many join), the query was granted 450 MB of workspace memory.

The second query has an estimated row count of 6,000 rows and an actual row count of 35 million. The memory grant that the query execution engine requested was based on that estimate, and was 1.5 MB. If the first query required 450 MB to do the hash join, the second is not going to be able to do it in 1.5 MB. So what happens? Figure 3-27 shows the result.

A hash spill happens. I won't go into the complexities of hash spills here because that's beyond the scope of this chapter, but in short, portions of the hash table are written to TempDB and then read back when necessary. This can happen once or it can happen repeatedly during the execution of the query.

```
Hash Warning
Hash Warning
SQL:BatchCompleted
```

*Figure 3-27. Hash warnings viewed via SQL Profiler.*

As I'm sure you can imagine, that's not going to be good for performance. Memory is many times faster than disk and having to write and re-read portions of what should be an in-memory structure is going to make the query run slower than it otherwise would. In this example, the query that didn't spill took on average 8 seconds to run and the query that did spill took on average 10 seconds. That's not a huge difference, but that was on a machine with a single user and no other appreciable I/O load.

In addition to the hash spill, there are other operations that can spill—sorts and exchanges being the most common. Spools also use TempDB, but that's not so much a spill as the fact that a spool is, by definition, a temporary structure in TempDB.

The obvious outstanding questions are how do you detect these spills, what do you do about them, and how do you prevent them?

Detecting hash spills is the easy part. There are three SQLTrace events that fire in response to hash spills, sort spills, and exchange spills. They are hash warnings, sort warnings, and exchange warnings, respectively.

Those trace events show only that a spill has happened; they don't say anything about how much data was spilled to TempDB. To detect that information, you need to turn to the Dynamic Management Views—specifically, to sys.dm_db_task_space_usage and sys.dm_db_session_space_usage. I'll use the second one because it is a little easier. The first one shows data only for currently executing queries. The second one shows data for currently connected sessions.

```
SELECT  es.session_id ,
        user_objects_alloc_page_count ,
        internal_objects_alloc_page_count ,
        login_name ,
        program_name ,
        host_name ,
        last_request_start_time ,
        last_request_end_time ,
        DB_NAME(dbid) AS DatabaseName ,
        text
FROM    sys.dm_db_session_space_usage AS ssu
        INNER JOIN sys.dm_exec_sessions AS es ON ssu.session_id = es.session_id
        INNER JOIN sys.dm_exec_connections AS ec ON es.session_id = ec.session_id
        LEFT OUTER JOIN sys.dm_exec_requests AS er ON ec.session_id = er.session_id
```

```
            CROSS APPLY sys.dm_exec_sql_text(COALESCE(er.sql_handle, ec.most_recent_sql_handle)) AS
dest
WHERE    is_user_process = 1
```

This query tells you how much space in TempDB any current connection has used, along with either the currently running command or the last command that was run.

Using that on the earlier example, I can see that the query that didn't spill had 0 pages allocated in TempDB. The query that did spill had 0 pages of user objects and 10,500 pages of internal objects—that's 82 MB. (A page is 8 KB.)

That query can be scheduled to check for any processes that are using large amounts of TempDB space and to log any excessive usage for further investigation. Large amounts of internal allocations don't necessarily indicate spills, but it's probably worth investigating such readings. (Large amounts of user allocations suggests temp table overuse.)

On the subject of fixing spills, the first and most important point is that spills cannot always be prevented. Some operations will spill no matter what. A sort operation is the poster child here. If you imagine a sort of a 50-GB result set on a server with only 32 GB of memory, it's obvious that the sort cannot be done entirely in memory and will have to spill to TempDB.

Tuning spills has three major aspects:

- Prevent unnecessary spills caused by memory grant misestimates.

- Minimize the number of operations that have to spill.

- Tune TempDB to be able to handle the spills that do happen.

Memory grant underestimates are often a result of row cardinality misestimates. These can be caused by stale statistics, missing statistics, non-SARGable predicates (as discussed in the first section of this chapter), or a few less common causes.

For more details on cardinality problems, see the following:

- http://blogs.msdn.com/b/bartd/archive/2011/01/25/query_5f00_tuning_5f00_ key_5f00_terms.aspx

- http://msdn.microsoft.com/en-us/library/ms181034.aspx

- *Microsoft SQL Server 2008 Internals* by Kalen Delaney (Microsoft Press, 2009)

Minimizing the number of operations that have to spill is mostly a matter of application design. The main points are not to return more data than necessary and not to sort unless necessary.

It's common for applications to fetch far more data than any user would ever read, retrieving millions of rows into a data set or producing a report with tens or even hundreds of pages of data. This is not just a waste of network resources and a strain on the client machine, but it can often also lead to huge joins and sorts on the SQL Server instance.

There's a fine line between a chatty application that calls the SQL Server instance too many times requesting tiny amounts of information and an application that fetches far too much data, wasting server and client resources.

When you are designing applications, it is generally a good idea to fetch all the data for a particular screen or page in the smallest number of calls possible. That said, don't err on the side of fetching the entire database. The user should be able to specify filters and limitations that restrict the data that is requested. Don't pull a million rows to the app and let the user search within that. Specify the search in the database call, and return only the data that the user is interested in.

On the subject of sorts, note that it's worthless to sort the result set in SQL Server if the application is going to sort it when displayed. It's also sometimes more efficient to sort the result set at the client rather than on the server, because the client is dealing only with the one user's requests and small amounts of data while the server is dealing with multiple concurrent requests. You should consider this during the application design and development phases. It's certainly not always possible to do this, but you should at least consider whether it can be done.

The last part is tuning TempDB for the cases that will spill. This is one of those areas where almost everyone has an opinion and none of them are the same. I won't go into huge amounts of detail; rather, I'll just give you some solid guidelines.

Unless you have a storage area network (SAN) large enough and configured to absorb the I/O requirements of TempDB and the user databases without degradation, the TempDB database should preferably be placed on a separate I/O channel from the user databases. This means putting them on separate physical drives, not on a partition on the same drive as the user databases. Preferably, you should use a dedicated RAID array.

TempDB should be on a RAID 10 array if at all possible. If not, RAID 1 might be adequate. RAID 5 is a bad choice for TempDB because it has slower writes than RAID 1 or 10 because of the computation of the parity stripe.

I've heard of suggestions to use RAID 0 for TempDB. In my opinion, this is a very dangerous suggestion. It is true that there is no persistent data in TempDB (or at least there shouldn't be) and, hence, losing anything in TempDB is not a large concern. However, RAID 0 has no redundancy; if a single drive in the array fails, the entire array goes offline. If the drive hosting TempDB fails, SQL Server will shut down and cannot be restarted until the drive is replaced or TempDB is moved elsewhere. Hence, although using RAID 0 for TempDB does not pose a risk of data loss, it does have downtime risk. Depending on the application, that might be worse for the app.

If Solid State Drives (SSD) are available, putting TempDB onto the SSD array should be considered— just considered, not used as an automatic rule. It might be that a user database has higher I/O latency than TempDB and would hence benefit more, but it is definitely worth considering and investigating putting TempDB onto an SSD array if one is available.

On the subject of the number of files for TempDB, much has been written. Some writers on the topic even agree.

There are two reasons for splitting TempDB into multiple files:

- I/O throughput

- Allocation contention

Allocation contention seems more common than I/O throughput, though it isn't clear whether that's just because it's talked about more or whether it occurs more. Allocation contention refers to frequent `PageLatch` waits (not `PageIOLatch`) seen on the allocation pages in TempDB, usually on page 3 in file 1 (appearing as 2:1:3). They also appear on page 1 and 2 (appearing as 2:1:1 and 2:1:2), though those are less common. These waits can be seen in `sys.dm_exec_requests` or `sys.dm_os_waiting_tasks`.

The contention happens because (very simplified) anything writing to TempDB needs to check those pages to find a page to allocate and then needs to update that page to indicate that the allocation has been done. The primary solution for allocation contention is to add more files to TempDB. How many, well, that depends. You can read more about this at the following website: `http://www.sqlskills.com/BLOGS/PAUL/post/A-SQL-Server-DBA-myth-a-day-%281230%29-tempdb-should-always-have-one-data-file-per-processor-core.aspx`.

Splitting for I/O throughput is less common. If the dedicated array that holds TempDB is not providing adequate I/O throughput and cannot be tuned, you might need to split TempDB over multiple dedicated arrays. This is far less common than splitting for allocation contention.

For further reading, see the white paper "Working with TempDB in SQL Server 2005" (`http://www.microsoft.com/technet/prodtechnol/sql/2005/workingwithtempdb.mspx`).

# Conclusion

All of the problems looked at in this chapter are subtle, hard to see, and very easy to miss, especially in the semi-controlled chaos that many of us seem to work in these days. I hope the details I provided give you valuable insight into some design and development choices that can influence the performance of your apps and systems in various ways. This chapter also described additional tools and processes you can examine and experiment with when faced with performance problems.

# CHAPTER 4

▨ ▨ ▨

# Dynamic Management Views

## By Kellyn Pot'vin

I've been working with Microsoft SQL Server since version 6.5 and was introduced to performance tuning and high-intensity database management in SQL Server 7 back in 2000. The environment at that time was a SQL Server 7 implementation clustered on a Compaq SAN and pulling in 1to 4 gigabytes (GB) per day, which was considered a great deal for a SQL Server back then. Performance tuning incorporated what *appeared* as voodoo to many at this time. I found great success only through the guidance of great mentors while being technically trained in a mixed platform of Oracle and SQL Server. Performance tuning was quickly becoming second nature to me. It was something I seemed to intuitively and logically comprehend the benefits and power of. Even back then, many viewed SQL Server as the database platform anyone could install and configure, yet many soon came to realize that a "database is a database," no matter what the platform is. This meant the obvious-: the natural life of a database is growth and change. So, sooner or later, you were going to need a database administrator to manage it and tune all aspects of the complex environment.

The days of voodoo ceased when SQL Server 2005 was released with the new feature of Dynamic Management Views (DMVs). The ability to incorporate a familiar, relational view of data to gather critical system and performance data from any SQL Server version 2005 or newer was a gigantic leap forward for the SQL Server professional. As an Oracle DBA who had access to V$* and DBA_* views for years, the DMV feature was a wonderful addition to Microsoft's arsenal of performance tools.

In this chapter, I will not just describe the views and how to collect the data, but I'll cover why collecting this data is important to the health and long performance of an MSSQL database. Performance tuning is one of the areas that I see often neglected in MSSQL, because it is often marketed as being easy to set up, yet it takes strong, advanced database knowledge to understand what can hinder performance and how to resolve that problem. The introduction of Dynamic Management Views gives you the ability to provide clear, defined performance data, whereas before they were introduced, incorrect assumptions were easily made and many mistakes resulted from them.

## Understanding the Basics

Dynamic Management Views must be used with Dynamic Management Functions (DMFs). There is no way around this: the views are the data, and the table functions offer you the additional processing capability required to view the data—specifically, using the OUTER and CROSS APPLY operators to present the results in a proper format for easy readability.

Table functions can perform more than a single select (that is, of a view). When that functionality is used with Dynamic Management Views, it offers more powerful logic choices than any view alone could offer.

Before you can use the techniques found in this chapter, you need to understand basic database administration, which includes knowing how to locate a database ID (DBID), how to query views with function calls, and the differences between SQL calls from `Procedure` object names.

# Naming Convention

The DMVs and DMFs reside in the SYS schema and can be located by their specific naming convention of `dm_*`. No aliases (synonyms) have been created for DMVs or DMFs, so you must prefix them with the `sys.` schema name. When DMVs are discussed, they often are referred to with the `sys.` in the name, but within this chapter, the `sys.` part will be assumed—for example, `sys.dm_exec_sql_text`.

These naming conventions can be confusing at times, depending on what type of dynamic-management object you are referring to. DMVs can be queried using a "simple" naming convention, whereas DMFs can be referenced only with the standard two-part and three-part names—that is, `<dbname>.<dbowner>.<view_name>`, not the four-part, fully qualified naming convention, which adds the `<dbserver>` prefix.

For example, if you want to query the Employee table from the HumanResources schema in the AdventureWorks2012 database that resides on ServerHost1, the naming convention breakdown looks like the following:

- **Four-part** `ServerHost1.AdventureWorks2012.HumanResources.Employee`

- **Three-part** `AdventureWorks2012.HumanResources.Employee`

- **Two-part** `HumanResources.Employee`

# Groups of Related Views

More views and functions have been added in each subsequent SQL Server release to support the dynamic-management features. These views are then grouped by usage. In SQL Server 2005, there were 12 initial groups; in 2008, there were 15; and in 2012, there are now 20 groups of views. These additional groups include ones to support the new disaster-recovery and high-availability feature: the AlwaysOn Availability Groups Dynamic Management Views and Functions group.

As of 2012, the DMVs are broken down into the following groups:

- AlwaysOn Availability Group Dynamic Management Views and Functions

- Index Related Dynamic Management Views and Functions

- Change Data Capture Related Dynamic Management Views

- I/O Related Dynamic Management Views and Functions

- Change Tracking Related Dynamic Management View

- Object Related Dynamic Management Views and Functions

- Common Language Runtime Related Dynamic Management Views

- Query Notifications Related Dynamic Management Views

- Database Mirroring Related Dynamic Management Views

- Replication Related Dynamic Management Views

- Database Related Dynamic Management Views

- Resource Governor Dynamic Management Views

- Execution Related Dynamic Management Views and Functions

- Security Related Dynamic Management Views

- Extended Events Dynamic Management Views

- Service Broker Related Dynamic Management Views

- Filestream and FileTable Dynamic Management Views (Transact-SQL)

- SQL Server Operating System Related Dynamic Management Views

- Full-Text Search and Semantic Search Dynamic Management Views

- Transaction Related Dynamic Management Views and Functions

To query DMVs and DMFs, the user must have the VIEW SERVER STATE or VIEW DATABASE STATE permission granted. Without this permission, users receive an error stating the object does not exist.

# Varbinary Hash Values

To query the data from a DMV, you need to use SQL Server's version of a system-generated hash value, called the *handle*. The handle replaces other options that could have been used but would have been more difficult, including data that is stored in XML formats. A handle is stored in a varbinary(64) datatype, and the performance benefits for doing this are apparent.

Varbinary is variable-length binary data. A varbinary value can be a value from 1 to 8,000. After creation, when measuring allocation, the storage size is the actual length of the data entered plus an additional 2 bytes.

Following are some characteristics of varbinary data:

- Varbinary is data that has inconsistent or varying entries.

- Varbinary is more efficient if any sorting is required because it does not require collation.

- Varbinary generally consumes fewer bytes on average than a varchar or other common datatype choices.

- Note that, as different datatypes are converted to varbinary, they can be padded or truncated on the left or right, depending on the datatype they are being converted from.

The two most widely used varbinary datatypes in DMVs are the following:

- plan_handle   Hash value of the execution plan for the sql_handle in question.

- sql_handle   Hash value of a given SQL statement. This is a unique value for a SQL statement that is produced by an algorithm that will guarantee that the same sql_handle will appear on any SQL Server server for a unique statement. This can be very useful in clustered environments or for comparisons between development, test, and production SQL Server servers.

You will find that there are a number of ways to query the sql_handle. The following code demonstrates how to pull the sql_handle for a procedure call:

```
DECLARE @HANDLE BINARY(20)
SELECT @HANDLE = SQL_HANDLE FROM SYSPROCESSES WHERE SPID = <SESSION ID>
```

The following code shows how to query the handle with a select command, with the results shown in Figure 4-1:

```
SELECT * from sys.sysprocesses
cross apply sys.dm_exec_sql_text (sql_handle)
```

| spid | kpid | block | waitty... | waittime | lastwaittype | waitresour... | d... | uid | c... | physical | memusa... |
|------|------|-------|-----------|----------|--------------|---------------|------|-----|------|----------|-----------|
| 51 | 0 | 0 | 0x0000 | 0 | MISCELLANEOUS | | 1 | 1 | 78 | 209 | 2 |
| 52 | 0 | 0 | 0x0000 | 0 | MISCELLANEOUS | | 1 | 1 | 31 | 5 | 2 |
| 53 | 10728 | 0 | 0x0000 | 0 | SOS_SCHEDULER_YIELD | | 1 | 1 | 0 | 0 | 3 |

*Figure 4-1. Results joining sys.processes and sys.dm_exec_sql_text.*

Each SQL Server performance-tuning DBA has its own suite of scripts to query DMVs in times of performance challenges. Included in this chapter is my own collection of scripts that I have pulled together through the years. Most of them are sourced from MSDN, various websites, and books. I made changes to some of them as was required for the environment I was working in, but I've often noticed that many DBAs query the data the same way to gather the same pertinent information.

# Common Performance-Tuning Queries

Performance tuning is an area that many have found more difficult to master in SQL Server than they might have in other database platforms. The DMVs covered in this section represent an incredible leap in the direction of performance control, understanding, and reporting that the SQL Server DBA didn't have access to in earlier days.

Because performance tuning is my niche, the *exec* DMVs are by far my favorite area of the featured DMVs. This section covers how to locate connection, session, and status information, and then moves on to actual query stats and performance metrics.

## Retrieving Connection Information

Query the sys.dm_exec_connections view to retrieve information about connections to the database. Table 4-1 lists the most commonly used columns in the view.

*Table 4-1. Columns commonly used by dm_exec_connections.*

| Column | Data Retrieved |
|--------|----------------|
| session_ID | Identifying ID (must be an integer) for the session |
| connect_time | Timestamp showing when the connection was established |
| client_net_address | Host address, can be an Internet Protocol (IP), only used for the Transmission Control Protocol (TCP) transport provider established. |

| | |
|---|---|
| `last_read` | Timestamp showing when the last read occurred |
| `last_write` | Timestamp showing when the last write occurred |
| `auth_scheme` | States whether SQL Server or Windows Authentication is being used |
| `most_recent_sql_handle` | As stated, it's the most recent SQL_HANDLE executed |

Following is an example query against the view. The query returns a list of current connections to the instance.

```
SELECT  session_id,
        connect_time,
        client_net_address,
        last_read,
        last_write,
        auth_scheme,
        most_recent_sql_handle
FROM sys.dm_exec_connections
```

Figure 4-2 shows my output from this query.

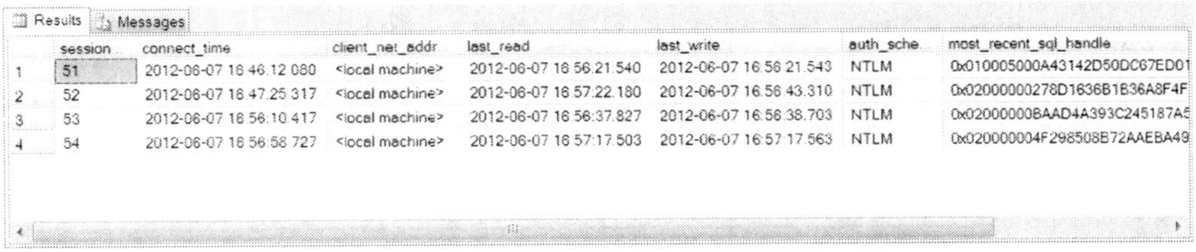

| | session | connect_time | client_net_addr | last_read | last_write | auth_sche | most_recent_sql_handle |
|---|---|---|---|---|---|---|---|
| 1 | 51 | 2012-06-07 16:46:12.080 | <local machine> | 2012-06-07 16:56:21.540 | 2012-06-07 16:56:21.543 | NTLM | 0x010005000A43142D50DC67ED01 |
| 2 | 52 | 2012-06-07 16:47:25.317 | <local machine> | 2012-06-07 16:57:22.180 | 2012-06-07 16:56:43.310 | NTLM | 0x02000000278D1636B1B36A8F4F |
| 3 | 53 | 2012-06-07 16:56:10.417 | <local machine> | 2012-06-07 16:56:37.827 | 2012-06-07 16:56:38.703 | NTLM | 0x02000000BAAD4A393C245187A5 |
| 4 | 54 | 2012-06-07 16:56:58.727 | <local machine> | 2012-06-07 16:57:17.503 | 2012-06-07 16:57:17.563 | NTLM | 0x020000004F298508B72AAEBA49 |

***Figure 4-2.*** *Example output showing currently connected sessions.*

# Showing Currently Executing Requests

For the `dm_exec_requests` DMV, the results show information about each of the requests executing in SQL Server at any given time. The results from this view will appear very similar to the `sp_who` view of years gone by, but the DBA should not underestimate the added value of this DMV.

Table 4-2 lists columns commonly used in this view.

***Table 4-2.*** *Columns commonly used by dm_exec_requests.*

| Column | Data Retrieved |
|---|---|
| `session_id` | The identifier for the session |
| `start_time` | Timestamp showing when the request arrived—not to be confused with login time. |

| status | Request status, which can be any of the following:<br>Background<br>Running<br>Runnable<br>Sleeping<br>Suspended |
|---|---|
| command | Identifies the type of statement (for example, DML or DDL type, including SELECT, INSERT, BACKUP, DBCC, and so forth) |
| sql_handle | The hash map identified for the SQL text |
| user_id | Identifies the user requesting the session |
| blocking_session_id | Blocking session ID, if one exists |
| wait_type | Blocking session wait type, which is a short 2-3 word definition of the type of wait occurring. |
| wait_time | Blocking session wait time |
| wait_resource | Blocking session wait resource |
| cpu_time | CPU time in milliseconds |
| total_elapsed_time | Total time that has elapsed since the request was received |
| reads | Number of reads performed |
| writes | Number of writes performed |
| query_plan_hash | Binary hash value assigned to the query execution plan |

The dm_exec_requests DMV can pull basic information or be joined to other views, such as dm_os_wait_stats, to gather more complex information about sessions currently executing in the database. Here's an example:

```
SELECT session_id,
       status,
       command,
       sql_handle,
       database_id
FROM sys.dm_exec_requests
```

Figure 4-3 demonstrates the output for the current requests.

Note that the background processes for MSSQL, (the session number is less than 51, which signifies a background system session) are displayed with the command type and purpose, along with what database (DBID) it belongs to.

| | session | status | command | sql_han | database |
|---|---|---|---|---|---|
| 1 | 1 | background | LOG WRITER | NULL | 0 |
| 2 | 2 | background | RECOVERY WRITER | NULL | 0 |
| 3 | 3 | background | LOCK MONITOR | NULL | 0 |
| 4 | 4 | background | SIGNAL HANDLER | NULL | 1 |
| 5 | 5 | background | LAZY WRITER | NULL | 0 |
| 6 | 6 | background | RESOURCE MONITOR | NULL | 0 |
| 7 | 7 | background | XE DISPATCHER | NULL | 0 |
| 8 | 8 | background | XE TIMER | NULL | 0 |
| 9 | 9 | background | BRKR TASK | NULL | 1 |
| 10 | 10 | sleeping | TASK MANAGER | NULL | 1 |
| 11 | 11 | background | TRACE QUEUE TASK | NULL | 1 |
| 12 | 12 | background | SYSTEM_HEALTH_ | NULL | 0 |
| 13 | 13 | background | RECEIVE | NULL | 0 |

*Figure 4-3. Example output showing current requests.*

Locating a blocked session and blocked information is simple with sys.dm_exec_requests, as the following example shows:

```
SELECT session_id, status,
     blocking_session_id,
     wait_type,
     wait_time,
     wait_resource,
     transaction_id
FROM sys.dm_exec_requests
WHERE status = N'suspended';
```

Figure 4-4 shows an example of results for a blocked session.

| | session_id | status | blocking_session_id | wait_type | wait_time | wait_resource | transaction_id |
|---|---|---|---|---|---|---|---|
| 1 | 56 | suspended | 54 | LCK_M_U | 7530 | KEY: 5 72057594045136896 (8194443284a0) | 23893 |

*Figure 4-4. Example output showing a blocking session.*

In the scenario shown in Figure 4-4, you can see that the blocked session (56) is blocked by session ID 54 on an update for the same row (LCK_M_U), and that it is suspended until the lock is either committed or rolled back. You now identify the transaction_id, which can also be used for further information in joins to secondary DMVs.

## Locking Escalation

Locking escalation is one of the enhanced features in SQL Server that Microsoft spent a lot of time on. When an issue does arise, it is important that the DBA understand what is occurring and how to address a lock-escalation issue. If you do experience a locking issue in one of your databases, the following query, using the dm_trans_lock DMV returns information regarding locking status from the database in question.

```
SELECT resource_type,
       resource_associated_entity_id,
       request_status,
       request_mode,
```

```
        request_session_id,
        resource_description
    FROM sys.dm_tran_locks
    WHERE resource_database_id = <DBID>
```

Figure 4-5 shows the results of this query.

| | resource_type | resource_associated_entity_id | request_status | request_mode | request_session_id | resource_description |
|---|---|---|---|---|---|---|
| 1 | DATABASE | 0 | GRANT | S | 58 | |
| 2 | DATABASE | 0 | GRANT | S | 55 | |
| 3 | DATABASE | 0 | GRANT | S | 52 | |
| 4 | DATABASE | 0 | GRANT | S | 56 | |
| 5 | DATABASE | 0 | GRANT | S | 54 | |
| 6 | DATABASE | 0 | GRANT | S | 53 | |
| 7 | PAGE | 72057594050707456 | GRANT | IU | 54 | 1:9295 |
| 8 | PAGE | 72057594045136896 | GRANT | IU | 54 | 1:1048 |
| 9 | PAGE | 72057594045136896 | GRANT | IX | 56 | 1:1048 |
| 10 | OBJECT | 1237579447 | GRANT | IX | 54 | |
| 11 | OBJECT | 1237579447 | GRANT | IX | 56 | |
| 12 | KEY | 72057594050707456 | GRANT | U | 54 | (a6896c7ab296) |
| 13 | KEY | 72057594045136896 | GRANT | X | 56 | (8194443284a0) |
| 14 | KEY | 72057594045136896 | WAIT | U | 54 | (8194443284a0) |

***Figure 4-5.*** *Demonstration of locking-escalation information shown in SQL Server.*

In Figure 4-5, you can see that there is a lock escalation in progress between session IDs 54 and 56. The "Page" escalation on `resource_associated_entity_id` (the Employee table) involves the index (IX, KEY) as well. Always be aware of object and key escalations. Lock escalation should work seamlessly in SQL Server and when issues arise, always inspect the code and statistics first for opportunities for improvement.

Identifying what type of locking status, including, the mode, the transaction state the lock is in, addressing a lock that has escalated and has created an issue are pertinent parts of the DBA's job. Gathering the information on locking is now simple—you do it by joining the `dm_tran_locks` DMV to the `dm_os_waiting_tasks` DMV, as shown here:

```
SELECT  dtl.resource_type,
        dtl.resource_database_id,
        dtl.resource_associated_entity_id,
        dtl.request_mode,
        dtl.request_session_id,
        dowt.blocking_session_id
    FROM sys.dm_tran_locks as dtl
    INNER JOIN sys.dm_os_waiting_tasks as dowt
        ON dtl.lock_owner_address = dowt.resource_address
```

# Finding Poor Performing SQL

As a performance-tuning DBA, I find the DMVs in the next section to be some of my favorites. These DMVs are the most commonly queried by any DBA looking for performance issues with the plan cache of SQL Server. With these queries, you can view aggregated data about execution time, CPU resource usage, and execution times.

How is this view an improvement over the voodoo that DBAs used to perform to locate issues in versions of SQL Server prior to 2005?

- It isolates each procedure and procedure call to identify how each one impacts the environment. This can result in multiple rows for the same procedure in the result set.

- It immediately isolates an issue, unlike the SQL Profiler.

- It produces impressive results when you use it with the DBCC_FREEPROCCACHE before executing queries against it.

- It can be used to create performance snapshots of an environment to retain for review when performance issues arise.

- It makes it easy to isolate top opportunities for performance tuning, allowing the DBA to pinpoint performance issues—no more guessing.

- Not all queries show up in this view. SQL that is recompiled at the time of execution can circumvent the view results. (You need to enable StmtRecompile to verify.)

- It can be used with a multitude of SQL Server performance tool suites (such as DB Artisan, Performance Dashboard, Toad, and so forth). However, these tools might not give you the full access that querying the view might grant to a DBA.

Here is what happens when performance data with DMVs isn't 100 percent accurate:

- Removing the compiled plan from cache will result in the corresponding rows for the query plan being removed from the DMV as well.

- Results will show in this DMV only *after* the query execution has successfully completed, so any SQL that is still executing or long-running queries can be missed because of this fact.

- Cycling the SQL Server or any interruption in service to the hardware will remove the corresponding rows from the DMV as well.

The most common method of locating performance issues with SQL is by using the dm_exec_sql_text, dm_exec_query_plan, and dm_exec_query_stats DMVs, which are joined together to give DBAs the most accurate information about the database. Tables 4-3 through 4-5 list the columns most commonly used of these DMVs.

**Table 4-3.** *Common columns used for dm_exec_sql_text.*

| Column | Data Retrieved |
|--------|----------------|
| dbid | The ID for the database |
| objectid | The identifying ID of the object |
| number | For a numbered stored procedure; check the system object sys.numbered_procedures |
| text | The actual text from the query |

**Table 4-4.** *Common columns used for dm_exec_query_plan.*

| Column | Data Retrieved |
|--------|----------------|
| dbid | The ID for the database |

| Column | Data Retrieved |
|---|---|
| objectid | The identifying ID of the object |
| number | For a numbered stored procedure; check the system object sys.numbered_procedures |
| query_plan | Contains the show plan at the compile time of the query execution plan with the plan_handle in XML format. |

*Table 4-5. Common columns used by dm_exec_query_stats.*

| Column | Data Retrieved |
|---|---|
| sql_hande | The identifying handle for the query or procedure |
| plan_handle | The identifying handle for the plan, which is often joined to the dm_exec_query_plan DMF to show the query plan |
| total_worker_time | The total amount of CPU time in microseconds |
| min_worker_time | The minimum CPU time in microseconds for an execution |
| max_worker_time | The maximum CPU time in microseconds for an execution |
| total_physical_reads | The total number of physical reads |
| total_elapsed_time | The total time elapsed in microseconds for completion |

## Using the Power of DMV Performance Scripts

Locating the top 10 performance challenges in any given database can be a powerful weapon to use when issues arise. Having this data at your fingertips can provide the DBA, developer, or application-support analyst with valuable data about where to tune first to get the best results.

```
SELECT TOP 10 dest.text as sql,
        deqp.query_plan,
        creation_time,
        last_execution_time,
        execution_count,
        (total_worker_time / execution_count) as avg_cpu,
        total_worker_time as total_cpu,
        last_worker_time as last_cpu,
        min_worker_time as min_cpu,
        max_worker_time as max_cpu,
        (total_physical_reads + total_logical_reads) as total_reads,
        (max_physical_reads + max_logical_reads) as max_reads,
        (total_physical_reads + total_logical_reads) / execution_count as avg_reads,
        max_elapsed_time as max_duration,
        total_elapsed_time as total_duration,
        ((total_elapsed_time / execution_count)) / 1000000 as avg_duration_sec
FROM sys.dm_exec_query_stats deqs
CROSS APPLY sys.dm_exec_sql_text(sql_handle) dest
CROSS APPLY sys.dm_exec_query_plan (plan_handle) deqp
ORDER BY deqs.total_worker_time DESC
```

There are two areas in this query, along with the subsequent ones in this section, that I want you to fully understand. The first is the initial column of SQL, followed by the XML output of the showplan, which you can see in Figure 4-6.

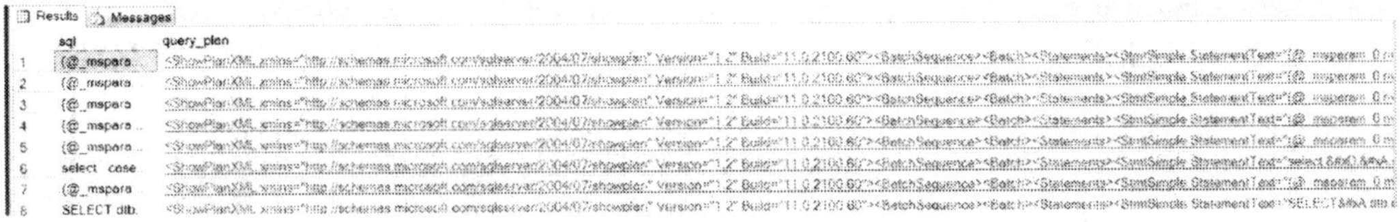

**Figure 4-6.** *Top 10 performance-challenging queries, arranged by total working time in the database.*

The example in Figure 4-6 shows the results of a CPU intensive environment. As helpful as this data is, the process of collecting this data can add CPU resource pressure to a production environment and the database professional should take care regarding when and how often this type of query is executed. The benefits of the resulting query are the links shown for the show plan data, which can then be clicked on to show the full SQL for the statement in row chosen.

When investigating further, the next area of focus is on how the quantity of execution counts corresponds to the impact to CPU, reads, durations and other pertinent data, as shown in Figure 4-7.

| exe... | avg_cpu | total_cpu | last_cpu | min_cpu | max_cpu | total_reads | max_rea... | avg_reads | max_durati... | total_durat... |
|---|---|---|---|---|---|---|---|---|---|---|
| 1 | 135100 | 135100 | 135100 | 135100 | 135100 | 37546 | 37546 | 37546 | 181251 | 181251 |
| 1 | 117582 | 117582 | 117582 | 117582 | 117582 | 81146 | 81146 | 81146 | 147781 | 147781 |
| 1 | 101602 | 101602 | 101602 | 101602 | 101602 | 80604 | 80604 | 80604 | 101815 | 101815 |
| 5 | 15435 | 77175 | 15196 | 15101 | 15797 | 0 | 0 | 0 | 15797 | 77177 |
| 1 | 60029 | 60029 | 60029 | 60029 | 60029 | 0 | 0 | 0 | 60088 | 60088 |
| 1 | 53720 | 53720 | 53720 | 53720 | 53720 | 17458 | 17458 | 17458 | 65005 | 65005 |
| 142 | 346 | 49181 | 309 | 281 | 2239 | 4101 | 32 | 28 | 2239 | 49194 |
| 1 | 29850 | 29850 | 29850 | 29850 | 29850 | 2059 | 2059 | 2059 | 29860 | 29860 |
| 3 | 7380 | 22140 | 6780 | 6590 | 8769 | 318 | 106 | 106 | 8769 | 22142 |
| 1 | 21528 | 21528 | 21528 | 21528 | 21528 | 0 | 0 | 0 | 21528 | 21528 |

**Figure 4-7.** *The response from this query results in a wide array of columns that can then identify SQL code with high execution counts, extensive physical reads and/or elapsed time.*

When any performance DBA is evaluating easy options for performance tuning, identifying the low-hanging fruit—that is, comparing the number of executions to the time they take and the impact they have on the CPU—is crucial. Identifying and tuning these can result in a quick performance gain by making small, efficient corrections to one to five offending top processes rather than creating a large, resource-intensive project to correct an environment.

Note also that the preceding queries and subsequent ones all have a common DMF call in them. You can use this DMF to retrieve a sql_handle for a given SQL statement, such as CROSS APPLY sys.dm_exec_sql_text(sql_handle) sql. As mentioned earlier, for performance reasons DMVs refer to SQL statements by their sql_handle only. Use this function if you need to retrieve the SQL text for a given handle. This DMF accepts either the sql_handle or plan_handle as input criteria.

Many of the performance DMFs won't complete in SQL Server environments if version 8.0 (SQL 2000) compatibility is enabled. The common workaround is to execute the DMF from a system database using the common fully qualified name—for example, CROSS APPLY <dbserver>.<dbname>. sys.dm_exec_sql_text(plan_handle).

# Divergence in Terminology

Terminology divergence is a common issue for many as new versions and features evolve. Note that DMVs that use the plan handle to execute results within the execution plan will also be referred to as the *showplan*. This now is often shown as a link in a user-friendly XML format. The links will only display plans that are executed or are still in cache. If you attempt to display plans other than these, a null result will occur upon clicking on the link.

- Execution plans in XML format are often difficult to read. To view execution plans graphically in Management Studio, do the following:

  - The function will return a hyperlink automatically for the showplan XML.

  - Click on the hyperlink to bring up the XML page in an Internet browser.

  - Click on File®Save As and save the file to your local drive using a .SQLPLAN file extension.

  - Return to SQL Server Management Studio. You can now open the file you just saved without issue.

- It is a best practice to retain an archive of the XML for execution plans of the most often executed SQL in each environment.

- The creation of XML for any execution plan uses a fair amount of CPU. I recommend performing this task at off hours if you are executing the XML on a production system.

- You can use the data in the show plan for comparisons when performance changes occur, allowing you to compare performance changes and pinpoint issues.

- The query plan is based on the parameters entered during the execution of the first query. SQL Server refers to this as *parameter sniffing*. All subsequent executions will use this plan whether their parameter values match the original or not.

- If a poor combination of parameters was saved to the base execution plan, this can cause performance issues not just for the original execution but for all subsequent ones. Because you can view this in the execution-plan XML, knowing how to view this data when you have concerns regarding a query can be very helpful.

- If you do suspect an issue, you can locate the correct plan and force its usage with the OPTIMIZE FOR hint.

# Optimizing Performance

There are many versions of queries joining the DMVs dm_exec_query_stats and dm_exec_sql_text to provide a DBA with information regarding poor performance. The following is a collection of queries that I retain in my own arsenal to locate and troubleshoot performance.

Top 1000 Poor Performing is a script that will generate a large report, showing the worst code executed in the environment, and for many environments, it will show some of the least offending code executed in the environment. This provides you with a solid understanding of what code is executed in the environment and how much is high impact and how much is standard processing and everyday queries.

```
SELECT  TOP 1000
        [Object_Name] = object_name(dest.objectid),
```

```
            creation_time,
            last_execution_time,
            total_cpu_time = total_worker_time / 1000,
            avg_cpu_time = (total_worker_time / execution_count) / 1000,
            min_cpu_time = min_worker_time / 1000,
            max_cpu_time = max_worker_time / 1000,
            last_cpu_time = last_worker_time / 1000,
            total_time_elapsed = total_elapsed_time / 1000 ,
            avg_time_elapsed = (total_elapsed_time / execution_count) / 1000,
            min_time_elapsed = min_elapsed_time / 1000,
            max_time_elapsed = max_elapsed_time / 1000,
            avg_physical_reads = total_physical_reads / execution_count,
            avg_logical_reads = total_logical_reads / execution_count,
            execution_count,
            SUBSTRING(dest.text, (deqs.statement_start_offset/2) + 1,
                (
                    (
                            CASE statement_end_offset
                                WHEN -1 THEN DATALENGTH(dest.text)
                                ELSE qs.statement_end_offset
                            END
                            - deqs.statement_start_offset
                    ) /2
                ) + 1
            ) as statement_text
FROM        sys.dm_exec_query_stats deqs
CROSS APPLY sys.dm_exec_sql_text(qs.sql_handle) dest
WHERE Object_Name(st.objectid) IS NOT NULL
            --AND DB_NAME(dest.dbid) = 5
ORDER BY    db_name(dest.dbid),
            total_worker_time / execution_count  DESC;
```

When you execute this query, it returns the top 1000 procedures or processes and it breaks down performance impacts by the actual procedural calls, listing the offending code from the procedure or complex process, as Figure 4-8 shows.

statement_text

INSERT INTO @media_set_id (media_set_id)    SELECT ...

DELETE msdb.dbo.backupmediafamily    FROM msdb.dbo...

DELETE msdb.dbo.backupmediaset    FROM msdb.dbo.b...

INSERT INTO @backup_set_id (backup_set_id)    SELEC...

SELECT @job_id = job_id,         @owner_sid = owner_s...

DELETE FROM msdb.dbo.restorehistory    WHERE restor...

INSERT INTO @restore_history_id (restore_history_id)    ...

DELETE FROM msdb.dbo.backupfile    WHERE backup_s...

*Figure 4-8. Results of the top 1000 SQL Statement text from the query.*

You can also take advantage of various joins between dm_exec_query_stats and dm_exec_sql_text to clearly identify the statement by average CPU and SQL text, two of the most important aspects to note when researching poorly performing SQL. Here's an example:

```
SELECT TOP 5 total_worker_time/execution_count 'Avg CPU Time',
    SUBSTRING(dest.text, (deqs.statement_start_offset/2)+1,
        ((CASE deqs.statement_end_offset
          WHEN -1 THEN DATALENGTH(dest.text)
          ELSE deqs.statement_end_offset
          END - deqs.statement_start_offset)/2) + 1)statement_text
FROM sys.dm_exec_query_stats deqs
CROSS APPLY sys.dm_exec_sql_text(qs.sql_handle) dest
ORDER BY total_worker_time/execution_count DESC;
;
```

The results are shown in Figure 4-9.

| | Avg CPU Ti... | statement_text |
|---|---|---|
| 1 | 135100 | SELECT SCHEMA_NAME(udf.schema_id) AS [Schema], u ... |
| 2 | 134706 | SELECT TOP 10 sql text as sql,        qp.query_plan, ... |
| 3 | 117582 | SELECT SCHEMA_NAME(sp.schema_id) AS [Schema], sp... |
| 4 | 101602 | SELECT SCHEMA_NAME(sp.schema_id) AS [Schema], sp... |
| 5 | 60029 | SELECT 'Server[@Name=' + quotename(CAST(      ser... |

***Figure 4-9.** The top five offending statements, ordered by average CPU time. This query is based on the "top 20," which results in a more defined report for the DBA to inspect and clear CPU-intensive resource data that is important in terms of performance.*

Always remember, CPU is everything in a SQL Server environment. The output from many of the performance queries in this section of the chapter gives the DBA a clear view of what statements are the largest impact on this important resource usage.

```
SELECT TOP 20 deqt.text AS 'Name',
        deqs.total_worker_time AS 'TotalWorkerTime',
        deqs.total_worker_time/deqs.execution_count AS 'AvgWorkerTime',
        deqs.execution_count AS 'Execution Count',
        ISNULL(deqs.execution_count/DATEDIFF(Second, deqs.creation_time, GetDate()), 0) AS
'Calls/Second',
        ISNULL(deqs.total_elapsed_time/deqs.execution_count, 0) AS 'AvgElapsedTime',
        deqs.max_logical_reads, deqs.max_logical_writes,
        DATEDIFF(Minute, deqs.creation_time, GetDate()) AS 'Age in Cache'
    FROM        sys.dm_exec_query_stats AS deqs
CROSS APPLY sys.dm_exec_sql_text(qs.sql_handle) AS deqt
WHERE deqt.dbid = db_id()
ORDER BY deqs.total_worker_time DESC;
```

The results of this query are shown in Figure 4-10.

| | Name | TotalWorkerTime | AvgWorkerTime | Execution Count | Calls/Second | AvgElapsedTime | max_logical_reads | max_logica ▲ |
|---|---|---|---|---|---|---|---|---|
| 1 | SELECT TOP 10 sql.text as sql. | 177846 | 177846 | 1 | 0 | 195945 | 0 | 0 |
| 2 | (@_msparam_0 nvarchar(4000).. | 14982 | 394 | 38 | 0 | 394 | 29 | 0 |
| 3 | (@_msparam_0 nvarchar(4000).. | 8096 | 4048 | 2 | 0 | 4593 | 47 | 4 |
| 4 | SELECT TOP 20 qt.text AS 'Name. | 6130 | 6130 | 1 | 0 | 6130 | 0 | 0 |
| 5 | (@_msparam_0 nvarchar(4000)) . | 4482 | 448 | 10 | 0 | 448 | 63 | 0 |
| 6 | (@_msparam_0 nvarchar(4000).. | 3369 | 1684 | 2 | 0 | 1892 | 29 | 0 |
| 7 | (@_msparam_0 nvarchar(4000).. | 3175 | 317 | 10 | 0 | 317 | 29 | 0 |
| 8 | (@_msparam_0 nvarchar(4000).. | 2001 | 2001 | 1 | 0 | 2001 | 391 | 0 |
| 9 | select case when cfg.configura.. | 1877 | 187 | 10 | 0 | 187 | 0 | 0 |
| 10 | (@_msparam_0 nvarchar(4000)) . | 1730 | 173 | 10 | 0 | 173 | 6 | 0 |
| 11 | (@_msparam_0 nvarchar(4000).. | 1177 | 585 | 2 | 0 | 588 | 61 | 0 |
| 12 | (@_msparam_0 nvarchar(4000).. | 897 | 448 | 2 | 0 | 1066 | 48 | 0 |
| 13 | SELECT db.name AS [Name]. ct. | 891 | 445 | 2 | 0 | 445 | 24 | 0 |
| 14 | (@_msparam_0 nvarchar(4000).. | 667 | 333 | 2 | 0 | 333 | 17 | 0 |
| 15 | (@_msparam_0 nvarchar(4000)) . | 419 | 209 | 2 | 0 | 210 | 4 | 0 |
| 16 | () select table_id. item_guid. opts | 207 | 18 | 11 | 0 | 19 | 0 | 0 |

*Figure 4-10. CPU usage, time, and reads, broken down by averages, minimums, and maximums.*

## Inspecting Performance Stats

Generating useful performance stats have been a common challenge for SQL Server DBAs. DMVs offer another option for extracting information that provides clear answers that can then be viewed in a user-friendly XML format.

Performance statistics can come in many forms- physical reads, logical reads, elapsed time and others. The following query is an excellent demonstration of high-level performance statistics in a MSSQL environment.

```
SELECT  dest.dbid
        ,dest.[text] AS Batch_Object,
        SUBSTRING(dest.[text], (deqs.statement_start_offset/2) + 1,
        ((CASE deqs.statement_end_offset
                WHEN -1 THEN DATALENGTH(sdest.[text]) ELSE deqs.statement_end_offset END
                    - deqs.statement_start_offset)/2) + 1) AS SQL_Statement
        , deqp.query_plan
        , deqs.execution_count
        , deqs.total_physical_reads
        ,(deqs.total_physical_reads/deqs.execution_count) AS average_physical_reads
        , deqs.total_logical_writes
        , (deqs.total_logical_writes/deqs.execution_count) AS average_logical_writes
        , deqs.total_logical_reads
        , (deqs.total_logical_reads/deqs.execution_count) AS average_logical_lReads
        , deqs.total_clr_time
        , (deqs.total_clr_time/deqs.execution_count) AS average_CLRTime
        , deqs.total_elapsed_time
        , (deqs.total_elapsed_time/deqs.execution_count) AS average_elapsed_time
        , deqs.last_execution_time
        , deqs.creation_time
FROM    sys.dm_exec_query_stats AS deqs
        CROSS apply sys.dm_exec_sql_text(deqs.sql_handle) AS dest
        CROSS apply sys.dm_exec_query_plan(deqs.plan_handle) AS deqp
WHERE   deqs.last_execution_time > DATEADD(HH,-2,GETDATE())
        AND dest.dbid = (SELECT DB_ID('AdventureWorks2012'))
ORDER BY execution_count
```

Figure 4-11 shows the results of this query.

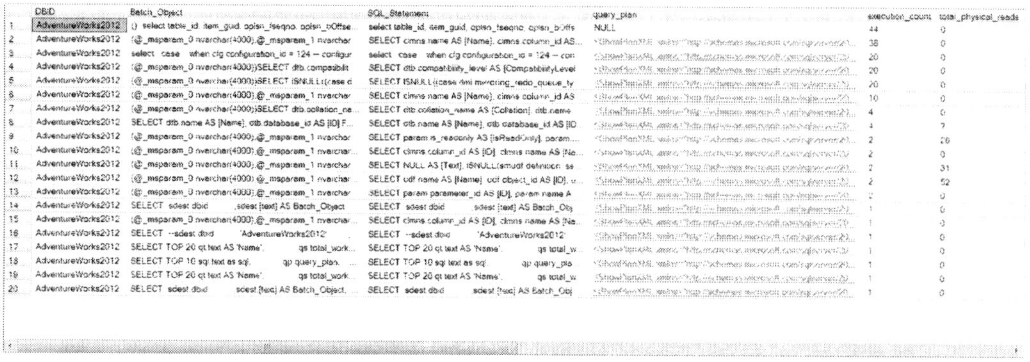

| | DBID | Batch_Object | SQL_Statement | query_plan | execution_count | total_physical_reads |
|---|---|---|---|---|---|---|
| 1 | AdventureWorks2012 | () select table_id, item_guid, oplsn_fseqno, oplsn_bOffse... | select table_id, item_guid, oplsn_fseqno, oplsn_bOffs | NULL | 44 | 0 |
| 2 | AdventureWorks2012 | (@_msparam_0 nvarchar(4000),@_msparam_1 nvarchar | SELECT clmns.name AS [Name], clmns.column_id AS... | <ShowPlanXML xmlns="http://schemas.microsoft.com/sqlserver/20... | 38 | 0 |
| 3 | AdventureWorks2012 | select case when cfg.configuration_id = 124 -- configur | select case when cfg.configuration_id = 124 -- con | <ShowPlanXML xmlns="http://schemas.microsoft.com/sqlserver/20... | 20 | 0 |
| 4 | AdventureWorks2012 | (@_msparam_0 nvarchar(4000))SELECT dtb.compatibilit | SELECT dtb.compatibility_level AS [CompatibilityLevel | <ShowPlanXML xmlns="http://schemas.microsoft.com/sqlserver/20... | 20 | 0 |
| 5 | AdventureWorks2012 | (@_msparam_0 nvarchar(4000))SELECT ISNULL((case d | SELECT ISNULL((case dmi.mirroring_redo_queue_ty | <ShowPlanXML xmlns="http://schemas.microsoft.com/sqlserver/20... | 20 | 0 |
| 6 | AdventureWorks2012 | (@_msparam_0 nvarchar(4000),@_msparam_1 nvarchar | SELECT clmns.name AS [Name], clmns.column_id AS | <ShowPlanXML xmlns="http://schemas.microsoft.com/sqlserver/20... | 10 | 0 |
| 7 | AdventureWorks2012 | (@_msparam_0 nvarchar(4000))SELECT dtb.collation_na... | SELECT dtb.collation_name AS [Collation], dtb.name | <ShowPlanXML xmlns="http://schemas.microsoft.com/sqlserver/20... | 4 | 0 |
| 8 | AdventureWorks2012 | SELECT dtb.name AS [Name], dtb.database_id AS [ID] F... | SELECT dtb.name AS [Name], dtb.database_id AS [ID | <ShowPlanXML xmlns="http://schemas.microsoft.com/sqlserver/20... | 4 | 7 |
| 9 | AdventureWorks2012 | (@_msparam_0 nvarchar(4000),@_msparam_1 nvarchar | SELECT param.is_readonly AS [IsReadOnly], param.... | <ShowPlanXML xmlns="http://schemas.microsoft.com/sqlserver/20... | 2 | 26 |
| 10 | AdventureWorks2012 | (@_msparam_0 nvarchar(4000),@_msparam_1 nvarchar... | SELECT clmns.column_id AS [ID], clmns.name AS [Ne... | <ShowPlanXML xmlns="http://schemas.microsoft.com/sqlserver/20... | 2 | 0 |
| 11 | AdventureWorks2012 | (@_msparam_0 nvarchar(4000),@_msparam_1 nvarchar | SELECT NULL AS [Text], ISNULL(smudf.definition, ss | <ShowPlanXML xmlns="http://schemas.microsoft.com/sqlserver/20... | 2 | 31 |
| 12 | AdventureWorks2012 | (@_msparam_0 nvarchar(4000),@_msparam_1 nvarchar... | SELECT udf.name AS [Name], udf.object_id AS [ID], u... | <ShowPlanXML xmlns="http://schemas.microsoft.com/sqlserver/20... | 2 | 52 |
| 13 | AdventureWorks2012 | (@_msparam_0 nvarchar(4000),@_msparam_1 nvarchar | SELECT param.parameter_id AS [ID], param.name A | <ShowPlanXML xmlns="http://schemas.microsoft.com/sqlserver/20... | 2 | 0 |
| 14 | AdventureWorks2012 | SELECT sdest.dbid ,sdest.[text] AS Batch_Object | SELECT sdest.dbid ,sdest.[text] AS Batch_Obj | <ShowPlanXML xmlns="http://schemas.microsoft.com/sqlserver/20... | 1 | 0 |
| 15 | AdventureWorks2012 | (@_msparam_0 nvarchar(4000),@_msparam_1 nvarchar... | SELECT clmns.column_id AS [ID], clmns.name AS [Ne... | <ShowPlanXML xmlns="http://schemas.microsoft.com/sqlserver/20... | 1 | 0 |
| 16 | AdventureWorks2012 | SELECT --sdest.dbid 'AdventureWorks2012' | SELECT --sdest.dbid 'AdventureWorks2012' | <ShowPlanXML xmlns="http://schemas.microsoft.com/sqlserver/20... | 1 | 0 |
| 17 | AdventureWorks2012 | SELECT TOP 20 qt.text AS 'Name', qs.total_work... | SELECT TOP 20 qt.text AS 'Name', qs.total_w... | <ShowPlanXML xmlns="http://schemas.microsoft.com/sqlserver/20... | 1 | 0 |
| 18 | AdventureWorks2012 | SELECT TOP 10 sql.text as sql, qp.query_plan, ... | SELECT TOP 10 sql.text as sql, qp.query_pla | <ShowPlanXML xmlns="http://schemas.microsoft.com/sqlserver/20... | 1 | 0 |
| 19 | AdventureWorks2012 | SELECT TOP 20 qt.text AS 'Name', qs.total_work... | SELECT TOP 20 qt.text AS 'Name', qs.total_w | <ShowPlanXML xmlns="http://schemas.microsoft.com/sqlserver/20... | 1 | 0 |
| 20 | AdventureWorks2012 | SELECT sdest.dbid sdest.[text] AS Batch_Object, ... | SELECT sdest.dbid sdest.[text] AS Batch_Obj | <ShowPlanXML xmlns="http://schemas.microsoft.com/sqlserver/20... | 1 | 0 |

***Figure 4-11.*** *XML query plan links offered through DMVs that open a browser to the showplan for each statement and provide more defined performance data.*

# Top Quantity Execution Counts

As any performance-oriented DBA knows, it's not just how long a query executes, but the concurrency or quantity of executions that matters when investigating performance issues. DMVs provide this information and, in more recent releases, inform you of how complete the data is with regard to concurrency issues, which can be essential to performing accurate data collection.

```
SELECT TOP 100 deqt.text AS 'Name',
           deqs.execution_count AS 'Execution Count',
           deqs.execution_count/DATEDIFF(Second, deqs.creation_time, GetDate()) AS
'Calls/Second',
           deqs.total_worker_time/deqs.execution_count AS 'AvgWorkerTime',
           deqs.total_worker_time AS 'TotalWorkerTime',
           deqs.total_elapsed_time/deqs.execution_count AS 'AvgElapsedTime',
           deqs.max_logical_reads, deqs.max_logical_writes, deqs.total_physical_reads,
           DATEDIFF(Minute, deqs.creation_time, GetDate()) AS 'Age in Cache'
    FROM sys.dm_exec_query_stats AS deqs
    CROSS APPLY sys.dm_exec_sql_text(deqs.sql_handle) AS deqt
    WHERE deqt.dbid = db_id()
    ORDER BY deqs.execution_count DESC
```

The results of this query are shown in Figure 4-12. They show that a process has performed a full scan on the HumanResources.employee table 10,631 times, and they show the average worker time, average elapsed time, and so forth.

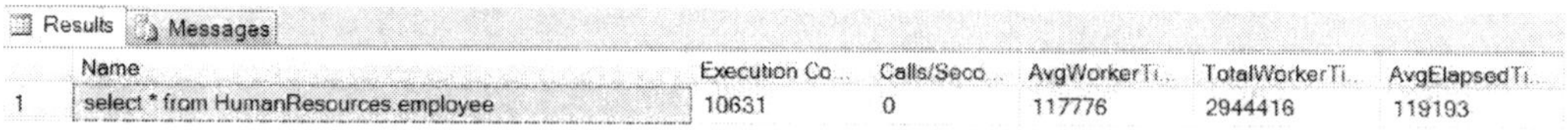

Results | Messages

| | Name | Execution Co... | Calls/Seco... | AvgWorkerTi... | TotalWorkerTi... | AvgElapsedTi... |
|---|---|---|---|---|---|---|
| 1 | select * from HumanResources.employee | 10631 | 0 | 117776 | 2944416 | 119193 |

***Figure 4-12.*** *Highly concurrent SQL; note the average elapsed time versus. the number of executions shown in the Execution Count column.*

## Physical Reads

Another area of high cost to performance is I/O. Having a fast disk is important, and as SQL Server moves deeper into data warehousing, having a faster disk and fewer I/O waits are both important to performance. There is a cost to all reads, regardless of whether they are physical or logical, so it is crucial that the DBA be aware of both.

```
SELECT TOP 20 deqt.text AS 'SP Name',
 deqs.total_physical_reads,
 deqs.total_physical_reads/deqs.execution_count AS 'Avg Physical Reads',
          deqs.execution_count AS 'Execution Count',
          deqs.execution_count/DATEDIFF(Second, deqs.creation_time, GetDate()) AS
'Calls/Second',
          deqs.total_worker_time/deqs.execution_count AS 'AvgWorkerTime',
          deqs.total_worker_time AS 'TotalWorkerTime',
          deqs.total_elapsed_time/deqs.execution_count AS 'AvgElapsedTime',
          deqs.max_logical_reads, deqs.max_logical_writes,
    DATEDIFF(Minute, deqs.creation_time, GetDate()) AS 'Age in Cache', deqt.dbid
    FROM sys.dm_exec_query_stats AS deqs
    CROSS APPLY sys.dm_exec_sql_text(deqs.sql_handle) AS deqt
    WHERE deqt.dbid = db_id()
    ORDER BY deqs.total_physical_reads
```

The results of this query are shown in Figure 4-13.

*Figure 4-13. Physical and logical read data generated by the preceding query.*

# Physical Performance Queries

Physical performance tuning involves indexing, partitioning and fragmentation unlike the queries in the previous section, which are often used to discover opportunities for logical tuning.

## Locating Missing Indexes

When SQL Server generates a query plan, it determines what the best indexes are for a particular filter condition. If these indexes do not exist, the query optimizer generates a suboptimal query plan, and then stores information about the optimal indexes for later retrieval. The missing indexes feature enables you to access this data so that you can decide whether these optimal indexes should be implemented at a later date.

Here's a quick overview of the different missing index DMVs and DMFs:

- `sys.dm_db_missing_index_details` (**DMV**)   Returns indexes the optimizer considers to be missing

- `sys.dm_db_missing_index_columns` (**DMF**)   Returns the columns for a missing index

- `sys.dm_db_missing_index_group_stats` **(DMV)** Returns usage and access details for the missing indexes similar to `sys.dm_db_index_usage_stats`.

The pertinent columns for these three DMVs and DMFs are covered in Tables 4-6 through 4-8.

For these DMVs to be useful, the SQL Server instance must have been in service for a solid amount of time. No set amount of time can be given, because the level of knowledge of the database professional's is what determines whether sufficient processing has occurred to provide the DMVs with accurate data. If the server has just been cycled, you will be disappointed with the results. The only way SQL Server can tell you if indexes are used or missing is if the server has had time to collect that information.

Take any recommendations on index additions with a grain of salt. As the DBA, you have the knowledge and research skills to verify the data reported regarding index recommendations. It is always best practice to create the recommended index in a test environment and verify that the performance gain is achieved by the new index. Indexes should always be justified. If you create indexes that are left unused, they can negatively impact your environment, because each index must be supported for inserts and updates on the columns that they are built on.

*Table 4-6. Common columns used in `dm_db_missing_index_groups`.*

| Column | Data Retrieved |
| --- | --- |
| `index_group_handle` | Identifies the missing index group |
| `index_handle` | Identifies a missing index within the missing index group |

*Table 4-7. Common columns used in `dm_db_missing_index_group_stats`.*

| Column | Data Retrieved |
| --- | --- |
| `group_handle` | Joined to the `index_group_handle` |
| `user_seeks` | Number of seeks that would benefit from the group |
| `user_scans` | Number of scans that would benefit from the group |
| `avg_user_impact` | Average percentage benefit that user queries could experience if the index group is implemented |
| `avg_total_user_cost` | Average cost of the user queries that could be reduced by the addition of the index group |

*Table 4-8. Common columns used in `dm_db_missing_index_details`.*

| Column | Data Retrieved |
| --- | --- |
| `index_handle` | Identifier for the missing index |
| `database_id` | Identification of the database with the missing index |
| `object_id` | Table that the missing index is from |
| `equality_columns` | Comma-separated list of columns that contribute to equality |
| `inequality_columns` | Comma-separated list of columns that contribute to inequality |
| `included_columns` | Comma-separated list of columns needed to cover the columns of the query |

Identifying missing indexes to improve performance is a well-designed and functional feature that DMVs offer. Note that the index recommendations that are needed are collected during the uptime of the database environment and are removed on the cycle of the database server. There is a secondary concern that needs to be addressed. Is this is a test environment or a new environment, where processing would not have accumulated the substantial time required to offer valid recommendations? Information must be accumulated in the DMV to provide accurate data, so a nonproduction or new environment might yield inaccurate results.

```
SELECT so.name
    , (avg_total_user_cost * avg_user_impact) * (user_seeks + user_scans) as Impact
    , ddmid.equality_columns
    , ddmid.inequality_columns
    , ddmid.included_columns
FROM sys.dm_db_missing_index_group_stats AS ddmigs
INNER JOIN sys.dm_db_missing_index_groups AS ddmig
ON ddmigs.group_handle = ddmig.index_group_handle
INNER JOIN sys.dm_db_missing_index_details AS ddmid
ON ddmig.index_handle = ddmid.index_handle
INNER JOIN sys.objects so WITH (nolock)
ON ddmid.object_id = so.object_id
WHERE ddmigs.group_handle IN (
    SELECT    TOP (5000) group_handle
    FROM sys.dm_db_missing_index_group_stats WITH (nolock)
    ORDER BY (avg_total_user_cost * avg_user_impact)*(user_seeks+user_scans)DESC);
```

The above query will only result in accurate results if you first run the Database Engine Tuning Advisor fromtheManagement Studio to determine your initial indexing needs. The simple wizard will take you through the steps needed to easily execute the analysis, and it will locate the new object readily, as shown in Figure 4-14.

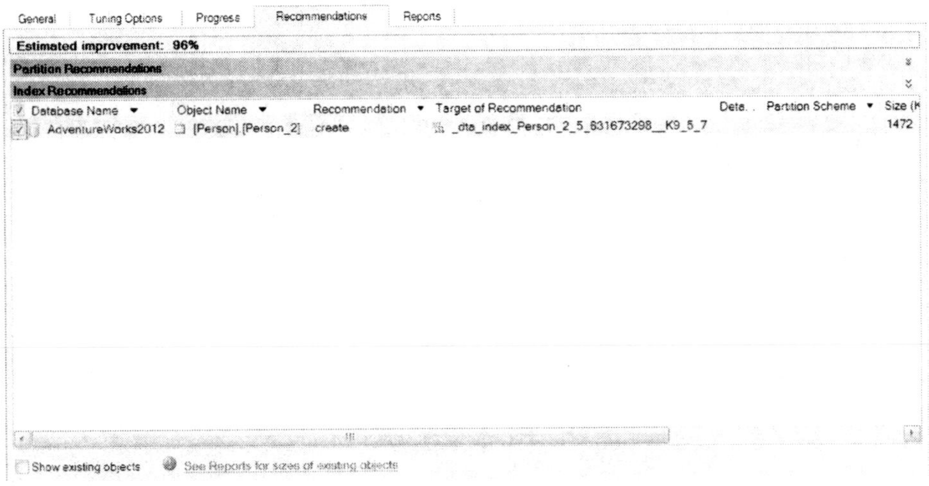

*Figure 4-14. Results of the Database Engine Tuning Advisor.*

Index performance challenges involve determining how the index is used and whether there is an index for a specific query to use. Reporting aggregated totals for all index usage in the current database—broken down by scans, seeks, and bookmarks—can tell you if your indexing is efficient or if changes are required. By using the dm_db_index_usage_stats DMV, you can find out exactly how an index is used. In the view, you will see the scans, seeks, and bookmark lookups for each index.

Removing unused indexes produced some of my largest performance gains in most SQL environments. It is common for many to mistakenly believe "If one index is good, more means even better performance!" This is simply untrue, and as I previously stated, all indexes should be justified. If they are unused, removing them can only improve performance.

Index usage should be established over a period of time—at least one month. The reason for this is that many environments have once-per-month or month-end processing, and they could have specific indexes created for this purpose only. Always verify the index statistics and test thoroughly before dropping any index.

You will know the index is unused when all three states—user_seeks, user_scans, and user_lookups—are 0 (zero).

Rebuild indexes based on the value in dm_db_index_usage_stats. Higher values indicate a higher need for rebuilding or reorganizing.

Return all used indexes in a given database, or drill down to a specific object. Remember that the following query returns only what has been used since the last cycle of the SQL Server instance.

Additionally, with a small change, using very similar columns to the dm_db_ missing_index_group_ stats view, you now have view results based on index usage rather than the results you got from previous queries, which focused on indexes that were missing:

```
SELECT sso.name objectname,
       ssi.name indexname,
       user_seeks,
       user_scans,
       user_lookups,
       user_updates
from sys.dm_db_index_usage_stats ddius
join sys.sysdatabases ssd on ddius.database_id = ssd.dbid
join sys.sysindexes ssi on ddius.object_id = ssi.id and ddius.index_id = ssi.indid
join sys.sysobjects sso on ddius.object_id = sso.id
where sso.type = 'u'
order by user_seeks+user_scans+user_lookups+user_updates desc
```

Figure 4-15 shows the results from the preceding query and that the Person_2, Employee, and Department tables are experiencing full scans. It is important for the DBA to understand why the scan is being performed. Is it due to a query, an update, or a hash join?

| | objectname | indexname | user_seeks | user_scans | user_lookups | user_updates |
|---|---|---|---|---|---|---|
| 1 | Person_2 | NULL | 0 | 14 | 0 | 0 |
| 2 | Employee | PK_Employee_BusinessEntityID | 0 | 1 | 0 | 6 |
| 3 | Employee | AK_Employee_NationalIDNumber | 0 | 6 | 0 | 0 |
| 4 | Department | PK_Department_DepartmentID | 0 | 1 | 0 | 0 |

***Figure 4-15.*** *Table scans versus different types of index scans.*

You can also use the missing views on indexing to view when you are not using an index. This is one of the most common tuning gains for a DBA: adding missing indexes to avoid table scans.

```
SELECT sso.name objectname,
       ssi.name indexname,
```

```
        user_seeks,
        user_scans,
        user_lookups,
        user_updates
from sys.dm_db_index_usage_stats ddius
join sys.sysdatabases ssd on ddius.database_id = ssd.dbid
join sys.sysindexes ssi on ddius.object_id = ssi.id and ddius.index_id = ssi.indid
join sys.sysobjects sso on ddius.object_id = sso.id
where ssi.name is null
order by user_seeks+user_scans+user_lookups+user_updates desc
```

Figure 4-16 shows the results of this query.

**Figure 4-16.** *Tables without indexes.*

As I stated before, locating unused indexes and removing them can be one of the quickest ways a DBA can produce performance gains, as well as achieve space-allocation gains. Executing the following query will join the dm_db_index_usage_stats DMV to sys.tables and sys.indexes, identifying any unused indexes:

```
SELECT st.name as TableName
     , si.name as IndexName
from sys.indexes si
inner join sys.dm_db_index_usage_stats ddius
on ddius.object_id = si.object_id
and ddius.index_id = si.index_id
inner join sys.tables st
on si.object_id = st.object_id
where ((user_seeks = 0
and user_scans = 0
and user_lookups = 0)
or ddius.object_id is null)
```

Figure 4-17 shows the results.

**Figure 4-17.** *Unused index on table Person.*

The index shown in Figure 4-17 was created by me for just this query. It's never been used and is on the column MiddleName of the Persons table. This might seem like a ridiculous index, but it would not be the worst I've identified for removal. The important thing to note is that you should monitor unused indexes for at least a month's time. As new objects and indexes are placed into an environment, they might not be called (that is, objects are released, but application code is to be released at a later date that will call upon the index, and so forth). These scenarios must be kept in mind when choosing indexes to remove, because removing a needed index can have a serious performance impact to the users or applications.

## Partition Statistics

Reporting on partition statistics can offer the DBA pertinent day-to-day data storage information, performance information, and so forth. Knowing how to join to system tables, such as sys.partitions, is important because it can give database professional more valuable data, as well as reviewing space usage and LOB info.

The DMVs will show only one row per partition. This allows the DMV to simplify partition count queries for any given object. Row overflow data, which is extremely important to maintenance work, can be pulled easily from the DMV, too.

Querying partition statistics DMVs offer high hit partitions with drill down lists, page and row-count information. The OBJECT_ID function can then be used to identify the objects from the views by name.

Retrieving information about used pages and the number of rows on a heap or clustered index can be challenging, but not if you use the following query:

```
SELECT SUM(used_page_count) AS total_number_of_used_pages,
    SUM (row_count) AS total_number_of_rows
FROM sys.dm_db_partition_stats
WHERE object_id=OBJECT_ID('Person.Person')
AND (index_id=0
or index_id=1)
```

Figure 4-18 shows the results.

| | total_number_of_used_pages | total_number_of_rows |
|---|---|---|
| 1 | 14697 | 1090313 |

*Figure 4-18. Statistics on a partitioned index.*

Locating partitions with the largest row counts can give you pertinent data about future partitioning needs. This data can be very helpful when deciding whether to create a subpartition.

```
SELECT OBJECT_NAME(object_id) AS
tableName,sys.dm_db_partition_stats.row_count
FROM sys.dm_db_partition_stats
WHERE index_id < 2
ORDER BY sys.dm_db_partition_stats.row_count DESC
```

The results are shown in Figure 4-19.

| | tableName | row_count |
|---|---|---|
| 1 | xml_index_nodes_1765581328_256001 | 301696 |
| 2 | SalesOrderDetail | 121317 |
| 3 | TransactionHistory | 113443 |
| 4 | TransactionHistoryArchive | 89253 |
| 5 | WorkOrder | 72591 |
| 6 | WorkOrderRouting | 67131 |
| 7 | SalesOrderHeader | 31465 |
| 8 | SalesOrderHeaderSalesReason | 27647 |
| 9 | BusinessEntity | 20777 |
| 10 | EmailAddress | 19972 |
| 11 | Password | 19972 |
| 12 | Person | 19972 |

*Figure 4-19. Row counts on partitions.*

# System Performance Tuning Queries

System requests are often joined with the operating system wait DMVs (referred to as *operating system waits*) to give DBAs a clear picture of what is occurring in a SQL Server environment. Where once the DBA was dependent on the information in sp_who and sp_who2, now they can use the information in DMVs and have defined control over the data regarding system information in a SQL Server environment.

## What You Need to Know About System Performance DMVs

Any database professional will have an appreciation for the replacement DMV queries for sp_blocker and sp_who2. You can now request the blocking session_ids and locate issues more quickly, along with extended data with DMVs.

During joins to dm_exec_requests, always verify the blocking session_id. As with any time-sensitive views, you need to know that you have the most up-to-date information in your blocking session results.

Percent_complete and estimated_completion_time can now be retrieved for tasks such as reorganizing indexes, backing up databases, and performing certain DBCC processes and rollbacks In the past, this data was unavailable.

Keep in mind that the data used by the following queries doesn't have to be cleared by a cycle of the database server or services. The data can also be cleared by running DBCC FREEPROCCACHE.

## Sessions and Percentage Complete

Being able to track sessions and obtain information about the logged-in session (such as whether it's active and, if so, how close to complete the process is) is a task most DBAs face daily. DMVs offer up this information in a simple, easy-to-read format, which is focused on the session ID and results that include the SQL statement text and the percentage complete:

```
SELECT der.session_id
    , sql.text
    , der.start_time
    , des.login_name
    , des.nt_user_name
    , der.percent_complete
```

```
        , der.estimated_completion_time
from sys.dm_exec_requests der
join sys.dm_exec_sessions des on der.session_id = des.session_id
cross apply sys.dm_exec_sql_text(plan_handle) sql
where der.status = 'running'
```

Figure 4-20 shows the result of this query.

| | session. | text | | | | start_time | login_name | nt_user_na. | percent_compl. |
|---|---|---|---|---|---|---|---|---|---|
| 1 | 53 | select e session_id | , sql text | , e st. | | 2012-05-29 14:13:25.843 | Kellyn_Zen-PC\Kellyn_Zen | Kellyn_Zen | 0 |

***Figure 4-20.*** *Locating all available requests with percentage complete.*

The following query locates all active queries, including blocked session information:

```
SELECT der.session_id as spid
    , sql.text as sql
    , der.blocking_session_id as block_spid
    , case when derb.session_id is null then 'unknown' else sqlb.text end as block_sql
    , der.wait_type
    , (der.wait_time / 1000) as wait_time_sec
FROM sys.dm_exec_requests der
LEFT OUTER JOIN sys.dm_exec_requests derb on der.blocking_session_id = derb.session_id
CROSS APPLY sys.dm_exec_sql_text(der.sql_handle) sql
CROSS APPLY sys.dm_exec_sql_text(isnull(derb.sql_handle,der.sql_handle)) sqlb
where der.blocking_session_id > 0
```

Figure 4-21 shows the result of this query.

| | spid | sql | | | block_spid | block_sql | wait_type | wait_time_sec |
|---|---|---|---|---|---|---|---|---|
| 1 | 53 | select er session_id as spid | , sql text as s. | | 0 | unknown | NULL | 0 |

***Figure 4-21.*** *Locating all active queries, including blocked-session information.*

The two DMVs—dm_os_tasks and dm_os_threads—can be joined to identify the SQL Server session ID with the Microsoft Windows thread ID. This has the added benefit of monitoring performance and returns only active sessions.

```
SELECT dot.session_id,
       dots.os_thread_id
   FROM sys.dm_os_tasks AS dot
   INNER JOIN sys.dm_os_threads AS dots
   ON dot.worker_address = dots.worker_address
   WHERE dot.session_id IS NOT NULL
   ORDER BY dot.session_id;
```

Figure 4-22 shows the results of this query.

| | wait_type | wait_time_seconds |
|---|---|---|
| 1 | LOGMGR_QUEUE | 21351.236 |
| 2 | DIRTY_PAGE_POLL | 21351.046 |
| 3 | HADR_FILESTREAM_IOMGR_IOCOMPLETION | 21350.687 |
| 4 | SQLTRACE_INCREMENTAL_FLUSH_SLEEP | 21348.257 |
| 5 | LAZYWRITER_SLEEP | 21348.145 |
| 6 | REQUEST_FOR_DEADLOCK_SEARCH | 21346.959 |
| 7 | XE_TIMER_EVENT | 21345.793 |
| 8 | XE_DISPATCHER_WAIT | 21240.495 |
| 9 | CHECKPOINT_QUEUE | 15379.700 |
| 10 | BROKER_EVENTHANDLER | 14794.565 |
| 11 | BROKER_TO_FLUSH | 10675.990 |

*Figure 4-22. Results of query showing session_id and the matching operating system thread ID in Windows.*

Of course, the most important session ID info most investigations need is the information for any session IDs less than 51.

Wait statistics are important in any database, and SQL Server is no different. The following DMV, dm_os_wait_stats, lists the wait type and also shows you the wait time in seconds. You'll find this very useful when looking for the top five wait statistics in any given environment.

```
SELECT wait_type, (wait_time_ms * .001) wait_time_seconds
    FROM sys.dm_os_wait_stats
    GROUP BY wait_type, wait_time_ms
    ORDER BY wait_time_ms DESC
```

Figure 4-23 shows the results of this query.

| | wait_type | wait_time_seconds |
|---|---|---|
| 1 | LOGMGR_QUEUE | 21351.236 |
| 2 | DIRTY_PAGE_POLL | 21351.046 |
| 3 | HADR_FILESTREAM_IOMGR_IOCOMPLETION | 21350.687 |
| 4 | SQLTRACE_INCREMENTAL_FLUSH_SLEEP | 21348.257 |
| 5 | LAZYWRITER_SLEEP | 21348.145 |
| 6 | REQUEST_FOR_DEADLOCK_SEARCH | 21346.959 |
| 7 | XE_TIMER_EVENT | 21345.793 |
| 8 | XE_DISPATCHER_WAIT | 21240.495 |
| 9 | CHECKPOINT_QUEUE | 15379.700 |
| 10 | BROKER_EVENTHANDLER | 14794.565 |
| 11 | BROKER_TO_FLUSH | 10675.990 |

*Figure 4-23. Results for different wait types in SQL Server.*

In Figure 4-23, there isn't any user processing, only background processes, so the wait time in seconds won't be the standard event times you would normally see.

Gaining insights into which operating-system processes have issues is sometimes left to the DBAs perception and assumptions. The DMV dm_os_workers takes the guesswork out of this task by listing each of the operating-system sessions, indicating whether there is an actual issue with any one of them.

```
SELECT dot.session_id,
       dow.is_sick,
       dow.is_in_cc_exception,
       dow.is_fatal_exception,
       dow.state,
       dow.return_code
    FROM sys.dm_os_workers dow,
sys.dm_os_tasks dot
where dow.worker_address= dot.worker_address
and dot.session_id is not NULL
```

The results are shown in Figure 4-24.

| session_id | is_sick | is_in_cc_exception | is_fatal_exception | state | return_code |
|---|---|---|---|---|---|
| 7 | 0 | 0 | 0 | RUNNING | 0 |
| 15 | 0 | 0 | 0 | SUSPENDED | 0 |
| 5 | 0 | 0 | 0 | SUSPENDED | 0 |
| 18 | 0 | 0 | 0 | SUSPENDED | 258 |
| 13 | 0 | 0 | 0 | RUNNING | 0 |
| 14 | 0 | 0 | 0 | SUSPENDED | 0 |
| 16 | 0 | 0 | 0 | SUSPENDED | 0 |
| 19 | 0 | 0 | 0 | SUSPENDED | 0 |
| 53 | 0 | 0 | 0 | RUNNING | 0 |
| 4 | 0 | 0 | 0 | SUSPENDED | 258 |
| 12 | 0 | 0 | 0 | SUSPENDED | 0 |
| 17 | 0 | 0 | 0 | SUSPENDED | 258 |

*Figure 4-24. Health results of operating-system processes on the database server.*

If any of the preceding processes were found to be in trouble (that is, they showed up as is_sick, is_in_cc_exception or is_fatal_exception), they would have returned a value of 1 in Figure 4-24. Here is a list of the values that indicate some sort of trouble:

| | |
|---|---|
| is_sick | Process is in trouble |
| is_in_cc_exception | SQL is handling a non-SQL exception |
| is_fatal_exception | Exception has experienced an error |

The meaning of the codes in the State column are as follows:

| | |
|---|---|
| INIT | Worker is currently being initialized. |
| RUNNING | Worker is currently running either non-pre-emptively or pre-emptively. |
| RUNNABLE | Worker is ready to run on the scheduler. |
| SUSPENDED | Worker is currently suspended, waiting for an event to send it a signal. |

And the meaning of the return codes are the following:

| 0   | Success          |
|-----|------------------|
| 3   | Deadlock         |
| 4   | Premature Wakeup |
| 258 | Timeout          |

The dm_os_volume stats view, which is new to SQL Server 2012, returns the disk, database-file, and usage information. There is no known way to collect this data for a pre-2012 version of SQL Server.

```
SELECT database_id as DBID,file_id as FileId,
       volume_mount_point as VolumeMount,
       logical_volume_name as LogicalVolume,
       file_system_type as SystemType,
       total_bytes as TotalBytes,available_bytes as AvailBytes,
       is_read_only as [ReadOnly],is_compressed as Compressed
FROM sys.dm_os_volume_stats(1,1)
UNION ALL
SELECT database_id as DBID,file_id as FileId,
       volume_mount_point as VolumeMount,
       logical_volume_name as LogicalVolume,
       file_system_type as SystemType,
       total_bytes as TotalBytes,available_bytes as AvailBytes,
       is_read_only as [ReadOnly],is_compressed as Compressed
FROM sys.dm_os_volume_stats(1,2);
```

For my little test hardware, there isn't much that's interesting to report on (as you can see in Figure 4-25), but this data could prove incredibly valuable in production environments when you want to inspect the I/O resources available to the database server.

| DBID | FileId | VolumeMo... | LogicalVolu... | SystemTy... | TotalBytes  | AvailBytes | ReadO... | Compress... |
|------|--------|-------------|----------------|-------------|-------------|------------|----------|-------------|
| 1    | 1      | C:\         | OS             | NTFS        | 111441604608 | 27464982528 | 0        | 0           |
| 1    | 2      | C:\         | OS             | NTFS        | 111441604608 | 27464982528 | 0        | 0           |

*Figure 4-25. Volume stats of mount points obtained through the dm_os_volume stats DMV.*

I included the transactional snapshot information because I find the virtual table generation an interesting feature of this view. It's not commonly used, but it demonstrates how easy it is to use these views and produce valuable information from them.

The following query reports transactions that are assigned a transaction sequence number (also known as an XSN). This XSN is assigned when a transaction accesses the version store for the first time.

```
SELECT
    transaction_id,
    transaction_sequence_num,
    commit_sequence_num,
    is_snapshot session_id,
    first_snapshot_sequence_num,
    max_version_chain_traversed,
    average_version_chain_traversed,
    elapsed_time_seconds
```

```
FROM sys.dm_tran_active_snapshot_database_transactions;
```

Keep the following in mind when executing this query:

- The XSN is assigned when any DML occurs, even when a SELECT statement is executed in a snapshot isolation setting.

- The query generates a virtual table of all active transactions, which includes data about potentially accessed rows.

- One or both of the database options `ALLOW_SNAPSHOT_ISOLATION` and `READ_COMMITTED_SNAPSHOT` must be set to ON.

The following is the output from executing the query:

| transaction_id | transaction_sequence_num | commit_sequence_num |
|---|---|---|
| 11630 | 59 | NULL |
| 11512 | 62 | NULL |
| 11622 | 68 | NULL |
| 11670 | 57 | NULL |
| 11580 | 66 | NULL |

| is_snapshot | session_id | first_snapshot_sequence_num |
|---|---|---|
| 0 | 62 | 0 |
| 0 | 53 | 0 |
| 1 | 61 | 66 |
| 1 | 56 | 63 |
| 1 | 57 | 69 |

| max_version_chain_traversed | average_version_chain_traversed |
|---|---|
| 0 | 0 |
| 0 | 0 |
| 1 | 1 |
| NULL | NULL |
| NULL | NULL |

| elapsed_time_seconds |
|---|
| 573 |
| 569 |
| 222 |
| 218 |
| 168 |

Here's how to read these result tables:

- The first group of columns shows information about the current running transactions.

- The second group designates a value for the is_snapshot column only for transactions running under snapshot isolation.

- The order of the activity of the transactions can be identified by the first_snapshot_sequence_num column for any transactions using snapshot isolation.

- Each process is listed in order of the transaction_id, and then by elapsed_time.

# Conclusion

Anyone database administrators who were troubleshooting performance-level or system-level issues before the existence of Dynamic Management Views faced unique challenges. The introduction of this feature has created a relational database management system environment with robust performance-tuning and system-metric-collection views that DBAs can use to figure out answers to the performance challenges that exist in their SQL Server environments.

# CHAPTER 5

■ ■ ■

# From SQL Trace to Extended Events

## By Mladen Prajdić

In this chapter we'll look at the currently existing tracing and diagnostic infrastructure in SQL Server 2012. There are three areas we'll cover: SQL Trace, Event Notifications, and Extended Events. SQL Trace is the oldest of the three and has been put on the deprecated features list in SQL Server 2012. This means that it will be removed from the SQL Server in a future version. Future version usually means current version + 2. Because of that I assume for this chapter that you're familiar with the terminology and basic use of SQL Profiler. Event Notifications were introduced in SQL Server 2005 and are an asynchronous eventing system based on SQL Server Service Broker. The events that are sent can be database or server scoped. Extended Events were introduced in SQL Server 2008 and are a completely new diagnostic and tracing infrastructure built directly inside SQLOS.

## SQL Trace

The SQL Trace infrastructure consists of 2 parts: the server side and the client side. The server side is the whole tracing infrastructure built into the SQL Server: the extended stored procedures that actually control the tracing capabilities and the trace points in SQL Server code from where the trace event data is collected from. In SQL Server 2005 we got introduced to SQLOS (SQL Operating System), the part of SQL Server that handles memory management, IO access, CPU scheduling, locking, exception handling, etc… Because SQLOS has an API that the other components of SQL Server use, SQL Trace is built on top of SQLOS and uses this API. The client side includes the SQL Server Profiler tool for creating and analyzing traces and the .NET object model that offers the same functionality as SQL Server Profiler but lets you automate the whole collect/analyze/store process that is usually present with continuous monitoring. Figure 5-1 shows the overview of the SQL Trace architecture.

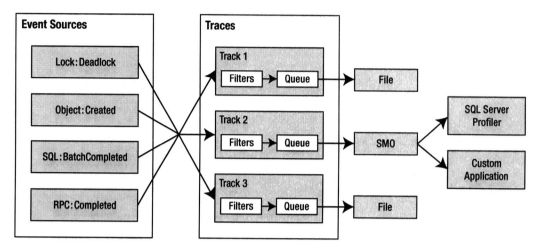

***Figure 5-1.*** *SQL Trace infrastructure: events fire, are sent to traces, filtered there and sent to the target provider (file or rowset)*

There are about 180 trace events (the exact number depends on the SQL Server version you're using) and 66 columns that contain various trace data. There are also 10 user configurable events that you can specify in your T-SQL code that are collected just as any other trace event. They are named UserConfigurable:0 to UserConfigurable:9 and are fired with the sp_trace_generateevent stored procedure. Because it requires ALTER TRACE permissions we must grant this permission to any account executing the stored procedure. The sp_trace_generateevent stored procedure is called like this:

```
DECLARE @msg NVARCHAR(128);
SELECT  @msg = N'Message that will be displayed in the SQL Trace or SQL Profiler';
-- user configurable events have ID's from 82 (UserConfigurable:0) to 91
(UserConfigurable:9)
EXEC sp_trace_generateevent 82, @msg;
```

There are two providers for collecting data: the file provider used by the server side tracing, and the rowset provider used by client side tracing. That means that there is *not* a built in direct-to-table provider. At first this can be confusing to people new to SQL Server tracing but if you think about it is quite logical. To have a direct-to-table provider you'd have to follow the rules of SQL Server data writing, transaction logs, locking, blocking, resources, etc… this way you just have a simple file or a memory buffer that the trace data gets written to and SQL Server is done with it. One important thing to note is that although you can use filters when creating traces, those filters are not applied in the data collection phase. Every single column for any event is fully collected and sent to the provider where it gets filtered down to the columns we specified in the trace definition. It is also better to have a few smaller traces than one huge trace. This is because each trace has its own target destination and you can put these targets on different drives spreading out the load.

All traces are managed inside the SQL Server in a thread called background management thread. This thread is started as soon as any trace starts running. You can view details about this thread in the sys. sysprocesses view or in sys.dm_exec_requests dynamic management view if you're on SQL Server 2005 and up. There is a default trace always running in SQL Server 2005 and up so this will always return at least one row, unless you explicitly turn off the default trace. We'll talk about the default trace later in the chapter. Code shows how to query the view and the DMV. The results will vary across machines and you can see what the columns contain in Books Online.

```
-- SQL Server 2000
SELECT  *
FROM    sys.sysprocesses
WHERE   cmd = 'TRACE QUEUE TASK';

-- SQL Server 2005 and up
SELECT  *
FROM    sys.dm_exec_requests
WHERE   command = 'TRACE QUEUE TASK';
```

The SQL Trace engine has what is known as an *event send buffer*. The trace event data is first collected into this buffer and then sent to the providers. The background management thread monitors the trace providers and for file providers it flushes them every 4 seconds. This is better for performance because it can then use large block writes (1 large continuous write to disk instead of many small ones) for faster IO write speed. For rowset providers it closes every provider that has been dropping events for more than 10 minutes. We'll talk more about event dropping shortly.

## Trace rowset provider

The SQL Server rowset provider sends trace data to SQL Server Profiler and .NET SMO (Server Management Objects) object model. You've probably heard of stories about the running SQL Profiler on the production box bringing the whole server to a standstill. You haven't? Well, they are true. This happens because the rowset provider is memory-based. It takes all the memory it needs and if you run it on a production server, it takes that valuable memory and makes in unusable to SQL Server. This is the reason why it's crucial that you run the SQL Profiler or a .NET SMO collector service (this is coded by a programmer to suit specific tracing needs, and not part of the SQL Server product) on a non-production machine.

The rowset provider uses internal buffers to process incoming trace data, and if those buffers get full, the events can be dropped from the trace output. The traces begin to be dropped after the internal buffers have been full for 20 seconds. After that, the rowset provider will drop them to get things moving again. When this happens, the SQL Server Profiler will show a special message that the events have been dropped. Internal buffers waiting to be flushed also increment the TRACEWRITE wait type. This way you can see if your rowset provider based traces are problematic for your system by using the sys.dm_os_wait_stats dynamic management view.

As mentioned there are 2 ways you can view the rowset provider, the SQL Profiler and SMO object model. We'll take a look at both starting with SQL Profiler.

## SQL Server Profiler

SQL Profiler is not available in SQL Express edition but there is a free open source project called SQL Express Profiler that fills that gap. SQL Profiler comes with 9 preinstalled templates that help with common tracing scenarios like tracing statement duration or taken locks. The default trace output is in the profiler window where you can see the traces being written. The more trace events you have, the more memory it will take. One thing to keep in mind is that even though the profiler UI shows the duration column in milliseconds, its value is actually in microseconds. This can be seen if you save the trace to a table. The duration value in the SMO object model is also in microseconds. In my conversations with people there seems to be a misconception that the same thing happened with the CPU column. This is not so. The CPU column is still in milliseconds.

When creating traces with SQL Profiler there might be some confusion about various options you can choose. Figure 5-2 shows the new trace dialog.

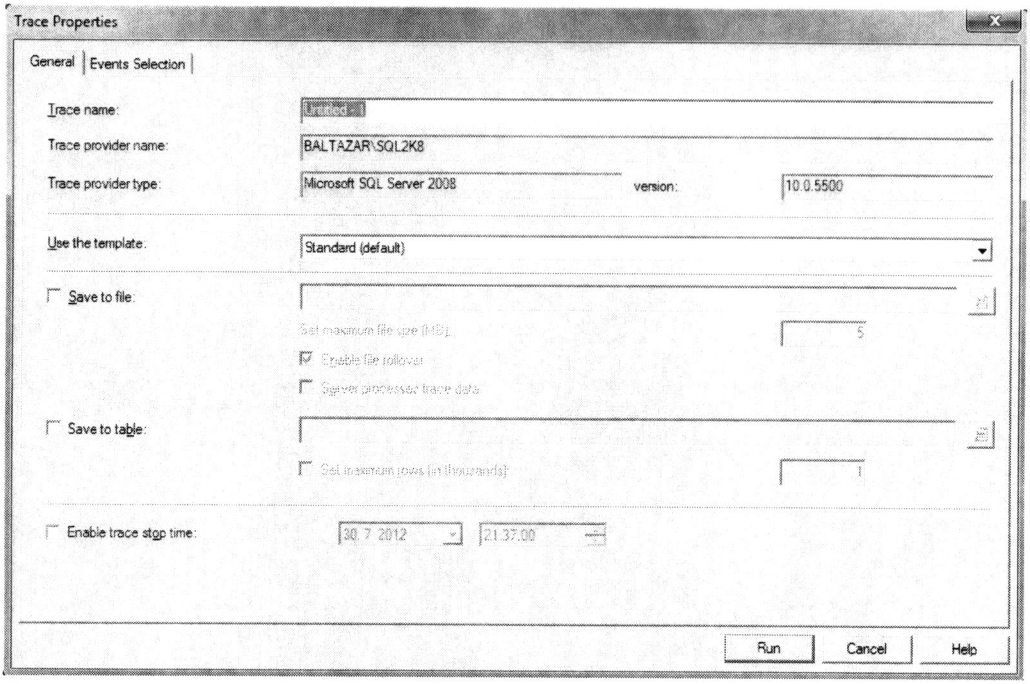

**Figure 5-2.** *The New Trace Properties dialog box*

At the top there are the standard input options like naming your trace and choosing a template. The interesting part is in the middle of the dialog. There are options like "Save to file" and "Save to table". If you remember from earlier there is no direct to-table provider and the rowset provider SQL Profiler uses is memory based. The catch here is that although those options do create a file and save to a table, the data first goes through the rowset provider memory buffer. Notice that there's an option "Server processes trace data". This is the worst thing you can choose. The name is a bit misleading as it makes you think that you're actually creating a server-side trace. What actually happens is you're creating two exactly identical traces. One goes through the rowset provider and the other through the file provider. Figure 5-3 shows the chosen options and the following code shows we really do have 2 traces running.

```
-- This query returns 2 rows.
-- The rowset provider has the
-- is_rowset column set to 1 and
-- NULL in the path column.
-- The file provider has the path column set
-- to the path we've set in options (E:\MyTrace.trc).
SELECT  *
FROM    sys.traces
WHERE   is_default != 1;
```

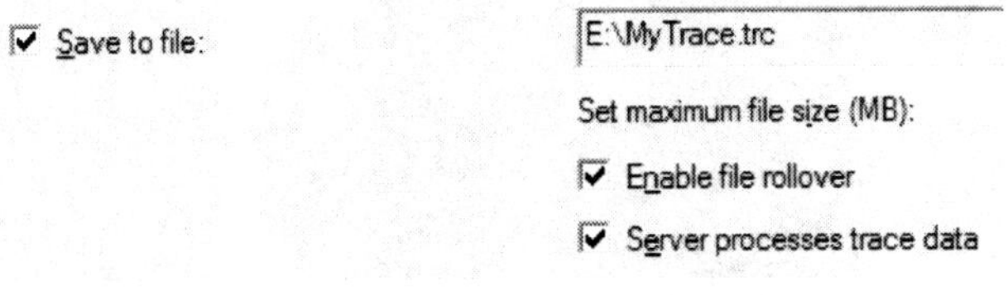

☑ Save to file:  E:\MyTrace.trc

Set maximum file size (MB):

☑ Enable file rollover

☑ Server processes trace data

*Figure 5-3. Save to file options that you should avoid*

If you choose the Save to table option, trace data still goes through the rowset provider and is then inserted into a table row by row. The Set maximum rows option lets you set the maximum row size for the table. After that size is reached the trace data is no longer stored into a table. Tracing however still continues. Another very useful and not well known feature of SQL Profiler is the ability to merge already saved traces with saved PerfMon binary (.blg) or text (.csv) data files. To do this, your trace must have StartTime and EndTime columns included so that it can be synchronized with the PerfMon data. PerfMon merging doesn't work on live traces, only on already saved ones. To merge them open the SQL Trace file, go to File->Import Performance Data and choose the PerfMon data file. Figure 5-4 shows what the correlated data looks like in SQL Profiler.

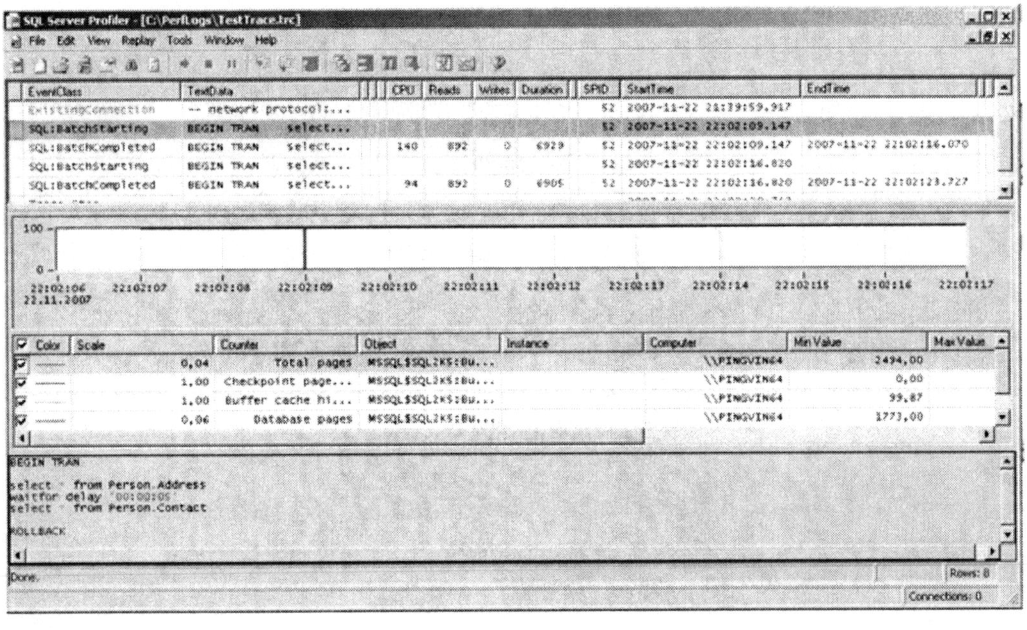

*Figure 5-4. A saved trace correlated with Performance Monitor data, displayed in SQL Profiler*

## .NET SMO objects

Now that we've looked at the SQL Profiler let's take a quick look at the .NET SMO object model. Its capabilities exactly match those of the SQL Profiler. Because of this it can be used for automated tracing, filtering and storing of the filtered traces into various tables or files. One example is to have all statements that last longer than 1 second saved into one separate file, and all the others into another one. Figure 5-5 shows what the object model looks like.

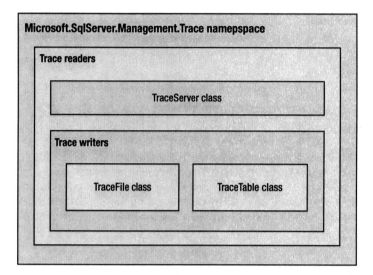

**Figure 5-5.** *The SMO Object Model*

The following code example shows how to read an existing trace file called `DurationTrace.trc` with SMO, and filter it so that only statements with duration longer than 500 ms are saved into a new file. The `DurationTrace.trc` file can be created by running SQL Profiler with Duration template for a few minutes. One thing to note is where the filtering takes place. The first time I used SMO for tracing I thought that since we have a reader and a writer class, we have to read a trace line, perform the filtering there, and then either send it to the writer or not. However this is not the case. You can stream the reader directly into the writer without any filtering. The writer class has a `WriteNotify` event. This event gets called every time a row from the reader is read. In this event you have to perform any filtering and determine whether to skip the record or let it be written. This way of doing things still seems a bit backwards to me, but since this is the case we have to live with it. The example is well documented and is not that hard to follow. By understanding how the classes fit together you can build powerful tracing solutions directly in .NET. However be aware that this still uses the rowset provider and can still drop events.

```
static void Main(string[] args)
{
        // create the reader that reads from the existign trace file
        TraceFile traceFileReader = new TraceFile();
        string traceFileReaderPath =
Path.Combine(Path.GetDirectoryName(Assembly.GetExecutingAssembly().Location),
"DurationTrace.trc");
        traceFileReader.InitializeAsReader(traceFileReaderPath);

        // create the trace writer class with the file destination
        string traceFileWriterPath =
Path.Combine(Path.GetDirectoryName(Assembly.GetExecutingAssembly().Location),
"DurationTraceFiltered.trc");
        TraceFile traceFileWriter = new TraceFile();
```

```
            traceFileWriter.InitializeAsWriter(traceFileReader, traceFileWriterPath);
            // add the event where the filtering occurs
            traceFileWriter.WriteNotify += new
WriteNotifyEventHandler(traceFileWriter_WriteNotify);

            // simply looping the writer until the end is enough.
            // Internally it reads from the reader and filters
            // through the WriteNotify event
            while (traceFileWriter.Write()) ;

            // close both to dispose of the resources
            traceFileReader.Close();
            traceFileWriter.Close();

        }

        static void traceFileWriter_WriteNotify(object sender, TraceEventArgs args)
        {
            try
            {
                object durationInMicroSeconds = args.CurrentRecord["Duration"];
                if (durationInMicroSeconds == null || (long)durationInMicroSeconds < (500
/*ms*/ * 1000 /* to get to microseconds*/))
                {
                    args.SkipRecord = true;
                    return;
                }
            }
            catch (Exception ex)
            {
                Console.WriteLine(ex.Message);
            }
        }
```

## Trace file provider

Unlike the rowset provider we discussed earlier, the file provider writes directly to files and guarantees lossless delivery of trace data. Just like rowset provider it uses internal buffers to dispatch the trace data. The buffers get flushed every 4 seconds to maximize the IO performance by using large block writes. It's less expensive to write one large continuous block of data than many small ones. Because the file provider guarantees lossless delivery, it can't drop events and if there are too many of them the whole system can stop. That can be seen with increasing SQLTRACE_LOCK and IO_COMPLETION waits in the sys.dm_os_wait_stats dynamic management view. To avoid this, never write your trace file to the same disk subsystem where your databases are. Use either a separate local physical disk or a UNC share. Keep in mind that whichever you choose the account under which SQL Server runs has to have write permissions on that folder.

The only parts of the SQL Trace that we can use are the extended stored procedures and functions. Those take care of creating, altering, starting, stopping and viewing trace files. Table 5-1 shows the extended stored procedures and functions names and what they do.

*Table 5-1. SQL Trace extended stored procedures and functions and descriptions about what they do*

| Extended Stored Procedure | Function |
|---|---|
| fn_trace_geteventinfo | Returns information about events included in a trace. |
| fn_trace_getinfo | Returns information about a specified trace or all existing traces. |
| fn_trace_getfilterinfo | Returns information about filters applied to a trace. |
| sp_trace_create | Creates a trace definition. The new trace will be in a stopped state. |
| sp_trace_generateevent | Creates a user-defined event. |
| sp_trace_setevent | Adds an event class or data column to a trace, or removes one from it. |
| sp_trace_setstatus | Starts, stops, or closes a trace. |
| sp_trace_setfilter | Applies a new or modified filter to a trace. |

If you look at these stored procedures and functions in greater detail you'll notice they're not the most intuitive things to work with. For example the trace events and columns are not referenced by their names but their ID's. This is where SQL Profiler comes to the rescue. It has the ability to export a defined trace to a .sql file that you can use to start the SQL trace on the server. This makes life much easier than having to code everything by hand. The created file does have to be checked and things like trace name and path have to be manually entered. To do this, start a trace, stop it, then go to File->Export->Script Trace Definition and choose the desired SQL Server version.

There are two out of the box traces that come with SQL Server: a blackbox trace and a default trace. The blackbox trace is not running by default. As its name suggests, it's a trace you can't modify in any way. Theirs is no adding of events, filtering, or changing the target file settings. You can either start it or stop it. You start it by using sp_trace_create with option 8, it contains only 4 events (RPC starting, Batch starting, Exception, Attention) and is saved to a 5 MB file at %SQLDIR%\MSSQL\DATA\blackbox.trc. When that file is full it creates a second rolled over filed called blackbox_1.trc. When the second file gets full it again starts writing into the first one and so on. It has been used for troubleshooting and auditing in SQL Server 2000 but now other functionality is used for that, such as the default trace and custom solutions.

The second built in trace is called the Default Trace. It was introduced in SQL Server 2005 as a lightweight diagnostic trace and unlike the blackbox trace, it runs by default unless you specifically turn it off by enabling advanced options with sp_configure. Like the blackbox trace it can't be modified. It uses 5 files of 20 MB that are rolled over. The following code shows how to see if the default trace is running and how to enable it if not.

```
-- See if the default trace is enabled
SELECT * FROM sys.configurations WHERE configuration_id = 1568
GO
-- See if the default trace is running
SELECT * FROM sys.traces WHERE is_default = 1
GO
-- if not start it
sp_configure 'show advanced options', 1;
GO
RECONFIGURE;
GO
sp_configure 'default trace enabled', 1;
GO
RECONFIGURE;
GO
```

It contains quite a few more events than the blackbox trace, 32 to be exact. They events are from 6 categories: Server, Database, Error and Warnings, Full Text, Object related, and Security audit. The complete set of events can be found in Books Online. As useful as the default trace is, if you have an application that creates, alters, or drops a lot of objects (like temporary tables in tempdb) the needed information may be quickly lost. The following code shows three events that get written to the default trace: the Sort Warning, the Missing Join Predicate and the Audit Addlogin Event with Add and Drop subclasses. If you're going to run this code, make sure to change the path to the Default Trace.

```
-- make a suboptimal plan that gets reused and creates a sort warning.
-- creates the Sort Warning event in the default trace
USE tempdb
-- create test table
IF (OBJECT_ID('TestSortWarning', 'U') IS NOT NULL)
    DROP TABLE TestSortWarning
GO
CREATE TABLE TestSortWarning
 (
    c1 NVARCHAR(100) NOT NULL,
    c2 NVARCHAR(40) NOT NULL
 )
GO
-- insert 100000 random rows
INSERT INTO TestSortWarning(c1, c2)
SELECT TOP 100000 c1.name, CAST(NEWID() AS NVARCHAR(40))
FROM    sys.all_columns AS c1,
        sys.all_columns AS c2
GO
CREATE CLUSTERED INDEX CI_TestSortWarning_c1 ON TestSortWarning(c1)
GO
-- Clear the cache
DBCC freeproccache
GO
-- returns 0 rows
EXEC sp_executesql N'SELECT * FROM TestSortWarning WHERE c1 LIKE @p1 ORDER BY c2',
                   N'@p1 NVARCHAR(20)',
                   @p1 = '#%'
GO
-- Sort warning because of suboptimal plan (see row count estimation for sort operator)
EXEC sp_executesql N'SELECT * FROM TestSortWarning WHERE c1 LIKE @p1 ORDER BY c2',
                   N'@p1 NVARCHAR(20)',
                   @p1 = 'B%'
GO
USE master
GO
SELECT  TE.name, T.DatabaseName, T.DatabaseID
FROM    sys.fn_trace_gettable('C:\Program Files\Microsoft SQL
Server\MSSQL11.SQL2012\MSSQL\Log\log.trc', DEFAULT) T
        JOIN sys.trace_events TE ON T.EventClass = TE.trace_event_id
WHERE   TE.name = 'Sort Warnings'
ORDER BY T.StartTime DESC
```

```
--------------------------------------------------------------------------------
--------------------------------------------------------------------------------
-- Make a CROSS JOIN between 2 columns.
-- creates the Missing Join Predicate event in the default trace
USE master
GO
SELECT  top 100 *
FROM    master..spt_values t1,
        master..spt_values t2
GO
SELECT  TE.name, T.DatabaseName, T.DatabaseID
FROM    sys.fn_trace_gettable('C:\Program Files\Microsoft SQL
Server\MSSQL11.SQL2012\MSSQL\Log\log.trc', DEFAULT) T
        JOIN sys.trace_events TE ON T.EventClass = TE.trace_event_id
WHERE   TE.name = 'Missing Join Predicate'
ORDER BY T.StartTime DESC
GO


--------------------------------------------------------------------------------
--------------------------------------------------------------------------------
-- Create a login and drop it.
-- This creates the Audit Addlogin Event: Add
-- and Audit Addlogin Event: Drop events in the default trace
USE master
CREATE LOGIN DT_LOGIN_TEST WITH PASSWORD = 'I_AM_PASSWORD!';
GO
DROP LOGIN DT_LOGIN_TEST
GO
SELECT  TE.name AS [EventName], TSV.subclass_name, T.DatabaseName, T.DatabaseID
FROM    sys.fn_trace_gettable('C:\Program Files\Microsoft SQL
Server\MSSQL11.SQL2012\MSSQL\Log\log.trc', DEFAULT) T
        JOIN sys.trace_events TE ON T.EventClass = TE.trace_event_id
        JOIN sys.trace_subclass_values TSV ON TSV.trace_event_id = TE.trace_event_id AND
TSV.subclass_value = t.EventSubClass
WHERE   te.name LIKE 'Audit Addlogin Event'
ORDER BY T.StartTime DESC
```

If you need to collect more data than the default trace, you should create another trace with just the extra data and correlate the two to reduce overhead. Even though the default trace is lightweight, one can never be too careful.

# Event Notifications

Event notifications were introduced in SQL Server 2005. They are based on Service Broker, a asynchronous addition to the database engine. Figure 5-6 shows the basic architecture of Service Broker. You can see the Service Broker building blocks: messages, services, queues and dialogs. Service Broker can send messages between databases and servers in transactional manner keeping the properties of ACID intact. The communication between two endpoints can be open or encrypted (transport security). Even messages themselves can be encrypted (dialog security). We'll cover just the very basics of Service Broker but for deeper understanding you can read about it in Books Online.

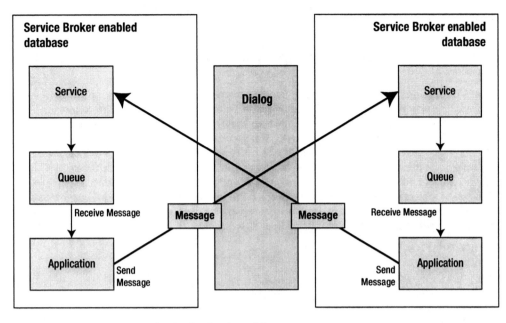

*Figure 5-6. SQL Server Service Broker basic architecture*

What you need to know about Service Broker to understand Event Notifications is that when an event you're interested in fires, a message with that event data is asynchronously sent in a dialog to a service that is backed by a queue where the actual message is stored until processed. The message is processed inside a custom stored procedure called *activation stored procedure* where we RECEIVE the messages from the queue and do with them whatever we want. RECEIVE is a new T-SQL keyword that is used to retrieve a message from the queue. It's basically a SELECT statement for messages in a queue. A message is always stored in an XML form that can also be validated with a schema if needed. Message size can be up to 2 GB. Because the messages are always in XML format there is a very small overhead of converting the event data into XML format and sending the event notification. Because of this Service Broker dependency you have to enable Service Broker on the databases you're going to use Event Notifications in.

There are 2 categories the Event Notifications events fall into: server-scoped and database-scoped. Server-scoped events are a subset of SQL Trace event classes, while database-scoped ones are all DDL events that can be used for either an event notification or a DDL trigger. Both have a fixed XML schema that they conform to and are validated against when creating a message for sending.

There are a few differences between SQL Trace and Event notifications though. If a DDL statement is rolled back, the message is not fired. That means that the event notifications get sent only after a transaction is successfully committed. While a transaction is running the messages are stored in internal Service Broker queues. The next difference is that the Event Notifications unlike SQL Trace traces (except default trace) persist across server restarts. They can also be received remotely to a different server for processing.

You can monitor anything related to Event Notifications with the following catalog views. You can find their details in Books Online.

- sys.event_notification_event_types: Contains all server and database scoped events. They are hierarchicaly grouped, which means you can subsribe to anything from a group of events to a single event. This kind of granularity provides a powerful tracing model.

- sys.server_event_notifications and sys.server_events: contains all server level event notifications and the events each notification contains

- sys.event_notifications and sys.events: contains all database level event notifications and the events each notification contains

Because Event Notifications are based on Service Broker, they fire an activation stored procedure each time an event is fired. This way you can have different activation stored procedures for different events. I have found this very useful and Event Notifications have become my number one way to get immediately notified about important events like deadlocks or blocks. You just have to subscribe to a DEADLOCK_GRAPH and BLOCKED_PROCESS_REPORT events, and when you get one, you can save the notification to a table and send an email to the person in charge. Sure beats constantly running a trace and events without immediate notifications. The following examples shows how to subscribe to a DEADLOCK_GRAPH server scoped event and a short stored procedure snippet to process it. The full code can be found in the book's code appendix. This is actually part of the code I use on my servers for immediate deadlock notificatios. They work great and let me investigate problems as soon as they happen.

```sql
-- INSTANT DEADLOCK NOTIFICATIONS
USE tempdb;
GO
-- this procedure will write our event data into the table and
-- send the notification email in this example the stored procedure
-- is missing error and transaction handling!
CREATE PROCEDURE usp_ProcessNotification
AS
    DECLARE @msgBody XML;
    DECLARE @dlgId uniqueidentifier;
    -- you can change this to get all messages at once
    WHILE(1=1)
    BEGIN
            -- receive messages from the queue one by one
            ;RECEIVE TOP(1)
                    @msgBody = message_body,
                    @dlgId   = conversation_handle
            FROM    dbo.EventNotificationsQueue;
            -- insert event data into our table
            INSERT INTO TestEventNotification(eventMsg)
            SELECT @msgBody;
            -- we can also send an email after processing the event
            -- DECLARE @MailBody NVARCHAR(MAX)
            -- SELECT @MailBody = CAST(@msgBody AS NVARCHAR(MAX));
            -- send an email with the defined email profile.
            -- since this is async it doesn't halt execution
            -- EXEC msdb.dbo.sp_send_dbmail
            --          @profile_name = 'your mail profile', -- your defined email profile
            --          @recipients = 'dba@yourCompany.com', -- your email
            --          @subject = 'occured notification',
            --          @body = @MailBody;
    END
GO
-- create the notification queue that will receive the event notification messages
-- add the activation stored procedure that will process the messages in the queue
```

```
-- as they arrive
CREATE QUEUE EventNotificationsQueue
    WITH STATUS = ON,
    ACTIVATION (
        PROCEDURE_NAME = usp_ProcessNotification,
        MAX_QUEUE_READERS = 1,
        EXECUTE AS 'dbo' );
GO
-- crete the notification service for our queue with the pre-defined message type
CREATE SERVICE NotificationsService
    ON QUEUE
EventNotificationsQueue(
[http://schemas.microsoft.com/SQL/Notifications/PostEventNotification]);
GO
-- create the route for the service
CREATE ROUTE NotificationsRoute
    WITH SERVICE_NAME = 'NotificationsService',
    ADDRESS = 'LOCAL';
GO
-- create the event notification for the DEADLOCK_GRAPH event.
CREATE EVENT NOTIFICATION ServerNotificationEvent
ON SERVER
FOR DEADLOCK_GRAPH
TO SERVICE 'NotificationsService',
            'current database'
-- CASE sensitive string that specifies USE OF server broker IN CURRENT db;
GO
-- check to see if our event notification has been created ok
SELECT * FROM sys.server_event_notifications WHERE name = 'ServerNotificationEvent';
GO
-- create the table that will hold our data
-- every time a deadlock happens its information will be written into this table
CREATE TABLE TestEventNotification(Id INT IDENTITY(1,1), EventMsg xml, EventDate datetime
default(GETDATE()));
```

The other example shows how to subscribe to a database scoped DDL_TABLE_EVENTS event group that consists of CREATE_TABLE, ALTER_TABLE, and DROP_TABLE events. Everything works exactly the same in regard to the activation stored procedures and message handling. The example is running in a tempdb that has service broker enabled by default. If you want to run it in another database, you have to enable service broker in it.

```
-- SUBSCRIBE TO DDL_TABLE_EVENTS EVENT GROUP
-- view the full DDL_TABLE_EVENTS event group we're going subscribe to
WITH cteEvents AS
(
    SELECT  0 AS LEVEL, *
    FROM    sys.event_notification_event_types
    WHERE   TYPE_NAME = 'DDL_TABLE_EVENTS'
    UNION ALL
    SELECT  LEVEL + 1 AS LEVEL, EN.*
    FROM    sys.event_notification_event_types EN
```

```
                    JOIN cteEvents C ON C.parent_type = EN.type
)
SELECT  *
FROM    cteEvents
ORDER BY TYPE;


-- create the event notification for the DDL_TABLE_EVENTS events.
-- send it to the same service that we used for the Server Events
CREATE EVENT NOTIFICATION DatabaseNotificationEvent
ON DATABASE
FOR DDL_TABLE_EVENTS
TO SERVICE 'NotificationsService',
           'current database';
-- CASE sensitive string that specifies USE OF server broker IN CURRENT db
GO
-- Test if it works
CREATE TABLE testEN (id INT);
GO
INSERT INTO testEN VALUES (1), (2);
GO
ALTER TABLE testEN ADD VALUE VARCHAR(20);
GO
DROP TABLE testEN;
GO
SELECT * FROM TestEventNotification;
```

# Extended Events

*Extended events* are a new addition to the SQL Server database engine in SQL Server 2008. They are a new lightweight high performance eventing system that is built directly inside the SQLOS. The extended events engine itself is just a pool of dispatchers that send event data to their targets. It contains no metadata and is fully pluggable. This way Microsoft can extended it without the need to modify other code. In SQL Server 2012 the SQL Trace infrastructure for the database engine was deprecated (however the SSAS part is not yet deprecated). Extended events are its replacement. As the data sizes and loads increase so does the need for tracing with as little overhead as possible. In SQL Server 2008, SQL Trace was still the main tracing engine and had more events. SQL Server 2012 fixed this and now an exact mapping exists between SQL Trace events and Extended events. Because they are more complete in SQL Server 2012 all code is based on that version. Since there have been various changes not all of it will be runnable on SQL Server 2008.

Figure 5-7 shows how all the pieces of extended events fit together. A module is dll or an exe file. Each module can contain multiple packages and each package contains its own extended events objects. This way a grouping can be done based on event functionality like auditing or SQLOS events or general SQL Server events. There are 4 packages in SQL Server 2008 and 9 in SQL Server 2012. They can be viewed by querying the sys.dm_xe_packages catalog view.

Not all of the packages can be used, and not all of them have entirely public objects. For example you can't use anything from SecAudit package since it's reserved for the built in auditing functionality. In the following sections, we'll take a short look at the objects that are in a package.

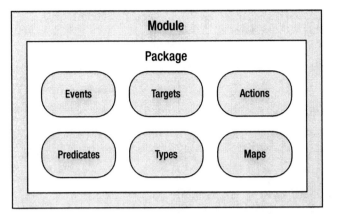

**Figure 5-7.** *Extended events architecture*

## Events

Events are points in code that we can trace. They are defined with the standard ETW (event tracing for windows) model that includes channel, keyword, and payload attributes. Channel tells the target audience for the event like an administrator or a developer. Keywords give us the ability to group events into extra categories. Events always execute synchronously but the extended events engine can forward them to their targets synchronously or asynchronously. The payload is just a fancy name for the data collected for the event. The cool thing about the events is that we can unlike with SQL Trace extend the collected data with actions. We'll look at those shortly. Existing events and their payload can be viewed with these SQL statements:

```
-- view all defined events in sql server
SELECT *
FROM sys.dm_xe_objects
WHERE object_type = 'event'
-- show only targets that we can use
    AND (capabilities IS NULL OR capabilities & 1 = 0)
ORDER BY name;

-- view all columns for each event - the event payload
SELECT    *
FROM      sys.dm_xe_object_columns
WHERE     -- show only targets that we can use
          (capabilities IS NULL OR capabilities & 1 = 0)
ORDER BY object_name, name;
```

## Predicates

Predicates are similar to filters in SQL Trace but much more powerful. They function like a WHERE clause in a SQL statement. They filter which events will be sent to the target, again unlike SQL Trace, which sends an event to all targets and leaves the filtering to them. Predicates fully support short-circuiting so it's a good idea to first specify simple predicates followed by more complex ones. All predicates are processed synchronously so be aware that heavy duty conditions can cause some performance degradation. It's best to keep predicates simple like filtering the event based on a transaction ID or object ID or something similar. Existing predicates can be viewed with this SQL statement:

```
SELECT *
FROM sys.dm_xe_objects
WHERE object_type in ('pred_compare', 'pred_source')
-- show only targets that we can use
    AND (capabilities IS NULL OR capabilities & 1 = 0)
ORDER BY name;
```

## Actions

Actions are commands that provide additional information for an event. You can view them as environment variables that give information about the current database engine state. However you can also perform a task with them inside the database engine, like inserting a breakpoint or collecting a mini dump. Just be careful with those breakpoints because they stop the SQL Server execution. They are bound to the event in the session definition and a few (such as database_name, event_sequence) are direct column mappings from SQL Trace. Any action can be linked to any event. They are also processed synchronously after all predicates have been evaluated and before the event is sent to its target. Actions reflect the global state of the database engine and they are not hard linked to an event. For example there's an action called sqlserver.sql_text that can be collected when an event fires. This action returns the same information as DBCC INPUTBUFFER command. A first time user will probably think (like I did) that it is collecting the SQL statement that fired the event. This is not the case.

Existing actions can be viewed with this SQL statement:

```
SELECT *
FROM sys.dm_xe_objects
WHERE object_type = 'action'
-- show only targets that we can use
    AND (capabilities IS NULL OR capabilities & 1 = 0)
ORDER BY name;
```

## Types and Maps

A *type* is a simple or complex data type that is used in the event payload. *Maps* are dictionaries that map some numeric value to a text. Existing types and maps can be viewed with these SQL statements:

```
SELECT *
FROM sys.dm_xe_objects
WHERE object_type in ('map', 'type')
-- show only targets that we can use
    AND (capabilities IS NULL OR capabilities & 1 = 0)
ORDER BY name;

SELECT *
FROM sys.dm_xe_map_values;
```

# Targets

Targets are the destinations where the extended event data is stored. A target can be a memory buffer or a file and can be either synchronous or asynchronous in the way it saves data. If a target is synchronous then the engine waits until the event data is successfully stored in the target. In both SQL Server 2008 and 2012 there are 6 targets. Because some target names and some of their properties have changed between versions I will use SQL Server 2012 names and properties.

First target is called the *Histogram*. It is memory based and asynchronous. It counts the number of occurrences that an event fires. The basis for a histogram group can be event data or an action. As this target only stored counts and has a low performance overhead it's a good choice to use when we're trying to find which events fire the most in the database engine.

The *Event Counter* target is a memory-based and synchronous target. It is similar to the Histogram but only in that it counts events. The difference is that it can't be modified or filtered in any way and counts all events that happen in the engine. Using this counter is a good way to find out the workload characteristics of your system.

The *Pair Matching* target is an interesting target because with it you can track events that are still happening. It takes an event pair, for example `sql statement starting` and `sql statement completed`, matches them on one or many columns in the event data and discards them from further processing if they match up. For each event it captures the whole event data and all the actions that have been specified for that event. It stores all this data in a memory buffer until the paired event has fired. This memory buffer can't be set, is internally handled by the extended events engine, and is based on available system resources. If there is memory pressure and the stored unpaired events have to be flushed, the incoming events that would be matched with the flushed ones will appear as unmatched in the target. There's one thing you have to be careful about here. Not all events can be paired up nicely. Lock Acquired is one of them. There is the Lock Released event that you might think fires for every Lock Acquired event but that is not the case. One such occurrence is when lock escalation happens from row to page to table. The Lock Acquired event fires for each of those but Lock Released fires only once when the page or table lock is released.

*Ring Buffer* is a memory based and asynchronous target. It stores events in a cyclical memory space that gets used over and over again. It can work in two modes. The first is strict FIFO (the default) in which the oldest event gets removed from the buffer when the buffer fills up. The second is per-event FIFO, in which, as the name suggest a number of the events of the same types are kept in memory. In this mode the last event of each type is removed from the buffer. The ring buffer memory size, the number of events to keep (all and for each type) are all configurable options.

*Event File* is a file based and asynchronous target. When the session buffer is full it writes its contents into a file. Like in SQL Trace you can specify a filename, the file size, whether the files can be rolled over, and by how much the file will grow once it's full. To read the contents of the event file we have to use the `sys.fn_xe_file_target_read_file` function. When specifying the file name you can use the * character anywhere in the name to read all the files that match the partial name. It works in the same way as the % character in a SQL LIKE comparison. To read the event file in SQL Server 2008 we also needed to provide a metadata file (created at session start) to the `sys.fn_xe_file_target_read_file` function. In SQL Server 2012 this isn't needed anymore.

The last target is called *Event Tracing for Windows – ETW* target. It's a file based synchronous target. To use this target successfully you have to have knowledge how the ETW works in Windows, which is out of the scope of this chapter. If you want to get more information about it search MSDN for "Event Tracing for Windows Target" article (http://msdn.microsoft.com/en-us/library/ff878411.aspx). The target is a singleton in the SQL Server process. This means that the events arriving to it will be processed one at a time no matter how many Extended Events sessions are sending the vents data. Once you enable the ETW target, an ETW session is created on the machine that SQL Server runs on. This session is shared across all instances installed on that machine. To use ETW target, the account SQL Server Service runs under must be a member of the Performance Log Users group.

After reading about ETW target, if you think it's confusing I would say you are completely right. In my opinion this target is too complex to use effectively in its current state.

Existing targets can be viewed with this SQL statement:

```
SELECT      *
FROM        sys.dm_xe_objects
WHERE       object_type = 'target'
    -- show only targets that we can use
    AND (capabilities IS NULL OR capabilities & 1 = 0)
ORDER BY name;
```

## Sessions

Sessions are just a grouping of events, actions and targets. There are no limits about which of those you can and cannot mix, except the ones that are private to the database engine by default like objects from SecAudit package. Sessions are not auto-started when created and can be changed while running.

There are quite a few configuration options that each session has. You can look all them up in Books Online but we'll name 3 most interesting ones. The first is EVENT_RETENTION_MODE which lets us control what's the event loss our session can handle. It has 3 options: ALLOW_SINGLE_EVENT_LOSS (the default setting), ALLOW_MULTIPLE_EVENT_LOSS, and NO_EVENT_LOSS. The names are pretty self-explanatory. But be careful if you set it to NO_EVENT_LOSS. For events that fire a lot, this can slow down the server considerably.

The second session option is TRACK_CAUSALITY. When turned ON it adds action package0.attach_activity_id to every event. This action is a combination of GUID and sequence number. With it we can track events that happen in a batch or across multiple threads in the parallel query execution. This option is OFF by default.

The third option is the MAX_DISPATCH_LATENCY which sets the number of seconds before the non-full session buffers are sent to the asynchronous target. The default is 30 seconds.

All information about Extended events objects and running sessions can be found in dynamic management views that start with sys.dm_xe_* and catalog views starting with sys.server_event_session*. Figure 5-8 from Books Online shows the lifecycle of a single event.

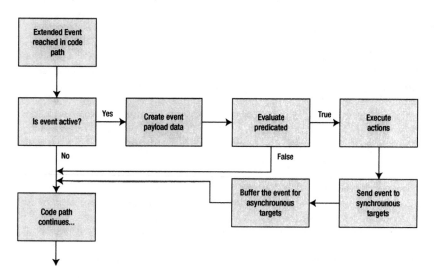

*Figure 5-8. Event life cycle*

Now that we've familiarized ourselves with the Extended Events objects let's talk about the format of the data in the targets. All events are stored in schemaless XML that is read with XQuery. We have to get familiar with the following XML functions:

- nodes() transforms XML to a relational form (rowset view of the XML)

- query() makes an XQuery lookup and returns XML

- value() makes an XQuery lookup for a scalar value of SQL data type and returns it

The following code example shows the quick school of XML. Make sure to read the comments.

```
use tempdb;
GO
IF (OBJECT_ID('TextXML', 'U') IS NOT NULL)
    DROP TABLE TextXML;
GO
CREATE TABLE TextXML
(
    ID INT IDENTITY(1,1),
    XmlColumn XML
) ;
GO
INSERT INTO TextXML(XmlColumn)
SELECT
'<root>
    <event name="Fast Event Name 1" timestamp="2012-05-19T11:53:06.395Z">
        <data name="TestComponent 1">
          <type name="TestType 1" />
          <value>100</value>
          <text>This is some Test Text 1</text>
        </data>
    </event>
    <event name="Fast Event Name 2" timestamp="2012-05-20T12:53:06.395Z">
        <data name="TestComponent 2">
          <type name="TestType" />
          <value>200</value>
          <text>This is some Test Text 2</text>
        </data>
        <data name="TestComponent 2 a">
          <type name="TestType a" />
          <value>2001</value>
          <text>This is some Test Text 2 a</text>
        </data>
    </event>
</root>';
-- node depth setting in cross apply
-- Get 2 rows from the XML, one for each event, in XML form
SELECT  Tbl.cols.query('.') as ShreddedXML
FROM    TextXML X
        -- we're saying to get all the event nodes
        CROSS APPLY X.XmlColumn.nodes('/root/event') Tbl(cols);
```

```
-- Get 2 rows from the XML, one for each event node.
-- Here we get the attributes for each event via .query().value() construct
-- notice the [1] indexer inside the .value(). It is one based, not zero based.
SELECT  Tbl.cols.query('.') as EventXML
        , Tbl.cols.query('.').value('(event/@name)[1]', 'nvarchar(100)') as EventName
        , Tbl.cols.query('.').value('(event/@timestamp)[1]', 'datetime') as
EventTimestamp
FROM    TextXML X
        -- we're saying to get all the event nodes
        CROSS APPLY X.XmlColumn.nodes('/root/event') Tbl(cols);
GO
-- Get 2 rows from the XML, one for each event node.
-- We get the attributes from the data nodes and
-- the values of data nodes children via .query().value() construct
-- Event 1 has just one data node so the query().value() returns null
-- when looking for values at index 2.
-- This can be viewed as denormalization of the XML
SELECT Tbl.cols.query('./data') as DataXML
        , Tbl.cols.query('./data').value('(data/@name)[1]', 'nvarchar(100)') as Data1Name
        , Tbl.cols.query('./data').value('(data/@name)[2]', 'nvarchar(100)') as Data2Name
        , Tbl.cols.query('./data/type').value('(type/@name)[1]', 'nvarchar(100)') as
Type1Name
        , Tbl.cols.query('./data/type').value('(type/@name)[2]', 'nvarchar(100)') as
Type2Name
        , Tbl.cols.query('./data/value').value('(value)[1]', 'int') as Value1
        , Tbl.cols.query('./data/value').value('(value)[2]', 'int') as Value2
        , Tbl.cols.query('./data/text').value('(text)[1]', 'nvarchar(100)') as Text1
        , Tbl.cols.query('./data/text').value('(text)[2]', 'nvarchar(100)') as Text2
FROM    TextXML X
        -- we're saying to get all the event nodes
        CROSS APPLY X.XmlColumn.nodes('/root/event') Tbl(cols);
GO
-- Get 3 rows from the XML, one for each data node.
-- The first event has one data node and the second event has two data nodes.
-- We get the attributes from the data nodes and the values of their children
-- There are no nulls here since we're selecting all the values that exist.
-- If the above was denormalization then this is normalization of the XML values
SELECT  Tbl.cols.query('.') as DataXML
        , Tbl.cols.query('.').value('(data/@name)[1]', 'nvarchar(100)') as DataName
        , Tbl.cols.query('./type').value('(type/@name)[1]', 'nvarchar(100)') as TypeName
        , Tbl.cols.query('./value').value('(value)[1]', 'int') as Value
        , Tbl.cols.query('./text').value('(text)[1]', 'nvarchar(100)') as [Text]
FROM    TextXML X
        -- we're saying to get all the data nodes from all the event nodes
        CROSS APPLY X.XmlColumn.nodes('/root/event/data') Tbl(cols);
```

Now that we know how to work with XML to parse the event data let's take look at a concrete example. We'll use the ring buffer target to trace all statements that take longer than 500ms.

```
USE master;
GO
```

```
IF EXISTS(SELECT * FROM sys.server_event_sessions WHERE name =
'RingBufferExampleSession')
    DROP EVENT SESSION RingBufferExampleSession ON SERVER;

CREATE EVENT SESSION RingBufferExampleSession
ON SERVER
    ADD EVENT sqlserver.sql_statement_completed
        (
            ACTION (sqlserver.session_id, sqlserver.username)
            WHERE sqlserver.sql_statement_completed.duration > 500000
            -- duration is in microseconds
        )
    ADD TARGET package0.ring_buffer
        (SET max_memory = 4096)
WITH (max_dispatch_latency = 1 seconds);

ALTER EVENT SESSION RingBufferExampleSession ON SERVER STATE=START;
GO
-- this takes longer than half a second
SELECT    TOP 100000 *
FROM      master..spt_values t1
          CROSS JOIN master..spt_values t2;

GO
SELECT  -- these are some of the event columns
        Cols.value('(data[@name="duration"]/value)[1]','BIGINT')/1000.0 as
duration_in_ms,
        Cols.value('(data[@name="cpu_time"]/value)[1]','BIGINT')/1000.0 as
cpu_time_in_ms,
        Cols.value('(data[@name="logical_reads"]/value)[1]','BIGINT') as logical_reads,
        Cols.value('(data[@name="row_count"]/value)[1]','BIGINT') as row_count,
        Cols.value('(data[@name="statement"]/value)[1]','NVARCHAR(MAX)') as
sql_statement,
        -- these are actions we specified for the event
        Cols.value('(action[@name="username"]/value)[1]','NVARCHAR(MAX)') as username,
        Cols.value('(action[@name="session_id"]/value)[1]','SMALLINT') as session_id
FROM    (
            SELECT  CAST(t.target_data AS XML) AS RingBufferInfo
            FROM    sys.dm_xe_session_targets t
                    JOIN sys.dm_xe_sessions s ON s.address = t.event_session_address
            WHERE   t.target_name = 'ring_buffer' AND s.name = 'RingBufferExampleSession'
        ) RB
        CROSS APPLY RingBufferInfo.nodes('/RingBufferTarget/event') AS Tbl(Cols);
GO
ALTER EVENT SESSION RingBufferExampleSession ON SERVER STATE=STOP;
```

## Built in Health Session

Like the default trace in SQL Server 2005, Extended Events provides an always-running session called health_sesion. This session holds the combination of events and actions that help us troubleshoot various problems like deadlocks which had no built in automatic detection system until now. A few things health_session tracks:

- sql_text, session_id for any error with severity >=20

- sql_text, session_id for any sessions that encounters a memory error (not all memory errors are severity >=20)

- A record of any "non-yielding scheduler" problems

- Any deadlocks

- Callstack, sql_text, session_id for sessions waiting on latches (or other interesting resources) for > 15 seconds

- Callstack, sql_text, session_id for sessions waiting on locks for > 30 seconds

- Callstack, sql_text, session_id for sessions waiting 5 seconds for "external" waits or "pre-emptive waits"

In SQL Server 2008 the only target for health_sesion was the Ring Buffer, but in SQL Server 2012 the targets are both the Ring Buffer and the Event File. Because we've previously shown how to read from the Ring Buffer target the following code example will read from the Event File.

```
-- just get a few columns from the XML report to show the principle of XML data retrieval
-- the whole XML deadlock report can be seen by viewing the XmlDeadlockReport column
SELECT    Col.query('.') as XmlDeadlockReport,
          Col.query('.').value('(/event/@timestamp)[1]', 'datetime') as EventTime,
          Col.query('.').value('(/event/data/value/deadlock/victim-
list/victimProcess/@id)[1]', 'NVARCHAR(100)') as VictimProcess,
          Col.query('.').value('(/event/data/value/deadlock/process-list/process/@id)[1]',
'NVARCHAR(100)') as Process1_id,
          Col.query('.').value('(/event/data/value/deadlock/process-list/process/@id)[2]',
'NVARCHAR(100)') as Process2_id,
          Col.query('.').value('(/event/data/value/deadlock/process-
list/process/@spid)[1]', 'NVARCHAR(100)') as Process1_spid,
          Col.query('.').value('(/event/data/value/deadlock/process-
list/process/@spid)[2]', 'NVARCHAR(100)') as Process2_spid,
          Col.query('.').value('(/event/data/value/deadlock/process-
list/process/@isolationlevel)[1]', 'NVARCHAR(100)') as Process1_isolationlevel,
          Col.query('.').value('(/event/data/value/deadlock/process-
list/process/@isolationlevel)[2]', 'NVARCHAR(100)') as Process2_isolationlevel,
          Col.query('.').value('(/event/data/value/deadlock/resource-
list/ridlock/@objectname)[1]', 'NVARCHAR(100)') as Resource1_objectName,
          Col.query('.').value('(/event/data/value/deadlock/resource-
list/ridlock/@objectname)[2]', 'NVARCHAR(100)') as Resource2_objectName
FROM    (
            SELECT    CAST(event_data AS XML) AS event_xml_data
            FROM    sys.fn_xe_file_target_read_file('C:\Program Files\Microsoft SQL
Server\MSSQL11.SQL2012\MSSQL\Log\system_health*.xel', null, null, null)
            -- because the event file returns event name and full event
            -- XML in tabular form it's easier to filter by event
            WHERE    object_name = 'xml_deadlock_report'
        ) EventFile
        CROSS APPLY EventFile.event_xml_data.nodes('/event') as Tbl(Col);
```

# Extended Events .NET provider

Just like SQL Trace has the .NET rowset provider, the Extended Events have the .NET object model for creating and reading sessions. Unlike the rowset provider, the extended events reader is not really live but rather asynchronous with the MAX_DISPATCH_LATENCY set to 3 seconds when connected. After it disconnects the sessions, MAX_DISPATCH_LATENCY is reset to the original value. If you have multiple readers connected to the same session the first one that disconnects will reset the MAX_DISPATCH_LATENCY to the original value. That means that all other connected readers will have that setting which is probably not the desired behavior. If the Extended Events engine detects any lag in the sending of data to the reader it disconnects that reader. This is because it follows the so called prime directive of diagnostic monitoring: The most important workload on the server is the customer workload; diagnostic systems should not prevent the customer workload from running.

Figure 5-9 shows the Extended Events .NET object model. We can see that it's split into the metadata information objects and the actual running session objects.

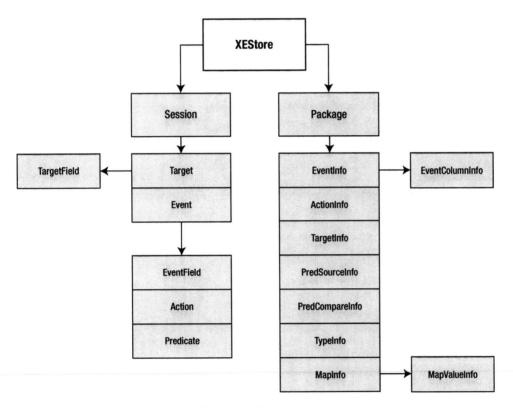

***Figure 5-9.** Extended Events .NET object model*

The following code example shows how to create the Extended Events session in .NET with the ring buffer target and how to read the built-in system_health session event file.

```
private static void CreateStatementTrackingSession()
{
    // The XEStore is a type of SFC store so we use the SqlStoreConnection
```

```
        // and a SqlConnection to pass to the XEStore.
        // Reference SFC and SqlServer.ConnectionInfo from SQL version specific directory,
        // eg: C:\Program Files (x86)\Microsoft SQL Server\110\SDK\Assemblies
        SqlConnectionStringBuilder conBuild = new SqlConnectionStringBuilder();
        // name of the SQL Server we're connecting to
        conBuild.DataSource = @"BALTAZAR\SQL2012";
        conBuild.InitialCatalog = "master";
        conBuild.IntegratedSecurity = true;
        // Create the actual SqlStoreConnection...
        Microsoft.SqlServer.Management.Sdk.Sfc.SqlStoreConnection server = new
    Microsoft.SqlServer.Management.Sdk.Sfc.SqlStoreConnection(new
    SqlConnection(conBuild.ConnectionString.ToString()));
        // ...and then create the XEStore
        XEStore xestore = new XEStore(server);
        // Create a session object and set session options.
        Microsoft.SqlServer.Management.XEvent.Session demoSession =
    xestore.CreateSession("XE_DOTNET_DEMO_SESSION");
        demoSession.MaxDispatchLatency = 20; // Set in seconds.
        demoSession.MaxMemory = 2048; // Set in KB
        demoSession.TrackCausality = true; // Turn on correlation tracking.
        // Add the sql_statement_completed event to the session and configure
        // the optional field to collect the statement
        Microsoft.SqlServer.Management.XEvent.Event evt =
    demoSession.AddEvent("sql_statement_completed");
        evt.EventFields["collect_statement"].Value = 1;
        // Add an action.
        evt.AddAction("session_id");
        // Add a predicate for this event.
        evt.PredicateExpression = @"duration > 5000";
        // Add a target to the session.
        Microsoft.SqlServer.Management.XEvent.Target targ =
    demoSession.AddTarget("ring_buffer");
        // set the max memory for the ring buffer
        targ.TargetFields["max_memory"].Value = 2048;
        // Add the session to the XEStore.
        demoSession.Create();
        demoSession.Start();

        // run some sql statements in your database here

        demoSession.Stop();
        // delete the session
        demoSession.Drop();
    }

    private static void ReadSystemHealthSessionFileWithAPIReader()
    {
        // the example processes:
        // - event data where kernel_mode_time greater than 150000
        // - event action where session_id >= 5
        Microsoft.SqlServer.XEvent.Linq.QueryableXEventData events =
```

```
            new QueryableXEventData(@"C:\Program Files\Microsoft SQL
Server\MSSQL11.SQL2012\MSSQL\Log\system_health*.xel");

    // Iterate through each event in the file.
    foreach (Microsoft.SqlServer.XEvent.Linq.PublishedEvent evt in events)
    {
        // do any event filtering by name here
        // if (evt.Name == "desiredFilter") ...

        // Iterate through each field in the current event and return its name and value.
        foreach (Microsoft.SqlServer.XEvent.Linq.PublishedEventField fld in evt.Fields)
        {
            if (fld.Name != "kernel_mode_time")
                continue;
            if ((ulong)fld.Value < 150000)
                continue;

            // any processing of the event is done here
        }
        // Iterate through each action in the current event and
        // return its name and value.
        foreach (Microsoft.SqlServer.XEvent.Linq.PublishedAction action in evt.Actions)
        {
            if (action.Name != "session_id")
                continue;
            if ((UInt16)action.Value < 5)
                continue;
            // any processing of the action is done here
        }
    }
}
```

# Extended Events UI

Since SQL Server 2008 had no UI for Extended Events, SQL Server 2012 got a UI for creating sessions and profiling. Unlike the SQL Server Profiler, the UI for both is built into SSMS.

## Session Creation UI

To access the session creation UI, you have to navigate to the Server node, then to the Management node, and finally go to the Extended Events node. Right click on the sessions node, and start the profiler from the context menu from. There are two options you can choose from: the New Session Wizard item and the New Session... item. The wizard lets you create a new session in wizard style, but it limits you to only the Ring Buffer and Event File targets. The New Session... option lets you unleash the full power of the Extended Events. Because the wizard UI is a subset of the New Session... UI we'll take a look at the latter. There are four main option pages that comprise the session creation UI.

The first page is the General page displayed in Figure 5-10. On it you can name a session, choose an existing template to base the session on, set session scheduling options, and turn on causality tracking.

There are nine built in templates and all the data you can see in the figures are based on the Connection Tracking template.

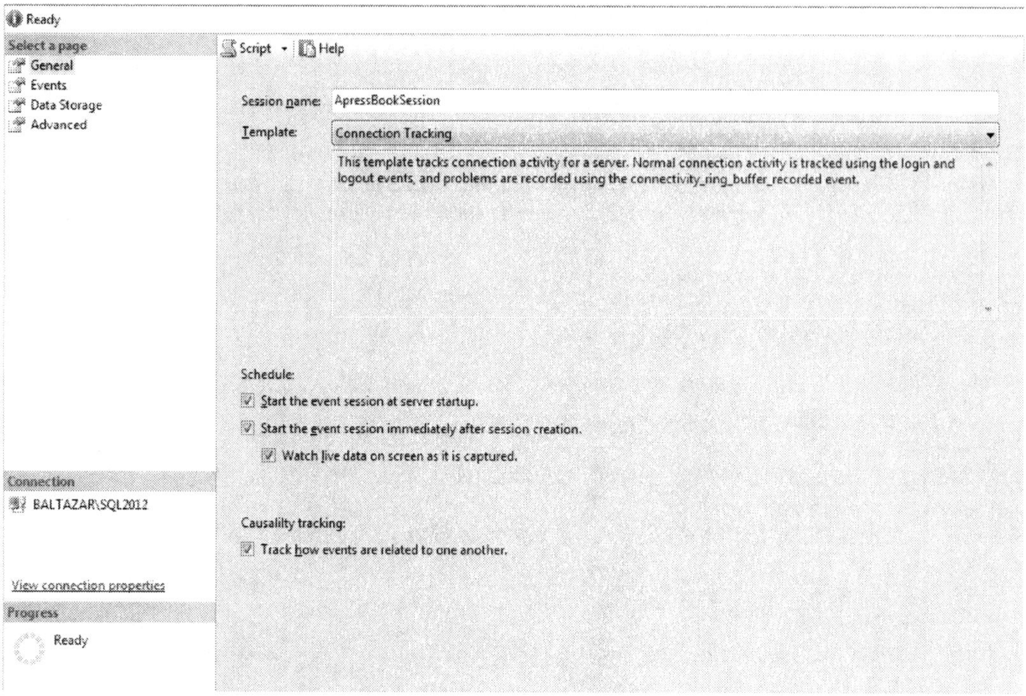

***Figure 5-10.*** *Extended Events Session creation page: General*

Figure 5-11 shows the first part of the Events page. This page is the heart of the session creation process. Here you choose the events you'll track, their fields, extra actions, and any event filters. You can filter the events by event names, their descriptions, their fields, or all of the above. This makes the job of finding the correct event much simpler. In the left grid there's a Category column which tells you which category the events falls under, and the Channel category tells you which Event Tracing for Windows (ETW) channel the event goes into. If you click on the Channel header you'll notice that the events in the Debug channel are not shown. This is because they aren't needed for normal DBA tracing. They are usually used when Microsoft support needs to troubleshoot a problem on your server. You can filter the events on both of these columns. Underneath the left grid there are descriptions of the events and their fields.

The grid on the right shows which events from the grid on the left have you chosen to track. The column with a small lightning bolt lists the number of actions we track for this event and the filter column indicates if a filter is present for this event.

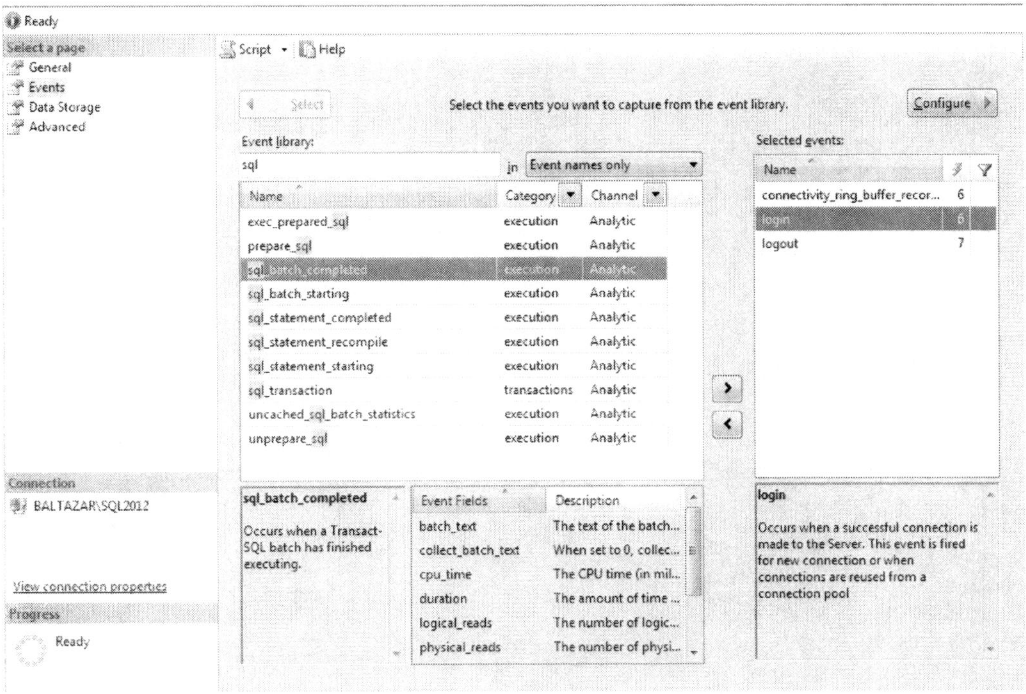

**Figure 5-11.** *Extended Events Session creation page: Events - part 1*

Figure 5-12 shows the second part of the Events page. You get to this part by clicking the Configure button in the upper right corner of the page shown in Figure 5-11. The events you selected are now shown in the grid on the left. Below the grid is the description of the selected event. The grid on the right has three tabs. The first one, called Global Fields(action), lets you choose the actions you want to collect for this event. The second tab, called Filter(Predicate), enables us to add various simple and complex filters. In the third tab, named Event Fields, you can see all the fields for the selected event. The fields that are not autocollected by defauld have a checkbox on their left side. In Figure 5-12 you can see the options_text field will be collected but the database_name won't be since you already have the database_id.

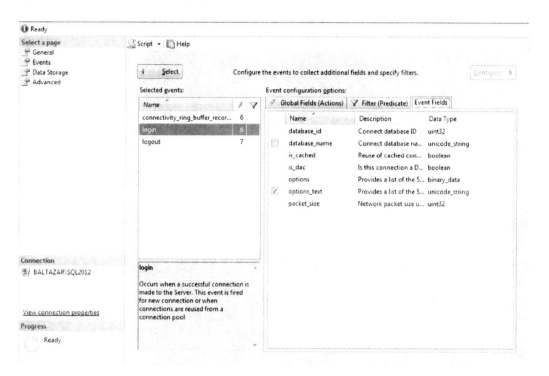

**Figure 5-12.** *Extended Events Session creation page: Events - part 2*

Figure 5-13 shows Data Storage page. Data Storage is just a different name for a target. You can see that the ring_bufer target is chosen in this figure. I've kept the default number (1000) of kept events in the buffer and set the maximum memory for the ring_buffer to 10 MB. Also I've created an all-event FIFO buffer, and not a per-event type FIFO buffer. You can add as many targets as you want on this page.

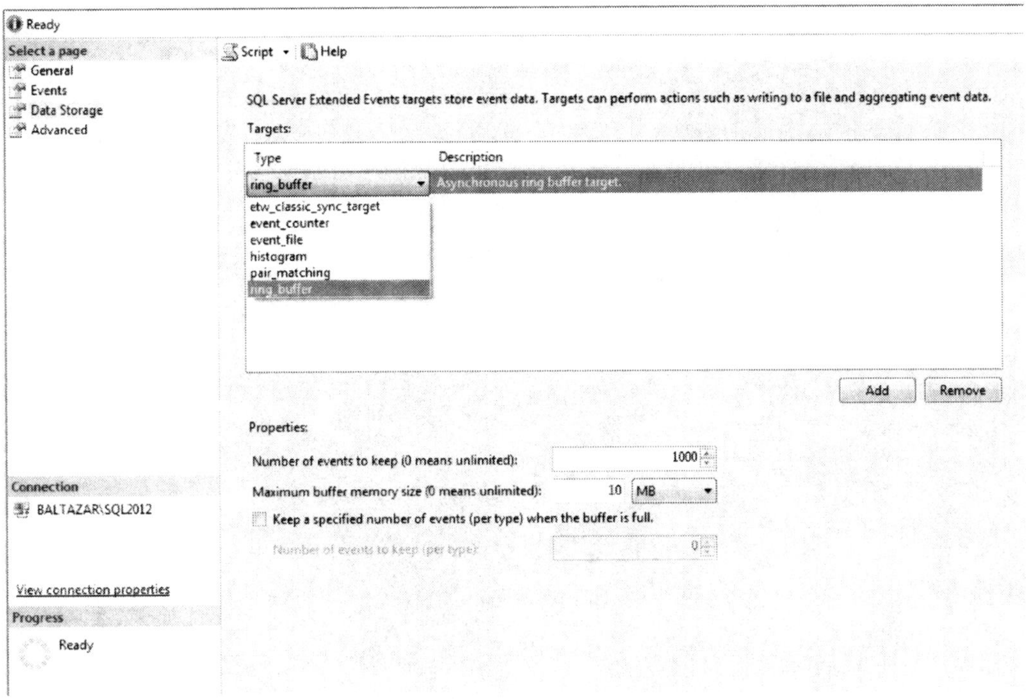

*Figure 5-13. Extended Events Session creation page: Data Storage (Targets)*

Figure 5-14 shows the Advanced session options, like the Event retention mode, the Maximum dispatch latency, Min and Max memory size, and Memory partition mode. For an explanation of these values, see the session part of the chapter. I've left all the options here to their default values.

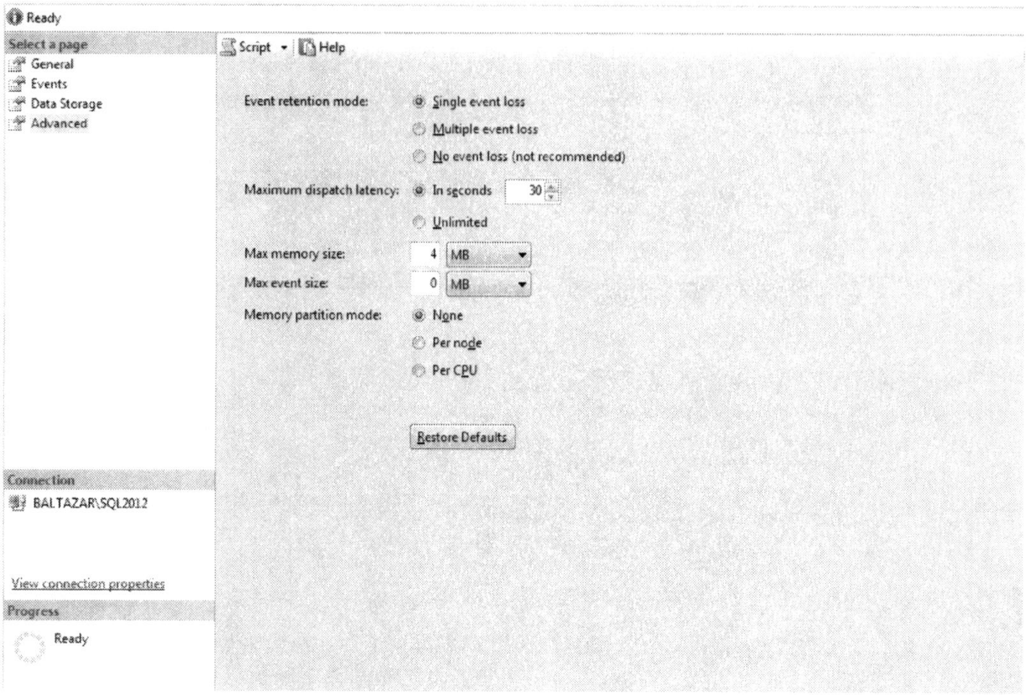

*Figure 5-14. Extended Events Session creation page: Advanced*

After you're done setting the Session options, click OK to create the sessions. The session autostarts after the dialog closes, if that option was set.

## Extended Events Profiler UI

For how the Profiler works, we'll look at a session called ApressBookSession, which tracks connections. As we set it to already watch live data we get the same window that we would get if we right clicked on the ApressBookSession node and clicked the Watch Live Data menu item. Open a few query windows and close them. That should give you output similar to what is shown in Figure 5-15. Notice that there is also a new toolbar called Extended Events. The top Events grid shows live events as they are being generated. This grid is limited to showing one million events. The extra events that aren't shown in the grid are not removed from the target though. The bottom Details grid shows each event's fields. We can add/remove any of those fields into/from the top grid.

If you stop the watching of live data via the Stop button in the toolbar (this does not stop the session) you can see that some options are now enabled in the toolbar. The Grouping button activates the Grouping window shown in Figure 5-16. You can use this window to add columns that you want to group output by.. Once we've grouped our data we can do various aggregations on these groups. Clicking the Aggregation toolbar button opens the window shown in Figure 5-17. Since we're already grouping by client_app_name, session_id, and logical_reads columns we can do aggregates only on timestamp and name columns. Here we'll only COUNT the name column and sort by it in ascending order. The result of the grouped and aggregated data is shown in Figure 5-18.

Displaying 104 Events

| name | timestamp | session_id | client_app_name |
|---|---|---|---|
| login | 2012-08-21 23:43:28.3414055 | NULL | Microsoft SQL Server Management Studio - Query |
| login | 2012-08-21 23:43:28.3852764 | NULL | Microsoft SQL Server Management Studio - Query |
| logout | 2012-08-21 23:43:28.3862016 | 59 | Microsoft SQL Server Management Studio - Query |
| login | 2012-08-21 23:43:29.6900994 | NULL | Microsoft SQL Server Management Studio - Transact-SQL IntelliSense |
| logout | 2012-08-21 23:43:29.6905398 | 59 | Microsoft SQL Server Management Studio - Transact-SQL IntelliSense |
| login | 2012-08-21 23:43:29.6931798 | NULL | Microsoft SQL Server Management Studio - Transact-SQL IntelliSense |
| logout | 2012-08-21 23:43:29.7072766 | 59 | Microsoft SQL Server Management Studio - Transact-SQL IntelliSense |
| login | 2012-08-21 23:43:29.7120995 | NULL | Microsoft SQL Server Management Studio - Transact-SQL IntelliSense |
| logout | 2012-08-21 23:43:29.7160006 | 59 | Microsoft SQL Server Management Studio - Transact-SQL IntelliSense |
| login | 2012-08-21 23:43:29.7196524 | NULL | Microsoft SQL Server Management Studio - Transact-SQL IntelliSense |
| logout | 2012-08-21 23:43:29.7273808 | 59 | Microsoft SQL Server Management Studio - Transact-SQL IntelliSense |
| login | 2012-08-21 23:43:29.7290756 | NULL | Microsoft SQL Server Management Studio - Transact-SQL IntelliSense |
| logout | 2012-08-21 23:43:29.7308942 | 59 | Microsoft SQL Server Management Studio - Transact-SQL IntelliSense |
| login | 2012-08-21 23:43:29.7328289 | NULL | Microsoft SQL Server Management Studio - Transact-SQL IntelliSense |
| logout | 2012-08-21 23:43:29.7331555 | 59 | Microsoft SQL Server Management Studio - Transact-SQL IntelliSense |
| login | 2012-08-21 23:43:29.7377350 | NULL | Microsoft SQL Server Management Studio - Transact-SQL IntelliSense |
| logout | 2012-08-21 23:43:29.7381036 | 59 | Microsoft SQL Server Management Studio - Transact-SQL IntelliSense |
| login | 2012-08-21 23:43:29.7434614 | NULL | Microsoft SQL Server Management Studio - Transact-SQL IntelliSense |
| logout | 2012-08-21 23:43:29.7451636 | 59 | Microsoft SQL Server Management Studio - Transact-SQL IntelliSense |
| login | 2012-08-21 23:43:29.7471685 | NULL | Microsoft SQL Server Management Studio - Transact-SQL IntelliSense |
| logout | 2012-08-21 23:43:29.7481153 | 59 | Microsoft SQL Server Management Studio - Transact-SQL IntelliSense |

Event: logout (2012-08-21 23:43:28.3862016)

Details

| Field | Value |
|---|---|
| attach_activity_id.guid | CEB60655-C66A-4EAD-B59D-71BC01E4AEE1 |
| attach_activity_id.seq | 1 |
| attach_activity_id_xfer.guid | 51D1B82E-4F3E-4354-9CF0-59B20F44292E |
| attach_activity_id_xfer.seq | 0 |
| client_app_name | Microsoft SQL Server Management Studio - Query |
| client_connection_id | 00000000-0000-0000-0000-000000000000 |
| client_hostname | BALTAZAR |
| context_info | 0x |
| cpu_time | 0 |
| duration | 0 |
| is_cached | False |
| is_dac | False |
| logical_reads | 0 |
| physical_reads | 0 |
| server_instance_name | BALTAZAR\SQL2012 |
| server_principal_name | |
| session_id | 59 |
| writes | 0 |

*Figure 5-15. Extended Events Watch Live Data window in stopped state*

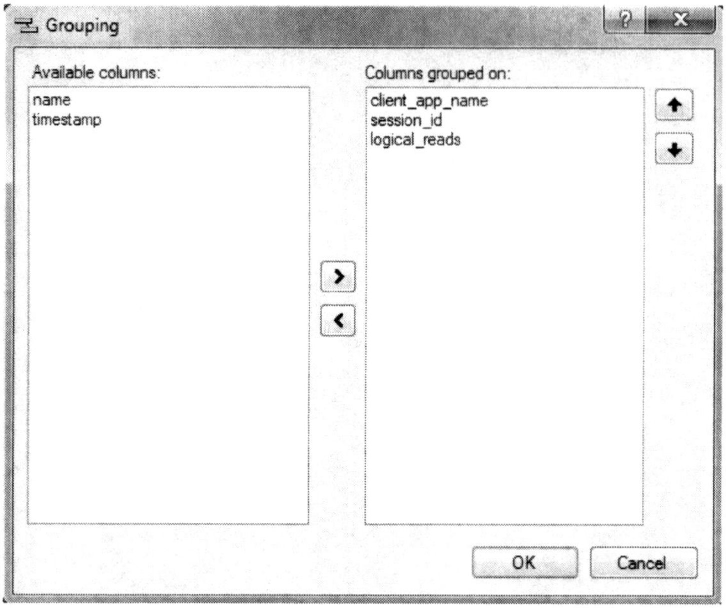

*Figure 5-16. Extended Events column grouping window.*

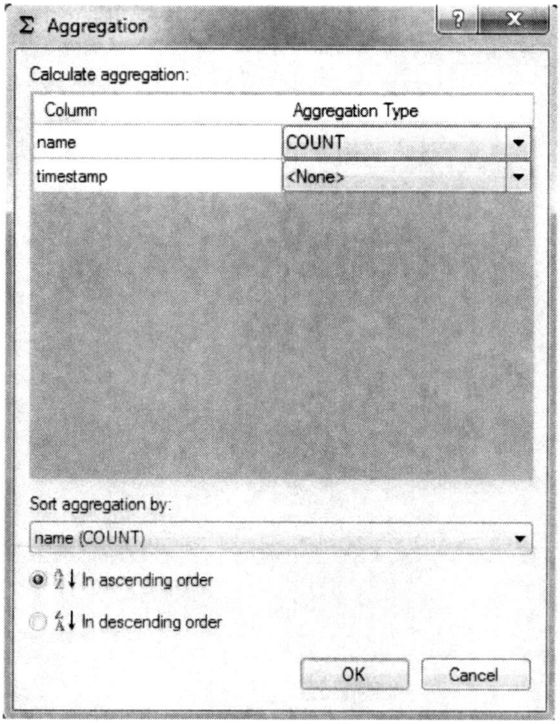

*Figure 5-17. Extended Events column aggregation window.*

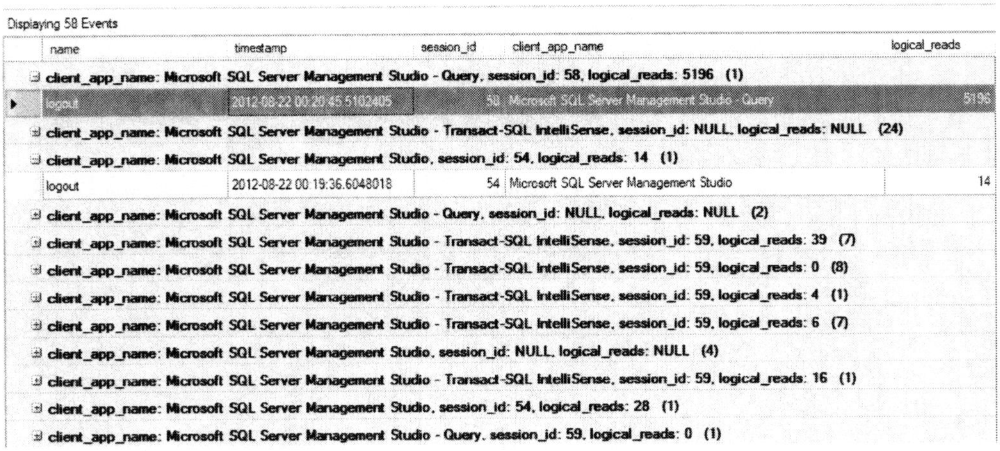

*Figure 5-18. Extended Events grouped and aggregated data*

This was a quick overview of the new Extended Events Profiler. It is really easy to use once you get the hang of it. Hopefully this chapter has made it a bit easier.

# Conclusion

In this chapter we've taken a look at the current state of tracing and diagnostic infrastructure in SQL Server. 5 years ago SQL Trace might have been sufficient to diagnose problems but faced with increased workload in clients' systems a new infrastructure was needed. That infrastructure was Extended Events, a completely new, highly customizable engine built directly into the SQLOS, that should be enough for the next few years. By actually deprecating SQL Trace in SQL Server 2012 Microsoft showed that we have to learn Extended Events and start using them in our daily troubleshooting and performance tuning endeavors.

■ ■ ■

# The Utility Database

## By Chris Shaw

Time and time again, I have been able to use my own custom database, named the *utility database*, to solve problems. This has shortened troubleshooting times by supplying additional insight into what the system has been doing historically, and what the system is doing now. The utility database has reduced my repetitive and time-consuming tasks, such as reviewing the error logs, by automating and using SQL Server Reporting Services (SSRS) to send reports on a daily basis to my e-mail. When you are able to record database history, it makes it much easier for you to identify certain database patterns, such as growth. The additional data eases the ability to forecast key issues, such as performance degradation or the volume of disk space required when new hardware needs to be ordered.

When you are responsible for the well-being of a database or a server, there are a number of key factors that you must pay attention to or your long-term system health and performance will be at risk. Some of these tasks require much time and manual effort to verify that the systems are behaving as expected.

As a consultant, one of my first experiences with a client had me diagnosing an error they received when the transaction log backups would fail overnight. The error message they were receiving indicated they didn't have enough disk space to store the backup file. There were some serious concerns as to why this happened each night, because when they came in the next morning and started to research the failure, there was plenty of disk space on the drive for the file. In addition, subsequent transaction log backups would complete without any problem.

My suspicion was that a file was being created on the drive, that would consume the required free space. Long before the morning shift would start, the file would be removed, leaving the space open and the appearance that the error message they received was incorrect.

I was able to create a utility database to track the disk free space to solve the issue. The process reviewed the amount of free space on the drive, and the results were then inserted into a table every five minutes. I then built a report off those results, which provided visibility as to what was happening.

It quickly became apparent that my hunch in this situation was correct. I was able to narrow down the time when the space was consumed, and again when the space was released, along with the list of files on that volume. With this data, we were able to find the source of the error, correct it, and give the client new visibility into the disk space usage.

Over the course of this chapter, we will review some of the strategies used to create the utility database and leverage the use of it, allowing you more time for necessary project-oriented tasks. The information in this chapter is designed to give you the fundamentals of how to retrieve, store, process, and report the information. This, in turn, allows you to move your work strategy to a proactive style rather than a reactive style where workers feel as if they are only there to chase down problems after they occur. Think of this as a style to *work smarter, not harder.*

# Start with Checklists

The key aspect to the utility database is that it is a collection of data that is designed by you, and contains data that is important to you and your environment. A way to look at a utility database is as a custom monitoring utility designed just for you, by you. I'll make a series of recommendations in this chapter on some of the trackable items that you might consider storing in your database. The examples can be used as is and should provide additional insight into the databases and database servers that it gathers data from. However, the usefulness is multiplied when the data is meaningful to the individual user or organization. Keep this in mind as you read through this chapter, and consider aspects of different information that might be critical to your database. As you review the examples provided, take note of the strategies we use to gather the information on those databases, and then think about how you can apply these strategies to your utility database. A strong argument can be made that the utility database should never stop gaining new features, and I urge readers to take this stance. If there is a task that you perform more than once, you should consider whether this is something that your utility database can automate.

Recently, while boarding a flight, I observed how the pilot walked around the plane. He looked at the engine, the wheels, and some other key components. He then entered the cockpit, retrieved a clipboard, and began to check off items while assessing the instruments on the control panel. As a nervous flyer, I was comforted by his due diligence in making sure the craft was ready for flight.

In like fashion, you should review the health of your servers each day. Check the backups to make sure they executed properly, and review the error logs to look for any looming issues, along with many other key points. Likewise, the company will be comforted in knowing that the database is ready for the upcoming operations. For the pilot, this was a lengthy process that included many people looking at multiple aspects of the plane. For a database administrator, many of these tasks can be automated after they have been identified.

Each server may utilize different features of SQL Server 2012; for example, some systems require AlwaysOn, while some do not. Some of your required features might need different checks on a regularly scheduled interval; for instance, if you're using AlwaysOn, you might want to validate the latency each day to ensure the network and the databases are performing to standards. The checklists that follow identify tasks that you might require for success with SQL Server 2012, including tasks that ensure the ability to recover your SQL Server. Each installation and feature usage may change the items that you require.

## Daily Checklist Items

The following items should be checked daily:

- Backups—Recovery means that a backup is required. Without a proper backup, the database could be lost for good. A backup plan is the best place to start, but ensuring it is running each time without failure is critical for long-term success.

- Automated Restores—The most effective way to validate a backup plan is to exercise it, but that can be time consuming and often forgotten about when staff is busy. Automating restores is common, but not complete unless the restore is being monitored for success or failure.

- Error Logs—Many issues present themselves in the error log, but similar to the automated restores, checking each one of these daily in a busy environment can quickly consume a large portion of the day. This check is often skipped to complete tasks that might be considered more pressing.

- SQL Server Jobs—SQL Server 2012 gives the user the ability to schedule jobs. These jobs could be maintenance or tasks that are critical to the operations of the business. The completion of these jobs needs to be reviewed each day.

- Disk Space/Database Growth—Databases should be checked to ensure they have plenty of space to accept new data. Depending on the options of the database, this could mean internal checking of the database to make sure the files have enough free space, or it could mean validating that there is enough drive space for the database to grow.

- Integrity Checks—The health of the pages inside the database can be verified by running a number of integrity checks. You must make sure that these checks yield error-free results each time they are executed.

- Index Health—Indexes to databases can be compared to an index of a book. As more pages (i.e., information) are added to the book, the index will need to be adjusted. Likewise, more information added to a table may result in adjustment to its indexes. The performance of the database relies on this task being done. If performance is critical to the SQL Server, you must review the indexes and their efficiency.

- Security—It is common to log failed attempts to access the databases. Logging is good, but it is equally important that you review the log so that you can take any necessary corrective action.

- Key Business Indicators (KBI)—Many organizations have indicators in the data that determine not only the health of the database, but the health of the business. For example, if the database was for support of an emergency 911 system, a KBI could be the number of calls in queue that need to be answered. Even though the number might not be directly related to the performance of the database, a high number of calls could indicate that the database cannot keep up on logging the information.

## Longer-Term Checklist Items

The following items don't need to be checked daily, but should be done periodically. Each environment (e.g., a nonprofit vs. a public company) has different requirements that could determine the frequency. I recommend completing these items no less then once a quater.

- Audits—Audits are starting to be required by more organizations each day. Even if it is not required, it is a good practice to audit your servers regulary. It might be as simple as a quick inventory audit, or you could need an in-depth security audit.

- Patches/Service Packs—SQL Server 2012 is a stable platform and is proving to be very reliable, but on occasion it might need a patch or a service pack to remove potential errors in the code or enable some features. Keeping track of what version the database server is and when these versions have changed can be critical in troubleshooting issues.

- Configurations—Validating the configuration of the SQL Server is as important as ensuring the configuration is correct the first time. In environments where more accounts are able to access and change the configuration, it is crucial to continually check that the proper configuration is in place.

- New SQL Servers—SQL Server has many versions, each with different features, prices, and licensing. Many applications install a version of SQL Server for the database support that they need. Checking to make sure that you are licensed correctly and that each of the servers is being maintained can be a difficult task to do once. Doing this task on a repeated basis can be overwhelming and time consuming, but critical.

What might appear to be an extensive checklist of tasks is really only a scratch on the surface. The items are too numerous to list, and as you work with SQL Server 2012 in your environment, new items will become obvious. The addition of other repetitive and time-scheduled tasks should fit into your utility database structure using the same design with some slight adjustments.

# Utility Database Layout

The structure of the utility database is key to the long-term ease of use; enterprise use of the utility database begins here. A good understanding of the structure eases the addition of new features and customization to ensure useful data is collected in each environment. Without a defined structure, upgrades and the organization of the database becomes complex. The utility database we will be working with in the examples is separated into the following three major categories:

- Category 1—Core installation specific

- Category 2—Feature specific

- Category 3—Domain specific (KBIs)

The first of these categories is the data that must be collected on all the SQL Server installations that will use the utility database. Data such as SQL Server version, inventory of SQL Servers, and index fragmentation fit into this category.

The second category is data that is dependent on features that may be implemented on the SQL Server, such as AlwaysOn and SQL Server Audits. This category of data provides a layer of history and monitoring that might not be available in other methods. For example, a table that I include in here often is the cluster node history; this provides information as to what node of a cluster was hosting the SQL Server historically.

This third category has been extremely helpful to me as a consultant. As discussed in the previous checklist section, each business has different key business indicators. Data that does not fit in a core install of SQL Server, and does not fit into the features of SQL Server, fits into this third category. For example, if we reuse the previous 911 call list queue example, a table in this category would store the date and time of how many calls were waiting in the queue. This data does not have to do with SQL Server core install nor SQL Server features; instead, it falls into the third category of domain-specific data.

## Data Storage

The data in your utility database fits into many different groups. Organizing the data based on the intent of how it will be used in the future, and how long the data is retained, helps in the determination of how the tables are designed.

- Group 1—Data in which historical content is being analyzed

- Group 2—Data that is reviewed for current health

- Group 3—Archived data

Data that is reviewed for historical trending, such as database growth, should be retained long term. An example of the benefits of grouping like data can be seen with database growth as the measured value. The primary benefit is to determine what the growth rate is and to measure that growth rate over the course of time. You could draw secondary benefits from this historical information as well; for example, the data footprint after a major release, or when a database growth pattern stopped or started, add valuable information when troubleshooting.

Data that has no long-term value, but might be part of a daily checklist report, might not need to be retained longer than 24 hours. An example of this data group could be the SQL Server error log. SQL Server error logs can be imported and then filtered each day by the utility database. When this data is reported, the report can include only the data that is relevant. The filtered data might not be relevant after the initial report of the data, and might not need to be kept. In the example of SQL Server error log filtering, the original source of the data (the error log), is not altered; therefore, keeping the data would create duplicate information.

There is a slight difference between archived data and historical data. The historical data is being kept around to identify long-term trends (such as growth). The archive data group gives you the option to log information that was sent in a report, but then removed. In the case of the SQL Server error log, there might be no need to keep detailed data because of the duplication of data, but a user might want to see what data was sent in a previous report. The archive data, if you choose to use it, would be the data that was sent in a report, but then deleted. This allows you to re-create reports that were sent in the past. Keep in mind that this might not be useful in each utility database implementation.

Figure 6-1 shows how a category can have one or more groups. The core install category (Category 1) collects information about the basic install, such as database growth and SQL Server error logs. After reporting, the SQL Server error logs table (filtered data) can be truncated, making it a Group 2. The database growth table would be retained long term for historical trending, making it a Group 1.

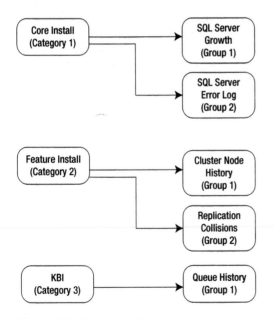

***Figure 6-1.*** *Data grouping*

# Using Schemas

When creating the objects that will reside in the utility database, consider using schemas to keep the tables organized by categories. In the past, I have found this helpful when I use the same Category 1 collection on multiple servers, but only use the relevant Category 2 collections on SQL Servers where the feature is installed. For example, if I am logging data about mirroring, I create a schema named Mirror. In addition, when working with KBI data, I use the company name as the schema name. You will see this practice being used throughout this chapter.

# Using Data Referential Integrity

Good database designs incorporate the proper use of data referential integrity (DRI) (i.e., the proper use of foreign keys and primary keys). This can also include default values or other constraints in the database to ensure that your data follows all the rules that are required.

Proper DRI is not difficult to implement, but with each deployment of a utility database, being flexible and custom to the environment that it is being deployed alters the requirements slightly. Don't let this be a reason to not use the proper DRI in your implementation.

For the purpose of the examples in this chapter, there might be places where you will see that some of the DRI is not being used when it should be. I might have excluded it in the examples to save on space, or to simplify some of the examples. In the examples where the data referential integrity is critical for the operations, it has been added in the example.

# Creating the Utility Database

The initial step in creating a utility database is creating the actual database itself. The configuration options of your individual database will depend on your environment. The options that I tend to use when creating my utility database include leaving the database on Full Recovery mode. Many times, KBI stored in the utility database can be extremely helpful for troubleshooting, so I tend to backup the database aggressively to allow for the least amount of data loss, in case of a restore.

If you are following along with the examples listed here in the rest of this chapter, they will be using the database named dbUtilities. The following create script will create the database in the default data and log directory that has been configured on the server. Make sure to test this and all other code in a test environment before pushing it to production servers.

```
USE [master]
GO

CREATE DATABASE [dbUtilities]
  GO

ALTER DATABASE [dbUtilities] SET COMPATIBILITY_LEVEL = 110
GO

ALTER DATABASE [dbUtilities] SET RECOVERY FULL
GO
```

After the database has been created, and the options have been set, the next step is to start gathering data. The next section will discuss some of the strategies that can be used to gather data, store data, and manage data.

# Table Structure

Categorizing and grouping the data that the utility database is going to be collecting will drive the design of the table that you will use to store the data. Predefining how the tables should be organized will ease the implementation of adding watched items to the utility database.

## Historical Data Tables

Historical data tables store the data that provide trends. A good example of this type of data collected is the standard baseline information you might want to review before the purchase of new hardware. Processor performance, disk space, database growth, and memory usage are just a few items where historical information can greatly impact decisions in the future. A standard table format that can be used for historical information can look like this:

```
USE [dbUtilities]
GO

CREATE TABLE [dbo].[Sample_Historical_Data](
    [PrimaryKeyID] [int] IDENTITY(1,1) NOT NULL,
    [Measureable] [varchar](100) NOT NULL,
    [MesuredItem1] [int] NOT NULL,
    [MesuredItem2] [int] NOT NULL,
    [MesuredItem3] [int] NOT NULL,
    [MesuredItem4] [int] NOT NULL,
    [ReadingDate] [datetime] NOT NULL,
CONSTRAINT [PK_PrimaryKeyID] PRIMARY KEY CLUSTERED
    ([PrimaryKeyID]))
```

A few items to note: each one of these tables should have a primary key, but depending on how you access the data, additional indexes may be required for the quickest database access. All the values in this example will not accept null values, and this might not always be appropriate for each of the historical table measures. The date that the data is gathered can be important for viewing proper trends, even though in this example, a sort could be done on the primary key. The reading date might not always be the date that a measure occurred. For example, when querying the stored procedure execution times, an average might be recorded for the prior week. The reading date could present the data of when the information was gathered and inserted into the table, and additional dates might be required.

## Current Health Tables

When creating the current health table, the purpose of the table is to keep information long enough so that an action can be taken on that data. This action could include tasks that should be completed, such as calling a stored procedure or even a report. Data that resides in the current health tables should be treated as temporary. An example of using a current health table to store data, until which time the collection is complete and a report is executed, is a daily checklist report. With these tables, the columns in the tables are not always specific and can represent many different items. Take a look at the following example:

```
USE [dbUtilities]
GO

CREATE TABLE [dbo].[Daily_Report](
    [ReportRowID] [int] IDENTITY(1,1) NOT NULL,
```

```
    [EventStatus] [varchar](50) NOT NULL,
    [EventDate] [datetime] NOT NULL,
    [EVENT] [varchar](2000) NOT NULL,
 CONSTRAINT [PK_Daily_Report_ReportrowID] PRIMARY KEY CLUSTERED
    (
    [ReportRowID]))
GO
```

The EventStatus is a value that I often use for grouping data in the right collection with the Event storing the data. Multiple rows in this table could contain the EventStatus of database growth, but the Event value would be different for each row of data, such as "Database 1 growth is 10%," and the next row containing "Database 2 growth is 2%." A report could group on the EventStatus so all of the database growth information is reported together.

## Archive Tables

A common use for the archive tables is to view a historical representation of a current health table as it was before the next collection of data was executed. Before each collection of data begins for a time frame, the current heath tables can have the content moved to the corresponding archive table.

```
USE [dbUtilities]
GO

CREATE TABLE [dbo].[Daily_Report_Archive](
    [ReportRowID] [int] NOT NULL,
    [EventStatus] [varchar](50) NOT NULL,
    [EventDate] [datetime] NULL,
    [EVENT] [varchar](2000) NOT NULL,
 CONSTRAINT [PK_Daily_Report_Archive_ReportrowID] PRIMARY KEY CLUSTERED
    (
    [ReportRowID] ASC
    )) ON [PRIMARY]
GO
```

An item of note: in this example, the identity attribute to the ReportRowID was removed. The following is an example of how to move data from the current health tables over to an archive table:

```
USE [dbUtilities]
GO

CREATE PROCEDURE [dbo].[Archive_Daily_Report]
AS
    INSERT INTO Daily_Report_Archive
    SELECT * FROM Daily_Report
IF @@error = 0
    BEGIN
        Delete dbutility..Daily_Report
    END
GO
```

# Gathering Data

Without understanding the options for data collection, the utility database is limited in what data is collected. As new versions of SQL Server are released, the inner workings of SQL Server become more accessible, providing further information that allows users to make more critical decisions than with the previous versions. In this gathering data section, we will look at some of the options available. In the last part of this section, examples will show how to take advantage of these options, maximizing the usefulness of the utility database.

In the earliest versions of SQL Server, a seasoned professional would spend time diving into the system tables, not only in the system databases, but the user databases as well. SQL Server 2005 introduced us to dynamic managed views, which have been expanded with each new release. In the most recent version, SQL Server 2012 extended events are easier to use than ever before. A key component to keep in mind when creating the utility database is the right method to collect data for the version of SQL Server that the utility database will be collecting data for.

If the utility database you are implementing supports multiple versions of SQL Server, a piece of code that could be helpful checks the version of SQL Server that is actively connected, like so:

```
SELECT @@Version
```

Or, you might find that checking the version of the database by using the serverproperty function provides a little more information. The serverproperty expression provides much information about your SQL Server and can be extremely helpful.

```
SELECT SERVERPROPERTY('productversion') AS 'Version Number',
    SERVERPROPERTY ('edition') AS 'Edition'
```

The results of the script will be similar to this:

```
11.0.2100.60
Developer Edition (64-bit)
```

## System Tables

Older versions of SQL Server used a number of system tables to manage the databases. Over the course of time, many of these tables have moved, or have been renamed. The amount of system information data has grown, as well as the need to access that data. The process that is implemented in the examples shows how the system tables can be queried. Keep in mind when looking at system tables that many of them have had system views added that provide more information.

## Extended Stored Procedures

Extended stored procedures are stored procedures that can make DLL calls outside of SQL Server to retrieve information. For example, using xp_cmdshell in older versions of SQL Server was the best way to complete tasks such as getting a directory listing, running batch files, or reading the error log. Be aware when using extended stored procedures that some of them are listed as deprecated, so they might not appear in future releases of SQL Server beyond 2012. For the extended stored procedures that are being deprecated, a replacement may be made with CLR.

---

▓ **Note**　IA list of deprecated features can be found on Microsoft's web site at http://msdn.microsoft.com/ en-us/library/ms143729.aspx. Keep in mind that each version of SQL Server has a new list of deprecated features, and that most features that are being removed have a new feature that improves upon the older deprecated feature.

# CLR

Common Language Runtime (CLR) integration provides an environment that enables SQL Server to execute managed code that, traditionally, Transact-SQL was not designed for. This CLR integration adds flexibility to SQL Server by allowing SQL Server to utilize the strengths of other programming languages. CLR can often be tricky to implement, and is not in the scope of this chapter; however, the example on collecting processor utilization uses this method. In some cases, altering processes to run in the CLR environment greatly improves the performance of that process.

# DMVs

Dynamic Management Views (DMVs) give the user a view into the current SQL Server state. Many features of SQL Server, such as replication, file stream, extended events, wait times, and AlwaysOn, have DMVs associated with them. When gathering data for the utility database, the DMVs are one of the more powerful sources of data because of the completeness of the data and the ease of access. DMVs are installed with the standard installation of SQL Server; because of this, it is easy to find ways to access the information. To find more information on DMV best practices, refer to Chapter 4.

> ■ **Note**    ISQL Server MVP Glenn Berry (the author of Chapter 15) has a collection of DMV queries that have proven to be extremely helpful time and time again. Many of the examples in this chapter are based on accessing data thought the DMVs, either in part or completely on the code he has written. Glenn's blog can be found at http://sqlserverperformance.wordpress.com.

# Storage

The amount of free space remaining on your database storage device and the amount of space that a database occupies are two pieces of information a database professional should be aware of. These two different and distinct numbers are not always related.

## Database File Sizes

The size of the databases on a SQL Server instance is a measurable quantity that should be tracked on each individual instance of SQL Server. Having the historical growth information over a long period of time will increase the odds of accuracy for future storage requirements. Defining the data as such helps determine a table structure that is logical for the utility database. Create the table with a model that is aimed at long-term retention of the data.

```
USE [dbUtilities]
GO
```

```
CREATE TABLE [dbo].[File_growth](
    [FileGrowthReadingID] [int] IDENTITY(1,1) NOT NULL,
    [Physical_Name] [nvarchar](200) NOT NULL,
    [Size_in_MB] [int] NULL,
    [Reading_date] [datetime] NULL DEFAULT GetDate(),
 CONSTRAINT [PK_FileGrowth_ReadingID] PRIMARY KEY CLUSTERED ([FileGrowthReadingID]))
GO
```

To populate the table with data that accounts for each file associated with each database on the managed server, perform a simple query of the system table. This will provide a page count for each file. Each page stores 8k worth of information. Therefore, to calculate the total size of a file (in megabytes), multiply the total page count by 8k pages. Divide the total size of the file by 1024 (the number of kilobytes per megabyte) to determine the file size in megabytes. There is more than one database on each instance (system databases), so to measure the size of each file in each database, the sp_MSforeachdb stored procedure can be used.

The stored procedure that retrieves this information can be created and compiled in the dbUtilities database, in the same schema as the table it is populating.

```
USE [dbUtilities]
GO

CREATE PROCEDURE [dbo].[Get_File_growth]
AS
DECLARE @RETURN_VALUE int , @command1 nvarchar(1000)
SET @command1 = 'Select
                Physical_name,
                Size_in_MB = (size * 8 / 1024)
                from ?.sys.database_files'

INSERT INTO File_growth (Physical_Name, Size_in_MB)
    EXEC @command1 = sp_MSforeachdb @command1 = @command1
GO
```

After the table and the stored procedure have been created, execute the stored procedure to gather all the current database sizes.

```
EXECUTE [dbUtilities].[dbo].[Get_File_growth]
```

The results can be seen by selecting the rows from the table.

```
SELECT * FROM [dbUtilities].[dbo].[File_growth]
```

The remainder of the examples in this chapter will not include the execution of the collections or the validation of the result statements because they are simply statements with different object names. The collection of the database file growth information is collected only when the stored procedure executes. Later in the chapter, methods and timing of the data collection will be reviewed.

## Finding the Amount of Free Space

Understanding the file growth rate of your databases is an important fact, but without the space to grow into, trouble can quickly arise. Understanding the amount of space that is left on a storage volume can be not only historically relevant for planning, but an alerting or monitoring point as well. When considering these traits, this data category matches the definition of a Category 1. The grouping of this data fits in both historical and current health. To keep track of the historical information, the table design echoes that of the database file growth table, discussed in the previous section.

```
USE [dbUtilities]
GO

CREATE TABLE [dbo].[Free_Drive_Space](
    [DriveSpaceReadingID] [int] IDENTITY(1,1) NOT NULL,
    [Drive] [char](1) NOT NULL,
    [MBFree] [int] NOT NULL,
    [ReadingDate] [datetime] NOT NULL,
 CONSTRAINT [PK_Free_Drive_Space_ReadingID] PRIMARY KEY CLUSTERED
    ([DriveSpaceReadingID]))
GO
```

Tracking this data is not only relevant to the historical health of the database; it also provides a point where the current health of the database can be reviewed. If the amount of free space decreases to a point where action needs to be taken to ensure future database stability, then the attention of the administrators needs to be raised. The results from the following stored procedure can be inserted into not only the Free_ Drive_Space table for historical reference, but also into the current health table, Daily_Report.

```
USE [dbUtilities]
GO

CREATE PROCEDURE [dbo].[Get_Drive_Space_Free]
AS
DECLARE @driveSpace TABLE (drive CHAR(2), MBFree int)
    INSERT INTO @driveSpace
        EXEC sp_executesql N'xp_fixeddrives'
INSERT INTO [dbUtilities].[dbo].[Daily_Report]
        SELECT 'Drive Space', GETDATE(), 'Free space on ' + drive +
' is ' + CONVERT (VARCHAR(20), MBFree/1024) + ' Gigs'
            FROM @driveSpace
INSERT INTO [dbUtilities].[dbo].[Free_Drive_Space]
        SELECT Drive, MBFree,GETDATE()
            FROM @driveSpace
GO
```

The Get_Drive_Space_Free stored procedure is an example of using extended stored procedures to gather information outside of SQL Server, and how to store that information.

## Processors

Understanding how hard the processors are working is also an important key data point, but accessing this information is not easy. One option to retrieve this information is to review the DVMs. This information, however, includes statistics on how SQL Server is using the processors, not the actual processor utilization numbers that you might need.

One method that can retrieve processor information from the operating system level is Windows Management Instrumentation (WMI). A great resource for WMI can be found in Microsoft's Script Center (http://technet.microsoft.com/en-US/scriptcenter/default.aspx). The compiled code that is used in this example was provided by a developer willing to help. Inside the .dll that was provided to me is a WMI call that starts monitoring the processor utilization, waits 10 seconds, and then determines the average over that time period. The utility database can call this .dll by enabling CLR and then addressing the information by a user-created function. As complex as it sounds, the code is not too difficult to put into place.

The first step is to create the table that will store this information. The table format will match other Category 1 tables as a core part of the utility database, and the retention of the data matches that of other data that should be retained historically.

```
USE [dbUtilities]
GO

CREATE TABLE [dbo].[Processor_UTI](
    [ProcessorReadingID] [int] IDENTITY(1,1) NOT NULL,
    [ReadingDate] [datetime] NOT NULL,
    [ProcessorUTI] [int] NOT NULL,
 CONSTRAINT [PK_Processor_UTI_ID] PRIMARY KEY CLUSTERED
([ProcessorReadingID])) ON [PRIMARY]
GO
```

Retrieving the information includes a number of steps that will adjust some of the server's configuration settings. The first step to enable the processor utilization collection is to enable CLR on your server.

```
sp_configure 'show advanced options', 1;
RECONFIGURE
GO
sp_configure 'clr enabled', 1;
RECONFIGURE
GO
```

SQL Server needs to be instructed that the contents within the database are trustworthy. The altering of the trustworthy status needs to be done with elevated permissions on the SQL Server instance. This step is to validate that the code being called from inside the database is trusted by the administrators.

```
ALTER DATABASE dbUtilities SET TRUSTWORTHY ON;
```

Once the server has been configured to allow the external calls to the .dll, it is important to make sure that the .dll exists where SQL Server can access it. Copy the .dll to the directory.

---

■ **Note**  I tend to put the .dll in directories where I store the data. This way, if the SQL Server is on a cluster, the .dll will be accessible on any node of the cluster.

---

SQL Server needs to register the location of the .dll. The create assembly statement addresses this need.

```
USE [dbUtilities]
GO

CREATE ASSEMBLY [dbUtilities.Database.CLRFunctions]
    FROM 'C:\Data\dbstats.Database.CLRFunctions .dll'
WITH PERMISSION_SET = UNSAFE
GO
```

SQL Server can execute the .dll through a function.

```
USE [dbUtilities]
GO

CREATE FUNCTION [dbo].[GetCPUUTI]()
    RETURNS [nchar](300) WITH EXECUTE AS CALLER
AS
EXTERNAL NAME [dbUtilities.Database.CLRFunctions].[UserDefinedFunctions].[GetCPUUTI]
GO
```

The final step is to create the stored procedure that the processes can use to retrieve the processor information to eventually store it.

```
USE [dbUtilities]
GO

CREATE PROCEDURE GetProcUTI
AS
Insert Into Processor_UTI (ReadingDate,ProcessorUTI)
    Select Getdate(),Isnull(Round(dbo.getCPUUTI(), 0),0)
GO
```

# Error Logs

There are a number of messages, warnings, and errors that show up in the error log. Regular reviews of these errors are required to ensure that no critical health messages get missed. Automating and filtering the error log can help with avoiding critical messages. The nature of the data is at the core of SQL Server and is relevant to the current health. There is no need to store the data outside of the messages that have been reported on. Filtering the error log works on the Daily_Report table that has already been created.

```
USE [dbUtilities]
GO

CREATE PROCEDURE [dbo].[Get_Filtered_Error_Log]
AS
    DECLARE @Errorlog TABLE (LogDate datetime, ProcessorInfo VARCHAR
(100),ErrorMSG VARCHAR(2000))
        INSERT INTO @Errorlog
EXEC sp_executesql N'xp_readerrorlog'
DELETE
    FROM @Errorlog
    WHERE ErrorMSG LIKE '%Log was backed up%'
DELETE
    FROM @Errorlog
    WHERE ErrorMSG LIKE '%Setting database option COMPATIBILITY_LEVEL%'
DELETE
    FROM @Errorlog
    WHERE ErrorMSG LIKE '%were backed up%'
DELETE
    FROM @Errorlog
    WHERE ErrorMSG LIKE '%without errors%'
```

```
INSERT INTO dbUtilities.dbo.Daily_Report
    SELECT 'Error Log',Logdate,SUBSTRING(ErrorMSG, 1, 2000)
    FROM @Errorlog
    WHERE LogDate > DATEADD(dd, -1, GETDATE())
GO
```

The core of this stored procedure uses an extended stored procedure to load a temporary table with the data in the error log. Because we don't want to review all the messages in the error log, and it is being used as a source review, messages of success and messages that have been identified as not needing review are then deleted from the temporary table. The data is then filtered for the last days' worth of data, and then inserted into the Daily_Report table.

---

■ **Note**  It is important to keep the error log for an extended time frame. By default, a new error log is created only when the SQL Server service is started. Log files can be a little more difficult to navigate with SQL Servers that are not restarted very often. Consider using sp_Cycle_Errorlog to keep your error logs manageable.

---

# Indexes

When tables have records inserted or updated, the indexes become fragmented. As a database administrator, part of your responsibilities will likely be ensuring that the database performs well. SQL Server 2012 offers maintenance plans where you can add reindexing; however, needs might exist that require you to create an indexing strategy outside of the maintenance plans.

---

■ **Note**  Different tables fragment at different rates; tables with many data changes fragment much quicker than tables with static data. This becomes important when the amount of data that is changing is critical, such as when you are using database mirroring over smaller bandwidth. As the index is rebuilt, the movement of the records becomes logged, and those transactions are pushed to the mirror. Why create unnecessary transactions and traffic when it might not be needed (such as when reindexing an index that doesn't require it)?

---

The table the utility database uses to keep track of index fragmentation has the following structure:

```
USE [dbUtilities]
GO

CREATE TABLE [dbo].[Index_Fragmentation](
    [IndexFragID] [int] IDENTITY(1,1) NOT NULL,
    [DatabaseName] [Sysname] NULL,
    [OBjectName] [Sysname] NULL,
    [IndexName] [Sysname] NULL,
    [Index_Type] [nvarchar](120) NULL,
    [Fragmentation] [float] NULL,
    [ReadingDate] [datetime] NULL,
 CONSTRAINT [PK_IndexFragID] PRIMARY KEY CLUSTERED
    ([IndexFragID]))
GO
```

149

Population of the Index_Fragmentation table is accomplished using the following stored procedure to query the sys.indexes table. The granularity in this example includes database, table, and index. With a few added lines, the procedure can be modified to look at partitions and all the databases on a server.

```
USE [dbUtilities]
GO

CREATE PROCEDURE Get_Index_Fragmentation
AS
DECLARE @objectID int
DECLARE @IndexID int
DECLARE @Index_Fragmentation TABLE ([DatabaseName] [Sysname], DB_ID int,
[OBjectName] [Sysname], ObjectID int, [IndexName] [Sysname], IndexId int,
[Index_Type] [nvarchar](120),[Fragmentation] [float])

INSERT INTO @Index_Fragmentation ([DatabaseName], [DB_ID], [OBjectName],
[ObjectID], [IndexName],  [IndexId], [Index_Type])
    Select
        db_name(), db_ID(), object_schema_name(indexes.object_id) + '.' +
object_name(indexes.object_id),OBJECT_ID, indexes.name, indexes.index_id,
indexes.type_desc
    FROM sys.indexes
    Where object_schema_name(indexes.object_id) not like 'sys'

DECLARE Get_Frag CURSOR FOR SELECT ObjectID, IndexID FROM
@Index_Fragmentation;
Open Get_Frag
WHILE 1=1
BEGIN
    FETCH NEXT from Get_FRAG Into @OBJECTID, @INDEXID;
    IF @@FETCH_STATUS < 0 BREAK
    UPDATE @Index_Fragmentation
        SET Fragmentation = avg_fragmentation_in_percent
            from
sys.dm_db_index_physical_stats(db_id(),@ObjectID,@IndexID, null, null)
    WHERE ObjectID = @ObjectID and IndexId = @IndexID
END
CLOSE Get_Frag
DEALLOCATE Get_Frag

INSERT INTO Index_Fragmentation
        ([DatabaseName], [OBjectName], [IndexName], [Index_Type],
[Fragmentation], [ReadingDate])
    Select [DatabaseName], [OBjectName], [IndexName], [Index_Type],
[Fragmentation], GETDATE()
    From @Index_Fragmentation
GO
```

After your utility database has the index fragmentation stored, index maintenance can be very strategic. Code can be written that includes decision factors in rebuilding or defragmenting and index based on fragmentation.

# Stored Procedure Performance

Tracking stored procedure performance can be critical in many complex environments. The flexibility of SQL Server and the demands on new features for applications that require database support can require hours of code reviews to validate performance before release. Often, this is not an option due to the time commitment; therefore, understanding the performance patterns on the stored procedures, historically, is critical.

```
USE [dbUtilities]
GO

CREATE TABLE [dbo].[Procedure_Execution_Times](
    [ProcExecutionReadingID] [int] IDENTITY(1,1) NOT NULL,
    [DatabaseName] [Sysname],
    [SPName] [Sysname] NULL,
    [ExeCount] [bigint] NULL,
    [ExePerSec] [bigint] NULL,
    [AvgWorkerTime] [bigint] NULL,
    [TotalWorkerTime] [bigint] NULL,
    [AvgElapsedTime] [bigint] NULL,
    [MaxLogicalReads] [bigint] NULL,
    [MaxLogicalWrites] [bigint] NULL,
    [TotalPhysicalReads] [bigint] NULL,
    [DateRecorded] [datetime] NULL,
 CONSTRAINT [PK_Procedure_Execution_Times_ID] PRIMARY KEY CLUSTERED
    ([ProcExecutionReadingID]))
GO
```

The stored procedure execution times can be retrieved by looking at the sys.dm_exec_query_stats DMV. When using a DMV as the source of statistics, it is important to understand the source of this information. With the sys.dm_exec_query_stats DMV, the data is based on the cache. When the execution plan is no longer in cache, the corresponding statistics are removed from the sys.dm_exec_query_stats DMV.

---

■ **Note**    I highly recommend looking at some of the other useful DMVs that Glenn Berry has on his blog at http://sqlserverperformance.wordpress.com.

---

```
USE [dbUtilities]
GO

CREATE PROCEDURE [dbo].[Get_Proc_Exection_Times]
AS
INSERT INTO dbUtilities..Procedure_Execution_Times
(DatabaseName,SPName, ExeCount, ExePerSec, AvgWorkerTime, TotalWorkerTime,
AvgElapsedTime, MaxLogicalReads, MaxLogicalWrites, TotalPhysicalReads,
DateRecorded)
SELECT
    DB_Name() AS dbname,
OBJECT_SCHEMA_NAME(qt.objectid, qt.dbid) + '.' + object_name(qt.objectid,
qt.dbid) AS spname,
```

```
    qs.execution_count AS 'Execution Count',
isnull(qs.execution_count,.0001)/Isnull(DATEDIFF(Second, qs.creation_time,
GetDate()),.0001) AS 'Calls/Second',
    isnull(qs.total_worker_time,1)/isnull(qs.execution_count,1) AS
'AvgWorkerTime',
    qs.total_worker_time AS 'TotalWorkerTime',
    isnull(qs.total_elapsed_time,1)/isnull(qs.execution_count,1) AS
'AvgElapsedTime',
    qs.max_logical_reads,
    qs.max_logical_writes,
    qs.total_physical_reads,
    GETDATE() AS RecordedDate
FROM sys.dm_exec_query_stats AS qs
        CROSS APPLY sys.dm_exec_sql_text(qs.sql_handle) AS qt
ORDER BY qs.execution_count DESC
GO
```

This information should help answer questions such as what stored procedure is executed the most often, and what stored procedures have the longest duration.

## Failed Jobs

Keep track of failed jobs over the last 48 hours by querying the system tables in the msdb database and inserting the results into the Daily_Report table. Because this data is used as an overview and notification to the report viewer of potential problems, minimum data is stored and there is no historical use, in this context. The stored procedure can be altered to keep a longer, more detailed history if it is a requirement, and the history in the msdb database does not meet the requirements.

```
USE [dbUtilities]
GO

CREATE PROCEDURE Get_Failed_Jobs
AS
INSERT INTO Daily_Report
(EventStatus, EventDate, Event)
    SELECT
    'Job Failed',
    msdb.dbo.agent_datetime(sjh.run_date, sjh.run_time),
    'SQL Server Job Failed ' + Name
    FROM msdb..sysjobs sj
        Join msdb..sysjobhistory sjh
            on sj.job_id = sjh.job_id and sjh.run_status = 0
    WHERE Enabled = 1 and step_id = 0
    AND msdb.dbo.agent_datetime(sjh.run_date, sjh.run_time) > Dateadd(dd,
-2,GetDate())
GO
```

---

▪ **Note**    You can modify the option for keeping longer history on SQL Server 2012 job and task history by adjusting the job history properties in the SQL Server Agent properties.

---

The visibility of information that SQL Server 2012 provides helps you get the important information required to manage the servers and databases. Up to this point, the examples have been focused on the core installation of SQL Server, so all the tables and stored procedures have been created in the dbo schema. In the next section, the examples focus on feature-specific counters. In your environment, you may use all, some, or none of the features. These examples use a different schema for each feature to help with the deployment of the code based on used features. I would recommend you consider using a like method to organize the information you are collecting.

# Reporting Services

SQL Server Reporting Services (SSRS) has made report authoring and deployment easy and common. Yet, a thorough understanding of how Reporting Services is used is not as common. With a few simple steps, question such as what is the most common report, what is the longest running report, and what step of building the report takes the most time can be answered with confidence.

---

▓ **Note**    Recently, I received a call that the reports were not performing well. After a few quick queries, I was able to isolate what reports were having issues, and was able to determine that the performance degradation was on the Reporting Services machine with the rendering time, rather than the database server and the data retrieval time. Having this information allowed me to focus my work where it could make the largest impact.

---

SQL Server Reporting Services uses two databases for the operations of reporting services. One of the two databases is used for storing temporary data (ReportServerTempDB), and the other database stores the report definitions (ReportServer). There are a number of tables and views inside the ReportServer database that contain information you might want to consider reviewing; however, there is one key view that contains some key information about your Reporting Services install and how it is being used. (This view only exists in SQL Server 2012, when reporting services is installed. If an older version of SQL Server Reporting Services has been installed, use the ExecutionLog 2 view, and alter the stored procedure.)

Reporting Services is not installed with the basic installation. Because this is an added feature, I created a new schema for the feature. In this case, I used the schema name rpt.

```
USE [dbUtilities]
GO

CREATE SCHEMA rpt
GO
```

After the schema is created, adding the stored procedure is done in the same prior method.

```
CREATE PROCEDURE [rpt].[Get_Report_Stats]
AS
DECLARE @Last24hours int
DECLARE @Reports TABLE (ItemPath VARCHAR(1000), UserName VARCHAR(100),
ReportExecution int)

SET @Last24hours = (SELECT COUNT(*) FROM ReportServer..ExecutionLog3
                        WHERE TimeStart > DATEADD(dd, -1, GETDATE()))

INSERT INTO @Reports
        (ItemPath, UserName, ReportExecution)
            SELECT TOP 10
```

```
                    ItemPath,
                    UserName,
                    COUNT(*) AS 'ReportExecution' FROM
ReportServer..ExecutionLog3
            WHERE TimeStart > DATEADD(dd, -1, GETDATE())
            GROUP BY ItemPath, UserName
            ORDER BY COUNT(*) DESC

INSERT INTO [dbo].[Daily_Report]
    (EventStatus, EventDate, EVENT )
            SELECT 'Total Reports', GETDATE(), 'Total number of Reports
Executed ' + CONVERT(VARCHAR(10), @Last24hours)

INSERT INTO [dbo].[Daily_Report]
    (EventStatus, EventDate, EVENT )
            SELECT 'Top Reports', GETDATE(), ItemPath + ' ' + UserName + '
' + CONVERT(VARCHAR(10),ReportExecution)
            FROM @Reports
            ORDER BY ReportExecution DESC
GO
```

## Mirroring

Database mirroring is a high-availability feature introduced in SQL Server 2005. This feature enables a database to be mirrored to a second database on another instance of SQL Server. This mirrored database can take over as the primary source of the data if a situation arises. When mirroring is configured, you have the option of using a witness server to help in the decision as to what database should be running as the principal. If a witness server is not used, a manual failover is required. Mirroring is easy to configure and easy to failover; however, if there are objects (e.g., user accounts or jobs) outside of the database that the database requires to be operational, a few extra steps are required.

Knowing what database is acting as the current primary is critical information. In addition, the value of knowing what server was acting as the principal host historically can be a key piece of information when troubleshooting. In similar fashion as the SQL Server Reporting Services data, I recommend a schema just for the mirroring objects.

```
USE [dbUtilities]
GO

CREATE SCHEMA Mir
GO
```

For the historical data, a table will be created to store our log information. A default is assigned on the ReadingDate column for a point in reference as to when a failover may have occurred. However the value is dependent on when the row was inserted; therefore, if the status is to be checked only once every ten minutes, the date could be off by almost ten minutes.

```
CREATE TABLE [Mir].[MirrorLogging](
    [MirrorLoggingID] [int] IDENTITY(1,1) NOT NULL,
    [HostName] [sysname] NOT NULL,
    [DatabaseName] [sysname] NOT NULL,
    [MirrorDescription] [varchar](10) NOT NULL,
```

```
    [ReadingDate] [datetime] DEFAULT getdate() NULL,
 CONSTRAINT [PK_MirrorLoggingID] PRIMARY KEY CLUSTERED
([MirrorLoggingID]))
GO
```

If you want to use the mirror logging table as a source of notification for when the database mirroring state changes, consider using a trigger or tying into the following stored procedure to send you an e-mail message when the state changes.

```
CREATE PROCEDURE Mir.Log_Mirroring_Status
AS
Set NOCOUNT ON
DECLARE @HostName SYSNAME
DECLARE @dbname SYSNAME
DECLARE @MirDesc VARCHAR(10)
DECLARE @CurrentStatusID INT
DECLARE dbname CURSOR FAST_FORWARD FOR
    SELECT
        CAST(SERVERPROPERTY ('MachineName') AS SYSNAME),
        DB_NAME(database_id),
        Mirroring_Role_Desc
    FROM sys.database_mirroring
            WHERE mirroring_state is not null
OPEN dbname
WHILE 1=1
BEGIN
    FETCH NEXT from dbname Into @hostname, @dbname, @MirDesc;
    IF @@FETCH_STATUS < 0 BREAK
-- Valdiate a record is there for the database,  If not insert it.
If Not Exists (Select HostName, DatabaseName From Mir.MirrorLogging
            WHERE HostName like @HostName
            AND DatabaseName like @dbname)
    Begin
        Insert Mir.MirrorLogging (HostName, DatabaseName,
MirrorDescription)
        VALUES (@HostName, @dbname, @MirDesc)
    END
-- Find the most recent status, if the status has changed
-- Insert a new entry
SET @CurrentStatusID = (Select Max(MirrorLoggingID) From Mir.MirrorLogging
            WHERE HostName like @HostName
            AND DatabaseName like @dbname)
IF @MirDesc not like (Select MirrorDescription from Mir.MirrorLogging
            WHERE MirrorLoggingID = @CurrentStatusID)        BEGIN
        Insert Mir.MirrorLogging (HostName, DatabaseName,
MirrorDescription)
        VALUES (@HostName, @dbname, @MirDesc)
        END
END
CLOSE dbname
DEALLOCATE dbname
```

```
GO
```

## AlwaysOn

The AlwaysOn feature set is new with SQL Server 2012, and is the next generation of database mirroring in combination with Windows clustering. A difficult and expensive aspect of Windows clustering has always been clustering machines that are not physically near each other. With database mirroring, the mirror is not easily readable for applications unless the mirror is using database snapshots. AlwaysOn allows the SQL Server to have multiple databases online and readable, while providing the functionality of the automated failover.

Monitoring and historical tracking of AlwaysOn can be accomplished in a very similar fashion as monitoring and historical tracking of database mirroring. By using the SERVERPROPERTY functions, you are able to get facts such as server names, database names, availability groups, and other key pieces of information. Additional views and functions have been added in SQL Server 2012 to assist in reaching valuable information. When implementing AlwaysOn, review the monitoring and historical tracking to ensure you are getting the information you need. The following is a short list of just a few of these objects:

- sys.availability_groups
- sys.availability_group_cluster
- sys.dm_hadr_availability_group_state
- sys.dm_hadr_database_replica_states
- sys.availability_replicas
- sys.fn_hadr_backup_is_preferred_replica

## Managing Key Business Indicators

The previous example case used to explain a Key Business Indicator (KBI) was that of a 911 service for the local town. If the call status is logged, and is important to the functions of the business that supplies the 911 server, the number of calls in a specific status could not only be a business performance indicator, but also a way to determine whether the business needs to make adjustments for critical times.

It is critical to gather historic trends and behaviors of the business data flow. This data is based on a design internal to databases that have been created after the install, and is not directly related to the installation of SQL Server as a feature. This data can also be used as a critical performance counter that can be acted upon; for example, if there was an emergency of some sort in an otherwise slow period of business, messages and warnings could be sent out to the organization informing them of the increase of 911 calls. As an example, assume there is a database named emergencyservice on the server. The table that tracks the phone queue might look similar to this:

```
USE [dbUtilities]
GO

CREATE TABLE CallStatus(
CallStatusID int identity(1,1) not null,
CallID int Not null,
CallStatus varchar(15) Not Null,
StatusChangeDateTime datetime Not Null,
CONSTRAINT [PK_CallStatusID] PRIMARY KEY CLUSTERED
```

```
([CallStatusID]))
GO
```

For example purposes, assume there is a foreign key pointed over to a Call table. Each call that comes into the 911 service had a header record created in the Call table, and then a record in the CallStatus table. Each call should have multiple call status records, which indicate when a call has entered into a new status. For instance, when a call first comes into the system, but has not yet been answered, the status may be "initial call." When it is answered, a new status record would be inserted with a CallStatus of "call answered." There are many call status options, such as hold, waiting police, waiting fire, lost, and closed. After a call has been marked in the closed status, it might be a short period of time before the data is archived out of the CallStatus table.

Even with few columns in the CallStatus table, many KBIs can be tracked. For example, you could track the amount of time the caller is waiting for the police, the average total length of calls, or the percent of calls that are lost. An important KBI for the 911 service company might be the number of calls that are lost. All the data with this KBI is directly related to the individual company, so use a new schema in the dbUtilities database to indicate it as such.

```
USE [dbUtilities]
GO

CREATE SCHEMA ES
GO
```

The table creation is similar to the other tables that we have created.

```
CREATE   TABLE ES.LostCall
(
LostCallID int identity(1,1) not null,
AvgLostCall_ByHour int not null,
ReadingDate DateTime not null,
CONSTRAINT [PK_LostCallID] PRIMARY KEY CLUSTERED
([LostCallID])
)
```

The historical data can be tracked for this in your utility database, with a stored procedure, like so:

```
CREATE PROCEDURE ES.Log_LostCallCount
AS
Insert Into ES.Log_LostCall (AvgLostCall_ByHour)
Select COUNT(CALLStatusID) from Emergencyservice..CALLStatus
WHERE Callstatus like 'lost'
AND StatusChangeDateTime > DATEADD(hour, -1, GETDATE())
GO
```

Each business is different, and understanding what is important to an organization is critical. A database professional that can help an organization get to pertinent information can dramatically improve his or her visibility within that organization. Often, when database administrators are doing job tasks well, their visibility is not as great; however, when the database administrators are not completing essential tasks, their visibility is achived, but in a negative light.

# Using the Data

Once the methods for collection and storing the data have been created, collection and reporting on the data completes the development cycle of your utility database. Monitoring the data can be automated, as well, by configuring alerts, triggers, and creating a SQL mail profile.

## Automating the Data Collection

The primary use of the utility database is to gather and store information on a consistent schedule, to determine the health and history of the SQL Server and databases located on the SQL Server. Collection data on a schedule makes automation easy. The first step in automating all the data collection points is to identify what collection points need to be collected, how often they should be collected, and when this collection should occur. If you use the stored procedures created during the examples of this chapter, you can isolate a few data points to collect each day.

- Get_Drive_Space_Free

- Get_Failed_Jobs

- Get_File_Growth

- Get_Filtered_Error_Log

- Get_Index_Fragmentation

A stored procedure can be created to execute each one of these stored procedures by nesting the individual executions. The calling stored procedure should be named something obvious that indicates the frequency of the collection.

```
USE [dbUtilities]
GO

CREATE PROCEDURE Daily_Data_Collection
AS
SET NOCOUNT on
-- Maintenance Work--
INSERT INTO [dbo].[Daily_Report_Archive]
    SELECT * FROM [dbo].[Daily_Report]
DELETE Daily_Report
-- Disk Space--
EXECUTE Get_Drive_Space_Free
EXECUTE Get_File_Growth
--Read Error Log--
EXECUTE Get_Filtered_Error_Log
--Get Failed Jobs --
EXECUTE Get_Failed_Jobs
--Get Index Frag --
EXECUTE Get_Index_Fragmentation
--Get Procedure Execution --
EXECUTE Get_Proc_Exection_Times
GO
```

The following are some notable items to consider:

- Error Handling—For space considerations, the error handling lines on the code has been removed.

- Archive—The Maintenance Work section of code clears the Daily_Report table after the data has been archived. If the examples are followed, the report wizard in Visual Studio 2010 is an easy way to build a report that can be subscribed to.

## Scheduling the Data Collection

To schedule the data collection, create a new SQL Server Agent job. After the job has been named and a description added, add a new task. For the command portion of the task, execute the calling stored procedure created in the previous example (see Figure 6-2).

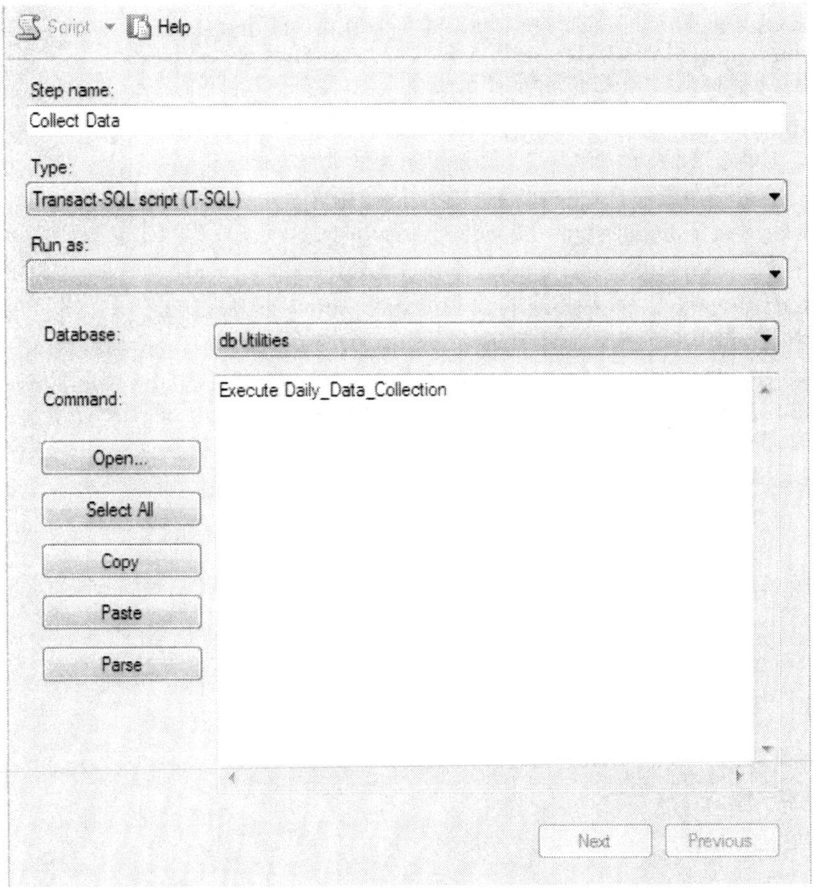

**Figure 6-2.** *Creating the job task*

The last step to automating the data collection is to schedule the job. The code in the examples has been created with the intention that the majority of the data collection steps would execute once a day.

The scheduling of the job for once a day is a natural fit, but not required; however, note that some of the stored procedures might need to be altered.

## Conclusion

We have focused on how to organize the data storage, different ways to retrieve your important data, and scheduling the collection of information. After you have started getting some data collected into your utility database, you should soon start seeing the benefits. The next steps to expand the usefulness of the utility database include the following:

- Use Visual Studio to build a report that can be deployed and subscribed to. This simple step-by-step wizard adds quite a bit to your custom utility database.

- Deploy your utility database to all the SQL Servers in your domain. With a few modifications to tables and stored procedures, tracking server names or instance names is an easy code change. With linked servers, SSIS or PowerShell data can be collected and centralized with little additional effort.

- Add additional counters by using the techniques discussed. At the time of authoring, I am working on reviewing server inventory tracking that was implemented by a friend of mine.

- Consider using PowerShell to deploy your utility database; the larger your environment, the more helpful this is.

- Most important, don't forget to back up your database. After putting all this effort into getting the data, make sure you keep your data.

If all of this information or code development appears overwhelming, start small. Add the dbUtilities database to you server, then add one counter. The database growth counter is a good one to start with because the value of the historical data is high, yet the complexity to add it is not.

# CHAPTER 7

## Indexing Outside the Bubble

### By Jason Strate

When it comes to indexing, there are many best practices we could adhere to. These practices help define how and when we should build our indexes. They provide a starting point for us, and help guide us through creating the best set of indexes on the tables in our databases. Some popular best practices include the following:

- Use clustered indexes on primary keys, by default.
- Index on search columns.
- Use a database-level fill factor.
- Use an index-level fill factor.
- Index on foreign key columns.

This list provides a glimpse of what we should be looking for when indexing a table. The one thing missing from this list is *context*. It is easy to take a query, look at the tables, and identify the index that is best suited for that query. Unfortunately, in most of our SQL Server environments, there will be more than one query run on the server. In fact, on most databases, there will be hundreds or thousands of queries written against each table. With all of that activity, there are numerous variations of indexes that can be added to the table to get the best performance for each query. This could lead to a situation where the number of indexes on the tables is unsustainable. An insert or update would require so much effort from the SQL Server that the resulting blocking and locking would make the table unusable.

For these reasons, you should not use a query alone as the sole motivation for building an index. Working in isolation like this is sometimes referred to as *working in a bubble*. The problem with this is that because any one index will affect the other queries that are executed against a table, you must consider them all. You must work outside the bubble of a single query and consider all queries.

Along the same lines, an index that provides the best improvement for a query will not always be justified. If the query is not executed frequently or doesn't have a business need sufficient to justify it, then it isn't always necessary to have the perfect index. In these cases, to borrow from how the query optimizer builds execution plans, the query needs a set of indexes that are "good enough" to get the job done.

In this chapter, we're going to look at how you can break out of the bubble and start indexing for all of the queries that are running against a table, and the database in which it resides. We'll look at at two general areas of justifications for indexes. The first will be the workload that a database is encountering.

Through this, we'll examine the tools available to investigate and analyze how to uncover and design the best indexes for the table. In the second part of the chapter, we'll examine how that workload isn't necessarily the only consideration when designing indexes.

# The Environment Bubble

The first bubble to break out of when indexing is the environment bubble. You must consider not only the query at hand, but the other queries on the table. Of the two bubbles, this will be the easier, or rather more straightforward, to break out of. In order to so, you should use the following two steps:

1. Identify missing indexes.

2. Evaluate a workload.

By following these steps, you will break out of the trap of indexing within a bubble and change your indexing practices to consider all of the tables and indexes in the database, rather than the narrow scope of a single query.

## Identifying Missing Indexes

The first place to start when indexing is with the missing index recommendations that are available within the SQL Server instance. The main reason to start here is that the SQL Server query optimizer has already determined that these indexing opportunities exist. While there might be other methods for improving query performance outside of adding the missing index, the addition of the index is one of the lowest risk activities you can do to improve performance.

A missing index recommendation can be created whenever a plan is generated for a query. If the statistics on the column are selective enough that an index could improve performance of the query, then the index schema is added to the list of missing index recommendations. However, be aware that there are a few situations where this won't happen. First, if there are already 500 recommendations, then no further recommendations will be made. Second, missing index recommendations won't include clustered, spatial, or columnstore indexes.

Each missing index recommendation includes a number of attributes that define the recommendation. Depending on the source of the recommendation, which we will discuss later in this chapter, the location of the attribute's values will differ. Table 7-1 lists all the attributes that will always be included for each source.

*Table 7-1. Missing Index Attributes*

| Attribute | Description |
| --- | --- |
| Statement | Name of the database, schema, and table where the index is missing. |
| Equality Columns | Comma-separated list of columns that contribute to equality predicates. These predicates are used when there is a specific value that is used for filtering. |
| Inequality Columns | Comma-separated list of columns that contribute to inequality predicates. An inequality predicate occurs when a range of values is filtered. |
| Included Columns | Comma-separated list of columns needed as covering columns for the query. |
| Impact | Average percentage benefit that user queries could experience if this missing index group had been implemented. |

There are some activities that can cause missing index recommendations to be dropped from the list of missing indexes. The first occurs whenever indexes are added to the affected table. Since the new index could potentially cover the columns in the missing index, the suggestions for that table are removed from the queue. In a similar note, when indexes are rebuilt or defragmented, the missing index suggestions will also be removed.

As we review some missing index scenarios, there are a few recommendation limitations that are important to keep in mind. First, the missing index is in regards to the plan that was created. Even if the index is created, there still could be a different missing index suggestion that provides a greater improvement that hadn't been considered by the current plan. Second, the costing information for the inequality columns is less accurate than that of the equality columns because the inequality columns are based on ranges.

With all of the considerations, you might think that using the missing index recommendations doesn't hold much value. Fortunately, that is quite far from the truth. The recommendations that are provided allow you to immediately begin identifying indexing opportunities with minimal work. When done on a regular basis, the information is fresh, relevant, and provides a window into indexes that can easily improve performance on your SQL Server database.

There are two ways within SQL Server to access the missing index recommendations: the dynamic management objects and the plan cache. In the rest of this section, we'll look at how to use these sources to obtain the indexing suggestions.

## Dynamic Management Objects

The first method for accessing missing index recommendations is through dynamic management objects (DMOs). Through the DMOs, the missing index information can be collected and viewed. The DMOs are as follows:

- `sys.dm_db_missing_index_details`: This returns a list of missing index recommendations; each row represents one suggested index.

- `sys.dm_db_missing_index_group_stats`: This returns statistical information about groups of missing indexes.

- `sys.dm_db_missing_index_groups`: This returns information about what missing indexes are contained in a specific missing index group.

- `sys.dm_db_missing_index_columns`: For each `index_handle` provided, the results returns the table columns that are missing an index.

The easiest manner to use the DMOs to return missing index information is by using the first three DMOs in this list (`sys.dm_db_missing_index_details`, `sys.dm_db_missing_index_group_stats`, and `sys.dm_db_missing_index_groups`). These three can be joined together to procedure a query that returns one row for every recommendation that has been identified. The query in Listing 7-1 uses these DMOs to return missing index recommendations.

While the DMOs provide quite a bit of useful information, keep in mind that when you review missing index recommendations, you should look beyond the statistics provided for the recommendation. You can also use those statistics to identify which recommendations would have the most impact on database performance.

The performance impact can be determined through two calculations included in the query. The first calculation, `total_impact`, provides an aggregate value of average impact to the queries, multiplied by the seeks and scans. This allows you to determine which indexes would have the highest percent impact if implemented. This helps you make judgments on whether an index that improves performance by 90 percent on one query is as valuable as an index that improves performance on 50 queries by 50 percent (where the total impact values would be 90 and 2,500, respectively).

The second calculation, index_score, includes avg_total_user_cost in the equation. Because the cost of a query relates to the amount of work that a query will perform, the impact of improving a query with a cost of 1,000 versus a cost of one will likely result in a greater visible performance improvement. Table 7-2 shows a full list of the columns and the information they provide.

---

■ **Note**  Occasionally, people will recommend adding indexes that have values in either the total_impact or index_score calculations that exceed one value or another. None of these recommendations should ever be taken at face value. The longer a set of recommendations is in the missing index recommendation list, the greater the chance the score will be high. A recommendation shouldn't be accepted just because it is high and has accumulated long enough; it should be accepted after consideration between the other recommendations and the indexes that exist on the table.

---

*Listing 7-1. Query for Missing Index DMOs*

```
SELECT
  DB_NAME(database_id) AS database_name
,OBJECT_SCHEMA_NAME(object_id, database_id) AS schema_name
,OBJECT_NAME(object_id, database_id) AS table_name
,mid.equality_columns
,mid.inequality_columns
,mid.included_columns
,migs.avg_total_user_cost
,migs.avg_user_impact
,(migs.user_seeks + migs.user_scans)
    * migs.avg_user_impact AS total_impact
,migs.avg_total_user_cost
    * (migs.avg_user_impact / 100.0)
    * (migs.user_seeks + migs.user_scans) AS index_score
,migs.user_seeks
,migs.user_scans
FROM sys.dm_db_missing_index_details mid
  INNER JOIN sys.dm_db_missing_index_groupsmig
    ON mid.index_handle = mig.index_handle
  INNER JOIN sys.dm_db_missing_index_group_statsmigs
    ON mig.index_group_handle = migs.group_handle
ORDER BY migs.avg_total_user_cost * (migs.avg_user_impact / 100.0)
    * (migs.user_seeks + migs.user_scans) DESC
```

*Table 7-2. Missing Index Query Columns*

| Column Name | Description |
| --- | --- |
| database_name | Name of the database where the index is missing |
| schema_name | Name of the schema for the table where the index is missing |

| | |
|---|---|
| table_name | Name of the table where the index is missing |
| equality_columns | Comma-separated list of columns that contribute to equality predicates |
| inequality_columns | Comma-separated list of columns that contribute to inequality predicates |
| included_columns | Comma-separated list of columns needed as covering columns for the query |
| avg_total_user_cost | Average cost of the user queries that could be reduced by the index in the group |
| avg_user_impact | Average percentage benefit that user queries could experience if this missing index group had been implemented |
| total_impact | Calculation of total user impact across seeks and scans that provides weighing of recommendations to determine which index recommendations would have the most effect across full use of the index recommendation |
| index_score | Calculation providing a measure of weighing to the total_impact calculation by multiplying the value by the avg_total_user_cost |
| user_seeks | Count of seeks in user queries that would have occurred if the missing index had been built |
| user_scans | Count of scans in user queries that would have occurred if the missing index had been built |

The final DMO, sys.dm_db_missing_index_columns, returns a row for every column in the missing index recommendation. Because this DMO is an inline table-valued function, the index handle for the missing index recommendation is required in any queries, such as the example in Listing 7-2. While not especially useful for retrieving the recommendations in a single row, it can be useful when needing the columns for the recommendations returned in separate columns, such as those in Figure 7-1.

*Listing 7-2. Query for sys.dm_db_missing_index_columns*

```
SELECT column_id
,column_name
,column_usage
FROM sys.dm_db_missing_index_columns(44)
```

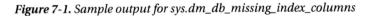

| | column_id | column_name | column_usage |
|---|---|---|---|
| 1 | 4 | DueDate | INEQUALITY |
| 2 | 3 | OrderDate | INCLUDE |

*Figure 7-1. Sample output for sys.dm_db_missing_index_columns*

To help you understand the recommendations you can retrieve from the missing index DMOs, we'll review the following two scenarios that create missing index recommendations:

- Equality Columns
- Inequality Columns

In the equality scenario, we want to look at the recommendation generated when there are specific value queries from the database. In this scenario, we'll look at the missing index recommendations for three queries, included in Listing 7-3. The first query selects and filters a date on the DueDate column. The second selects the OrderDate column and filters a date on the DueDate column. Finally, the third selects the AccountNumber column while filtering a value on both the DueDate and AccountNumber columns.

After running the query in Listing 7-1 to obtain the missing index recommendations, we see that there are two recommendations based on these three queries, shown in Figure 7-2. The first two queries resulted in the first recommendation, which is evident by the inclusion of two user seeks on the recommendation. This recommendation is for an index with the DueDate column as the index key. The second recommendation includes two columns for the index. This recommendation correlates to the third query in the script, which has two columns (DueDate and AccountNumber) as predicates.

**Listing 7-3.** *Equality Columns Scenario*

```
USE AdventureWorks2012
GO

SELECT DueDate FROM Sales.SalesOrderHeader
WHERE DueDate = '2005-07-13 00:00:00.000'
GO

SELECT OrderDate FROM Sales.SalesOrderHeader
WHERE DueDate = '2010-07-15 00:00:00.000'
GO

SELECT AccountNumber FROM Sales.SalesOrderHeader
WHERE DueDate = '2005-07-13 00:00:00.000'
AND AccountNumber = '10-4020-000676'
GO
```

| | database_name | schema_name | table_name | equality_columns | inequality_co | core | user_seeks | user_scans |
|---|---|---|---|---|---|---|---|---|
| 1 | AdventureWorks2012 | Sales | SalesOrderHeader | [DueDate] | NULL | °0337887333 | 2 | 0 |
| 2 | AdventureWorks2012 | Sales | SalesOrderHeader | [DueDate], [AccountNumber] | NULL | ¡58070973333 | 1 | 0 |

**Figure 7-2.** *Missing index recommendations for the Equality Columns scenario*

An important aspect to missing index recommendations can be discovered while looking at the second of the recommendations from the first scenario. In that recommendation, the columns for the equality are DueDate and AccountNumber, and it appears they are recommended in that order. The order of the columns in the recommendation does not have any bearing on the most useful order of the columns in the index. As you might already know, indexes should be designed with the most unique columns at the leftmost side of the index. In this case, using the code in Listing 7-4, we are able to determine that there are 1,124 unique DueDate values and 19,119 unique AccountNumber values. The index would be better served with the AccountNumber column leading on the left side of the index. While the index recommendations provide value, you must always check to verify the most useful order of the columns in the index.

**Listing 7-4.** *Column Uniqueness*

```
USE AdventureWorks2012
GO
```

```
SELECT COUNT(DISTINCT DueDate) AS UniquenessDueDate
FROM Sales.SalesOrderHeader

SELECT COUNT(DISTINCT AccountNumber) AS UniquenessAccountNumber
FROM Sales.SalesOrderHeader
```

The second scenario with indexes found in the recommendations is for those that include inequality columns. These are situations where a range of values or multiple values are used in the predicate of a query. In this scenario, we'll examine the effect on missing indexes for four more queries, shown in Listing 7-5. The first query in the list executes on a range of values for the OrderDate and the DueDate columns, and returns the DueDate column. The second query is the same as the first, except the select portion also includes the CustomerID column. The third filters on range of dates on the DueDate column, and returns the DueDate and OrderDate columns. The last query is identical to the third with the exception that it also returns the SalesOrderID, which is the clustered index key column for the table.

***Listing 7-5.*** *Inequality Columns Scenario*

```
USE AdventureWorks2012
GO

SELECT DueDate FROM Sales.SalesOrderHeader
WHERE OrderDate Between '20010701' AND '20010731'
AND DueDate Between '20010701' AND '20010731'
GO

SELECT CustomerID, OrderDate FROM Sales.SalesOrderHeader
WHERE DueDate Between '20010701' AND '20010731'
AND OrderDate Between '20010701' AND '20010731'
GO

SELECT DueDate, OrderDate FROM Sales.SalesOrderHeader
WHERE DueDate Between '20010701' AND '20010731'
GO

SELECT SalesOrderID, OrderDate, DueDate FROM Sales.SalesOrderHeader
WHERE DueDate Between '20010701' AND '20010731'
GO
```

To analyze the recommendations for these queries, execute the missing index query from Listing 7-1. Similar to the equality scenario results, the results for the inequality scenario, included in Figure 7-3, provide some valuable suggestions. Even so, they cannot be taken at face value and require further analysis.

To begin with, the recommendations include two recommendations in which the inequality columns are OrderDate and DueDate. The difference between the two is the inclusion of the CustomerID in the second recommendation. If you were implementing these recommendations, the two would be better consolidated into a single index, since it would cover both queries.

The second item to note is the similarity between the third and fourth suggestions. In these, the only difference is the addition of the SalesOrderID in the fourth index as an included column. Because the SalesOrderID column is the clustering key for the table, there is no reason to include it in the index; it is already there.

| | database_name | schema_name | table_name | equality_columns | inequality_columns | included_columns | avg_total | | user_seeks | user_scans |
|---|---|---|---|---|---|---|---|---|---|---|
| 1 | AdventureWorks2012 | Sales | SalesOrderHeader | NULL | [OrderDate], [DueDate] | NULL | 0.5911282 | .36667 | 1 | 0 |
| 2 | AdventureWorks2012 | Sales | SalesOrderHeader | NULL | [OrderDate], [DueDate] | [CustomerID] | 0.5911283 | .36667 | 1 | 0 |
| 3 | AdventureWorks2012 | Sales | SalesOrderHeader | NULL | [DueDate] | [OrderDate] | 0.5722493 | .3333 | 1 | 0 |
| 4 | AdventureWorks2012 | Sales | SalesOrderHeader | NULL | [DueDate] | [SalesOrderID], [OrderDate] | 0.5722493 | | 1 | 0 |

*Figure 7-3. Missing index recommendations for Inequality Columns scenario*

Through both of these scenarios, it should be evident that the missing index recommendations do have an opportunity to provide value. While the recommendations will not always be perfect, they provide a starting point that gives an advantage over those starting from scratch to index the database.

## Plan Cache

The second method for identifying missing index recommendations is to retrieve them from cached execution plans. For many readers, it is probably somewhat common to see a missing index recommendation at the top of execution plans (see the example in Figure 7-4). These happen to be the same missing index recommendations as those that appear in the missing index DMOs. The chief difference is that these are associated with specific execution plans and T-SQL statements.

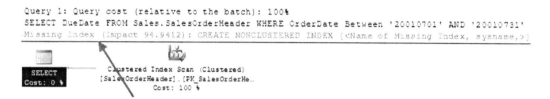

*Figure 7-4. Missing index recommendation in a query plan*

As is to be expected, it isn't practical to collect all of the execution plans as they are created and used on your SQL Server instance to look for missing index recommendations. Fortunately, that activity isn't required to obtain the information. Instead, the information can be found in the execution plans that are stored in the plan cache. Within these plans, the T-SQL statements that would benefit from missing index recommendations have a `MissingIndex` node stored in the SHOWPLAN XML for the execution plan, similar to Figure 7-5.

```
<MissingIndex Database="[AdventureWorks2012]" Schema="[Sales]" Table="[SalesOrderHeader]">
  <ColumnGroup Usage="INEQUALITY">
    <Column Name="[OrderDate]" ColumnId="3" />
    <Column Name="[DueDate]" ColumnId="4" />
  </ColumnGroup>
</MissingIndex>
```

*Figure 7-5. Missing index node in SHOWPLAN XML*

With the `MissingIndex` node, you are able to retrieve missing indexes suggestions from the plan cache and associate them with the T-SQL statements that would be directly impacted with the creation of the index. Retrieving the missing index information requires the use of an xquery SQL statement, similar to the one provided in Listing 7-6. In this query, the plans with missing index nodes from the plan cache are identified. With this list, the plans are parsed to retrieve the SQL statements and the database, schema, and table names. Along with that, the impact, equality, inequality, and included columns are retrieved. Since the plan cache is being accessed, the use counts for the plan and the execution plan can also be included, such as in the example script. When executed after the queries from Listing 7-6, the results from Figure 7-6 should be returned.

*Listing 7-6. Query for Missing Index from Plan Cache*

```
WITH XMLNAMESPACES  (DEFAULT 'http://schemas.microsoft.com/sqlserver/2004/07/showplan')
,PlanMissingIndexes
AS (
    SELECT query_plan, cp.usecounts
    FROM sys.dm_exec_cached_plans cp
        OUTER APPLY sys.dm_exec_query_plan(cp.plan_handle) tp
    WHERE tp.query_plan.exist('//MissingIndex')=1
)
SELECT
stmt.value('(//MissingIndex/@Database)[1]', 'sysname') AS database_name
,stmt.value('(//MissingIndex/@Schema)[1]', 'sysname') AS [schema_name]
,stmt.value('(//MissingIndex/@Table)[1]', 'sysname') AS [table_name]
,stmt.value('(@StatementText)[1]', 'VARCHAR(4000)') AS sql_text
,pmi.usecounts
,stmt.value('(//MissingIndexGroup/@Impact)[1]', 'FLOAT') AS impact
,stmt.query('for $group in //ColumnGroup
for $column in $group/Column
where $group/@Usage="EQUALITY"
return string($column/@Name)
        ').value('.', 'varchar(max)') AS equality_columns
,stmt.query('for $group in //ColumnGroup
for $column in $group/Column
where $group/@Usage="INEQUALITY"
return string($column/@Name)
        ').value('.', 'varchar(max)') AS inequality_columns
,stmt.query('for $group in //ColumnGroup
for $column in $group/Column
where $group/@Usage="INCLUDE"
return string($column/@Name)
        ').value('.', 'varchar(max)') AS include_columns
,pmi.query_plan
FROM PlanMissingIndexes pmi
    CROSS APPLY pmi.query_plan.nodes('//StmtSimple') AS p(stmt)
```

| | database_name | schema_name | table_name | sql_text | usecounts | impact | equality_columns | inequality_columns | include_columns | query_plan |
|---|---|---|---|---|---|---|---|---|---|---|
| 1 | [AdventureWorks2012] | [Sales] | [SalesOrderHeader] | SELECT ... | 1 | 94.0173 | | [DueDate] | [SalesOrderID] [OrderDate] | ShowPla... |
| 2 | [AdventureWorks2012] | [Sales] | [SalesOrderHeader] | SELECT ... | 1 | 94.7939 | | [DueDate] | [OrderDate] | ShowPla... |
| 3 | [AdventureWorks2012] | [Sales] | [SalesOrderHeader] | SELECT ... | 1 | 94.2083 | | [OrderDate] [DueDate] | [CustomerID] | ShowPla... |
| 4 | [AdventureWorks2012] | [Sales] | [SalesOrderHeader] | SELECT ... | 1 | 94.9602 | | [OrderDate] [DueDate] | | ShowPla... |

*Figure 7-6. Missing index nodes obtained from plan cache*

In many respects, the results returned from the plan cache for missing indexes is identical to querying the missing index DMOs. There are, of course, a few key and important differences between the two. With the missing index DMOs, you have information on whether the query would have used a seek or scan with the missing index. On the other hand, using the plan cache provides the actual plan and T-SQL statement that generate the missing index recommendation. Where the DMOs help you know how a new index will be used, the plan cache is where you want to go to determine what will be affected. And by knowing what code will be affected, you know what the testers need to test, where the performance improvements will be, and have the opportunity to consider whether an index is really the best way to mitigate the performance issue uncovered by the missing index recommendation.

---

▨ **Note**    Since the plan cache is critical to the performance of queries in your SQL Server instances, be cautious when querying the plan cache. While there will often be no impact when it is queried, be careful when using any plan cache query in a production environment and be on alert for unexpected behavior.

---

## Index Tuning a Workload

After looking at the missing indexes recommendations, the next place to look for index suggestions is to use the Database Engine Tuning Advisor (DTA). The DTA is an indexing tool included with SQL Server that can be used to evaluate a workload, or collection of queries, to determine what indexes would be useful for those queries. This activity goes beyond the recommendations made by the missing index processes discussed in previous sections. Where the missing index processes can identify statistics that would be best materialized as indexes, the DTA can do much more. As examples, the DTA is capable of the following:

- Suggesting changes to clustered indexes
- Identifying when partitioning would be of value
- Recommending nonclustered indexes

By using the DTA with some automation, you can start identifying early when to make changes to more than just missing nonclustered indexes. Instead, you can begin to dig deep into indexing with minimal effort. Instead of time spent imagining new indexes, you can shift your focus to validating suggestions and digging into more complicated performance issues that are outside the boundaries of where DTA functions.

---

▨ **Note**    The Database Engine Tuning Advisor (DTA) is often shunned by senior-level database administrators and developers. For various reasons, it is seen as an unwelcomed crutch to indexing and performance tuning. While not all recommendations will make it to production environments, the work that it can do and effort that it replaces is of high value. Ignoring the value of DTA is akin to the stories from American folklore of the railroad workers trying to beat the steam powered tools. In the end, this tool frees us from menial work so we can expand our horizons and skills.

---

# Collecting a Workload

In order to test a series of queries, to determine whether they are in need of additional indexes, you must first collect the queries in which you wish to discover indexing opportunities. There are a few ways that a workload can be gathered. In many situations, you could ask peers what queries they think need performance improvements, you could check with developers to see what they believe the applications are using most frequently, or you could ask the business to identify the most important queries in the database.

The chief issue with all of these methods is that they often bear relationship to the queries that the SQL Server instance is actually processing. Your peers will know what they think the problems are, but what about the smaller, more frequently run queries that are bleeding the server with small performance issues? While application developers know what an application does, they don't necessarily know what the users are using and how often. Also, the features and functionality important to the business users might not be the activity on the database that needs the most assistance or should be the primary focus.

An alternative method to using the resources already discussed is to have the SQL Server instance or database tell you the queries that are most often used. In that way, you can look at those queries and determine what indexes, through DTA, are needed on the database. Ideally, you will want to collect a sample of queries from times in which the applications are generating activity that matches common portions of the application life cycle. If the business's peak activity occurs from noon to 5 P.M., then you will want to capture the workload from that time period. Capturing activity overnight or in the morning won't provide the information necessary to adequately build indexes for your databases.

There are a few ways to collect your workload. In this chapter, we'll look at two of the most common methods. These methods are by using SQL Profiler and Extended Events. With each of these methods, we'll look at how the process for collecting information can be set up and configured, and then how the workload collection itself can be automated.

SQL Trace

The most often recommended approach for collecting a workload for DTA is to use the Tuning template from SQL Profiler (see Figure 7-7) and launching it as a SQL Trace session. The Tuning template is specifically designed for use with the Database Engine Tuning Advisor to provide the queries necessary for a workload. Within the template are the following three events, shown in Figure 7-8:

- RPC: Completed

- SP: Completed

- SQL: Batch Completed

For these events, information on the SQL statements, SPID, DatabaseName, DatabaseID, and others are collected. This template provides all of the information necessary for DTA to be able to provide recommendations.

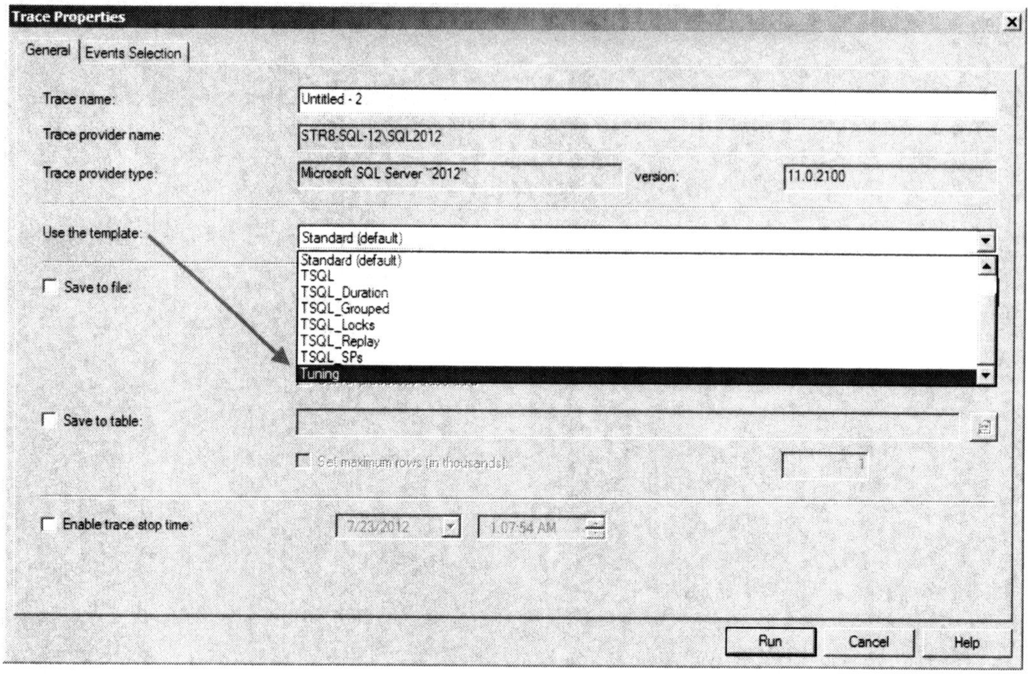

**Figure 7-7.** *Select the Tuning SQL Profiler template*

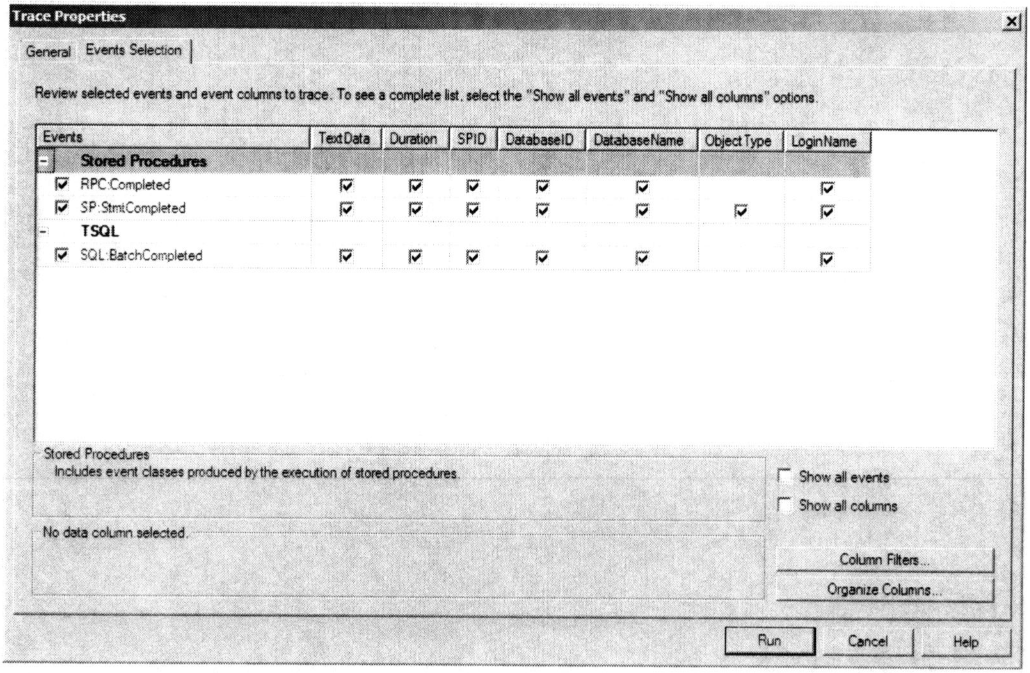

**Figure 7-8.** *Tuning template configuration*

One piece not included in the Tuning template is a filter for the workload export. In some cases, you might want to only examine a single database at a time with the DTA. If that is the case, you'll also want to limit the workload collected down to that database. You can do so by adding a filter to the Profiler session. For example, in the upcoming scenario, the DTA will be used against AdventureWorks2012. To filter the workload, add a filter to the DatabaseName column in the Like category, as shown in Figure 7-9.

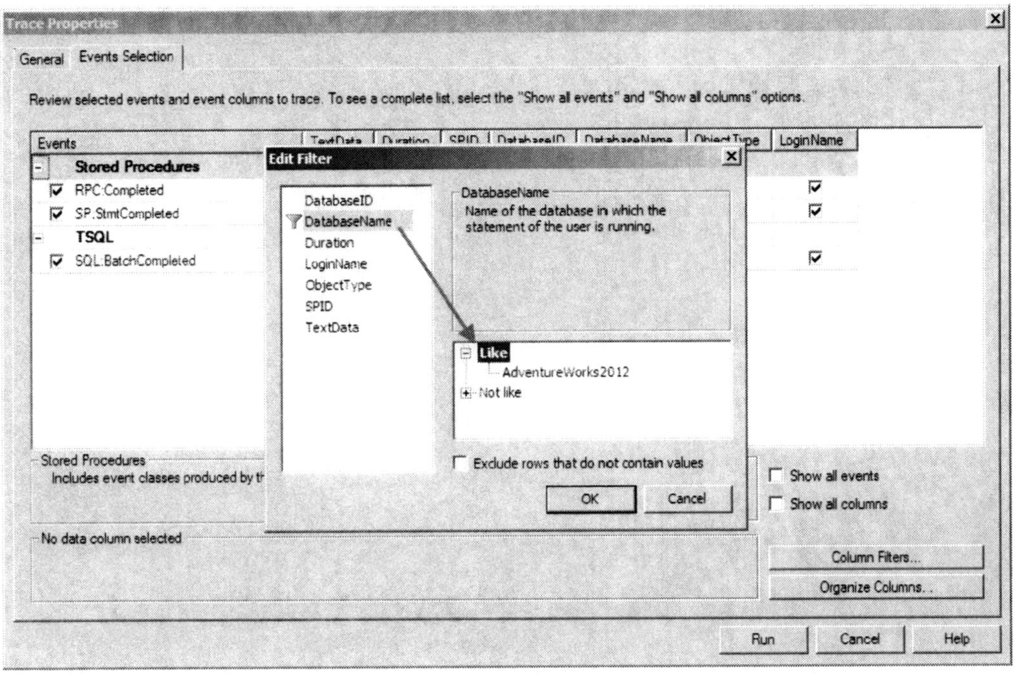

*Figure 7-9. Filtering the workload export to a single database*

If you are familiar with SQL Profiler, you'll likely already know that collecting a workload using SQL Profiler can be burdensome. With SQL Profiler, all of the events need to be passed from SQL Server to the workstation running the trace. Also, the information is stored only in the GUI, which can't be used by DTA when running the workload.

To get around these issues, you will want to create a SQL Trace session identical to the Tuning temple. Using the code in Listing 7-7, you can create this session. Alternatively, you can also export a SQL Profiler session to a file and obtain a script similar to the one provided. The primary difference between the script provided and the one available through SQL Profiler is the variable for the trace file and increased size (50 MB) for the trace files in the provided script.

*Listing 7-7. SQL Trace Session for Tuning Template*

```
-- Create a Queue
declare @rcint
declare @TraceIDint
declare @maxfilesize BIGINT
DECLARE @tracefile NVARCHAR(255) = 'c:\temp\index_workload'
set @maxfilesize = 50
```

```
exec @rc = sp_trace_create @TraceID output, 0, @tracefile, @maxfilesize, NULL
if (@rc != 0) goto error

-- Set the events
declare @on bit
set @on = 1
exec sp_trace_setevent @TraceID, 10, 1, @on
exec sp_trace_setevent @TraceID, 10, 3, @on
exec sp_trace_setevent @TraceID, 10, 11, @on
exec sp_trace_setevent @TraceID, 10, 12, @on
exec sp_trace_setevent @TraceID, 10, 13, @on
exec sp_trace_setevent @TraceID, 10, 35, @on
exec sp_trace_setevent @TraceID, 45, 1, @on
exec sp_trace_setevent @TraceID, 45, 3, @on
exec sp_trace_setevent @TraceID, 45, 11, @on
exec sp_trace_setevent @TraceID, 45, 12, @on
exec sp_trace_setevent @TraceID, 45, 13, @on
exec sp_trace_setevent @TraceID, 45, 28, @on
exec sp_trace_setevent @TraceID, 45, 35, @on
exec sp_trace_setevent @TraceID, 12, 1, @on
exec sp_trace_setevent @TraceID, 12, 3, @on
exec sp_trace_setevent @TraceID, 12, 11, @on
exec sp_trace_setevent @TraceID, 12, 12, @on
exec sp_trace_setevent @TraceID, 12, 13, @on
exec sp_trace_setevent @TraceID, 12, 35, @on

-- Set the Filters
declare @intfilter int
declare @bigintfilter bigint

exec sp_trace_setfilter @TraceID, 35, 0, 6, N'AdventureWorks2012'
-- Set the trace status to start
exec sp_trace_setstatus @TraceID, 1

-- display trace id for future references
select TraceID=@TraceID
goto finish

error:
select ErrorCode=@rc

finish:
go
```

When you're ready, run the script to start collecting the workload. After a while, you will need to stop the trace session so that you can use the trace data that is output. Be certain to run the workload long enough to collect enough queries to represent a worthwhile workload from your environment. To stop the session you can use the sp_trace_setstatus stored procedure.

Extended Events

One of the possible sources for the DTA is a table that contains SQL statements; you can also use extended events to collect your workload. Generally, this will provide the same information as the SQL Trace session. There are a few differences that make the use of extended events a bit more appealing.

First, you have more control on what is collected for the event. Each event comes with a number of base columns, but you can add more to fit your needs. Of course, you can add more events to use the session for additional activities. Second, you have more control over the targets, such as being able to determine whether you want all events, no matter what, or some events can be dropped to just capture a sample of the events. Finally, many events within extended events perform substantially better than the similar event does in SQL Trace. Through the lower overhead, you are able to investigate more often with less concern over the impact of your activities.

As already mentioned, to use extended events with the DTA, the events will need to be stored in a table. The table definition, provided in Listing 7-8, matches the definition of a table that would be created when saving the SQL Profiler session based on the Tuning template. The table contains a RowNumber column and then a column for each of the attributes of the trace being collected.

**Listing 7-8.** *Table for Extended Events Workload*

```
CREATE TABLE dbo.indexing_workload(
    RowNumber int IDENTITY(0,1) NOT NULL,
    EventClassint NULL,
    TextData nvarchar(max) NULL,
    Duration bigint NULL,
    SPID int NULL,
    DatabaseID int NULL,
    DatabaseName nvarchar(128) NULL,
    ObjectType int NULL,
    LoginName nvarchar(128) NULL,
    BinaryData varbinary(max) NULL,
PRIMARY KEY CLUSTERED (RowNumber ASC))
```

With the table in place, the next step is to create the extended event session. To start, we'll build the session through SQL Server Management Studio (SSMS), and then script out the session to allow it to be customized as you require. Begin by browsing through SSMS to the Management à Extended Events node in the Object Explorer. From here right-click on Sessions and select the option for New Session Wizard, as shown in Figure 7-10.

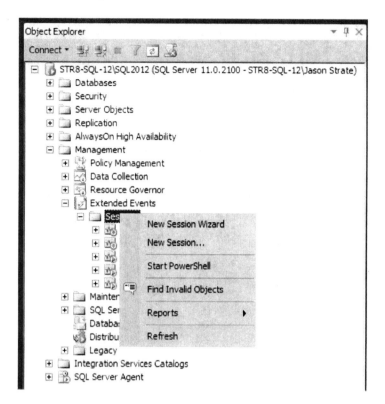

*Figure 7-10. Browse Object Explorer for extended events*

The session wizard will launch an introduction screen. From this screen, select the Next option. If you would like, you can select the "Do not show this page again" option to avoid this screen in the future.

The next screen in the wizard is the Set Session Properties screen, which is shown in Figure 7-11. Here, you will name the extended events session. For this example, type *indexing_workload*; this matches the activities that you are planning to perform. Also, select "Start the event session at server startup" to make certain that when the server stops for maintenance or a instance failover that the data is still collected. This functionality of extended events makes using extended events as the workload source superior to SQL Trace, because a SQL Trace session will have to be re-created to be used after a SQL Server instance restart. Click Next to continue.

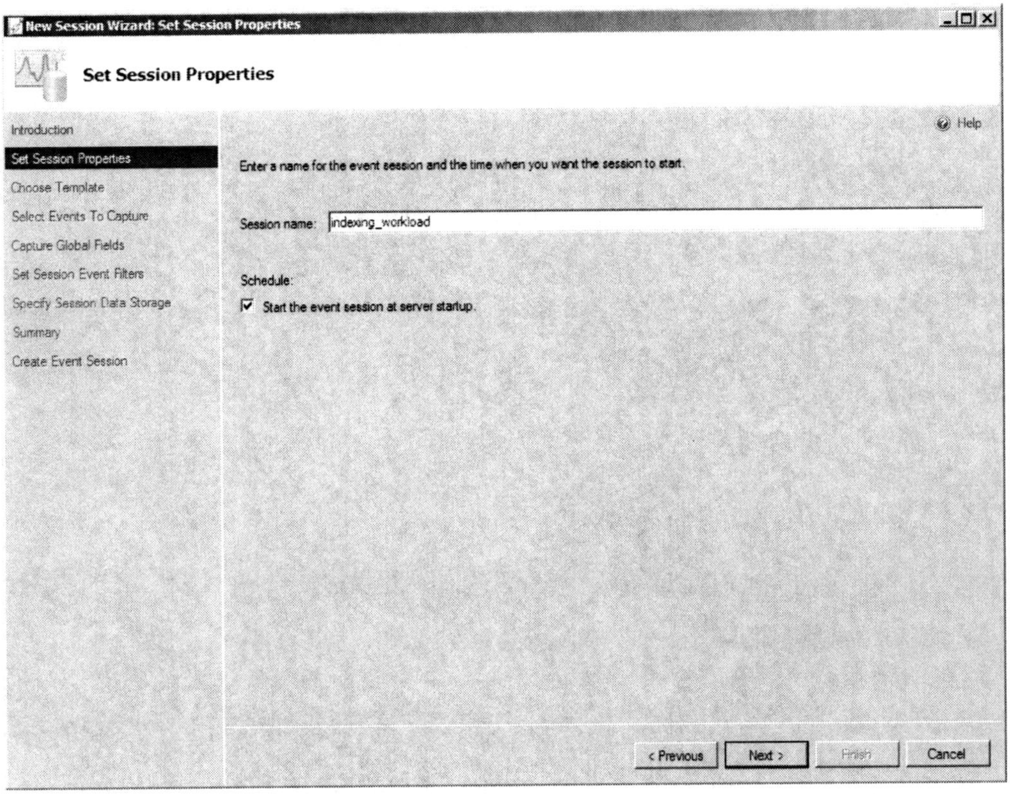

*Figure 7-11. Extended events wizard Set Session Properties screen*

The next screen of the wizard contains the options for choosing a template, as shown in Figure 7-12. There are a number of templates available, but we are looking for specific events in our trace and will not use a template. Select the option "Do not use a template" and then select Next.

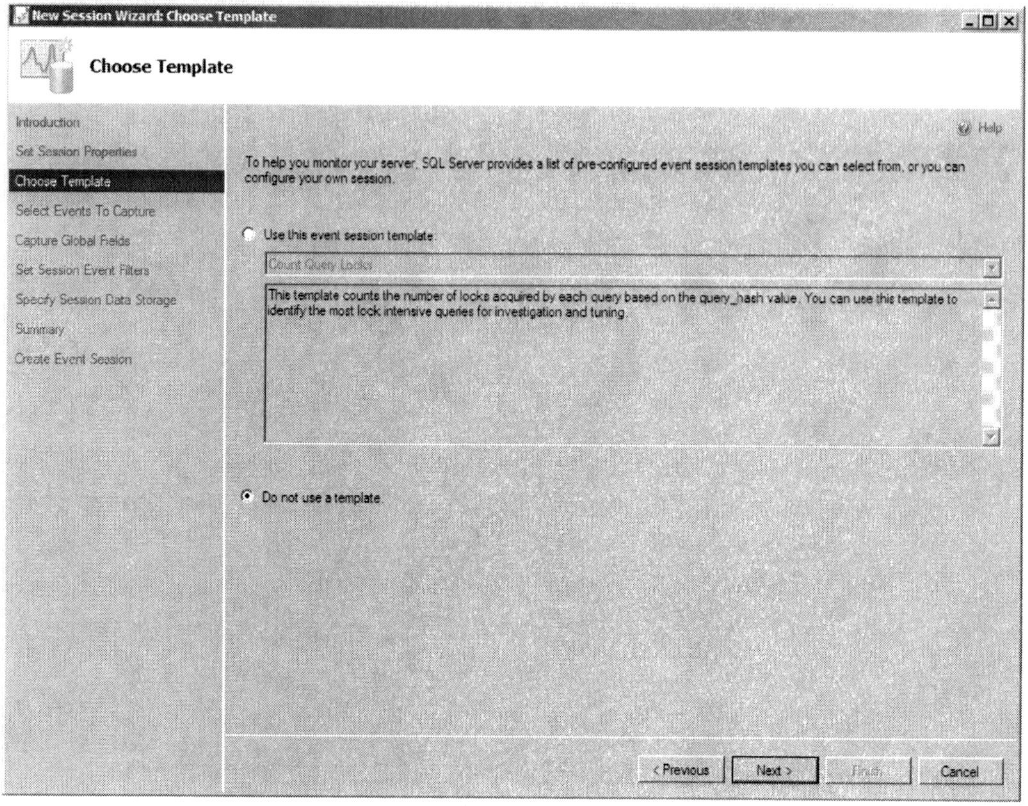

*Figure 7-12. Extended events wizard Choose Template screen*

The next step is to select the events that will be captured through the extended events session. These are configured on the Select Events To Capture screen of the wizard. To configure the session similar to the SQL Profiler Tuning session, you need to select the events in extended events that match the RPC: Completed, SP: Completed, and SQL: Batch Completed events. The easiest way to discover these events is to use the event filter and retrieve all of the events with the word *completed* in their names, as shown in Figure 7-13. The events to select are `rpc_completed`, `sp_statement_completed`, and `sql_statement_completed`. After you've selected these events, click the Next button to continue.

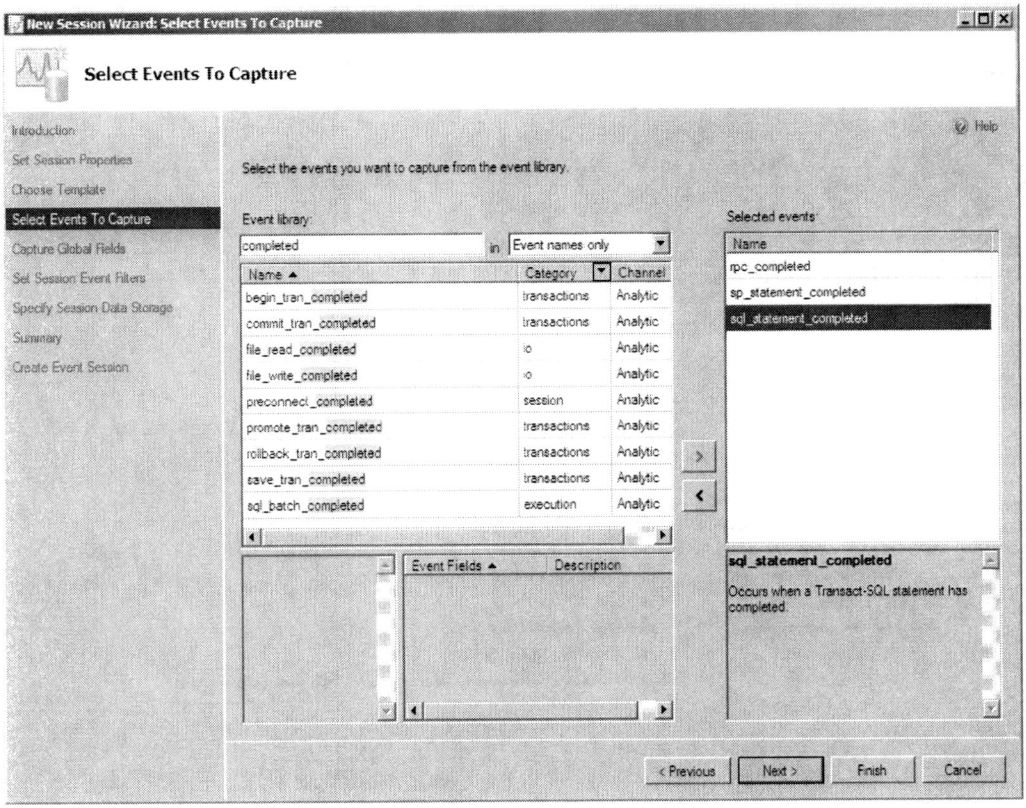

*Figure 7-13. Extended events wizard Select Events To Capture screen*

Each extended event has its own set of columns, but these don't cover all of the columns required for matching the extended event session to the SQL trace session. To accomplish this, you need to add some additional columns to the session on the Capture Global Fields screen of the wizard. The additional fields to include, which are shown in Figure 7-14, are as follows:

- `database_id`
- `database_name`
- `session_id`
- `username`

After selecting the global fields, click the Next button to continue to the next screen of the wizard.

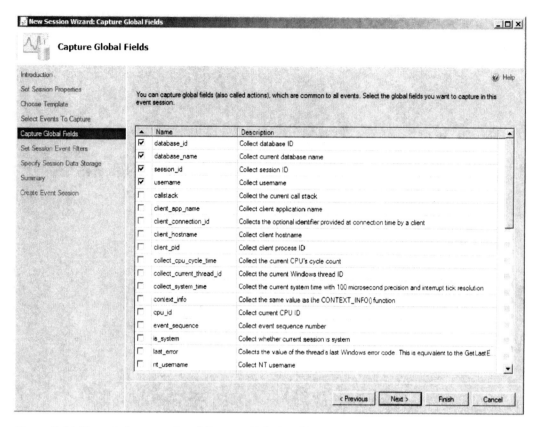

*Figure 7-14. Extended events wizard Capture Global Fields screen*

The next step in building the session is adding filter criteria to the session via the Set Session Event Filters screen, shown in Figure 7-15. There are two filters that will be worthwhile for most loads. The first removes system activity using the `is_system` field filter, since we won't be indexing any system tables. The second limits the events only to those that are occurring in the database in which we want to look at improving indexing. In this case, it is only the AdventureWorks2012 database, which has the database ID of 18 on the demonstration server used for this chapter.

You can use either the `database_name` or `database_id` columns for the filtering. It is typically preferred to use the `database_id` column because the data types for the filtering are smaller. On the other hand, using the `database_name` for the filter is easier to port between servers, which would likely not have identical `database_id` values. When building filters, it is important to configure them in the order of highest selectivity, as extended events filtering supports short-circuiting.

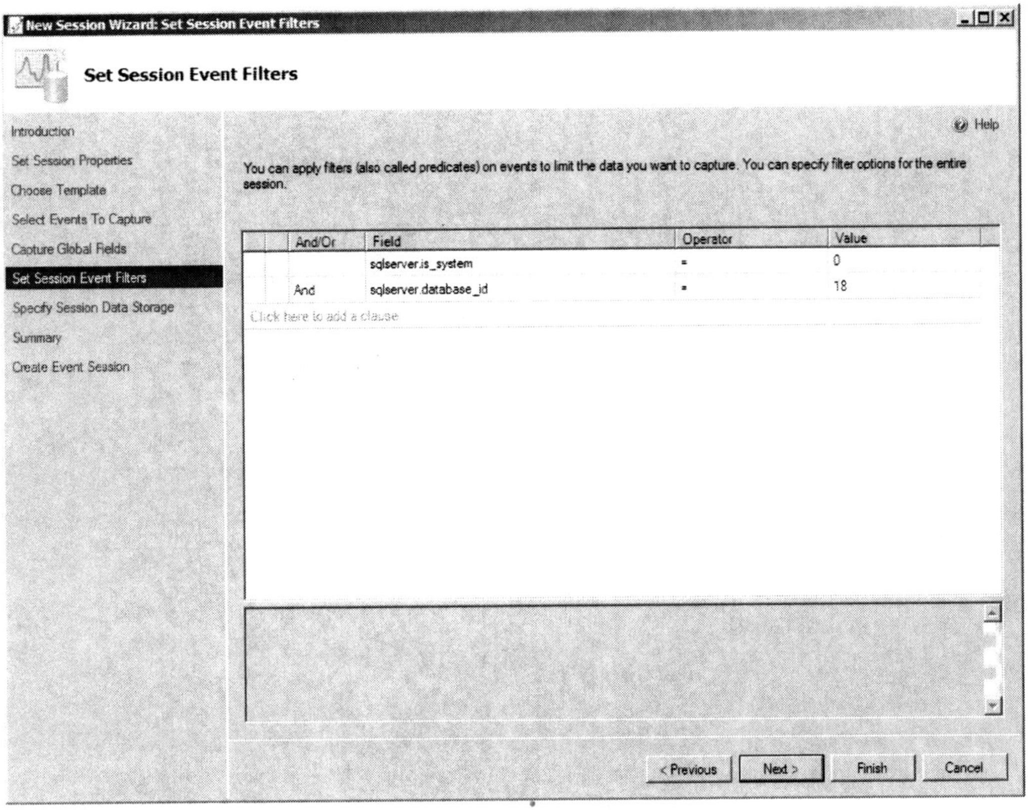

*Figure 7-15. Extended events wizard Set Session Event Filters screen*

The last step in configuring the extended events session is to configure the target for the events. On the Specify Session Data Storage screen, shown in Figure 7-16, select the option for "Save data to a file for later analysis (event_file target)." You can use the default file location, but you should be certain that it is a location that will not conflict with other more important I/O activity, such as tempdb and transaction files. Click Next to continue, or Finish to build and start the session. The next screen in the wizard summarizes the session and builds the session.

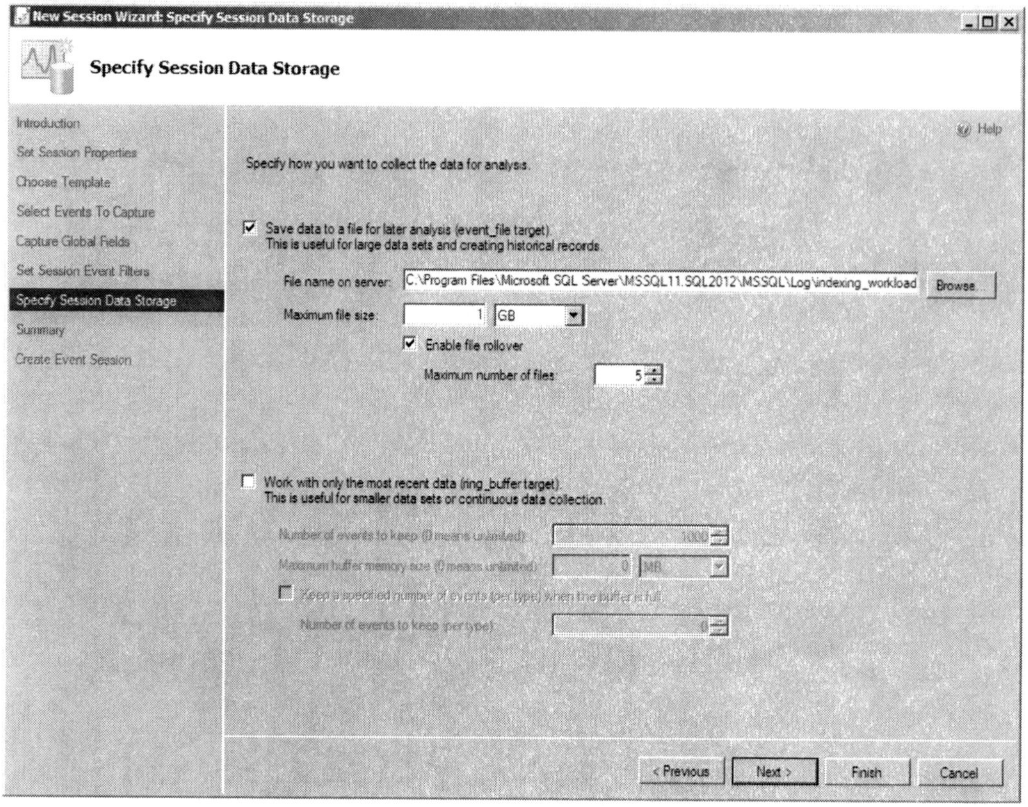

*Figure 7-16. Extended events wizard Specify Session Data Storage screen*

Alternatively to building the extended event session through the wizard, you can also build the session through T-SQL DDL commands. To do this, you will use the CREATE EVENT SESSION statement, provided in Listing 7-9, which includes event, action, predicate, and target information in a single statement.

Using DDL is much easier when you want to build and create the sessions on many servers, and allows you to avoid using the wizard time and again. One difference between the wizard-created session and the one provided in Listing 7-9 is the inclusion of the EVENT_RETENTION_MODE=ALLOW_SINGLE_EVENT_LOSS option in the session. The use of this option is advised, as it will allow the extended event session to drop events in situations where the server is taxed with other activities. In general, this should be the case, but you will likely want to allow for this.

*Listing 7-9. Create Extended Events Session*

```
CREATE EVENT SESSION [indexing_workload] ON SERVER
ADD EVENT sqlserver.rpc_completed(
SET collect_data_stream=(1),collect_statement=(1)
ACTION(sqlserver.database_id,sqlserver.database_name
,sqlserver.session_id,sqlserver.username)
WHERE (([sqlserver].[is_system]=(0))
AND ([sqlserver].[database_id]=(18)))),
ADD EVENT sqlserver.sp_statement_completed(
```

```
ACTION(sqlserver.database_id,sqlserver.database_name
,sqlserver.session_id,sqlserver.username)
    WHERE (([sqlserver].[is_system]=(0))
AND ([sqlserver].[database_id]=(18)))),
ADD EVENT sqlserver.sql_statement_completed(
ACTION(sqlserver.database_id,sqlserver.database_name
,sqlserver.session_id,sqlserver.username)
    WHERE (([sqlserver].[is_system]=(0))
AND ([sqlserver].[database_id]=(18))))
ADD TARGET package0.event_file(
SET filename=N'C:\temp\indexing_workload.xel')
WITH (STARTUP_STATE=ON,EVENT_RETENTION_MODE=ALLOW_SINGLE_EVENT_LOSS)
GO
```

After the session has been created, you will need to start the session for it to begin collecting events. The session should be run for the period that was determined at the start of this section. The code provided in Listing 7-10 can be used to start and stop the session.

*Listing 7-10. Start and Stop the Session*

```
--Start Session
ALTER EVENT SESSION indexing_workload ON SERVER STATE = START
GO

--Stop Session
ALTER EVENT SESSION indexing_workload ON SERVER STATE = STOP
GO
```

When the extended event session has been stopped, the data from the session will need to be inserted into the table dbo.indexing_workload, which was created in Listing 7-8. Listing 7-11 shown how we accomplish this. Because the extended event session was output to a file target, the function sys.fn_xe_file_target_read_file is used to read the data back into SQL Server. One of the benefits of using the file target in this scenario, is that the files can be read into any server; this means you can perform the analysis on any server and, specifically, not on the production server.

*Listing 7-11. Insert Extended Event Session into dbo.indexing_workload*

```
WITH indexing_workload AS (
    SELECT object_name as event
,CONVERT(xml, event_data) as XMLData
FROMsys.fn_xe_file_target_read_file
    ('C:\temp\indexing_workload*.xel'
    , 'C:\temp\indexing_workload*.xem'
    , null, null))
INSERT INTO dbo.indexing_workload
  (
EventClass
  , TextData
  , Duration
  , SPID
  , DatabaseID
  , DatabaseName
```

```
  , ObjectType
  , LoginName
  , BinaryData
  )
SELECT
  CASE event
    WHEN 'sp_statement_completed' THEN 43
    WHEN 'sql_statement_completed' THEN 12
    WHEN 'rpc_completed' THEN 10
    END
  , XMLData.value('(/event/data[@name=''statement'']/value)[1]','nvarchar(max)')
  , XMLData.value('(/event/data[@name=''duration'']/value)[1]','bigint')
  , XMLData.value('(/event/action[@name=''session_id'']/value)[1]','int')
  , XMLData.value('(/event/action[@name=''database_id'']/value)[1]','int')
  , XMLData.value('(/event/action[@name=''database_name'']/value)[1]','nvarchar(128)')
  , XMLData.value('(/event/data[@name=''object_type'']/value)[1]','bigint')
  , XMLData.value('(/event/action[@name=''username'']/value)[1]','nvarchar(128)')
  , XMLData.value('xs:hexBinary((/event/data[@name=''data_stream'']/value)[1])'
,'varbinary(max)')
FROM indexing_workload
ORDER BY XMLData.value('(/event/@timestamp)[1]','datetime') ASC
GO
```

With all of the steps in this section complete, you will have the information collected for your indexing workload. The next steps will be to prepare a database for the workload to analyze indexes against and then to run the Database Engine Tuning Advisor.

## Sample Workload

We'll next look at a sample workload that will help demonstrate some the value of using the Database Engine Tuning Advisor. Prior to running the workload, we'll make one change to the AdventureWorks2012 database to allow DTA to identify a clustering index issue. We'll change the clustering key on Sales. SalesOrderDetail from SalesOrderID and SalesOrderDetailID to just SalesOrderDetailID. The code in Listing 7-12 will perform this change.

*Listing 7-12. Change the Clustering Key on Sales.SalesOrderDetail*

```
ALTER TABLE Sales.SalesOrderDetail
    DROP CONSTRAINT PK_SalesOrderDetail_SalesOrderID_SalesOrderDetailID
GO

ALTER TABLE Sales.SalesOrderDetail ADD CONSTRAINT
    PK_SalesOrderDetail_SalesOrderID_SalesOrderDetailID PRIMARY KEY NONCLUSTERED
    (
    SalesOrderID,
    SalesOrderDetailID
    )

GO

CREATE CLUSTERED INDEX CLUS_SalesOrderDetail ON Sales.SalesOrderDetail
```

```
(
SalesOrderDetailID
)
GO
```

The workload, provided in Listing 7-13, contains scripts that accomplish the following:

- Query Sales.SalesOrderHeader filtering on DueDate.

- Query Sales.SalesOrderHeader filtering on DueDate and AccountNumber.

- Query Sales.SalesOrderHeader filtering on DueDate and OrderDate.

- Execute stored procedure dbo.uspGetBillOfMaterials.

- Query Sales.SalesOrderDetail filtering on SalesOrderDetailID.

*Listing 7-13. Sample AdventureWorks2012 Query*

```
USE AdventureWorks2012
GO

SELECT DueDate FROM Sales.SalesOrderHeader
WHERE DueDate = '2005-07-13 00:00:00.000'
GO 10

SELECT OrderDate FROM Sales.SalesOrderHeader
WHERE DueDate = '2010-07-15 00:00:00.000'
GO 10

SELECT AccountNumber FROM Sales.SalesOrderHeader
WHERE DueDate = '2005-07-13 00:00:00.000'
AND AccountNumber = '10-4020-000676'
GO 15

SELECT DueDate FROM Sales.SalesOrderHeader
WHERE OrderDateBetween '20010701' AND '20010731'
AND DueDateBetween '20010701' AND '20010731'
GO 10

SELECT CustomerID, OrderDate FROM Sales.SalesOrderHeader
WHERE DueDateBetween '20010701' AND '20010731'
AND OrderDateBetween '20010701' AND '20010731'
GO 10

SELECT DueDate, OrderDate FROM Sales.SalesOrderHeader
WHERE DueDateBetween '20010701' AND '20010731'
GO 10

SELECT SalesOrderID, OrderDate, DueDate FROM Sales.SalesOrderHeader
WHERE DueDateBetween '20010701' AND '20010731'
GO 10

EXEC [dbo].[uspGetBillOfMaterials] 893, '2004-06-26'
```

```
GO 10

EXEC [dbo].[uspGetBillOfMaterials] 271, '2004-04-04'
GO 10

EXEC [dbo].[uspGetBillOfMaterials] 34, '2004-06-04'
GO 10

SELECT sod.*
FROM Sales.SalesOrderHeadersoh
INNER JOIN Sales.SalesOrderDetail sod ON soh.SalesOrderID = sod.SalesOrderID
WHERE OrderDateBetween '20010701' AND '20010731'
GO 100
```

## Preparing the Database

In an ideal world, you will have unlimited space and servers for testing that exactly match your production environment. We don't all live in an ideal world, and that means that when it comes to finding a database that is identical to production for indexing, we are often left with a server that has significantly less space in it than the production database has. For this reason, there needs to be a method to test a workload against a database as similar as possible to production so that the recommendations will match the same recommendations that you would received if the test were run in production.

We can find a solution to the problem through a process commonly referred to as *cloning* the database. A cloned database is one that contains the exact schema of the source database on the destination, along with the statistics and histogram information from the source in the destination. In this case, the execution plans generated in the destination database will be identical to those generated in the source database. Because the same execution plans will be generated in both databases, the indexes used or needed will be the same.

There are various means to clone a database. You can use the generate scripts wizard in SSMS. You can restore a database, disable stats updates, and then delete all of the data. Or you can leverage PowerShell and Server Management Objects (SMO) to build a script. The advantage to using a PowerShell script is the ability to build the process once and run it over and over again. Because you will want to run multiple workloads over time, the best option is to use a solution that is easily repeatable.

Using PowerShell to clone a database takes just a few steps. These steps are as follows:

1. Connect to source instance and database.

2. Connect to destination instance and validate that database does not exist.

3. Create destination database.

4. Set database scripting options on the source database.

5. Create clone script from source database.

6. Execute clone script on destination database.

While there are various ways to accomplish each of these steps, the script in Listing 7-14 provides one means of doing so. The script executes each of the steps and includes variables that can be used to change the SQL Server instance and database names.

*Listing 7-14.* *PowerShell Script to Clone Database*

```
$version = [System.Reflection.Assembly]::LoadWithPartialName( "Microsoft.SqlServer.SMO")
if ((($version.FullName.Split(','))[1].Split('='))[1].Split('.')[0] -ne '9') {
[System.Reflection.Assembly]::LoadWithPartialName("Microsoft.SqlServer.SMOExtended") |
out-null}

$SourceServer = 'STR8-SQL-12\SQL2012'
$SourceDatabase= 'AdventureWorks2012'
$DestinationServer= 'STR8-SQL-12'
$DestinationDatabase = 'AdventureWorks2012'

$SourceServerObj = new-object("Microsoft.SqlServer.Management.SMO.Server") $SourceServer
if ($SourceServerObj.Version -eq  $null ){Throw "Can't find source SQL Server instance:
$SourceServer"}
    $SourceDatabaseObj = $SourceServerObj.Databases[$SourceDatabase]

if ($SourceDatabaseObj.name -ne $SourceDatabase){
    Throw "Can't find the source database '$SourceDatabase' on $SourceServer"};

$DestinationServerObj = new-object ("Microsoft.SqlServer.Management.SMO.Server")
$DestinationServer
if ($DestinationServerObj.Version -eq  $null ){
Throw "Can't find destination SQL Server instance: $DestinationServer"}
    $DestinationDatabaseObj = $DestinationServerObj.Databases[$DestinationDatabase]

if ($DestinationDatabaseObj.name -eq $DestinationDatabase){
    Throw "Destination database '$DestinationDatabase' exists on $DestinationServer"};

    $DestinationDatabaseObj = new-object
('Microsoft.SqlServer.Management.Smo.Database')($DestinationServerObj,
$DestinationDatabase)
    $DestinationDatabaseObj.Create()

#Required options per http://support.microsoft.com/kb/914288
$Options = new-object ("Microsoft.SqlServer.Management.SMO.ScriptingOptions")
$Options.DriAll = $true
$Options.ScriptDrops = $false
$Options.Indexes = $true
$Options.FullTextCatalogs = $true
$Options.FullTextIndexes = $true
$Options.FullTextStopLists = $true
$Options.ClusteredIndexes = $true
$Options.PrimaryObject = $true
$Options.SchemaQualify = $true
$Options.Triggers = $true
$Options.NoCollation = $false
$Options.NoIndexPartitioningSchemes = $false
$Options.NoFileGroup = $false
$Options.DriPrimaryKey = $true
$Options.DriChecks = $true
```

```
$Options.DriAllKeys = $true
$Options.AllowSystemObjects = $false
$Options.IncludeIfNotExists = $false
$Options.DriForeignKeys = $true
$Options.DriAllConstraints = $true
$Options.DriIncludeSystemNames = $true
$Options.AnsiPadding = $true
$Options.IncludeDatabaseContext = $false
$Options.AppendToFile = $true
$Options.OptimizerData = $true
$Options.Statistics = $true

$transfer = new-object ("Microsoft.SqlServer.Management.SMO.Transfer") $SourceDatabaseObj
$transfer.options=$Options
$output = $transfer.ScriptTransfer()

$DestinationDatabaseObj.ExecuteNonQuery($output)
```

## Performing Analysis

At this point, you will have the sample workload from your database environment and a cloned database to use with the Database Engine Tuning Advisor. The next step is to pull these together into a tuning session and review the results. There are two basic methods to execute a workload against a database. You can use the GUI that comes with DTA, which is probably the most familiar method for using DTA; or you can use the same tool, but through a command-line interface. We will use the command-line interface with dta.exe in this chapter. The primary reason is that it easily ties into the theme of scriptable actions that have been used for the previous activities.

---

■ **Note**    More information on indexing and using DTA can be found in *Expert Performance Indexing for SQL Server 2012* by Jason Strate and Ted Krueger (Apress, 2012).

---

Through dta.exe, you'll provide the tool with an XML configuration file which will provide all of the information needed to run the workload against the database. The XML configuration files provided in Listings 7-15 and 7-16 can be used to configure dta.exe to run against either SQL Profiler .trc files or the dbo.indexing_workload table, respectively. The other options in the XML input file configure the following attributes:

- SQL Server instance name set to STR8-SQL-12

- Database name set to AdventureWorks2012

- Workload set to either files or table

- Tune clustered and nonclustered indexes

- Do not consider additional partitioning

- Keep none of the existing clustered and nonclustered indexes

Through these options, the DTA will be able to do more than what is possible through the missing indexes feature. Where missing indexes provide suggestions for where statistics could be made into nonclustered indexes that will improve performance, the DTA can suggest when to consider partitioning or, even, when to move the clustered index.

*Listing 7-15. Sample XML Input File for DTA Using .trc Files*

```
<?xml version="1.0" encoding="utf-16" ?>
<DTAXML xmlns:xsi="http://www.w3.org/2001/XMLSchema-instance"
xmlns="http://schemas.microsoft.com/sqlserver/2004/07/dta">
<DTAInput>
<Server>
<Name>STR8-SQL-12</Name>
<Database>
<Name>AdventureWorks2012</Name>
</Database>
</Server>
<Workload>
<File>c:\temp\index_workload.trc</File>
</Workload>
<TuningOptions>
<StorageBoundInMB>3000</StorageBoundInMB>
<FeatureSet>IDX</FeatureSet>
<Partitioning>NONE</Partitioning>
<KeepExisting>NONE</KeepExisting>
</TuningOptions>
</DTAInput>
</DTAXML>
```

*Listing 7-16. Sample XML Input File for DTA Using dbo.indexing_workload Table*

```
<?xml version="1.0" encoding="utf-16" ?>
<DTAXML xmlns:xsi="http://www.w3.org/2001/XMLSchema-instance"
xmlns="http://schemas.microsoft.com/sqlserver/2004/07/dta">
<DTAInput>
<Server>
<Name>STR8-SQL-12</Name>
<Database>
<Name>AdventureWorks2012</Name>
</Database>
</Server>
<Workload>
<Database>
<Name>tempdb</Name>
    <Schema>
<Name>dbo</Name>
<Table>
<Name>indexing_workload</Name>
</Table>
</Schema>
</Database>
</Workload>
<TuningOptions>
```

```
<StorageBoundInMB>3000</StorageBoundInMB>
<FeatureSet>IDX</FeatureSet>
<Partitioning>NONE</Partitioning>
<KeepExisting>NONE</KeepExisting>
</TuningOptions>
</DTAInput>
</DTAXML>
```

After building the XML input file for the tuning session, save the file as WorkloadConfig.xml, or any other appropriate name that you can remember. The next step is to execute the session against dta.exe using command-line arguments, such as those provided in Listing 7-17. To pass in the input file, you will use the ix argument. For the report outputs, you will need to use the ox argument to determine where to place the reports and the rl argument output format. Table 7-3 shows a list of available report outputs. Along with those arguments, you will also need the s argument to specify a name for the session. Session names must always be unique.

**Listing 7-17.** *DTA Command with XML Input File*

```
dta -ix "c:\temp\WorkloadConfig.xml" -ox "c:\temp\Output.xml" -rl ALL -s Workload
```

**Table 7-3.** *DTA Analysis Report List*

| Value | Report |
|---|---|
| ALL | All analysis reports |
| STMT_COST | Statement cost report |
| EVT_FREQ | Event frequency report |
| STMT_DET | Statement detail report |
| CUR_STMT_IDX | Statement-index relations report (current configuration) |
| REC_STMT_IDX | Statement-index relations report (recommended configuration) |
| STMT_COSTRANGE | Statement cost range report |
| CUR_IDX_USAGE | Index usage report (current configuration) |
| REC_IDX_USAGE | Index usage report (recommended configuration) |
| CUR_IDX_DET | Index detail report (current configuration) |
| REC_IDX_DET | Index detail report (recommended configuration) |
| VIW_TAB | View-table relations report |
| WKLD_ANL | Workload analysis report |
| DB_ACCESS | Database access report |
| TAB_ACCESS | Table access report |
| COL_ACCESS | Column access report |

When the execution completes, you will be presented with an XML report that details the indexing recommendations. You can use these to identify potential new indexes to add, along with information on indexes that can be removed from the database. From a high level, the output report will contain all of the individual reports that are requested from tuning sessions. This will look like the XML document shown in Figure 7-17. Examining the individual recommendations, the results will include items such as the index recommendation that is shown in Figure 7-18.

While there is still work to be done to validate the results, the key with using the DTA is that the heavy lifting has already been done. You aren't going to be using your time to consider and test new index configurations; rather, you'll be spending your time validating and applying the indexes. The heavy lifting can be done with minimal effort.

```xml
<?xml version="1.0" encoding="UTF-16"?>
<DTAXML xmlns="http://schemas.microsoft.com/sqlserver/2004/07/dta" xmlns:xsi="http://www.w3.org/2001/XMLSchema-instance">
    <DTAOutput>
        + <TuningSummary>
        + <Configuration>
          <AnalysisReport/>
        </DTAOutput>
</DTAXML>
```

*Figure 7-17. DTA output report sample*

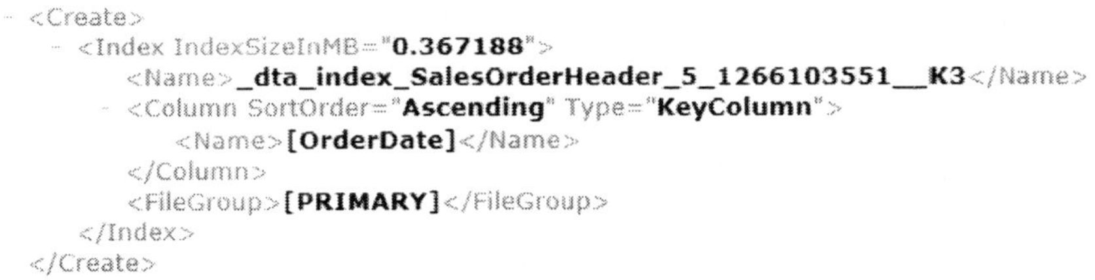

```xml
<Create>
  <Index IndexSizeInMB="0.367188">
      <Name>_dta_index_SalesOrderHeader_5_1266103551__K3</Name>
      <Column SortOrder="Ascending" Type="KeyColumn">
          <Name>[OrderDate]</Name>
      </Column>
      <FileGroup>[PRIMARY]</FileGroup>
  </Index>
</Create>
```

*Figure 7-18. DTA index recommendation*

---

■ **Caution**    Never run DTA on a production server. When evaluating a workload, the tool uses algorithms that will, in essence, use a brute-force process to investigate as many indexing options as possible on the database. While no physical indexes or database changes will be made, there are hypothetical objects created that the tool uses to make its recommendations.

---

# The Business Bubble

Besides the overall impact on the total performance of an index on a table and the queries that utilize the table, there is another area and reason that helps dictate whether an index is of value to a database. In the context of this chapter, we refer to this other reason as the *business bubble*. The business bubble is all of the nonstatistical reasons to index a table that can dictate the need for an index. Sometimes supporting the most important queries in a database defines the queries that are run most often. At times, they will be supporting the queries that are important because of the business value that they provide.

## Index Business Usage

Probably the most often overlooked part of indexing is investigating the purpose or use of an index. There are not many easy ways to identify why an index is used. While that might be the case, there is one method you can use that will tell you how an index has been recently used—this is by querying the plan cache. Within the SHOWPLAN XML for every cached plan, all of the indexes and tables used are documented. Because of this, by querying the plan cache for index use, you can identify where an index is being used.

While the use of an index can be determined through the plan cache, what is the point of determining where an index is used? The point of this is to be able to identify the reasons in which an index is providing value. By knowing this, you can determine which business process that the index supports and, thus, know whether the index is being used to populate value lists or to calculate your next quarter bonus. When you know what is being supported, you will best be able to identify where the impact of changing or dropping an index will occur and know how and where to test for the changes made to the index.

As an example, we'll investigate the demonstration server from this chapter to see what queries are using the PK_SalesOrderHeader_SalesOrderID index. Using the code in Listing 7-18, we can see that by investigating the Object node of the SHOWPLAN XML, the index is stored in the attribute @IndexName. We can query for this directly or through a variable, which is used in the query. The results of this query, shown in Figure 7-19, show you that there are eight plans in the cache that are using the index, along with the counts of use and the execution plan that you'd use to further investigate how it is being used.

**Listing 7-18.** *Query Plan Cache for Index Usage*

```
SET TRANSACTION ISOLATION LEVEL READ UNCOMMITTED
GO

DECLARE @IndexName sysname = 'PK_SalesOrderHeader_SalesOrderID';
SET @IndexName = QUOTENAME(@IndexName,'[');
WITH XMLNAMESPACES (DEFAULT 'http://schemas.microsoft.com/sqlserver/2004/07/showplan')
,IndexSearch
AS (
SELECT qp.query_plan
,cp.usecounts
,ix.query('.') AS StmtSimple
FROM sys.dm_exec_cached_plans cp
OUTER APPLY sys.dm_exec_query_plan(cp.plan_handle) qp
CROSS APPLY qp.query_plan.nodes('//StmtSimple') AS p(ix)
WHERE query_plan.exist('//Object[@Index = sql:variable("@IndexName")]') = 1
)
SELECT StmtSimple.value('StmtSimple[1]/@StatementText', 'VARCHAR(4000)') AS sql_text
,obj.value('@Database','sysname') AS database_name
,obj.value('@Schema','sysname') AS schema_name
,obj.value('@Table','sysname') AS table_name
,obj.value('@Index','sysname') AS index_name
,ixs.query_plan
FROM IndexSearch ixs
CROSS APPLY StmtSimple.nodes('//Object') AS o(obj)
WHERE obj.exist('.[@Index = sql:variable("@IndexName")]') = 1
```

| | sql_text | database_name | schema_name | table_name | index_name | query_plan |
|---|---|---|---|---|---|---|
| 1 | SELECT Sales | [AdventureWorks2012] | [Sales] | [SalesOrderHeader] | [PK_SalesOrderHeader_SalesOrderID] | <ShowPlanXM... |
| 2 | SELECT DueD... | [AdventureWorks2012] | [Sales] | [SalesOrderHeader] | [PK_SalesOrderHeader_SalesOrderID] | <ShowPlanXM... |
| 3 | SELECT Custo... | [AdventureWorks2012] | [Sales] | [SalesOrderHeader] | [PK_SalesOrderHeader_SalesOrderID] | <ShowPlanXM... |
| 4 | SELECT DueD... | [AdventureWorks2012] | [Sales] | [SalesOrderHeader] | [PK_SalesOrderHeader_SalesOrderID] | <ShowPlanXM... |

**Figure 7-19.** *Results from plan cache query*

**Note**   In one situation, I worked with a database that had indexes on a number of tables. These indexes were used on average once or twice a week. During an indexing assessment, it was determined that these weren't used often enough to justify keeping the indexes. Once removed, the import process that they supported degraded substantially and the import time went from under an hour to many hours. This is a near perfect example of why it is critical to know how your indexes are used, and what they are used for. Had the research into the purpose of the indexes been done, then the process using the indexes would not have regressed in performance.

# Data Integrity

The other piece of the business value for an index relates to the data integrity, or rather the rules that are placed on the database to validate and ensure data integrity. The chief method for this is the use of foreign keys. With foreign keys, we are able to ensure that a value placed on one table is a value that is in another table, which contains reference information. While it might not seem important to index this information, it is often critical to do so. The reason for this need is that if the column being validated is not indexed, then any validation check will require a scan of the column. If the column has thousands or millions of rows, this scan can cause performance issues, and could lead to deadlocks.

The best way to determine whether there are missing indexes on foreign keys is to check the metadata for the foreign keys against and indexes. All of the information needed is included and can be easily queried. The key thing to remember is to be certain the that indexes and foreign keys are compared from the left edge of the index. If the foreign key does not match to that edge, then it cannot be used to validate values in the index. Using the query shown in Listing 7-19 provides the list of foreign keys that are not indexed in a database. The results from this query, shown in Figure 7-20, show that there are 33 foreign keys in the AdventureWorks2012 database that are not indexed.

After the unindexed foreign keys are identified, the next step is to create indexes that cover those foreign keys. The table that the index needs to be built on is in the fk_table_name column in Figure 7-20; the key columns for the index will be from the fk_columns column. As an example, the index to cover the missing foreign key index for FK_BillOfMaterials_Product_ComponentID would use the code in Listing 7-20.

*Listing 7-19. Query for Unindexed Foreign Keys*

```
SET TRANSACTION ISOLATION LEVEL READ UNCOMMITTED

;WITHcIndexes
AS (
    SELECT i.object_id
,i.name
,(SELECT QUOTENAME(ic.column_id,'(')
        FROM sys.index_columnsic
        WHERE i.object_id = ic.object_id
        AND i.index_id = ic.index_id
        AND is_included_column = 0
        ORDER BY key_ordinal ASC
        FOR XML PATH('')) AS indexed_compare
    FROM sys.indexesi
), cForeignKeys
AS (
```

```
    SELECT fk.name AS foreign_key_name
,fkc.parent_object_id AS object_id
,STUFF((SELECT ', ' + QUOTENAME(c.name)
            FROM sys.foreign_key_columnsifkc
            INNER JOIN sys.columns c ON ifkc.parent_object_id = c.object_id
AND ifkc.parent_column_id = c.column_id
            WHERE fk.object_id = ifkc.constraint_object_id
            ORDER BY ifkc.constraint_column_id
            FOR XML PATH('')), 1, 2, '') AS fk_columns
,(SELECT QUOTENAME(ifkc.parent_column_id,'(')
            FROM sys.foreign_key_columnsifkc
            WHERE fk.object_id = ifkc.constraint_object_id
            ORDER BY ifkc.constraint_column_id
            FOR XML PATH('')) AS fk_columns_compare
    FROM sys.foreign_keysfk
    INNER JOIN sys.foreign_key_columnsfkc ON fk.object_id = fkc.constraint_object_id
    WHERE fkc.constraint_column_id = 1
), cRowCount
AS (
    SELECT object_id, SUM(row_count) AS row_count
    FROM sys.dm_db_partition_statsps
    WHERE index_id IN (1,0)
    GROUP BY object_id
)
SELECT fk.foreign_key_name
,OBJECT_SCHEMA_NAME(fk.object_id) AS fk_schema_name
,OBJECT_NAME(fk.object_id) AS fk_table_name
,fk.fk_columns
,rc.row_count AS row_count
FROM cForeignKeys fk
INNER JOIN cRowCount rc ON fk.object_id = rc.object_id
LEFT OUTER JOIN cIndexes i ON fk.object_id = i.object_id AND
i.indexed_compare
LIKE fk.fk_columns_compare + '%'
WHERE i.name IS NULL
ORDER BY OBJECT_NAME(fk.object_id), fk.fk_columns
```

| | foreign_key_name | fk_schema_name | fk_table_name | fk_columns | row_count |
|---|---|---|---|---|---|
| 1 | FK_BillOfMaterials_Product_ComponentID | Production | BillOfMaterials | [ComponentID] | 2679 |
| 2 | FK_CurrencyRate_Currency_FromCurrencyCode | Sales | CurrencyRate | [FromCurrencyCode] | 13532 |
| 3 | FK_CurrencyRate_Currency_ToCurrencyCode | Sales | CurrencyRate | [ToCurrencyCode] | 13532 |
| 4 | FK_Customer_Person_PersonID | Sales | Customer | [PersonID] | 19820 |
| 5 | FK_Customer_Store_StoreID | Sales | Customer | [StoreID] | 19820 |
| | FK_Do...mployee_Own... | ...oduction | Document | ...wn... | ...3... |
| 29 | FK_SalesPerson_SalesTerr...ry_...erritoryID | Sales | SalesPerson | [Ter...ry...] | 17 |
| 30 | FK_SalesTerritory_CountryRegion_CountryReg.. | Sales | SalesTerritory | [CountryRegionCode] | 10 |
| 31 | FK_SalesTerritoryHistory_SalesTerritory_Territo.. | Sales | SalesTerritoryHistory | [TerritoryID] | 17 |
| 32 | FK_ShoppingCartItem_Product_ProductID | Sales | ShoppingCartItem | [ProductID] | 3 |
| 33 | FK_StateProvince_CountryRegion_CountryRe.. | Person | StateProvince | [CountryRegionCode] | 181 |

*Figure 7-20. Results from foreign key query*

*Listing 7-20. Example Foreign Key Index*

```
CREATE INDEX FIX_BillOfMaterials_ComponentID ON Production.BillOfMaterials (ComponentID)
```

# Conclusion

Indexing your databases is an important aspect of maintaining performance for your applications. While we often build our indexes by hand and make decisions on their value based on their frequency of use, there are other things to consider. The totality of the indexing for a table and the purposes of those indexes often outweigh the value in adding one index for one purpose. Though, sometimes the one index for one purpose is needed to to support a business process.

In this chapter we looked at how to use the missing index DMOs and DTA to perform some of the heavy lifting with indexes and get a head start with less manual work. We also looked at a few reasons outside statistics that can necessitate an index. When going forward with your indexing strategies, it will be important to consider all of these facets to index your databases as a whole.

■ ■ ■

# Release Management

## By TJay Belt

The very nature of a database system is to be dynamic, rarely static. The applications that use databases tend to change, thus requiring changes within the associated databases. The totality of pieces and parts that comprise this "change" will be combined into a "release" that will be applied to the system. Controlling this change is not rocket science, but it is not without its complexities. In this chapter, we will discuss various terms, processes, and ideas, and suggest tools to assist you in performing this necessary function, while minimizing risk, and impacting your system in a graceful fashion.

While there are many factors that influence a system, we will specifically discuss changes to databases. There are several concerns that we need to keep in mind as we contemplate making changes in our databases. There is always a risk to making a change to a system. Changes typically will come in the form of newly released features, or fixes to existing features. Assuming that your system is in a preferred state and running as designed, any new changes should, hopefully, be for the best. As we delve into how to create your own release management process, remember that minimizing risk will be the goal of this chapter.

## My Release Management Process

The following information has come to you via many years of release process executions, and will impart details learned over a few hundred separate releases, some even being heralded as successful. In the beginning, when I first embarked on this journey of release management, I had no idea what I was doing. I simply knew that changes needed to occur.

I took it upon myself to look at the process as a whole and try to make it better. It was a difficult road, and had many late nights, early mornings, and other frustrations. Having to speak to my company, both within and outside of my department, was a difficult task. Getting them to commit to a process that they didn't understand or care about was even more difficult.

Slowly, we made progress. We started by implementing small changes, such as a rule disallowing ad-hoc queries. The reasoning behind this was sane, and though it generated frustrations from others, its enforcement was successful. This lead us to the need to wrap our changes into stored procedures that we could introduce into our system, execute, and then drop. This allowed us to minimize human involvement at release time.

Soon, we discovered that we needed many additional steps in the process. Eventually, I started keeping track of everything we did to prepare for a release. This led me to the realization that many of the tasks were unknown to many people, and I was able to share these with others via documentation. Once folks realized how complex a release was, they were more inclined to be open and helpful, especially when I would show them that their release would require hundreds of steps. No more were they shy about being available and helping me out. They learned that their simple request (or so it seemed to them) required multiple people to work many hours to prepare and perform. When they saw the level of documentation that we requested them to review, they suddenly caught the vision. This vision spread and was infectious.

In the beginning, we would hold our breath as we embarked upon a release. Often, we would hold our breath through the entire release. Many of our initial releases failed, had to be rolled back, or had some otherwise undesirable outcome. Soon, through the careful implementation of this release process, we started becoming proficient at not only planning, but also executing the releases. Soon, we could scarcely recall a failed release. Well, that's a bit of an exaggeration. We always remembered the failed releases, but we started putting time between us and them. This experience made us happy, but ever vigilant.

One release, well into our successful period, showed us that even though we had been doing a good job, we were not beyond error. An unforeseen functionality occurred immediately after the release, and the decision to rollback was made. However, in our confidence, we had started skimping on the rollback procedures. In this case, it was left to the release engineer to decide how to rollback, and the choice that was made turned out to be a bad one. Who was at fault? Was it the individual that rolled back in an improper way? No. Was it the developer that released the bad code? No. It was me, the creator of the release plan. Because I had not spent time creating and documenting the rollback process sufficiently, the onus rested upon me. I still feel the sting of this experience, and I use that feeling to remain more diligent.

By sharing such experiences with you, I intend to show you that the release management process isn't a new idea; it has been in practice in various organizations for quite a while. I have continued to perfect and alter this process over time. Each time the process iterates, it gets stronger. It might never be perfect, but as long as the process evolves to meet needs, it will greatly benefit us.

# A Change Is Requested

As you can probably guess, a change will eventually be requested in your application and/or database system. How this request comes into existence is not important. The request will come, and it will need to be dealt with. We want to determine the best ways we can deal with them, control them, and gracefully introduce them into our respective systems.

Unfortunately, many release processes might be similar to the one detailed in Figure 8-1. This shows a process that contains very few steps, very few tests, very little verification, and a large chance of failure. Granted, for certain releases, success could be achieved with this simplistic process.

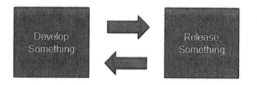

**Figure 8-1.** *A typical (and ineffective) release process*

The following basic steps are involved in this minimalistic release process:

1. A change is requested.

2. T-SQL code is created to support this change.

3. T-SQL code is tested.

4. T-SQL code is deployed.

---

■ **Note** When we refer to T-SQL code, this could be T-SQL that creates or alters functions, tables, stored procedures, data, and so on.

---

The minimum tasks from the preceding steps could be steps 2 and 4: create and deploy the code. The actual request (step 1) might not come as an official request; it might be received in a variety of unofficial ways. Unfortunately, testing (step 3) does not often occur. This leaves us with only two core tasks transpiring.

Saying this out loud should make you realize that this greatly increases our risk to an unacceptable level. To mitigate this risk, we should apply a series of tasks to a *release management process*. These tasks need not be cumbersome. We should apply them to our process to simply ensure the safety of our individual systems. It is up to you to find the balance in making sure that your tasks are sufficient, yet not cumbersome. This will take time, and involves creating a flexible process. Add some tasks, take some away. Let's talk about how to get achieve that balance. This is our goal.

## Release Process Overview

As we discuss this large topic of release management, there will be many considerations, documents, and tasks that will come to light. In fact, these are the three areas of concentration for the rest of this chapter. We will dig into considerations that you should put at the forefront of your thought. This will help you develop documents that detail tasks. As you read the ideas that follow, please contemplate how you can apply them to your topology and system. Remember that no process is absolutely perfect for everyone, or for every situation. Take those ideas that fit and add them to your release management process. If you do not have a process currently, this chapter will help you create one.

## Considerations

While there are many considerations in planning a release management strategy, we will delve into some specific ones and, hopefully, bring to light some of the reasons why you should consider them. Our goal is to create a balanced process that will allow you create your release in a controlled fashion, without negative incidents. As this discussion occurs, please take into account the particulars of your system. The following is an overview of the considerations we will discuss:

- **Goals:** Define the goals for your release process.

- **Environments:** Detail your environments, from top to bottom, from development to production.

- **Release Process:** Define a release process to share with all involved and get their commitment.

- **Players Involved:** Indicate who will be involved in the process.

- **Version Control:** Determine a safe place to keep track of your code.

- **Rollback Process:** Always have a way to revert back to a known state.

# Goals

First and foremost, you should detail what your goals are for release management. My goals may differ from yours. Your goals might change as time passes and you might need to alter them with the introduction of new ideas, new managers, and so on. Regardless of what your current goals are, continue to review them, and discuss them with others as you perform your release process. If speed is of vital importance, this will help you streamline your tasks and procedures for your release process. If safety is your goal, other tasks may grow and entwine themselves in your process. Let's minimize the goals down to a few simple ones and further define those terms. I consider the following items to be a core set of goals for my release management process:

- Reduce risk

- Control change

- Perform successful change

- Follow best practices

- Architect/design changes

- Review changes

### Reduce Risk

Your system exists and functions for a purpose, so reducing risk to it should be an obvious goal. Not allowing a change to occur that would impact your system is more easily said than done. Keeping it stagnant is not an option, so let's face the inevitable, and attempt to reduce the risk that change will introduce.

We need to take measures to create a process that is molded to each system, with elements borrowed from other iterations of release management processes to find that perfect one that will suit you, protect you, and reduce your risk. As you review code, test your release process, and perform other tasks, always keep in mind that you need to do all tasks with an eye on reducing risk. This doesn't mean that you shouldn't implement change; rather, it attempts to wrap that change into a process that will be graceful, controlled, and successful.

### Controll Change

Controlling change simply means that whatever change occurs in your system follows a process that has been vetted, agreed upon, detailed, and documented. In other words, the right people performing the right tasks, in the right order, at the right time. You need to define all this. Others can give you suggestions, even plan out the process for you and with you; however, you will be the ultimate authority on what is actually decided upon. Remember that you are the data professional and it falls to you to ensure your system is secure, available, and properly used.

In order to control this change, you should take the time to understand your entire topology. Understand how data flows in and out. Learn as much as you can about your system. Knowing how your system functions, how it is secured, and how data moves within it will better enable you to control how changes will impact it.

## Perform Successful Change

A successful change can be defined as one that was executed as expected, with no negative impact. No exceptions were raised once the change was introduced to your system and there was no unforeseen degradation of system functionality. This does not mean that the change contains flawless code or perfect functionality. We have seen before that functionality can be introduced that is not expected or simply performs differently than expected. A successful change is one that simply introduces a change in a successful manner, requiring no rollback of code to a previous state. Even though the goal is to perform successful change, it behooves you to take the steps necessary to ensure that you include proper testing and a foolproof rollback process. We will discuss this later in this chapter.

## Follow Best Practices{"

Determine and document what your best practices will be for releases. You should refer to Microsoft for published best practices (for example, some can be found at http://msdn.microsoft.com/en-us/practices/ff921345). You should also look for best practices in books, blogs, training, and so on. Search out sources that can impart what others believe to be best practices. There are many examples available from which you can pick and tailor those that make sense for your system. You will probably already have some best practices that are alive and well within your organization. Use these practices as well.

Whatever the source, include these rules into your release management process and documentation. Do not be afraid to add to them, or remove from them, as you repeat iterations of your release management process. Always review your process and continually tweak it. When you find something that will help you perform better releases, integrate it into your process.

When you implement best practices, ensuring that these rules are followed is the next logical step. If you choose to go this extra mile, you can include a means to monitor your system to prevent changes that would violate your chosen best practices. Policy Based Management (PBM) is a solution that is available with SQL Server that does just that. PBM allows you to define and enforce policies on your SQL Server systems, thus preventing unwanted changes. This chapter will not delve into how to implement PBM. Homegrown solutions can prevent and track changes as well. Using tools to control change will also help.

Best practices can also be found in various SQL Server books. Joe Celko has written a book called *SQL Programming Style* (Morgan Kaufmann, 2005) and Louis Davidson has a book called *Pro SQL Server 2012 Relational Database Design and Implementation* (Apress, 2012). Both these resources will help you find best practices. Look to your managers, teammates, and other coworkers to determine what best practices are already being followed, and find where they can fit into your release process.

Let us assume that you have decided to implement a best practice that prohibits the use of ad-hoc queries in your system. If such a rule exists and all parties agree upon it, then when a review is performed of a proposed release, the code can be kicked back for redesign because it contains ad-hoc queries. This leaves the reviewer out of the mess of explaining why this is a bad thing. It has been agreed upon already, added to your process, and simply becomes a checkmark to look for upon review.

A suggestion that has helped me time and time again is to create stored procedures that actually contain a database change. Let us assume that a change to be released will perform an alter table statement, adding a column to an existing table. This change will be an ALTER TABLE T-SQL statement that adds a column. You can put this code within a stored procedure. The stored procedure can contain code that performs validations. Maybe there should be a validation that checks for the existence of this column, prior to performing the ALTER TABLE statement. After the statement has been performed, you can check for the existence of this column. I would suggest that this entire T-SQL code be wrapped with a transaction, so that the post validation can either commit or roll back your change, based on the validation results. As part of your release, you would create this stored procedure, execute it, and then drop it. When the stored procedure is executed, it will perform the ALTER TABLE command for you.

You can bundle all the changes into a single stored procedure or multiple stored procedures. These stored procedures are what you actually release. Then you execute them, which executes the changes, and finally you drop them. So, they exist for a short period within your environment. They perform a task and are removed. This allows for a controlled change, and will ensure that when executed, they perform their desired tasks only. Saving these scripts into a release storage location will allow you to keep track of these in the future. You could also save these scripts in your favorite source control system. We will discuss this further, later in the chapter.

By executing changes via a controlled method, as previously explained, you will limit the quantity of ad-hoc changes that can be introduced into your system. Once you reach the stage of releasing code changes, you can easily execute the changes via a tool that will perform the executions for you, which further removes the human element from the change process. You would click the button; it would perform all the tasks possible, and commit them or roll back, depending on the result. You could also save the performed steps within a historical collection system. Remember that this is one of our goals.

Other best practices that you might want to include could be naming conventions, transaction levels limiting quantity of data changes, coding a breakout point in automated processes, and so on.

Naming conventions will help your database objects be cleaner and better understood. Well chosen and followed naming conventions will help with navigating and understanding your database. I would venture to say that even a bad standard, as long as it is followed, is better than choosing random standards and following them all simultaneously. Take some time to research the naming conventions that you already have in place, and ensure that going forward you have a documented naming standard and follow it completely.

When changes involve large quantities of data, implementing a cap on how many changes will occur at once, and wrapping this quantity within a transaction, can help speed up the overall process. This is much more efficient than applying all data changes at once and then committing, or worse yet, applying them one at a time. You might need to do some research to find the proper quantity for each large data change. Some data changes might not need a transaction and quantity. You will have to test this out in a nonproduction environment. You can and should ensure that you compare appropriate quantities of data in your testing. Testing a small version of similar data will not help you when you actually perform the change in production.

Some changes might take a long time to perform. While the change is churning on and on, if you had the ability to stop it midstream, gracefully, you could easily halt a potentially long-running process. For example, you could implement a loop that checks a table for a certain value. Then, based on the result of this value, you could continue or halt the change, thereby giving you an out. This is a feature that is not usually implemented in changes. However, you can implement this, and instill a breakpoint in long-running processes or updates.

## Architect/Design Changes

The earlier that you can be involved in the change process, the better you will be able to mitigate risk. It's not to say that you are the subject matter expert (SME) in all things database. However, being an expert in this field does allow you the ability to weigh in on decisions early on that could impact the final product. Just as you are the expert in databases, lean on other SMEs in other areas, and ensure that you are all involved in the change process as early on as possible. Take the time necessary to learn as much as you can about your respective systems, and how they interact with data and, especially, with your databases. Be as involved as you can with all things database, and you will be better prepared for a successful release.

You might be hesitant at stepping into this stage of the process. It might seem to you, your managers, and to others that this is not your place or job description. Simply remind yourself and others that you have experience with databases. Remind them all that you are a resource. Get in there. Force yourself in on the development process. Do it gingerly, respectfully, but do it. If you can gain access to this stage of development, you will be armed to impact changes all through the development process and into the actual release period.

**Review Changes**

It is imperative that each piece of code be reviewed, hopefully by multiple parties, along the route to becoming part of your permanent topology. If you ensure that you and others, with the necessary skills, perform a thorough review of changes, you'll be better armed to reduce risk to your system. It takes time. You must schedule this time. You must take the time necessary that will allow you and others to appropriately review the code, weigh its changes against the entire topology, and proceed accordingly. Even a simple change is a "change" and needs to be given proper attention. The process that you ultimately create will likely have several steps. Even if these steps take little time, make sure you take them, in their respective order, so as to reduce risk.

Don't be afraid to reject code that you feel might negatively impact your system. You will be the one that gets in trouble for it, not the creator of the code. Be firm, but be respectful. Back up your concerns with good information and best practices. Share with others the the agreements you've reached. Let them know that you are simply trying to protect your system, and minimize impact for the entire organization.

Involving others as you review code will be an excellent opportunity for team and cross-team unity. Do not be afraid of letting others help you out and helping others out as well. Peer reviews will let you get more folks involved, more eyes on the code, and many more chances to perfect the code and minimize risk to your system.

# Environments

Take the time to detail all vital pieces of your environment that will receive change. This may start at the development layer, and work its way up through many layers of various systems that influence your release management process. As a way to reduce risk, take time to create various testing ground environments through which your code can pass, allowing for various forms of testing, as well as testing of the actual release plan (we will discuss release plans in a bit). Only through properly tested iterations, can we truly reduce risk.

Involve your development group in your discovery and documentation of environments. They might already have various environments in play that allow them to test their changes prior to reaching any other environments. They might also have tools that can help with unit testing. If not, together you need to find such tools and add them to your arsenal. Together, you can discuss the best ways you can determine how to test code in these early stages of change development. You can pull out each new change and test it separately, but make sure you test the completed code as it would behave in a live, production environment.

At a minimum implement a development environment and a testing environment before your actual production environment. Beyond the minimum, implement as many layers as you feel comfortable implementing without adding burden to the process. Ensure that each layer is understood, managed, and controlled. I would suggest that you do not implement an environment that will become a burden, or be skipped, or become out of date and cause problems with your release testing. Each environment needs to provide a playground for you to perform tests within, yet remain valid and viable.

Ensure that no change enters the actual production environment without passing through the lower levels first. Ensure that only properly authorized individuals can access production and push out changes in a controlled manner. In fact, ensure that each layer of environment is secured to only those that should access it. By minimizing the quantity of individuals that have access to your production (and prior) environment, as well as having environments through which validations occur, you will more easily reach the goals we are striving for.

Realize also that this will create tasks for other individuals in your organization besides yourself. You will need to take the time to get their commitment on this process so that it is used, and not just dreamt about. This will take time and force you to show that having these other environments will greatly decrease your risk to change.

Some possible environments to consider are shown in Figure 8-2.

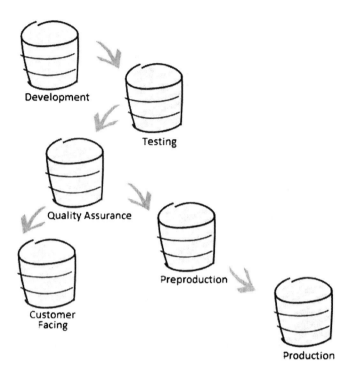

*Figure 8-2. Possible database environments*

The development environment may be a single environment or multiple environments. This area will be the playground for developers to make changes at their whim. You should ensure that they have sufficient quantities of data to approximate a production environment. Ensure that the development environments match in structure and objects with the production environment. If you have a development environment that has differences in objects, missing indexes, or only small amounts of data, you are setting yourself up for future problems.

The testing environment can be used by development, and even the DBAs that perform the release, to start testing the release plans. This environment, like others, should match production as closely as possible. Performing release plan testing is a vital step that needs to be performed to ensure that the plan you have created is accurate. The environment needs to be valid enough to be a good test for the release plan.

The quality assurance environment will be used primarily by the QA group for their own testing procedures. This environment also needs to match production and provide a decent playground for them to perform valid tests. You may or may not be involved in keeping this environment intact.

A customer facing environment would be used to provide a place where folks outside your company can preview changes. This environment will provide you very valuable data about how others perceive your product. There will be many opportunities for information to be collected about how a small change can affect your system as a whole. You will need to ensure that this environment has very up-to-date data compared to production. Your external users will want this to be as close to production as possible.

The preproduction environment is very similar to the customer facing environment, except that it is internally facing. This environment is the last stage before the change is released into the wild, into production. By this stage, your release plan should have been buttoned down and tested through the other environments. The steps to successfully perform the release will have been put to the test through the various environment releases. This last phase will let you test it one last time, and should include all pieces and parts, including replication, and so on. Do not skimp on this environment. Ensure it matches production in as many ways as you can implement. Having matching hardware and storage can only help you in the minimization of risk while testing your process and the actual release of the change.

The production environment doesn't need an introduction or explanation. This is the goal environment. All the others exist simply to allow you to prepare to push a change out to production.

## Release Process

The end goal of this chapter is that you will have created a release process that encompasses the necessary tasks to accomplish our goals of release management. Document this process and know that it will change over time to encompass any future possibilities. It must be rigid and always followed as its design intended. This means that, at any given time, the rules that you have created for this process must be followed. To ensure that all involved know the process, it must be discussed with the proper individuals; it must be accepted and agreed upon by all involved. Keep in mind that this process may change over time. Allowing it to be malleable will help you to improve your process as time marches on and your needs change.

This chapter provides many pieces and parts that you will be able to implement within a process. If you can automate pieces of this process, or even the entire process, you will greatly minimize risk. Humans are fallible. No matter how careful we are, we can make mistakes. As you review your process and as you perform a release, keep a wary eye on each step and make attempts to perfect it. Performing the steps manually initially will help you to understand what is needed to accomplish said task. But as you continue performing these steps, you will see ways to automate them. Automation is your friend, and will minimize risk if performed properly.

An example of automating release steps can be shown when a release involves replication. There will be a few steps to perform replication changes. These changes can be scripted out beforehand and tested in other environments. The actual scripts that you create to perform a step, such as adding an article to a publication, can be encapsulated into a tool and executed when you reach that step of the release plan.

Soon you will see other parts of your release plan that can also be automated.

## Players Involved

Because you are not an island, and change processes don't occur within a vacuum, you will need to be involved with multiple people throughout the entire release process. As you are planning your own release process, ensure that you have involved all the appropriate players. In this section, you will find some suggested groups that might need to be involved. Keep in mind that you may involve more than one person from each group.

Meet with the teams and managers that will ultimately be involved with the process. Start with your manager and team, and branch out to the other teams and managers. Get them to commit to this process, get them involved, spread the ownership, and the goals that you are pursuing.

Identify the potential individuals that should be involved from the following list:

- Project managers

- Product managers

- Development

  - Developers

- Development managers

  - Development team leads

  - Development subject matter experts

- Quality assurance

  - QA engineers

  - QA managers

  - QA team leads

  - QA subject matter experts

- Database administrators (DBAs)

  - Development

  - Tech ops

  - Infrastructure engineers

  - Production

- Network engineers

- Storage area network (SAN) engineers

- IT staff

## Version Control

If you do not currently have version control to contain a golden copy of your code and database objects, it is strongly suggested that you do so going forward. You should begin implementing a solution to keep different versions of code protected. There are many different ways to implement a comprehensive version control process, depending on your needs. At a minimum, you need to store versions of objects and other T-SQL code externally from your database, so that in the event of a change disrupting your systems, you can revert to the original version of said objects.

An easy way to implement version control is to capture a snapshot of the database schema before and after changes have occurred. If data changes are involved, those changes should be snapshotted as well. Keeping track of these changes before and after a release will also allow you to document what changed and reconcile it with the actual release plan that was created.

You could use PowerShell or SMO to script out objects to files or scripts. Third-party tools are also available, such as Git, Mercurial, SVN, Red Gate's SQL Source Control, and Microsoft's Team Foundation Server, among others. Each of these options affords you the opportunity to collect database objects and store them outside your database.

Keep in mind that the simplest way to perform version control is to create a backup of your database moments before you perform a release. I would suggest that you perform a backup each and every time that you release. Regardless of what version control system you implement or currently have, creating backups prior to a release will give you a failsafe. This process, like all others, should be malleable and allow you to change it from time to time, thus improving the process along the way.

Keeping track of your database objects and data is often difficult, but is worth it.

## Rollback Process

Just as you are preparing a process to ensure that your changes occur cleanly, you must be prepared to roll back your changes. Each time that you produce a change, ensure that you have created the proper scripts that will allow you to roll back those changes. You can rely on snapshots prior to a release, version-controlled objects, scripts generated, database backups, among other options.

You may implement a drop command that removes objects that you will be releasing. As mentioned earlier, you can use SMO and PowerShell to generate scripts of objects. You will also notice on most windows in SQL Server Management Studio (SSMS) that you can click on a scripting menu to generate a script of various objects, changes, and so on. You can generate these scripts on the fly via SSMS, and then save them as potential rollback scripts. You might need to create a script that adds or removes data. You must always be prepared to quickly recover your system to a state prior to the beginning of your release process execution.

Even if the change you are to introduce is one that "shouldn't affect anything," you should still create a rollback process. This means always, no matter how small of a change! You should accompany *any* change with a rollback process. Realize that you might need to involve other individuals in the creation of the process, or it could simply be you alone. Either way, be involved to ensure that it gets done. Before the release is the best time to have a cool head and plan appropriately. During the stress of a failed release, when your brain is inevitably compromised with emotion, you will be less likely to create a clean and graceful rollback. Do it when your head is clear, when you have the time to interact and get answers to the many questions you might have. I know from experience that in the heat of the moment, it seems that my brain seems less able to think clearly.

# Documents

Remembering that the goal is to create a balanced process that will allow you to create releases in a controlled fashion and without incident, we will now go over several documents that you can create and use to reach that goal. These documents will help you with the release process, as well as help you keep track of where you are within the process. Some of these documents will be templates that will quicken your steps to creating a release.

- Release notes
- Release plan template
- Release plan(s)

At a basic level, it is a good idea to keep a simple record of each requested change that is made, and keep a list of tasks associated with your release management process as they are accomplished. Keeping track of these tasks, and the dates performed or reperformed, will allow you to measure the success of the actual release. Collecting this information will help with future releases as well as help fine-tune your release management tasks. Allowing your process to change and refine will ensure that you create a successful release management process, filled with appropriate tasks.

Two documents that will help out are a release notes document and actual release plan documents. The release notes will be a single document that contains summary information about each release, and the tasks associated with said releases. Dates and other information will be gathered and saved within this document to help you plan better for each new release. The actual release plan documents will be created, filled out, tested, and ultimately performed, releasing change to your production environment. As each release is performed, keep track of these pieces of information for future review. As your steps within your release management process change, update future versions of your release plan. It's a good idea to have a template of this release plan on hand, which will receive any changes as you see fit to update it. This template will help you in the creation of each release plan by providing a starting point with much of the information already filled in.

# Release Notes

Keep a record of each release request. Keep a record of each date associated with each task you have performed. As you perform a release, and the next release, and the next, you will soon have a document with quite the collection of information. You can use this information to not only remember past releases, but review how they were performed, how many steps were repeated, what steps had a tough time, what steps were not as useful, and even holes in your process where steps are missing. Keeping track of where you are in the process as you prepare to release each change will also be made easy as you keep accurate information in these release notes.

An easy way to accomplish this task is to start an Excel document, similar to that shown in Figure 8-3. This document can continue to grow with each change request that comes in, and will help you keep track of each one along with its tasks.

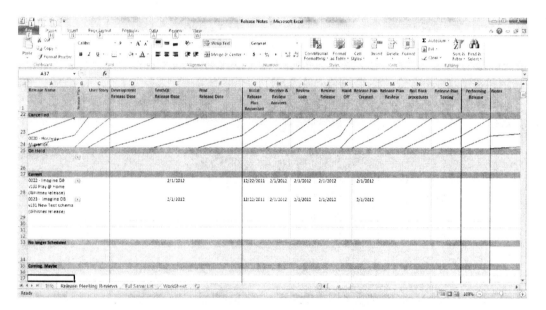

***Figure 8-3.*** *Release notes sample document*

The information that you can keep track of within these release notes will contain information, tasks, and dates. For example:

- Release name

- Release plan (reference to this document)

- Dates released to various environments

- Initial release plan requested

- Receive and review answers

- Review code
- Review release
- Hand off
- Release plan created
- Release plan review
- Rollback procedures
- Release plan testing
- Performing the release

## Release Name

A release name will be associated with each release. How you name each release will be up to you, but keep in mind that a unique naming convention will assist in keeping track of each individual release.

## Release Plan

You should create a document that contains all information and steps to perform the actual release. You will refer to this document as a *release plan*. Within your release notes, keep a link or reference to this release plan. While you are in the midst of preparing and performing a release, this information will be at your fingertips. When the release has been completed and some time has passed, having this reference will be valuable for your future releases.

## Dates Released to Various Environments

Keep track of the dates that the release has been executed in each of your environments. Performing these in order is vital, and keeping track of each of these executions as they occur in the proper order will also help you keep your process in order. Ensure that you do not leapfrog your ordered environments by skipping to another environment before its proper time.

## Initial Release Plan Requested

When a change has been requested, log this date in your release notes as the initial date that the release was requested. This will become your starting point. The end goal will be a successful release. You might never release it, which is fine. Keeping track of these dates will help you keep organized and follow your process. When you have received a request for change, at this point you can use a template to create a release plan and start to populate it with the information you are collecting and creating.

## Receive and Review Answers

As you prepare the release plan document and fill it with information, and as you review the code that is proposed for change, you will inevitably have questions that need answering. This iterative process can involve many cycles before you and the others involved are satisfied. Allow this cycle to occur, and continue to seek out answers to your questions. Keep track as you traverse each of the iterations, noting the dates associated with the receipt of answers.

## Review Code

Ensure that you review the code thoroughly; especially weighing how these changes will impact your system and topology. Each time that you touch the code, keep track of the dates, your observations, your progress, any notes, and any other information that you can gather during this process. Keep this information within your release notes. Share this information with all involved. You might have to plan various meetings between yourself and other individuals involved in the release process. As you collect information, ensure that you reference this information during and after the release process.

## Review Release

As you collect all this information, inevitably you will be creating a release plan that has great information, all the moving parts of the release, as well as various steps to perform. Ensure that you review this plan. If possible, perform a dry run of the release plan in another environment to validate the steps. Review these steps with the developers and architects of the change. Review these steps with your teammates and any others involved. Validating that these steps are appropriate will ensure that your release will perform successfully.

## Hand Off

Once the release plan has reached the point in which all the steps have been mapped out, and you have reviewed the steps, information, and code, you have reached a point in which you can consider the release "handed off" from development. Ensure that you have done your due diligence to get the release to this point. Do not accept a release as "handed off" until it has been vigorously vetted. If it has not reached this point, repeat any of the previous steps that are yet unfulfilled. Repeat these steps until you are satisfied.

## Release Plan Created

Now that you have created a release plan, note the date that this occurred in your release notes. This information will come in handy to help you create a baseline for future releases. Knowing the dates that a release is requested, knowing the length of time it takes to perform the various tasks, and knowing all the necessary parts needed to ensure a successful release will help you plan future releases. Saving this information and reviewing after your successful release will assist you.

## Release Plan Review

As mentioned before, reviewing the release plan can be an iterative process. Keeping track of each date you alter the plan will help you baseline and plan for future releases. Some of these future releases could entail similar steps, and your plan could be reused, which should save you time.

## Rollback Procedures

In addition to meticulously planning all the steps to perform a release, reviewing code, augmenting your documentation with notes and information, you should also painstakingly create rollback procedures. Just as there are steps to create a change, you should always have steps to back out of that change. This might entail a snapshot of your schema, and a process to revert object changes to original state. It might entail scripts that can be executed to reverse data changes, insertions, updates, or deletions. Ensure that you add this information to your release plan, so that if the inevitable happens and you are forced into a situation in which you must roll back a change, you will be prepared. You will have the steps, will have tested the steps as part of your release plan testing phase, and will have the knowledge to easily and gracefully perform the rollback procedures. You will certainly be happy you have these steps in place on the day you need it. As with all other steps within this release plan, these need to be vetted, tested, and approved by others.

## Release Plan Testing

It has been alluded to before, but let's say it again: test your release plan. Test and test and retest. Create a sandbox environment that mimics your production environment to the best of your ability, and perform the release in this environment. Doing so will also allow you to test the rollback procedures to return the environment's previous state. Perform your pre- and postvalidations. Perform any quality assurance tasks necessary in this environment. Use this environment as your testing ground. Giving yourself the ability to perform an actual release, and vet all the steps prior to the actual production release, will help you. Having to perform it multiple times when something goes wrong (and it might go wrong) will make you better prepared for the real release to production.

## Performing the Release

At this point you have done a lot of work, and all that is left is that fateful day, release day. All your ducks are in a row. Others have done their parts. You have performed countless tests on your release plan. It's ready. You can actually say with a level of certainty what the outcome will be. Hopefully, you will not be saying, "I hope that this works." You should know at this point. However, be wary and don't be over confident. Perform the release as you have outlined it in your release plan steps. Don't run the risk of skipping steps because you have performed them previously and probably know them by heart. Be meticulous, follow your plan, and perform the release as outlined.

While you perform the release, ensure that there is proper monitoring occurring on your environments. There should be many folks meticulously watching your processes for any falters in functionality, various monitoring results, and any alerts that might occur. These individuals should be aware that a release is occurring, and be able to indicate that something is awry. This awareness will allow you to halt the release and perform any rollback procedures you have in place, if necessary.

Just after the release has been performed, you might think that you are done. You could quit here. But why not take a little extra time to make any notes about the actual release? Detail any issues that you or others had while performing the steps. Maybe something was off in the execution that was not found in the previous iterations of testing. If you note those details now, making action items for the next release, your process will be that much more fine-tuned next time. Don't be afraid to make notes about what others could do better. Be even less afraid to make those same notes about yourself. The only way you get better is through practice and observation of the technique. Often, a root cause analysis will be performed after an error has occurred in an IT system, in order to investigate the causes and possible fixes. Why not do this on a positive note to your release process. Each performed iteration of a release, no matter how small or complex, can provide tips to make the next iteration more stable. Recall that our goal was to reach that perfect balance where the tasks are at once sufficient, yet not cumbersome. This will take you time and most likely involve various iterations of this malleable release process. Taking notes along the way is crucial to making your next release a more streamlined success.

# Release Plan Template and Release Plans

You will notice that in the documents that we have discussed, several tasks were intermingled among the information. Let's discuss the actual tasks that will go into a release plan. Here, I do not mean the tasks to create the release plan, rather the tasks that will be performed in the actual release, which you should document within a release plan.

You should create a release plan template to keep track of the generic tasks you want to perform for each release. Each release will have specific tasks, skipping some of the generic tasks, saving some, and maybe even adding unique tasks for that particular release. Using this template document as a launch pad into each release plan will greatly help your effectiveness, as well as be able to allow you to control your release, matching similar tasks to past releases. As your release management tasks evolve, so should this document.

My release plan template has three major sections. The first section contains generic information about a release. The next section has various questions that should be asked for each release. The last section will be the actual steps to be performed to execute the release. This last section will be created once, and then duplicated for each environment that will receive the changes.

## Generic Release Information

Within the template for release plans, as well as the actual release plans, you should document the generic information about the release. For the template, simply leave sections of the document ready to be filled in with the information shown in Figure 8-4.

In the actual release plan that you create for a given release, fill in this information as you collect it. This information will paint a picture of what these changes will impact. It will require you to go out and talk to people, to understand your topology, and find out the needed information. Do not skimp when you fill out these answers. Really dig into the questions and ask the appropriate people to glean as much information as you can. Collect this information in this section of the document so that you can refer to it during release preparation and after. Figure 8-4 is an example spreadsheet that has been used to collect this information.

| | A | B | C | D | E |
|---|---|---|---|---|---|
| 1 | | **Release Synopsis** | | | |
| 2 | | Release Name | **The Name of this Release** | | |
| 3 | | | | | |
| 4 | | Date and Time of release | | | |
| 5 | | Development | 8/29/2012<br>8/30/2012 | | |
| 6 | | Testing | 9/3/2012 | | |
| 7 | | Quality Assurance | 9/10/2012 | | |
| 8 | | Customer Facing | 9/17/2012<br>9/19/2012 | | |
| 9 | | Preproduction | 9/21/2012 | | |
| 10 | | Production | 10/1/2012 | | |
| 11 | | | | | |
| 12 | | Project Overview | | | |
| 13 | | New Database | Yes / No | | |
| 14 | | New Objects | Yes / No | | |
| 15 | | Replication impact | Yes / No | | |
| 16 | | Will the creation of this object cause issues? | Yes / No | Prove that this will not impact production | |
| 17 | | Schema Changes | Yes / No | | |
| 18 | | list all tables impacted by schema change | | | |
| 19 | | create/review schema change script | | | |
| 20 | | what activity do these tables experience? | | | |
| 21 | | Replication impact | Yes / No | | |

***Figure 8-4.*** *Release plan template—release synopsis*

The following list explains some of the information detailed in Figure 8-4. Do not stop here; add to these as your system and topology reveals questions you should be asking to prepare for a successful release. This list is meant to be a quick reference guide that is filled out with quick answers.

- The release name
- The dates to release to each environment
    - Each environment should get a date Multiple dates can be added for each attempt
- Project Overview
    - Will there be a new database?
    - Will there be new objects?
        - Will these objects affect replication?
        - Will the creation of this object cause issues? (It's important to prove this while testing this release.)
    - Will there be schema changes?
        - List all tables impacted by schema changes
        - Ensure that you create or review the schema change script
        - Detail the activity that these tables experience
    - Will there be replication impact?
        - Detail the quantity of impact to be expected
    - Will there be data updates?
    - Will there be DTS package updates? (similar for SSIS)
    - Will there be changes to Scheduled Jobs?
- Notes
    - General notes about the release
    - Notes from any preproduction environments
    - Notes about replication
    - Notes about data changes
    - Handoff notes

## Questions and Answers

You should also keep track of various questions and answers that you typically ask of the developers. Keep these questions within the release plan template. As you fill out individual release plans, you can reference these questions and fill in the answers, as well as any others that arise. These will help you to collect the information necessary to prepare for the releases. Figures 8-5 show an example spreadsheet of several questions that I have used in the preparation of my releases.

| | A | B | C | D |
|---|---|---|---|---|
| 1 | Database (new or existing) | | | |
| 2 | Questions | Answers | Notes | |
| 3 | Name | | | |
| 4 | Capacity Requirements? | | | |
| 5 | Size | | | |
| 6 | Type of activity (high read, high write, etc...) | | | |
| 7 | Growth projection | | | |
| 8 | | | | |
| 9 | New Objects | | | |
| 10 | Questions | Answers | Notes | |
| 11 | Table | | | |
| 12 | Name | | | |
| 13 | Capacity Requirements | | | |
| 14 | Size | | | |
| 15 | Type of activity (high read, high write, etc...) | | | |
| 16 | Growth projection | | | |
| 17 | Triggers | | | |
| 18 | | | | |
| 19 | SP, View, Function | | | |
| 20 | Name | | | |
| 21 | Business Function | | | |
| 22 | Verify Query Plan / efficient use of indexes | | | |
| 23 | Understand potential impact to systems. | | | |
| 24 | | | | |
| 25 | Altered Objects | | | |
| 26 | Questions | Answers | Notes | |
| 27 | Table | | | |
| 28 | Name | | | |
| 29 | Capacity Requirements | | | |
| 30 | Changes? | | | |
| 31 | Size | | | |
| 32 | Type of activity (reads, writes, etc......) | | | |

***Figure 8-5.*** *Release plan template—release questions*

The following list goes into detail about the information shown in Figures 8-5. These are all questions you should pose to the developers within your organization.

- Does this release create a new or alter an existing database?
  - What is the name of the affected/new database?
  - What are the capacity requirements?
  - What is the database size?
  - What type of activity occurs?
    - Read only
    - Write only
    - Highly transactional
    - Reporting
    - Periodic lookup
  - What are the growth projections?
    - Detail how many rows will be created, how often, and so on
- Does this release create new objects?
  - If the object is a table, ask the following:
    - What is the name of the new or affected object?
    - What are the capacity requirements?

- What is the size of this object?

- What type of activity occurs?

- What are the growth projections?

- Are there triggers involved with this object?

- If the object is a stored procedure, view or function, ask the following:

  - What is the name of the object?

  - What is the businesss function? (This might be a political hot button. Ensure that you find out as much as possible as why this needs to exist and how it will help your system.)

  - Have you verified the query plan or efficient use of indexes?

  - Do you understand the potential impact to your system?

- Does this release contain alterations to objects?

  - If the object is a table, ask the following:

    - What is the name of the new or affected object?

    - What are the capacity requirements?

    - What are the changes to the table?

    - What is the size of this object?

    - What type of activity occurs?

    - What are the growth projections?

    - What will the transactional activity be?

    - Can the table remain quiet during release?

    - Does the proposed schema change lock the table for an extended period of time?

    - Are there triggers involved with this object?

  - If the object is a stored procedure, view, or function, ask the following:

    - What is the name of the object?

    - What are the changes to the object?

    - Have you verified the query plan or efficient use of indexes?

    - Do you understand the potential impact to your system?

- Are there data updates?

  - What is the business need to have data changed?

  - What is the excpected quantity of changes?

  - What will the lock impact be?

  - What will the transaction size be?

- Does data need to be replicated to other systems? If so, why?
- Is there an impact to replication?
    - What tables will be involved?
    - What will the security impact be?
    - Why does this change need to occur?
- Is there impact to regular database maintenance tasks?
    - Will this change impact indexes?
    - Will there be any data purge? If so, understand the expected growth rate and any processes to maintain
- Is there any impact to SQL Server Agent Jobs?
    - Explain the requirements for this job change
    - Detail the schedule for this job
- Are there changes/new SSIS/DTS packages?
    - Detail the configuration requirements for these packages.
    - Detail the purpose and implementation steps
    - Understand the tables involved
        - What read activity will occur?
        - Detail the write / update / deletes that will occur.
        - Verify the the transaction boundries are small.

Obviously, your environment will be different and might require additional questions. These are only samples to get you thinking about the possible questions you should ask before each release. Ask these or similar questions to determine what this change will entail, so that you can properly plan for it. Some of the preceding questions are just the tip of the iceberg, and depending on the answers receive, you might need to dig deeper.

For example, if a new object is to be introduced as part of the change, you will want to follow up with questions about the name of the object, the capacity requirements if it is a database or table, the size it should start out at and possibly grow to, the type of activity it will experience, and what interactions it will have with other objects within your database.

Or, if the change requires an alteration to an existing object, you might need to know about its type of activity, and if the proposed change will impact it, lock it, or otherwise cause the object to be inaccessible for a period. If so, how can you ensure that the rest of your topology, system, applications, and so forth are minimally impacted? You might have to gracefully shut down services prior to this change being released to production, and finding this out early on will help you create the proper steps to perform this graceful shutdown.

When a change impacts replication, you might have to take special precautions to ensure that replication continues functioning as currently designed and implemented. There could be extra steps that need to be performed to introduce this change into a replicated environment that would not be necessary in a nonreplicated environment. Maybe you rely on a third-party replication scheme that is difficult to maintain and could generate many extra steps. In any event, knowing the impact to replication as you create your release plan will help.

The point is that there is always room for more digging to find out as much as you possibly can. Think about how this change could affect your regular, automated, or even manual maintenance of your database systems. You will need to plan this into the release plan as well. If you are introducing a new database to your system, ensure that your regular maintenance processes pick up this new database and perform the necessary tasks upon it. You might need to create or alter backup jobs. Other maintenance processes will likely be impacted. Identify and plan for these changes.

If you are changing any jobs, ensure that you collect the details about the job. Review the schedule that it will execute. You will want to make sure that this doesn't conflict with other existing jobs. Review the details of the job to see what the job will affect. It would be bad for new or existing jobs to be negatively impacted through a change.

If your change affects any DTS packages or SSIS packages, there will be many details that you should investigate. There will be configurations and steps that you should review, as well as determining which objects will be affected with the various steps of the packages.

## Release Steps

As you create the steps to perform a release, realize that these steps will be repeated for most environments. Some of the steps might not occur in some environments, and some environments might need extra steps. This will depend on how you have set up each of these environments. I suggest that you create these steps for a single environment, and then make adjustments for each of the other environments as needed. This means that general steps could be created for all environments, and then multiple environments can be copied from the original, creating unique steps for each. Ensure that you detail the steps necessary for each environment. Be methodical and list them all. I find it imperative to create individual step lists for each environment and check off each task as they are performed. Figure 8-6 shows the release steps portion of the plan template.

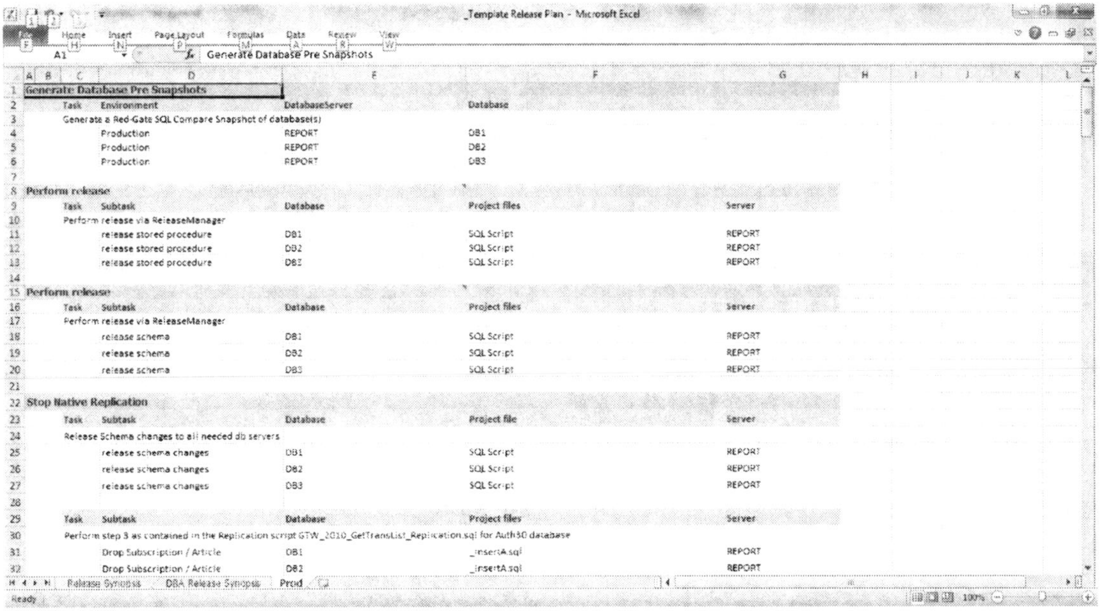

*Figure 8-6. Release plan template—release steps*

List each database that will be touched by the release, and the people who work on those databases that need to be informed of the impending release. This is important to keep things organized. This database list will also become a series of steps you will take to ensure snapshots are taken for each affected database. Generating a snapshot of each database schema will give you a baseline to compare against before, during, and after the release.

There will be many options to generate these snapshots. Third-party applications can perform this task, scripting objects directly from Management Studio, SMO, or PowerShell. One of my favorite tools is Red Gate SQL Compare, which lets you generate a snapshot as a single file containing the schema of the selected database. You can then compare this snapshot to another snapshot of that same database at a later time. Comparisons will show the different objects that were altered by your change. The main point is that it's an important step to perform. Generating a before-and-after snapshot of your various database schemas, and using this comparison to show what was affected, can assist with rollback, if necessary.

Along with generating a snapshot, there might be other steps that you need to perform to get ready for the release. These could include a graceful shutdown of other services or application, or you might need to make changes to your replication configuration to properly prepare for the release. Each of these steps needs to be detailed, thought out, and planned. You should identify and document preparatory tasks as individual steps.

At some point, you will need to list all the objects and/or scripts that will be executed to affect the needed changes. You could simply execute these changes directly in Management Studio, which will require someone to generate a script.

You could also use a tool to perform a compare between production and a lower environment, and affect the changes via this generated script. You can use a release tool that controls the execution of changes, documenting each step, with ability to roll back failed changes. Creating this tool will take some time and effort, but it will help you gracefully release change into your environment. Using a comparison tool will let you manually decide which objects will be compared and ultimately altered.

Whether you use a comparison tool or Management Studio, a script that details the changes will need to be created by someone intimately involved with the requested changes. A script will need to be generated that can perform a rollback as well. Creating a single script with all changes, or multiple scripts with individual changes will be your prerogative. Single or multiple scripts will also impact the rollback process. How you execute this change will be an important factor in your release process, allowing for a graceful and controlled change.

If you have replication involved in your topology, your release might need some extra steps. You might need to drop subscriptions and/or articles, add articles back, stop distribution agents, refresh subscriptions, and maybe even resnapshot publications. These steps will need to be tested in a similarly replicated environment, to ensure that the steps taken will succeed.

Just as you detailed all the steps to gracefully shut down applications and services, you will now want to detail the reverse of those steps that will need to be taken to seamlessly turn them back on. List each of these steps, in the proper order.

After everything has been released, generate another schema snapshot and use it to compare to the original snapshot. This should prove which objects where altered. This can be used to generate reports to show what was accomplished for the release.

As you perform each step within the release plan, mark it as completed. Even though this is just for you, you will be able to refer to this document on many occasions in the future, and it will certainly help in planning future similar releases. Use this as proof of what steps were taken, or what steps were not taken. Let this documentation validate that your release process steps were executed in the proper order. You can always refer to these and make alterations to your process and your release plan template to accommodate new information, new knowledge, and new ways of accomplishing successful releases.

Create this document with the intent that you may hand it over to another individual to perform all the steps themselves, without your involvement. This will force you to include a level of detail and explanation that will make the steps easily accomplished. Being as thorough as possible with all the steps will foster success.

## Document Repository

Because we have been creating several files, including the release plan and release plan template documents, a folder structure to contain all of these files will assist you in organizing your releases. Acquire a central location that everyone involved with the release process can access to store documents associated with each release. You will be generating pre and post snapshots of each database to be affected, the actual scripts that will effect change, and other files. All these files can reside in the following folder structure to easily help:

- Release name
- Pre snapshots
- Post snapshots
- Database objects
- Web objects
- Application objects
- Release plan
- Other

As soon as you receive the request to make a change, create a location (similar to the previous suggestion) to store all the relevant files and information. Keep adding to this repository as you create files. You could store these files in your version control system as well. Ensure that you store them somewhere that is secure and can allow you and others to access them during the release period, as well as before and after.

This will ultimately be the location from which you pull all relevant information to perform the production release. If done properly, you will have used these files for release to each environment as you march this release to production. Keep all these files as proof and reference of the actual release. You can even refer your supervisor to this location to review your work for year-end reviews.

## Conclusion

Accept change, embrace it, plan for it, and then gracefully introduce it into your environment. And then repeat. As you repeat, you will learn how to modify your release process to achieve that perfect balance where change is introduced into your topology, yet risk is minimized and the impact is graceful. You can do this, though you probably can't do this alone. You will need to include others along the way. Realize that there are quite a few tasks, several documents, and many considerations that have been discussed—quite a few, indeed! Please take the necessary time to dig into all these and formulate your own release process. Do it for your systems. Do it for yourself. Become the hero.

# CHAPTER 9

■ ■ ■

# Compliance and Auditing

## By Jonathan Gardner

In the United States, the Health Insurance Portability Accountability Act (HIPAA), Sarbanes-Oxley, and Payment Card Industry Data Security Standard (PCI DSS) make up just a sampling of the regulatory issues faced by today's businesses. Today's database professional is on the front lines of ensuring compliance with these regulations. Database administrators (DBAs) can use auditing to monitor and document access and changes to databases that are subject to these regulations. While auditing is only part of ensuring compliance, many times it is the only tool that a database professional has control over.

Microsoft introduced auditing in SQL Server 2008 as a feature to satisfy requirements related to regulatory compliance with the laws mentioned earlier and others. SQL Server 2012 provides even more granular audit controls, making it an indispensable addition to the DBA's toolset.

This chapter will detail the some of the major laws DBAs must ensure their organizations comply with, including how they are enforced and what that means for database professionals. The chapter will also cover the new auditing features introduced in SQL Server 2012 and walk step by step through setting up auditing.

## Compliance

Compliance laws rarely go into detail about how to protect or audit data. Understanding the law and what it is trying to protect arms database professionals with the knowledge to properly align their organization with the law's mandate.

## Sarbanes-Oxley

The Sarbanes-Oxley Act of 2002 (SOX) was established in the wake of the accounting scandals at Enron, WorldCom, and others. United States public companies and accounting firms are subject to SOX. While the bill contains new corporate governance rules, Section 404 "Management Assessment of Internal Controls" is the section that database professionals need to understand.

Section 404 states that an annual report must be generated to show "management's responsibility for establishing and maintaining an adequate internal control structure and procedures for financial reporting". It also requires management to perform "an assessment of the effectiveness of the internal control structure and procedures for financial reporting."

It is difficult for these statements to be any more vague regarding how the database professional should ensure compliance. The actual law does not define what needs to be done to ensure compliance. It simply states that "internal controls" are required and must be audited on an annual basis.

Since no specific definition is provided in the law, the parties responsible for enforcing and monitoring SOX should provide the necessary guidance. Therefore, the U.S. Securities and Exchange Commission (SEC) and the Public Company Accounting Oversight Board (PCAOB) are charged with ensuring SOX compliance.

The SEC issued a final ruling on how compliance with the law should be ensured. This ruling stated that the framework defined by the Treadway Commission—in the Committee of Sponsoring Organizations (COSO) report "Internal Control – Integrated Framework"—should be used. The COSO report does not define the specifics of an IT Framework. Instead, it states "Policies and procedures that help ensure the continued, proper operations of computer information systems. They include controls over data-center operations, systems software acquisition and maintenance, access security, and application system development and maintenance. General controls support the function of programmed application controls. Other terms sometimes used to describe general controls are general computer controls and information technology controls." The report defines effective internal controls as including the following:

- Control Environment

- Risk Assessment

- Control Activities

- Information and Communication

- Monitoring

---

■ **Note**   The full, SEC-issued final ruling on how compliance should be ensured can be found at `http://www.sec.gov/rules/final/33-8238.htm`.

---

The PCAOB released Auditing Standard No. 2: An Audit of Internal Control Over Financial Reporting Performed in Conjunction with an Audit of Financial Statements. While this report discusses IT controls, it refrains from mentioning which IT controls need to be implemented.

For the readers still following along at this point, both the PCAOB and the COSO mention the need for IT controls and an IT framework. However, they fail to actually recommend one.

In 1996, the Information Systems Audit and Control Association (ISACA) released an IT framework called Control Objectives for Information and Related Technologies (COBIT). While the release of the COBIT framework occurred long before the 2002 scandals, the framework is aligned with those that the PCAOB and COSO require. The COBIT 4.1 framework has been widely adopted as the framework used to comply with SOX requirements. For database professionals, this still does not provide clarity because there is little outlined in the framework that is specifically directed at them.

---

■ **Note**   More information regarding COBIT can be found at `http://www.isaca.org/Knowledge-Center/COBIT/Pages/Overview.aspx`.

---

While neither the law nor the organizations charged with enforcing it give a directive to database professionals, what they do define is the intent of the law. SOX is focused on the accuracy of reporting, meaning that it is not concerned with who has seen the data, but with what has been added, modified, or deleted. Thus, database professionals need to be concerned mainly with write events and who has access to do perform them.

Table 9-1 shows the areas that should be audited on SQL Server instances containing SOX-regulated data.

*Table 9-1. Areas of attention for servers containing data regulated by SOX.*

| Area | Audit Group |
|------|-------------|
| Role Changes | SERVER_ROLE_MEMBER_CHANGE_GROUP |
| Ensure Auditing | AUDIT_CHANGE_GROUP |
| Database State | BACKUP_RESTORE_GROUP<br>DATABASE_CHANGE_GROUP<br>DATABASE_OBJECT_CHANGE_GROUP |
| Logins and Security | SCHEMA_OBJECT_CHANGE_GROUP<br>SCHEMA_OBJECT_PERMISSION_CHANGE_GROUP<br>DATABASE_PRINCIPAL_IMPERSONATION_GROUP |

■ **Note** A full list of SQL Server audit action groups and actions can be found here: http://technet.microsoft.com/en-us/library/cc280663.aspx.

The main focus of SOX is accuracy of reporting and the ability to audit how and when data is entered or changed. Auditing these events is done through the database audit actions and is covered later in this chapter. The actions that need to be audited are UPDATE, INSERT, and DELETE. These audits are specific to database schema or objects, and they need to be planned out for any SOX-regulated database.

# Health Insurance Portability and Accountability Act

The Health Insurance Portability and Accountability Act of 1996 (HIPAA) is a United States law designed to streamline and standardize the way electronic healthcare transactions are conducted. With this standardization taking place around the use of electronic health records, the security and privacy of the data was a concern. The law attempted to address this issue through the Privacy Rule.

The Privacy Rule is used to regulate how Protected Health Information (PHI) is used or disclosed. Not all health information is classified as PHI, but the definition is held to be any part of a medical record or payment history. A database professional might be in charge of hundreds of databases, but it's possible that only one database or server in that group is subject to HIPAA.

The Department of Health and Human Services (HHS) is responsible for enforcement of HIPAA. Just like the agencies overseeing SOX, HHS has outlined that an entity must mitigate the accidental or illegal exposure of health information but has not given guidelines on how to do it.

The differences between HIPAA and SOX can be seen in the intent of the laws. SOX is intended to ensure the accuracy of financial data. This means that database professionals need to audit who the data has been accessed by. HIPAA is concerned with keeping health information private. This means that database professionals need to audit who the data has been accessed by.

Table 9-2 shows the areas that should be audited on SQL Server instances containing HIPAA data.

*Table 9-2. Areas of attention for servers containing data regulated by HIPPA*

| Area | Audit Group |
|---|---|
| Logons and Security Changes | SUCCESSFUL_LOGIN_GROUP<br>FAILED_LOGIN_GROUP<br>LOGOUT_GROUP<br>LOGIN_CHANGE_PASSWORD_GROUP |
| Role Changes | SERVER_ROLE_MEMBER_CHANGE_GROUP |
| Access to Databases | APPLICATION_ROLE_CHANGE_PASSWORD_GROUP<br>DATABASE_CHANGE_GROUP<br>DATABASE_OBJECT_ACCESS_GROUP<br>DATABASE_OBJECT_CHANGE_GROUP<br>DATABASE_OBJECT_OWNERSHIP_CHANGE_GROUP<br>DATABASE_OWNERSHIP_CHANGE_GROUP<br>DATABASE_PERMISSION_CHANGE_GROUP<br>DATABASE_PRINCIPAL_CHANGE_GROUP<br>DATABASE_PRINCIPAL_IMPERSONATION_GROUP<br>DATABASE_ROLE_MEMBER_CHANGE_GROUP |
| Ensure Auditing | AUDIT_CHANGE_GROUP |
| Changes to the Server or Access to the Server | SERVER_OBJECT_CHANGE_GROUP<br>SERVER_OBJECT_PERMISSION_CHANGE_GROUP<br>SERVER_OBJECT_OWNERSHIP_CHANGE_GROUP<br>SERVER_PERMISSION_CHANGE_GROUP<br>SERVER_PRINCIPAL_CHANGE_GROUP<br>SERVER_PRINCIPAL_IMPERSONATION_GROUP<br>SERVER_STATE_CHANGE_GROUP<br>DBCC_GROUP |
| Server Operations | SERVER_OPERATION_GROUP<br>SERVER_STATE_CHANGE_GROUP<br>BACKUP_RESTORE_GROUP |

With the focus of HIPAA on controlling access to data, database-level audit actions need to be created. The SELECT action should be audited on database schema or objects that have access to PHI. Because these database-level audit actions are specific for each database, they need to be planned out for each database containing PHI.

While both SOX and HIPAA are laws governing companies in the United States, other countries have similar standards, such as Canada's Bill 198, Japan's J-SOX, or Germany's Corporate Governance Code. Global industry-specific standards like the Payment Card Industries Data Security Standard exist as well. These standards will dictate what needs to be audited to meet the law's compliance requirements.

# New Auditing Features in SQL Server 2012

With the release of SQL Server 2012, Microsoft has made improvements and additions to its Auditing feature, including adding or improving audit filtering and user-defined auditing, and bringing some auditing features to the Standard edition. These features will be coved in detail in the following sections.

# Server-Level Auditing for the Standard Edition

When SQL Server Auditing was introduced in SQL Server 2008, it was an Enterprise-only feature. While fully granular auditing remains an Enterprise-only feature in SQL Server 2012, server-level auditing is available in the Standard edition. This allows companies running SQL Server Standard to audit server access, database backups, and restored, security-related events.

# Audit Log Failure Options

To ensure compliance requirements are met, some companies might mandate that information be audited. A new feature of auditing in SQL Server 2012 allows database professionals to define what the server should do if it cannot log events. This is defined in the server option ON_FAILURE in the Server Audit. Three options are available. The server can be shut down, the single operation can be failed, or the server can be allowed to continue operating.

The ON_FAILURE and QUEUE_DELAY options can be set both in SQL Server Management Studio and through T-SQL. These options syntax will be covered later in this chapter.

# Maximum Rollover Files

Auditing can generate a large volume of data, so the ability to set the maximum file size and the maximum number of rollover files allows an organization to control the amount of space auditing will consume. These controls are specified through the MAXSIZE and MAX_ROLLOVER_FILES options. The MAXSIZE option defines the maximum file size for each audit log file. The MAXSIZE option can be set in megabytes (MB), gigabytes (GB), or terabytes (TB). The MAX_ROLLOVER_FILES option defines the size for the audit file. Once the MAX_ROLLOVER_FILES limit is reached, the oldest additional file over that size will be deleted and the server will continue to run.

In SQL Server 2008, there were options to roll over the log files after they reached a defined size or have an infinite number of log files. SQL Server 2012 allows for the log files to be rolled over and for a limit to be placed on the number of log files. The MAXSIZE and MAX_ROLLOVER_FILES options can be set both in SQL Server Management Studio and through T-SQL. Examples of both options will be shown later in this chapter.

# User-Defined Auditing

SQL Server 2012 now allows database professionals to write applications that send information to the Audit Log. This gives database administrators the flexibility to log custom application information for auditing along with standard SQL Server audit information. Examples of using the User-Defined Auditing feature will be covered later in this chapter.

# Audit Filtering

SQL Server 2012 now allows for events to be filtered *before* they are written to the audit log. This allows database professionals to have more granular control over what events are audited. Examples of using Audit Filtering will be covered later in this chapter.

# Auditing

SQL Server Auditing is made up of three components: a server audit, server audit specification, and database audit specification. A server audit and an audit specification (either for the server or the database) are required to actually audit any events. The following sections will cover how to create these through both SQL Server Management Studio and T-SQL.

---

■ **Note**    Some examples in this chapter will use the AdventureWorks 2012 sample databases. The databases can be found on CodePlex: `http://msftdbprodsamples.codeplex.com/releases/view/55330`.

---

# Server Audit

The server audit defines where audit data is stored. Server audit information can be stored in a binary log file, the Windows Application log, or the Windows Security log. The Server audit is specific to a single instance of SQL Server but more than one Server Audit can exist per instance. This allows for different audit information to be stored in different locations.

Some organizations require a separation of duties between auditors and database professionals. The ability to create multiple server audits satisfies the separation of duties and allows for both parties to conduct audits. The danger with this separation of duties is when the ON_FAILURE option is set to shut down the server if it cannot write to the audit file location. If the database professional cannot access or monitor the file location, and it runs out of space or goes offline, the server will shut down unexpectedly.

The server audit can be created using T-SQL or SQL Server Management Studio. Running the following code will create a server audit that outputs data to a binary file located in the C:\AuditLogs\ folder. This binary file can be located on a local drive, on attached storage, or at a network location. The file should be located on a drive that will not create disk contention with SQL Server data or log files.

```
--Create a server audit called Corp_Audit in the folder C:\AuditLogs\.
    CREATE SERVER AUDIT Corp_Audit
    TO FILE (FILEPATH = 'C:\AuditLogs\', MAXSIZE = 500MB, MAX_ROLLOVER_FILES = 10)
    WITH (QUEUE_DELAY = 0, ON_FAILURE = SHUTDOWN)
```

The QUEUE_DELAY option defines the time delay that can occur between the action being audited and failure to write to the audit log

By default, the server audit is disabled. To enable it, run the following T-SQL statement:

```
--Enable the Server Audit
    ALTER SERVER AUDIT Corp_Audit
    WITH (STATE = ON)
    GO
```

To create the server audit in Management Studio, expand the Security, Audits folder and right-click the Audits folder. Select the New Audit option to open the Create Audit dialog box, which is shown in Figure 9-1.

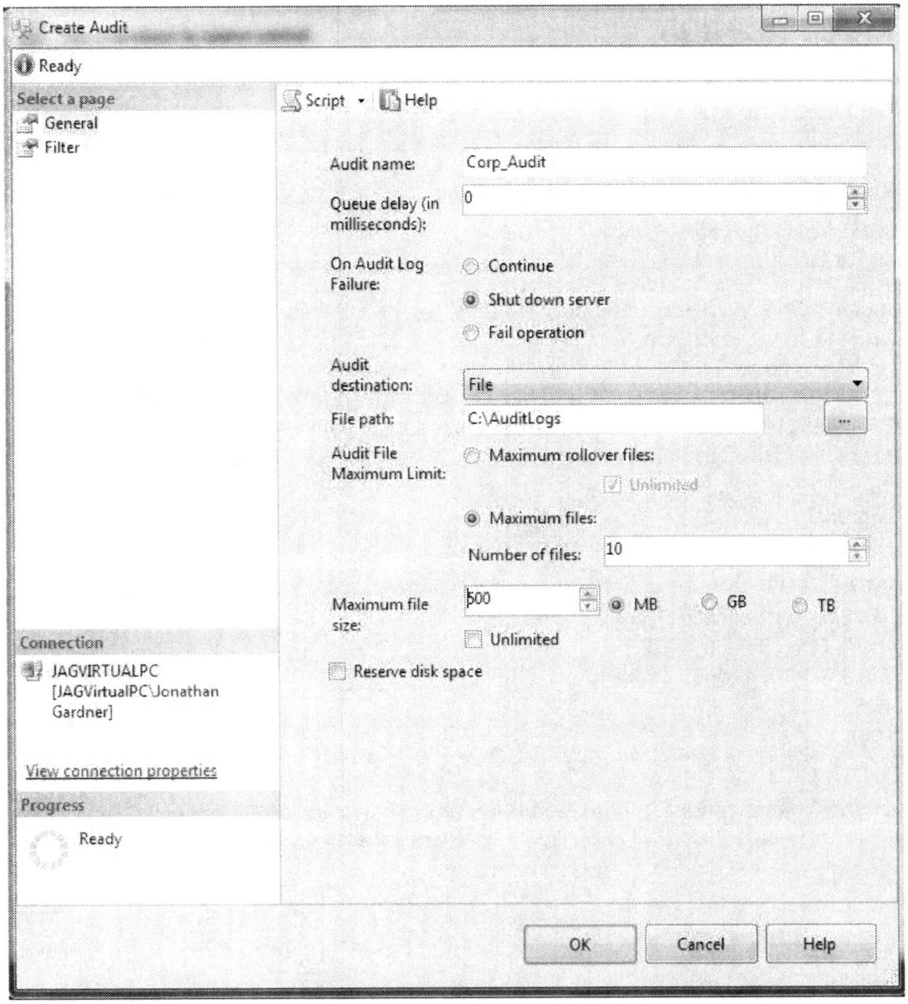

**Figure 9-1.** *The Create Audit dialog box showing the creation of the server audit with a queue delay set to 0, shutdown on audit log failure, with anan audit destination of a file specified, and a maximum number of rollover files defined, and a file size of 500 MB specified.*

Just like the T-SQL code, the server audit created through SQL Server Management Studio is disabled by default after it is created. To enable the server audit, right-click on the newly created audit and select Enable Audit from the menu. Once the server audit is created, SQL Server is ready to begin auditing, but nothing will be captured until a server audit specification or database audit specification has been defined. How to set up server audit specifications and database audit specifications will be covered in the following sections.

# Server Audit Specification

The server audit specification defines server-level events to be audited. These events include backups, restores, failed logins, and more.

---

▓ **Note**    A full list of the SQL Server Audit action groups and actions can be found here: `http://msdn.`
`microsoft.com/en-us/library/cc280663.aspx`.

---

The server audit specification can be created using T-SQL or SQL Server Management Studio. The following code will create the server audit specification Corp_Server_Audit_Spec for the server audit Corp_Audit created in the previous section. This audit will capture the server-level audit groups BACKUP_RESTORE_GROUP, DATABASE_OBJECT_CHANGE_GROUP, DATABASE_PRINCIPAL_CHANGE_GROUP, DATABASE_ROLE_MEMBER_CHANGE_GROUP, and FAILED_LOGIN_GROUP. Unlike the server audit, the server audit specification can be created and enabled in the same transaction through the STATE option.

```
--Create and enable the Server Audit Specification
    CREATE SERVER AUDIT SPECIFICATION Corp_Server_Audit_Spec
    FOR SERVER AUDIT Corp_Audit
      ADD (BACKUP_RESTORE_GROUP),
      ADD (DATABASE_OBJECT_CHANGE_GROUP),
      ADD (DATABASE_PRINCIPAL_CHANGE_GROUP),
      ADD (DATABASE_ROLE_MEMBER_CHANGE_GROUP),
      ADD (FAILED_LOGIN_GROUP)
    WITH (STATE = ON)
    GO
```

To create the server audit specifications in Management Studio, right-click on the Security, Server Audit Specifications folder and select the New Server Audit Specifications menu option. The Create Server Audit Specification dialog box will be opened, as shown in Figure 9-2.

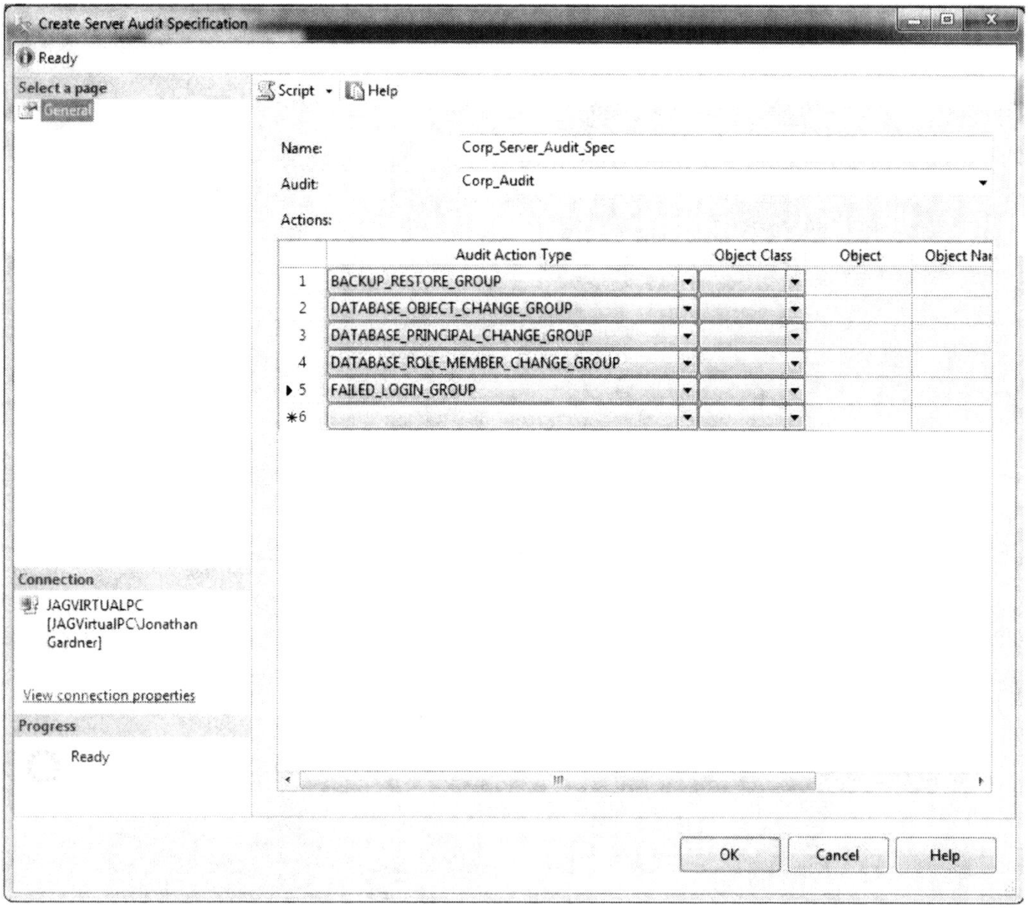

**Figure 9-2.** *The Create Server Audit Specification dialog box, showing a server audit specification created based on the* Corp_Audit *and defining the audit action types.*

If the server audit specification is created through T-SQL, it can be enabled at the same time it is created. If the server audit specification is created through SQL Server Management Studio, an additional step is needed to enable it. Select the newly created server audit specification, right-click and select Enable Server Audit Specification. The server audit specification can be enabled with the following T-SQL code:

```
--Enable Corp_Server_Audit_Spec
ALTER SERVER AUDIT SPECIFICATION Corp_Server_Audit_Spec
WITH (STATE = ON)
GO
```

# Database Audit Specification

Database audit specification captures database-level events on individual database objects. Database-level events include SELECT, UPDATE, INSERT, and DELETE on a table. A database audit specification needs to be created for each database that is to be audited.

The database audit specification can be created through T-SQL or SQL Server Management Studio. The code in the following example will create a database audit specification on the AdventureWorks2012 database. This database audit specification will audit any SELECT, UPDATE, INSERT, or DELETE events on the HumanResources.EmployeePayHistory table by user dbo. The database audit specification can be created and enabled at the same time through the STATE option.

```
--Create and enable the Database Audit Specification
USE AdventureWorks2012
GO
CREATE DATABASE AUDIT SPECIFICATION  Corp_AdventureWorks2012_Database_Audit_Spec
FOR SERVER AUDIT Corp_Audit
    ADD (SELECT, UPDATE, INSERT, DELETE ON HumanResources.EmployeePayHistory BY dbo)
    WITH (STATE = ON)
```

Database audit specifications are unique to each database, so they will need to be added to the Security, Database Audit Specification folder of each database in Management Studio. Right-clicking on the Database Audit Specification folder and selecting New Database Audit Specification will open the Create Database Audit Specification dialog box seen in Figure 9-3.

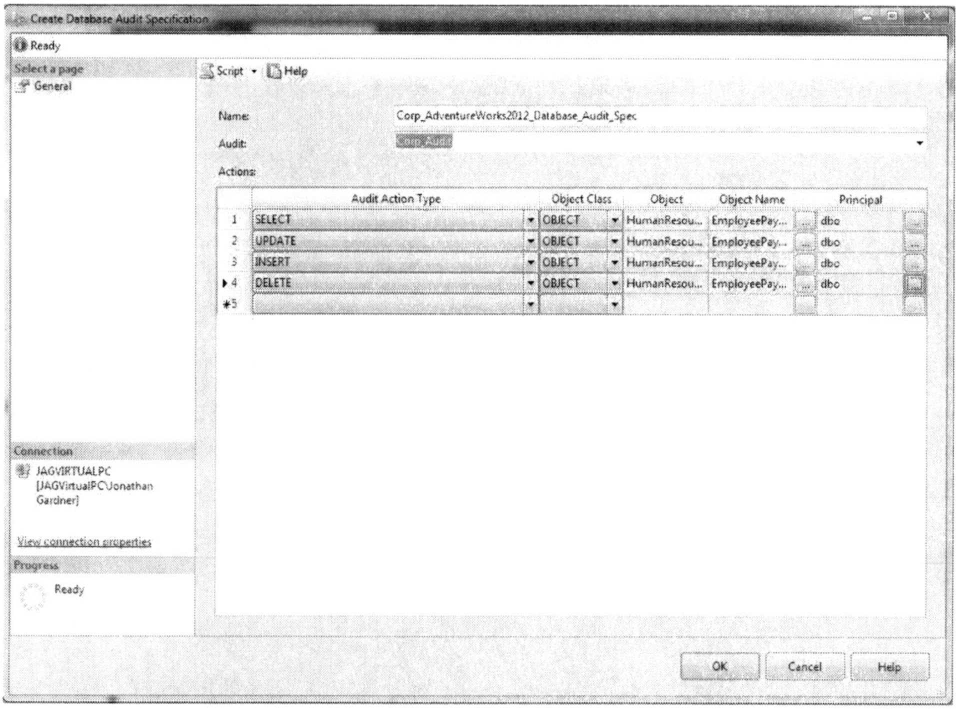

*Figure 9-3. The Database Audit Specification dialog box shows the definition based on the Corp_Audit and defines the audit action types.*

The T-SQL command can enable the database audit specification in a single command, but this cannot be done through Management Studio. To enable it, right-click and select Enable Database Audit Specification.

# Query the Audit File

If the server information is logged to a binary audit file, you can review this information in two ways: querying the file through SQL Server or viewing the Audit Log via SQL Server Management Studio. The binary audit file cannot be viewed as a plain text file. The fn_get_audit_file function is used to query the audit file. The following T-SQL code will return all the information that has been audited:

```
--Query the audit file
SELECT *
 FROM sys.fn_get_audit_file('C:\AuditLogs\Corp_Audit_*.sqlaudit',DEFAULT,DEFAULT )
 GO
```

Individual audit files can be queried, but if multiple files have been created, a wildcard in the file path is supported to return results across multiple audit files.

To view the audit log from SQL Server Management Studio, right-click on the audit and select View Audit Logs from the menu. This will open the SQL Server Log File Viewer. From this window, the audit log can be filtered or exported.

If audit events are logged to the Security log or the Windows Event log, they can be viewed through the respective logs or through the SQL Log File Viewer. Each event that is logged will be an information-level event and have a source of MSSQLSERVER. The SQL Log File Viewer can be found under the Management, SQL Server Logs folder. The SQL Log File Viewer will display SQL Server logs by default, but selecting the Application log will show the Windows Application log as well.

The SQL Log File Viewer, shown in Figure 9-4, can be filtered for the date, the source, event information, and more. The filter can be configured by clicking the Filter button on the SQL Log File Viewer screen. The SQL Log File Viewer can also export the log file for an auditor to review.

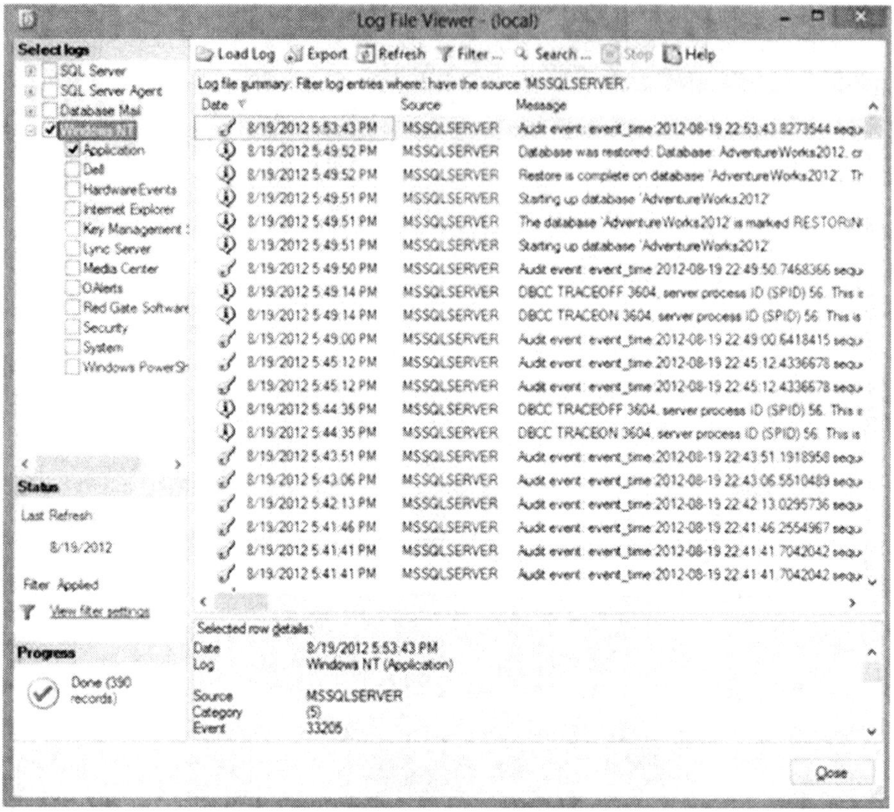

*Figure 9-4. The Log Viewer can be filtered to show just audit events in the Windows Application log*

The Windows Event logs can also be accessed through Start, All Programs, Administrative Tools, Event Viewer.

# Pro Tip: Alert on Audit Events

Auditing is not designed to send an alert or notify anyone if an audit event occurs. Although SQL Server is not designed to send these alerts, there is a solution that will allow this to happen. The caveats to this solution are that audits must be sent to the Windows logs and it leverages SQL Server alerts.

During normal operation, SQL Server generates events and writes them to the Windows Application log. The SQL Server Agent is continuously reading the Application log and can trigger an alert based on an event. If an audit is configured to write audit events to the Windows Application log, an alert can be configured to notify an administrator or auditor of the event.

---

■ **Note**   Setting up alerts requires the audit events to be written to the Windows Application log, Database Mail to be configured, and an operator to be created.

---

Alerts can be created with both T-SQL code and through SQL Server Management Studio. The following code will create an alert to notify Jonathan Gardner when a database is backed up:

```
USE [msdb]
GO
EXEC msdb.dbo.sp_add_alert @name=N'BackupAlert',
        @message_id=18264,
        @severity=0,
        @enabled=1,
        @delay_between_responses=60,
        @include_event_description_in=1,
        @job_id=N'00000000-0000-0000-0000-000000000000'
GO
EXEC msdb.dbo.sp_add_notification @alert_name=N'BackupAlert', @operator_name=N'Jonathan Gardner',
@notification_method = 1
GO
```

In SQL Server Management Studio, alerts are located in the Alerts folder under the SQL Server Agent. To create a new alert, right-click on the Alerts folder. The New Alert dialog box will open, as shown in Figure 9-5. The name of the alert, the error number to be monitored, and the specific database can all be set in this dialog box.

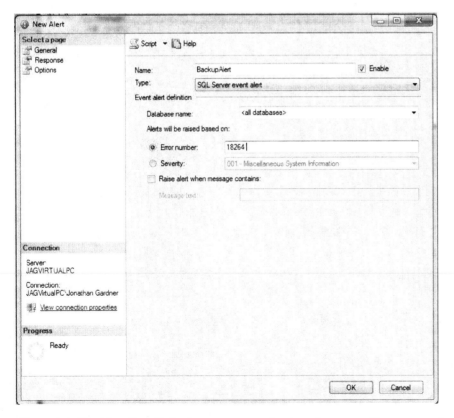

*Figure 9-5. The New Alert dialog box creates an alert based on a specific error number.*

You can select the operator and the method of notification by clicking on the Response tab and choosing from the options that appear on it.

The Options tab, shown in Figure 9-6, is where the alert can be configured to include the error text and the delay between the responses. The Delay Between Responses option provides a waiting period, which you can use to control how often the alerts are generated. In the example, only one alert will be sent out every minute, even if more audit events have been created for Application log activity.

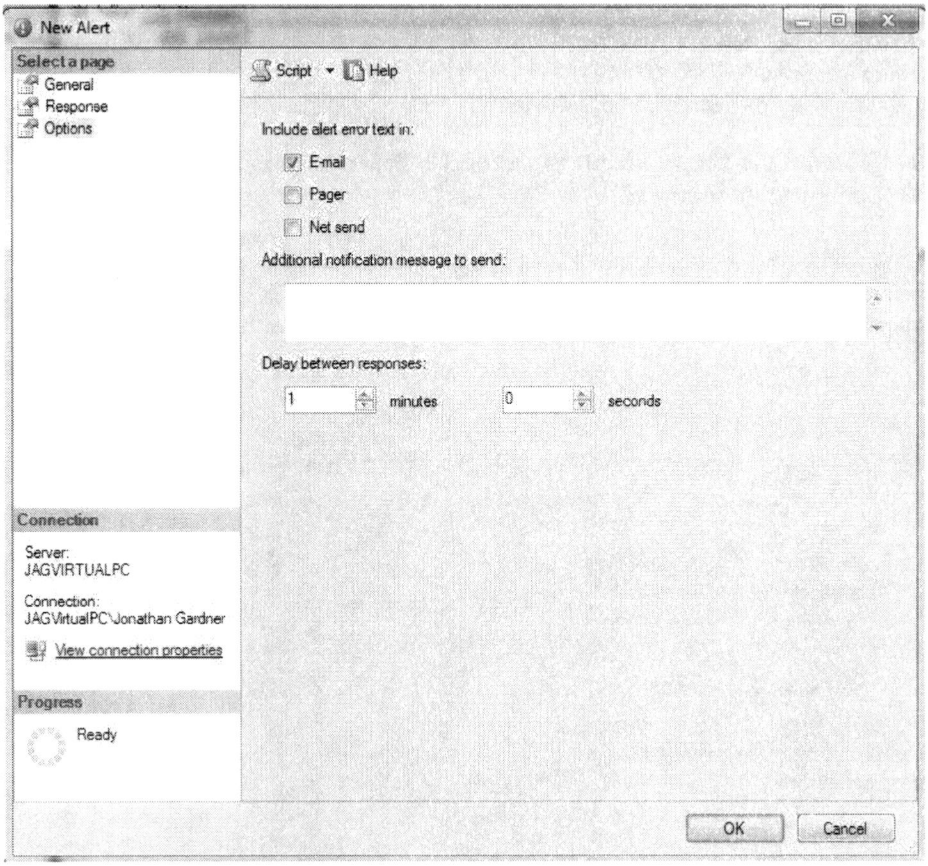

*Figure 9-6. The Options tab on the New Alert page is where you configure alerts.*

# Conclusion

Today's regulatory environment requires organizations to track and monitor who is accessing and changing data in the environment. Database professionals need to work with management to understand what laws the business is subject to so that they understand what information needs to be audited.

SQL Server 2012 provides database professionals with the tools to fully comply with laws and regulations. Database professionals can quickly and easily set up auditing for the environments that they manage. With the new SQL Server auditing capabilities, even SQL Server Standard instances can be monitored.

■ ■ ■

# Automating Administration

## by Jes Borland

For the past few decades, computers have been replacing humans for tasks in manufacturing and other industries. Robotics and computers have advanced to the point that they can perform many tasks people used to do. Automation can help you prevent problems, do your job faster, be proactive, be more productive, scale your environment, and result in cost savings.

It is unlikely that computers will replace database administrators, but we can learn how to be more efficient and productive by automating our techniques. You might ask, "Why?" Your current manual processes and third-party tools are getting the job done.

As a database administrator, your job is not merely to react to problems, but also to help prevent them. Automating common tasks such as backups and restores ensures these critical steps are done, regularly and consistently. You can make many of these tasks faster by automating as well, because you won't need to start them every day or week—you can schedule them. Once you have automated monitoring to watch your environment, you can catch problems before they get out of control.

Automation can help you scale your environment, without the company needing to hire additional staff. In the business world, time is money. Every minute or hour you create by automating a task means that time can be spent working on a project, maintaining other systems, catching up on a backlog of report requests, or furthering your professional development.

The main points to consider about automation are the tools to enable it, and what tasks in your environment can and should be automated.

## Tools for Automation

SQL Server provides several tools useful for automation. These are described in the following subsections. They include utilities such as Perfmon and scripting languages like PowerShell .

### Performance Monitor

A tool available in Windows is Performance Monitor, or Perfmon. This is an operating system tool, not a SQL Server tool. There are general counters, and those specific to SQL Server.

With SQL Server, the resources you'll want to watch most closely are server memory, disk, and processor. The following are a few frequently used counters:

- **Memory - Available Mbytes**: Shows the physical memory available for allocation to a process or the system.

- **Physical disk - Disk reads/sec**: Shows the number of read operations on the disk.

- **Physical disk - Disk writes/sec**: Shows the number of write operations on the disk.

- **Physical disk - Avg. disk sec/Read**: Shows the average number of seconds a read takes to complete.

- **Physical disk - Avg. disk sec/Write**: Shows the average number of seconds a write takes to complete.

- **Processor - % Processor Time**: Shows the percentage of time the processor spends executing a thread.

- **SQL Server: Buffer Manager - Page Life Expectancy**: Shows the number of a seconds a page will live in the buffer pool.

The counters for disks and processors should be used to monitor each disk and processor separately, not the total. The total will provide an overall value for the server, but won't show you which disks or processors are consuming the most resources.

To access Performance Monitor and its data, open it in Windows Server 2008R2 by going to Start, then Run, and entering perfmon.exe. When this graphical tool opens, you can create a data collector set, define the data counters you want to collect, and start executing it. Counters are logged to a binary or comma-separated value file for you to parse later.

To create a data collector set, expand Data Collector Sets and right-click on User Defined, then New, then Data Collector Set. Assign a name, select Create manually, and click Next. With Create data logs selected, choose Performance counter and click Next. On the Performance counters screen, choose Add to select counters.

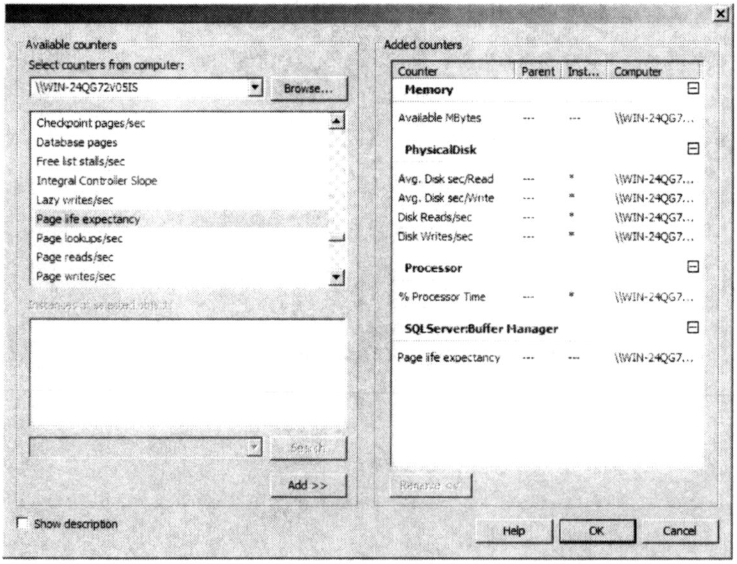

***Figure 10-1.*** *Adding counters to a performance monitor data collector set*

Figure 10-1 shows the screen you will see to select the counters. Select the appropriate server name, and add your counters. When you have chosen the counters, click OK to save, choose your sample interval, and click Next. Select a location to save your log files and select Next. Choose Start this data collector set now and click Finish. The data will be captured starting from that point forward.

After you have created the data collector set, you can start and stop the collection by clicking on the name of it under User Defined, and using the Play and Stop buttons. It is best practice to set up the data collector set and save the logs to a computer other than the database server, such as your workstation or another designated computer. Doing so prevents additional workload on the server.

# Dynamic Management Views

SQL Server Dynamic Management Views (DMVs) provide a wealth of information about the server, the instance, the individual databases, and the activity occurring at any given moment. Capturing this information on a regular basis and reporting on it can help you establish a performance baseline, and troubleshoot errors when they occur.

Memory, processor, and disk can be monitored through DMVs. There is also much more that can be captured, such as what an instance is waiting on, what execution plans are in the plan cache, and index usage. There are DMVs for AlwaysOn Availability Groups, mirroring, replication, and more.

Memory can be monitored through a combination of DMVs. To start, use `sys.dm_os_sys_memory` to check the configuration of the memory on the server. Listing 10-1 shows a query to view the total and available memory on the server, and the state of that memory. You do not want the `system_memory_state_desc` column to show "Available physical memory is low," as this indicates memory pressure.

*Listing 10-1.* Query to View System Memory Configuration

```
SELECT total_physical_memory_kb,
    available_physical_memory_kb,
    system_memory_state_desc
FROM sys.dm_os_sys_memory;
```

Processor usage can be monitored by querying the `sys.dm_exec_requests` DMV to see the current CPU time used by each session. The view shows you how much time is being used by the processor, in milliseconds, on each session. Listing 10-2 shows a query to view this information. You want to sort it by the amount of CPU time in descending order, and look at the query text that is returned for the queries with the highest amount. There is no specific threshold in milliseconds that indicates a good or bad query; that is something you need to set a baseline for in the instance and weigh the queries against.

*Listing 10-2.* Query to See CPU Time Used by Session

```
 SELECT ER.session_id,
   ER.request_id,
   ES.host_name,
   ES.login_name,
   DB_NAME(ER.database_id) AS dbname,
   ER.start_time,
   GETDATE() as currenttime,
   ER.cpu_time,
   ER.total_elapsed_time,
   EST.text as query_text
FROM sys.dm_exec_requests ER
   INNER JOIN sys.dm_exec_sessions ES on ER.session_id = ES.session_id
```

```
    OUTER APPLY sys.dm_exec_sql_text(ER.sql_handle) EST
    OUTER APPLY sys.dm_exec_query_plan(ER.plan_handle) EQP
ORDER BY ER.cpu_time DESC;
```

Disk reads and writes can be monitored through the sys.dm_exec_requests DMV. The reads and writes columns will tell you how many of each have been performed by each session. Listing 10-3 gives you a query to view the sessions, sorted by reads. Like processor times, there is no set answer for how many reads or writes are bad, or too much. An established baseline will tell you what is normal for your database.

*Listing 10-3.* *Query to view sessions sorted by reads.*

```
SELECT ER.session_id,
    ER.request_id,
    ES.host_name,
    ES.login_name,
    DB_NAME(ER.database_id) AS dbname,
    ER.start_time,
    GETDATE() as currenttime,
    ER.total_elapsed_time,
    ER.reads,
    ER.writes,
    EST.text as query_text
FROM sys.dm_exec_requests ER
    INNER JOIN sys.dm_exec_sessions ES on ER.session_id = ES.session_id
    OUTER APPLY sys.dm_exec_sql_text(ER.sql_handle) EST
    OUTER APPLY sys.dm_exec_query_plan(ER.plan_handle) EQP
ORDER BY ER.reads DESC;
```

Be aware that the information in the DMVs is cleared each time SQL Server restarts. Later in this chapter, I will show you how to create a SQL Server Agent job that will gather this information on a schedule and insert it into a database for review.

## SQL Server Agent

SQL Server Agent is a service that executes jobs as an external process to the SQL Server Engine. This is a very simplistic explanation for a tool that has many features and uses. You begin by creating a task, or series of tasks. Your task or tasks constitutes a *job,* which can be called on demand, on a schedule, or from an alert. You can perform actions such as notifying operators or running another job on success or failure. SQL Agent is a multilayered, flexible tool that easily enables automation.

To get the most from SQL Agent, it is helpful to have Database Mail set up and enabled, which allows SQL Server to send e-mail through an SMTP server.

---

■ **Note**   Database Mail can be found in Books Online at http://msdn.microsoft.com/en-us/library/ms190658.aspx.

---

After Database Mail has been enabled, you can configure operators to notify users via e-mail.

# Operators

Operators hold contact information for people that notifications and alerts can be sent to. You can set them up for any e-mail address. For many functions, it is recommended to have a general mailbox for a team that the alerts can be sent to, rather than one individual.

To access operator information, go to SSMS Object Explorer. Connect to an instance and expand SQL Server Agent. To create an operator, right-click and select New Operator. The operator general setup screen is shown in Figure 10-2. The necessary fields here are Name and E-mail name. (Microsoft states the net send and pager options will be removed in a future version of SQL Server, and advises not to use them.)

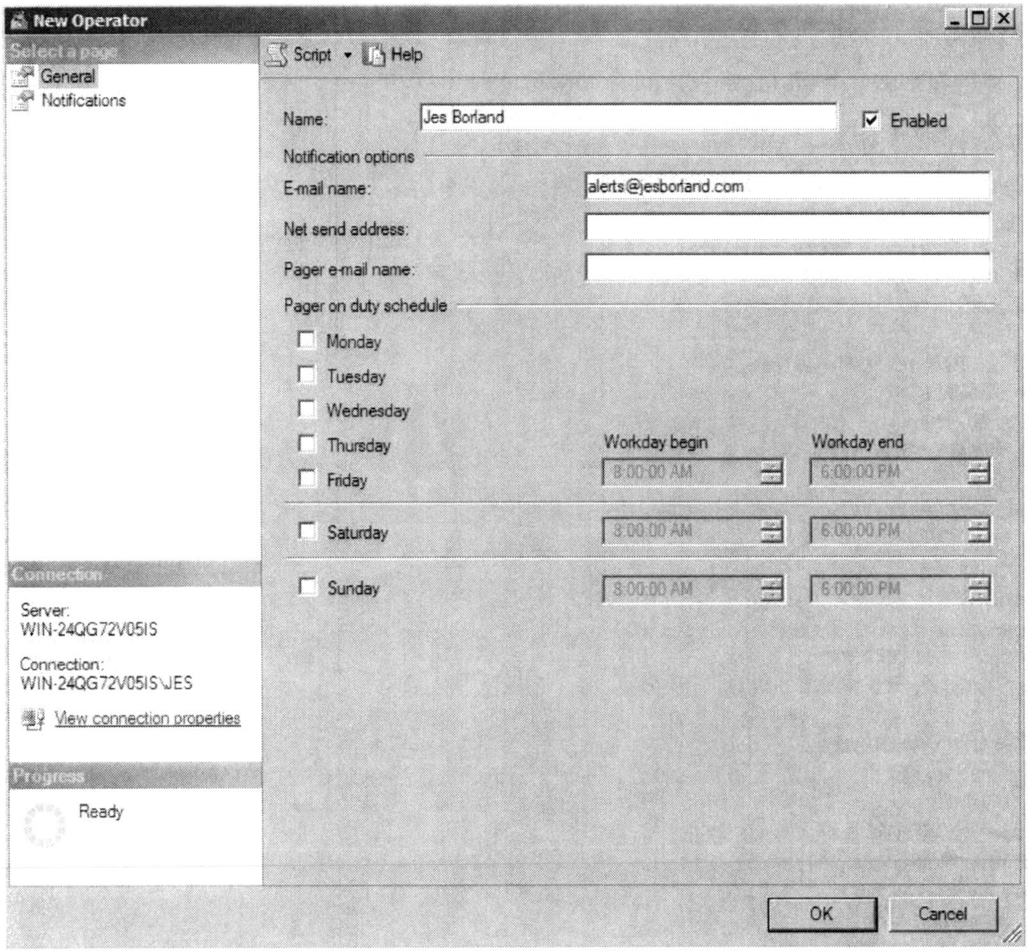

*Figure 10-2. Configuring an operator*

# Jobs

SQL Server Agent allows you to create jobs, which are an action or series of actions performed against the instance. The job can be run once, or multiple times. A job will have several components. These components are the job steps, the schedule, and the notifications.

An example of a job is monitoring the memory, processor, and disk information discussed in the DMV section. To begin, you will create a database to hold tables to log the information. This query is shown in Listing 10-4.

***Listing 10-4.*** *Creating the DBAInfo Database*

```
CREATE DATABASE DBAInfo;
```

Next, you will create a table to hold the information for each DMV query, as shown in Listing 10-5.

***Listing 10-5.*** *Creating Tables to Hold Monitoring Information*

```
CREATE TABLE MemoryDMVHistory
(total_physical_memory_kb BIGINT,
    available_physical_memory_kb BIGINT,
    system_memory_state_desc NVARCHAR(256),
    collection_date_time DATETIME);

CREATE TABLE ProcessorDMVHistory
(session_id SMALLINT,
    request_id INT,
    host_name NVARCHAR(128),
    login_name NVARCHAR(128),
    db_name NVARCHAR(128),
    start_time DATETIME,
    currenttime DATETIME,
    cpu_time INT,
    total_elapsed_time INT,
    query_text NVARCHAR(MAX),
    collection_date_time DATETIME);

CREATE TABLE DiskDMVHistory
(session_id SMALLINT,
    request_id INT,
    host_name NVARCHAR(128),
    login_name NVARCHAR(128),
    db_name NVARCHAR(128),
    start_time DATETIME,
    currenttime DATETIME,
    total_elapsed_time INT,
    reads BIGINT,
    writes BIGINT,
    query_text NVARCHAR(MAX),
    collection_date_time DATETIME);
```

To view existing jobs open SSMS, connect to an instance, expand SQL Server Agent, and expand Jobs. To create a new job, right-click Jobs. The General screen, shown in Figure 10-3, allows you to configure basic information such as the job name, category, and description. Name the job "Gather DMV performance metrics," select Data Collector as the category, and add a description.

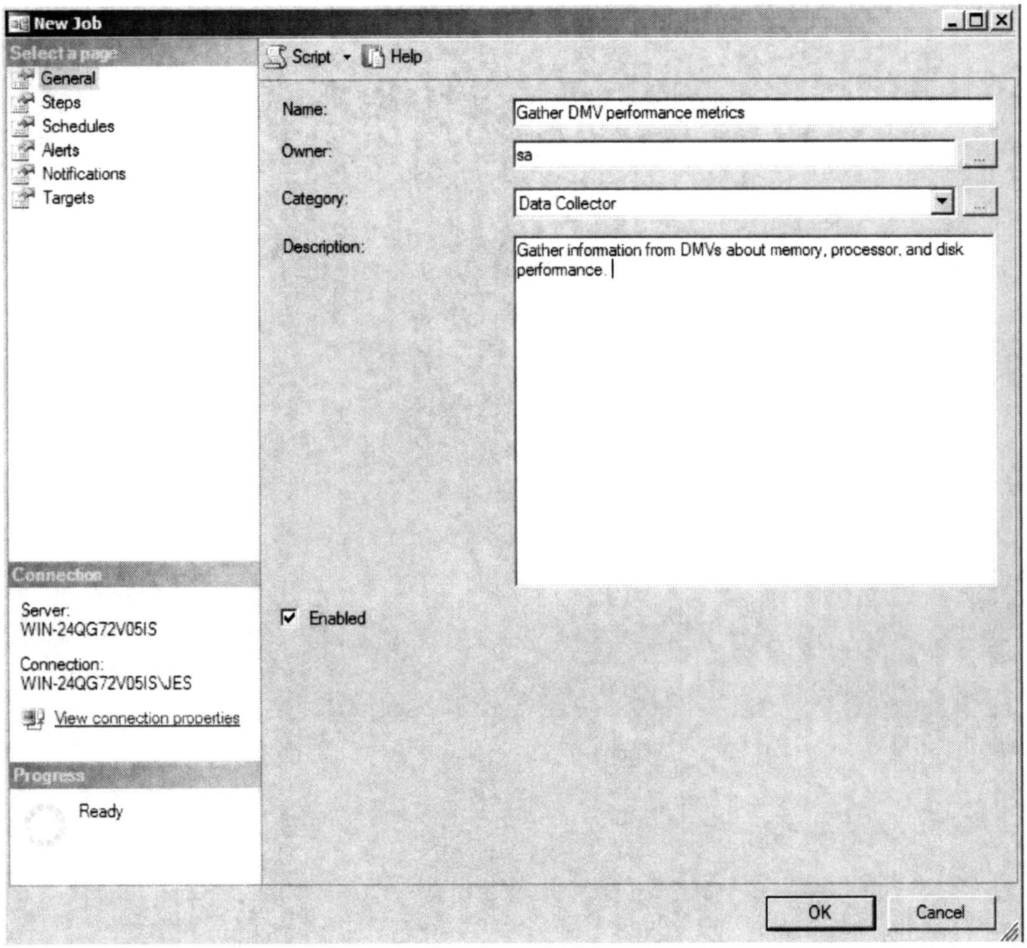

*Figure 10-3. The General properties of a SQL Server Agent job*

## Job Steps

Each job is comprised of one or more steps. To create a step, click Steps on the left of the job screen, as shown in Figure 10-4. When creating a job step, at minimum you will supply a step name, type, and command. The step name is how you will see the steps referenced in the Job Activity Monitor and error logs. Pick a clear name that makes it obvious what the step does.

The most common type of command used is T-SQL, but you are also able to specify ActiveX Script, CmdExe, PowerShell, Replication agents, Analysis Services commands or queries, or Integration Services packages. These options greatly extend the functionality of the jobs. T-SQL can do many tasks, but some tasks are better done by other tools.

If your SQL Agent service account doesn't have enough permission to execute a T-SQL script, you can include the EXECUTE AS command in the code. For steps other than T-SQL, the Run As option allows you to designate another account to execute the step. Being able to pass in a different set of credentials can help you circumvent a lack of permissions, without your having to grant the Agent account additional permissions.

The following are a few steps required to set up the Run As option correctly:

- You must first add a credential to the server with the username and password information. The setup for doing so can be accessed under Security > Credentials.

- Then, create a proxy linked to those credentials. Proxy setup is under SQL Server Agent > Proxies.

- After you have created a credential, create a proxy. Assign the proxy to the type of steps it can be associated with.

You will now be able to choose an account to run any associated steps.

To continue creating the job that executes the DMVs, add a step that executes the query shown in Listing 10-6.

*Listing 10-6. Query to Insert the Results of the DMV Queries into Tables*

```
INSERT INTO MemoryDMVHistory
SELECT total_physical_memory_kb,
    available_physical_memory_kb,
    system_memory_state_desc,
    GETDATE()
FROM sys.dm_os_sys_memory;

INSERT INTO ProcessorDMVHistory
SELECT ER.session_id,
    ER.request_id,
    ES.host_name,
    ES.login_name,
    DB_NAME(ER.database_id) AS dbname,
    ER.start_time,
    GETDATE() as currenttime,
    ER.cpu_time,
    ER.total_elapsed_time,
    EST.text as query_text,
    GETDATE()
FROM sys.dm_exec_requests ER
    INNER JOIN sys.dm_exec_sessions ES on ER.session_id = ES.session_id
    OUTER APPLY sys.dm_exec_sql_text(ER.sql_handle) EST
    OUTER APPLY sys.dm_exec_query_plan(ER.plan_handle) EQP;

INSERT INTO DiskDMVHistory
SELECT ER.session_id,
    ER.request_id,
    ES.host_name,
    ES.login_name,
    DB_NAME(ER.database_id) AS dbname,
    ER.start_time,
```

```
    GETDATE() as currenttime,
    ER.total_elapsed_time,
    ER.reads,
    ER.writes,
    EST.text as query_text,
    GETDATE()
FROM sys.dm_exec_requests ER
    INNER JOIN sys.dm_exec_sessions ES on ER.session_id = ES.session_id
    OUTER APPLY sys.dm_exec_sql_text(ER.sql_handle) EST
    OUTER APPLY sys.dm_exec_query_plan(ER.plan_handle) EQP;
```

The step should appear the same as the screen in Figure 10-4.

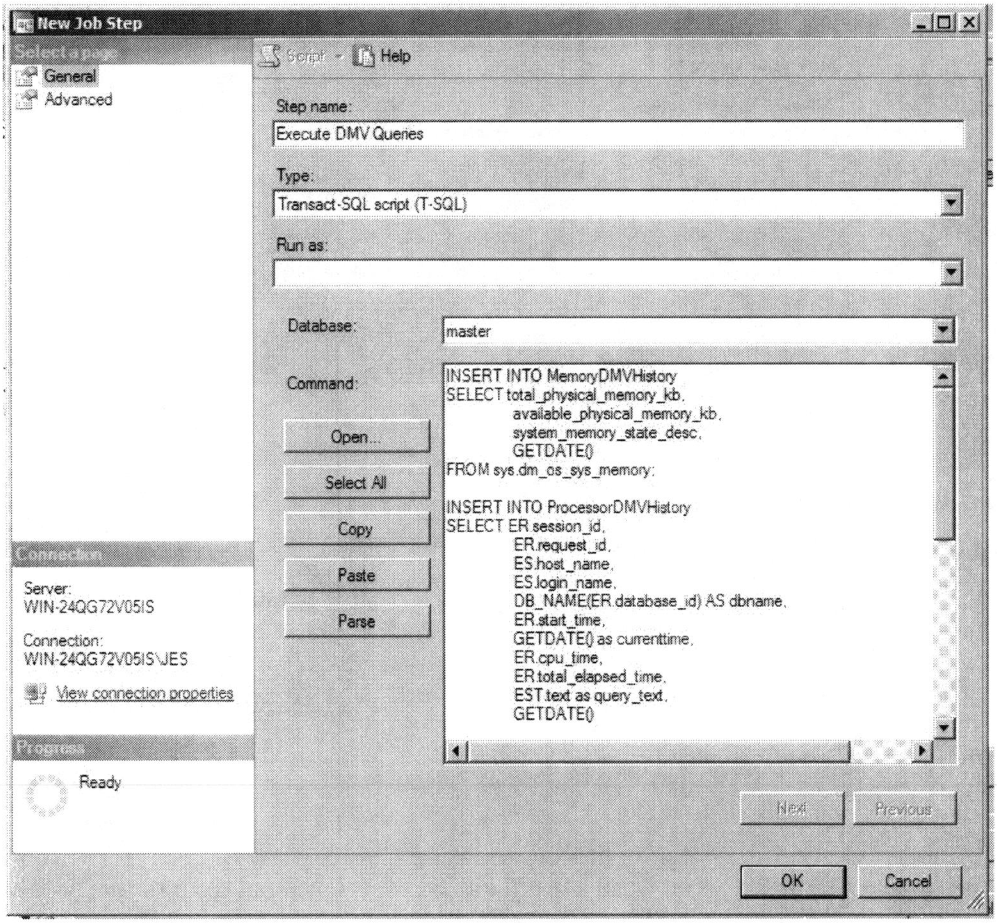

*Figure 10-4. A job step*

Each step also offers advanced options, as seen in Figure 10-5. If successful, you can continue to another step, quit reporting success, or quit reporting failure. If a step fails, you can choose to retry it. If it fails after the specified number of retries, you have the same options: continue to another step, quit reporting success, or quit reporting failure.

Additional error logging options are shown in Figure 10-5 as well. You can choose to output the information about an error to a file, or to a table in a database.

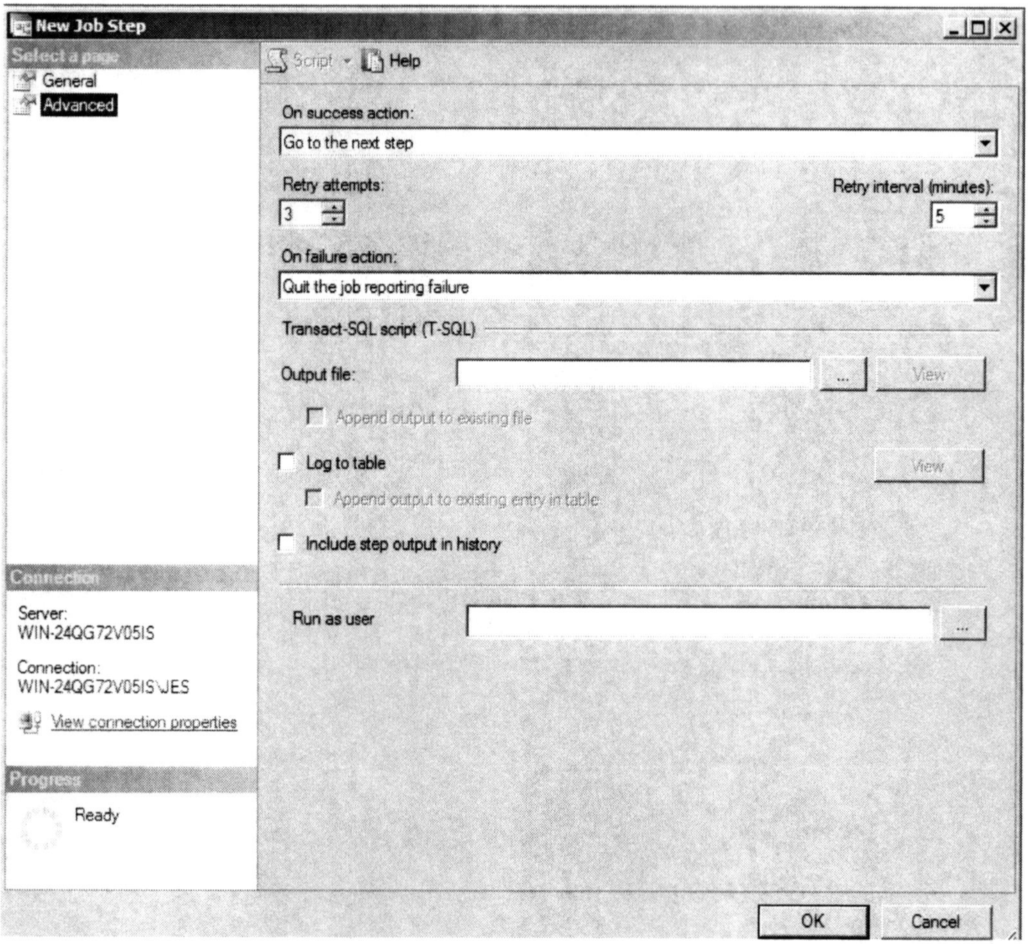

**Figure 10-5.** *Advanced options of a job step*

## Schedules

The real power of automation in SQL Server Agent jobs is the ability to set schedules. You no longer need to start the execution of jobs as you leave the office, or worry about logging in on a weekend to start a one-time job.

The screen for scheduling is shown in Figure 10-6. The first time you establish a schedule, you give it a name. Try to make this schedule name as descriptive as possible, so the type and frequency of the schedule are clear. For schedule type, you can pick from the following:

- Recurring: Jobs that need to run multiple times, such as database backups, transaction log backups, index reorg or rebuilds, or queries to populate report tables.

- One time: Jobs that only need to run once, such as for a scheduled data load.

- When SQL Server Agent starts: Jobs that need to execute only when the Agent service is started, perhaps to send a notification or run a specific stored procedure.

- Whenever the CPUs become idle: Jobs that can take advantage of CPU idle time and don't need to be run at a specific time, such as batch processing.

Frequency can be daily, weekly, or monthly. If daily, pick the number of days between recurrences. For example, you can run a job every day, every five days, or every ten days. If weekly, pick the number of weeks between recurrences, and the day(s) of the week the job will run. If monthly, you can choose a specific day of the month. Another option is to pick the X day of each Y months (such as the second Thursday of every month, or the last day of every third month). Figure 10-6 shows the schedule screen. The DMV gathering job will run every day, every 15 minutes.

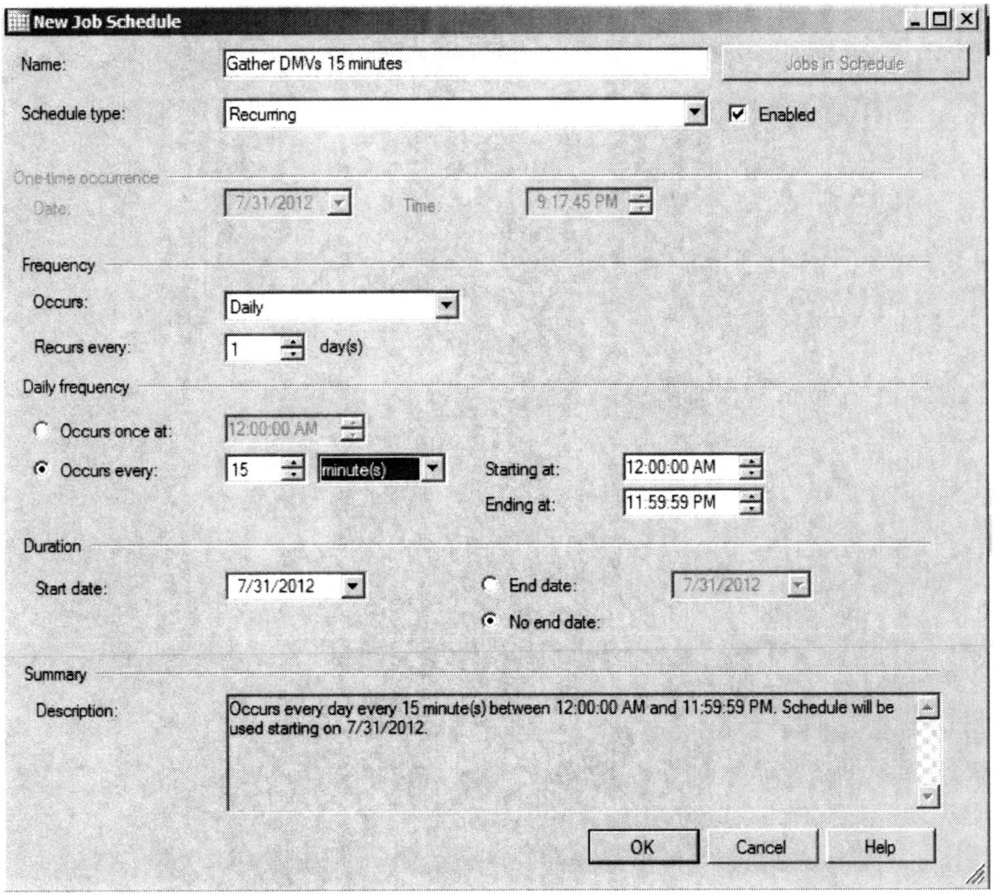

*Figure 10-6. Setting up a job schedule*

Another benefit is that once a schedule is established, it can be reused. When you're looking at the Schedules screen for a job, select Pick instead of New to choose an existing schedule.

---

▪ **Note** You can also create a job based on an alert, which will be covered later in this chapter.

---

## Notifications

Notifications allow you to perform an action when a job completes. As shown in Figure 10-7, you can send an e-mail to any of the operators you have set up. The e-mail can be sent when the job fails, when the job succeeds, or when the job finishes, regardless of outcome.

You also have the option to write to the Windows Application event log. Deleting a job upon completion is also an option, which is useful if the job is a one-time operation and you don't want to worry about coming back to clean it up later. For the DMV execution, notification will be via e-mail and the Windows Event log if the job fails.

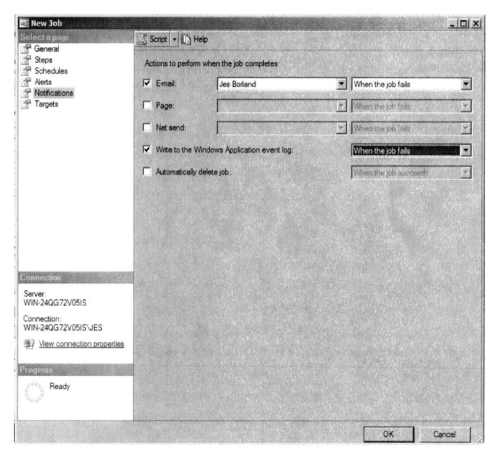

*Figure 10-7. Selecting the notifications for job completion*

# Alerts

As already discussed, there are many levels of logging set up in SQL Server. There are error numbers and messages written to the event log. Errors are assigned a severity, which determines how critical they are. Many times, an error indicating that something might be going wrong can be buried in the log. Reading through, say, the error log on every server every day can be time-consuming, and that sort of thing is exactly what we are trying to avoid through the process of automation.

Setting up alerts that can notify an operator or kick off a job is a very helpful way to proactively let someone know about an error, or to take corrective action. When an alert is defined, SQL Server will monitor the error logs, looking for a match to a condition you have defined. When a match is found, SQL Server will perform the action you have set up in the alert.

Alerts can be defined on a specific error number, a severity level, a performance condition, or a WMI event. To view existing alerts or generate a new one, open SSMS, connect to an instance, open Object Explorer, expand SQL Server Agent, and click on Alerts.

## Errors and Severity Levels

The first type of alert is for a specific error number, or a severity level, as shown in Figure 10-8. The general information required for setting up an alert is a name, a type, and a definition.

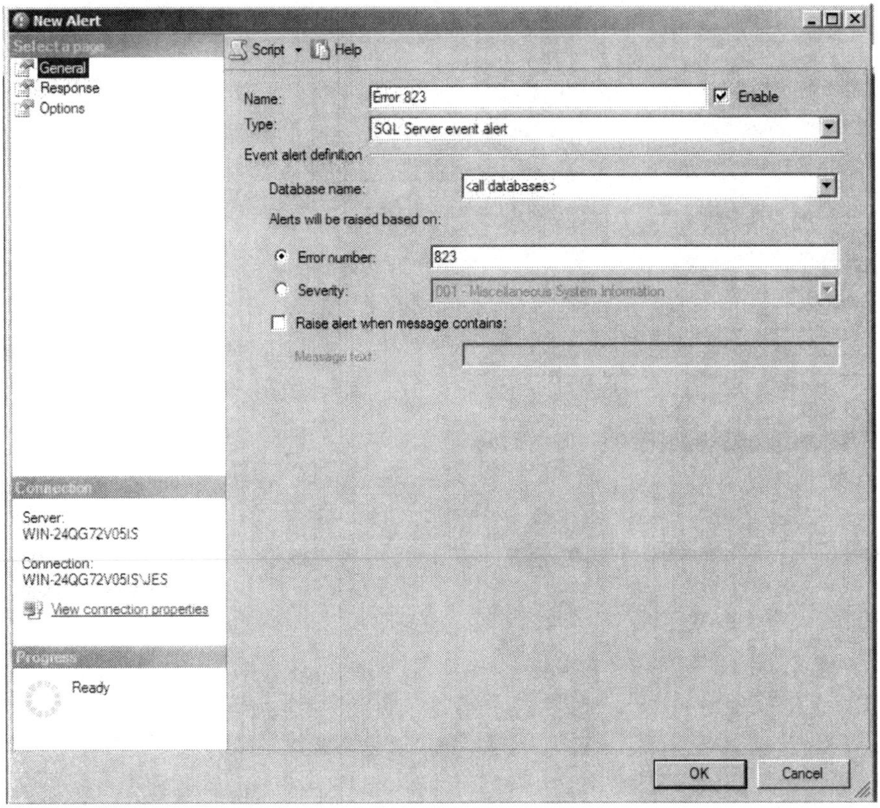

**Figure 10-8.** Setting up a SQL Server event alert

Give the alert an easily identifiable name. "Corruption Alert" isn't nearly as specific as "Error 823." Choose the database the alert is for carefully. For each event alert, you can choose to monitor one database, or all databases on the instance. Be aware that some events, such as database restores, cannot take place in the database they are executing an action in, and must be set against another database.

There are thousands of error numbers in SQL Server, and setting up an alert for each one is not necessary. However, some errors are very critical and can warn you of impending disaster, such as disk corruption. Errors 823, 824, and 825 are good examples. These three errors indicate that SQL Server cannot read pages off your disk. These are errors for which you want to set up an alert.

There are also several severity levels. Levels 017 through 025 indicate hardware or software errors, and should be monitored. Levels 017 through 019 are for software errors, such as running out of resources, which a user can't fix. Levels 020 through 025 indicate fatal errors, and will terminate client connections. It is very important a system administrator be notified if a fatal error occurs.

The example in Figure 10-8 shows an alert for all databases on the instance, for error 823.

## Performance Conditions

The second type of alert is based on a performance condition. These are SQL Server–specific counters from Performance Monitor. You choose an object, its counter, and an instance (if applicable). Then, you need to define the specific counter—it must fall below, rise above, or become equal to a specific value.

The example alert shown in Figure 10-9 would be raised if the number of active transactions in the AdventureWorks2012 database rises above 500. This is just one of many conditions that are available.

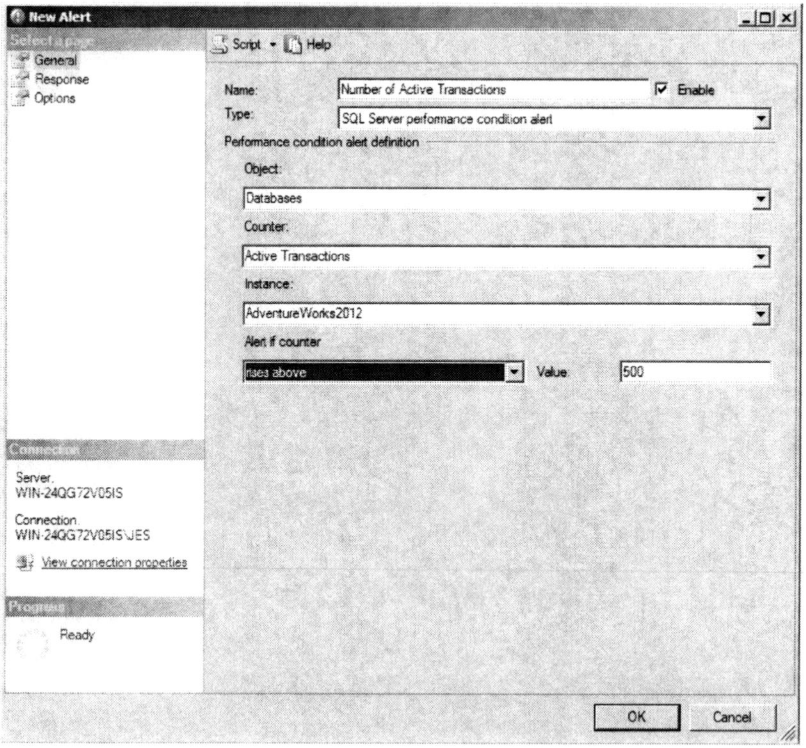

*Figure 10-9. A SQL Server performance condition alert*

# WMI Events

The third type of alert is based on a Windows Management Instrumentation (WMI) event. WMI is a framework to carry out common server management tasks with a programming or scripting language. Agent will use the Windows Management Instrumentation Query Language (WQL), which is similar to SQL. To create this alert, you specify the namespace and a query.

In Figure 10-10, a WMI event alert has been set up to capture a DEADLOCK_GRAPH event. The default SQL Server namespace is used, and the query is using WQL.

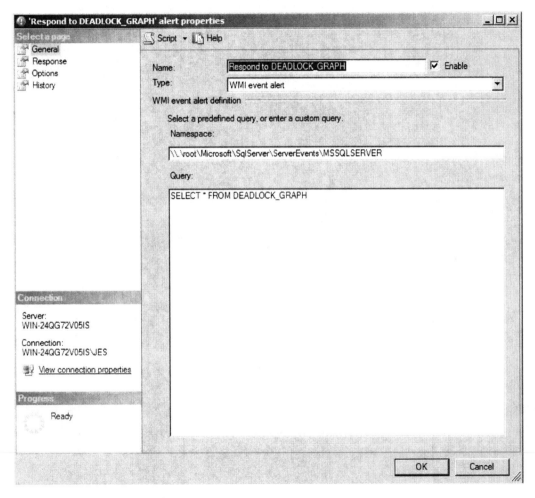

*Figure 10-10. A WMI event alert*

When a deadlock occurs, a SQL Server Agent job is started, as shown in Figure 10-11. The job that was set up, Capture Deadlock Graph, will insert the current date and time and the deadlock graph into a table for further review.

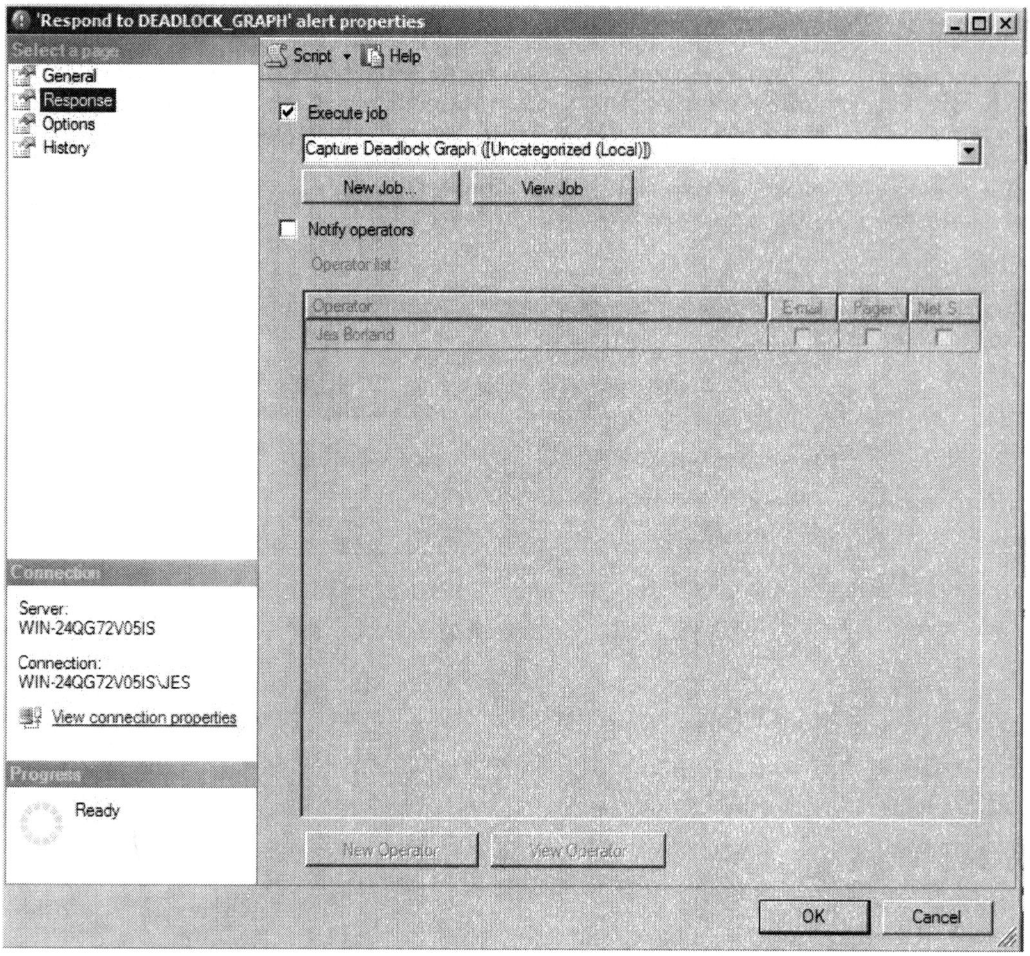

*Figure 10-11. The response to this WMI event alert is to execute an Agent job*

## Responses

For all alert types, after selecting the type of event, the next step is to define a response when the condition you established is met. As seen in Figure 10-12, you can choose to execute an existing SQL Server Agent job, notify existing operators, or do both.

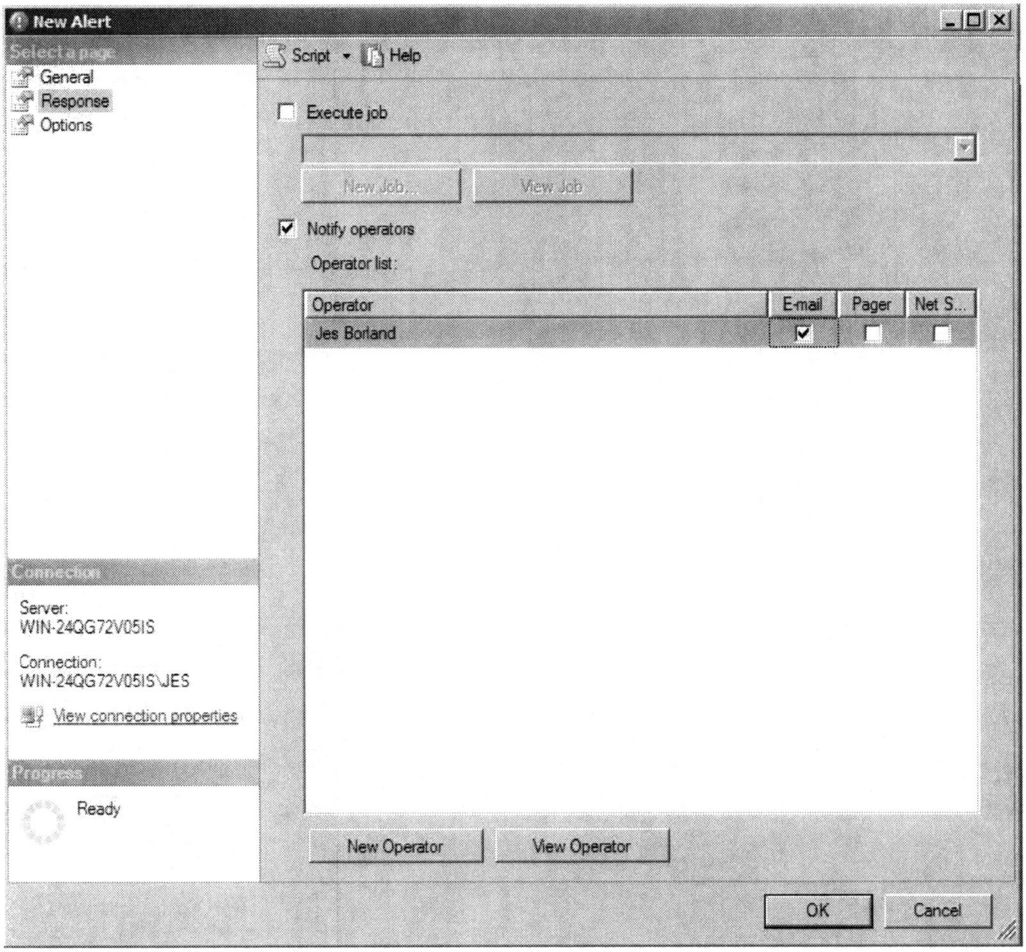

**Figure 10-12.** *The response options for an alert*

## Options

The third step is to set options, as seen in Figure 10-13. You can choose to include the error text in the alert, so you know exactly what the problem is. Including the error text is also beneficial when someone who might not be familiar with error numbers and severity levels is assigned to receive the notifications, such as a junior DBA. You can choose to add your own additional, custom messages here as well.

Most importantly, you can set a delay between the responses that are sent. When something is going wrong, there could potentially be thousands of errors and alerts being generated per minute. To keep this manageable, set a delay between the responses. On average, 30 to 60 seconds is enough of a delay to not get an overwhelming amount of alerts, but still be aware there is a problem.

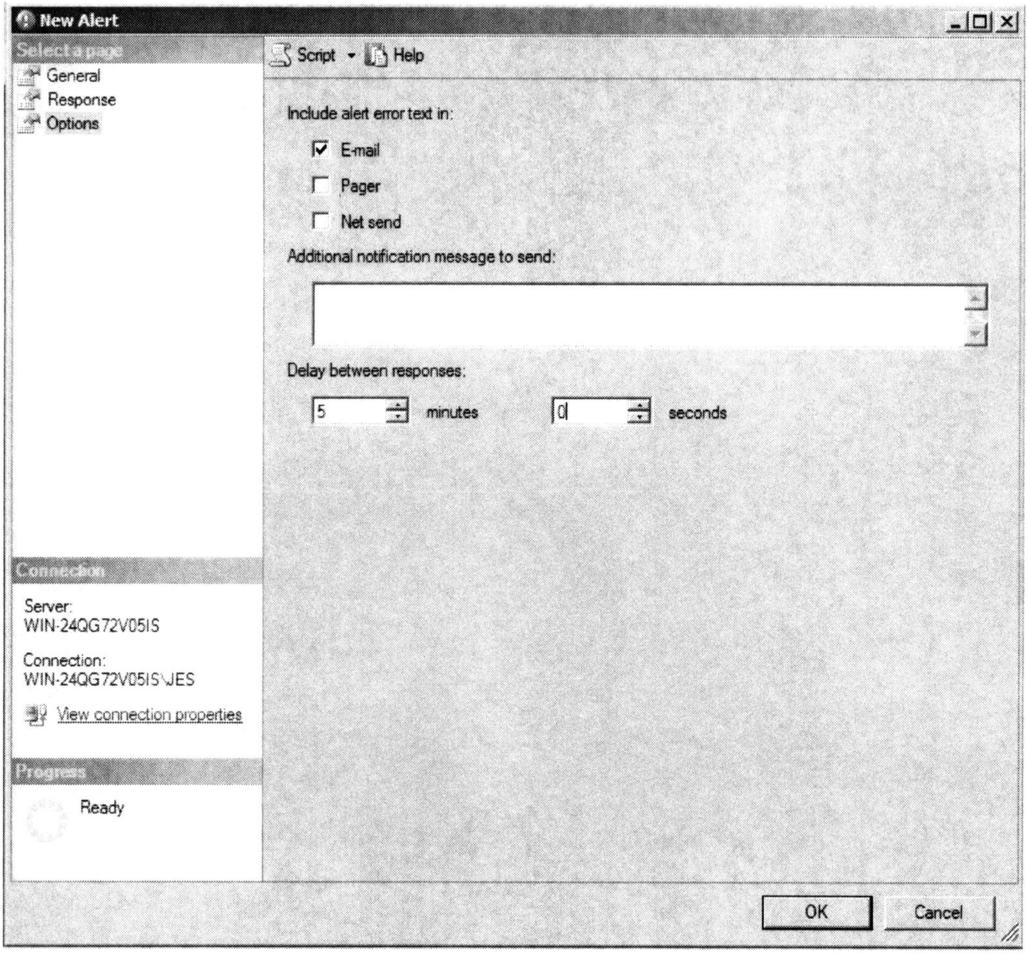

**Figure 10-13.** *Additional options for an alert*

## Maintenance Plans

SQL Server gives you a convenient way to manage many common administration tasks, such as backups, restores, and index maintenance. Maintenance plans are workflows based on SQL Server Integration Services (SSIS) packages

To access this functionality in SSMS, expand Management and look for Maintenance Plans. From here, you can create the maintenance plans manually, or use the built-in wizard. The first decision you will make when putting a plan together is deciding which tasks to include. There are eleven available in SQL Server 2012.

## Tasks

The tasks available in maintenance plans include Back Up Database, Check Database Integrity, Execute SQL Server Agent Job, Execute T-SQL Statement, History Cleanup Task, Maintenance Cleanup Task, Notify

Operator, Rebuild Index, Reorganize Index, Shrink Database, and Update Statistics, as shown in Table 10-1. Some of these tasks should be approached with great care or avoided because of default options. For example:

- History Cleanup Task: Do not delete too much or too recent of information. Backup and restore history can be used to determine a recovery strategy if needed. Agent job and maintenance plan history can help troubleshoot failed jobs or errors.

- Maintenance Cleanup Task: Do not delete backup files you need. If your standards are to save full backups for two full weeks and transaction log backups for three full days, ensure you are not deleting those files with this step.

- Rebuild Index and Reorganize Index: The tasks do not allow you to specify a fragmentation threshold for an object at which to perform the action. If the object is selected, it will be rebuilt or reorganized, perhaps unnecessarily. It might be tempting to choose all objects in a database, but that can result in unnecessary rebuild and reorganize operations, which lead to increased I/O activity on the server.

- Shrink Database: DBCC SHRINKDATABASE is performed, which moves pages in the database. This causes fragmentation, which leads to performance problems. This task should not be performed on any database on a regular basis. Your data files should be sized for the amount of data they will need.

For each of these tasks, as you are building plans and selecting options, you can select the View T-SQL button at the bottom of the Edit screen to see what SQL Server is really doing behind the scenes.

*Table 10-1. Available Maintenance Plan Tasks*

| Task | Description |
| --- | --- |
| Back Up Database | Perform a full, differential, or log backup. You have the option to pick all databases, all system databases, all user databases, or select just one or more. You select where you want to save the backup files. An option is included to verify the backup file's integrity, which performs a RESTORE VERIFYONLY. Compression level can also be set. |
| Check Database Integrity | This task will perform a DBCC CHECKDB on the database(s) you select. You can choose to check all pages, or exclude indexes. |
| Execute SQL Server Agent Job | After you have created Agent jobs, you can include them in a maintenance plan. SQL Server uses a system stored procedure, sp_start_job, to run the job. |
| Execute T-SQL Statement | This task will allow you to enter any T-SQL statement or script. If you have developed custom scripts, this can be a way to incorporate and automate them. |
| History Cleanup Task | SQL Server stores the history of many operations in the msdb database. This includes backup and restore information, Agent job history, and maintenance plan history. These tables, if left unattended, can grow very large. The history cleanup task allows you to pick one or more types, and a time frame, and will delete information older than that from the msdb tables. |

| | |
|---|---|
| Maintenance Cleanup Task | Just as some operations will take up space in msdb, other operations will take up space on disk. This task allows you to clean up backup files and maintenance plan reports that are older than a certain date. Be very careful with this option, particularly when used with backup files. You want to ensure you are not deleting any files that you need for your disaster recovery plans. |
| Notify Operator | This task will use the operators you have defined in SQL Server Agent, so that service must be enabled and running. The task allows you to configure your plan to send information to the operator. You can customize the subject and body of the notification. |
| Rebuild Index | An ALTER INDEX…REBUILD statement will be built and executed using the options you choose. Select one or more databases and one or more tables or views. There are advanced options available here, such as sorting results in tempdb and keeping the indexes online. However, make sure you understand the implications of these before selecting them. |
| Reorganize Index | To perform the less-intensive ALTER INDEX…REORGANIZE operation, use this task. Select the databases and objects against which the task will be executed. |
| Shrink Database | When this task is configured, databases, size limits, and free space percentages are chosen. The database will be shrunk to the target size with the specified free space remaining. Use caution when enabling the task. The DBCC SHRINKDATABASE command that is executed can cause fragmentation of the database, thus degrading performance. |
| Update Statistics | This task will build and execute an UPDATE STATISTICS statement. You choose the database(s), tables(s), and column or index statistics. You can also select to a full scan, or a percentage of the rows to sample. |

## Creating a Maintenance Plan

The Check Database Integrity task is important to run on a regular basis, and simple to set up as a maintenance plan. This task performs a DBCC CHECKDB on one or more databases to validate the data consistency on each page.

To start creating the plan, right-click Maintenance Plans, then select Maintenance Plan Wizard. The starting screen is shown in Figure 10-14. Give the plan a descriptive name and enter a description. Choose the account to run the job. Use the Change button to set a schedule (the options will be the same as an Agent job).

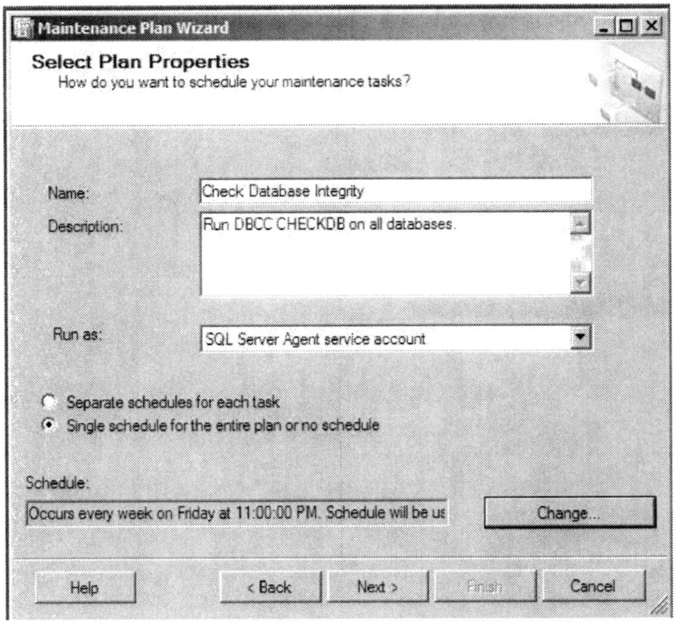

**Figure 10-14.** *Creating a maintenance plan*

On the Select Maintenance Tasks, shown in Figure 10-15, choose the tasks you want to complete in this plan. For this example, choose Check Database Integrity.

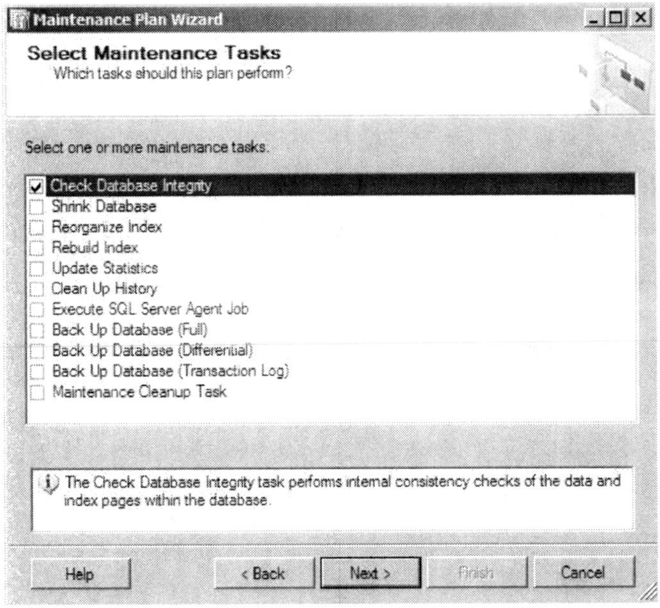

**Figure 10-15.** *Select maintenance tasks in the wizard*

The Select Maintenance Task Order screen, shown in Figure 10-16, will allow you to choose the order of the tasks you select. If you choose only one task, like in this example, the sort options are not available.

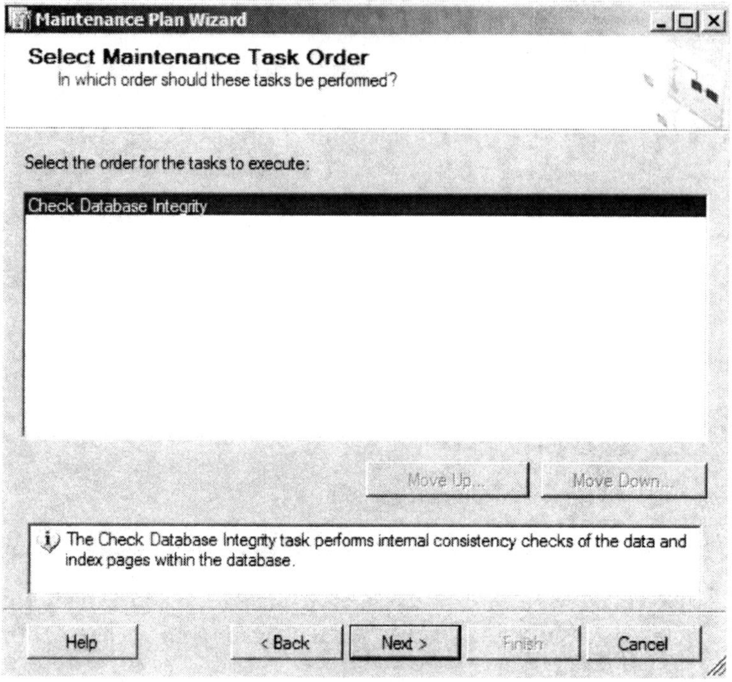

**Figure 10-16.** *Choose the order of the tasks in your plan*

The next step is to pick the databases you want to perform the task on, shown in Figure 10-17. Your options are as follows:

- All databases

- System databases: Master, model, msdb, and tempdb.

- All user databases: All databases except master, model, msdb, and tempdb.

- These databases: choose one or more databases

Unless one database is very large or has other special requirements, it is best to check all databases. Checking the "Include indexes" option will check the index pages in the database, which is also recommended.

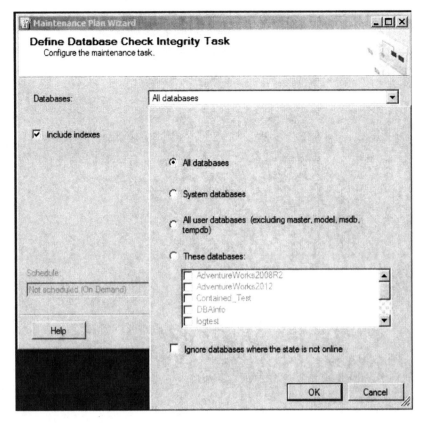

*Figure 10-17. Choosing the databases for the Check Database Integrity task*

The Select Report Options screen, shown in Figure 10-18, is where you will set logging options for the plan. "Write a report to a text file" will generate a `.txt` file each time the plan is run, including details such as steps executed and errors. The default option is to save these to the server the plan is run on, which will take up space on the storage. Choose a disk used for logging purposes, or choose a different server or network location to save the logs. "Email report" will send an e-mail to an operator when the plan completes.

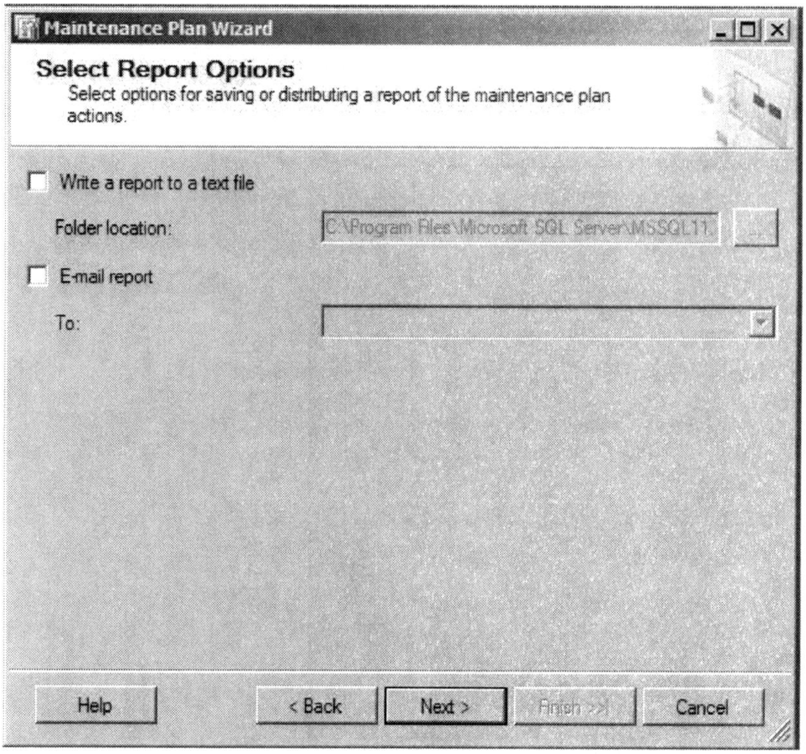

*Figure 10-18. The Select Report Options screen*

After you complete the wizard, the plan will be created, and will begin executing using the schedule you created. To view the details of the plan, double-click the plan name under Maintenance Plans.

## Other Options

Choosing your tasks is only the first step in a plan. After it's created, you have options to control the flow of tasks. Flow control allows you to link two or more tasks together, and one can be dependent on the success or failure of the previous. As an example, you could set up a plan to reorganize your indexes and then update statistics. Because these two are related, having one plan instead of two can ease administration.

There is a maintenance plan log file viewer also, to help you monitor the jobs. In SSMS, right-click Maintenance Plans and choose View History. You can see the success or failure of jobs, along with execute time, and errors if it failed. If you have plans set up, make sure you are monitoring them!

## Possible Pitfalls

Maintenance plans are an easy way to set up basic administration of your instances. However, like any other feature, make sure you understand the options you have selected, and the implications. For example, choosing to rebuild all the indexes of a database is quite easy in the Rebuild Index task, but performing that task could impact the availability of the database to users due to locking and resource consumption while the task executes.

# SQL Server Integration Services

SQL Server Integration Services is a tool designed for Extract, Transform, and Load (ETL) operations. It is frequently used to take data from a source such as a spreadsheet, a flat file, or another database system and import it into SQL Server. It's also used to transfer data from one SQL Server database to another, whether that be from a production environment to a QA environment, or from an OLTP database to an OLAP database.

SSIS works on the concept of packages. A package will have one or more tasks associated with it. Many of the tasks that are available in maintenance plans are available in SSIS. You'll find the Back Up Database Task, Check Database Integrity Task, Rebuild Index Task, Reorganize Index Task, Transfer Database Task, and Update Statistics Task. Tasks can be configured, grouped together as a package, and set to execute automatically. As a matter of fact, SSIS is the foundation of maintenance plans!

Other tasks are available in SSIS that are not available anywhere else, such as the following:

- Transfer Database Task: Copies or moves a database, within an instance or to a different instance.

- Transfer SQL Server Objects Task: Copies objects such as tables, views, and stored procedures from one instance to another.

- Execute SQL Task: Executes T-SQL statements or stored procedures.

A common administration task is transferring logins from one instance to another. Logins may be transferred from development to QA, or QA to production, as a database is tested and released. If a database needs to be upgraded, or moved to a different server, logins will need to be moved or re-created. Writing or downloading a script is a common way to perform this task, but using SSIS can be more efficient.

To build an SSIS package, you will need to install SQL Server Data Tools, an environment for creating SSIS packages, SSAS cubes, and SSRS reports. SSDT should never be installed on a database server, because developing and running packages will consume CPU, memory, and disk resources. Install the software on your workstation to develop the packages; deploy them to the server when they are complete.

Once installed, created a new SQL Server Integration Services Project. You will see a Toolbox that contains the tasks and containers, and the Control Flow screen. Find the Transfer Logins Task and drag it on to the Control Flow. Right-click the task and select Edit to open the Task Editor, as shown in Figure 10-19. Enter a name and description.

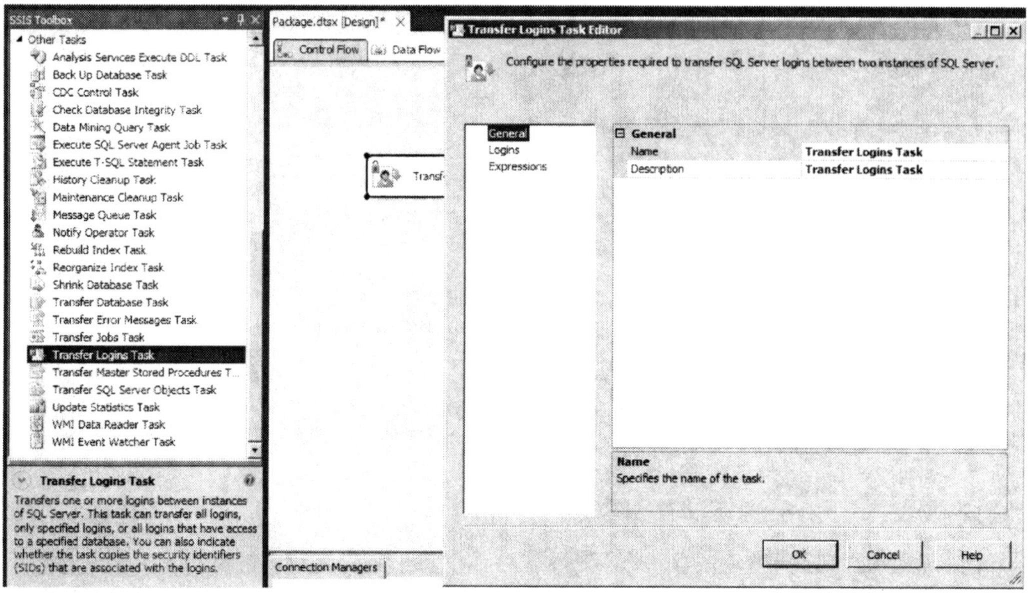

**Figure 10-19.** *The Transfer Logins Task Editor screen!*

Click the Logins option on the left to set the source connection, destination connection, logins to be transferred, and other options, shown in Figure 10-20. Choose a source connection (where the logins currently reside) and a destination connection (where you want to move the logins). You can choose to move all logins, only selected logins, or only logins from selected databases. These choices are as follows:!

- All Logins: All logins on the source server will be transferred to the destination server.

- Selected Logins: All logins you choose will be transferred. Windows and SQL Server logins can be moved.

- All Logins From Selected Databases: All the logins from all databases you choose will be transferred.

The IfObjectExists property allows you to specify what will happen if the login already exists on the destination server. These choices include the following:

- Fail Task: The task will not complete.

- Overwrite: The login information at the destination will be overwritten with the information from the source.

- Skip: If the object exists on the destination server, it will remain intact and the task will move on to the next login.

The option to Copy Sids determines whether the security identifiers (SIDs) that are assigned to the logins are moved with the logins. If you do not move the SID, the databases on the destination server that use the login won't recognize it.

There are some additional constraints to consider. The one login that can't be transferred is sa. Also, when a login is transferred, it is disabled on the destination server, and the password is set to a random password. You will need to have a process for re-enabling the logins, and if they are Windows logins, resetting the passwords.

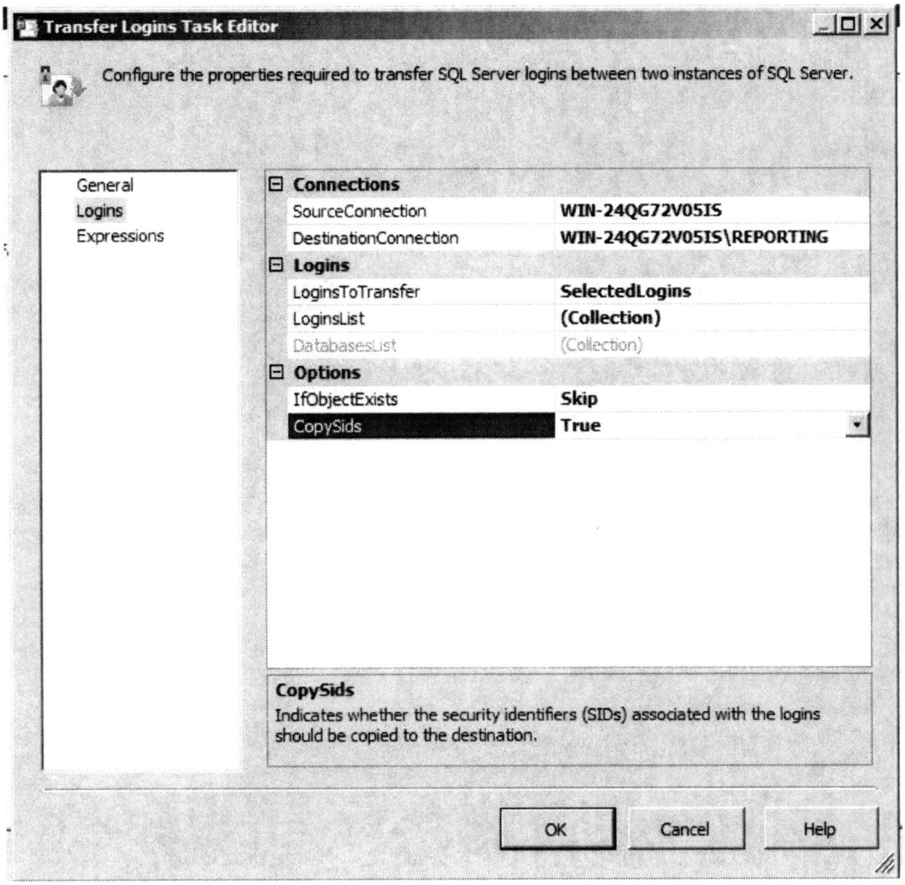

*Figure 10-20. Configuring the options of the Transfer Logins task*

When done configuring, you can test the package by running it from your computer. Be aware that this will transfer the logins! To test it, click the green play button to debug. If successful, a green circle with a checkmark and the message, "Package execution completed with success" will appear, as seen in Figure 10-21.

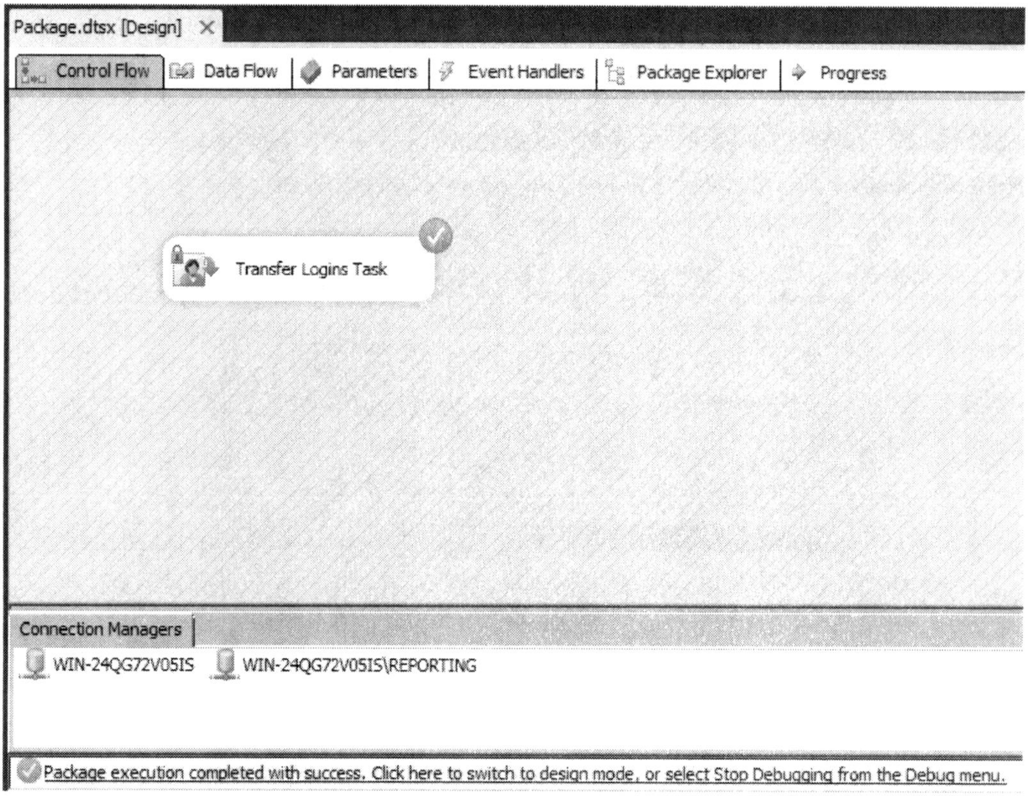

***Figure 10-21.*** *A successfully executed package in BIDs*

When the package has been tested and meets your requirements, it can be deployed to a SQL Server instance and executed on-demand, or it can be scheduled with a SQL Server Agent job. This package is one example of the capabilities SSIS has to make SQL Server administration simpler.

## PowerShell

PowerShell is a powerful, .NET-based scripting language created by Microsoft. It makes management of Windows Server and programs that run on it, like SQL Server, much easier.

What are some of the benefits of using PowerShell? The environment it is built on can access parts of the OS and file system that T-SQL can't. It is an object-oriented programming language, unlike VBscript or Perl. It has many advanced programming constructs, such as looping and error handling. There are many tasks that are difficult or not possible with T-SQL but are simple with PowerShell.

To understand PowerShell, you must first understand cmdlets. These are lightweight .NET classes that perform the work you tell them to. All cmdlets are in a verb-noun format, such as Get-Help. While many of these are powerful on their own, the ability to take the results of one cmdlet as an object, pass it to another cmdlet, and continue to work is invaluable.

Specific to the database engine are Invoke-Sqlcmd, which runs T-SQL and XQuery queries; Invoke-PolicyEvaluation to evaluate Policy Based Management policies; Encode-Sqlname and Decode-Sqlname to allow special characters allowed in SQL Server but not PowerShell; and Convert-UrnToPath to translate SQL SMO resource names to the provider paths.

## Launching PowerShell

From your workstation or a server, you can run powershell.exe to launch the environment. In SQL Server, you can right-click an object in Object Explorer and select Start PowerShell. The difference is that if you open it from SSMS, it automatically opens with the sqlps utility, meaning the SQL Server provider and cmdlets are already loaded and ready for use.

## Using PowerShell

Using PowerShell can be as simple as opening it and executing one cmdlet. You can also create a more detailed script that passes in variables, reads files from disk, and writes to tables. Any commands or scripts can be saved as a PowerShell script file (.ps1) for future use.

An example of this is using PowerShell to check the space available on your disks. PowerShell can use WMI to access this information. The Get-WmiObject cmdlet will call WMI objects, and can be used on a local or remote computer. If you are using it on a remote computer, your credentials must have access to it.

The script in Listing 10-7 will allow you to enter a computer name variable, and check the available disk space on that computer. The size and freespace are in bytes.

***Listing 10-7.*** *PowerShell Script to View Total and Available Drive Space*

```
#Checking available disk space
$Server = 'dev01'
get-wmiobject -query '
"Select DeviceID, Size, Freespace From Win32_logicaldisk Where drivetype=3" '
-computer $Server | select-object DeviceID, Size, FreeSpace
```

## Automating PowerShell

With the ability to create a script and save it for future use comes the ability to automate the running of the scripts. Windows Task Scheduler, if in use in your environment, can be set to run a script on a schedule.

You can also schedule a PowerShell job through SQL Server Agent. There are two things to note here. First, each time the Agent service runs the step, a PowerShell instance will be launched, which will use memory. Second, running PowerShell from SQL Server requires that you create a credential that has access to any resources in your environment, and then create a SQL Server Agent proxy for PowerShell using that credential. In the job, you must specify the proxy in the RunAs field.

# What to Automate

With an understanding of the tools you have available to help you automate tasks, the next decision to make is which tasks you should automate. Start by making a list of the tasks you perform on a daily, weekly, monthly, and annual basis. Any task you perform more than once is a candidate for automation. Choose one task with which to start.

As with any change in IT, don't change more than one process at a time. Implement one new process or schedule, test it, work out the bugs, and refine it. This helps ensure that if something goes wrong, you can pinpoint the cause and work to correct it as quickly as possible. When you are certain the process is working the way you want it to, then you can pick another task on your list.

The second step is to create a baseline of the amount of time you spend on tasks today. How much time do you spend reading through error logs, manually restoring databases, and fixing index fragmentation? After you change a process, measure the time again. Doing so can give you, and the business, an accurate picture of the time saved.

# Monitoring

Monitoring your servers for existing problems or the signs of future problems is one of the most critical aspects of being a successful DBA. There are many sources that contain information you can mine to understand the health of a server—Windows event logs, SQL Server error logs, and SQL Server Agent logs are a few of the valuable resources at your disposal. Being able to automate the searching of these for everything from impending potential disk corruption to failed login attempts is incredibly valuable.

## Windows Event Viewer

The Windows Event Viewer contains the application and system logs. The application log will list events, logged by programs installed on the computer. The various internal and external features and processes of SQL Server (such as the Engine, Agent, and Reporting Services) will write entries to this log. Information such as the date and time, the source of the error, the event ID, and an explanation of the item or an error message is included in the log entry. Each item is also assigned a level of importance. You should focus on the items of highest importance, which are marked Critical, Error, or Warning.

The system log will list events logged by the operating system and its components. If a service fails to start when the server starts up, you will see an error and error message.

The application log and system log differ by the level at which an event is logged. An event logged can be anything involving an exception, informational event, or critical systems failure. Note that systems failures are logged, but in some cases, such as critical dump exceptions, dump files are utilized to ensure the exception is captured for later review. This means some events may not be logged to the system log. Each logged event has a signature. The signature is either an OS-level component, or an application-level signature. Depending on where the event comes from, it is logged appropriately in order to be related in a logical container, either in the system or application log.

Reviewing the logs daily for items marked Critical, Error, or Warning will help you be proactive. A great tool to help you collect logs from a server, filter them down, and search for errors is PowerShell.

## SQL Server Error Log

You can gain some information about how SQL Server interacts with the operating system and other applications through Event Viewer. However, to truly understand what is going on in SQL Server, you'll want to regularly review, and capture important information from, the SQL Server error logs.

To access the logs in SSMS, expand Management, and then SQL Server Logs. You will see a list of all logs kept by SQL Server, as shown on the left side of Figure 10-22. To view a specific log, double-click the entry. You can also view the logs by going to <drive letter>:\Program Files\Microsoft SQL Server\ InstanceDirectory\MSSQL\Log.

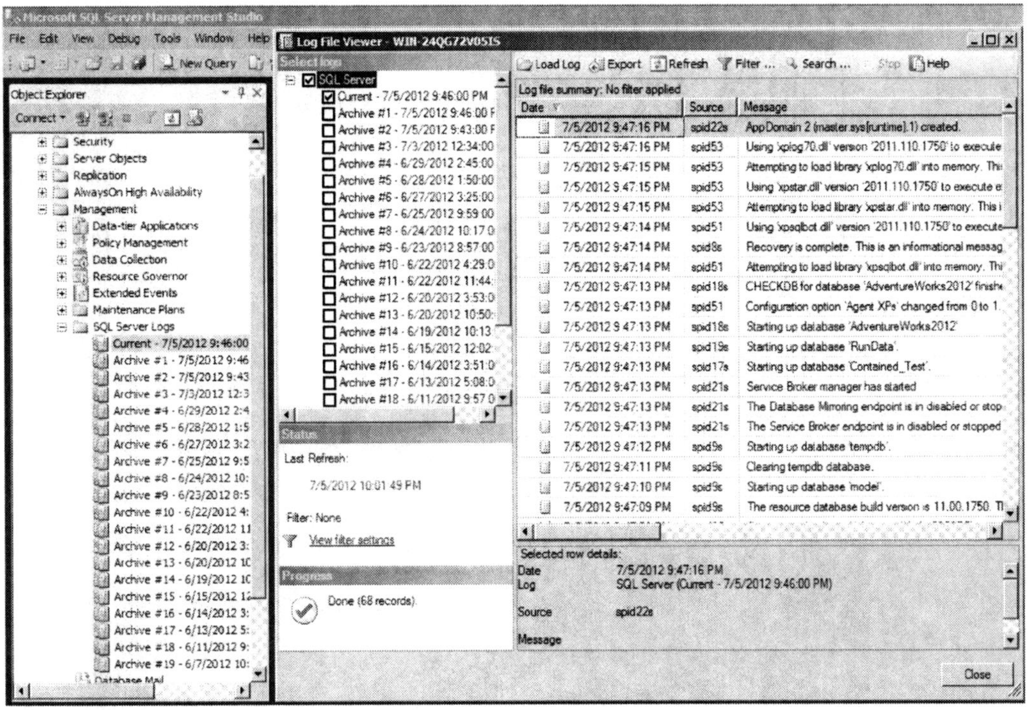

*Figure 10-22. Viewing SQL Server error logs*

Upon startup, the authentication mode, service account, startup parameters, port number, and other information are captured. Normal operations are logged, including, but not limited to, databases starting up, database backups, restores of data files and log files, failed logins, DBCC commands, deadlocks, data or log files reaching maximum capacity, and more.

Why is this important? You want to regularly check the error logs to catch potential problems before they arise, or soon after. You can log into the server, open SSMS, and read the error logs each day, but this gets tiring and tedious. It is much better to automate the reading and searching of them. Setting up Agent alerts for high-priority errors, or those you want to ensure don't cause problems in your environment, is a great way to accomplish this.

## SQL Server Agent Logs

SQL Server Agent has its own set of error logs. To view Agent jobs, logs, and more, open SSMS and expand SQL Server Agent. To view the logs, expand Error Logs and double-click one to view it. You can see this in Figure 10-23. To view the log of a specific job, double-click Job Activity Monitor to open it. Right-click a specific job and select View History.

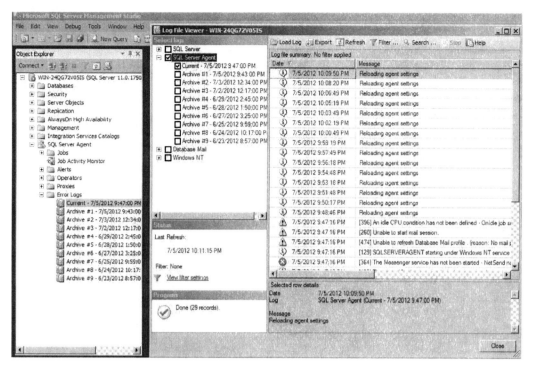

***Figure 10-23.*** *Viewing the history for SQL Agent jobs*

## Failed Jobs

One of the first things you will want to look for is jobs that have failed. This can happen for a variety of reasons, depending on what the job does. A backup may fail if it is being written across the network and loses connection. An index job may fail because you run out of space in tempdb to sort. A job can fail if the database is a state in which it cannot be accessed. You want to monitor the jobs that are failing, and determine why. After analysis, you can determine if it was a one-time or recurring failure. If it's a one-time occurrence, you can decide if you need to rerun it or wait until the next scheduled job. If the job consistently fails, you can decide if the timing is incorrect, or perhaps the job needs to be rewritten. This is the power of automation: you can be more proactive.

## Long-Running Jobs

Another element you can track in the Agent logs is the duration of a job. You will soon become familiar with the average length of time it takes to execute. Some jobs (backups, restores, index rebuilds, etc.) you will expect to take longer as the database grows in size. However, what if you have a normal amount of growth but an abnormal run time? Seeing this information and tracking it can help you prevent a problem from occurring in the future. You are also able to track the job history by step, so if a failure occurs, you know at exactly what point it happened.

# Drive Space

Something that is almost certain with every database is that it will grow in size. Depending on the application and the data stored, that growth could be slow or quick. Both the data and the log files will grow. In addition to user databases, you also need to be watchful of the system databases, especially tempdb, as it is used for many operations.

The first thing to automate with databases is their autogrow settings. You will want to verify these are configured appropriately for each database created on your server, and monitor both data and log files. I also recommend checking the settings in model on each server you manage, to ensure that any databases created follow your standards. This will ensure that you do not have to manually expand every database and every log file as they grow. These settings can be found by connecting to SQL Server through SSMS, expanding Databases, right-clicking the database name, selecting Properties, and selecting Files. The Autogrow/Maxsize column will tell you the settings for that database, and you can click the ellipses on the right of that field to change the settings.

You'll also want to ensure your databases are in the correct recovery model for your environment, and if in Full or Bulk-Logged that you are automating log backups. You can check the recovery model in Properties, on the Options tab, and reviewing Recovery Model at the top. Remember, each user database is unique and requires unique settings given the data storage purposes it has been created for.

# Disk Space

The saying is that disk space is cheap. However, it's still finite. You need to set up a process that will notify you if your drives are approaching their limits. You can then plan whether you need to move a database to another server or drive, separate data and log files onto different drives, set up partitioning, or remove databases that are no longer needed. A combination of DMVs and PowerShell can be used to monitor disk space.

# Database File Limits

You'll also want to know if your data and log files are approaching their maximum sizes. Setting the autogrow limits will help you manage this growth. Being alerted when files are nearing their limits makes you proactive. You can expand a file before a user gets an error saying the database is out of space and contacts you to fix the problem.

One way to manage getting advance notice that a file is approaching its limit is to have a weekly report that sends the DBA team the list of data and log files that are within 10 percent of their maximum. Then, you can expand the files and double-check autogrow settings. Even databases that are set for unlimited growth should be monitored and manually changed, so you are in control of the process. Conversely, you can also report databases that are large and not using much space. Perhaps they were very large once for a data load, or a log file grew for an operation. Reducing the size saves disk space and money.

# Backups and Restores

SQL Server backups are the cornerstone of your disaster recovery plan, because a company's data is its business. You need to back up your databases to ensure that if anything were to happen—whether it be a natural disaster that destroys your data center or a developer dropping a database—you can recover the data to the point of the last backup.

## Backups

You could come into work each day, open SSMS, connect to each server, and back up each database. But what happens when you get so many databases or servers that you don't have the time to do that every day? How do you manage to regularly back up transaction logs? How do you take a day off work and still ensure backups are taken? Automation is the key. Creating an Agent job that runs a T-SQL script to back up your databases on a schedule is the best choice for backups.

There are three database recovery model options in SQL Server: Simple, Full, and Bulk-Logged. Simple requires you to back up the data files. Full and Bulk-Logged require you to back up the data and transaction log files. Simple allows you to recover the data to the point of the last full backup. Bulk-Logged allows you to back up to the point of the last log backup, but without point-in-time recovery. Full allows you to recover to a point in time, as long as it is covered by a complete backup. Carefully choose the recovery model for each database, balancing the amount of data you can lose with the amount of space required for backups.

For each database, you'll need to decide the type of backup to be performed, and on what schedule. A full backup will contain all the data in the database. A differential backup will capture any changes made since the last full backup. A transaction log backup, applicable only to Full or Bulk-logged databases, contains all log records not in a previous backup.

Deciding where to save your backups is another consideration. Saving backups to the same storage as the data and log files is not recommended. First, there will be heavy I/O operations as SQL Server reads the data and writes it to the backup. Second, if there is a drive failure in that storage array, you will lose both your database and your backup—the worst scenario! Saving the backups to the same server, but perhaps a different storage array, might be quick but doesn't offer much protection if there is an issue with the server. Saving to a different location on the network, such as a file server, offers a good mix of speed and safety, as the likelihood of two servers going down at the same time is less. An offsite backup is best, and it is common to back up the file server to tape and then ship the tapes off site.

Once you have determined the recovery model for your database and selected the location to save the files, you can set the schedule, mixing in full, differential, and log backups as necessary.

## Restores

Backing up your databases is the first step in a disaster recovery plan, but realize there is no guarantee that the backup worked correctly every time. Disks and networks are still fallible. The second and equally important step is restoring the database so you know you can access your data if needed.

Where should you restore the database to test the validity of your backups? It might be tempting to restore it to the same instance. If there was an actual disaster, that is exactly what you would need to do. However, remember that this will increase the I/O load on the server and that might not be desirable. It's best to find a different, but identical or similar, server for the restore.

How often should you perform these restores? This is a question you will need to consider carefully. A mission-critical database that holds essential business information might need to be tested daily. On another database, it might be acceptable to do an actual restore one day a week and a RESTORE VERIFYONLY the other days.

You also want to ensure that you are restoring all the necessary files. If you are performing full and differential backups, make sure you are restoring both backups. If you have transaction log backups, make sure you can restore those also.

# Database Integrity

Despite anyone's best intentions, even with the writing of good code, regular backups, and periodic restores, data can be corrupted. It will happen to you, at some point in your career. You can be proactive by running DBCC CHECKDB.

This is a process that performs several steps to check the integrity of the data. The system catalogs are first checked for integrity. Then, allocation consistency checks are performed, followed by a check of tables, indexes, and views. Additional data may be checked, such as Service broker, indexed views, XML indexes, and spatial indexes. As a whole, this process makes sure the data is readable and usable.

How often you run this, and against which copy of your database, is something to be considered carefully. The larger your database becomes, the longer this task will take to run. The task is performed on a snapshot of the database, not the database itself, and the operation can take extra resources on the server. You may want to consider options such as creating a database snapshot on separate storage and running DBCC CHECKDB against that, or combining this task with the previous by restoring a backup on a secondary server, then running DBCC CHECKDB. However you go about it, it's vital to check the health of the database on a regular basis. This can easily be automated with a SQL Server Agent Job.

# Index Maintenance

SQL Server relies on indexes to efficiently find data and return it in queries. Properly applied indexes can greatly increase the performance of applications and reports. These are not something you can create and forget about, however. Proper maintenance is essential to make sure they continue to be of benefit.

Clustered indexes order data pages. As records are inserted, updated, or deleted, the amount of space taken up by a record can increase or decrease. This leads to additional pages inserted, and unused gaps on other pages. The logical ordering may not match the physical ordering of the pages. This is called fragmentation. Left unattended, fragmentation can cause queries to run slowly, affecting the performance of applications, and can result in calls to the DBA. By proactively monitoring index fragmentation and fixing it, you can reduce those calls.

To combat fragmentation, you want to perform index maintenance. You can reorganize or rebuild indexes. Reorganizing will physically reorder the leaf-level pages to match the logical order in order to fill unused areas and better use the space allocated. Rebuilding will drop the index and re-create it. During this operation, a lock is taken on the index. If the index is a clustered index, the table is unavailable for that time, unless you use the ONLINE option, which is only available in Enterprise edition. Rebuilding is much more intensive than reorganization, but will reclaim space as pages are compacted, and reordered. If you choose to rebuild indexes, you'll need to determine a maintenance window and schedule rebuilds to execute during that time. For example, if that window is Saturday at 2:00 am, you don't want to be responsible for logging into the server and starting a rebuild task. Again, automation is the key. (More information about indexes can be found in Chapter 7.)

You probably don't want to rebuild each index every time fragmentation is detected. Doing so can cause unnecessary amounts of work. First, establish what an unacceptable amount of fragmentation is for your indexes. Once you determine what an unacceptable level is, decide if you will reorganize or rebuild the index. You may even take a tiered approach by reorganizing indexes that are between A% and B% of fragmentation, and rebuilding those between B% and C% of fragmentation. Identify all the indexes that fall within each threshold and then perform maintenance on them as indicated by the thresholds you've set.

## Statistics Maintenance

Statistics go hand-in-hand with indexes. Statistics keep track of the distribution of data in a column. Essentially, they tell the query optimizer how many of each value are in a column. This helps the optimizer pick the best plan for a query. As data is added, updated, and deleted, the distribution of data, and thus the statistics about the data, changes.

SQL Server can maintain the statistics automatically. One of the database settings you can choose is AUTO UPDATE STATISTICS. If this is set, once the number of changes to a column reaches the threshold set by the database engine, statistics are updated. However, if you want more control over this, you can schedule a job to execute commands that you provide, that run on the schedule that you set, and that update statistics in the ways that you wish.

The UPDATE STATISTICS command in SQL Server allows you to specify how many rows you want scanned as a sample, in either a number or a percentage. You can update statistics for an entire table, or only one statistic on the table. The stored procedure sp_updatestats will update out-of-date statistics for all tables in a database. There are some drawbacks to the command and the procedure, such as query plans recompiling, so they are best used with caution.

# Conclusion

There are many opportunities for you to automate SQL Server administration tasks, and many tools with which to do so. Automating gives you many benefits such as preventing problems, working faster, being proactive, being more productive, scaling your environment, and cost savings. With a goal in mind, you can set out a plan to automate your environment, implement it, and measure the results.

# CHAPTER 11

■ ■ ■

# The Fluid Dynamics of SQL Server Data Movement

## By Wendy Pastrick

One of my favorite tasks as a database administrator (DBA) is configuring and administering solutions that get data from one place to another. Very early in my career, I was fortunate to work in an environment where we had to replicate data all over the globe. Supporting a system where I was responsible for data redundancy across seven major geographic hubs was very exciting, and it was a new challenge for me to tackle. Only later did I realize moving data is seen as a daunting task to many. Over the years, I have seen how the need for data replication has become more widespread

Since I started with Microsoft SQL Server, I have used numerous methods to achieve data redundancy. However, what I do depends on the task I am trying to accomplish. Is the copy of data for reporting? High availability? Disaster recovery? In this chapter, I will give practical advice on how to choose the right feature to get your data from point A to point B based on my experience, and I will let you know about the pros and cons of each method as well.

## Why the Need for Replicating Data?

The need to have multiple copies of the same data in more than one place is ever-increasing. Companies both large and small are bombarded from all directions with requests for access to their data stores from both internal and external users. Everyone wants to see the data, and they want to see the data as quickly as possible. Often, that data needs to be current and clean. Here is a short list of reasons why an organization might need replicas of its data:

- To use production data in development, test, or staging

- To move data closer to users—geographical displacement

- To satisfy reporting needs

- To process data before it goes into production

- For high availability (HA)

- For disaster recovery (DR)

This list is, of course, not comprehensive, and I'm sure you can come up with a few additional scenarios that are not shown here and specific to your company's needs. The point is that there is a lot more to data replication than just having copies for HA or DR. Although those are the most common reasons people have redundant copies of data elsewhere, the other reasons might be just as important.

For example, if your company has its own team of developers, there will be at least one development environment in your datacenter, and possibly others for testing, quality assurance, or pre-production release reviews. As a database administrator, you will be responsible for refreshing this data on some type of scheduled basis. I have seen everything from yearly to nightly refreshes, and even the need for on-demand capabilities.

How about overcoming issues with latency in data retrieval? There have been two key jobs where I worked for global companies, and both had similar issues with geographically dispersed offices maintaining current data stores locally. While both companies worked with replication models to distribute their data, they each went about it in completely different ways. For both companies, though, the key was to have the data physically closer to the users to ease the long synchronization times associated with connecting to a single data store that could be on the other side of the world.

A similar problem occurs when many users are attempting to create or run reports against a single data store. Too many connections simultaneously trying to access the same pieces of information can result in apparent latency issues for your users. Additionally, if your company allows ad-hoc reporting or has departments that access your databases through Microsoft Excel or Access data sources, you cannot control any bad querying of the data. One poorly written query can have a serious impact on your system. In this case, having a copy of the data available for those reports that are not using the same system resources as the true production source could alleviate much of that resource contention.

What do you do if you need to run batch processes against your data, but you need to ensure there is no negative impact on your daily business functions? You might choose to set up a secondary copy of your data to test the effect of the batch processes before pushing those changes to production.

Before I move on, let me say a few words about high availability and disaster recovery. A highly available system is one that is ready to use as instantly as possible with as little data loss as possible in the event of a single hardware failure. Some of the technologies I will describe here are great for providing highly available systems. Disaster recovery, on the other hand, is your company's contingency plan in the event of a major disaster. Think of earthquakes, atom bomb explosions—the types of events we pray never come to pass but could knock out entire communities, or your entire facility. If faced with a true disaster situation, could your company still recover and be back up and running in a matter of hours, days, or weeks? I will leave discussions about planning for those types of contingencies to other sources, because they are quite complex. One thing is guaranteed, though, and that is the fact you will need to account for a replica of your core data stores in the event of a disaster.

Let's examine a few scenarios that illustrate the need for different data-distribution implementations.

> **SCENARIO 1: Global Organization**    Consulting Firms R Us is a global professional services company. They have a headquarters in Chicago, Illinois (USA) with two datacenters. One is located onsite at their main facility, and the other is in Columbus, Ohio (USA) at a co-hosting facility. They have business offices across the globe in Mexico City, Rio de Janeiro, Sydney, Tokyo, Istanbul, London, and Johannesburg. Worldwide, business operations must be online 24 hours a day, with a short available outage window on Saturday mornings.

> **SCENARIO 2: High-Volume Reporting Needs**    The firm has several databases that are accessed for reports. A number of users attempting to query these databases concurrently are causing issues with data access.

**SCENARIO 3: Overnight Processing Jobs**   With a particularly large database, taking a nightly backup has started to cause issues with overnight processing jobs. These jobs are critical to starting business the next morning and are required to finish before the employees arrive at 8 a.m.

**SCENARIO 4: Hardware Failure**   The main database server has failed due to a hardware issue. The vendor, while providing prompt service, cannot guarantee a subsequent failure without upgrading to the newest hardware it offers. Everything appears to be running smoothly, but having more than just the nightly backup to rely upon is now a number 1 priority.

# SQL Server Solutions

Without having a clear understanding of the technology you want to use, it is easy to work yourself into trouble. SQL Server provides a variety of options for data replication. Shown here are various methods available to you just by using the product:

- Replication
  - Snapshot
  - Transactional
  - Peer-to-Peer
  - Merge
- Log shipping
- Database mirroring
  - Asynchronous
  - Synchronous
- AlwaysOn (requires Windows Server Failover Cluster)
  - Availability groups
  - Failover cluster instance (FCI)
- Custom ETL (Extract, Transform, Load) using SQL Server Integration Services
- Bulk copy process (BCP)

Each of these methods has certain benefits and limitations compared to the others, and certain ones are better suited to different needs. The flexibility gained by having so many choices can be daunting. Once you are familiar with the strengths of each, it becomes easier to determine which is best for the purpose at hand.

The sections that follow provide descriptions of each option, along with the benefits offered by each. Also covered are some potential hurdles you should be aware of with a given solution. Keep in mind as you read, though, that nothing is ever "set and forget." You will always need to monitor and tune as your servers continue to support your company's applications.

# Replication

Many data professionals, upon hearing the word "replication," get a wary look and start moving away from you. I have yet to understand why people can be so antireplication—unless they haven't worked with it since SQL Server version 6.5 "back in the day." Today's options for using SQL Server replication cover a wide variety of scenarios and offer a lot of flexibility.

---

■ **Note**   In general, replication involves three players: the publisher, the distributor, and one or more subscribers.

---

The main use for replication is for redundancy and geographic distribution of data. There is no tenet for failing over services or applications when using replication. However, subscribers can be used to support outages of other subscribers when needed.

## Snapshot

Just as the name implies, a snapshot is a point-in-time picture of the data. The snapshot method can be good for making quick copies that do not need to be updated frequently. Snapshots are typically used to initialize other replication topologies, but they can also be useful for creating mainly read-only copies of an entire database. The process is comparable to a backup/restore operation that runs on a scheduled basis—for example, daily, weekly, or monthly.

---

■ **Note**   Snapshot replication uses the same topology as transactional replication, which is described in the next section.

---

If you decide to implement snapshot replication, the size of the data being replicated is a paramount concern. If the amount of data is too large and takes a long time to replicate to the subscribers, the frequency of snapshots should be limited significantly.

## Transactional

Picture a three-ring circus consisting of a publisher database, distribution database (DB), and at least one subscriber database, all brought together with the use of the SQL Server Agent as the ringmaster. (Figure 11-1 illustrates the topology.) There are several options for configuring transactional replication that make this solution scalable by parceling off each component. Another strength of this solution is that you can choose to replicate portions of your data, whether it's a single table, a few columns in a table, or even a subset of data from a table.

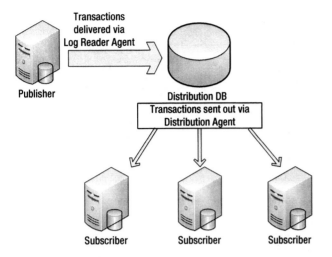

**Figure 11-1.** *Transactional replication.*

Additionally, you can have multiple subscriber databases, so you have the ability to create many copies of the data and keep them synchronized with the data from the publisher. By using stored procedures to apply data changes, you can gain even greater flexibility because you can create your own custom logic if needed.

Another win here is the option to not only pass along data changes, but also pass along changes to the objects themselves. Data Definition Language (DDL) changes to tables, views, stored procedures, and so on can also be replicated. Multiple databases can be set up as publishers, subscribers, or both on any given server.

In the transactional replication setup, data changes are made at the publisher database. Then the transaction details are sent to the distribution database, which in turn sends those changes to all of the subscriber databases. SQL Server Agent jobs called *log readers* facilitate the collection and delivery of transactions.

The benefits include the following:

- Flexibility in the topology so that you can use it in a wide variety of environments

- Customizability through the implementation of stored procedures for insert, update, and delete transactions

- Ability of the distribution agent to push changes out to subscribers, or to allow each subscriber to have its own distribution agent to pull changes from the distribution database

- Availability in all versions of SQL Server

- Table-level data replication, with options for partitioning and filtering

- Ability for a subscriber to have a completely different set of data replicated to it

The limitations include the following:

- Every table included in a replication topology must have a Primary Key defined.

- There is potential for varied degrees of latency due to network traffic or significant or frequent data changes.

## Peer-to-Peer

In the peer-to-peer topology, all database servers—referred to as *nodes*—act as both publishers and subscribers. The distribution agents facilitate the delivery of all changes to all nodes, essentially making peer-to-peer a hybrid of transactional and merge replication.

There is an option for conflict detection. If conflict detection is enabled, conflicts are handled at the distribution database and will cause a failure of the distribution agent until the conflict has been manually resolved.

The benefits of peer-to-peer replication are the following:

- Can be useful in load-balancing architectures

- Possibility to fail over to any node (application level)

The price you pay is that you have to deal with a somewhat longer list of limitations:

- Every table included in a replication topology must have a Primary Key defined.

- Row and column partitioning is not supported.

- Snapshots cannot be used for the initialization of a new node.

- Conflict detection requires manual intervention.

- The recommended setup is to have only one node updateable due to conflict-detection intervention.

- Peer-to-peer replication is an Enterprise edition–only feature.

## Merge

Merge is the granddaddy of the replication topologies (shown in Figure 11-2), allowing updates of the data to originate from any source (publisher or subscriber). These updates are then consolidated by the publisher. By using conflict-resolution rules, the publisher ultimately determines the state of each data point and then replicates those to other subscribers. Instead of log readers, merge replication uses table triggers and system tables plus the merge agent, which tracks table changes and then logs actions to the distributor.

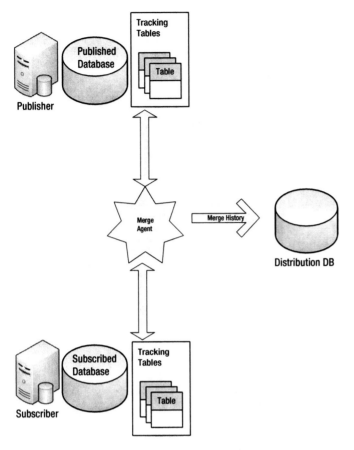

*Figure 11-2. Merge replication.*

So what is the difference between peer-to-peer and merge replication, then? The key is in conflict detection and management. With peer-to-peer replication, the entire distribution process is halted until someone manually resolves the conflict. With merge replication, custom business rules for resolving conflicts can be implemented without any interruption of service.

Merge replication provides numerous benefits:

- It is ideal for use in systems where you are working with point of sale (POS) data or a remote sales force.

- Conflict detection does not cause any interruption of service.

- Synchronizations can be pushed out to subscribers, or subscribers can pull from the publisher.

- You can perform table-level data replication, with options for partitioning and filtering.

- Each subscriber can have a completely different set of data replicated to it.

Yet you cannot completely escape limitations, such as the following:

- Each table participating in merge replication must have a globally unique identifier (GUID) value for each record.

- Subscriptions that expire require full reinitialization, which can be time consuming.

## Replication Examples

Following are examples of how replication can be applied to the four scenarios introduced earlier in the chapter:

**SCENARIO 1: Global Organization**    This is a good scenario for replication. Choose one server as the publisher (transactional replication)—let's say Chicago—and set up each other city as a subscriber. Data can be shared among all of the major hubs. You can implement a peer-to-peer setup that allows data updates from any major city. You can use merge replication to manage data updates from any of the subscribers.

**SCENARIO 2: High-Volume Reporting Needs**    Consider the reporting requirements first. If up-to-the-minute data is needed for reporting, transactional replication could be a good fit. Another bonus to having a subscriber copy of the database is that you can set up different indexing strategies on each subscriber, thereby giving you the ability to performance tune for individual reporting needs. Alternatively, peer-to-peer replication can be configured with only one node updateable, allowing for read-only access at a given node and no possibility for conflicts to occur.

**SCENARIO 3: Overnight Processing Jobs**    If your subscribers are exact copies of your publisher, replication might help out here. Ensure that all objects in the database are identical (table definitions, indexing, stored procedures—everything!), and set your backups to run against a subscriber. Your doing so will enable the overnight processing to run against the publisher, and replication will then distribute any changes made to the subscriber or subscribers. Alternatively, peer-to-peer replication can be configured with only one node updateable , allowing backups to be performed on the nonupdateable node.

**SCENARIO 4: Hardware Failure**    Replication is not ideal in the case of a hardware failure. Having said that, if you have multiple subscribers and one of those fails, you might be able to use a second subscriber in its place until the first one is recovered. Your application will need to be configured to have that flexibility of connecting to an alternate subscriber. If, however, you lose your publisher, replication will not help. Peer-to-peer replication is an option here, and it can be useful as long as your application can easily switch to using another node and all nodes are updateable.

# Log Shipping

A log-shipping solution (shown in Figure 11-3) involves taking transaction log backups of a primary database, copying them, and applying them to a secondary database located on another server. The SQL Server Agent services on the primary and secondary servers manage the process flow of backups, file copy, and restore. There is a mandatory delay between when the backup is taken on the primary and when it is then applied to the secondary. At a minimum, this delay is the time it takes for the backup operation to complete and the file copy to occur before the restore operation begins. The delay prior to a restore can be configured for specific time intervals—for example, 15 minutes, 2 hours, and so forth.

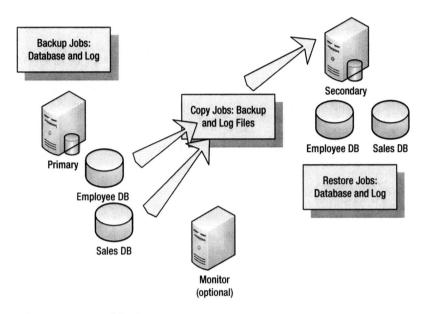

**Figure 11-3.** *Log shipping.*

There are several benefits to implementing log shipping. First, you can copy the logs to multiple destinations, much like having multiple subscribers in replication. Second, the secondary database or databases can be used for read-only activity when the logs are not being actively applied. Finally, the delay in applying the transaction log backups on the secondary database can allow for data recovery in the event of a mass data update or a delete applied accidentally. An optional monitor instance can be used to detect any failures in the log backup/delivery/restore process and send out a notification of the need for a failover.

Log shipping is most often used for disaster-recovery scenarios, because the built-in latency is often not desired for other data-replication needs.

Benefits from log shipping include the following:

- Multiple secondaries are allowed.

- Limited, read-only use of secondary databases is allowed.

- The entire database is sent to the other instance.

The limitations include the following:

- A database cannot be used while log files are being restored.

- Failover to a secondary database is a manual process.

- There is no support for partitioning or filtering data.

Following are examples of how replication can be applied to the four scenarios:

**SCENARIO 1: Global Organization**  Log shipping will not help distribute the data across the globe for daily use. Because the database will be repeatedly taken offline to apply log backups, even having a read-only copy in each of the major cities would not be of any benefit. However, if you need read-only activity during an upgrade or outage window, you might want to set up log shipping and perform a role change for your applications to the secondary database while performing maintenance. This is not a perfect solution, but it could provide some uptime for users globally.

**SCENARIO 2: High-Volume Reporting Needs**  Log shipping might be useful here. There would need to be a more sizable delay in applying the log backups to the secondary database, however. For example, if a secondary is set up to apply logs only once or twice per day (perhaps at 7 a.m. and 7 p.m.), the times when users are accessing the data will not be interrupted. Data will be up to 12 hours old, depending on when it is accessed.

**SCENARIO 3: Overnight Processing Jobs**  Log shipping is not a viable option for distributing the load because of the high-volume tasks.

**SCENARIO 4: Hardware Failure**  In the event of a hardware failure, log shipping can be useful but should not be seen as a permanent solution. The primary should be repaired or rebuilt as needed. While this is in process, the secondary database can be brought online and fully recovered. At this point, it will no longer be secondary. The application using the database needs to be configured to access the new database source. Once the primary database is ready to be brought back online, the secondary database can be backed up and restored to the primary database. Log shipping needs to be reconfigured and restarted so that it can be ready for the next failover occurrence.

# Database Mirroring

Database mirroring has a tendency to be confused with log shipping (I still can't figure out why), but really it has nothing in common with log shipping. The use of mirroring takes you back to applying changes at the transaction level; however, unlike replication, the transactions are batched together and applied as quickly as possible without the use of a distributor. With mirroring, there is a single principal server and there can only be a single mirror server. An optional witness server also can be used to verify communication to both the principal and the mirror.

If you are looking to implement some type of data replication in your environment—and you have a shiny, new installation of SQL Server 2012—I would not recommend setting up database mirroring. This feature has been deprecated and eventually will not be available in future versions of the product. The upgrade is to convert a mirroring configuration to an AlwaysOn availability group.

If you currently need to support mirroring in a SQL Server 2008 or 2008 R2 version that will be upgraded to 2012, there is no problem with keeping mirroring in place. Remember when a technology is deprecated, you have a grace period in which to make changes and plan for replacements. But having that grace period doesn't mean you should continue to encourage the use of the deprecated feature for new systems!

The single-most important feature of mirroring is the ability to easily fail over when communication to the primary database is lost or interrupted. Additionally, with the options for data "safety," you can control the amount of potential data loss on failover. Following are the two options:

**High-Performance Mode (Asynchronous)**   Transactions are batched up and applied on the mirror as they come in. There is the possibility on failover that some transactions have not yet been applied on the mirror. This option is available only with the Enterprise edition.

**High-Safety Mode (Synchronous)**   Transactions are applied to the mirror before being committed to the primary. The ensures no data is lost on failover. There is a potential for latency when using synchronous mode. With high-safety mode, you can also have automatic failover if a witness server is configured.

The benefits from mirroring include the following:

- Compression when delivering the transactions

- The entire database is mirrored.

- There is support for automatic failover.

- On failover, the roles of the principal and mirror are swapped.

- No data loss occurs with synchronous mirroring.

- Early detection of corruption in your database is possible.

The imitations form a rather long list this time:

- Mirroring requires the FULL recovery model.

- The mirror copy is not online and cannot be used until failover.

- There is no support for data partitions or filtering.

- Mirroring requires Transmission Control Protocol (TCP) endpoints for communication.

- Mirroring cannot support cross-database transactions or distributed transactions.

- You cannot mirror any system databases (for example, master, msdb, tempdb, or model).

- Mirroring's asynchronous option is only available only in the Enterprise edition.

- You might need to manually set applications to use the mirror in the event of failover.

Following is how you might benefit from mirroring in the four scenarios we've been considering so far in this chapter:

**SCENARIO 1: Global Organization**   Using mirroring here would not provide a benefit in terms of distributing the user load, because mirroring is more useful for HA/DR scenarios. Because the mirror database cannot be used until failover, only the principal is in use at any given time.

**SCENARIO 2: High-Volume Reporting Needs**   Much like Scenario 1, mirroring is of limited use here. Having said that, I have seen setups that use mirroring, coupled with log shipping on top of the mirror instance, to provide users with a read-only copy of the database.

**SCENARIO 3: Overnight Processing Jobs**    Mirroring will not provide any benefit in this scenario, because the mirror is not accessible for data reads or writes.

**SCENARIO 4: Hardware Failure**    Here is where mirroring can shine. If a hardware failure happens, failover is immediate. Applications might still need manual intervention to point to the new data source, however, depending upon how those applications are designed. Once the failover condition has been cleared, failing the database back over to the principal is simple.

---

■ **Note**    In Scenario 4, failover is immediate when synchronous mirroring is used. Asynchronous mirroring brings the possibility of delay while the target database clears the redo queue.

---

# AlwaysOn

"AlwaysOn" is an umbrella term that covers two features are in SQL Server 2012:

- Availability groups
- Failover clustering instance (FCI)

## Availability Groups

Availability groups (shown in Figure 11-4) incorporate the best of database mirroring, but they are enhanced beyond that. Availability groups require that the servers hosting the SQL Server instances are part of a Windows Server Failover Cluster (WSFC). SQL Server can also be installed as a standalone instance on a server in a WSFC with no shared storage requirement; it is not required to be a failover cluster instance (FCI) to implement availability groups. To review all of the prerequisites needed for using AlwaysOn, see the documentation from Microsoft here: http://msdn.microsoft.com/en-us/library/ff878487.aspx.

Once you have installed a SQL Server instance and the AlwaysOn feature has been enabled, you can configure availability groups. Each availability group serves as a host to a number of user databases (availability databases) in a primary replica, and up to four additional secondary replicas can be configured, for a total of up to five replicas. This is different from mirroring, where only a single principal database can be configured to a single mirror.

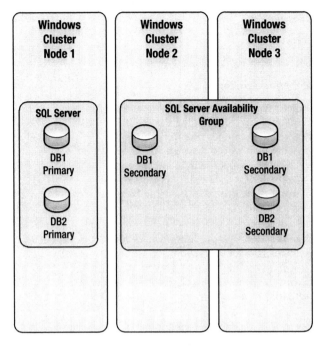

*Figure 11-4. AlwaysOn availability groups.*

The primary replica and all secondary replicas are kept in sync by a process called *data synchronization*, where the transaction log entries from the primary are applied to each secondary. Each database in the availability groupwill have its own data-synchronization process. Data is not synchronized for the entire availability group, but for each individual database. As with mirroring, synchronization can be synchronous or asynchronous per database. Recall that with synchronous replicas, latency might occur while the primary replica database waits for the secondary replica database transaction to be committed. Unlike mirroring, secondary replicas can be configured for read-only access and can also be used to support full (copy-only) or transaction log backups.

In the event of a failover, one of the secondary replicas will become the primary and the original primary replica will become a secondary. There can only be one primary replica for any given availability group. All databases in a replica will be failed over together.

One of the biggest benefits of availability groups is that you have the ability to configure a *listener name*, which acts as a single point of entry for applications that stays the same name no matter where it lives (which is always where the primary replica is). As with an FCI, this allows applications to not worry about connecting after a failover to a different name.

Benefits include the following:

- Availability groups allow for more than one database to fail over as a group if they are configured that way.

- Automatic failover can be configured.

- Secondary replicas can be configured for read-only access by users and applications.

- Secondary replicas can be used for some backup operations.

Limitations are the following:

- Availability groups are an Enterprise edition feature.

- They require endpoints for communication.

- Availability groups cannot be used for server instance-level protection.

You can apply availability groups to our four scenarios as follows:

**SCENARIO 1: Global Organization**   Availability groups can be used to enable particular offices to connect to read-only secondary copies of the database. However, there might still be significant issues with latency due to the time it takes for the data request and delivery to occur as it would be in any dispersed scenario. Think of this scenario as having three copies of the data in Chicago, and everyone still has to connect to Chicago to access the data. In countries where the network infrastructure is poor, availability groups provide no help with problematic access.

**SCENARIO 2: High-Volume Reporting Needs**   Here is a possible case for using availability groups. Allowing reporting tools to connect to a specific secondary database could alleviate database contention, but it might impact that replica's ability to meet specific RTO and RPO needs. If separate indexing strategies are needed for data retrieval, however, that would not be supported.

**SCENARIO 3: Overnight Processing Jobs**   Another possible case for using availability groups. Backup procedures could be pointed at a secondary database for full (copy-only) and transaction log backup while processing continues to occur on the primary database. Differential backups on a secondary database are not supported. Find complete information on support for backups on a secondary replica here: *http://msdn.microsoft.com/en-us/library/hh245119.aspx.*

**SCENARIO 4: Hardware Failure**   Availability groups can be used to failover in this situation. Much like mirroring, when an issue with the primary replica is detected, failover to one of the secondaries can take place. Unlike mirroring, no manual intervention is needed to redirect your application if you configure a listener name and your application uses the right client utilities. If you want the highest protection, you can combine availability groups with FCIs.

# Failover Clustering

SQL Server can be installed as a clustered instance that runs on top of a Windows Server Failover Cluster (shown in Figure 11-5). It provides instance-level protection and automatic failover to another node due to how the underlying Windows clustering feature works. An FCI is not a solution that provides a redundant copy of the data; there is only one copy of the data for databases in an FCI. The databases are then stored on a shared-storage solution such as a storage area network (SAN).

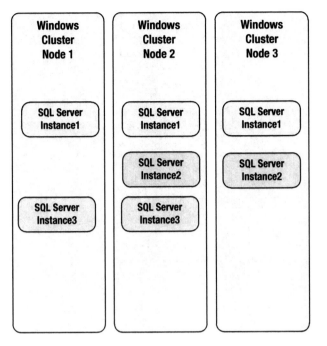

*Figure 11-5. AlwaysOn failover clustering.*

Failover can happen in a variety of circumstances, but the two most common scenarios are service or hardware failures and loss of quorum. Failures in services and issues with hardware are fairly obvious: the service or the hardware experiences a fatal failure and cannot recover. Loss of quorum can be a bit more confusing, but it boils down to answering this question: Are a majority of the servers in the cluster actually functioning? If the answer is yes, the cluster continues to run. If the answer is no, the entire cluster can go offline. This is certainly not a preferred state, and the configuration of your cluster should consider a loss of quorum situation.

The benefits from failover clustering include the following:

- For high-availability, failover clustering is one of the best features SQL Server has to offer.

- Failover clustering in SQL Server 2012 supports the multisubnet feature of WSFC and does not require a virtual local area network (VLAN) like in previous versions.

- The entire SQL Server instance is protected in event of a hardware or service failure.

- You get fast and automatic failover from the use of shared storage.

The imitations are as follows:

- Additional hardware resources are needed for multiple nodes.

- You need to work closely with other teams—such as teams working with storage, security, and network—to configure and support the Windows Server Failover Cluster.

- Loss of quorum in a WSFC can result in everything going down, which would then require manual intervention.

And following are some examples of how failover clustering might be applied in our four scenarios:

**SCENARIO 1: Global Organization**    An FCI is intended for recovery from a hardware failure, so it will not cover a globally dispersed scenario. Although you can span multiple data centers with an FCI configuration, it still does not provide the data redundancy. The data redundancy needed to be able to switch between data centers underneath the cluster is provided by a storage-based solution.

**SCENARIO 2: High-Volume Reporting Needs**    An FCI is intended for recovery from a hardware failure. It provides no redundancy of data. An FCI can house a reporting database, but typical methods to make it scale need to be employed.

**SCENARIO 3: Overnight Processing Jobs**    Similar to Scenario 2, an FCI can be used for batch processing, but it would be a database in an instance—nothing more, nothing less.

**SCENARIO 4: Hardware Failure**    Install SQL Server on a Windows Server Failover Cluster to provide immediate failover in this situation.

# Custom ETL Using SQL Server Integration Services

SQL Server Integration Services (SSIS) is an incredibly powerful tool in the SQL Server stack, allowing for the utmost flexibility in creating processes for moving or copying data from one source to another. Commonly called *ETL processing* (Extract, Transform, Load), SSIS is most often used for loading data warehouses. Through the use of custom control-flow and data-flow tasks, any data source can be copied or moved to another location. Business logic can also be used to limit or change the data in any way needed.

If you have ever used the Data Import/Export Wizard in SQL Server Management Studio and saved the package at the end, you have created an SSIS package. The interface for working with SSIS is either Microsoft Visual Studio or Business Intelligence Development Studio (BIDS), a lighter weight version of Visual Studio. By using a single control flow that can branch out into multiple data-flow tasks, you take a dataset from its original format and location, massage the data to get it to look the way it needs to, and then save it in a new location.

The benefits are that Integration Services does the following:

- Provides for the highest level of customization

- Incorporates business logic if needed

- Allows secondary databases to be made available for use

Its limitations are these:

- You must rely on manual scheduling for execution.

- Integration Services might require extended development resources for design, coding, and testing.

- No troubleshooting or maintenance tools are included.

Following are ways you can apply custom ETL solutions developed using Integration Services to our four scenarios:

**SCENARIO 1: Global Organization** Creating a customized ETL for global distribution can be a tedious project. If your satellite offices require only copies of the data, or subsets of the data, replication is likely a better option. However, if your offices need data that is based on the data at the primary location, but not the raw data itself, an SSIS project might be worthwhile.

**SCENARIO 2: High-Volume Reporting Needs** Depending on the types of reports being run, you might want to create aggregate tables in a separate data store to support those. A custom ETL can be created to build a set of aggregations on a secondary server. Moving this data manipulation to a server with its own storage and memory capacity could make tedious reports much more accessible.

**SCENARIO 3: Overnight Processing Jobs** Custom ETL will not alleviate resource contention in this case.

**SCENARIO 4: Hardware Failure** Custom ETL would not be of any use in the event of a service or hardware failure.

# Bulk Copy Process

Bulk Copy Process (BCP) is a utility that enables data to be copied from a data source to or from a file. Run at the command line, simple parameters are enabled to state the source and destination locations for the data. Optional use of a format file can be added to map the source and target more easily.

Let's say you have a table with a million rows and 200 columns and you need to move that data somewhere or share it with multiple users rather quickly. Or maybe you have 50 tables that need to be shared and their combined data size is in the hundreds of Gigabytes. How will you get that data distributed? For initial loads, BCP is often a viable option when dealing with large amounts of data.

Using BCP is simple. You create and execute a BCP command at either the target or the source, depending on whether you are creating a data file for export or importing a data file. A host of options are available to customize the processing, including the ability to indicate a query for a subset of data from a table.

The benefits of using BCP include

- Simple, command-line execution

- Provision for reading and generating XML and text formats for ease in mapping data fields

Its limitations are

- A BCP command applies to a single table only.

- Manual mapping is required if you're not using a format file.

- No troubleshooting or maintenance tools are included.

Following are ways in which to apply BCP in our four scenarios:

**SCENARIO 1: Global Organization** If satellite offices require subsets of the data only on an occasional basis, BCP might be an option for transferring those limited datasets. Data files for export could be created on a scheduled basis (ex: weekly) and offices could import those files as needed. BCP is used under the covers for applying snapshots in replication.

**SCENARIO 2: High-Volume Reporting Needs**   BCP would not help in this scenario.

**SCENARIO 3: Overnight Processing Jobs**   BCP would not help in this scenario.

**SCENARIO 4: Hardware Failure**   Although BCP would not provide any help in the event of a service or hardware failure, it could be used to create files for all tables in a database. Those files could be used to "restore" the data for any table, but a format file for each table would also need to be used.

# Choosing the Right Deployment

There will be times when one solution seems to be the perfect fit for the needs of your company or process, and you have the resources at hand to implement it easily. Treasure those times! More often, there will be compromises and concessions that need to be made along the way. I have seen it happen that management decides it needs one implementation, but in reality, once all of the requirements and resources have been laid out, it turns out a different implementation is needed.

Tables 11-1a and 11-1b—actually, one table split into two in order to fit onto the page—can help you decide which approach to take in a situation in which data needs to be replicated to or from another database. Choose your database edition and the features you need in the left column. Look for occurrences of "Yes" in the other columns to help you identify which of the solutions talked about in this chapter will cover your needs.

*Table 11-1a. Replication Decision Factors, Part 1*

| | Replication | | | | |
|---|---|---|---|---|---|
| | **Transactional** | **Peer-to-Peer** | **Merge** | **Custom ETL** | **BCP** |
| SQL Express Edition | Subscriber only | | Subscriber Only | Yes | Yes |
| SQL Standard Edition | Yes | | Yes | Yes | Yes |
| SQL Enterprise Edition | | Yes | | Yes | Yes |
| SQL BI Edition | | | | Yes | Yes |
| Scope: | | | | | |
|   Table | Yes | Yes | Yes | Yes | Yes |
|   Database | Yes | Yes | Yes | Yes | Yes |
|   Instance | | | | | |
| Partition Support (Columns) | Yes | | Yes | Yes | Yes |
| Filtering Support (Values) | Yes | | Yes | Yes | Yes |
| Copies available for read-only | Yes | Yes | Yes | Yes | Yes |
| Copies available for write or read | Yes* | Yes | Yes | | |

| | Replication | | | | |
| | Transactional | Peer-to-Peer | Merge | Custom ETL | BCP |
|---|---|---|---|---|---|
| Conflict Detection | | Yes | Yes | | |
| Immediate Failover | | | | | |
| Monitoring | Yes | | | | |

*It is possible to have updateable subscribers in a transactional replication.

*Table 11-1b. Replication Decision Factors, Part 2*

| | Log Shipping | Mirroring | AlwaysOn Availability Groups | Failover Cluster Instance |
|---|---|---|---|---|
| SQL Express Edition | | | | |
| SQL Standard Edition | | | | |
| SQL Enterprise Edition | | | | |
| SQL BI Edition | | | | |
| Scope: | | | | |
| Table | | | | |
| Database | Yes | Yes | Yes | |
| Instance | | | | Yes |
| Partition Support (Columns) | | | | |
| Filtering Support (Values) | | | | |
| Copies available for read-only | Yes | | Yes | |
| Copies available for write or read | | | | |
| Conflict Detection | | | | |
| Immediate Failover | Yes | Yes | Yes | Yes |
| Monitoring | Yes | Yes | | Yes |

The key to a successful deployment is to ensure all parties involved have bought in and signed off on the requirements and the process to be used to achieve the goal. Problems arise when managers or executives are expecting one thing and they end up with something different. Managing those individual expectations will go a long way toward a successful deployment. Additionally, verify that all key personnel understand what the process implemented will actually be doing. If you have spent a considerable sum of money setting up a Windows Failover Cluster with SQL, and management expects to have a second copy of the data ready for reporting, you are going to have a lot of explaining to do later.

Keep in mind the following:

> **Edition of SQL Server**  Several features are available only with the Enterprise edition, which incurs greater licensing costs than the Standard edition.

> **Latency**  Determine whether or not latency will negatively impact your system. In many cases, a copy of the data that is 15-minutes to 1-hour old might be more than sufficient for the business needs.

> **Overall goal**  When the needs of data redundancy are for high availability or disaster recovery, log shipping, mirroring, and failover clustering are more likely the place to begin building your implementation plan. When searching for load-balancing, reporting, or distributed systems solutions, replication or AlwaysOn availability groups might be better places to start.

Keep in mind that there are always situations in which management might choose to go with a choice you don't fully agree with or that you feel is suboptimal. Often, that is due to cost considerations, resource considerations, or both. For example, management might prefer to avoid the high cost of the Enterprise edition. Don't dig in your heels in these cases. Work with what you have.

# Keeping the Data Consistent

We've now created a picture of what each technology can do and have created a roadmap to help determine the best course of action. It's time to talk about keeping the resulting solution running smoothly.

First and foremost, you need to monitor your systems. Some features, such as replication, come with built-in monitoring tools. These can be a starting place for troubleshooting in the event of failures. Other features, however, have nothing unless you build it yourself—BCP, for example.

If you build an automated system, remember to include error-handling and notification mechanisms too. The worst thing that can happen to your environment is to discover hours or days later that your data was not in sync!

If you discover inconsistencies in your data, you need to be prepared to fix them quickly. Notifying your superiors and users is crucial to keeping the situation from spiraling out of control. Have a plan for communication in the event of failures. Timing is very important. Plan for fast communication ahead of time.

Let's go through our list once again and look at what is offered in terms of monitoring and recovery for each data-redundancy technology.

Monitoring and recovery options for replication include

- Monitoring
  - Replication Monitor
  - Custom Errors
- Recovery:
  - Re-apply failed transactions
  - Manually edit the data at the subscriber
  - Reinitialize

Also helpful are the articles "Monitoring Replication with System Monitor" and "Monitoring Replication," which you can read for information about using system tools in replication solutions. You'll find these on the Microsoft Developer Network website (*http://www.msdn.com*). Just search for their titles.

Options for log shipping are as follows:

- Monitoring

  - Notification upon failure of the Transaction Log backup

  - Notification upon failure of the Copy job

  - Notification upon failure of the Restore

- Recovery

  - Restart failed jobs

  - Manually apply log backups at the secondary

  - Reinitialize

Again, MSDN is your friend. See the MSDN article "Monitor Log Shipping" for a list of system tables and stored procedures you can use to help stay on top of log-shipping solutions.

For database mirroring, your options are the following:

- Monitoring

  - Notification upon failover

  - Performance counters (see http://technet.microsoft.com/en-us/library/ms189931.aspx)

- Recovery

  - GUI interface for failback

  - Reinitialize

The list is very short for AlwaysOn availability groups:

- Monitoring

  - The AlwaysOn dashboard in SQL Server Management Studio (SSMS)

  - Extended events

  - Windows PowerShell

- Recovery

  - Failover and failback of the primary replica

Custom ETL using SQL Server Integration Services offers the following options for monitoring and recovery:

- Monitoring

  - Scheduled ETL jobs can be configured to notify on failure.

  - Error handling in the package can be configured.

- Recovery

  - You might be able to manually correct data.

- Reinitialization could be complex.

And finally, for Bulk Copy Process (BCP), you have the following options:

- Monitoring

  - Scheduled BCP jobs can be configured to notify on failure.

  - More robust scripting can include some error handling.

- Recovery

  - When BCP fails on importing data, the entire batch is rolled back so that no data inconsistency can come from a partial load.

Keep in mind that you can take advantage of Extended Events and PowerShell to create your own custom monitoring. These two tools can actually be applied to any of the data-replication techniques described in this chapter.

# Conclusion

You might end up using one or more of the methods described in this chapter, or a combination of two or more. They all have their strengths. They all have drawbacks, too. If you plan well and communicate that plan to the right team members, you are well on your way to successful deployment. Make sure your senior managers also are aware of what the technology you choose can and cannot do. With their understanding, you are less likely to be asked later, "Why doesn't it do X? We thought it would do X."

---

▧ **Note**  Don't forget to use all of the valuable resources available to you, most are available for free on YouTube, Twitter, and many SQL Server support sites.

---

As with everything related to SQL Server, your mileage might vary because your experiences can be vastly different from mine. The examples provided here have all come from real-life scenarios I have had to support. They are not intended to be all encompassing, and even though my company went in one direction for a solution, yours might choose another. A few things are certain, though: the technology will continue to advance, and database administrators and developers will continue to find creative solutions using those tools.

# CHAPTER 12

■ ■ ■

# Windows Azure SQL Database for DBAs

## By Herve Roggero

Microsoft entered the cloud-computing space a few years ago with the vision to provide organizations a set of services they could use to build applications faster, with reduced maintenance requirements and with as much transparent scalability and availability as possible. As part of this vision, Microsoft created Windows Azure SQL Database (or SQL Database for short), a relational database service for the cloud, which delivers configuration-free high availability and scalability at a reasonable cost.

Although you can easily install and configure a full instance of SQL Server on virtual machines in the cloud, SQL Database is one of the most interesting cloud technologies because it provides many features of SQL Server and high availability without the burden of complex configuration settings. Think of SQL Database as a subset of SQL Server for the most part; I will explore some key differences and explain how this technology works throughout this chapter to give you a solid foundation to understand and manage this platform.

Before diving into the details of this technology, I should set an expectation upfront: SQL Database is not SQL Server in the cloud. This is perhaps the number one misconception about this technology and the source of much confusion about what SQL Database should and should not do. Because SQL Database instances run on shared hardware and infrastructure, SQL Database is a "one size fits all" environment from a configuration standpoint. For example, everyone gets a database that is fully redundant with 99.95 percent monthly availability, and everyone gets roughly the same share of computing resources on any given server. Conversely, no one can modify the disk subsystem, modify memory allocation, or have direct access to the physical server on which SQL Database instances are running.

So if there are no configuration options to worry about and, as a result, no hardware and database-level tuning options, why are we even discussing this technology at all in this book? Because, as a DBA, you will inevitably be asked about the capabilities of SQL Database at some point, how this technology could be leveraged by your organization, what its strengths and weaknesses are, and even possibly how to support it as part of your daily responsibilities. And as you will see in this chapter, there is no shortage of opportunities for businesses to leverage SQL Database.

> ■ **Note**   The formal name of this technology is *Windows Azure SQL Database*. However, for simplicity, I refer to it as *SQL Database* in this chapter. Also, a user database in SQL Database is referred to as a *SQL Database instance* .

# SQL Database Architecture

Let's first take a look at the SQL Database underlying architecture and discuss some of its implications. As you will see, SQL Database was designed as a cloud database, and not simply as a database in the cloud.

## Infrastructure

One of the primary drivers of this architecture is to favor availability and scalability rather than raw performance. When you connect to a SQL Database instance, you are in fact connecting through a layer of routers and proxies that will find the server on which your database is currently located. That's right, your database can move around from server to server. There is no way for you to know on which server your database is located; Microsoft reserves the right to move SQL Database instances around based on current workload requirements and other factors.

When an application connects to a SQL Database instance, the connection request first goes through a layer of gateways that route the connection request to the correct underlying server holding your database, as shown in Figure 12-1. The gateway has additional responsibilities, including security and protocol parsing.

From a security standpoint, the gateway determines if the connection request comes from an approved Internet Protocol (IP) address. Indeed, SQL Database comes with its own built-in IP firewall. If the connection comes from a client IP address that's not specifically authorized, the connection will be rejected. Also, if too many requests are coming in at the same time, the gateway might deny access to the database in an attempt to block Denial of Service (DoS) attacks.

If the connection is authorized, the gateway also parses the statement coming in to determine if a special command is coming through, such as CREATE DATABASE. Creating a new database is handled by another component within the SQL Database infrastructure because it impacts billing.

Once the connection is authorized and the T-SQL statements can be forwarded to the actual database, the proxy layer forwards the Tabular Data Stream (TDS) packets to the correct underlying SQL Server instance for processing.

You should also note that there is no physical master database available through SQL Database. Although you can connect to the master database and execute T-SQL statements, you actually are communicating with the proxy layer. As a result, the master database is read-only and removed from billing considerations. In fact, to create a new database, you must be connected to the master database; and to change firewall settings, you also need to be connected to the master database.

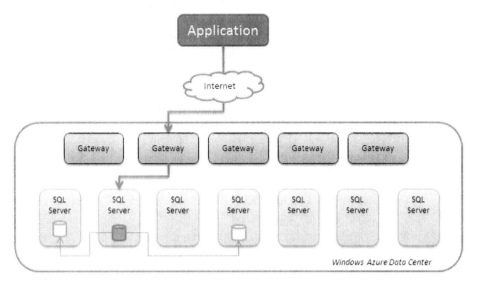

*Figure 12-1. Simplified SQL Database infrastructure and replication topology.*

## Availability and Failover

You might have noticed in Figure 12-1 that three databases are depicted in the diagram. The SQL Database instance you are connecting to is called the *primary instance*. To ensure high availability, every SQL Database instance is replicated to two other instances (called *secondary instances*). Every operation performed on a SQL Database instance involves a two-phase commit; at least one of the secondary instances must be successfully committed before the operation completes, which by nature slows down write access. This is an example of high availability taking precedence over pure performance.

Another implication of this architecture is that failing over is very quick and virtually transparent. Because each SQL Database continuously updates two copies of the primary instance, failing over in case of severe failure of the primary server can be performed very quickly; one of the secondary instances becomes the new primary instance. The proxy layer can detect the failover and redirect all new connection requests to the newly upgraded primary database. As you can imagine, applications need to account for connection loss and perform connection retries whenever necessary; for this and many other reasons, database connection retry logic is now part of normal coding practices in the cloud.

---

■ **Note**   The underlying SQL Database architecture gives Microsoft the liberty to roll out critical updates and enhancements virtually unnoticed.

---

## Hardware

You might wonder what the physical servers are made of, how much memory is available, and so on. At the time of this writing, each server is configured with 32 GB of RAM, 8 cores, and 12 disks. The server configuration is the same for all servers running SQL Database and even Windows Azure, making it easy for Microsoft to swap resources when needed.

As mentioned previously, this infrastructure is a shared environment, so you are effectively sharing the available resources on each machine with many other customers. Because your SQL Database instances are running on commodity hardware in a shared infrastructure, scaling applications up (by adding resources to the server) is not possible anymore. However, SQL Database is designed for scaling out with a feature called Federations. A federation is a set of SQL Database instances that work together to distribute data horizontally over multiple servers, similar to a shared-nothing configuration in which each resource has its own set of CPU, memory and disk subsystem. I will review federations in more detail later in this chapter.

# Differences with SQL Server

You now know that SQL Server is the underpinning technology of SQL Database. However, this doesn't mean SQL Database offers all of the features of SQL Server. Let's review the major differences between the two platforms.

## Database Components

SQL Database offers a limited subset of the components that make up a typical SQL Server installation. For example, SQL Server Integration Services is not included with SQL Database. However, you can connect to SQL Database using a locally installed copy of SQL Server Integration Services. So for the most part, although many of the components provided by SQL Server are not available in the cloud with SQL Database, you can use the ones installed on a local SQL Server installation and connect to a SQL Database instance in the cloud.

Table 12-1 shows a summary of the components supported in SQL Database. *Partially Supported* means that some or most of the features of the component can be used with SQL Database. *Not Included* means that there is no Windows Azure equivalent. *Included* means that there is a Windows Azure equivalent but the component itself can use SQL Database if needed. *Replaced* means that the component itself is not supported at all but Windows Azure offers an equivalent.

*Table 12-1. SQL Server component support in SQL Database*

| SQL Server Component | SQL Database |
|---|---|
| Relational Engine | Partially Supported |
| SQL Server Reporting Services | Included |
| SQL Agent | Not Included |
| SQL Server Integration Services | Not Included |
| SQL Server Analysis Services | Not Included |
| SQL Profiler | Not Supported |
| Replication | Replaced |

Windows Azure includes its own version of Reporting Services. The Windows Azure SQL Reporting service allows companies to deploy and manage reports in the cloud with high availability and scalability automatically configured. So you can either use a local SQL Server Reporting Service to connect to a SQL Database remotely or use the one provided as part of Windows Azure. However, if you use the Reporting service in Windows Azure, certain limitations apply. For example, the only data source supported from Windows Azure SQL Reporting is SQL Database.

Replication is not supported with SQL Database. However, another feature called Windows Azure SQL Data Sync offers a way to transfer data between two or more SQL Database instances and even between a SQL Server database and a SQL Database instance. Data changes can be propagated both ways.

# Management Platform

With SQL Server, you depend on SQL Server Management Studio (SSMS) to manage your databases. However, SQL Database comes with online tools to manage cloud databases. At the time of this writing, the Windows Azure Management Portal is used to provision databases and manage both Windows Azure SQL Reporting and Windows Azure SQL Data Sync. Because they are both part of the Windows Azure Management Portal, you do not need to log in again.

The SQL Database Management Portal (SDMP) is a bit different. Because it was built as a separate portal entirely, you do need to log in again even if you are already logged in to the Windows Azure Management Portal. There are links available from the Windows Azure Management Portal to access the database portal. The various portals and high-level security requirements are shown in Figure 12-2.

---

■ **Note**    Because Windows Azure is a fast-evolving platform, managing resources in Windows Azure continues to improve. At the time of this writing, a new Windows Azure Management Portal is available as a Preview and is also shown in Figure 12-2.

---

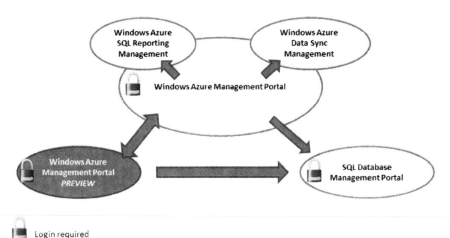

*Figure 12-2. Windows Azure portals.*

Table 12-2 presents a quick summary of the functions provided by each portal. Certain functions do not have a user interface yet, such as managing users and object-level security. For the time being, the functions that cannot be performed in the SQL Database Management Portal need to be performed in SSMS.

*Table 12-2. High-level functions performed by each portal*

| Portal | Functions Provided |
| --- | --- |
| Windows Azure Management | Create or drop a database. Manage firewall rules. View a database connection string. Export or import data. |
| Windows Azure SQL Reporting | Upload and manage reports. Manage user security. View log files. |
| Windows Azure SQL Data Sync | Create and manage data synchronization between databases. View log files. |
| SQL Database Management | Manage database objects (such as views, tables, and stored procedures). View database usage and poorly performing queries. Run T-SQL statements. View execution plans. Manage federations. |

You can also use SSMS to manage your SQL Database instances. As long as you adhere to the supported T-SQL syntax and use version 2008 R2 SP1 or higher, you can perform all the functions offered by the SQL Database Management Portal. You can check the SQL Database T-SQL reference on MSDN at http://msdn.microsoft.com/en-us/library/windowsazure/ee336281.aspx.

For example, to create a 5-GB SQL Database instance in SSMS, you would execute the following statement while connected to the master database:

```
CREATE DATABASE mydb1 (MAXSIZE=5GB)
```

## Security

When it comes to security, SQL Database provides only a few features, but they're important ones. However, at this time, SQL Database does not support certificates for encryption at rest. Although the lack of encryption of data at rest has been identified as a notable gap in the platform, this gap is currently unavoidable because you would need to give Microsoft all the keys necessary to decrypt the data.

Even when considering the limitation about encryption, SQL Database remains a very secure database and offers advanced security mechanisms, as listed in Table 12-3.

*Table 12-3. Summary of security features in SQL Database*

| Security Feature | Description |
| --- | --- |
| Database Login | The only authentication available against SQL Database is a database login. Network-level authentication is not currently available. |
| Hashing | The same level of hashing that SQL Server has is supported. |
| SSL Traffic | All traffic to a SQL Database is encrypted using Secure Sockets Layer (SSL) certificates. This security feature cannot be turned off. |
| Object-Level Security | All the traditional object-level security mechanisms are available on the objects supported by SQL Database, such as schema-level security. |
| Firewall | SQL Database comes with its own firewall that is configured in the master database. The firewall works before database authentication and prevents unwanted connections from IP addresses that are not authorized. |

# Other Important Information

So far, I outlined some key differences between SQL Server and SQL Database. There are a few additional things you need to know while we are on this topic.

## Database Sizes

SQL Database instances come in specific sizes that map to either the Web Edition or the Business Edition. For the time being, there is no functional difference between the editions; only the database sizes available under each edition vary, as enumerated in Table 12-4.

*Table 12-4. SQL Database maximum sizes by edition*

| SQL Database Edition | Database Max Sizes Available |
| --- | --- |
| Web Edition | 1 and 5 GB |
| Business Edition | 10, 20, 30, 40, 50, 100, and 150 GB |

## Database Version

If you check the version of a database, you will see that SQL Database is running as SQL Server 2012; however, if you check the compatibility mode of a database, you will soon realize that the database instance itself is running in SQL 2008 backward-compatibility mode. This means that while SQL Database is running on the SQL Server 2012 platform, it cannot use the new features of SQL Server 2012 at the moment. Nevertheless, a few programmability features specific to SQL Server 2012 are available in SQL Database, such as new date and time related functions (like DATEFROMPARTS, EOMONTH), new logical functions (IIF and CHOOSE), and a few more.

## Support for T-SQL

Although the vast majority of T-SQL operations are supported by SQL Database, there are a few notable exceptions and many limitations. Generally speaking, system views that can provide information from other customers located on the same server are not available, and neither are the statements that depend on hardware knowledge (such as the location of files) or features that are not available (such as the use of certificates and encryption). Because the list of these limitations is likely to change rapidly and is somewhat large, you should look on MSDN for the latest information about which statements are supported, partially supported, or not supported. Check out http://msdn.microsoft.com/en-us/library/windowsazure/ee336253 for the list of unsupported T-SQL statements.

## Backup and Restore

There are no backup and restore commands in the traditional sense in SQL Database. However, there are multiple ways to recover from the accidental loss of data that usually follows erroneous operations on a database, such as an accidental truncate operation. These options are shown in Table 12-5. Note that the Export/Import functionality does not offer transactional consistency unless the operation is performed on a copy of the original primary SQL Database instance.

*Table 12-5. Summary of data copy and restore operations that can be performed against a SQL Database instance*

| Operation | Transactional Consistency | Comment |
|---|---|---|
| COPY operation | Yes | Use the `CREATE DATABASE AS COPY OF` command to create a clone of a SQL Database instance. |
| Import/Export | No | Copies both the data and schema of a database to a blob so that they can be restored through the Import process. Certain limitations apply. |
| Point in Time Restore | Yes | Future capability of SQL Database that provides a point-in-time restore option. Certain limitations apply. |

▪ **Note**   The Point in Time Restore functionality is not yet available publicly at the time of this writing.

# Federations

As mentioned previously, SQL Database instances run on commodity hardware with virtually no hardware or environment configuration options. This makes a SQL Database instance a poor choice for applications and systems that have very demanding workloads and need a scale-up environment. However, you can scale with SQL Database, using a feature unavailable on SQL Server called *Federations*.

You can use federations with SQL Database to partition one or more tables across multiple databases, and developers can use federations to access the data in a somewhat transparent manner through code. Because SQL Database instances can be created programmatically without any hardware configuration or environment settings, adding new SQL Database instances to a federation is simple and requires very little administration. The simplicity of SQL Database becomes its strength when it comes to scalability.

▪ **Note**   *Scale up* is usually a term used to refer to database systems that scale by adding more processing power, more memory, or more disks to a single server. *Scale out* is a term used to refer to database systems that scale by adding more servers for improved response time.

## Key Terms

Before we go any further, let's review the terms related to the SQL Database Federations feature. A SQL Database instance is called a *root database* when one or more federations have been created in it. Because many federations can be created in a root database, a few system views were added so that you can easily find out how many federations were created.

A federation is created by specifying a *distribution name* and contains one or more *federation members*. The distribution name is a typed identifier used by SQL Database to determine which type of field a table can be federated on. You specify which field a table will be federated on by linking it to the federation distribution name. (See "T-SQL Changes for Federations" later in this chapter for further details.) The field in the federated table used to partition the data is called the *federated column.* The distribution name and the *federated column* must be of the same type.

A federation member is a SQL Database instance that contains a slice of data for the federated tables it contains, based on its allocated range. If a federation member is responsible for holding records from 1 to 100 on the distribution name called `CustomerID`, all the tables in that federation member that are federated on `CustomerID` can store only values in that range. Records that fall outside of that range are stored in other federation members. Note, however, that a federation member can contain more than federated tables; it can also contain stored procedures, views, and most database objects supported by SQL Database.

A federated member can also contain *reference tables.* Reference tables are tables that are not federated and are used to store the same data on all the federated members for referential integrity and performance. However, reference tables are not synchronized, meaning that once they are created in the federated members, changing records in a reference table in one federation member does not automatically change the reference tables in other federation members.

Figure 12-3 represents a sample federation called `FederationCust` with two federation members split at `CustomerID = 1000`. In this example, the `Customers` table contains the first 999 customers in the first federation member and the remaining records in the second federation member. The `Countries` table is used as a reference table and contains the same records.

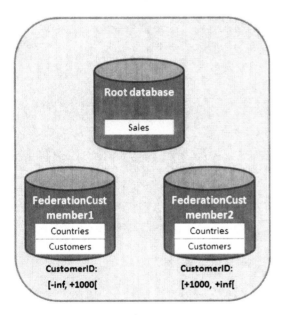

**Figure 12-3.** *Sample federation in SQL Database.*

# T-SQL Changes for Federations

Because Federations are a fully supported feature of SQL Database, certain T-SQL commands were created and others modified to manage them. Table 12-6 provides a summary of the most important statements and views used with federations.

*Table 12-6.* *Summary of important federation commands and system views*

| T-SQL Statement | Comment |
|---|---|
| CREATE FEDERATION | This new statement is executed on a SQL Database instance to create a new federation. This statement also specifies the distribution name that will be used during the CREATE TABLE statement to determine which field the table will be federated on. The SQL Database instance on which this command is used becomes the root database. |
| DROP FEDERATION | The federation to drop. All the federation members (databases) that make up this federation will be dropped as well. |
| ALTER FEDERATION | Future capability of SQL Database that provides a point-in-time restore option. Certain limitations apply. |
| USE FEDERATION | Allows a session to change its database context from one federation member to another, or back to the root database. |
| CREATE TABLE  FEDERATED ON | The CREATE TABLE statement was modified to accept the FEDERATED ON option. This option tells SQL Database which field in that a table will serve as the federated column and will be used to distribute the data across federation members. |
| sys.federations | Provides access to the list of federations created in a root database. |
| sys.federation_members | Provides a list of federation members that make up all the federations in a root database. |

# Federation Example

Let's review a simple scenario in which I am creating a federation called FederationCust that will hold two tables: Customers and Countries. My Customers table is being federated because it will contain many records and will be the cause of performance and scalabilities issues in my SQL Database instance as my database grows. My Customers table will contain a CustomerID field as a unique identifier, which is being used as the key to federate the table. The Countries table doesn't need to be federated; however, I want to include that table as a reference table in my federation for data integrity. The following steps show how I create the federation, as depicted in Figure 12-4:

1. I create a federation called FederationCust using the CREATE FEDERATION statement, specifying a distribution name called CustomerID. This creates an empty database. I switch context to that database by using the USE FEDERATION statement and create my two tables: Countries and Customers. However, when I create my Customers table, I specify this table will be federated on its ID field (the federated column) using the CREATE TABLE … FEDERATED ON statement. Because my federation has only one member database at the moment, all the records will be stored in this database.

2. At some point in the future, I realize that my federation is growing and I want to store my Customers table on two member databases (also referred to as *federation members*, or simply *members*) for increased application performance. So I decide to split the federation with the ALTER FEDERATION … SPLIT command, specifying that the CustomerID distribution name will be split at 1000. In the background, SQL Database creates two new member databases and copies the customer records from the original member database so that the first new

member will contain all the records with an ID less than 1000, and the second new member with an ID of 1000 or greater. Because the Countries table is not federated, it will be copied in its entirety. If other objects were created in the original member, such as stored procedures, they would be copied too.

3. Once the copy operation is completed, the original member will be dropped and only two members will remain. The SPLIT operation can be performed online with limited performance impact, and the databases will be transactionally consistent at the end of the operation. I can further split my federation over time as needed to scale my database.

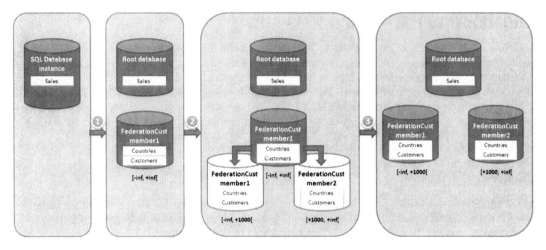

*Figure 12-4. Steps to create a SQL Database federation.*

## Limitations

SQL Database Federations are becoming more popular because they answer an important scalability need in cloud computing. However, certain limitations apply that developers and database administrators should know about. Some of these limitations might be lifted over time, so I encourage you to verify whether the following limitations still apply:

- **Data types**   The timestamp and rowversion data types are not supported in federation members.

- **Identity**   The identity column is not supported in federation members.

- **Merge**   It is not currently possible to merge federation members at this time. This feature is planned but not yet available.

- **Fan-out support**   From a development standpoint, it is not possible to issue requests across federation members in a single call. Developers are responsible for issuing requests and processing the results of the client side.

- **Database copy**   The database copy operation is currently not supported against a root database or a federated member.

- **Isolated schema changes**   Changes to the schema of a federation member stay within that federation member.

- **User interface**   For the time being, the only interface that supports managing SQL Database Federations is the SQL Database Management Portal.

- **Other**   Other limitations apply, such as indexed views not being supported, additional limitations on the federated columns, and more. Check MSDN for a complete list of limitations: http://msdn.microsoft.com/en-us/library/ windowsazure/hh597469.

# Troubleshooting Performance Issues

If you are experiencing performance issues with SQL Database, the first thing to do is follow traditional database-tuning techniques, such as evaluating your indexes, tuning T-SQL statements, limiting the use of triggers, and minimizing database roundtrips and the volume of data being returned to the consumers.

Unfortunately, as mentioned previously, SQL Database does not support the use of SQL Trace. That's because the system stored procedures used by SQL Trace are not accessible on a SQL Database instance. The good news is that you do have access to certain Dynamic Management Views (DMVs). You also have access to execution plans either through SSMS or through the SQL Database Management Portal.

## DMVs Available

DMVs are invaluable system views provided by SQL Server and SQL Database to troubleshoot the inner workings of the database engine. SQL Database offers a subset of the DMVs available under SQL Server because of security reasons. The following DMVs are available in SQL Database:

- `sys.dm_exec_connections`   Returns the list of connections established in a SQL Database instance.

- `sys.dm_exec_query_plan`   Returns the XML execution plan of a SQL query or a batch.

- `sys.dm_exec_query_stats`   Returns aggregate performance information for cached query plans.

- `sys.dm_exec_requests`   Returns information about the statements being executed by a SQL Database instance.

- `sys.dm_exec_sessions`   Returns the current session opened, along with performance information about that session. However, it doesn't return last-login information, such as the `last_successful_logon` column.

- `sys.dm_exec_sql_text`   Returns the text of a SQL batch.

- `sys.dm_exec_text_query_plan`   Returns the execution plan in text format for a SQL query or batch.

# Execution Plans

Execution plans are another powerful tool you can use to understand and troubleshoot performance issues. You can also view execution plans with the SQL Database Management Portal (SDMP). However, the portal provides a somewhat different experience than SSMS does in a few different areas.

First of all, the symbols provided in the graphical representation are different and not as granular. For example, the symbol for Index Seek operations looks different on the portal than it does in SSMS. (See Table 12-7 for a few symbols displayed in SDMP.).Also, the same symbol is provided in the portal for Clustered Index Seek and Non-Clustered Index Seek operations. Although some symbols might not be as granular in the portal as in SSMS, their descriptions are granular enough.

**Table 12-7.** *Partial list of execution plan symbols shown in SQL Database Management Portal*

| Operation | SDMP Symbols |
|---|---|
| Seek | |
| Scan | |
| Nested Loop | |
| Sort | |
| Table Spool | |
| Filter | |

Similarly to SSMS, you can zoom in and out of execution plans in SDMP and you can view batched execution plans. SDMP also gives you quick search options and different views without having to re-execute the T-SQL statement. For example, you can search expensive operations by clicking on the CPU icon, which automatically finds the most expensive CPU operations in the batch and highlights them, as shown in Figure 12-5.

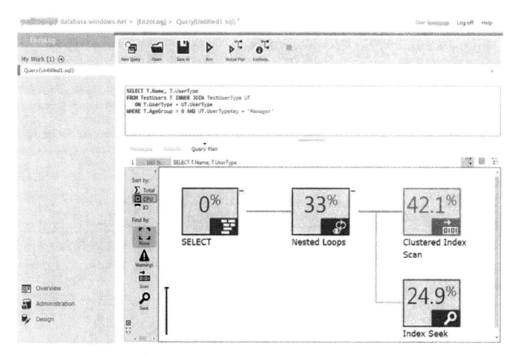

**Figure 12-5.** *Execution plan in SDMP sorted by the CPU cost*

## Performance Dashboard

The SQL Database Management Portal also provides a handy performance dashboard showing current activity and detailed performance information in a secondary screen. When you first log in to the portal, you will see a summary of the database you logged in to. To view a summary of the performance dashboard, click on Query Performance on the top of the screen. You will see a screen similar to Figure 12-6. This screen shows you a list of queries with performance metrics, including resource consumption per second. For example, the statement SELECT * FROM EnzoUsers consumed 2 physical reads per second and had a duration of 11 millisecond (ms) per second on average. These metrics are obtained by using the sys.dm_exec_query_stats table and provide an average burn rate per second, which is displayed on the screen. Although this might sound a bit complicated, this screen is designed to list in decreasing order the statements that are the most active and consuming the most resources at any point in time.

*Figure 12-6. Query Performance summary dashboard.*

Clicking on a specific query opens another screen, shown in Figure 12-7, which provides execution details, including most of the statistics provided by sys.dm_exec_query_stats. This screen shows you resource consumption and query plan information, such as when the query plan was cached, the plan handle, and more. You can also look at the execution plan directly from this screen if you click on Query Plan.

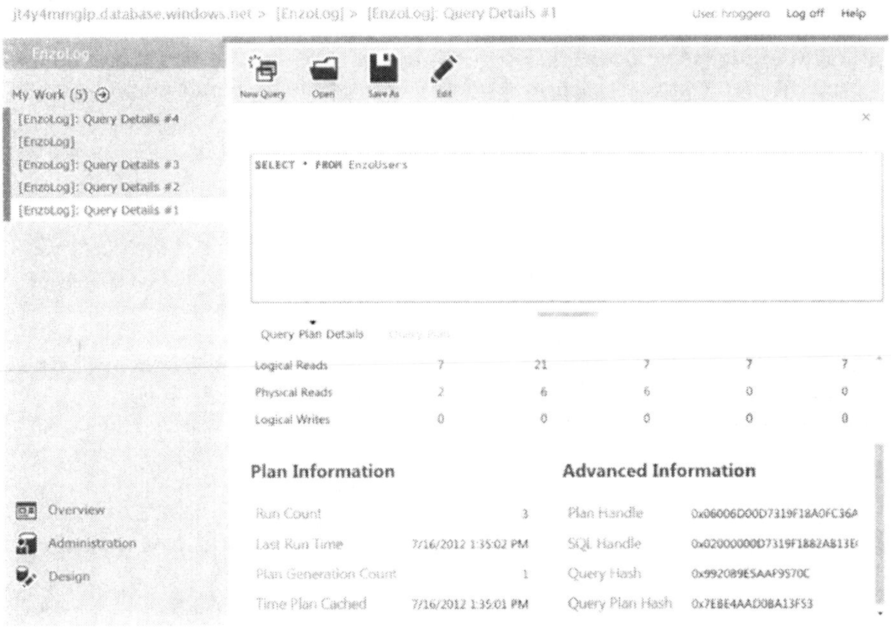

*Figure 12-7. Query Performance detailed view.*

# Related Services

Windows Azure SQL Database comes with a few related services, including Windows Azure SQL Reporting, Windows Azure SQL Data Sync, and the Export/Import feature. As mentioned previously, Windows Azure SQL Reporting has its own management portal, while the other features are accessible through the Windows Azure Management Portal.

## Windows Azure SQL Reporting

Windows Azure includes a cloud service you can use to deploy reports with minimal effort and allow these reports to be run from traditional Windows applications, from web applications, or directly from a browser by giving users the URL of the report.

Working with Windows Azure SQL Reporting (or SQL Reporting) is much simpler than working in an on-premises Reporting Service environment because there are no configuration settings to worry about, other than user and application access control. As with any other service provided in the cloud, SQL Reporting is designed to scale to demand and automatically handle the back-end configuration settings necessary to provide a highly scalable service.

SQL Reporting is currently a fully supported service; however, there are a few limitations you should know about. First and foremost, SQL Reporting can connect only to SQL Database instances. This means that at the time of this writing you cannot use SQL Reporting with internal data sources or other cloud data sources, such as Azure Tables. Another important limitation is related to user management; you need to create and manage each user individually in the management portal created specifically for SQL Reporting. Also, custom assemblies are not supported; indeed, you do not have access to the servers running this service, so your reports cannot use custom extensions. Other limitations do apply, so make sure to check MSDN for a complete list.

From the Windows Azure Management Portal, you can access the SQL Reporting portal directly by selecting Reporting from the left bar as shown in Figure 12-8. A menu showing available options appears and provides access to user-management screens, reports created in Visual Studio 2008 Reporting Services, execution logs, and usage statistics. Reports are accessed using HTTPS, so the data shown on the report is encrypted over the network for stronger security. Note that at this time a separate administrator account needs to be created to manage the reports in the SQL Reporting portal.

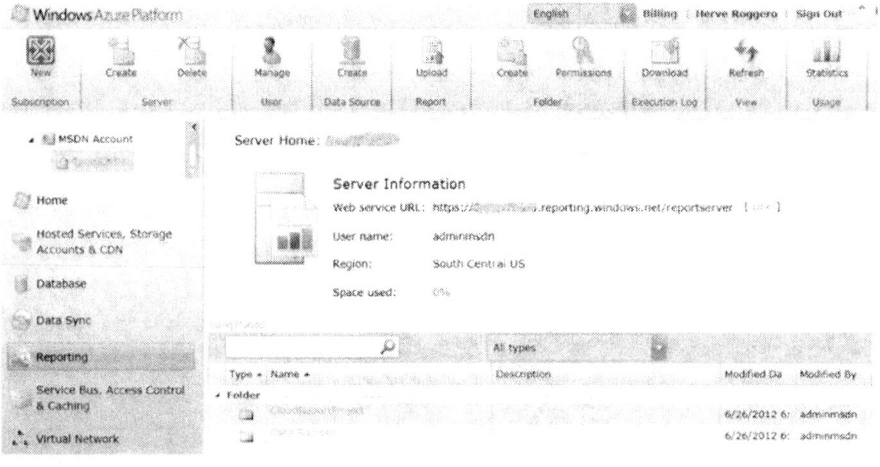

**Figure 12-8.** *Windows Azure SQL Reporting management portal.*

# Windows Azure SQL Data Sync

Because many companies need to synchronize data between on-premises databases and SQL Database, or even between SQL Database instances, Windows Azure provides a data-synchronization service called Windows Azure SQL Data Sync (SQL Data Sync, for short). This service offers schedule-based, data-synchronization capabilities between multiple databases and is designed with high resiliency in mind.

When working with SQL Data Sync, you first create a Sync Group, in which multiple on-premises and cloud databases are added. On-premises SQL Server databases are optional in any given Sync Group; however, a Sync Group must have at least one SQL Database instance that serves as the hub. Because the SQL Data Sync functions as a hub-and-spoke architecture, the hub serves as the central database against which all data changes from individual member databases are copied to, and then successful changes are copied back to the relevant member databases. Each Sync Group defines its own conflict-resolution strategy: either the hub wins or the client wins. (The *client* is another term used to refer to a member database.) Normally, you choose the hub database based on its location compared to the other databases in a manner that minimizes data-transfer cost and optimizes performance.

When configuring a Sync Group with on-premises SQL Server databases, you must install and configure a client agent that will manage data synchronization on the database servers. Once the client agent has been installed and properly configured, you will see it added to the Sync Group in the Windows Azure Management Portal.

Synchronization errors are clearly visible; an operation log file can be viewed from the portal directly by clicking the Log Viewer button. You can also force synchronization to take place at any time. Figure 12-9 shows a failed synchronization.

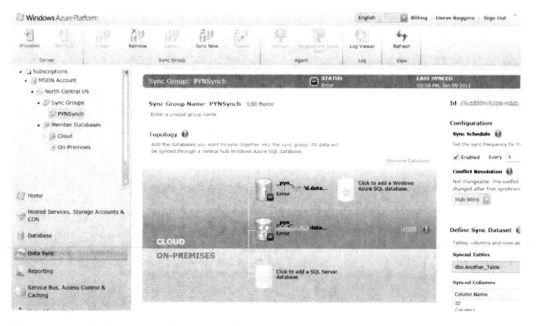

***Figure 12-9.*** *Windows Azure SQL Data Sync management portal.*

SQL Data Sync also has a few limitations worth noting. Perhaps the most important limitation of this feature is that the data is not copied with transactional consistency. Also, keep in mind that to synchronize two databases, a full synchronization must first be completed. Depending on the location of the database and the amount of data being synchronized, the first sync operation could take some time. Finally, certain properties cannot be changed after the Sync Group has been created; for example, you cannot change the hub once the Sync Group has been created.

## Import/Export Feature

SQL Database also comes with an interesting feature called Import/Export. It is designed to export a database schema and data in a single blob that can be later imported into a SQL Server instance or another SQL Database instance. This feature creates a logical backup file called a *data-tier application* (DAC) file. When the file is created on a local disk, it has a .bacpac extension, so it is also referred to as a BACPAC file. You can use the BACPAC file to copy databases from the cloud to your on-premises SQL Server databases, and back. Because the BACPAC file contains objects specific to the release of the database being backed up, you might experience errors when importing a BACPAC file on a version of SQL Server prior to SQL Server 2012.

When you are exporting a SQL Database instance to a BACPAC, you are essentially creating a blob device in a Windows Azure Storage Account you own. Figure 12-10 shows you the information you need to provide when exporting a database. In addition to providing the database credentials, you need to provide the path of the blob that will be created and the access key needed to access your storage account. The blob path contains the storage account and the blob name (mystorageaccount and blobbackup001, respectively, in my example).

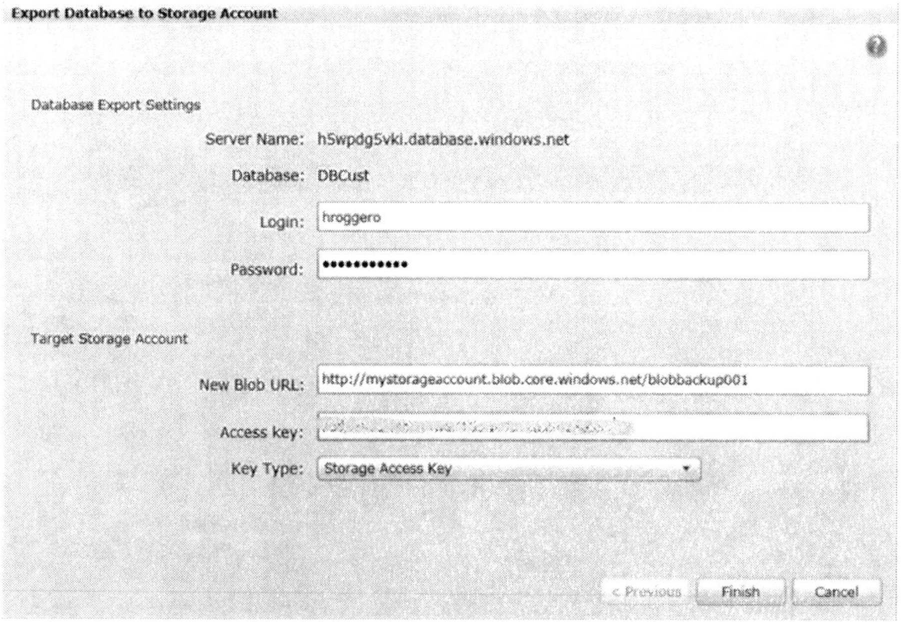

*Figure 12-10. Exporting a database using the Import/Export feature.*

If you want to create another database in the cloud with this blob, you need to create an empty SQL Database instance and run the Import Wizard from the Windows Azure Management Portal. If you want to create a database on a local SQL Server instance, you first need to download the blob to a local machine and then use SQL Server Management Studio to import this file into a newly create database.

■ **Note** You should know that the export process does not create a backup file; it creates a copy of a database and does not ensure transactional consistency. If you want to create a blob with transactional consistency, you first need to use the CREATE DATABASE … AS COPY OF… command, and then export the copied database after the copy operation has completed.

# Cost of SQL Database

The SQL Database service can cost you just a few dollars a month to hundreds or even thousands of dollars, depending on your needs. Generally speaking, you pay for what you use; the more database space you need and the more network traffic you generate, the more you will pay. The total cost for using SQL Database is made up of a flat rate that varies based on the amount of data stored and the outbound network traffic generated in a given month.

At the time of this writing, a 1-GB SQL Database instance costs $9.99 per month, plus 12 cents for each GB of outbound bandwidth consumed. The minimum amount you can pay for a SQL Database is $4.99 per month if you consume only 100 MB of storage in a 1-GB database instance. A 150-GB SQL Database instance costs $225.78 per month, excluding the bandwidth cost. As you can probably guess, the price per GB goes down with a larger database, as you can see in Figure 12-11.

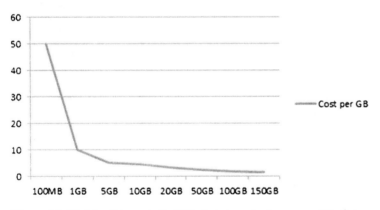

*Figure 12-11. Monthly cost of a SQL Database instance per GB of storage in US dollars.*

In the case of a federated environment, you might need multiple database instances; each federated database instance incurs its own cost. So if you have 25 federated members of 1 GB each and a root database of 100 MB, you would pay about $254.75 (25 * $9.99 + $4.99) plus the combined outbound bandwidth generated by all your databases.

■ **Note** Make sure to check the latest pricing on the Microsoft website. Visit http://www.microsoft.com/azure, and use the price calculator provided on this website.

# Conclusion

This chapter introduced you to the basics of the Windows Azure SQL Database platform offered on the Microsoft cloud. I provided you with an overview of the underlying architecture of this platform so that you can better understand the inner workings of this technology. I also provided an overview of the major differences between SQL Server and SQL Database, gave you a quick introduction of the various management portals available online, and gave you a quick tour of the various services provided by the Azure platform that leverage SQL Database.

SQL Database is designed to serve the needs of a wide variety of projects, from smaller applications to very large systems, by leveraging the recent federation features built to deliver a shared-nothing architecture and support larger workloads in a distributed fashion. With its simple configuration and provisioning model, SQL Database is poised to become a very popular database platform over time.

Because this technology is continuously evolving, I encourage you to learn more about it and other Azure-related services online on the Microsoft website, where you can find additional information on the topics covered in this chapter and more.

# CHAPTER 13

## I/O: The Untold Story

### By Jeremy Lowell

We are living in an age when data growth is being measured in factors over the previous decade. There's no indication that the rate of growth will subside. This pace is here to stay, and it presents companies and data professionals with new challenges.

According to Gartner (`http://www.gartner.com/it/page.jsp?id=1460213`), data growth is the largest challenge faced by large enterprises. Not surprisingly, system performance and scalability follow close behind.

In an unscientific study based on conversations I've had with many database administrators (DBAs) and other personnel in companies I have the honor of working with, I've found that they are struggling to keep up with this data explosion. It's no wonder that DBAs share one of the lowest unemployment numbers in the technical field. The purpose of this chapter is to provide DBAs with the knowledge and tools to drive this conversation with your company, your peers, and that wicked smart storage guru in the corner office.

How many times have you entered a search in Google related to I/O and come up with either a trivial answer or one so complex that it's hard to fully understand? The goal of this chapter is to help bridge that gap and fill in the blanks in your knowledge regarding your database environment and the correlating I/O.

I/O is often misunderstood with respect to its impact within database environments. I believe this is often due to miscommunication and a lack of foundational understanding of how to measure I/O; what to measure; how to change, modify, or otherwise alter the behavior; and perhaps more importantly, how to communicate and have the conversation about I/O with peers, management, and of course the storage and server gurus whom we all rely on. As you delve into this chapter and learn how to better measure, monitor, communicate, and change your I/O patterns, footprint, and behavior, it's important to begin from a common definition of "I/O."

A distilled version of I/O, as it relates to this chapter, is "Data movement that persists in either memory or on disk." There are any number of additional types of I/O, all of which are important but fall outside of the context and focus of this chapter.

The untold story of I/O is one you have likely struggled with before—either knowingly or unknowingly—and it contains within it a number of very important data points for your database health, consistency, performance, and availability. This chapter will focus on two primary types of I/O: memory (logical I/O) and disk (physical I/O). Although they are intimately related, they follow different patterns, and different approaches are required for measuring, monitoring, and resolving issues with each of them.

# The Basics

The beginning of this quest starts with preparation. In this case, with understanding what your database system requires of your disk subsystem during normal operations, peak loads, backups, subsystem (SAN) maintenance, and what appear to be idle periods.

Baselining your database, server or servers, and environment is critical to understanding the I/O characteristics of your system. More importantly, it helps you to determine if there's an issue and where its origin might lie. There are a handful of metrics you need to obtain and whose trends you need to monitor over time. Table 13-1 shows sample output from the counters you can use for this, and they will be explained in further detail as you dive deeper into the chapter.

*Table 13-1.* *Illustration of counters that will be the basis for further discussion throughout this chapter.*

| LogicalDisk | _Total | C: | D: |
|---|---|---|---|
| Avg. Disk Bytes/Read | 64,810.127 | 65,536.000 | 64,771.413 |
| Avg. Disk Bytes/Write | 4,289.730 | 4,174.769 | 4,352.000 |
| Avg. Disk sec/Read | 0.000 | 0.000 | 0.000 |
| Avg. Disk sec/Write | 0.001 | 0.000 | 0.001 |
| Disk Bytes/sec | 10,416,951.109 | 579,574.335 | 9,837,376.774 |
| Disk Read Bytes/sec | 10,257,952.840 | 525,207.185 | 9,732,745.655 |
| Disk Reads/sec | 158.277 | 8.014 | 150.263 |
| Disk Write Bytes/sec | 158,998.269 | 54,367.150 | 104,631.119 |
| Disk Writes/sec | 37.065 | 13.023 | 24.042 |

The source for the data in Table 13-1 is Performance Monitor. Performance Monitor is a utility found in Microsoft operating systems which graphs performance related data. In the "Tactical" section of this chapter, you can find details on how to configure counters in Performance Monitor.

There are two primary counters found in Performance Monitor for the counters referenced in Table 13-1: the Logical Disk counter and the Physical Disk counter. I prefer the counter Logical Disk for a number of reasons, but an understanding of the primary difference between the two can be found in the description of the counters, which in part reads, "The value of physical disk counters are sums of the values of the logical disks into which they are divided." As such, the Logical Disk counter provides you with a lower level of granularity, and I'd argue it gives a more accurate depiction of how the server—and thus, the database—is performing on that drive. It's also a more intuitive way to look at the disks on the server because most DBAs know which database files live on which drives.

# Monitoring

The counters I prefer to base decisions on have changed over time. Years ago, I relied on the Disk Queue Length counter. This counter measures the queued requests for each drive. There is a common rule which states that a sustained value above 2 could be problematic. The challenge with this value is that it must be a derived value. To derive the correct number, the quantity of disks or spindles involved must be taken into account as well. If I have a server with 4 disks and a queue length of 6, that queue length appears to be three times higher than the threshold value of 2. However, if I take that value of 6 and divide it by the quantity of disks (4), my actual value comes out to 1.5, which is below the threshold value of 2. Over the years, storage vendors have done some wonderful work, but it has left others wondering how to adapt to the changes. This is the reason that I leave out the counter I relied on many years ago and now my primary counters deal with how much data the database is moving to the storage subsystem (Disk Bytes/sec), what type of bytes (read or write) they are, how many of them there are (Disk Reads/sec) and (Disk writes/sec), the size of the I/O request (in and out requests per second) (Avg. Disk Bytes/Read) and (Avg. Disk Bytes/Write), and finally how quickly the storage subsystem is able to return that data (Avg. Disk sec/Read) and (Avg. Disk sec/Write).

This set of counters yields interesting data, all of which happen to be in a language your server administrator or your storage guru can relate to. Note that when your operating system (OS) reports a number, it might not be the same number that the storage device is reporting. However, it shouldn't be far off. If it is, it's often due to the sample interval that each of you are independently working from. Traditionally, storage area network (SAN) metrics and reporting aren't sampled at a frequency of one second. However, servers are often sampled at this frequency, and for good reason. The sample set is typically sourced from Performance Monitor, and it's only captured during times of interest at that poll frequency. The result is that when the conversation begins, you need to ensure that everyone is talking about the same apples—this includes the same server, logical unit number (LUN), frequency of the sample (sample interval), and of course time frame. Time frame is certainly important here, because averages have a way of looking better over time.

There's an interesting relationship between all of these counters which helps to explain the I/O behavior on a database server. As you can imagine, if the Disk Reads/sec (read In/Out Per second, IOPs) increased, one would expect the Disk Read Bytes/sec counter to increase. Typically, this is true, but what if, at the same time, a different profile of data were accessing the database server and the Disk Bytes/Read decreased? In this manner, you certainly could have more I/O requests per second, at a smaller size, resulting in the same Disk Bytes/second measure. It's for this reason that knowing and understanding your specific I/O footprint and pattern is so important. There are times of the day that your system will behave in a certain fashion and other times of the day when it's significantly different.

## Considerations

Imagine that your database server supports an online retail store where 99 percent of the orders and the web traffic occur between 8:00 AM and 5:00 PM. During that time of the day, your I/O pattern will be indicative of what the web application needs in order to fulfill orders, look up item information, and so forth. Of course, this assumes you don't run database maintenance, backups, Database Console Command's (DBCCs), and so forth during the day. The only thing running on the database server during those hours are applications that support the online web application. Once you have an understanding of what that I/O profile looks like, it will give you a solid foundation to begin from.

At this point, if you are anything like me, you are thinking to yourself, "Can't you just show me a picture, already?" Indeed, often it can be easier to visualize the relationship between counters to see why they matter. Figure 13-1 shows that relationship.

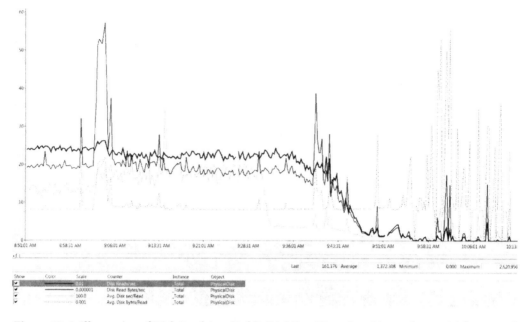

**Figure 13-1.** *Illustration of Disk Reads/sec (Bold), Disk Read Bytes/sec (Normal), Avg. Disk sec/Read (Light), and Avg. Disk Bytes/Read (Dash)*

This is an interesting view of the logical disk because it shows that the relationship of IOP size (Avg. Disk Bytes/read), disk throughput (Disk Read Bytes/sec), and the quantity of IOPs (Disk Reads/sec). The Disk Reads/sec counter (the bold line) shows a very steady trend for the majority of the sample, but as you can see early on, there was an increase in the size of the I/O, which translated into nearly a threefold increase in disk throughput.

This means, in short, that not all I/Os are created equal. As you can see in Figure 13-1, a variation in the size of the IOP can have a noticeable effect on the environment. One of the primary reasons I look for this and make note of it is so that I'm not surprised when this occurs in an environment. Imagine that you are working diligently on providing scalability numbers for your environment and one of the key performance indicators (KPIs) is "business transactions." In this context, the application group makes a statement along the lines of "You do 1,000 transactions per hour during the day and 100 transactions per hour at night," and you are asked what that means at a database level. In this scenario, the business also wants to know what it would mean if the transaction rate remained the same yet native growth of the database continued over the period of a year. They also want to ensure that the next hardware purchase (the server and SAN, specifically) will provide enough horsepower to further the native growth of the database and also a potential transaction increase from 1,000 per hour to 2,000 per hour.

At first blush, this scenario seems simple: double what you have and you will be OK. But what if that simple math didn't actually pan out? What if, due to "wall-clock" time and service times on the SAN, there suddenly weren't enough hours in the day to update your statistics, rebuild your indexes, execute DBCCs, or keep up with the backup window?

Typically, there's not a linear increase with data growth over time. For many businesses, the customer base is expanding, not contracting. These additional customers will slowly add to the size of your database and require additional I/O that you cannot see a need for in your data today. Even in the scenarios where the customer base is contracting, it's common that data is kept for the old customers. This happens for a variety of reasons, including regulatory, marketing, financial, and so on. The result is that, while it's tempting to rely on the simple math, doings so can result in some complications down the road.

For this reason, understanding your I/O profile over time and knowing which data is in the mix is critical.

---

■ **Note**   The type of I/O is perhaps more important than the overall quantity of I/O operations.

---

The type of I/O will change based on the type of business transaction or the operation you have written or scheduled. Backups, for instance, have a very different I/O profile than traditional business transactions, and even business transactions are not created equal. Consider a company that sells widgets online and via an outbound call center. The type of I/O for the online web store might have differing characteristics than the client-server application that's used by the outbound call center employees.

Another interesting example is determining what type of reporting occurs against your OLTP database server and even the times that the reports are run. Often, operational types of reporting occur during the day, while summarized information or rolled-up data reporting occurs during the evening hours. But what if users have the ability to run the larger, more I/O-intensive rollup types of reports at, say, the end of each month in the middle of the day? What if that coincides with a marketing push and your web store traffic increases by 50 percent?

What if your environment is configured in such a manner that you have a multinode cluster in which all clusters reside on the same SAN? In that scenario, when you are doing your nightly maintenance (backups, index maintenance, DBCCs, updating statistics, user processes, and so forth), the job to populate your data warehouse is also pulling large amounts of data from your OLTP database into your staging environment, and then munging that data into your star schema. You can see that during that time, no single server will appear overloaded; however, they all share the same storage array and, likely, the same controllers and, many times, the same spindles (disks). Suddenly, your scheduling takes on new meaning. Ensure that your scheduling is thought through from an environment perspective, not just at a server level. Every shared component needs to be taken into account.

# Tactical

As you go through the process of measuring, monitoring, and trending your IOP profile, bear in mind the ever-important Avg. Disk sec/Read and Avg. Disk sec/Write counters because they are critical to your I/O performance. They measure the duration it takes to read and write that specific IOP request to the disk. In Table 13-1, you can see that the disk I ran a test on is very fast, taking 0.000 seconds (on average) to read from the disk and only .001 seconds to write to the disk.

In my experience, it's difficult to find an authoritative source for what these numbers should be. This is due to the quantity of variables involved with reading from and writing to disk. There are different speeds of disks, sizes, manufacturers, seek times, scan times, throughput metrics, SAN cards, SAN card configurations, SAN configurations, OS configuration, LUN layout, and database settings. Most importantly, there are also differences in your database, its access patterns, data types, and size, to name a few. I believe it's due to those variables that vendors, SAN manufactures, server manufacturers, Microsoft, and even experts in the field hesitate to provide hard-and-fast answers. With all of that said, the numbers in Table 13-2, in part, are subject to the variables I just listed, as well as any number of additional items that I have yet to come across.

Table 13-2 represents a best-case scenario for how long it should take your subsystem (disk) to return data to the OS based on the counters Avg. Disk sec/Read and Avg. Disk sec/Write.

*Table 13-2. Table of times (in seconds) for reading from and writing to disk as reported from Performance Monitor.*

| Avg. Disk sec/ Read | Avg. Disk sec/ Write | Condition |
|---|---|---|
| .000 to .005 | .000 to .005 | Potentially underutilized |
| .005 to .010 | .005 to .010 | Healthy |
| .010 to .015 | .010 to .015 | Healthy |
| .015 to .035 | .015 to .035 | Healthy - Busy |
| .035 to .050 | .035 to .050 | Busy—some request are likely waiting for Page I/O |
| .050 to .100 | .050 to .100 | Very Busy—many requests are likely waiting for Page I/O |
| .100 to .250 | .100 to .250 | Very Busy—OK only for shorter durations |
| .250 to .500 | .250 to .500 | Very Busy—OK only during known, high-I/O operations |
| > .500 | > .500 | Potentially some serious issues |

The numbers in Table 13-2 are given in fractions of one second, and it's often easier to have this illustrated and communicated in milliseconds. By multiplying the values shown in the table by 1,000, the time will be displayed in milliseconds (ms). Throughout this chapter, when disk read and write time is referenced, it will be shown in milliseconds.

Armed with this as a guideline, be aware that there are additional variables to take into account that can and should be taken into account when you're striving to better understand your I/O footprint or resolve a potential issue in your environment. The specific variables are TempDB and transaction logs. You also should keep your application in mind. If you support an ultra-low latent application—such as those found in the credit card industry or trading industry, such as the stock market or energy market—these numbers are likely not applicable. Alternatively, if your application supports a mail order catalog, which has no user front end and is predominately batch in nature, these numbers could be too aggressive. Again, it's all relative. The intent of providing the numbers in Table 13-2 is to give you a gauge of what I've commonly seen over the years with a variety of applications and I/O requirements.

Logs are more impacted by long write times and, depending on the environment, can become problematic by having long read times as well. Each transaction in a database that requires an element of data modification (Insert, Update, or Delete) is a logged operation. This is always the case, regardless of the recovery model in place. As such, ensuring that the write time for your transaction logs is as low as possible is perhaps one of the most important things you can do within your database environment.

A practical way to think about this is in terms of write transactions per second. This counter is interesting to look at in combination with transactions per second because it illustrates how many transactions are dependent on the write time to the transaction log. If you couple this value with the Avg. Disk sec/Write, you can often find a correlation. The reason that this matters is that if your database environment is adding 20 unnecessary milliseconds to each write transaction, you can multiply the quantity of write transactions by the quantity of milliseconds to further understand how much "wall clock" time is being spent on waiting for the storage array to tell the OS it has completed its operation. As you do that math, watch your blocking chains and scenarios and you will likely see that you have a higher number of blocks during the longer-duration log write events.

■ **Note** I've seen the Avg. Disk sec/Read and Avg. Disk sec/Write times as high as five seconds. Conversely, I've seen this value as low as 10 ms with Disk Bytes/sec measuring higher than 1,400 MB/sec. Each of those two scenarios are extremes, and although we all want over 1 GB per second in throughput, with our read and write times below 10 ms, very few of us have the budget to accomplish that. However, we all should have the budget and tools to keep us from having requests taking longer than a second. If you aren't in that scenario, perhaps it's because you haven't helped to build the case for the additional capital expenditure. Keep in mind that while numbers are numbers, people are people and they might not be as passionate about the numbers you are passionate about. The old adage of "Know your customer" is very relevant to the I/O discussion because the conversation typically involves pointing out that a meaningful amount of money needs to be spent based on your findings and recommendation.

---

The size of the I/O request also plays a part. The size refers to how much data exists for each request. Traditionally, read IOPs will have larger blocks than write IOPs. This is due, in part, to range scans and applications selecting more data than they write. This is another area where understanding your I/O profile is very important. For instance, in the evenings when re-indexing occurs, you'll likely see higher values for the size of your IOP request than you will see during the day. This is because the sizes of the transactions you are working with are much larger than individual inserts or updates, which are traditionally very small. Imagine the scenario where you have a solid understanding of your I/O pattern yet you notice that your Disk Bytes/sec counter varies. The problem here is likely the size of the I/O request. It's important to understand that these counters work in concert with one another and, in their completeness, the full picture can be seen and your true I/O pattern can be realized.

At this point, you should have a good understanding of how to monitor your I/O. Over the course of this chapter, a harder portion of the equation will be factored in as well. The aforementioned equation includes some of the variables mentioned previously, specifics unique to your environment and database, and, of course, some suggestions for what can be done about decreasing or changing your I/O footprint and/or pattern.

To monitor your I/O, open Performance Monitor, expand Data Collector Sets, right-click User Defined, and select New. That will bring up the screen you see in Figure 13-2.

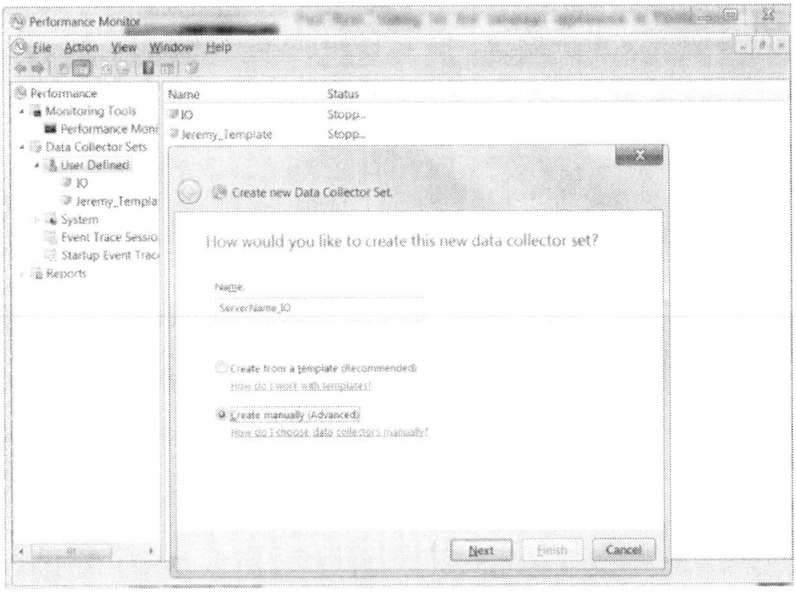

*Figure 13-2. Creating a new data collector set using Performance Monitor.*

Choose Create Manually, click Next, and then choose Create Data Logs and select Performance Counter, as shown in Figure 13-3.

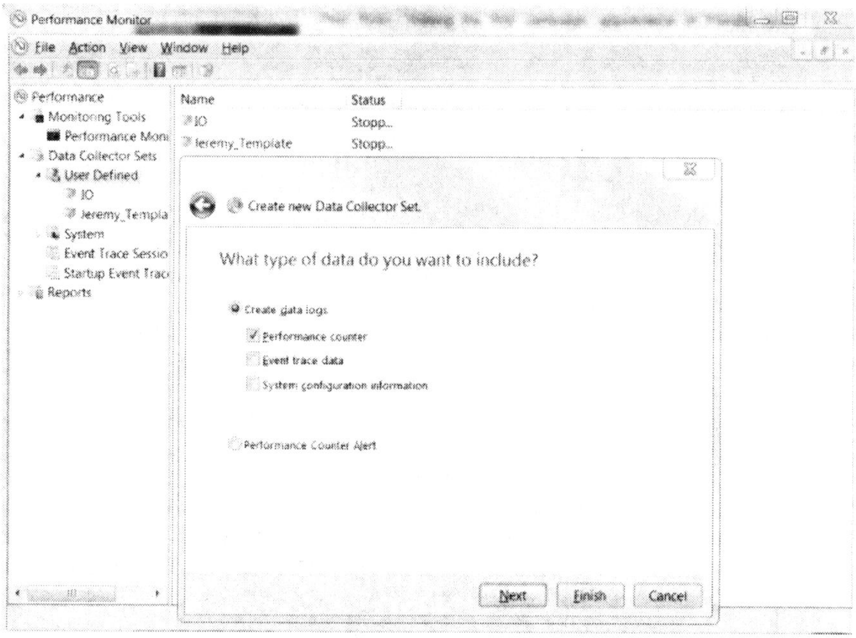

**Figure 13-3.** *Specifying the type of data to collect with Performance Monitor.*

Click Next, set the sample interval to one second, and then click Add. Then choose Logical Disk and, for the sake of simplicity, choose All Counters and <All Instances>, as shown in Figure 13-4.

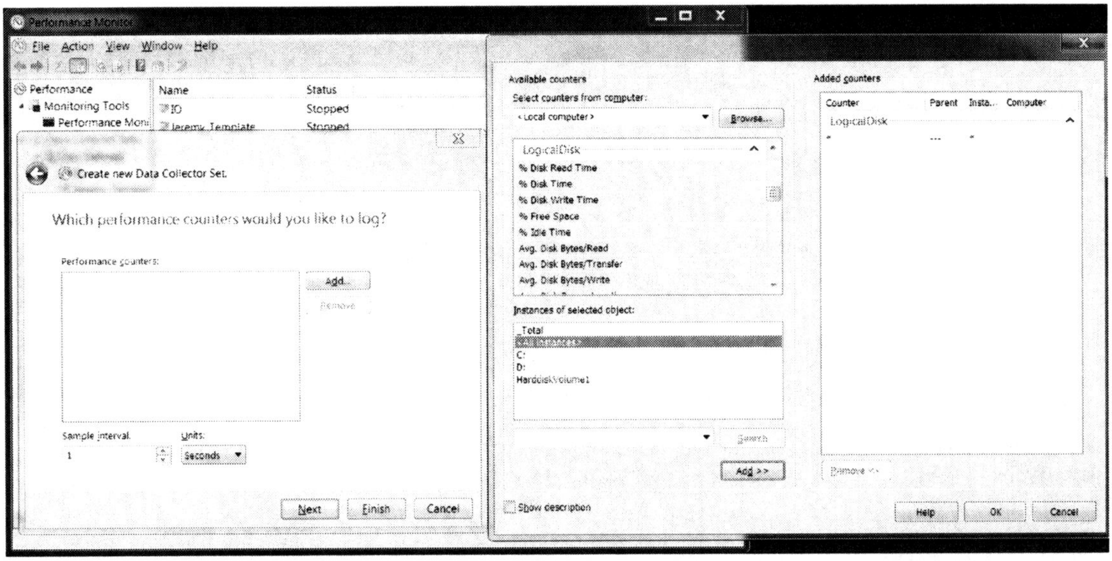

*Figure 13-4. Specifying which counters to use in Performance Monitor.*

You will then choose where you want the file written to. As you become more familiar with Performance Monitor, you will find that Log Format, Log Mode, and additional options that can be helpful depending on your needs.

Now that you have numbers in hand… (Oh, didn't I mention earlier that there would be some required work associated with this chapter?) If you don't yet have your IOP numbers, go get them—I'll hang out and watch another episode of Mickey Mouse Clubhouse with my daughter.

Later, you can work on refining your process, your data-collection times, your reporting for this data, and so on; for now, know what your numbers are. Without knowing your I/O profile inside and out, how can you ever know if it's good, bad, or an issue at 3:30 AM on a Saturday morning after a fun night out on the town? Trying to figure this out while in the midst of a performance meltdown of your .com server on Super Bowl Sunday is not only a way to develop ulcers, it could be the demise of your tenure at FillInTheBlank.com.

# Code or Disk?

I've read many articles and books over the years that state, in part, that not having backups is an inexcusable offense for a DBA. I couldn't agree more with that sentiment, but honestly, that bar is pretty low and I think we're all up for raising it a few notches. So let's throw I/O into that mix as well.

One of the questions I often receive is along the lines of "Is this bad code or bad IO?" I love that question because the answer is typically "yes." Of course your system has bad code. Of course your environment has bad I/O. There's no such thing as "good I/O" in a database system, where I/O is the slowest portion of the database environment. Well, it should be. If it isn't, read other chapters in this book!

So what's to be done about this? Let's begin with the I/O pattern, which was covered earlier. In most database environments, the I/O pattern will look very familiar day to day and week to week. Often, this I/O pattern looks the same during different times of the month as well, (Think about a retail store that is open from 8 AM to 5 PM and records inventory or reconciles its balances once per month or a traditional financial institution that sends out monthly statements at the end of each fiscal month.) The examples could go on forever, and you have an example of your own that you should be aware of, based on the business your database supports.

The I/O pattern is a valuable and actionable data set. With it, scheduling can encompass much more than just your database server because most environments contain shared storage (SANs or NASs) and these shared-storage appliances have their own maintenance windows, their own peak windows, and so forth.

---

▓ **Note**    I cannot count, on both hands, how many times the "I/O data set" has been the key common component to working with the SAN admits, application owners, and system administrators.

---

Once we are all working from the same sheet of music, it's much easier and more effective to communicate challenges. These challenges aren't experienced by you alone. This is very important to understand. If you are on a shared storage device, other application owners are encountering the same challenges that you are. The difference here is that you can be the one to drive the conversation for everyone because you are armed with data and you know your schedule and when you need certain IOP throughput from your shared storage device. I cannot emphasize enough the importance that this conversation will have within the various groups in your organization. This will build bridges, trust, and confidence. It will enable the SAN gurus to better understand your needs and why they matter, and it will enable the server administrators to change their system backup windows or virus scans to a different time. In short, it enables communication and collaboration because having such discussions without data, without the facts, it can come across as finger pointing or an attempt to shift the blame.

One of my favorite conversations with clients revolves around this topic because it's easy to take ownership of your database being "hungry" for IOPS. If the value and necessity of it can be clearly communicated with hard-and-fast data points, well, how can you go wrong? How can your organization go wrong?

Moving on, the point of the previous section was to introduce you to the metrics and to explain why they matter, what can be done with them, and how to obtain them. Now that you have them, let's talk about a few of the finer points.

In your I/O profile, you will likely see that during different times of the day your I/O pattern changes. Take, for example, the Disk Bytes/sec counter. If you see significant and sustained changes in this counter, check the related counter, Disk Bytes/Read(Write). You'll likely see a change in the size of the I/O because different types of IOPS are used for varying database loads. While looking at this, go ahead and look at the Disk Reads(Writes)—the correlation should be pretty clear. You will see that during your backup window, the quantity of I/Os are decreased while the throughput is increased, and the size is likely elevated as well. The same will be true for re-indexing activities.

Consider changing your backups, re-indexing, or statistic updates to times when your subsystem can better handle that type of load. When you contemplate changing this, you should communicate it with your system administrator and SAN guru, because they will appreciate the communication and might change something on their side to accommodate your need.

Now on to more specifics because, as they say, the devil is in the details and there's nothing like having your environment, including your I/O pattern pretty well understood and then being surprised. One of the key elements with this monitoring and analysis is to do it by LUN. Ideally, your database files are broken out on different LUNs. For example, having the log file on a separate drive makes monitoring easier, so is having TempDB broken out to a different drive. This is because the I/O pattern and type vary with these specific workloads, unlike the user databases in your environment. The log files, for example, will require the lowest possible write latency because every transaction is dependent on this file. If you have replication enabled, note that there will be some reads as well, but the more important aspect with your transaction log is that the writes need to be as fast as they can be. TempDB is a different beast, and it's used for a number of different functions within the RDBMS, such as for table variables, temp tables, global temp tables, sorts, snapshot isolation, and cursors. Because of the dynamic usage of TempDB and the elements which are enabled in your environment, you need to not only tune TempDB from a file management perspective, but also from an I/O perspective. This takes two forms: decreasing latch contention, and increasing throughput in TempDB. After all, the intent of having multiple data files for TempDB is to increase throughput in TempDB, which translates to increased throughput to the disk. If the disk cannot adequately support that throughput, the intended gain cannot be realized. TempDB usage, due to the quantity of operations that can occur in this database, can be more challenging to identify a known I/O pattern. Keep in mind that if you find slow I/O in TempDB, the scenario is similar to a slow log write except that your primary impact are to reads.

# Times Have Changed

Many years ago, the predominate method of attaching storage to a server was to procure a server with enough bays, find a controller that could support your redundant array of independent disk or disks (RAID) considerations and throughput requirements, and then find the drives that were the correct speed and size for what you needed.

As a simple example, suppose you have three hard drives. Believe it or not, this was a common configuration years ago, and often these three drives would be provisioned as a RAID-5 array, often with two logical drives partitioned.

Understanding the types of RAID will help you develop a solution that's in the process of being designed or configure an existing solution that is either being refactored or scaled up. In today's world, the ticky-tack details of RAID inside of current SANs is a bit different than it used to be, but you need to understand some of the underpinnings of the technology to better appreciate what the storage gurus do in your company. Developing such an understanding might build a communication bridge when they learn that you know a thing or two about their world.

You can think of RAID, in its simplest form, as taking the three disk drives, pushing the magic "go" button, and transforming them into one viewable disk from the operating system and by extension, SQL Server. Now that you have a drive with three disks, you can have bigger LUNs and more easily manage the OS and the databases that reside on the server. At this point, you are probably thinking the same thing I thought when I wrote that, which is "That's what those storage gurus get paid for?" Clearly, there's a bit more to it than pushing the magic "go" button. Just imagine if the storage gurus always gave you what you asked for. In this case, you would have one "drive" with your logs, data, OS, TempDB, and any third-party software you use on your server. Suddenly, the file structure on your server looks like the one on your laptop, and most folks aren't happy with the performance of their laptop when they are saving a big file or unzipping a .blg they just copied from their server to get to know their I/O pattern.

The primary purpose for the drives on your servers implementing a type of RAID is fault tolerance. In today's world, anyone can walk into a big-box electronics store and buy a terabyte of hard-drive space for less than $100. Compared to commercial-grade drives, that is a very good bargain—but somewhere you hear your grandfather's wisdom whispering, "You get what you pay for." While the quantity of storage per dollar reaches historically low levels year after year, the performance and availability of those hard drives hasn't had a similar increase. This means that if one terabyte of storage cost $1000 US dollars just five years ago and now it's $100 US dollars—a tenfold decrease—the availability, durability, and speed of that terabyte of data has not increased tenfold.

You also need to have a good grasp on the types of RAID. RAID 5 was the primary RAID configuration that I learned about, and it's still one of the most frequently used type in the industry. The concept of RAID 5 is akin to striping a file across all of the drives involved and then adding parity. In this manner, any singular drive in a three-drive configuration can fail and the data will still be available until such time as the drive is replaced and the data is then written to the new drive. This is perfect when the intent is to have fault tolerance with a hard drive. However, it comes at a price. In this case, that price is performance. For

RAID 5 to be successful, it must read the data you are accessing, and if you modify it, it must re-read the block to recalculate the parity, write the data, and then rewrite the data to maintain parity. This becomes a performance bottleneck rather quickly, and it's why you will see many blogs recommend that SQL Server transaction logs and TempDB be located on RAID 1+0 (10).

RAID 10 is arguably a better form of RAID for database systems because this form of RAID obtains its fault tolerance from mirrors of information and its performance from striping the data across all of the spindles (disks). Due to the definition of the word "mirror," the three-disk configuration I mentioned earlier wouldn't work for RAID 10, but if you had a fourth disk, you could implement RAID 10. This mean that the write penalty wouldn't be as significant as with RAID 5 but the usable space is now only roughly half as much as the storage you purchased, because the data is being mirrored. In our configuration with RAID 10, two of the drives simply mirror the other two, which means that our footprint for available data is half of the storage purchased. From a performance perspective, this is a much better way to go because the mirrors can be read from, and to support your data footprint, more spindles need to exist.

There are additional types of RAID. I could attempt to explain them all in this chapter , but your eyes are likely rolling back right in their sockets at this point and you are probably wondering, "Why do I care?"

You need to care because if your storage guru asks what you want, you can confidently say "I'd like a quarter pounder with cheese and a….". Back up—you aren't that cozy with your storage guru, yet. Arming yourself with knowledge about RAID and your specific SAN is invaluable when it's time for your storage guru to assign you LUNs for your database. It provides you with the opportunity to have an educated conversation with him and request what your database longs for: fast I/O. It was mentioned earlier that Transaction Log files and TempDB are both susceptible to slow I/O, and I/O waits are the bane of a well-performing database system.

In the majority of environments today, SQL Server database storage is often found on shared disk (SAN or NAS). Many of these appliances will have hundreds of spindles. If you consider the example we've been discussing with three disks, you can see how much this changes the landscape for your environment. One would immediately think "Yahoo! I have more spindles." Yes, you do—but with that, you typically have other applications on those same spindles.

For instance, what if the storage appliance your database is on also houses your Microsoft Exchange environment, SharePoint, middle-tier servers, web servers, and file shares? Suddenly, you find yourself competing for I/O with the shared-storage appliance and controller or controllers on that appliance. This not only changes the landscape, it also introduces some complexity in monitoring and measuring the performance of your database. This means you need to dive a bit deeper than just Performance Monitor numbers. If you have data points in hand and knowledge about your storage guru's world, you can better communicate what your database needs in order to support your SLA or the businesses expectations with regard to performance.

# Getting to the Data

With the Performance Monitor data you have in hand, you can see the impact that slow disk-access time has on your database by querying the Dynamic Management Views (DMV) in SQL Server. SQL Server offers a number of DMVs that can be used to dig deeper into the causes of your I/O, in conjunction with external data such as that provided by Performance Monitor.

The data set from the DMVs, in the query referenced next, can be queried, and it will return what's known as *disk stalls*. This result set is significant because it begins to narrow down which of your data files (databases) is driving your I/O.

In traditional Online Transactional Processing (OLTP) databases, the majority of I/O is consumed via reads. The percentage of reads compared to writes in most OLTP workloads follows the 90/10 rule. This is to say that 90 percent of the data your database server will present is for read operations and only 10 percent will be written. This number, however, is significantly skewed (in a good way) due to RAM. The more RAM you have, the more data you have in cache and, as such, the less data you have that needs to be retrieved from disk. The ratio of how much data is read from disk or written from disk varies significantly based on the usage patterns, access paths, indexing, available memory, workload, and so forth. As a result, it's important for you to know what your database server's ratio is. Again, keep in mind that backup operations, DBCC CheckDB, reindexing tasks, updating of statistics, and any number of additional database maintenance tasks can significantly alter the result set because this data is cumulative since SQL Server was last restarted.

Without further ado, the following query will begin to answer these questions for you:

```
SELECT sys.master_files.name as DatabaseName,
       sys.master_files.physical_name,
         CASE WHEN sys.master_files.type_desc = 'ROWS' THEN 'Data Files'
              WHEN sys.master_files.type_desc = 'LOG' THEN 'Log Files'
         END as 'File Type',
       ((FileStats.size_on_disk_bytes/1024)/1024)/ 1024.0 as FileSize_GB,
       (FileStats.num_of_bytes_read /1024)/1024.0 as MB_Read,
       (FileStats.num_of_bytes_written /1024)/1024.0 as MB_Written,
        FileStats.Num_of_reads, FileStats.Num_of_writes,
       ((FileStats.io_stall_write_ms /1000.0)/60) as
         Minutes_of_IO_Write_Stalls,
       ((FileStats.io_stall_read_ms /1000.0)/60) as
         Minutes_of_IO_Read_Stalls
FROM sys.dm_io_virtual_file_stats(null,null) as FileStats
         JOIN sys.master_files ON
              FileStats.database_id = sys.master_files.database_id
         AND FileStats.file_id = sys.master_files.file_id
```

Sample output for this query can be found in Table 13-3.

*Table 13-3. Table containing a sample output of the referenced DMV query.*

| Database Name | Physical_ Name | File Type | FileSize_ GB | MB_ Read | MB_ Written | Num_ of_ reads | Num_ of_ writes | Minutes_ of_IO_ Write_ Stalls | Minutes_ of_IO_ Read_ Stalls |
|---|---|---|---|---|---|---|---|---|---|
| tempdev | D:\Tem... | Data Files | 0.14 | 1.34 | 123.03 | 24 | 561 | 0.11 | 0.11 |
| templog | D:\Tem... | Log Files | 0.13 | 0.92 | 244.75 | 147 | 4846 | 0.84 | 0.84 |
| TEST | C:\Test... | Data Files | 0.21 | 66.76 | 123.19 | 238 | 643 | 0.1 | 0.1 |
| TEST_log | C:\Test... | Log Files | 0.49 | 1.14 | 362.15 | 204 | 9645 | 1.99 | 1.99 |

This is an interesting data set because it helps to illustrate which specific database is driving your IOPS higher.

The result set columns that aren't apparent are as follows:

- `FileSize_GB`   This is the size of the file as persisted in the `dm_io_virtual_file_stats` DMF.

- `MB_Read`   The quantity of MB read from this data file.

- `MB_Written`   The quantity of MB written to this data file.

- `Number of Reads`   The quantity of reads from this data file.

- Number of Writes   The quantity of writes to this data file.

- Minutes of IO Write Stalls   The aggregated total of all of the waits to write to this file.

- Minutes of IO Read Stalls   The aggregated total of all of the reads to this data file.

---

■ **Note**   The numbers are all aggregated totals since the instance was last restarted. This will include your higher, known I/O operations.

---

The values in this table are certainly useful, yet they contain information since the instance was last restarted. Due to this, the values reported are going to contain your backup I/O, your re-indexing I/O, and, of course, normal usage. This tends to skew these numbers and makes it challenging to know when the reported waits are occurring. One option is to create a job that persists this data at an interval. In this manner, it is easier to tell which databases are consuming the majority of I/O and, more importantly, identify the related stalls. I/O stalls are not a bad thing, and they will occur. However, if you see a significant deviation between your files and find that your log files have a high number of stalls associated with them, you need to determine if they are related to checkpoints or normal operations. A good way to tie this information together is via the wait statistics, per server, which are available via the sys.dm_os_wait_stats DMV. This DMV is also cumulative and provides some excellent information about your overall wait types. Armed with data in this DMV, you can begin to figure out what's causing the I/O stalls.

Even with that subset of information, it might not be clear what you need to address. That's where the session-level information begins to be of value.

---

■ **Note**   There are times when I dive straight to the session-level information, but that information can also be misleading. IOP patterns change over the course of the day, week, month, or even year in your environment.

---

The following query will begin to provide the actual T-SQL that is driving your I/O, as long as it's a query. It's certainly possible that external events can drive I/O, but those items are typically secondary to what drives I/O on a dedicated SQL Server server.

```
SELECT
        Rqst.session_id as SPID,
        Qstat.last_worker_time,
        Qstat.last_physical_reads,
        Qstat.total_physical_reads,
        Qstat.total_logical_writes,
        Qstat.last_logical_reads,
        Rqst.wait_type as CurrentWait,
        Rqst.last_wait_type,
        Rqst.wait_resource,
        Rqst.wait_time,
        Rqst.open_transaction_count,
        Rqst.row_count,
        Rqst.granted_query_memory,
        tSQLCall.text as SqlText
FROM sys.dm_exec_query_stats Qstat
JOIN sys.dm_exec_requests Rqst ON
```

```
        Qstat.plan_handle = Rqst.plan_handle AND Qstat.query_hash = Rqst.query_hash
CROSS APPLY sys.dm_exec_sql_text (Rqst.sql_handle) tSQLCall
```

Now we're getting somewhere. In the result set in Table 13-4, you see which SPIDs are driving the I/O at this moment in time.

*Table 13-4. Table containing a sample output of the referenced DMV query*

| SPID | total_ physical_ reads | total_ logical_ writes | last_ logical_ reads | CurrentWait | last_wait | wait_time | SqlText |
|------|------|------|------|------|------|------|------|
| 51 | 0 | 1802482 | | WAITFOR | WAITFOR | 7958 | exec prc... |
| 63 | 18549821 | 741189 | 12594554 | NULL | NULL | 0 | insert tab... |
| 86 | 0 | 0 | 158 | NULL | NULL | 0 | exec prc... |
| 99 | 0 | 79589 | 170794575 | NULL | NULL | 0 | exec prc... |
| 100 | 7266 | 126 | 1100403 | CXPACKET | CXPACKET | 2197599 | DECLARE @ Var... |
| 104 | 0 | 0 | 3 | WRITELOG | WRITELOG | 15 | DECLARE @ Var... |
| 111 | 51810 | 11352 | 11352 | ASYNC_IO_ COMPLETION | ASYNC_IO_ COMPLETION | 1962692 | BACKUP db.. |
| 122 | 0 | 0 | 0 | WRITELOG | WRITELOG | 15 | IF @@TRAN |

In this example, the database server is rebuilding a clustered index, running some long-running stored procedures with complex logic, deleting data from a table with blobs in them, and backing up a large database. Some of these tasks require a significant amount of I/O. As a result, you see in the wait types that the wait type for the backup SPID (111) is `ASYNC_IO_COMPLETION,` which is SQL Server waiting for an I/O completion event. SPID 104 and 122 are actually of more concern because they are waiting for their respective data to be committed (written) to the transaction log. In this event, it would have been wise to not run backups and stored procedure calls known to have high I/O while rebuilding a clustered index.

Figure 13-5 shows the quantity of bytes per second read and written and the response time to the SAN. As you can see, the response time ranges from 11 to 27 ms. In this environment, that's a very long time. Coupled with the query results from Table 13-4, it illustrates that the server was very busy during this time.

| Read (B/sec) | Write (B/sec) | Total (B/sec) | I/O Priority | Response Time (ms) |
|------|------|------|------|------|
| 236,124,525 | 0 | 236,124,525 | Normal | 26 |
| 235,736,347 | 0 | 235,736,347 | Normal | 27 |
| 223,678,756 | 0 | 223,678,756 | Normal | 27 |
| 217,374,884 | 0 | 217,374,884 | Normal | 26 |
| 131,255,285 | 22,790,528 | 154,045,813 | Normal | 21 |
| 3,277 | 64,438,067 | 64,441,344 | Normal | 13 |
| 23,127,722 | 23,126,909 | 46,254,631 | Normal | 11 |
| 0 | 23,095,027 | 23,095,027 | Normal | 17 |
| 0 | 23,050,098 | 23,050,098 | Normal | 16 |
| 104,001 | 4,360,376 | 4,464,377 | Normal | 13 |

*Figure 13-5. Illustration of server activity on a SAN under load.*

In the result set, it's helpful to know exactly what this query was doing. With that information, you can begin to dig deeper into your specific environment and address the I/O contention on two fronts: hardware and software (T-SQL). From here, you can choose to tune a particular query or take a broader view and interrogate the system tables about which indexes might be driving your I/O.

The following query provides usage statistics for your indexes:

```
SELECT
a.name as Object_Name,
b.name as Index_name,
b.Type_Desc,
c.user_seeks,
c.user_scans,
c.user_lookups,
c.user_updates,
c.last_user_seek,
c.last_user_update
 FROM sys.objects AS a
        JOIN sys.indexes AS b ON a.object_id = b.object_id
        JOIN sys.dm_db_index_usage_stats AS c ON b.object_id = C.object_id
        AND b.index_id = C.index_id
WHERE  A.type = 'u'
ORDER BY user_seeks+user_scans+user_updates+user_lookups desc
```

This data set can help narrow down which of the tables in the query or stored procedure returned is the most or least used. Additional overhead could be due to a missing index, a fragmented index, index scans, or RowID lookups (bookmark lookups).

Another interesting query can be found by interrogating the sys.dm_os_schedulers object like this:

```
SELECT MAX(pending_disk_io_count) as MaxPendingIO_Current,
               AVG(pending_disk_io_count) as AvgPendingIO_Current
FROM sys.dm_os_schedulers
```

Unlike the previous queries in the chapter, the results of this query are solely based on current activity and do not represent historical data.

# Addressing a Query

What you've just gone through can produce a lot of data, perhaps an overwhelming amount. However, perhaps you found that there's a particular query that is the most expensive from an IO perspective. Perhaps you opened this chapter with one already in mind. The question is, how to address it. Before that however, you first must understand some characteristics around this query.

There are many good books on execution plans and I'm not going to spend time in this chapter discussing them as there's an alternate manner to evaluate physical reads for a specific query or T-SQL batch. By using the statement SET STATISTICS IO ON, you can view some valuable characteristics about where a query is obtaining its data (disk or memory).

The following query was written for the AdventureWorksDW2008R2 database:

```
DBCC DROPCLEAN BUFFERS -- ensures that the data cache is cold
DBCC FREEPROCCACHE -- ensures that the query plan is not in memory
--*Warning, running this in a production environment can have unintended consequences.
Additional details on these DBCC commands can be found at: http://msdn.microsoft.com/
en-us/library/ms187762.aspx and http://msdn.microsoft.com/en-
```

us/library/ms174283(v=sql.105).aspx

```
SET STATISTICS IO ON;

USE AdventureWorksDW2008R2
GO

declare @ProductKey int = (select MIN (ProductKey) from dbo.FactInternetSales)

SELECT
SUM(UnitPrice) as Total_UnitPrice, AVG(UnitPrice) as Average_UnitPrice,
MIN(UnitPrice) as Lowest_UnitPrice, MAX(UnitPrice) as HighestUnitPrice,
SUM(OrderQuantity) as Total_OrderQuantity, AVG(OrderQuantity) as Average_OrderQuantity,
MIN(OrderQuantity) as Lowest_OrderQuantity, MAX(OrderQuantity) as HighestOrderQuantity,
SUM(SalesAmount) as Total_SalesAmount, AVG(SalesAmount) as Average_SalesAmount,
        MIN(SalesAmount) as Lowest_SalesAmount, MAX(SalesAmount) as HighestSalesAmount,
P.EnglishProductName, D.EnglishMonthName, D.FiscalYear,
AVG(P.ListPrice) / AVG(FIS.UnitPrice))  as ProductListPriceVersusSoldUnitPrice
FROM dbo.FactInternetSales FIS
        INNER JOIN dbo.DimProduct P ON FIS.ProductKey = P.ProductKey
        INNER JOIN dbo.DimDate D on FIS.OrderDateKey = D.DateKey
WHERE FIS.ProductKey = @ProductKey
GROUP by P.EnglishProductName, D.EnglishMonthName, D.FiscalYear
```

The output of this query isn't relevant, but if you click on the messages tab you should see something similar to the following:

```
Table 'FactInternetSales'. Scan count 1, logical reads 2, physical reads 2, read-ahead
reads 0,
lob logical reads 0, lob physical reads 0, lob read-ahead reads 0.

(13 row(s) affected)
Table 'Worktable'. Scan count 0, logical reads 0, physical reads 0, read-ahead reads 0,
lob logical reads 0, lob physical reads 0, lob read-ahead reads 0.
Table 'DimDate'. Scan count 1, logical reads 21, physical reads 1, read-ahead reads 22,
lob logical reads 0, lob physical reads 0, lob read-ahead reads 0.
Table 'FactInternetSales'. Scan count 1, logical reads 1036, physical reads 10, read-
ahead reads 1032,
lob logical reads 0, lob physical reads 0, lob read-ahead reads 0.
Table 'DimProduct'. Scan count 0, logical reads 2, physical reads 2, read-ahead reads 0,
lob logical reads 0, lob physical reads 0, lob read-ahead reads 0.
```

This output shows us some very interesting items. If you focus on the results for physical reads and read-ahead reads, you can begin to figure out how to better optimize this query or the objects it's pulling data from.

The most interesting result I see here is the second reference to the object FactInternetSales. It has a physical read count of 10 and read-ahead reads of 1,032. In total, 1,042 data pages were retrieved from disk and placed into cache to satisfy the query. That's a lot of data for a result set of only 13 rows. Granted, there is a GROUP BY involved, so it needed more rows in order to satisfy the WHERE clause, which alone returns 2,230 records.

So the question is, how can you make this query better with this data alone? If I run the statement sp_help FactInternetSales, part of the output for reads looks like Figure 13-6.

| | index_name | index_description | index_keys |
|---|---|---|---|
| 1 | IX_FactIneternetSales_ShipDateKey | nonclustered located on PRIMARY | ShipDateKey |
| 2 | IX_FactInternetSales_CurrencyKey | nonclustered located on PRIMARY | CurrencyKey |
| 3 | IX_FactInternetSales_CustomerKey | nonclustered located on PRIMARY | CustomerKey |
| 4 | IX_FactInternetSales_DueDateKey | nonclustered located on PRIMARY | DueDateKey |
| 5 | IX_FactInternetSales_OrderDateKey | nonclustered located on PRIMARY | OrderDateKey |
| 6 | IX_FactInternetSales_ProductKey | nonclustered located on PRIMARY | ProductKey |
| 7 | IX_FactInternetSales_PromotionKey | nonclustered located on PRIMARY | PromotionKey |
| 8 | PK_FactInternetSales_SalesOrder… | clustered, unique, primary key located on PRIMARY | SalesOrderNumber, SalesOrderLineNumber |

*Figure 13-6. Illustration of the output of sp_help FactInternetSales.*

This alone tells me that the query optimizer might try to use the index IX_FactInternetSales_ProductKey to satisfy the WHERE criteria, and it will most certainly use the clustered index PK_FactInternetSales_SalesOrderNumber_SalesOrderLineNumber. At this point, it doesn't matter which one it's using because I'm certain that, based on the columns in the index, the clustered key is where the majority of reads are coming from.

What if you took the simplest route with this query and simply added a covering index? A covering index is an index that satisfies the WHERE criteria and the join criteria, as well as the select columns in the query.

---

■ **Note**    Covering indexes can be a terrific solution for some queries, but they are typically much larger than indexes with singleton columns and require more overhead to maintain.

---

The index creation statement looks like this:

```
CREATE NONCLUSTERED INDEX [IX_Query1_Covering]
ON [dbo].[FactInternetSales] ([ProductKey])
INCLUDE ([OrderDateKey],[OrderQuantity],[UnitPrice],[SalesAmount])
GO
```

With that in place, the STATISTICS IO output for the query is as follows:

```
Table 'FactInternetSales'. Scan count 1, logical reads 2, physical reads 2, read-ahead
reads 0,
lob logical reads 0, lob physical reads 0, lob read-ahead reads 0.

(13 row(s) affected)
Table 'Worktable'. Scan count 0, logical reads 0, physical reads 0, read-ahead reads 0,
lob logical reads 0, lob physical reads 0, lob read-ahead reads 0.
Table 'DimDate'. Scan count 1, logical reads 21, physical reads 2, read-ahead reads 30,
lob logical reads 0, lob physical reads 0, lob read-ahead reads 0.
Table 'FactInternetSales'. Scan count 1, logical reads 17, physical reads 3, read-ahead
reads 8,
lob logical reads 0, lob physical reads 0, lob read-ahead reads 0.
Table 'DimProduct'. Scan count 0, logical reads 2, physical reads 2, read-ahead reads 0,
lob logical reads 0, lob physical reads 0, lob read-ahead reads 0.
```

That's much better. The count of pages necessary for the same query with that index in place dropped from a total of 1,042 to 11.

If this was a frequently run query, the potential IO savings are significant, as well as the potential memory savings. Instead of placing 1,302 pages of the table into memory, this query had a read-ahead count of only 8 pages.

To take it one step further, what if this index were compressed via row compression? This is a bit of a challenge because this table is relatively small and the dataset you are after is also small, but let's see what happens.

An index can be rebuilt and row compression can be added in the following manner:

```
CREATE NONCLUSTERED INDEX [IX_Query1_Covering]
ON [dbo].[FactInternetSales] ([ProductKey])
INCLUDE ([OrderDateKey],[OrderQuantity],[UnitPrice],[SalesAmount])
WITH (DATA_COMPRESSION = ROW, DROP_EXISTING = ON)
GO
```

When the query is re-run, the STATISTICS IO output reads as follows:

```
Table 'FactInternetSales'. Scan count 1, logical reads 2, physical reads 2, read-ahead reads 0,
lob logical reads 0, lob physical reads 0, lob read-ahead reads 0.

(1 row(s) affected)

(13 row(s) affected)
Table 'Worktable'. Scan count 0, logical reads 0, physical reads 0, read-ahead reads 0,
lob logical reads 0, lob physical reads 0, lob read-ahead reads 0.
Table 'DimDate'. Scan count 1, logical reads 21, physical reads 2, read-ahead reads 30,
lob logical reads 0, lob physical reads 0, lob read-ahead reads 0.
Table 'FactInternetSales'. Scan count 1, logical reads 10, physical reads 2, read-ahead
reads 8,
lob logical reads 0, lob physical reads 0, lob read-ahead reads 0.
Table 'DimProduct'. Scan count 0, logical reads 2, physical reads 2, read-ahead reads 0,
lob logical reads 0, lob physical reads 0, lob read-ahead reads 0.
```

It did help—a little. The total physical reads counter decreased from 3 to 2, but the logical reads (memory) decreased from 17 to 10. In this case, it had a minor impact on phsyical I/O but a more noticeable impact on memory I/O.

Additional resources for SET STATISTICS IO ON can be found at http://msdn.microsoft.com/en-us/library/ms184361.aspx. If you aren't familiar with this option, I recommend reading up on it and adding it to your tool box. More information on read-ahead reads can be found at http://msdn.microsoft.com/en-us/library/ms191475.aspx.

With the simple statement SET STATISTICS IO ON, a very valuable set of data can be obtained about how SQL Server is trying to access your data and that statement will also point you to which object to focus on in a specific query.

# Environmental Considerations

Earlier in this chapter, I mentioned a number of variables that come into play and will vary widely, even in your own environment. This portion of the chapter will cover the more common variables at a high level.

Depending on the version of the operating system and SQL Server, granting access to "Lock Pages in Memory" for the SQL Server service account will prevent the operating system from paging data in SQL Server's Buffer Pool. This can have a marked impact in your environment. In my experience, I've seen this most often with virtualized SQL Server instances.

Another setting that can improve I/O throughput is "Perform volume maintenance tasks." This permission allows the SQL Server process to instantly initialize files, which at start-up will decrease the time it takes to create TempDB. It also helps during incremental data-file growths or when new databases are being created. Note that this setting does not have an impact on transaction logs—only data files qualify for instant (zero fill) initialization.

I've discussed SANs at length in this chapter and, although the technology is continually changing, there are a couple of primary considerations to be aware of. The first is how the cache is configured on the controller. Typically, SANs contain memory, which is often backed up by battery power and enables that memory to be used as a write store. In this manner, your transactions won't have to wait for the data to actually be persisted to disk. Instead, the data makes its way through the server, the host bus adapter (HBA), and then the controller. Depending on the specific SAN vendor, controller, and configuration, it's likely that your data is only written to memory and then later flushed to physical spindles. What's important here is how the memory is configured in your environment. Many vendors have an auto-balance of sorts, but for traditional database workloads the primary usage of cache is best used in a high-write configuration. For instance, if your controller has 1 GB of memory, it's preferred, from a database workload, that the majority of that cache be allocated to writes rather than reads. After all, your database server has memory for read cache, but it does not contain write cache.

Another closely related setting to this is the queue depth on your HBA card. This is the piece of hardware that enables the server to connect to your SAN. The recommendations for configuring the HBA card vary and are based on your specific card, SAN, server, and workload. It's worth noting, though, that increasing the queue depth can improve performance. As with anything of this nature, ensuring that you test your specific environment is critical. The good news, at this point, is that you have known IOP characteristics in hand about your environment and you can use these to configure a test with SQLIO. This utility measures your disk throughput and can be configured for the type of I/O you are interested in testing (read or write), the number of threads, the block size in KB (IOP size), among many other factors. It will test contiguous reads and/or writes and random reads and/or writes. Running this is intrusive to your disk subsystem—don't run it in the middle of your business day. If you run this test, modify your queue depth, and then run it again, you can find the ideal balance for your specific workload on your specific hardware. The download for this can be found here: http://www.microsoft.com/en-us/download/details.aspx?id=20163.

Considerations about your I/O workload differ when working with virtual environments because the operating system is often running on the same set of spindles as your data files. These additional considerations can present opportunities for you to work with your virtualization expert and your storage guru to perhaps isolate the I/O required for the operating systems in the environment from your database files. A good way to illustrate the I/O required is with the Performance Monitor data discussed earlier and by using the SQLIO tool I just discussed.

Features of SQL Server will also impact your I/O. A great example of this is backup compression. When you use backup compression, fewer I/O requests are required to write the data file because it's compressed in memory before it writes to the disk. Another SQL Server feature is Snapshot Isolation, which enables SQL Server to use optimistic locking rather than the default pessimistic locking scheme. The difference is considerable. Pessimistic locking can be considered *serialized*, meaning that modifications can occur for only one column at a time. With optimistic locking, Microsoft introduced a way for multiple requests to modify the same column. The reason that it's important in this context is that the row version store required for Snapshot Isolation is in the TempDB database and can use TempDB aggressively, thereby increasing your I/O footprint. Again, this is an excellent feature, but one that must be tested in your specific environment.

> ▓ **Note** I've had success with increasing throughput and concurrency in TempDB with Snapshot Isolation by implementing trace flag –T1118 at startup. You can find out more at `http://support.microsoft.com/kb/2154845`.

Over the past several years, a few companies have risen to the forefront of I/O performance. I've had the pleasure of working with products from Fusion-io that provide very fast I/O throughput. I've used Fusion-io cards for TempDB, file stores, and even transaction logs. The throughput you can achieve with a Fusion-io card far exceeds that of traditional spindles, but the real value comes from the decreased latency. The latency of their entry-level product is measured in microseconds. This is pretty impressive considering that you measure I/O time in milliseconds. If you are considering purchasing this product or have a product similar to this, data files that require ultra-low latency benefit from this type of storage.

Compression is another feature that can benefit your I/O throughput and overall database performance, as it relates to I/O. There are two primary types of compression to be aware of. The first is *backup compression*. When creating a backup, you can choose to compress the backup. This decreases the amount of data that has to be written to disk. The second is *data compression*. Data compression comes in two primary forms: row and page. Chapter 14 dives into the details of data compression, but what you need to know for the purpose of this chapter is that data compression, if applied correctly, can significantly increase your database throughput, decrease your latency (read and write time), and improve the response time of your database server. It can also decrease memory pressure that you might be experiencing. There are many caveats to the case for using data compression and deciding which tables and index to compress in which fashion is critical. So be sure that you read the chapter on this topic and that you spend time to test.

Partitioning is another excellent avenue for decreasing your IOPS. Partitioning, in a nutshell, is akin to breaking your table up into many different tables. A quick example of this will help you understand the value of partitioning and, more importantly, the concept of *partition elimination*.

A simple illustration with the Transactions table that has a `TransactionDate` column will help. In this table, let's say that you have one million records ranging from 2005 to 2010 (five years). For the purpose of this example, assume that the data distribution across each year is identical. For each year, there are 250,000 transactions (rows). When you run a query similar to `SELECT COUNT (*)`, `Convert(date, TransactionDate) as TransactionDate FROM Transactions where TransactionDate BETWEEN '06/01/2005'` and `'06/01/2006'`, the database engine will need to access $n$ pages at the root and intermediate levels.

If partitioning is implemented on this table—specifically, on the `TransactionDate` column—you can decrease the footprint of the data that SQL Server needs to evaluate your particular query. Another way to think about this partitioning concept is akin to one of having multiple tables which contain the data in the Transaction table. In this example, if you had a Transactions table for each year, SQL Server's work would be significantly less. It would also make for some challenging T-SQL or implementation of a distributed partition view (DPV), but let's keep it simple and just partition the table and allow SQL Server to eliminate what it doesn't need to read. There are many good resources available to learn more about this subject, and one of my favorites can be found here: `http://msdn.microsoft.com/en-us/library/dd578580(v=sql.100).aspx`. Details specific to SQL Server 2012, including a change from previous versions of SQL Server as it relates to the quantity of partitions a table can contain, can be found here: `http://msdn.microsoft.com/en-us/library/ms190787.aspx`.

## Conclusion

At times, there are no easy answers for dealing with the increase in data volumes that many of you experience on a daily basis. However, there are tools at your disposal to help you define and then articulate your specific situation. There are also design considerations you can help introduce or implement in your environment. It all begins with knowing your IOP pattern and being able to discuss it at a moment's notice. Then work on the ideas you have gleaned from this chapter. Your IOP pattern will change over time and with new features and functionality. Keep your IOP profile up to date, take your storage guru out to lunch, build the bridge of communication and trust with your peers. Before you know it, you will be able to look this 800-pound I/O gorilla in the eye and not blink.

# CHAPTER 14

■ ■ ■

# Page and Row Compression

## By Bradley Ball

The first question that needs to be answered about page and row compression is the most important. Why should you use it? After all, hard-drives and disks are cheap, right?

You hear that all the time—disks are cheap, or storage is cheap. It certainly isn't as expensive as it was 10 years ago. You can walk down to your nearest retailer on Black Friday, an American Shopping holiday, and purchase a 2-terabyte (TB) hard drive for under $100. In some cases, you can find solid-state disks of the same size for a little more. I would wager a guess that you do not go out and buy the hard drives for your production servers on Black Friday, or any other shopping holiday. Even if you did, these disks are not designed to work in storage area network (SAN), devices. When you purchase a SAN, you're typically looking at an expense of thousands of dollars. If you have multiple SANs, you might have a SAN administrator or two. Before you know it, those disks start to add up.

Then you have the databases you manage. You probably don't manage just one database or one SQL instance. You might have the same database in Production, Staging or QA, or Development, or you might have a Continuation of Operations Planning/Disaster Recovery (COOP/DR) server. Administrators often strive to eliminate data duplication within a database, but it is a necessary part of proper content management to have duplicated copies of data in multiple environments. When you start thinking about all of that data for all of the many systems you manage, you quickly see how compression can save you space—not just on a single table in a single database, but across your entire corporate SQL Server enterprise.

Space savings in your database are just one reason to consider using page and row compression. You also reduce the memory footprint required for you database, the logical IOs from queries, your backup size, and your backup time.

---

■ **Tip** I cannot tell you how many times I give a presentation on compression and afterwards someone says something along the lines of, "Is it bad if I compress my entire database?".

Yes, Dear Reader, it is. However, I like to reply with a question and ask if they would compress their entire C: drive on their laptop? Sure it will save you space, but unless you're on a powerful computer it will drag down your whole operating system, because you're performing compression operations on all data regardless of whether it is suited for compression or not.

Similarly, you don't want to compress the entire contents of a database unless that data is compatible with compression. The cost of compression is additional CPU cycles and most servers have cycles to spare, but you don't want to waste them needlessly. Rarely will you find a database where compressing every single table is a good idea. 99.99 percent of databases should not be fully compressed. You might be in the 00.01 percent, but I wouldn't bet on it. Wasting CPU cycles can cause scalability issues for your database at a future date.

As we will discuss, there are certain specific things you can do to find what you should and should not compress in your database.

# Before You Get Started

Before you can begin enabling page and row compression, there are a couple of basic considerations to think about. First you need to use an edition of SQL Server 2012 that supports page and row compression, and you need to ensure that you will not need to restore that database on a lower version, such as Microsoft SQL Server 2012 Standard Edition. Once the basic compatibility issue is out of the way, you also need to consider exactly what data to compress and how to do it.

Most importantly: Know Thy Data! Knowledge of the data types that are used on tables, and the type of data that is stored within them, can make a big difference in determining what you should compress.

## Editions and Support

Compression is an enterprise-level feature. This means that you must be using SQL Server 2012 Enterprise Edition or Developer Edition for page and row compression to be available to you. This also means that if you enable compression on an Enterprise Edition SQL instance and try to restore that database to a standard-level instance, it will fail.

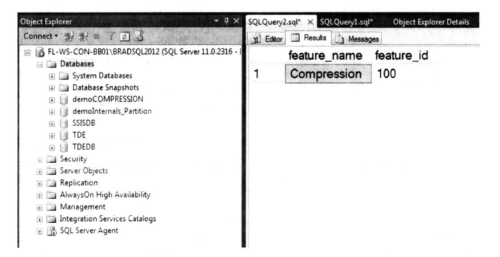

***Figure 14-1.*** *You can use DMV sys.dm_persisted_sku_features to find what Enterprise Edition features are enabled on your database.*

If you need to move an Enterprise Edition database to a lower edition, you can run the following query to see if there are any Enterprise Edition features currently enabled on the database.

```
SELECT
    feature_name
        ,feature_id
FROM
    sys.dm_db_persisted_sku_features;
```

Running this will not only tell you if compression is enabled, but it will inform you of any other Enterprise Edition feature that is enabled, as you can see from Figure 14-1.

## What to Compress and How to Compress It

So what can you compress inside of your database? You can compress heaps (base tables without a clustered index), clustered indexes (base tables ordered by a clustered index), nonclustered indexes, and objects by partition.

You might be wondering what I mean by "objects by partition" This means that if you have a table that uses multiple table partitions, you can compress each partition using a different level of compression: Page, Row, or None. In addition, if you have a partitioned nonclustered index, you can also compress each partition using a different level of compression. See Figure 14-2 for more details.

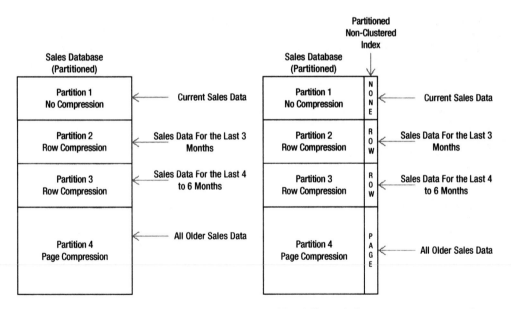

***Figure 14-2.*** *You can compress your partitioned tables differently by partition. You can also compress partitioned nonclustered indexes by partition as well.*

So you can compress heaps, clustered indexes, nonclustered indexes, and objects by partition, but *how* do you compress them? There are two different ways to apply compression. First, you can specify the level of compression you want to use upon creation of the object. Second, you can rebuild a heap, clustered index, or nonclustered index and specify the level of compression you want to use. The ability to rebuild a heap was first introduced in SQL Server 2008. The concept is the same as rebuilding an index.

When a heap is rebuilt, the structure is completely re-created on new data pages. While this occurs, any fragmentation or forwarding pointers caused by inserts, updates, or deletes are eliminated, and the specified compression level is fully applied.

```
ALTER TABLE dbo.heap
REBUILD WITH(data_compression=Page)
GO
```

Once an object is rebuilt using compression, the compression-level selection is inherited in any future rebuild operation. The only time the compression level changes is when you specify a new compression level in a rebuild command. From then on, that new setting will be inherited.

There are three different levels of compression: Page, Row, and None. None is the regular noncompressed format that you are used to using every day. But it is important to know that if you can compress your data, you can uncompress it as well. As far as page and row compression is concerned, let's dive a little deeper.

# Row Compression

We'll start our dive into data compression with row compression. Row compression is the lowest level of compression that will be applied to a SQL Server table, regardless of the compression level specified. Later, when I discuss page compression, I'll detail how it is a superset of row compression.

When I think about compression, I find it helps to think of the hierarchy in which data is stored inside of SQL Server as a map of a shopping mall. (For a full hierarchy, see Figure 14-3.) When you go to a mall, you see a lot of little signs that read "You Are Here." Compression directly affects the way that data is stored, and to understand it you need to start at the bottom and work your way up. Row compression affects the way that data is stored at the Record level. At the very bottom of the hierarchy are records—specifically, data records.

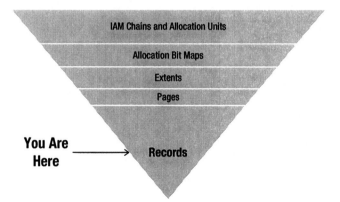

*Figure 14-3. Compression affects the way data is stored on disk. Row compression specifically alters the way data is stored at the record level.*

To help you understand what happens when changes are made to a data record, I'll start by examining a regular record. First I'll make a database and a table so that I can create a data record and insert a record:

```
IF EXISTS(SELECT NAME FROM SYS.DATABASES WHERE NAME='demoInternals')
BEGIN
```

```
        DROP DATABASE demoInternals
END
GO
USE master
GO
CREATE DATABASE demoInternals
GO
USE demoInternals
GO
IF EXISTS(SELECT NAME FROM sys.tables WHERE NAME='dataRecord')
BEGIN
        DROP TABLE dataRecord
END
GO
CREATE TABLE dataRecord
            (myID INT
            ,myfixedData CHAR(4)
            ,myVarData1 VARCHAR(6)
            ,myVarData2 VARCHAR(9)
            ,myVarData3 VARCHAR(6)
            )

GO
INSERT INTO dataRecord(myID, myfixedData, myVarData1, myVarData2, myVarData3)
VALUES (7, 'XXXX', 'SSS', 'WWWWWWWW', 'BB')
GO
```

A regular data record is made up of tag bytes, the NULL bitmap offset, the fixed data portion of the record, the NULL bitmap, the variable offset array, the variable array, and special information (used for the snapshot isolation level or forwarding pointers in heaps). I will now use the undocumented commands DBCC IND and DBCC PAGE to peek underneath the covers and see the data record on disk. (See Figure 14-5.)

```
DBCC IND(demoInternals, 'dataRecord',  1)
GO
--*Note your Page IDs may vary from mine
--We want to get the Page Number which
--has the column value of PageType  =1
```

| | PageFID | PagePID | IAMFID | IAMPiD | ObjectID | IndexID | PartitionNumber | PartitionID | iam_chain_type | PageType | IndexLevel |
|---|---|---|---|---|---|---|---|---|---|---|---|
| 1 | 1 | 277 | NULL | NULL | 245575913 | 1 | 1 | 72057594039042048 | In-row data | 10 | NULL |
| 2 | 1 | 276 | 1 | 277 | 245575913 | 1 | 1 | 72057594039042048 | In-row data | 1 | 0 |

**Figure 14-4.** *Output of DBCC IND.*

As you can see from Figure 14-4, two rows have been returned. We want to look at the data record. If you look at the PageType column, you'll see one row has a value of 10 and the other has a value of 1. Value 10 is an allocation page. Whenever a table is created, it receives an allocation page, and this is that page for our table, while value 1 indicates a data page. If you then look at column PagePID for the row that has a PageType value of 1, you see the data record is found on page 276. Now set Trace Flag 3604 to ON to send the output of DBCC Page to the SQL Server Management Studio, SSMS, window. If you don't enable Trace Flag 3604, you get only the message "Command completed successfully" and no additional output. Next I'll use DBCC Page to view the record. The output of DBCC Page will give us a lot of metadata. I strip that down just to the data that is relevant for us to examine the data record. See Figure 14-5 to see the data record output of DBCC Page.

```
DBCC TRACEON(3604)
GO
DBCC PAGE('demoInternals', 1, 276, 1)
GO
```

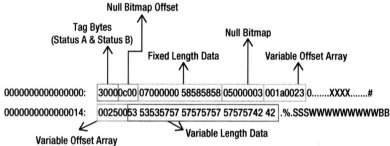
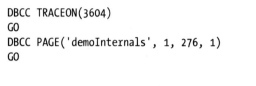
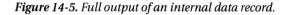

**Figure 14-5.** *Full output of an internal data record.*

In a normal data record, you have tag bytes, a NULL bitmap offset, fixed-length data, the NULL bitmap, our variable offset array, and our variable length data.

SQL Server has five transaction isolation levels: Read Committed, Read Uncommitted, Repeatable Read, Snapshot, and Serializable. The default transaction isolation level for SQL Server is Read Committed. If you use Read Uncommitted or Snapshot, you enable versioning on your data records. A full discussion of transaction isolation levels is beyond the scope of this chapter; see Microsoft Books Online to read more on transaction isolation levels at http://msdn.microsoft.com/en-us/library/ms173763.aspx.

If you have Snapshot or Read Uncommitted isolation level turned on or are using any feature that uses the Snapshot isolation level, such as Online Index or Table Rebuilds, you'll have an additional portion that contains a date timestamp of when the record was last changed.

Row compression works on the fixed-length data types in the data record. What are fixed-length data types? Anything that is decimal, numeric, smallint, int, bigint, bit, smallmoney, money, float, real, datetime, datetime2, datetimeoffset, char, binary, timestamp/rowversion, nchar, nvarchar, and introduced in SQL 2012 for the first time, Spatial Data Types Geometry and Geography.

So how does it work? Row compression stores fixed-length data that contains variable-length data as variable-length data. That's a bit of a tongue twister, but let me explain. If I took a Char(50) field and put in the value "Bradley Ball," I would be using only 12 bytes out of 50. A regular data record wastes those 38 bytes. Row compression stores just the 12 bytes. If I had a datetime field—normally, 8 bytes—and inserted the value "1/25/1977," a compressed record would store that as a 4-byte field, giving us 4 bytes of savings. Our variable-length identifiers, the variable offset array, are reduced from 4 bytes to 4 bits each. There is also special handling for NULL values and zeros, which reduces storage from bytes to bits.

Now that you've looked at a normal data record and read about the changes row compression will make, try compressing the record. After you rebuild the table, you need to use DBCC IND to get the data page again (as you can see in Figure 14-6), because the rebuild operation creates a new page with a new page number.

```
ALTER TABLE dataRecord
REBUILD WITH (DATA_COMPRESSION=ROW)
GO
DBCC IND(demoInternals, 'dataRecord',  1)
GO
```

| | PageFID | PagePID | IAMFID | IAMPID | ObjectID | IndexID | PartitionNumber | PartitionID | iam_chain_type | PageType |
|---|---|---|---|---|---|---|---|---|---|---|
| 1 | 1 | 321 | NULL | NULL | 949578421 | 0 | 1 | 72057594040811520 | In-row data | 10 |
| 2 | 1 | 320 | 1 | 321 | 949578421 | 0 | 1 | 72057594040811520 | In-row data | 1 |

*Figure 14-6. Output of DBCC IND.*

Now use DBCC Page to get the Row Compressed record. The results are shown in Figure 14-7. Once again, I strip out the metadata details and list only the data record, but as you examine the output of DBCC Page, you'll see that the record type is now listed as compressed.

```
DBCC PAGE('demoInternals', 1, 320, 1)
GO
```

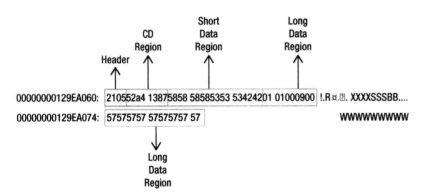

*Figure 14-7. Row-compressed data record.*

Now that the record is row-compressed, you can see that the structure of the record has changed quite a bit. You have a header, CD region, a short data region that stores all data shorter than 9 bytes, and a long data region with all data that is 9 bytes and longer. Once again, if you had the Snapshot isolation level turned on or if you had a forwarding pointer from a heap, they would be at the end of the record in an area called Special Information.

It is important to understand row compression because it is the default level of compression that will be applied when compression is turned on. Furthermore, index pages beyond the leaf level will only be row-compressed even if you're using Page-level compression.

# Page Compression

The next step on our tour of SQL compression internals is page compression, as shown in Figure 14-8.

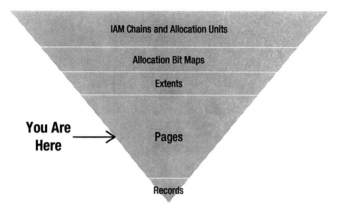

*Figure 14-8. Page compression rearranges structures at the page level.*

Page compression is a superset of row compression. As I mentioned before, at the lowest level once compression is turned on, everything is at least row compressed. Page compression contains row compression, column prefix compression, and page dictionary compression. Page compression is always applied in the order of row, column, and then dictionary. Note that you can specify only row and page compression settings on a database object. Column prefix and page dictionary compression are internal subsets of page compression. You cannot specify which portions of page compression to use—SQL Server makes that determination internally. To help you fully understand page compression, I need to cover each step that occurs when it is applied, which I will do shortly. First I'll create a table I can use to demonstrate the power of page compression.

```
USE demoInternals;
GO

/*
Let's create a Clustered Index
*/
IF EXISTS(SELECT NAME FROM sys.tables WHERE name=N'compressedDataRecord')
BEGIN
    DROP TABLE dbo.compressedDataRecord
END
CREATE TABLE compressedDataRecord(
    myID INT IDENTITY(1,1)
    ,productName char(500) DEFAULT 'some product'
    ,productDescription CHAR(1000) DEFAULT 'Product Description'
    ,PRIMARY KEY CLUSTERED(myID)
) ;
/*
Let's insert some data
*/
DECLARE @i INT, @myID INT
SET @i=0
WHILE (@i<383)
BEGIN
        SET @myID=(SELECT (MAX(myid)+1) FROM dbo.compressedDataRecord)
```

```
        INSERT INTO dbo.compressedDataRecord(productName, productDescription)
        VALUES(
    (REPLICATE('a', (500- LEN(@myID))) + CAST(@myID AS VARCHAR(3)))
    (REPLICATE('b', (1000- LEN(@myID))) + CAST(@myID AS VARCHAR(3)))
            )
    SET @i=@i+1
END
```

When we looked at row compression, it was important to look at one data row and see the changes. Page compression requires an understanding of not just the changes to the data page, explained shortly, but an understanding of how data storage changes. When you used the preceding script to insert data, you're taking fixed-length data fields and stretching them to the point that row compression can save you little to no storage space. You're packing these fields as full as you can. If you use DBCC IND to get a page count, you'll see that you're currently storing data on 79 different pages. Subtract the PageType 10 allocation page and the PageType 2 index page and you're at 77 total pages for the table:

```
DBCC IND(demoInternals, 'compressedDataRecord', 1)
GO
```

So now let's apply page compression, perform another DBCC IND, and see how this changes our storage structure:

```
/*
Rebuild our table applying Page Compression
*/
ALTER TABLE dbo.compressedDataRecord
REBUILD WITH (DATA_COMPRESSION=Page)
GO
DBCC IND(demoInternals, 'compressedDataRecord', 1)
GO
```

After running the commands, you should find that you now have only two data pages on disk. The PageType 10 allocation page and the PageType1 data page are all that is left. You just reduced 77 pages to 1. These results are not typical; you're working with a data set that is optimized to display the power that page compression *can* potentially have on your data.

When I discussed row compression, I talked about how it worked only on fixed-length data types. Page compression occurs at the binary level across the entire data page, so it is data-type agnostic. Meaning,

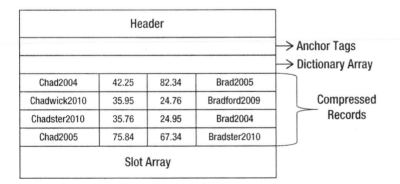

*Figure 14-9. Page compression starts with a page being row-compressed.*

simply, that if your data is in an IN_ROW_DATA page, it can be page-compressed. I'll say more about that a little later when I discuss allocation units.

So let's walk through how data is compressed at the page level. I find that it is easier to explain at a text level instead of at a binary level. The important thing to take away is an understanding of the difference of the structures between a regular data page and a compressed data page. When you look at Figure 14-9, you'll see a regular row-compressed data page. At this point, you can assume that row compression has been applied and all of the extra space has been removed from the records. You'll see boxes for anchor tags and the dictionary array, and I'll discuss these as we apply column prefix and dictionary compression, respectively.

Now if you look at Figure 14-10, you see a page that has had column prefix compression applied. The way that it works is it goes through each row at a record level and finds the common prefix values. For column one, you can see the values Chad2004, Chadwick2010, Chadster2010, and Chad2005. The common prefix in each column is (Chad). Column prefix compression takes the longest value with the matching pattern, (Chad), and places it in the anchor tag—in this case, Chadwick2010.

A special 2-bit value, symbolized by a NULL, takes the place of Chadwick2010, on Row 2 Column 1 of Figure 14-10. In that portion of the record, the NULL points to the anchor tag as the home of the data for that column. All the remaining rows are also altered, putting a numeric value in place to symbolize the number of characters to be read from the anchor tag to be applied to all of the other records in that column in order to be properly read, as shown in Figure 14-10.

If you look at the other columns, you can begin to see the matching patterns. In Column 2, the only values that match are 35.95 and 35.76. The common pattern is (35.), so 35.95 is placed in the anchor tag and the values in that column are replaced. There are two records in that column that do not have any values matching (35.): 42.25 and 75.84. These columns will still get a value placed before them—in this case, a zero—which tells the read process that it does not need to go to the anchor tag to retrieve any data for this row.

The same logic that applied to Column 2 is now applied to Column 3, with the matching value being (24.). Column 4 receives the same logic that was used on Column 1 with the matching value being (Brad).

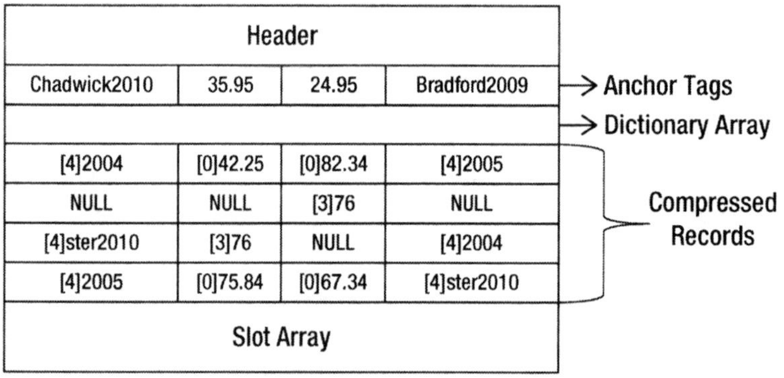

| Header | | | |
|---|---|---|---|
| Chadwick2010 | 35.95 | 24.95 | Bradford2009 |
| | | | |
| [4]2004 | [0]42.25 | [0]82.34 | [4]2005 |
| NULL | NULL | [3]76 | NULL |
| [4]ster2010 | [3]76 | NULL | [4]2004 |
| [4]2005 | [0]75.84 | [0]67.34 | [4]ster2010 |
| Slot Array | | | |

→ Anchor Tags
→ Dictionary Array

Compressed Records

*Figure 14-10. A page-compressed record with column prefix compression applied.*

Now that row and column prefix compression have been applied, it is finally time for dictionary compression. Figure 14-11 shows a page that is fully compressed, having had dictionary compression applied.

Dictionary compression populates a dictionary array at the top of the page. The dictionary array is a 0-based multidimensional array. It will look across the entire page to find matching binary patterns and place them in the dictionary array. When you look across the page, the first two common values you come

| Header | | | | |
|---|---|---|---|---|
| Chadwick2010 | 35.95 | 24.95 | Bradford2009 | → Anchor Tags |
| [4]2004 | [4]ster2010 | [4]2005 | [3]76 | → Dictionary Array |
| 0 | [0]42.25 | [0]82.34 | 2 | |
| NULL | NULL | 3 | NULL | Compressed Records |
| 1 | 3 | NULL | 0 | |
| 2 | [0]75.84 | [0]67.34 | 1 | |
| Slot Array | | | | |

*Figure 14-11.* A page fully compressed, with dictionary compression applied.

across are [4]2004 in Row 1 Column 1 and Row 3 Column 4. Each value will be replaced with a 0 (zero) pointing to the array position in the dictionary array.

The next value encountered is [4]Ster2010 in Row 3 Column 1 and Row 4 Column 4 for array position 1. Then the value [4]2005 from Row 4 Column 1, and Row 1 Column 4 will be replaced by array position 2. Finally [3]76, from Row 3 Column 2 and Row 2 Column 3 will be replaced by array position 3.

When you look at the contents of a regular data page compared to a compressed data page, you can see that the contents are wildly different. So different that you might wonder between SQL Server 2005 and SQL Server 2008, where compression was first introduced, how Microsoft developers had time to make the Relational Engine read from two different sets of pages. The answer is they didn't.

When page or row compression is turned on, the data is stored on disk in a compressed format, and it is read into memory in a compressed format. However, when it is read out from memory from the buffer pool before the access methods return the data to the relational engine, the compressed data is rewritten in an uncompressed format. The uncompressed pages are not stored in memory. The pages are translated at the cost of CPU operations. To examine this more closely, take a look at Figure 14-12 to see how a select operation works in SQL Server against a compressed table.

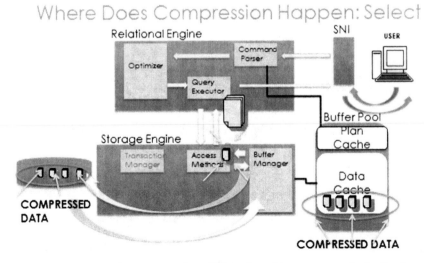

*Figure 14-12.* Data is compressed on disk and read into memory in the Pool compressed; only when it leaves the Storage Engine for the Relational Engine is it uncompressed.

When a query initially comes from the user, it connects through the SQL Network Interface (SNI), which translates the data to a Tabular Data Stream protocol that is proprietary to Microsoft. The query then reaches the Command Parser. You have interacted with the Command Parser if you've ever received an error on a query where the syntax is not correct. SQL Server checks to see if the query has a cached plan so that it can skip optimization; in our case, it does not, and the query is handed to the optimizer. After a plan is created for retrieving the data, the query goes to the Query Executor. The Query Executor asks the access methods for a copy of the data needed to satisfy the query and hands it the direction to go to find the data. The access methods ask for the required pages from the buffer manager, which checks the data cache to see if the pages are there. The pages for our query are not, so the buffer manager retrieves them from disk, in a compressed format, and reads them into memory in the data cache in a compressed format. The buffer manager then gives the required pages to the access methods. The access methods translate page-compressed pages to an uncompressed format. Row-compressed pages are uncompressed by a "landing pad" in the Relational Engine block of code before being handed back to the Query Executor. The Query Executor sends the data back through the SNI, which translates it for the client.

This is an oversimplification of the process. Weeks and months of courses are taught on the specific internal components of the Relational and Storage engines. The important information here is data is compressed on *disk* and in *memory*. So you receive space-savings benefits in both locations.

The amount of CPU overhead is directly related to the level of compression you use and the type of load on your server. If you have a CPU-bound server with average sustained CPU usage around 60 percent or higher, you might not want to use compression, at least not on volatile tables that have a lot of inserts and updates.

---

■ **Tip**  Page compression is a very interesting feature. Every page in a page-compressed table or index automatically receives row compression, but for column prefix or page dictionary compression to be applied, either or both must be able to accomplish 20 percent space savings across the page—otherwise, the page will receive only row compression. This means on a table that has had page compression applied, some pages could be only row-compressed while others are page-compressed. This is internally managed by SQL Server and is not something that can be changed by the user.

Index pages receive page compression only at the Leaf level. At the Root and Intermediate levels, they will be only row compressed.

When page compression is enabled, new data is inserted only in a row-compressed format. When a page fills to the point that a page split occurs in a clustered index, the page-compression calculation fires off.

In a heap, new data is always inserted in a row-compressed format even if 20 percent space savings can be achieved. The only way to get page compression to fully apply to a heap is to rebuild the heap.

---

# What Do You Compress?

Now that you have a better understanding of compression and how it works with your data, you can start to look at your data to figure out what you should and should not compress. The factors that will play the largest part in your compression decision are table size, allocation units, and scan and update patterns on your tables.

You want to get the biggest bang for your buck, and I understand that. When you go to your boss and say, "We can save X amount of space using SQL Server compression," you want to say it proudly. So the first thing you want to know is this: what are the largest tables in our database? There are multiple ways to get your table space usage in SSMS: you can right-click on your database, select reports, and select Disk Usage by Table. You could also use DMV sys.dm_db_partition_stats. It would take a little finesse to get the same output, but the data is there. Normally, to get that I like to run a script I have that uses the undocumented sp_MSforeachtable and that inserts the data from sp_spaceused into a table variable and returns a list of tables and their sizes.

The command sp_MSforeachtable is a function that does a cursor loop through all user tables in a user database, and all tables in a system database. The command sp_spaceused is a documented function that gives you the table name, rows, reserved space, data space, index size, and unused space per table.

```
DECLARE @myTable AS TABLE(
                        [Name] varchar(1000)
                        ,[Rows] int
                        ,[Reserved] varchar(500)
                        ,[Data] varchar(500)
                        ,[Index_Size] varchar(500)
                        ,[Unused] varchar(500)
                        );

INSERT INTO @myTable
EXEC ('sp_msforeachtable @command1="sp_spaceused [?]"');

SELECT
    NAME
    ,ROWS
    ,RESERVED
    ,(cast(LEFT([reserved],(LEN([reserved])-3)) as int)/1024) as ReservedMB
    ,((cast(LEFT([reserved],(LEN([reserved])-3)) as int)/1024)/1024) as ReservedGB
    ,DATA
    ,INDEX_SIZE
    ,UNUSED
FROM
    @myTable
ORDER BY
    (cast(LEFT([reserved],(LEN([reserved])-3)) as int)/1024) DESC;
GO
```

Now that you know what the largest tables are, you need to know what kind of allocation units they are made up of. SQL Server has three types of allocation units: IN_ROW_DATA, ROW_OVERFLOW_DATA, and LOB_DATA. Allocation units are responsible for tracking how many pages have been allocated and what types of pages have been allocated for a particular table. The data type you select to use in your table determines the type of allocation units SQL Server uses. See Table 14-1 for a list of which data types are associated with which types of allocation units.

The only allocations units that can be compressed are data types that use only IN_ROW_DATA pages. Luckily, as long as you're not using Large Object (LOB) types such as Text, Image, XML, or any of the MAX types—(VARCHAR(MAX), BINARY(MAX), NVARCHAR(MAX))—the data will be on IN_ROW_PAGES. If your data record contains less than 8,000 bytes of data, you can have LOB data types on IN_ROW_DATA pages. In those cases, row compression doesn't give you space savings, because you have variable-length columns and that do not waste extra unused space. Page compression might save you space if the binary data matches the criteria I previously covered with regard to meeting page-compression requirements for being applied to a page. As long as the data can exist on IN_ROW_DATA pages, it can be compressed. In a moment, I'll validate this statement with an example, but first let's continue on with allocation units.

**Table 14-1.** *Types of allocation units and their data types. Remember, only IN_ROW_DATA can be compressed.*

| Allocation Unit Type | Data Types | Description |
|---|---|---|
| IN_ROW_DATA | SMALLINT, INT, TINYINT, BIT, BIGINT, CHAR, NCHAR, NVARCHAR, NVARCHAR(MAX), VARCHAR, VARCHAR(MAX), DECIMAL, NUMERIC, SMALLMONEY, MONEY, FLOAT, REAL, DATE, DATETIME, DATETIME2, DATETIMEOFFSET, SMALLDATETIME, TIME, BINARY, VARBINARY, VARBINARY(MAX), XML, GEOGRAPHY, GEOMETRY TIMESTAMP/ ROWVERSION, UNIQUEIDENTIFIER, CLR User Defined Types, or SQL_VARIANT | Regular data pages, with a combined record size of 8,000 bytes. Most data types that can exist on other allocation-unit pages can also be on IN_ROW_DATA pages as well, as long as the total record size is under 8,000 bytes. |
| ROW_OVERFLOW_DATA | VARCHAR, NVARCHAR, VARBINARY, CLR User Defined Types, or SQL_VARIANT | Variable-length data that can start out on an IN_ROW_DATA page. Once the record exceeds 8,000 bytes, the largest variable-length field is moved into a ROW_OVERFLOW_DATA page. |
| LOB_DATA | XML, TEXT, IMAGE, NTEXT, VARCHAR(MAX), VARBINARY(MAX), NVARCHAR(MAX) | Stands for "Large Object Data." |

The first thing I would do is run a query against the database to get back all the page counts for allocation unit types. To do this, I run the following query to get a list of tables and indexes by page count, focusing on the tables with IN_ROW_DATA.

```
SELECT
    OBJECT_NAME(sp.object_id) AS [ObjectName]
    ,si.name AS IndexName
    ,sps.in_row_data_page_count as In_Row_Data
    ,sps.row_overflow_used_page_count AS Row_Over_Flow_Data
    ,sps.lob_reserved_page_count AS LOB_Data
FROM
    sys.dm_db_partition_stats sps
    JOIN sys.partitions sp
        ON sps.partition_id=sp.partition_id
    JOIN sys.indexes si
        ON sp.index_id=si.index_id AND sp.object_id = si.object_id
WHERE
    OBJECTPROPERTY(sp.object_id,'IsUserTable')    =1
order by sps.in_row_data_page_count desc
```

Now let's validate that the data type doesn't matter as long as the data is located on IN_ROW_DATA pages. We'll use the following script to create a table in our database that has the VARCHAR(MAX) data type, but we will use only 4,037 characters of data and apply page compression:

```
/*
Select our demo database
to use
*/
USE demoInternals
GO
/*
Create our table
*/
IF EXISTS(SELECT name FROM sys.tables WHERE name='vmaxTest')
BEGIN
    DROP TABLE dbo.vmaxTest
END
GO
CREATE TABLE vmaxTest(myid int identity(1,1)
    , mydata varchar(max) default 'a'
    ,CONSTRAINT pk_vmaxtest1 PRIMARY KEY CLUSTERED (myid))
GO
/*
Insert 5000 rows
*/
DECLARE @i INT
SET @i=0
WHILE (@i<5000)
BEGIN
    INSERT INTO vmaxTest(mydata)
    VALUES(replicate('a',4032)+cast(@i AS VARCHAR(5)))
    SET @i=@i+1
END
GO
/*
Check our space before we compress
*/
sp_spaceused 'vmaxTest'
GO
/*
Rebuild our table with
Page Compression
*/
ALTER TABLE dbo.vmaxtest
REBUILD WITH(DATA_COMPRESSION=PAGE);
GO
/*
Check our space after we compress
*/
sp_spaceused 'vmaxTest'
GO
```

As you can see from Figure 14-13, the space used before we compressed our table was 40,200 KB, or roughly 40 MB. Not a large data set, but enough to show what we want to test. The storage size was reduced to 320 KB after applying page compression.

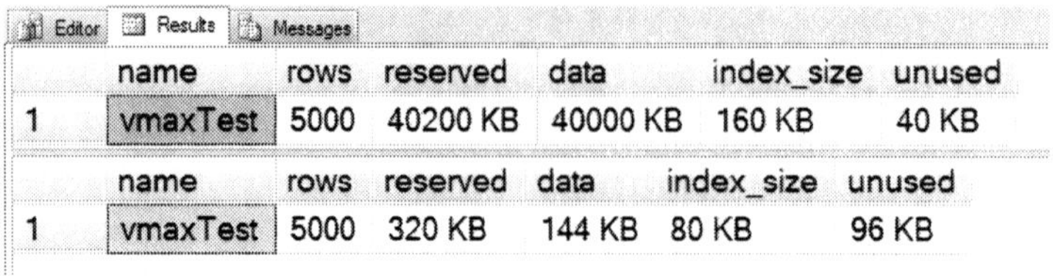

| | name | rows | reserved | data | index_size | unused |
|---|---|---|---|---|---|---|
| 1 | vmaxTest | 5000 | 40200 KB | 40000 KB | 160 KB | 40 KB |

| | name | rows | reserved | data | index_size | unused |
|---|---|---|---|---|---|---|
| 1 | vmaxTest | 5000 | 320 KB | 144 KB | 80 KB | 96 KB |

***Figure 14-13.*** *Looking at the results of page compression against a* VARCHAR(MAX) *data type that was in an* IN_ROW_DATA *page.*

This validates that we can compress VARCHAR(MAX) on an IN_ROW_DATA page, but it validates only half of our premise. To test this, we need to create data allocated by something other than IN_ROW_DATA and see that it doesn't compress. We'll use the same script as last time, but we'll add another VARCHAR(MAX) field and force some of the data to LOB_DATA pages. See Figure 14-14 for the page counts prior to compression. After that, we'll take a look at the allocation units, validate that the pages have been created, and then compress the data still in the IN_ROW_DATA pages. See Figure 14-15 for the page counts after compression has been applied.

```
/*
Select our demo database
to use
*/
USE demoInternals
GO
/*
Create our table
*/
IF EXISTS(SELECT name FROM sys.tables WHERE name='vmaxTest')
BEGIN
    DROP TABLE dbo.vmaxTest
END
GO
CREATE TABLE vmaxTest(myid int identity(1,1)
    , mydata varchar(8000) default 'a'
    ,mydata2 varchar(max) default 'b'
    ,CONSTRAINT pk_vmaxtest1 PRIMARY KEY CLUSTERED (myid))
GO
/*
Insert 5000 rows
*/
DECLARE @i INT
SET @i=0
WHILE (@i<5000)
BEGIN
    INSERT INTO vmaxTest(mydata, mydata2)
    VALUES(replicate('a',2016)+cast(@i AS VARCHAR(5)), replicate('b',2016)+cast(@i AS
VARCHAR(5)))
    SET @i=@i+1
END
GO
```

```
/*
create some row overflow data by
inflating the size of our mydata2
varchar(max) field to 7000 characters
*/
UPDATE dbo.vmaxTest
SET mydata=replicate('a',3900),
 mydata2=replicate('b', 5000)
GO
/*
Validate our Allocation Unit Makeup
and get page counts
*/
SELECT
    OBJECT_NAME(sp.object_id) AS [ObjectName]
    ,si.name AS IndexName
    ,sps.in_row_data_page_count as In_Row_Data
    ,sps.row_overflow_used_page_count AS Row_Over_Flow_Data
    ,sps.lob_reserved_page_count AS LOB_Data
FROM
    sys.dm_db_partition_stats sps
    JOIN sys.partitions sp
        ON sps.partition_id=sp.partition_id
    JOIN sys.indexes si
        ON sp.index_id=si.index_id AND sp.object_id = si.object_id
WHERE
    OBJECTPROPERTY(sp.object_id,'IsUserTable')     =1
order by sps.in_row_data_page_count desc
```

| | ObjectName | IndexName | In_Row_Data | Row_Over_Flow_Data | LOB_Data |
|---|---|---|---|---|---|
| 1 | vmaxTest | pk_vmaxtest1 | 5000 | 0 | 5009 |

*Figure 14-14. Page count by allocation unit before applying page compression.*

```
/*
Rebuild our table with
Page Compression
*/
ALTER TABLE dbo.vmaxtest
REBUILD WITH(DATA_COMPRESSION=PAGE);
GO

/*
Validate our Allocation Unit Makeup
and get page counts
*/
SELECT
    OBJECT_NAME(sp.object_id) AS [ObjectName]
```

```
        ,si.name AS IndexName
        ,sps.in_row_data_page_count as In_Row_Data
        ,sps.row_overflow_used_page_count AS Row_Over_Flow_Data
        ,sps.lob_reserved_page_count AS LOB_Data
FROM
    sys.dm_db_partition_stats sps
    JOIN sys.partitions sp
        ON sps.partition_id=sp.partition_id
    JOIN sys.indexes si
        ON sp.index_id=si.index_id AND sp.object_id = si.object_id
WHERE
    OBJECTPROPERTY(sp.object_id,'IsUserTable')    =1
order by sps.in_row_data_page_count desc
```

| | ObjectName | IndexName | In_Row_Data | Row_Over_Flow_Data | LOB_Data |
|---|---|---|---|---|---|
| 1 | vmaxTest | pk_vmaxtest1 | 46 | 2 | 5009 |

*Figure 14-15. Page count by allocation unit before after applying page compression.*

I once had a client who had just upgraded from SQL Server 2000 to SQL Server 2008 R2. They wanted to look at using compression on their main production database. They had a particular table in mind, one that had 132 GB of data in it. The first thing I did was look at the allocation units, and they were 1 percent IN_ROW_DATA 99 percent LOB_DATA. Upon asking what was stored in the table, I learned that it had an Image column and was used to hold PDF documents. I immediately told the client that SQL Server data compression was not something they should use on this table, because the majority of the data, the vast majority, was not compressible. The best thing about knowing what type of allocation units make up your table is that not only will it help you choose what *to* compress, but it will help you choose what *not to* compress. We could have used FILESTREAM to store the PDF documents or, in SQL Server 2012, FileTable also was an option to consider, to give them greater flexibility on how they store and searched their data.

As long as your data is in IN_ROW_DATA pages, you can compress it. Know what your allocation unit for your data is before deciding what to compress. I wouldn't normally compress a table with just a 50-50 ratio, like I did in our second example, without taking a couple steps. First find the queries or stored procedures that access this table. Extract the query plans in XML format and examine them. Compress the data, and extract the query plans again. Now did the plans change? How was performance impacted? Answering these questions can go a long way in determining what you will want to compress.

The scan and update patterns, on your tables, are the next thing to consider when determining what to compress. The more a table is updated, the less likely you should be to compress it. Writes cause extra CPU activities. SQL is constantly translating writes to data pages to compressed and uncompressed format. Updates can cause page splits, which then cause the page compression to be recalculated on all updated pages. Notice that I said "updates" and not "inserts." Inserts might cause an issue, but updates speak to the volatility of the data in your table. Our queries will look for scans and updates, and we will filter inserts out of each.

You use the DMV sys.dm_db_index_operational_stats to determine your scan and update patterns. This DMV returns low-level I/O details for a number of range and table scans, as well as update, insert, and delete activity. The query you'll use was originally two separate queries. I used a Common Table Expression (CTE), which is a temporary derived result set based on a simple query, to combine them so that you could look at scans and updates for indexes side by side.

You use the range_scan_count column to get all scans that have occurred against a heap, clustered index, or nonclustered index. You then multiply that number by 100.0 and divide the result by the total scans, inserts, updates, and deletes that have occurred on the system. This gives you a percentage of scan activity on all the indexes in all the tables in your database.

If you perform only selects, you'll always have returned 100 percent. If you issue some updates, deletes, or inserts, you'll see the scan percentage begin to drop.

You use the leaf_update_count column to get all update activity for your heaps, clustered indexes, and nonclustered indexes. Figure 14-16 shows the results of your scan and update query from some of our demo tables; your results might vary based on select, update, and insert statements that you have run. All scan and update data for an object will be cleared when rebuilding an object by applying compression.

Ideally, your updates should be under 40 percent and your scans should be 60 percent or higher, in order to select a table for compression. Neither of these percentages will add up to 100 percent—we are simply getting an average of these two activities out of all the other operations that could be performed on them.

So now let's run a query that will look at each table in your database and let you see what the allocation unit makeup is for each one.

```
WITH IndexUsage(tableName, IndexName, [Partition], IndexID, IndexType, USAGE, Percentage)
AS(
SELECT
    (ss.name + '.' + so.name)
    ,si.name
    ,ios.partition_number
    ,ios.index_id
    ,si.type_desc AS indexType
    ,'SCANS'
    , case ios.range_scan_count
    when 0 then 0
    else

 (ios.range_scan_count *100.0/
    (ios.range_scan_count +
    ios.leaf_delete_count +
    ios.leaf_insert_count +
    ios.leaf_page_merge_count +
    ios.leaf_update_count +
    ios.singleton_lookup_count)) end AS percentScan
FROM
    sys.dm_db_index_operational_stats(DB_ID(),NULL,NULL,NULL) ios
    JOIN sys.objects so
    ON so.object_id=ios.object_id
    JOIN sys.indexes si
    ON si.object_id = ios.object_id AND si.index_id = ios.index_id
    JOIN sys.schemas ss
    ON so.schema_id = ss.schema_id
WHERE
    OBJECTPROPERTY(ios.object_id, 'IsUserTable')=1
UNION ALL

SELECT
    (ss.name + '.'+ so.name)
    ,si.NAME
    ,ios.partition_number
```

```
        ,ios.index_id
        ,si.type_desc
        ,'UPDATES'
        , case ios.leaf_update_count
          when 0 then 0
          else
     (ios.leaf_update_count *100/
        (ios.range_scan_count +
        ios.leaf_insert_count +
        ios.leaf_delete_count +
        ios.leaf_update_count +
        ios.leaf_page_merge_count +
        ios.singleton_lookup_count)) end
FROM
        sys.dm_db_index_operational_stats(DB_ID(), NULL, NULL, NULL) ios
        JOIN sys.objects so
        ON so.object_id = ios.object_id
        JOIN sys.indexes si
        ON ios.object_id=si.OBJECT_ID AND ios.index_id=si.index_id
        JOIN sys.schemas ss
        ON so.schema_id=ss.SCHEMA_ID
WHERE
        OBJECTPROPERTY(ios.object_id, 'IsUserTable') =1
)
SELECT
        iu.tableName
        ,iu.IndexID
        ,iu.IndexType
        ,iu.USAGE
        , cast(iu.Percentage as decimal(12,2)) as Percentage
FROM
        IndexUsage iu
ORDER BY
        iu.tableName
        ,iu.IndexName
        ,iu.Percentage DESC
GO
```

| | tableName | IndexID | IndexType | USAGE | Percentage |
|---|---|---|---|---|---|
| 1 | dbo.datarecord | 0 | HEAP | UPDATES | 42.00 |
| 2 | dbo.datarecord | 0 | HEAP | SCANS | 14.56 |
| 3 | dbo.vmaxTest | 1 | CLUSTERED | SCANS | 100.00 |
| 4 | dbo.vmaxTest | 1 | CLUSTERED | UPDATES | 0.00 |

*Figure 14-16. The scan and update patterns on the tables in my demo database.*

This query uses the statistics in use on your database since the last reboot to determine these patterns. To get solid data, you should run this on a server that has been online for as long as possible. The higher the number of scans, the more the table is suited for compression. The lower the number of scans and higher the number of updates, the more you want to consider either row compression or no compression.

Look at Figure 14-16 and examine our usage patterns. You'll see that vmaxTest is a good candidate for compression. You'll also see that dbo.datarecord is not. Get a baseline of the statements run against the database to validate this decision.

Another thing to consider regarding indexes is the rebuild time. When you enable row compression index, rebuilds on that particular index should take 1.5 times what the rebuild rate is for the same -index in a noncompressed format. Page compression takes that up even further to 2 times the rebuild rate for the same index in an uncompressed format.

So now that you have selected a table based on the table size, allocation unit makeup, and a compression setting based on the scan or update patterns, you're ready to run sp_estimate_data_ compression_savings. This is the built-in procedure for estimating compression space savings. You can focus this procedure by providing the Schema Name, Object Name, Index ID, and Partition Number parameters and specifying the type of compression you want to estimate. You can specify Row, Page, or None. If you have an uncompressed object, you can see the estimated space savings by specifying the type of compression you would like to apply. If you would like to uncompress a compressed object, you can specify None and find out what the estimated size of the uncompressed object will be. Before you do that, I want to issue a big warning.

The system stored procedure sp_estimate_data_compression_savings works by placing 5 percent of the table in your Tempdb and performing the compression operation. Based on the rate of compression, it then extrapolates the data and estimates, based on the size of your table, what your savings might be for the type of compression you specified.

For most people, this will not be a problem. Estimating the compression savings of a 100-MB table will take 5 MB of Tempdb space. However, estimating the compression savings of a 100-GB table will take 5 GB of Tempdb space. If you have a 500-GB table, you need 25 GB of free Tempdb space for the operation. If you fill up Tempdb, activity on your server will grind to a halt. So be careful and only use sp_estimate_ data_compression_savings as your last step.

There are tools on Codeplex and scripts all over the Internet that put sp_estimate_data_compression_ savings in a cursor and run it for every table in your database. I do not recommend this approach because all it does is give you a possible savings *estimate*. It doesn't tell you what the allocation unit makeup of your tables are, nor does it help you determine what level of compression to use.

So before you use sp_estimate_data_compression_savings, take a look at your Tempdb and make sure you have enough free space to estimate the compression savings safely.

After doing this, make sure you take performance baselines before and after compression is applied. Compression will reduce the amount of data cache used by the buffer pool, and reducing the number of pages in a table could move some queries from scans to seeks, thus improving query performance. The only way to be sure is to have a baselines review.

# Fragmentation and Logged Operations

One of the great things about compression is that it efficiently uses all available space on a data page. One of the bad things about compression is it is very easy to create fragmentation from insert, update, and delete operations because compression uses all available space on a data page. Whenever you pack records tightly on a page, this is bound to occur. It is also one of the reasons why you should look at scan and update patterns before determining what to compress.

When you rebuild a heap, clustered index, nonclustered index, or object by partition and apply compression, you can still use all of the wonderful index options the way you have with noncompressed objects. Fill Factor, Pad Index, Sort_in_Tempdb, Online, and all other index options can still be used. Remember though, all rebuilt data records will receive the full amount of compression possible. If you set a Fill Factor of 60, 40 percent of every data page will be left empty and ready for new records. Those new records will receive only row compression even if you have specified page compression until they fill to the point that a page split would occur. This excludes heaps, which get forwarding pointers and not page splits. Heaps need to be completely rebuilt before they can compress new records to a compression level lower than Row.

This means you can use the power of compression with additional index hints to prevent fragmentation, while still getting space savings.

Another thing you might wonder is what this does this to database logging. If your database is in the Full recovery model, all transactions are logged operations that can be cleared only by transaction log backups. In this situation, you might wonder how much overhead compression adds. The answer to that is that compression applies very minimal changes in logging regardless of the recovery model.

But don't just take my word for it, let's prove it. First create a database you can test against:

```
USE master;
Go
IF EXISTS(SELECT name FROM sys.databases WHERE Name=N'demoCOMPRESSIONInternals')
    BEGIN
        DROP Database demoCOMPRESSIONInternals
    END
CREATE DATABASE demoCOMPRESSIONInternals
GO


USE demoCOMPRESSIONInternals
go
IF EXISTS(SELECT NAME FROM sys.tables WHERE name=N'myTableC1')
BEGIN
    DROP TABLE dbo.myTableC1
END

CREATE TABLE myTableC1(
    myID INT IDENTITY(1,1)
    ,productName char(500) DEFAULT 'some product'
    ,productDescription CHAR(1000) DEFAULT 'Product Description'
    ,PRIMARY KEY CLUSTERED(myID) WITH (DATA_COMPRESSION=PAGE)
) ;
```

I'll use a named transaction so that you can search the transaction log and find the logged operation easily:.

```
/*
Look at the Transactions within
The Transaction Log
*/
BEGIN TRAN Compressed
INSERT INTO dbo.myTableC1(productName, productDescription)
        VALUES(
                (REPLICATE('a', 499) + CAST(1 AS VARCHAR(1)))
                ,(REPLICATE('b', 999)+ CAST(1 AS VARCHAR(1)))
            )


DECLARE @a CHAR (20)
```

```
SELECT @a = [Transaction ID] FROM fn_dblog (null, null) WHERE [Transaction Name]='Compressed'

SELECT * FROM fn_dblog (null, null) WHERE [Transaction ID] = @a;
GO
```

We are using the undocumented function fn_dblog. This function allows us to see and query the contents of the transaction log. When you look at Figure 14-17, you will find, in the Transaction Log, that there are no logged operations outside of what you would find in a normal insert.

| | Current LSN | Operation | Context | Transaction ID | LogBlockGeneration | Tag Bits | Log Record Fixed Length |
|---|---|---|---|---|---|---|---|
| 1 | 0000001f:0000007c:0005 | LOP_BEGIN_XACT | LCX_NULL | 0000:000002fc | 0 | 0x0000 | 76 |
| 2 | 0000001f:0000007c:0006 | LOP_LOCK_XACT | LCX_NULL | 0000:000002fc | 0 | 0x0000 | 24 |
| 3 | 0000001f:0000007c:001b | LOP_INSERT_ROWS | LCX_CLUSTERED | 0000:000002fc | 0 | 0x0000 | 62 |

*Figure 14-17. Looking at the output from fn_dblog produced during the insert on a compressed table.*

So row compression, the default for inserts on pages that have not yet split on clustered indexes, did not produce any logged operations. You know that until the page is full and a split occurs you will not get a page-compression operation. So let's commit the transaction and try inserting some more rows to see what we find:

```
COMMIT TRAN

/*
Let's Add 5000 Rows!!!!
*/

BEGIN TRAN Compressed2
DECLARE @i INT
SET @i=1

WHILE (@i<5000)
    BEGIN
        INSERT INTO dbo.myTableC1(productName, productDescription)
        VALUES(
                (REPLICATE('a', (499-LEN(@i))) + CAST((@i +1) AS VARCHAR(5)))
                ,(REPLICATE('b',(999-LEN(@i))) + CAST((@i+1) AS VARCHAR(5)))
                )


        SET @i = @i +1

    END


DECLARE @a CHAR (20)

SELECT @a = [Transaction ID] FROM fn_dblog (null, null) WHERE [Transaction Name]='Compressed2'

SELECT * FROM fn_dblog (null, null) WHERE [Transaction ID] = @a;
```

GO

You see the same logged operations as before—LOP_BEGIN_XACT, LOP_LOCK_XACT, and LOP_
INSERT_ROWS—repeated over 4999 times. You do not see any compression operations inside of a
transaction because they occur outside of the scope of the transaction. This means there is no additional
overhead in transactions to account for compressed operations, which is very efficient.

If the overhead is a concern, there are two ways you can track this. If you're in the Full recovery model
or the Bulk Logged recovery model and are performing regular transaction log backups (and if you don't,
your transaction log will grow until it fills up the drive it is on and prevent any new data from being
inserted into your database), you can examine the size of your log files and track that size once you turn
compression on. If you notice significant growth, you can use the undocumented function fn_dump_dblog
to query your transaction log backups and see how many LOP_COMPRESSION_INFO logged events you have.
Use your favorite search engine to search for more information on fn_dump_dblog because that is beyond
the scope of this chapter.

If your recovery model is Simple, you can watch the overall growth of your transaction log and watch
your baselines for changes. As long as the Virtual Log Files (VLFs, which are the inner structures of the
transaction log), that contain compression operations have not been overwritten, you can use fn_dblog to
query them as well. You cannot use fn_dump_dblog because you cannot take transaction-log backups in the
Simple recovery model.

To find these transactions, I originally took the entire content of the transaction log and dumped it
into a spreadsheet and sorted by type until I could identify each operation. Because these operations did
not occur within the context of our named transactions, it means that compression operations do not add
overhead to user transactions. I found one in particular that stood out: LOP_COMPRESSION_INFO. Let's take a
look:

```
/*
first don't forget to commit
your transaction
*/
COMMIT TRAN


SELECT * FROM fn_dblog(NULL, NULL) dl
WHERE Operation='LOP_COMPRESSION_INFO'
```

You will find this logged operation frequently. The LOP_COMPRESSION_INFO operation is the logged
event that is called when a data page compression attempt is made. If the attempt has failed, it points to a
bitmap that contains the different reasons that the page would not be compressed. You also have the
columns Compression Info and Compression Log Type. Compression Info contains a copy of the data
record in its compressed format. If you use the commandDBCC Page, that you used earlier, and compare
the data record contents to that of the Compression Info column from the logged operation, they will
match exactly. If you look at the Compression Log Type column, you'll see it is a bit field that is set to 1
when the record has been paged-compressed and 0 when it has not. Some reasons why a record would not
be compressed is that you have not reached the 20 percent space-savings requirement, the page is not yet
full to the point of a page split (in a clustered index), or the data or the page changed and no new
compression savings could be found.

One important note is that when data is modified and committed in SQL Server, it is logged in the
transaction log. When that data is in a compressed state, it takes up less room. Depending on your data
and how it is used, that can translate into space savings within the transaction log. You should not be
afraid of transaction-log overhead when it comes to compression—in fact, quite the opposite.

# Conclusion

Page and row compression are powerful tools. If you're paying for an Enterprise license you should be taking advantage of them. As with indexes, there is not a one-size-fits-all solution to compression. Instead, the more you know about it, the better you will be able to apply it in your environment. Turning it on and walking away is never a good idea. Monitor your systems, and make sure there are not any changes or spikes in CPU usage that will catch you off guard. "Know Thy Data" is not just a catchy phrase. The more you know about your environment, the more you can apply SQL Server internal knowledge to help you manage it effectively.

Remember the criteria to consider: The larger the table, the more likely you are to see a benefit. Get accurate baselines so that you know how compression affects query performance. Look at your allocation-unit structure: tables with 100 percent IN_ROW_DATA pages are great candidates for compression. You want to tread carefully with anything lower than 50 percent. Tables and indexes with greater than 45 percent scan usage patterns are candidates for compression; for update patterns lower than 45 percent (down to 20 percent), use row compression. For 20 percent and lower, use page compression, get a baseline, and test again.

███

# Selecting and Sizing the Server

## By Glenn Berry

With the release of SQL Server 2012, Microsoft has moved to a new licensing model that is quite different from previous releases. Because of this, it is quite important to revisit how you go about selecting database server hardware in order to get good performance and scalability while still keeping your SQL Server 2012 license costs under control. SQL Server 2012 Enterprise Edition uses core-based licensing, where you pay for licenses based on physical processor cores, with a minimum of four physical core licenses required for each physical processor. This is quite a change from the socket-based licensing used by SQL Server 2008 R2 and all previous releases of SQL Server.

This new model came as an unpleasant shock to many people when it was first revealed in November 2011, causing some database professionals to immediately assume a worst-case scenario of a fourfold price increase for SQL Server 2012 licenses. This chapter will show you how to properly select your database server hardware to maximize your performance and scalability, while keeping your SQL Server licensing costs under control.

Depending on your workload type, you will want to make different hardware choices to get the best performance and scalability for your workload.

---

**Tip**    Read the entire chapter before you actually spec out any hardware. The interaction between workloads, hardware, and SQL Server licensing is a complex subject. It is easy to make an expensive mistake if you don't understand the concepts involved.

---

The hardware I look at in this chapter is specifically the server itself, meaning the form factor, and also the CPU and memory. Your CPU choice most strongly affects your licensing costs, and I spend a good deal of time looking at CPU choices with respect to SQL Server's new licensing model. Microsoft's new pricing scheme changes the game, and it's important to revisit assumptions you might be holding that are no longer valid.

## Understanding Your Workload

SQL Server places different demands on its underlying hardware depending on what type of database workload is running against the instance of SQL Server. Database engine workloads are quite different than file server, web server, or application server workloads. SQL Server instances that are running the database engine generally see one of two main types of workloads. One type is an online transaction processing (OLTP) workload, while the other type is a relational data warehouse (DW) workload.

OLTP workloads are characterized by a high number of short-duration transactions and queries that are usually executed on a single thread of execution. They can have a higher percentage of write activity, and the data in some tables can be extremely volatile. These characteristics have important implications for the hardware selection and configuration process. For example, you would want a processor with excellent single-threaded performance, as most queries use only a single thread of execution. You would also want an I/O subsystem that can supply a high number of input/output operations per second (IOPS), and one that has excellent write performance because of the volatility of the data and the high transaction log write activity.

DW workloads are characterized by longer running queries against more static data. These queries are often parallelized by the query optimizer, so having a higher number of physical cores in your processors can be very beneficial. Having a large amount of physical RAM is very useful for DW workloads, because you will be able to have more data in the SQL Server buffer cache, which will reduce the read pressure on the I/O subsystem. Outside of data loads, there tends to be very little write activity with a DW workload, which means the I/O subsystem would be provisioned and configured differently than for a typical OLTP workload. Many DW-type queries read large amounts of data as they calculate aggregates, so good sequential read I/O performance is very important. There is much less write activity (outside of data loads), which will also affect how you configure your I/O subsystem in terms of storage type and RAID level.

You should try to determine what type of workload your server will be supporting before you decide what type of hardware and storage subsystem to purchase. You also have to keep in mind that very few database workloads are pure OLTP- or pure DW-type workloads, so you will often have to deal with mixed workload types. You also might have to host multiple databases on a single SQL Server instance, where each database has a different type of workload. Another possibility is multiple databases on a single SQL Server instance where each database has the same type of workload, but the aggregate workload on the server ends up looking quite different from what you might expect. Given all of this, how can you determine your expected workload type?

If you have an existing server, running a production workload, you can run a number of Dynamic Management View (DMV) and Dynamic Management Function (DMF) queries, and monitor some key PerfMon counters to get a better idea about your existing workload type. For example, you can query the `sys.dm_os_wait_stats` DMV to see your top cumulative wait types since the last time that SQL Server was restarted (or the wait statistics were cleared) to get a better idea of your current bottlenecks.

For a new application that is under development, you can run these same queries and counters on your development and test servers, along with reviewing documentation and talking to the developers, business analysts, and end users to get a better idea about the expected workload type. The point of all this detective work is to have a better idea of the type of workload your hardware and storage subsystem is going to be dealing with, so you can make the best hardware selection and configuration decisions.

# SQL Server 2012 Enterprise Edition Consideration Factors

One critical question that you must answer early on in the design process is whether you are going to be able to use SQL Server 2012 Enterprise Edition, or whether you will be forced to use a lower-end edition, such as SQL Server 2012 Standard Edition or SQL Server 2012 Business Intelligence Edition. Speaking as a database professional, I strongly believe that Enterprise Edition is very much worth the extra license costs, but I know that it can be a tough sell when you have a limited budget. Following is a listing of some of the more valuable features that you get in SQL Server 2012 Enterprise Edition:

- Data compression

- Enhanced read ahead
- Advanced scanning for reads
- Automatic use of indexed views
- Table partitioning
- Distributed partitioned views
- Scalable shared databases
- Asynchronous database mirroring
- AlwaysOn Availability Groups
- Online index operations
- Fast recovery
- Parallel index operations
- Database snapshots
- Hot-add CPU and RAM
- Online restore
- Resource governor
- SQL Server Audit
- Change data capture
- Mirrored backups
- Oracle replication publishing
- Peer-to-peer replication
- Transparent database encryption

Many of these features are extremely useful for improving the performance and availability of your SQL Server instance, so you should make a determined effort to convince your organization to purchase Enterprise Edition.

If you must use SQL Server 2012 Standard Edition, then you will be restricted to using no more than 64 GB of RAM for the database engine. You will also be restricted to using the *lesser* of four processor sockets or 16 physical processor cores in your database server. If that is the case, you do not want to make the mistake of specifying a big database server that is a four-socket server with 40 physical cores and 256 GB of RAM, because the SQL Server 2012 database engine will only be able to use a fraction of those hardware resources.

Don't forget about the operating system version and edition as part of this decision process. There are licensing limits for maximum RAM, number of processor sockets, and total number of logical processors that are enforced by the operating system.

Windows Server 2008 R2 Standard Edition has a RAM limit of 32 GB and cannot use more than four processor sockets, while Windows Server 2008 R2 Enterprise Edition has a RAM limit of 2 TB and can use up to 256 logical processors. Windows Server 2012 Standard Edition has a RAM limit of 4 TB, and can use 640 logical processors. Windows Server 2012 Datacenter Edition has the same limits, but has higher virtualization limits.

# Server Vendor Selection

Before you can start looking at specific server models and components, you need to determine what server vendor you will be dealing with. There are a number of what I consider "first-tier" server vendors out there, including the following (in alphabetical order):

- Dell
- Fujitsu
- HP
- IBM
- NEC
- Unisys

Each of these server vendors has advantages and disadvantages, depending on what your priorities are. Some vendors have less expensive hardware, while others have proprietary technologies that extend their capabilities beyond what is seen in a reference design from Intel or AMD (for a higher price). Some vendors (such as Dell) target the low- and mid-range market, so if you really need an eight- or sixteen-socket server, you will not be able to buy a Dell server because they sell only four-socket and smaller servers.

I am not going to recommend any specific server vendor in this chapter. Most companies and organizations have a single preferred hardware vendor that they deal with, for a number of valid reasons. For example, it is easier for your IT staff to support servers from a single vendor, as they are familiar with the models and how they are serviced. They can also take advantage of any cold spares or common components in the event of an emergency. If you are a large enough customer, you will also probably be able to get discounted pricing and expedited sales and service from your preferred server vendor.

If you are working at an "HP shop" or "IBM shop" (or any other vendor shop), it is usually fairly difficult to convince your management and the rest of the technical organization that you should buy a new server from a different server vendor. You might be able to play server vendors against each other by requesting quotes from multiple vendors for roughly equivalent equipment, and then use these quotes to get better pricing from your regular preferred vendor.

Despite all this, you should keep an open mind about server vendors, and try to stay current with what they offer for the types of servers that you commonly buy. It could be that you will discover some truly compelling features in a particular model from a different vendor that would make it worth it to try to convince your organization to buy that particular model server instead of something from your regular server vendor. In most cases, you will probably have to pick a server model from your preferred vendor, whether you like it or not.

# Server Form Factor Selection

After you know the server vendor, you must decide whether you will be purchasing a rack-mounted server, a tower server, or a blade server. There are some pros and cons for each form factor that you should consider.

Rack-mounted servers are probably the most common form factor in data centers. They are a standard width and length, and are available in a number of standard vertical heights, which are known as *rack units* (as in 1U, 2U, 4U, etc.). They are usually mounted on rails and have cable management arms in the back that allow you to gently pull the server out of the front of the rack while it is running, without unplugging any of its cables. This lets you service many components while the server is powered on or do more major work while the server is powered off.

One small disadvantage of rack-mounted servers is that they are densely packed with various components, which can make them a little more difficult to service and somewhat harder to cool. Because of this, rack-mounted servers typically have a number of loud, small-diameter, high-velocity fans that pull cool air in through the front of the chassis and push the resultant hot air out of the back of the chassis. This is why data centers are arranged with alternating cold aisles and hot aisles between the server racks. The cold aisles have air conditioned cold air flowing up though holes in the raised floor of the server room that flows into the front of the server and then exits out through the back of the server. The hot aisles have air returns in the ceiling where the warm air rises and then exits the server room.

Tower servers are usually in tall and wide enclosures that sit on shelves instead of racks. They have more room inside the case and they are easier to work on once you have opened the enclosure. They do not usually have rails, so they often sit on the floor or on shelves in a rack. Some tower servers can be fitted with rails and mounted sideways in a rack, but this is not that common because it wastes vertical space in the rack compared to an actual rack-mounted server. Tower servers are usually considered to be entry-level servers that are more commonly used by smaller organizations because they can be less expensive than rack-mounted servers.

Blade servers are even smaller and denser than rack-mounted servers. They have a rack-mounted, blade enclosure chassis that holds common components for power, cooling, network connectivity, I/O connectivity, and management functionality. Multiple, individual blade servers are installed in a single blade enclosure, allowing you to have more individual servers and overall computing capacity in a smaller amount of physical rack space. While this sounds attractive, there are several issues you should be aware of if you are considering using blade servers for database servers. One problem is that the blade enclosure is a single point of failure for all of the blade servers that are installed inside the enclosure. If the blade enclosure has any hardware failures, it can affect all of the blade servers in the enclosure. This means that you would not want to have multiple nodes in a Windows Server failover cluster instance in the same blade enclosure chassis. The same caution holds true for multiple nodes in a SQL Server 2012 AlwaysOn Availability Group or for both sides of a database mirroring partnership.

The common infrastructure in the blade enclosure, especially the I/O interface between the blade servers and the actual storage subsystem, can become a performance bottleneck, especially as the number of blades increase. This is another reason not to use blade servers as mission-critical database servers.

It is standard practice for most database servers to use conventional rack-mounted servers. The main decision you will have to make is which vertical unit size (1U, 2U, 4U, or larger) that you want for your rack-mounted server. This choice is somewhat dictated by how many processor sockets are going to be in your server. Single-processor socket and dual-processor socket servers are available in a 1U vertical size. You can also get dual-processor socket servers in a taller, 2U vertical size that lets you have more internal storage drive bays in the chassis. You can get quad-processor socket servers in both 2U and 4U vertical sizes, with the larger size giving more space for internal storage drive bays. Finally, you can get higher processor socket counts in 4U or larger vertical sizes.

One thing to keep in mind is the overall power and cooling demands of multiple 1U and 2U rack-mounted servers in a single server rack. Dual-processor socket servers that are fully populated with internal drives, large amounts of physical RAM, and many PCI-E expansion cards can use a large amount of electrical power and generate a great deal of heat. This means that you can sometimes exceed the overall power capacity of a single 42U server rack if you populate the entire rack with 42 1U rack-mounted dual-processor socket servers. This problem is not as common as it was a few years ago as more modern processors that use less power and other more energy-efficient components become available. You should still check with your data center to see how much power and cooling capacity is available for each server rack.

# Server Processor Count Selection

One huge decision that you have to make is how many physical processors will be in your database server. The number of physical processors in the server has a somewhat indirect relationship to the performance, scalability, and overall load capacity of the server. With SQL Server 2012 core-based licensing, the number of physical processor cores (which is related to the number of processor sockets) has a huge effect on the overall cost (including software licensing) of the server. It is very easy to spend far more on the SQL Server 2012 core licenses than you will spend on the actual server hardware and storage subsystem.

One common mistake that many database professionals make is to assume that a "bigger" server (in terms of physical processor count) is a faster server compared to a smaller server. In most cases, this is simply not true. As explained in detail later in the chapter, the specific processors used in dual-socket servers often perform much faster for single-threaded performance than their contemporary four-socket processor counterparts.

Traditionally, it has been quite common to use four-socket servers for database server usage because they had more total processor cores, more memory slots, and more expansion slots than a contemporary two-socket server. Two-socket servers that were available before roughly 2008–2009 were limited to about eight total processor cores, 32 GB of RAM, and two or three PCI-E expansion slots (used by things like RAID controllers, Host Bus Adaptors, and network interface cards), which meant they simply could not handle higher-intensity database server workloads.

Since then, processor core density has increased, so you can have between 16 and 32 physical processor cores in a two-socket server. Memory density has increased, with two-socket servers having up to 24 memory slots that can each hold a 32-GB DIMM, giving a total RAM capacity of 768 GB in a two-socket server. You can also have up to seven PCI-E 3.0 slots in a new, two-socket server, which is a significant increase in total I/O capacity over what was available several years ago.

The main point here is that a modern two-socket server has enough CPU capacity, memory capacity, and I/O capacity to handle a very high percentage of SQL Server workloads, so you should strongly consider selecting a two-socket server instead of a traditional four-socket server. An exception would be if you absolutely need more than 16 to 32 physical processor cores, or more than 768 GB of RAM, or more than seven PCI-E expansion slots in a single server, and you are unable to split your workload between multiple servers. If any of those conditions are true, you could be forced to move up to a slower and more expensive four-socket database server. Most people will probably be able to run most of their workloads on a modern, two-socket database server.

# Dell 12th Generation Server Comparison

In order to make this discussion a little more concrete, it is useful to look at the various 12th generation, rack-mounted server models available from Dell, comparing them from a SQL Server perspective. There are currently seven models in this line, ranging from an entry-level, single-socket server to a four-socket server. All of these servers use the Intel Xeon E5 processor, but different models use different series of that processor family, which is a very important detail to pay attention to for SQL Server 2012 usage. You could easily compare the available server models from another vendor in the same way.

## Dell PowerEdge R320

This model server has a 1U form factor, one processor socket, uses the Intel Xeon E5-2400 series processors, has six memory slots (96 GB total RAM with 16-GB DIMMs), has eight 2.5-inch drive bays, and has one PCI-E 3.0 x8 and one PCI-E 3.0 x16 expansion slots. It has a total of four, six, or eight physical cores for SQL Server 2012 core licensing purposes. It has a total of eight, twelve, or sixteen logical cores with Intel hyper-threading enabled.

The R320 is an interesting option for some smaller workloads because it uses the Xeon E5-2400 series Sandy Bridge-EN processor (that is usually used in two-socket systems) instead of the Xeon E3-1200 Sandy Bridge or Xeon E3-1200 v2 series Ivy Bridge processor that is used in most new single-socket servers. This lets you use up to 96 GB of RAM instead of being limited to 32 GB of RAM, and it lets you have up to eight physical processor cores instead of being limited to four physical processor cores. The downside of this is being limited to slower processor clock speeds with the E5-2400 series compared to the E3-1200 series processors, which means you will see slower single-threaded performance. The R320 might be a good choice for a DW type of workload, where the extra processor cores and higher memory capacity would be more useful. A single-socket server with an Intel E3-1200 v2 series processor would be better for a small OLTP workload. Keep in mind that SQL Server 2012 Standard Edition is limited to 64 GB of RAM.

## Dell PowerEdge R420

This model server has a 1U form factor, two processor sockets, and uses Intel Xeon E5-2400 series processors. It also has twelve memory slots (192 GB total RAM with 16-GB DIMMs), has eight 2.5-inch drive bays, and has two PCI-E 3.0 x16 expansion slots. It has a total of eight, twelve, or sixteen physical cores for SQL Server 2012 core licensing purposes. It has a total of sixteen, twenty-four, or thirty-two logical cores with Intel hyper-threading enabled.

This model is a bad choice for SQL Server 2012. The Xeon E5-2400 series Sandy Bridge-EN processor is very limited compared to the Xeon E5-2600 series Sandy Bridge-EP processor. It has slower clock speeds, less memory bandwidth, and less memory capacity. Since you pay the same amount for each SQL Server 2012 core license regardless of what type of physical core is in the processor, the E5-2400 series is a bad choice compared to the E5-2600 series. Another problem with this model server is the fact that it has only two PCI-E expansion slots and eight internal drive bays, which limits your overall I/O capacity and performance.

## Dell PowerEdge R520

This model server has a 2U form factor, two processor sockets, and uses Intel Xeon E5-2400 series processors. It also has twelve memory slots (192 GB total RAM with 16-GB DIMMs), has eight 3.5-inch drive bays, and has three PCI-E 3.0 x8 and one PCI-E 3.0 x16 expansion slots. It has a total of eight, twelve, or sixteen physical cores for SQL Server 2012 core licensing purposes. It has a total of sixteen, twenty-four, or thirty-two logical cores with Intel hyper-threading enabled.

This model is also a bad choice for SQL Server 2012 because it uses the same Intel Xeon E5-2400 series processor as the R420. It does have four PCI-E expansion slots, which is a little better for I/O capacity and performance. Still, I would steer clear of both the R420 and R520 models for SQL Server usage.

## Dell PowerEdge R620

This model server has a 1U form factor, two processor sockets, and uses Intel Xeon E5-2600 series processors. It has twenty-four memory slots (384 GB total RAM with 16-GB DIMMs), has ten 2.5-inch drive bays, and has one PCI-E 3.0 x8 and two PCI-E 3.0 x16 expansion slots. It also has a total of eight, twelve, or sixteen physical cores for SQL Server 2012 core licensing purposes. It has a total of sixteen, twenty-four, or thirty-two logical cores with Intel hyper-threading enabled.

The R620 is a much better choice for SQL Server 2012 than either the R420 or R520 because it uses the Intel Xeon E5-2600 series Sandy Bridge-EP processor. This processor series gives you higher clock speeds, higher memory bandwidth, and higher memory capacity compared to the Xeon E5-2400 series Sandy Bridge-EN processor. The R620 is limited to three PCI-E expansion slots, but it does have ten internal drive bays. Overall, it is a good model for use as an entry-level, two-socket database server.

## Dell PowerEdge R720

This model server has a 2U form factor, two processor sockets, and uses Intel Xeon E5-2600 series processors. It has twenty-four memory slots (384 GB total RAM with 16-GB DIMMs), has sixteen 2.5-inch drive bays, and has six PCI-E 3.0 x8 and one PCI-E 3.0 x16 expansion slots. It has a total of eight, twelve, or sixteen physical cores for SQL Server 2012 core licensing purposes. It has a total of sixteen, twenty-four, or thirty-two logical cores with Intel hyper-threading enabled.

The R720 is one of my favorite models in the Dell 12th generation line. It uses the same Intel Xeon E5-2600 series processor as the R620, but it has seven PCI-E expansion slots and sixteen internal drive bays, which combine to give you a lot of potential I/O capacity and performance. It does cost a little more than the R620, and it is in a 2U vertical size, so there are some scenarios where I would prefer an R620. An example scenario would be an OLTP workload where I knew that I would have external storage area network (SAN) storage with very good random I/O performance, and I wanted to be able to use 1U database servers instead of 2U database servers.

## Dell PowerEdge R720xd

This model server has a 2U form factor, two processor sockets, uses Intel Xeon E5-2600 series processors, has twenty-four memory slots (384 GB total RAM with 16-GB DIMMs), has twenty-six 2.5-inch drive bays, and has four PCI-E 3.0 x8 and two PCI-E 3.0 x16 expansion slots. It has a total of eight, twelve, or sixteen physical cores for SQL Server 2012 core licensing purposes. It has a total of sixteen, twenty-four, or thirty-two logical cores with Intel hyper-threading enabled.

The R720xd is similar to the R720, except that it has twenty-six internal drive bays and only six PCI-E expansion slots. This model could be a good choice if you can run your I/O workload on twenty-six internal drive bays, some or all of which could be solid state drives (SSDs). This could let you avoid the expense of an external direct-attached storage (DAS) enclosure or a SAN.

## Dell PowerEdge R820

This model server has a 2U form factor, four processor sockets, and uses Intel Xeon E5-4600 series processors. It has forty-eight memory slots (768 GB total RAM with 16-GB DIMMs), has sixteen 2.5-inch drive bays, and has five PCI-E 3.0 x8 and two PCI-E 3.0 x16 expansion slots. It also has a total of sixteen, twenty-four, or thirty-two physical cores for SQL Server 2012 core licensing purposes. It has a total of thirty-two, forty-eight, or sixty-four logical cores with Intel hyper-threading enabled.

The R820 has four processor sockets in a 2U vertical size. It uses the Intel Xeon E5-4600 series processor, which has lower clock speeds than the Xeon E5-2600 series. There is also some nonuniform memory access (NUMA) scaling loss as you move from a two-socket to a four-socket server (i.e., a four-socket server does not have twice the scalability as a two-socket server with the exact same processor). The R820 does have sixteen internal drive bays and seven PCI-E expansion slots, so it has good I/O capacity and performance potential. It also has twice the total RAM capacity compared to an R620, R720, or R720xd. In spite of all these factors, I would tend to prefer two R720xd servers instead of one R820 server, assuming you can split your workload between two servers. You would have faster, less expensive processors, over three times as many internal drive bays, and nearly twice as many PCI-E expansion slots, while paying the same SQL Server 2012 license costs.

## Dell Comparison Recap

I really like the R720xd, with its 26 internal drive bays. I suspect that a very high percentage of SQL Server workloads would run extremely well on an R720xd. If 26 internal drives did not give you enough I/O performance and capacity, you could always add some internal solid state storage cards or use some form of external storage.

As a database professional, I would be actively lobbying against using the R420 or R520 models, since they have the entry-level Intel Xeon E5-2400 series processors, which have lower clock speeds and less memory bandwidth compared to the Intel Xeon E5-2600 series processors that are used in the R620, R720, and R720xd. They also have half of the total memory capacity and far fewer PCI-E slots compared to the higher-end models. They are a little less expensive, but the hardware cost delta is pretty small compared to the SQL Server 2012 license costs. Remember, you are paying for SQL Server 2012 core licenses based on physical core counts, so you want to get the best package you can as far as the rest of the server goes. One nice fact is that the Intel Xeon E5 processor family is available in four-core, six-core, and eight-core models, with specific four-core models having higher base clock speeds than the "top-of-the line" eight-core model processor. If you wanted to minimize your SQL Server 2012 core-based licensing costs and were willing to give up some scalability and capacity, you could pick one of these faster base clock speed four-core model processors for your server and actually see very good single-threaded performance.

# Processor Vendor Selection

In the Microsoft Windows and SQL Server world, you will have to pick between an Intel Xeon processor-based server or an AMD Opteron processor-based server. Your choice here directly dictates which model servers are available from your preferred server vendor, as only certain server models are available with an Intel or an AMD processor. Especially with the change to SQL Server 2012 core-based licensing, it is nearly impossible to recommend an AMD processor-based server for use with SQL Server 2012, especially for OLTP workloads.

There are a number of reasons for this rather strong assertion. First are the relatively high physical core counts in modern, high-end AMD Opteron processors, with models available with 12 or 16 physical cores. Each of these physical processor cores requires a relatively expensive SQL Server 2012 processor core license. That would perhaps be acceptable if each one of those physical cores provided excellent single-threaded performance, but sadly, that is not the case. You can easily check the relative performance per physical processor core for OLTP workloads by performing some simple arithmetic against official TPC-E OLTP benchmark scores. You can simply divide the actual TPC-E score for a system by the number of physical processor cores in the database server of the system under test (SUT), to get a score per physical processor core for a particular model of processor. This is a valid method, because the TPC-E benchmark is processor bound as long as you have sufficient I/O performance to drive the workload, which is a fairly safe assumption given the cost and time for a hardware vendor to develop and submit an official TPC-E benchmark submission.

For example, on July 5, 2012, Fujitsu submitted a TPC-E score of 1871.81 TpsE for a PRIMERGY RX300 S7 system that had two Intel Xeon E5-2690 processors that have a total of 16 physical cores in the system. Dividing 1871.81 by 16 physical cores gives you a score per physical processor core of 116.98.

On November 14, 2011, HP submitted a TPC-E score of 1232.84 TpsE for a Proliant DL385 G7 system that had two AMD Opteron 6282 SE processors that have a total of 32 physical cores in the system. Dividing 1232.82 by 32 physical cores gives you a score per physical processor core of 38.52. The score per physical processor core of the Intel system is 3.03 times as high as the score per physical processor core of the AMD system.

To make matters worse for AMD in this comparison, the SQL Server 2012 license costs for the AMD-based system are twice as high as for the Intel-based system, because you have to purchase 32 core licenses versus 16 core licenses.

The retail cost for SQL Server 2012 Enterprise Edition core licenses is $6,874. That means that you would pay $219,968 for 32 SQL Server 2012 Enterprise Edition core licenses for the two-socket AMD Opteron 6282 SE database server versus $109,984 for 16 SQL Server 2012 Enterprise Edition core licenses for the Intel Xeon E5-2690 database server. This means that you are paying twice the SQL Server 2012 core license costs for about one-third of the relative single-threaded performance.

Perhaps recognizing how bad this situation was for AMD, Microsoft released a document called the "SQL Server Core Factor Table" on April 1, 2012. This table allows you to adjust your physical core counts for licensing purposes for certain AMD processors, including AMD 31XX, 32XX, 41XX, 42XX, 61XX, 62XX Series Processors with six or more cores by multiplying your actual physical core count by 0.75, which essentially gives you a 25 percent licensing discount if you use an eligible AMD processor. In our earlier example, the SQL Server 2012 core licensing cost would be reduced from $219,968 to $164,976, which is a significant reduction. Still, it does not compare very favorably to the $109,984 license cost for the faster Intel-based system. Choosing the AMD-based system for SQL Server 2012 OLTP workloads would be fairly hard to defend to an intelligent CTO in your organization.

Another piece of evidence for this argument is the fact that there have been only four AMD-based TPC-E submissions out of a total of 54 total TPC-E benchmark submissions over the past five years. I honestly wish the evidence was not so grim for AMD, since healthy competition between AMD and Intel is good for everyone. If AMD cannot close this performance gap, Intel is very likely to slow down its pace of innovation and delay its release cycles to earn more profits out of its existing processor models for a longer period of time.

# Processor Model Selection

Let us assume that you are convinced that you should choose an Intel processor for your SQL Server 2012 database server. The next step would be choosing which exact processor your new server should use. This is a very important decision, as it will have a huge effect on your SQL Server 2012 core license costs, and it will have a direct effect on the performance, scalability, and capacity of your database server. You are also likely to be stuck with your processor choice for the next several years. It is possible to upgrade the processor(s) in an existing database server, by buying a "processor kit" from your server vendor. The problem with this is that the server vendors typically charge several times the retail cost of a bare processor for a processor kit, so that it is often more affordable to buy a brand new database server rather than to upgrade the processors in an existing database server.

In fact, I have never seen anyone actually upgrade the processors in an existing database server in my entire career. I have seen people buy additional processors to fill empty processor sockets. The point of this is that you will, in fact, be using those original processors for the entire life of the server, which is another reason to choose wisely.

Prior to SQL Server 2012, my advice was to simply select the "top-of-the-line," most expensive processor available for the particular model server that you were considering for purchase. This was because older versions of SQL Server used socket-based licensing, where you did not pay anything extra, regardless of how many physical cores were in a particular processor. It was foolish not to get that "top-of-the-line" processor back then, since your socket-based licensing cost was the same regardless of your processor choice. Despite this, I saw many people select low-end to mid-range processors to use with their very expensive (roughly $27,000 each) SQL Server 2008 R2 Enterprise Edition processor licenses, in order to save a few hundred dollars per processor but take a very noticeable performance and scalability penalty.

With the licensing changes in SQL Server 2012, you will have to rethink this old processor selection strategy. Depending on your budget and objectives, you can go in one of two directions. First, if your organization is running mission-critical applications that will be using your database server, and you have sufficient budget to work with, you are still going to want to pick that "top-of-the line" processor anyway, despite the added SQL Server 2012 core licensing costs. Those extra licensing costs might seem like a lot of money to you, personally, but to many large organizations, these costs can be quite trivial.

As a negotiating strategy, I try not to negotiate with myself. I will always ask for what I really want, and then come down only if it is really necessary. If you start out with a mid-range processor, and then end up getting a lower-end processor to save on hardware and licensing costs, you are the one that will get the blame if you have performance or scalability problems in the future. You will also have to live with the reduced performance and capacity over the life of the server, and the users of your application will also have to suffer with that reduced performance. After all, I have never heard anyone complain that their database server was too fast, but I have often heard complaints that it was too slow.

Second, if your application is not mission critical, or your organization *honestly* cannot afford to buy a larger number of SQL Server 2012 core licenses, then you can purposely select a lower core count processor that might have a higher base clock speed. This method can save a lot of money on SQL Server 2012 core licenses, at the cost of scalability and capacity headroom. If you go down this route, you should make sure everyone knows what you are doing and why you are doing it, and is in agreement with what you are doing. This can help you avoid being blamed if you have scalability or capacity issues in the future.

Walking through an example of how this might work, you could buy a two-socket database server that had two Intel Xeon E5-2690 processors that have eight physical cores each, for a total of sixteen physical cores in the server. The SQL Server 2012 Enterprise Edition core licensing cost for this one database server would be sixteen times $6,874 for a total of $109,984. If you wanted to focus on reducing your license costs for this server, you have two viable alternatives. One option would be to select two Intel Xeon E5-2643 processors that have four physical cores each, for a total of eight physical cores in the server. The SQL Server 2012 Enterprise Edition core licensing cost for this one database server would be eight times $6,874 for a total of $109,984.

A second option would be to select only one Intel Xeon E5-2690 processor that has eight physical cores, for a total of eight physical cores in the server. The SQL Server 2012 Enterprise Edition core licensing cost for this one database server would be eight times $6,874 for a total of $109,984.

There are some key differences between these two lower-cost options. The E5-2643 processor runs at a higher base clock speed of 3.3 GHz, with the ability to use Intel Turbo Boost to increase the clock speed of individual cores to 3.5 GHz (when all of the cores are not running at full speed already). This compares to the E5-2690 processor with a base clock speed of 2.9 GHz and a maximum Turbo Boost speed of 3.8 GHz. A heavily loaded system with E5-2643 processors will be running the processor cores at 3.3 GHz most of the time, with occasional bursts to 3.5 GHz for individual cores. A heavily loaded system with the E5-2690 processor will be running the processor cores at 2.9 GHz most of the time, with occasional bursts up to 3.8 GHz for individual cores. Some of the relevant specifications for these two processors are shown in Table 15-1.

*Table 15-1. Comparison of Two Intel Xeon E5 Series Processors*

| CPU | Base Clock | Turbo Clock | Cores | L3 Cache | Price |
| --- | --- | --- | --- | --- | --- |
| E5-2690 | 2.9 GHz | 3.8 GHz | 8 | 20 MB | $2,057 |
| E5-2643 | 3.3 GHz | 3.5 GHz | 4 | 10 MB | $885 |

Purposely leaving one socket empty would leave you with a lot of reserve capacity that you could take advantage of by purchasing a second processor in the future (and paying for the extra SQL Server 2012 core licenses). Having both sockets populated with the four-core processor would force you to replace both processors with something better if you ever needed to upgrade. That would be a harder proposition to sell in my experience, especially since the system vendor would likely charge a premium for the processor kits. You would also have the two original processors that would most likely end up in a drawer somewhere as rather expensive paperweights.

A two-socket system with either one of these processors would support 384 GB of RAM using 16-GB DIMMs if both processor sockets were populated. If only one processor socket were populated, the maximum RAM amount would be reduced to 192 GB using 16-GB DIMMs.

If I had to choose between these two alternatives, I would likely lean toward having one E5-2690 processor instead of two E5-2643 processors, as the upgrade path would be easier and less expensive.

# Memory Selection

Generally speaking, I like to specify database servers with a large amount of RAM. Currently, all new Intel- and AMD-based servers use error correcting code (ECC) DDR3 RAM, but ECC DDR4 RAM will start to be used in new servers by 2014. Over time, ECC DDR3 RAM prices have steadily declined to the point where this type of RAM is extremely affordable.

Having a large amount of physical RAM in your database server allows SQL Server to have a larger buffer pool, which is used for caching data that has been read into memory from the storage subsystem. Any data that is in the SQL Server buffer pool can be retrieved with a logical read instead of requiring a physical read from the storage subsystem. Logical reads are much faster than physical reads, even if you have flash-based storage.

Ideally, your entire database would fit into RAM, which would dramatically reduce the read I/O pressure on your storage subsystem. Having a large amount of RAM will also reduce how often the SQL Server lazy writer has to run, which can reduce the write I/O pressure on your storage subsystem. Buying more RAM is much less expensive than upgrading your storage subsystem.

Given all of this, how much RAM should buy for your new database server? The first decision point is whether you have SQL Server 2012 Enterprise Edition or not, as this directly affects how much RAM you can actually use for SQL Server.

SQL Server 2012 Standard Edition is limited to using 64 GB of RAM for the database engine and 64 GB of RAM for SQL Server Analysis Services (SSAS), so you could theoretically use 128 GB of RAM between the two (even though it is not a best practice to run the database engine and SSAS on the same instance for performance reasons).

SQL Server 2012 Business Intelligence Edition will let you use the operating system maximum for SSAS, and up to 64 GB of RAM for the database engine.

SQL Server 2012 Enterprise Edition can use up to the operating system maximum for the database engine, and up to the operating system maximum for SSAS. The operating system maximum is 2 TB for Windows Server 2008 R2 and it is 4 TB for Windows Server 2012. It is currently possible to get 2 TB of RAM in a commodity four-socket machine if you are willing to pay the premium for 32-GB DIMMs. The current sweet spot for memory module size is 16 GB, as you get a relatively large memory module for an affordable price.

If you will be running SQL Server 2012 Standard Edition, I don't see any reason to get less than 64 GB of RAM in your database server. I would strongly consider getting 80 GB using ten 8-GB DIMMs, so that you can set the instance level Maximum Server Memory setting to 64000 and still leave plenty of RAM for the operating system.

With SQL Server 2012 Enterprise Edition, I would want to fill up every available memory slot in the server with 16-GB DIMMs if at all possible, since server RAM is so affordable and so effective for improving performance. Because your organization has already spent the money for Enterprise Edition, it is foolish to hobble the performance and scalability of the server by saving a relatively small amount of money on RAM. For example, a two-socket database server with two Intel Xeon E5-2600 series processors can use 24 memory slots. The current cost for 24 16-GB ECC DDR3 DIMMS would be $6,240, which is a very small fraction of the SQL Server 2012 Enterprise Edition license cost for that database server.

Table 15-2 shows the relative prices for various sizes of memory modules in late 2012.

*Table 15-2. Relative Prices for ECC DDR3 RAM (Late 2012)*

| Module Size | Price | Price/GB |
| --- | --- | --- |
| 32 GB | $1,498 | $47/GB |
| 16 GB | $260 | $16/GB |
| 8 GB | $90 | $11/GB |

| 4 GB | $60 | $15/GB |
| 2 GB | $30 | $15/GB |

One last factor to consider is the effect of different memory configurations on the memory bandwidth of the memory. As you add more DIMMs to a system to populate more of the available memory slots, the bandwidth of the memory can decrease, which can hurt memory access performance somewhat. This effect varies based on the processor and the associated, integrated memory controller that is being used. The latest Intel processors are much less susceptible to this problem. Regardless of this, I still favor using large amounts of RAM, because even "slower" RAM is much, much faster than your storage subsystem. If you are concerned about this, you should consult the documentation for your server to see the recommendations for how you should configure your memory.

# Conclusion

This chapter has covered a lot of ground about a very complex subject. In order to get the best performance and scalability possible from your database server without spending a small fortune on SQL Server 2012 core license costs, you need to make wise choices, especially when it comes to the exact model of processor that you select for your database server. Because SQL Server 2012 uses core-based licensing, it is very important that you choose a processor that has very good single-threaded performance so that you get the most performance possible for each of those expensive core licenses. You also want to minimize your total physical core counts to minimize your licensing costs.

Two-socket servers are typically one generation ahead of their four-socket contemporary counterparts when it comes to processor technology. They also have much higher memory density and more PCI-E expansion slots than they did in the past, so they are an extremely attractive choice for many database server workloads.

You need to know whether you will be using SQL Server 2012 Enterprise Edition or whether you will have to use a lower edition, as this will affect how much RAM you can use and how many sockets and physical cores that you can use for SQL Server 2012.

You should take advantage of the extremely low pricing for ECC DDR3 server RAM by buying a larger amount of RAM for your new server. There is really no longer any excuse to have a new server with only 16 GB or 32 GB of RAM.

Finally, you need to understand your workload so that you can make the right hardware choices to get the best performance and scalability for that type of workload.

## CHAPTER 16

# Backups and Restores Using Availability Groups

## By Grant Fritchey

With the release of Microsoft SQL Server 2012, a whole new mechanism for ensuring continuous availability of databases in your system was introduced: AlwaysOn Availability Groups. Availability Groups provide a mechanism for failing over a database, or a group of databases, from a primary replica onto between one and four secondary replicas. This ability to keep a database online with little to no data loss and without the requirements of the old Failover Cluster shared disks and matching hardware makes for a great way to help ensure the continuity of access to data in your systems. Further, secondary replicas can be set up as read-only replicas, allowing you to offload some of the data access from your production system, hosting the primary replica, to one or more of the secondary replicas. If all this isn't enough, you also get the ability to remove the server load required for running part of the backup process and put that into the secondary replicas as well. The ability to change where and how you back up your databases without negatively affecting your ability to recover a database is a major improvement in the capabilities available for disaster recovery, and it provides performance improvements.

This chapter provides a very basic overview of how Availability Groups are set up and configured to allow you to get your own Availability Group going. From there, we'll explore how you can configure your Availability Group to support different mechanisms of backing up a SQL Server instance. Finally, because your backup is only as good as your last restore, we'll cover how you can restore your databases from these backups. All this will help you provide a more versatile disaster-recovery setup in your environment. You'll also receive some performance benefits when you remove things like backup compression overhead from your primary replica on your production servers.

One point is worth noting right away. You can't run a FULL BACKUP on the Availability Group. You can run only log backups and a COPY_ONLY backup. You also don't get DIFFERENTIAL backups either. So while we'll look at saving the cost of some backup processing, we're not talking about saving the cost of all backup processing.

# Setting Up an Availability Group

It's a fairly straight forward task to get an Availability Group up and running. But that's only for a simple setup. If you have a complex network topology, this task becomes more involved. I'll assume a simple setup in order to outline this process and move on to the backups.

You have to configure your Windows servers to take part in the Availability Group first. You also have to configure the SQL Server instance to support Availability Groups. Once these tasks are complete, you'll be able to add one or more databases to an Availability Group. First, you have to set up the Windows server.

## Configuring the Windows Server

Availability Groups require that you have a Failover Clustering service running and all the replicas are nodes within that group. Installing this is pretty simple. You just have to use the Features Wizard from the Server Manager as shown in Figure 16-1.

Getting the service onto the server is about the easiest step in the whole process. You are not required to have matching machines or a shared hard drive. You just need the service installed on each of the machines. The Windows Failover Clustering Service (WFCS) has a very long list of requirements for exactly how you need to configure your servers for it to work properly. You can access that list online here: http:// technet.microsoft.com/en-us/library/cc732035. The good news is that you don't have to go through this list and validate that your systems are ready for clustering. Instead, you can take advantage of the built-in tools that are installed as part of the clustering service.

Before proceeding to attempting to set up a cluster, you need to install the service on all the machines you're going to use to manage replicas within your Availability Group. You can create the cluster and then

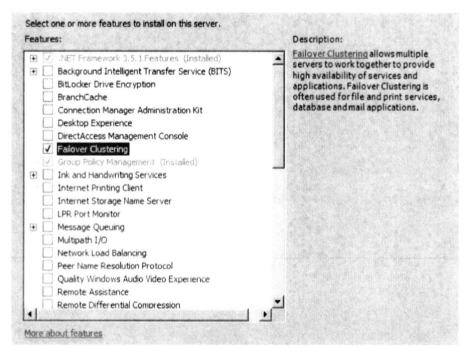

*Figure 16-1. Installing the Failover Clustering service.*

add machines to it, but that can be confusing. Further, if you already configured a cluster and put it into your production environment, you're risking downtime by choosing to add servers at a later date. It's better to install and configure what you need up front.

Once you have the clustering service installed on your servers, you can connect to one and use the Failover Clustering Manager software to set up your cluster. But first, you should validate that your servers will support the cluster. You do this by running the Validate A Configuration Wizard. This interface requires you to simply supply the servers that are going to take part in your cluster. The wizard will validate all the requirements for a cluster for you. Errors will prevent the success of your cluster, and by extension, your Availability Group. These must be addressed directly. Warnings are just indications that one or more of the servers taking part in the cluster might have configuration or hardware issues that will preclude it from being always available as a part of the clustering service. You should understand the implications of the warnings, but these will not prevent you from creating a cluster.

After completing the steps in the validation wizard, you can begin creating a cluster. Because you're not setting up all sorts of shared resources between these machines, you need to supply only the connection information, as you did during the validation process, for each server.

## SQL Server Availability Group

With the cluster set up and all the servers that you require made members of it, you need to set up SQL Server to create and support Availability Groups. The first thing you need to do is run the SQL Server Configuration Manager. You need to make one modification to the SQL Server service itself. Open the properties for the service from the Configuration Manager window, and click on the AlwaysOn High Availability tab, which is shown in Figure 16-2.

Select the Enable AlwaysOn Availability Groups check box. This enables this server to take part in Availability Groups. It does require a restart for the machine, so if you are adding this capability to a production server, plan for some downtime. Each server that is going to take part in your Availability Group needs to be configured in the same manner.

Now, with the server designated as a node in a cluster and AlwaysOn High Availability enabled, you're ready to start creating an Availability Group. You need to open SQL Server Management Studio (SSMS) and connect it to one of the servers in your clustered environment. Availability Groups can be managed through SSMS or through T-SQL. If you're going to be setting up and maintaining lots of these environments, you'll want to get very familiar with the T-SQL method of doing things. For simplicity's sake

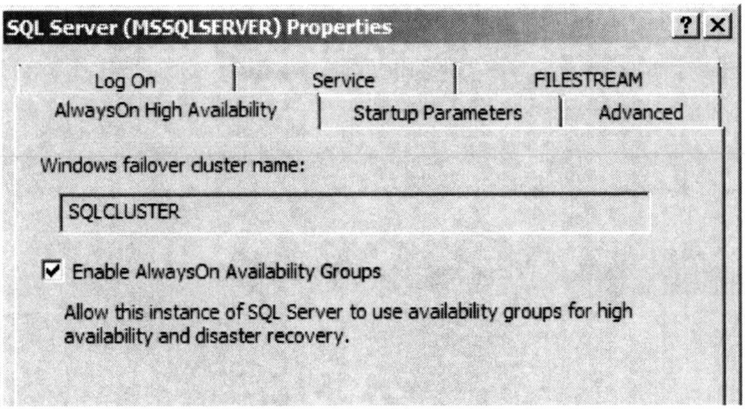

*Figure 16-2. Enabling AlwaysOn High Availability.*

here, I'll show you how to use SSMS to accomplish the same thing. There is a complete management interface for creating and maintaining your Availability Groups. Navigate to the AlwaysOn High Availability folder within the Object Explorer. After expanding this, you'll see a folder for Availability Groups. Within here, if you have Availability Groups already configured, you can see them, see their status, and make modifications to them. But, since at this point, you don't have one created, I suggest using the Availability Group Wizard to get started.

Right-click on the Availability Group folder, and select New Availability Group Wizard from the context menu. A standard wizard introduction window explaining things will open. Click the Next button and you'll be required to supply a name for your Availability Group. Select a name that meaningfully defines the group and its purpose. For this set of tests, I'll use the name "AgBackup" as the name for the group. After you define a name, click the Next button again. You are presented with a list of databases. These databases will be validated and marked as to whether or not they can take partake in an Availability Group. You can see an example of this in Figure 16-3.

There are four databases currently on the server referenced in Figure 16-3. From that list, the AdventureWorks2008R2 .database has its check box grayed out. The status shows that it has 2 required actions. Basically, that database is not currently valid for use in an Availability Group. The possible reasons are varied. You can click on the Status header to get a definition. Some of the possible reasons are that the database is not in Full Recovery mode, which is required for a database to be used in an Availability Group, or because no full backup has been run on this database, which is another requirement. You can see that the AOTest. database doesn't meet the criteria because it's already part of a different Availability Group. The database with the name. MirrorMe is being mirrored and therefore can't be put into an Availability Group. That leaves the MovieManagement database, which has passed all the validation requirements and therefore can be selected for inclusion.

If there are groups of databases you want to treat as a unit for the purposes of High Availability, you can. If they pass validation, add them to the group. With the database, or databases, selected for the group, click the Next button. This brings up the Specify Replicas page of the wizard. This is where you define the primary and secondary replicas for managing the Availability Group. You can specify between one and five different servers to create within the group, as shown in Figure 16-4.

For this example, I included five replicas and maxed out each of the different options: two replicas have automatic failover, and three replicas have synchronous commit. Automatic failover means that when the primary replica is taken offline for any reason, one of the secondary replicas will automatically become the primary replica. Transactions are transferred between the primary replica and the

**Select user databases for the availability group.**

User databases on this instance of SQL Server:

| Name | Size | Status |
| --- | --- | --- |
| ☐ AdventureWorks2008R2 | | 2 actions required |
| ☐ AOTest | 4.1 MB | Already part of an availability group |
| ☐ MirrorMe | 4.0 MB | Database is mirrored |
| ☑ MovieManagement | 4.0 MB | Meets prerequisites |

*Figure 16-3.* *A list of databases and information about whether or not they meet the criteria for use in an Availability Group.*

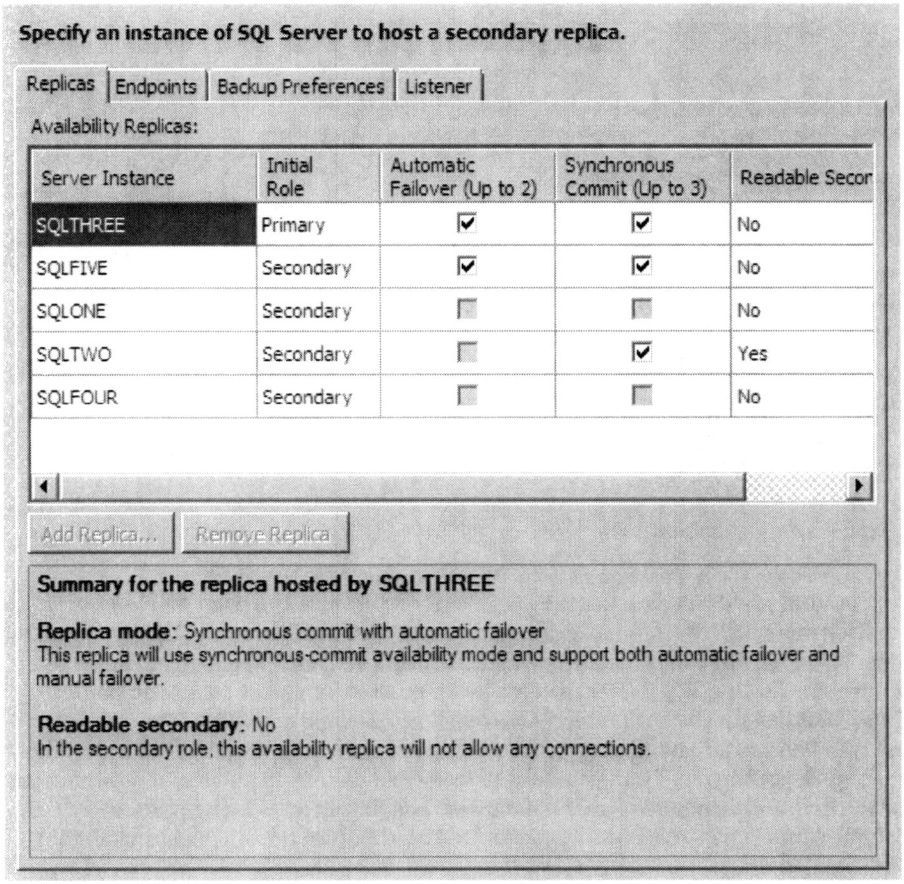

**Specify an instance of SQL Server to host a secondary replica.**

Replicas | Endpoints | Backup Preferences | Listener |

Availability Replicas:

| Server Instance | Initial Role | Automatic Failover (Up to 2) | Synchronous Commit (Up to 3) | Readable Secon |
|---|---|---|---|---|
| SQLTHREE | Primary | ☑ | ☑ | No |
| SQLFIVE | Secondary | ☑ | ☑ | No |
| SQLONE | Secondary | ☐ | ☐ | No |
| SQLTWO | Secondary | ☐ | ☑ | Yes |
| SQLFOUR | Secondary | ☐ | ☐ | No |

◄        ►

Add Replica...    Remove Replica

**Summary for the replica hosted by SQLTHREE**

**Replica mode:** Synchronous commit with automatic failover
This replica will use synchronous-commit availability mode and support both automatic failover and manual failover.

**Readable secondary:** No
In the secondary role, this availability replica will not allow any connections.

*Figure 16-4. Specifying the replicas in the Availability Group.*

secondaries. When you choose to make these transactions synchronous, it means that the Availability Group management will commit transactions to those replicas before those transactions can be removed from the primary replica. Asynchronous commits will separate the transactions on the secondaries from those on the primary replica and won't affect the primary's log. I also made one of the replicas a readable secondary. This means that queries can be run against that secondary even as it gets updated from whichever of the replicas is currently acting as the primary.

In addition to the replicas, this page offers three other tabs for setting up pieces of the Availability Group. On the Endpoints tab, you can modify the location information and connection strings for the servers. This is especially useful if you are building an Availability Group with servers in different physical locations requiring special settings in order to make the remote connection. You can click on the Backup Preferences tab to modify the backup preferences for the replicas, but I'll cover that in some detail later in the chapter. Finally, on the Listener tab, you can set up a listener for the Availability Group. This acts as a standard connection point for applications so that you don't have to write code that determines which server an application can connect to. Your application code connects to the listener and that directs your code to the appropriate replica.

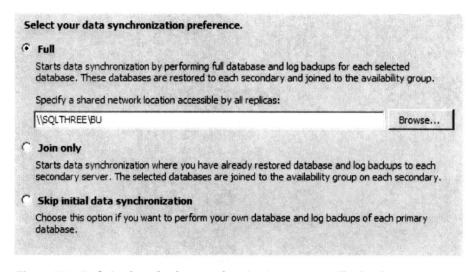

*Figure 16-5. Defining how the data-synchronization process will take place.*

If you click the Next button, you'll be taken to the Select Data Synchronization page. You use the options on this page to determine how the database, or databases, in your Availability Group get moved to the replicas in the group. There are three basic options, which are displayed and explained in Figure 16-5.

Your choices boil down to allowing SQL Server to manage the process for you or setting up the databases yourself. If you're setting up your Availability Groups within a single network without major physical separation, and the bandwidth and latency problems that brings with it, you might want to allow SQL Server to manage the process for you. If not, you need to restore a full backup and the appropriate log backups to ensure that the data and structures for your databases are completely in sync prior to initializing your Availability Group. Once this is done, clicking the Next button runs the next step in the wizard, which deals with validations.

The validations ensure that your servers and databases are all correctly configured and can communicate appropriately to support your Availability Group. If any of the validations fail, you will receive notice on the screen. Clicking on the notice will provide you with a detailed explanation. You can leave this screen in place to address the issues directly. Once they are fixed, you just have to click the Re-Run Validation button that you see on the bottom of Figure 16-6.

As you can see in Figure 16-6, there was a warning from the listener configuration for my Availability Group. This is because I did not define a listener on the previous page. You don't have to have a listener for Availability Groups to work, although it makes a huge difference in how you connect to the group from your applications. But you can set up and test the Availability Group first, and then add a listener when you're ready to work with applications.

After you complete the wizard, the next step of the process is to move the database onto each of the replica servers so that it's available for use. You can check the status of the Availability Group by using the Availability Group dashboard. This can be accessed from any server within the Availability Group. In Object Explorer, right-click on the AlwaysOn High Availability folder. You can then select Dashboard from the menu. Selecting this will show a listing of all Availability Groups on your server. If you select one of the groups, you'll see its current status. Figure 16-7 shows how my Availability Group, AgBackup, is currently configured.

The information is divided into three basic areas. Across the top is the status of the Availability Group itself. On the left, you can see that the current status of this group is Healthy, that the primary instance is

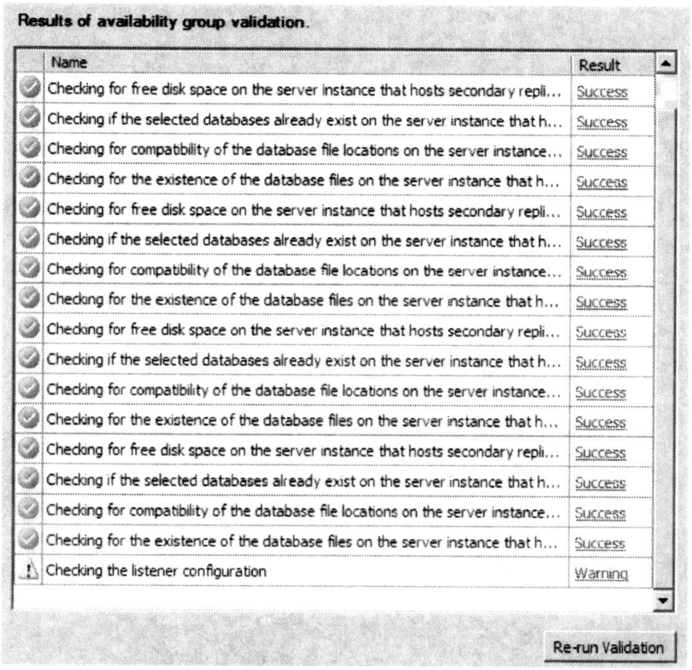

Results of availability group validation.

| | Name | Result |
|---|---|---|
| ✓ | Checking for free disk space on the server instance that hosts secondary repli... | Success |
| ✓ | Checking if the selected databases already exist on the server instance that h... | Success |
| ✓ | Checking for compatibility of the database file locations on the server instance... | Success |
| ✓ | Checking for the existence of the database files on the server instance that h... | Success |
| ✓ | Checking for free disk space on the server instance that hosts secondary repli... | Success |
| ✓ | Checking if the selected databases already exist on the server instance that h... | Success |
| ✓ | Checking for compatibility of the database file locations on the server instance... | Success |
| ✓ | Checking for the existence of the database files on the server instance that h... | Success |
| ✓ | Checking for free disk space on the server instance that hosts secondary repli... | Success |
| ✓ | Checking if the selected databases already exist on the server instance that h... | Success |
| ✓ | Checking for compatibility of the database file locations on the server instance... | Success |
| ✓ | Checking for the existence of the database files on the server instance that h... | Success |
| ✓ | Checking for free disk space on the server instance that hosts secondary repli... | Success |
| ✓ | Checking if the selected databases already exist on the server instance that h... | Success |
| ✓ | Checking for compatibility of the database file locations on the server instance... | Success |
| ✓ | Checking for the existence of the database files on the server instance that h... | Success |
| ⚠ | Checking the listener configuration | Warning |

Re-run Validation

*Figure 16-6. A successful set of validations, along with one warning.*

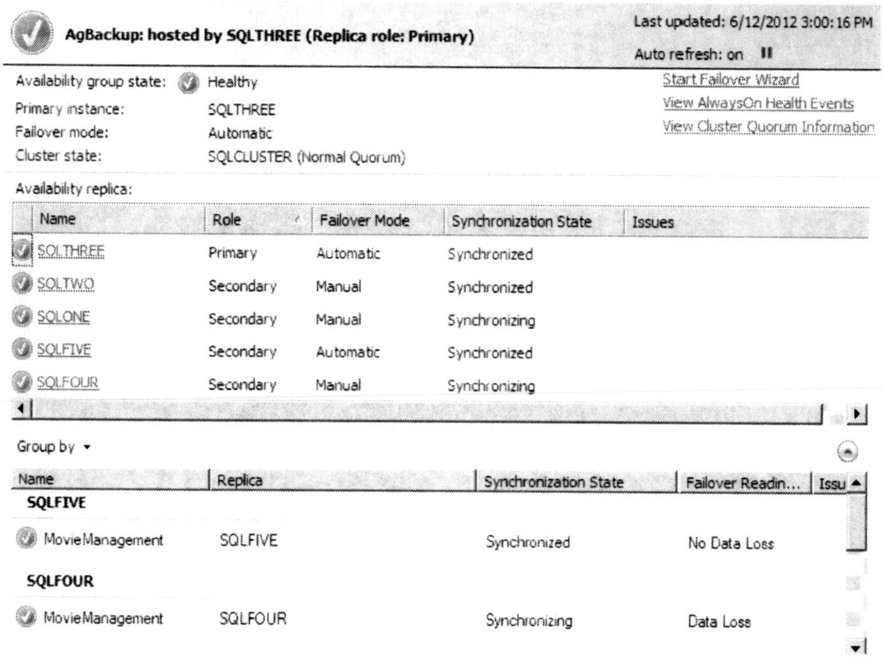

✓ **AgBackup: hosted by SQLTHREE (Replica role: Primary)**

Last updated: 6/12/2012 3:00:16 PM
Auto refresh: on  ❚❚

| | |
|---|---|
| Availability group state: | ✓ Healthy |
| Primary instance: | SQLTHREE |
| Failover mode: | Automatic |
| Cluster state: | SQLCLUSTER (Normal Quorum) |

Start Failover Wizard
View AlwaysOn Health Events
View Cluster Quorum Information

Availability replica:

| Name | Role | Failover Mode | Synchronization State | Issues |
|---|---|---|---|---|
| ✓ SQLTHREE | Primary | Automatic | Synchronized | |
| ✓ SQLTWO | Secondary | Manual | Synchronized | |
| ✓ SQLONE | Secondary | Manual | Synchronizing | |
| ✓ SQLFIVE | Secondary | Automatic | Synchronized | |
| ✓ SQLFOUR | Secondary | Manual | Synchronizing | |

Group by ▼

| Name | Replica | Synchronization State | Failover Readin... | Issu... |
|---|---|---|---|---|
| **SQLFIVE** | | | | |
| ✓ MovieManagement | SQLFIVE | Synchronized | No Data Loss | |
| **SQLFOUR** | | | | |
| ✓ MovieManagement | SQLFOUR | Synchronizing | Data Loss | |

*Figure 16-7. The Availability Group dashboard showing the current status of all the replicas.*

SQLTHREE, and that the failover mode is set to Automatic and the cluster state is a normal quorum, meaning enough servers are available to determine which of them is currently the primary. You also get a few links on the right side of the dashboard. You can click Start Failover Wizard, View AlwaysOn Health Events, or View Cluster Quorum Information. The second section shows more details about the Availability Group replicas. The links for each server allow you to drill down on the appropriate server. The final section shows more detailed information about the servers in the Availability Group. This is how you quickly determine what the status of your Availability Group is. But to manage the settings of the group, you need to go to a different window.

Right-clicking on the Availability Group in the Object Explorer allows you to access the Properties window in the context menu. This is where you can modify the decisions you've made regarding the setup of the Availability Group. The options are similar to those you were offered during the steps through the wizard, but you'll get quite a bit less guidance. You can adjust the primary replica and the secondary replicas and their roles within the group all as shown in Figure 16-8.

With this last screen, you have the basics for how to set up and manipulate the Availability Group. There are a lot more details on how to configure groups between different physical locations, with varying degrees of security and a number of other things, but now we're going to move on to setting up backups using the Availability Groups.

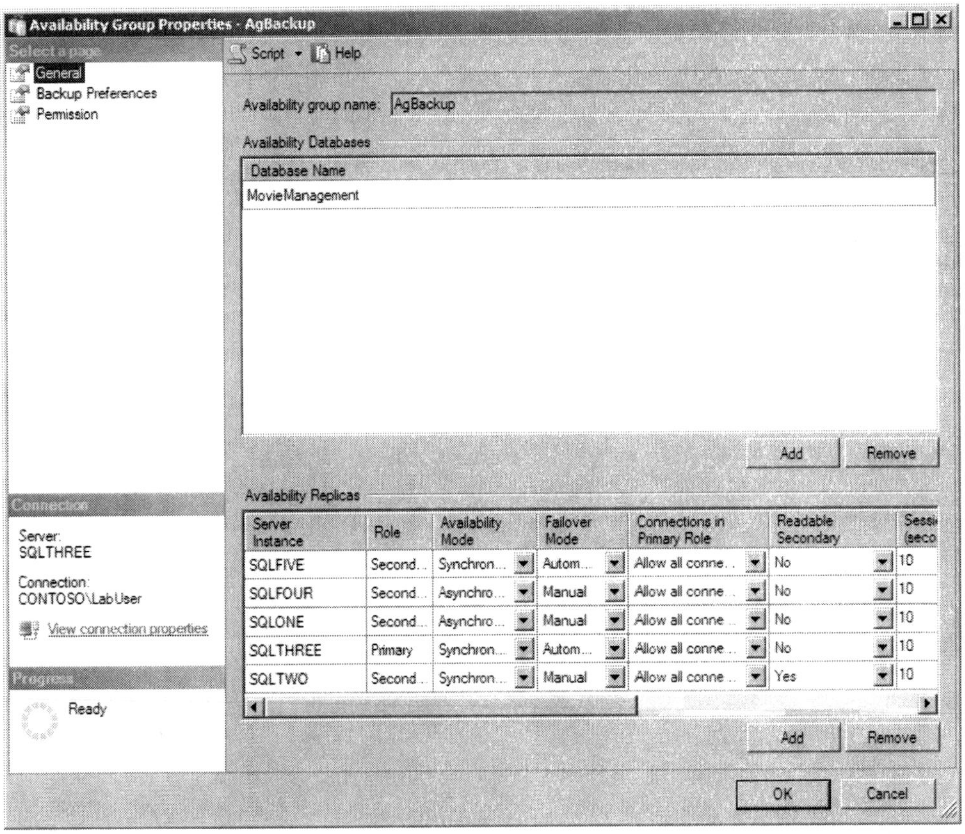

*Figure 16-8. Properties for the Availability Group that you can use to take control of the group.*

# Enabling Backups on Availability Groups

The only backups that are available on your Availability Group are log backups and full-database backups that are set to use COPY_ONLY. Full backups are not allowed nor are differentials. But even with the log backups, you can't simply run a backup. There are a number of configuration choices you have to make to ensure that you're going to get a set of backups you can use for recovery. To start with, you need to determine where your backups are going to occur. You can decide to run them only on the primary, only on secondaries, only on some secondaries, or all sorts of variations in between. Finally, you can set the priority value for each of your replicas if there is one in particular where you'd like to see the backups run.

The settings for your backup processes are available in the Properties dialog box for the Availability Group. You can access it exactly as described in the preceding section.

## Backup Location

Determining which of the replicas should be used for backup is entirely a part of your system and the requirements there. But the manipulation of where backups occur is done from the Properties dialog box for your Availability Group, as shown in Figure 16-9.

The most resilient mechanism for running the automated backups is to have them use the default option, Prefer Secondary. This ensures that as long as some part of the Availability Group is online and hasn't been removed from the backups entirely (more on that in the next section), you'll get a log backup from one of the replicas. This will tend to take the group away from the primary replica, but not eliminate it from consideration. If you really are trying to offload the process of running backups, you can choose the Secondary Only option. This will exclude the primary replica, wherever it might be when the backups are run. Or, if you need to, you can make it so that backups are only ever run from the primary server. Finally, you can just choose the Any Replica option. Choosing this will cause the automated backup simply to fall back on whichever replica is online, included in backups, and currently has the priority.

You can determine programmatically if a server has the backup priority. There's a system function called sys.fn_hadr_backup_is_preferred_replica. It's a function that just returns a Boolean. It can be called as part of an IF statement or simply as a SELECT:

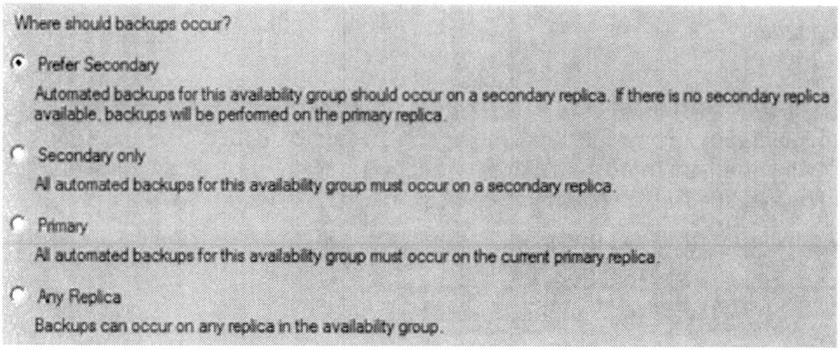

*Figure 16-9. Determining where to perform automated backups in an Availability Group.*

*Figure 16-10. The current server is not the preferred backup replica.*

```
SELECT sys.fn_hadr_backup_is_preferred_replica('MovieManagement');
```

If I ran this on the current primary replica and the backup location was set to the default option, Prefer Secondary, my output would look like Figure 16-10.

We'll do more with this function later.

Speaking of T-SQL, you can use T-SQL commands to take charge of the Availability Groups, including setting up the backup location. Here's how you could modify the AgBackup group to use the Secondary Only option for the backups. (Although individual database commands can be run within the database, most of the management commands for Availability Groups must be run from the master database.)

```
USE master;
GO
ALTER AVAILABILITY GROUP AgBackup
SET (AUTOMATED_BACKUP_PREFERENCE = SECONDARY_ONLY);
```

Now the primary, regardless of which server is the primary, cannot be used to run automated backups. But simply setting which type of replica you want to be able to control the backups is not the only way to control where the automated backups take place. You can also remove replicas from the list and adjust the priority of the replicas.

## Backup Priority

As with modifying which types of replicas can do the backups, backup priority is controlled through both the GUI and T-SQL. We'll start the GUI approach by looking at Figure 16-11.

You can specify the replicas that you want excluded. When a replica is selected, it cannot run a backup, regardless of what the other settings are. The Backup Priority is a number between 1 and 100. The default is to have all servers set to the same, midrange, priority of 50. You can adjust them up and down to provide a level of control over which of the servers is more likely to run the backup. All of this depends, of course, on the availability of the server. Although a replica might have the lowest priority, if it's the only server available for a backup, that's where the backup will occur.

Adjusting the priority level through T-SQL follows some of the mechanisms you saw earlier. To modify the priority level of a replica, you do this:

```
ALTER AVAILABILITY GROUP AgBackup
MODIFY REPLICA ON 'SQLTWO'
WITH (BACKUP_PRIORITY = 2);
```

This code will change the Availability Group specified, modifying the replica SQLTWO to make its priority extremely low at 2. Having numbers more than simply 1-5 allows you a more granular level of control over which replica or replicas are likely to receive priority.

| Replica backup priorities: | | |
| --- | --- | --- |
| Server Instance | Backup Priority (Lowest=1, Highest=100) | Exclude Replica |
| SQLFIVE | 50 | ☐ |
| SQLFOUR | 50 | ☐ |
| SQLONE | 50 | ☐ |
| SQLTHREE | 50 | ☐ |
| SQLTWO | 50 | ☐ |

*Figure 16-11. Setting the backup priorities and removing replicas from the automated backup process.*

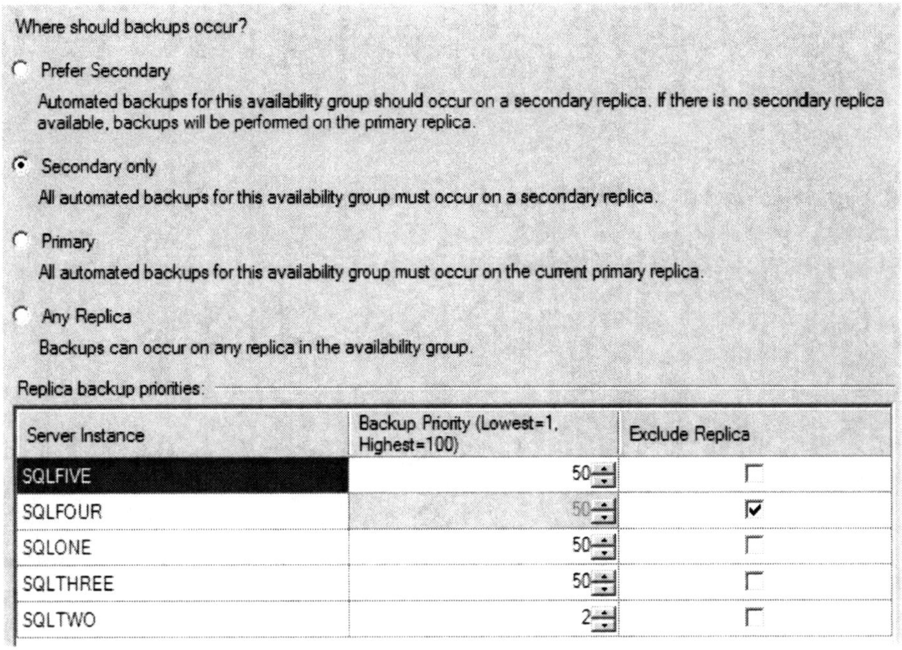

Where should backups occur?

○ Prefer Secondary

Automated backups for this availability group should occur on a secondary replica. If there is no secondary replica available, backups will be performed on the primary replica.

◉ Secondary only

All automated backups for this availability group must occur on a secondary replica.

○ Primary

All automated backups for this availability group must occur on the current primary replica.

○ Any Replica

Backups can occur on any replica in the availability group.

Replica backup priorities:

| Server Instance | Backup Priority (Lowest=1, Highest=100) | Exclude Replica |
|---|---|---|
| SQLFIVE | 50 | ☐ |
| SQLFOUR | 50 | ☑ |
| SQLONE | 50 | ☐ |
| SQLTHREE | 50 | ☐ |
| SQLTWO | 2 | ☐ |

***Figure 16-12.*** *The properties showing modifications made to where backups occur and which replicas support them.*

To completely remove the replica from the list of available replicas for backups, you adjust the backup priority down to zero using the T-SQL code:

```
ALTER AVAILABILITY GROUP AgBackup
MODIFY REPLICA ON 'SQLFOUR'
WITH (BACKUP_PRIORITY = 0);
```

That will change the replica specified and remove it from the Availability Group list of backups entirely. It means that if you ran the preferred backup function, sys.fn_hadr_backup_is_preferred_ replica, it could never return a positive value for that server. If you refresh the properties window, you can see the changes made graphically represented, as shown in Figure 16-12.

You can see that the automated backups now would run only on secondary servers, never on the primary. The replica SQLFOUR can't support automated backups because it has been excluded. Finally, the SQLTWO replica has had its priority changed to 2, making it the least likely replica to support the automated backup.

This is how you can control what kind of replica is performing the backup and where the backup is occurring. But how do you set up the backups themselves? I'll cover that in the next section. Before we move on though, I'll reset the Availability Group back to the default values:

```
ALTER AVAILABILITY GROUP AgBackup
SET (AUTOMATED_BACKUP_PREFERENCE = SECONDARY);

ALTER AVAILABILITY GROUP AgBackup
MODIFY REPLICA ON 'SQLTWO'
WITH (BACKUP_PRIORITY = 50);
```

```
ALTER AVAILABILITY GROUP AgBackup
MODIFY REPLICA ON 'SQLFOUR'
WITH (BACKUP_PRIORITY = 50);
```

# Automating Backups on Availability Groups

You can run a backup manually from any of the Availability Group replicas. To automate backups, though, you have to do some extra work because you'll never know which group is available to perform the backup, although you do get to set a bias as to which of the replicas will perform the action, as I discussed in the previous section. To use Availability Groups for this process, you need to configure a common set of scripts on each of the servers.

The backups themselves can be done using normal T-SQL commands or even using maintenance plans. You just have to make sure of two things. First, make sure that every replica that has not been excluded from the possibility of backups through setting the priority has an automated backup in place. Second, make sure that each of the backups you set up determines first if that server has the current priority through the use of sys.fn_hadr_backup_is_preferred_replica. This is included for you automatically if you're using maintenance plans.

The most important thing to understand is that the log cleanup that normally occurs with a database in the Full recovery model still occurs with your primary replica. The log backups that take place on a secondary cause the primary's log to be cleaned up. If the process didn't work this way, it would be pointless.

## Maintenance Plans

To provide you with an example, I chose to set up my automated log backups on the SQLTHREE server using maintenance plans. Figure 16-13 is the basic dialog box showing how the log backups have been configured.

Note that there are no options you can set in the standard dialog box that specify whether or not this backup process is configured for use with an Availability Group. You can select the For Availability Databases, Ignore Replica Priority For Backup And Backup On Primary Settings check box to ignore the replica priority, but this isn't a good choice for setting up a log backup that is meant to work regardless of which server is online. However, if you click the View T-SQL button at the bottom of the dialog box, you'll see a script that looks like this:

```
DECLARE @preferredReplica int

SET @preferredReplica = (SELECT
[master].sys.fn_hadr_backup_is_preferred_replica('MovieManagement'))

IF (@preferredReplica = 1)
BEGIN
    BACKUP LOG [MovieManagement] TO  DISK = N'C:\Program Files\Microsoft SQL
Server\MSSQL11.MSSQLSERVER\MSSQL\Backup\MovieManagement_backup_2012_06_25_144225_8512689.trn'
WITH NOFORMAT, NOINIT,  NAME = N'MovieManagement_backup_2012_06_25_144225_8512689', SKIP,
REWIND, NOUNLOAD,  STATS = 10
END
```

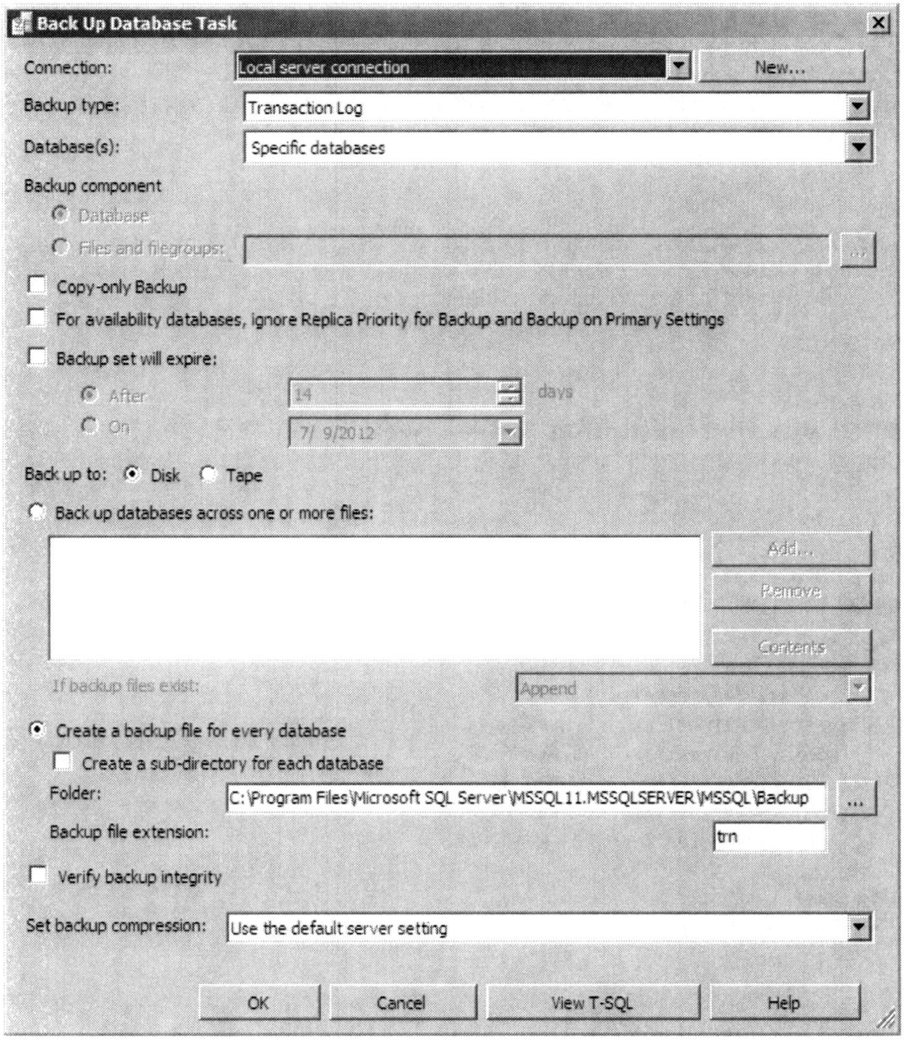

*Figure 16-13. The maintenace plan window you use to configure log backups.*

The script declares a variable, @preferredReplica, and then uses the sys.fn_hadr_backup_is_preferred_replica function to determine if the server currently calling the backup process is the replica in the Availability Group where the backup will currently run.

To show you this in action, I'm going to set up the maintenance plan on this server, SQLTHREE, so that it runs a log backup every 15 minutes. Currently, none of the other replicas have a backup process and SQLTHREE is the primary. When the job fires, it completes successfully, without error. However, that's only because it's getting to the priority check and finding that it's not currently the server with priority, which causes it to exit gracefully, but it means I don't have a log backup. I can validate that by going to the location specified to see if a backup file was created. There is none.

To get this to work, I need to perform two tasks. First, I need to create this same maintenance plan on all my other servers. Second, I need to create a schedule that executes the plan on each of the servers. Because only one will be selected by the sys.fn_hadr_back_is_preferred_replica function, I'm placing extremely little load on all the servers because they will only check to see if they are the preferred replica currently. If the server in question is not the preferred replica, the process will close out. If the server is the preferred replica, the log backup will be run.

I'm not a fan of using maintenance plans, because they don't offer enough granular control over how processes are run. Setting up a similar log-backup process using scripts is extremely easy.

## T-SQL Scripts

First, I need to establish the backup script that I want to use on each of the servers. My script will be slightly different than the one created for the maintenance plan:

```
DECLARE @preferredReplica INT

SET @preferredReplica = (SELECT
[master].sys.fn_hadr_backup_is_preferred_replica('MovieManagement')
                        )

IF (@preferredReplica = 1)
BEGIN
    DECLARE @Location NVARCHAR(50);
    DECLARE @CurrentTime DATETIME = GETUTCDATE();


    SET @Location = 'C:\bu\MovieManagement_log_'
        + CAST(DATEPART(year, @CurrentTime) AS NVARCHAR) + '_'
        + CAST(DATEPART(month, @CurrentTime) AS NVARCHAR) + '_'
        + CAST(DATEPART(day, @CurrentTime) AS NVARCHAR) + '_'
        + CAST(DATEPART(hour, @CurrentTime) AS NVARCHAR) + '_'
        + CAST(DATEPART(minute, @CurrentTime) AS NVARCHAR) + '.bak'

    BACKUP LOG MovieManagement
        TO DISK = @Location
        WITH INIT;
END
```

I can create a SQL Agent Job with a schedule that runs this backup every three minutes. That's probably more frequently than you would want to run a backup in a production system, but I'm just setting this up for testing purposes. Then I can easily script that job out and run it on each of my servers. Because I'm using a specific location for the backups, I need to make sure that each server does have that file location available. My finished Agent Job looks like this:

```
USE [msdb]
GO

/****** Object:  Job [LogBackups]     Script Date: 7/6/2012 6:05:56 PM ******/
BEGIN TRANSACTION
DECLARE @ReturnCode INT
SELECT @ReturnCode = 0
/****** Object:  JobCategory [[Uncategorized (Local)]]]     Script Date: 7/6/2012 6:05:56 PM
******/
IF NOT EXISTS (SELECT name FROM msdb.dbo.syscategories WHERE name=N'[Uncategorized (Local)]' AND
```

```
category_class=1)
BEGIN
EXEC @ReturnCode = msdb.dbo.sp_add_category @class=N'JOB', @type=N'LOCAL', @
name=N'[Uncategorized
(Local)]'
IF (@@ERROR <> 0 OR @ReturnCode <> 0) GOTO QuitWithRollback

END

DECLARE @jobId BINARY(16)
EXEC @ReturnCode =  msdb.dbo.sp_add_job @job_name=N'LogBackups',
        @enabled=1,
        @notify_level_eventlog=0,
        @notify_level_email=0,
        @notify_level_netsend=0,
        @notify_level_page=0,
        @delete_level=0,
        @description=N'No description available.',
        @category_name=N'[Uncategorized (Local)]',
        @owner_login_name=N'CONTOSO\LabUser', @job_id = @jobId OUTPUT
IF (@@ERROR <> 0 OR @ReturnCode <> 0) GOTO QuitWithRollback
/****** Object:   Step [Backup MovieManagement]     Script Date: 7/6/2012 6:05:56 PM ******/
EXEC @ReturnCode = msdb.dbo.sp_add_jobstep @job_id=@jobId, @step_name=N'Backup MovieManagement',
        @step_id=1,
        @cmdexec_success_code=0,
        @on_success_action=1,
        @on_success_step_id=0,
        @on_fail_action=2,
        @on_fail_step_id=0,
        @retry_attempts=0,
        @retry_interval=0,
        @os_run_priority=0, @subsystem=N'TSQL',
        @command=N'DECLARE @preferredReplica INT

SET @preferredReplica = (SELECT
[master].sys.fn_hadr_backup_is_preferred_replica(''MovieManagement'')
                    )

IF (@preferredReplica = 1)
BEGIN
    DECLARE @Location NVARCHAR(50);
    DECLARE @CurrentTime DATETIME = GETUTCDATE();


    SET @Location = ''C:\bu\MovieManagement_log_''
        + CAST(DATEPART(year, @CurrentTime) AS NVARCHAR) + ''_''
        + CAST(DATEPART(month, @CurrentTime) AS NVARCHAR) + ''_''
        + CAST(DATEPART(day, @CurrentTime) AS NVARCHAR) + ''_''
        + CAST(DATEPART(hour, @CurrentTime) AS NVARCHAR) + ''_''
        + CAST(DATEPART(minute, @CurrentTime) AS NVARCHAR) + ''.bak''
```

```
    BACKUP LOG MovieManagement
    TO DISK = @Location
    WITH INIT;
END',
        @database_name=N'master',
        @flags=0
IF (@@ERROR <> 0 OR @ReturnCode <> 0) GOTO QuitWithRollback
EXEC @ReturnCode = msdb.dbo.sp_update_job @job_id = @jobId, @start_step_id = 1
IF (@@ERROR <> 0 OR @ReturnCode <> 0) GOTO QuitWithRollback
EXEC @ReturnCode = msdb.dbo.sp_add_jobschedule @job_id=@jobId, @name=N'Every Two Minutes',
        @enabled=1,
        @freq_type=4,
        @freq_interval=1,
        @freq_subday_type=4,
        @freq_subday_interval=2,
        @freq_relative_interval=0,
        @freq_recurrence_factor=0,
        @active_start_date=20120706,
        @active_end_date=99991231,
        @active_start_time=0,
        @active_end_time=235959,
        @schedule_uid=N'70996e43-6c73-41f2-be5a-143853fdd5dd'
IF (@@ERROR <> 0 OR @ReturnCode <> 0) GOTO QuitWithRollback
EXEC @ReturnCode = msdb.dbo.sp_add_jobserver @job_id = @jobId, @server_name = N'(local)'
IF (@@ERROR <> 0 OR @ReturnCode <> 0) GOTO QuitWithRollback
COMMIT TRANSACTION
GOTO EndSave
QuitWithRollback:
    IF (@@TRANCOUNT > 0) ROLLBACK TRANSACTION
EndSave:

GO
```

With that script run on every single server, all that remains to be done is to test the process. To see changes in the database I've been using, I'm going to create a table for the database:

```
CREATE TABLE dbo.ChangingData
    (ID INT IDENTITY(1, 1),
     Val VARCHAR(50)
    );
```

Then I'm going to add a row, wait until a log backup has been run, and then add another row:

```
BEGIN TRANSACTION
INSERT  INTO dbo.ChangingData
        (Val)
VALUES  ('First Row');
COMMIT TRANSACTION

WAITFOR DELAY '00:04';
```

| | | | |
|---|---|---|---|
| MovieManagement_log_2012_7_6_22_10 | 7/6/2012 6:10 PM | File | 85 KB |
| MovieManagement_log_2012_7_6_22_12 | 7/6/2012 6:12 PM | File | 85 KB |
| MovieManagement_log_2012_7_6_22_14 | 7/6/2012 6:14 PM | File | 85 KB |
| MovieManagement_log_2012_7_6_22_16 | 7/6/2012 6:16 PM | File | 85 KB |
| MovieManagement_log_2012_7_6_22_18 | 7/6/2012 6:18 PM | File | 85 KB |
| MovieManagement_log_2012_7_6_22_20 | 7/6/2012 6:20 PM | File | 85 KB |
| MovieManagement_log_2012_7_6_22_22 | 7/6/2012 6:22 PM | File | 150 KB |
| MovieManagement_log_2012_7_6_22_24 | 7/6/2012 6:24 PM | File | 85 KB |

*Figure 16-14. Log backups completing on one of the replicas.*

```
BEGIN TRANSACTION
INSERT  INTO dbo.ChangingData
        (Val)
VALUES  ('Second Row');
COMMIT TRANSACTION
```

With all that in place, I can identify which of the replicas is currently my primary. In my case, it's SQLFIVE. I can see the log backups that have been running by looking at the drive on that server. as you can see in Figure 16-14.

And that's all it takes to set up the backups on an Availability Group. You can see the backups occurring, but the only way to know for sure that a backup has worked is to recover the database.

# Recovery on Availability Groups

The entire purpose of the Availability Group is to provide a mechanism whereby the databases that have been configured to be a part of the group are always available. This is done primarily through the process of automatic failover from one of the replicas to another. The very concept suggests that you no longer need backups at all. Keep in mind, though, Availability Groups are a means of maintaining high availability. They supplement your disaster recovery (DR) plans, but they cannot completely replace the fundamental beginning of all DR efforts, backups. You're still need to run your standard sets of backups.

There is one problem with placing a database in an Availability Group. Once that database is a part of the group, you can no longer run a restore on that database. In fact, as far as the Availability Group is concerned, you wouldn't want to. If a server went offline, a database was corrupted, or some other action caused the loss of connectivity to that replica, your other replicas are there to take up the load. And you can simply recover the system by getting it back online and rejoining the Availability Group. You'll resynchronize with the Availability Group and continue on happily.

However, what if you do need to go to the full-blown disaster recovery plan. You need to restore that database. Well, your processes haven't changed much. Let's walk through this.

I have a full database backup that I took from my primary replica. I also have a series of backups taken against one of my secondaries. In a normal DR scenario, you can move these backups off-site from your primary location to protect them. In this case, I bring together my full backup and my log backups, both taken on different replicas, and combine them to restore a database to a point in time on a different server as a different database.

First, I'll restore the full backup:

```
RESTORE DATABASE MMCopy
```

```
FROM DISK = 'c:\bu\moviemanagement.bak'
WITH NORECOVERY, MOVE 'MovieManagement' TO 'c:\data\moviemanagement.mdf',
MOVE 'MovieManagement_Log' TO 'c:\data\moviemanagement_log.ldf';
```

Now I can use some of the log backups that were created to recover this database to a point in time prior to the insertion of the second row of data:

```
RESTORE LOG MMCopy
FROM DISK = 'c:\bu\MovieManagement_log_2012_7_6_22_44'
WITH NORECOVERY, STOPAT = '7/6/2012 18:45';

RESTORE LOG MMCopy
FROM DISK = 'c:\bu\MovieManagement_log_2012_7_6_22_46'
WITH NORECOVERY, STOPAT = '7/6/2012 18:45';

RESTORE DATABASE MMCopy
WITH RECOVERY;
```

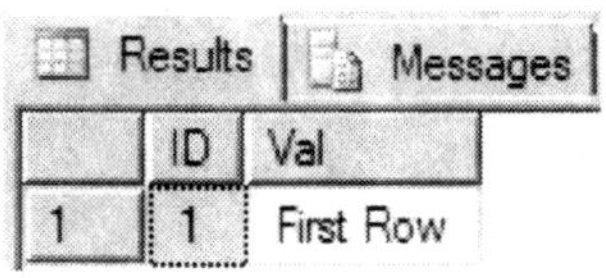

*Figure 16-15. The data returned after restoring to a point in time prior to the second insert.*

I can verify that I recovered the database to a point prior to the second insert by simply selecting data from the restored database:

```
USE MMCopy;
SELECT * FROM dbo.ChangingData;
```

The data returned looks like Figure 16-15.

Restoring to a point in time is no big deal. But you have to remember that the full backup that was used was from one server—specifically, my current primary replica, SQLTHREE. The log backups that were used were from a completely different server, SQLFIVE. I was able to take backups across multiple machines from within the Availability Group and then combine those backups at another location to restore a database.

# Conclusion

The advanced capabilities offered by Availability Groups within SQL Server 2012 provide a much wider array of high-availability solutions. But they also create additional opportunities for your disaster-recovery planning. You will be able to move part of your backups off to the secondary replicas without having to worry about which replica is currently the primary or even which of the secondary replicas is available. Just make sure that you always check against the sys.fn_hadr_backup_is_preferred_replica function to be sure that the correct replica is running the backups. Although you can't restore directly over databases within the Availability Group, you can use these log backups in combination with full backups from a primary replica to restore a database to another location. The best part is that you're not limited in how you run your backups. You can use maintenance plans or your own custom scripts without impacting how your Availability Group functions or negatively affecting your ability to later restore the databases that take part in that group.

■ ■ ■

# Big Data for the SQL Server DBA

## By Carlos Bossy

By now you've all heard about "Big Data," and the way people talk about it, you might think it's as overwhelmingly large as the universe. If you're like most database administrators, you likely already work with data that is big. You probably spend your professional time managing multiple databases that are terabytes in size or larger, and continue to grow. The size of data has exceeded Moore's Law, more than doubling every 24 months and making the DBAs job a challenge, to say the least. There's never been anything small about what you do. So, why is data now "big"?

This chapter will explain the meaning and significance of Big Data by comparing and contrasting it to the SQL Server relational database environment. It will also demonstrate the value a Big Data ecosystem can provide to your technology infrastructure by using it to complement your existing data architecture and having it co-exist in effective ways with your SQL Server databases. If hearing about Big Data has mystified you and made you wonder if it is nothing more than irrational exuberance, by the end of this chapter you'll have a better sense of how to make the best use of it and why it could benefit you and your organization.

For SQL Server–centric DBAs, what exactly does Big Data mean? It's still a nebulous area, not yet well-defined and without accepted practices or standards. If there wasn't already enough to know in the demanding job of a DBA, learning, understanding, and managing yet another technology can certainly add to an already stressful workday. Throughout this chapter, I'll present some definitions and descriptions that gradually introduce Big Data, present several business cases for taking advantage of Big Data, and show some practical working examples of actual code you can execute in Big Data database environments.

If you're not certain what Big Data is, you're not alone. Putting a wrapper around it isn't easy, and there is no precise industry standard definition. So, let's start by looking at some statements about Big Data that should provide some clarity.

---

■ **Note**   Big Data is a class of data that requires CPU and disk resources that exceed the power of stand-alone computer hardware to be retrieved efficiently. Processing it effectively requires multiple distributed computers working in parallel. This data is difficult to process in a traditional relational database management system (RDBMS). Therefore, it is beneficial to define the schema for this data at retrieval time, after it is stored on disk.

---

The "three Vs" that define Big Data are *volume* of data measured in at least terabytes and into petabytes; *variety* of data that includes media files, images, text, streams, logs, sensors, and more; and *velocity* of data, which is the speed with which it is collected.

---

For the SQL Server DBA, Big Data means managing and processing data that forces you to think beyond SQL Server's ample set of features. This approach includes solutions that are difficult to implement with the core database engine, partitioning, Service Broker, Analysis Services, and many other tools you commonly utilize to make SQL Server process high volumes of assorted data types.

A Hadoop implementation of Big Data is a mechanism for handling data that can and must be distributed for massive scalability beyond what SQL Server can do (and more than it was meant to do). Hadoop is also good at handling large data types, data without a well-defined schema, and data that is generally difficult for traditional databases, such as SQL Server, to handle. Big Data is about massive volumes of data, and a Hadoop infrastructure may be in your future if you have to deal with any of the following types of data:

- Unstructured data such as images, video, and free-form text

- Data you would have thrown away to save space or maintain performance

- Data you might need later for analysis, audits, or for an unplanned purpose

- Anything you don't want in your OLTP databases or data marts because it doesn't really belong there

- Data that doesn't relate precisely to any other data

Without immense data volumes or special data types, it's likely that a traditional SQL Server database solution will suit you just fine and will handle your data adequately without the complexity of introducing new technology. SQL Server OLTP relational databases start transactions, get data, lock it, change it, and commit the changes to the database. This is a proven, reliable, and well-understood process that has been developed and fine-tuned since the 1970s.

In addition to relational database technology, you also have other options for storing data. An Analysis Services cube and Tabular models are great for reporting, ad-hoc analysis, dashboards, and other metrics-based visualization. You can also partition data, use file tables, scale out with Service Broker, and more, making every data architecture uniquely its own. These techniques provide you with a multitude of choices, with the arrival of Big Data being one more weapon in your arsenal.

Big Data is nonrelational, yet the relational data model has proven itself to be very useful for more than 30 years. It's easy for technologists to understand, and if you understand the model, it's a good bet that you understand the application. It describes the entities in the database in a very familiar way; as we talk about the entities, we also describe the real world. A customer *has an* address. A store *contains* products. A supervisor *is an* employee. Developers can easily interpret its visual representation, and then use that as a guide for how to handle data within an application. For example, you can scan a data model diagram and immediately get a great understanding of the data. You could even post this diagram on a wall for reference and discussion.

The drawback of implementing data architecture primarily with the relational engine as a comprehensive, one-size-fits-all solution is that you often have difficulty making every data model work the way you would like. Often, you might use the relational engine for data that doesn't quite fit, but you do so because it's what you have available and it's what you know. To use all of SQL Server correctly can take a highly experienced professional who has expertise with every feature, property, and setting of the DBMS to get it done. For most professionals in the SQL Server world, the relational engine is a typical and undeniable solution for all data types and structures, including logs, archives, BLOBs, text, star schemas, staging data, and streaming data. That has now changed with Big Data. You'll have to choose where data will reside and dropping it in an OLTP database won't necessarily be the only (or default) choice. This is a new realm that the enterprise DBA will have to work within as they develop this architecture.

Should all of your data be stored in a Big Data cluster? It could be, but in a Microsoft SQL Server environment, the answer is very clear, "Never!" Remember, you still have SQL Server and it meets most (or all) of your needs already. It's a solid, reliable, full-featured package with a quality database engine, and any ACID (atomicity, consistency, isolation, durability) requirements you have in a high-volume environment will still be better served by SQL Server.

# Big Data Arrives with Hadoop

Now that we've established that Big Data doesn't replace SQL Server or your database infrastructure but complements it, let's look at the software and hardware that you will install, configure, and work with, and business cases that can make it useful for you. When you make the leap to Big Data, you are committing to developing a new type of data architecture that typically involves adding a Hadoop cluster to your environment, either internally within your network or in the cloud. This chapter will work with Hadoop on Azure, the cloud-based solution available from Microsoft in 2012. As of this writing, Microsoft has provided a Community Technology Preview (CTP) edition that we'll make use of to show working code. As a follow-on product, Microsoft will release Hadoop for Windows sometime in the future, but because this edition isn't publicly available yet, we won't discuss it here.

*Hadoop* is a framework, or an ecosystem, not a database. The framework is made up of various pieces of software that allow for the distributed, parallel, and redundant storing of data. The key parts of Hadoop are HDFS and MapReduce.

- **HDFS:** The Hadoop Distributed File System is the main file storage system used by the Hadoop framework software and applications.

- **MapReduce:** This is a software framework for processing large amounts of data in parallel on a cluster of servers in a reliable, fault-tolerant manner.

Hadoop gets its processing power by being able to write data in parallel to a large set of distributed machines, which in the Hadoop ecosystem are called *nodes*. When we talk about a large set of machines, consider that a small cluster might have 50 nodes. A cluster of this size would have all 50 machines processing data simultaneously in a coordinated manner. The redundancy of the data is baked in to this process, as it works by writing every piece of data to three nodes simultaneously.

A Hadoop cluster has three types of machines: Clients, Master Nodes, and Slave Nodes. There are two types of Master Nodes: Job Trackers and Name Nodes. The Name Node coordinates the data storage in HDFS, while the Job Tracker organizes the parallel processing of data using MapReduce. The majority of the machines in a Hadoop deployment are Slave Nodes, which do the work of storing data and running computations. Each Slave runs both a Data Node and Task Tracker daemon that communicate with and receive instructions from their Master Nodes. The responsibility of the Client machines is to load data into the cluster, submit MapReduce jobs, and retrieve the results of the jobs when they finish.

Figure 17-1 shows the Client–Master–Slave relationship and how the Name Node works with the data nodes to store and get data in HDFS. In smaller clusters of 50 nodes or less, you could have a single physical server playing multiple roles, such as both Job Tracker and Name Node. With medium to large clusters, you will often have each role operating on a single server machine.

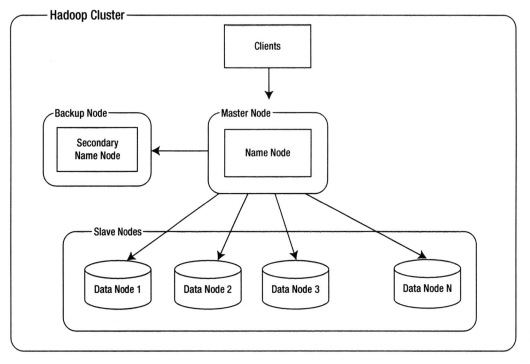

**Figure 17-1.** *A Hadoop cluster with N data nodes*

## MapReduce: The Nucleus of Hadoop

The reason for Hadoop's surge in popularity is its ability to retrieve and process large amounts of data faster than any other means available, and MapReduce is the key to making this happen. Consequently, the best way to understand Hadoop is to know how MapReduce works. To do this, you'll walk through an example of how MapReduce crunches data to solve a high-volume problem. Although writing code for MapReduce programs won't typically be the DBA's job, knowing how the data is processed will be as important to them as knowing how transactions are handled by a web application.

---

■ **Note**   Hadoop is written in the Java programming language, so MapReduce code is most often written in Java even though there is support for other languages, such as C++ and Python. An interesting development introduced by Microsoft to the Hadoop ecosystem is the addition of JavaScript as a MapReduce programming language. You'll use JavaScript to walk through an example of MapReduce in this section, and later in the chapter you'll execute a MapReduce job with your own code in the "JavaScript" section. For many software and database developers with experience using Microsoft development tools, JavaScript will be familiar and a viable option for MapReduce development.

---

To see how MapReduce processes data, you'll now work through a business scenario of an online retailer that is doing more than $2 billion in sales per year and has accumulated a large volume of sales data over the past three years. Assume the number of sales transactions processed over the three-year period has grown to more than 1 billion, and the company has used Hadoop to store a record of each transaction. Some of the data recorded for each transaction is shown in Table 17-1. The full set of data is spread across a cluster of 100 data nodes.

Keeping a record of the data in so much detail allows you to retrieve and analyze it in any way you choose. You know a lot about each sale, including customer details, product characteristics, and promotion information. The data is stored in CSV format by Hadoop in HDFS, so you can analyze this data over the full three-year period by computing sales metrics in numerous ways using the geography, product, promotion, customer, and sales data in your dataset. For your first task, you'll calculate the average sale amount by product line.

*Table 17-1.* *Ten Purchases in Your Sample HDFS Dataset*

| Country | Product | Product Line | Gender | Total Children | Order Quantity | Sale Amount |
|---------|---------|------|--------|----------------|----------------|-------------|
| USA | Road-650 Black | R | M | 4 | 1 | 699.09 |
| USA | Mountain-100 Silver | M | F | 5 | 1 | 3399.99 |
| France | Hydration Pack-70 oz. | M | F | 3 | 1 | 54.99 |
| Canada | Road-150 Red | R | M | 5 | 1 | 1777.77 |
| Australia | Short-Sleeve Classic Jersey | S | F | 0 | 1 | 35.99 |
| Australia | Mountain-350 Orange | M | M | 4 | 1 | 899.99 |
| USA | LL Touring Frame-Yellow | T | M | 0 | 1 | 874.99 |
| Australia | Hitch Rack-4-Bike | S | F | 0 | 1 | 120.00 |
| USA | Road-250 Red | R | M | 1 | 1 | 3528.99 |
| USA | Mountain-150 Silver | M | M | 0 | 1 | 1578.27 |

MapReduce has two important functions: map and reduce. The map function takes as input a dataset, filters out any data that is dirty or unwanted, and assigns a user-defined key to each row before outputting it. The Hadoop framework groups the data together by the user-defined key and sorts it before sending it to the reduce function. In this example, the key you'll use is Product Line. The only other data you'll need is Sale Amount, so ignore the rest. Here's a quick explanation of the important terms:

- **MapReduce Job:** This is a process run by the MapReduce framework that includes input data, custom MapReduce code, and configuration settings. One MapReduce job executes both map tasks and reduce tasks. The MapReduce work flow is shown in Figure 17-2.

- **Map Task:** The input to a MapReduce job is split into equal-sized units of work called *map tasks* by the framework. Each task processes a subset of a whole dataset and ideally executes on a node that contains that subset on its local disk.

- **Reduce Task:** Reduce tasks are made up of custom code and configuration settings that take as input the output of the map tasks. The map tasks group and sort the data by key and their output is fed into reduce tasks for further processing.

- **Map Function:** This is the custom program code that is executed by a map task whose main purpose is to filter data and identify a key field.

- **Reduce Function:** This is the custom program code that is executed by a reduce task that normally performs aggregations and other calculations.

■ **Note**    The number of map tasks does not have to equal the number of reduce tasks. Often, there will be multiple map tasks and only one reduce task if the Hadoop framework decides that using a single reduce task is the most efficient way to process the data. You can limit the number of map and reduce tasks running in parallel per data node (which by default is set to 2 and 1, respectively) by editing the `mapred-site.xml` config file under the `conf` directory of Hadoop. These parameters set only an upper boundary, and the Hadoop framework may use less tasks than the maximum if it determines it can complete the job with less resources.

*Figure 17-2. MapReduce work flow*

The data is read from the file system as input to the map function, and is passed in as a key-value pair with the key being a file offset for each row. The file offset isn't important to you here, so ignore the input in this example. Ordinarily, the file offset will never be useful because you're not interested in the data's location within the file. However, the value is important here, as it's the actual data that you want to process. The input to the map function will have complete rows, so it's the MapReduce developer's job to identify the data you're interested in and parse the input so you retrieve only the Product Line and Sale Amount. Table 17-2 has an example of data that is being sent to the map function as input.

*Table 17-2. Input to map Function with Key As Row Offset, and Value As Data Row*

| Key | Value |
| --- | --- |
| 0 | USA,Road-650 Black,R,M,4,1,699.09 |
| 33 | USA,Mountain-100 Silver,M,F,5,1,3399.99 |
| 74 | France,Hydration Pack-70 oz.,M,F,3,1,54.99 |
| 119 | Canada,Road-150 Red,R,M,5, 1,1777.77 |
| 157 | Australia,Short-Sleeve Classic Jersey,S,F,0,1,35.99 |
| 209 | Australia,Mountain-350 Orange,M,M,4,1,899.99 |
| 254 | USA,LL Touring Frame-Yellow,T,M,0,1,874.99 |
| 299 | Australia,Hitch Rack-4-Bike,S,F,0,1,120.00 |
| 344 | USA,Road-250 Red,R,M,1,1,3528.99 |
| 377 | USA,Mountain-150 Silver,M,M,0,1,1578.27 |

At this point in the process, the developer can also look for dirty data by checking for nulls or other inconsistencies and cleanse it or toss it out. This is an example of a simple map function using JavaScript:

```
var map = function (key, value, context) {
    var aryValues = value.split(",");
    var pattern = /[A-Za-z]/;
    var productLine;
    var salesAmount;
```

```
    productLine = aryValues[2];
    salesAmount = aryValues[6];

    if (pattern.test(productLine) && productLine.toString() != "null")
    {
        context.write(productLine.toUpperCase(),salesAmount.toString());
    }
};
```

Even though it's a small function, you'll see how it can be very worthwhile without being large and complex. The value portion of the key-value pair that is sent in as input to the function is a row of text data that you parse by splitting, using a comma as the delimiter because your data is comma-delimited. Then, you get the column values you're interested in by accessing them using array offsets. So, in our example, Product Line is at offset 2 and Sales Amount is at offset 6.

The map function's main purpose is to have a way to define your own key-value pairs for later processing. You use the context.write function to return a key-value pair as output, with Product Line being the key and Sale Amount being the value. The identification of the new key-value pair is made by the developer based on the problem being solved, and must be done correctly for MapReduce to get the desired results. Table 17-3 has an example of what this data looks like when it comes out of the map function.

*Table 17-3. Output of map Function with Key Set to Product Line, and Value Set to Sale Amount*

| Key | Value |
| --- | --- |
| R | 699.09 |
| M | 3399.99 |
| M | 54.99 |
| R | 1777.77 |
| S | 35.99 |
| M | 899.99 |
| T | 874.99 |
| S | 120.00 |
| R | 3528.99 |
| M | 1578.27 |

In between the map and reduce function, the MapReduce framework helps by doing some work for you. It groups and sorts the key-value pairs by key in a process known as the *shuffle* and passes the results on to the reduce step. Because your data has Product Line as the key, it is input into the reduce function grouped and sorted by Product Line. Each Product Line has every Sale Amount value associated with it. These new key-value pairs are written to local disk on each data node so the reduce function can read them. The key value pairs look like what is shown in the four rows below.

```
{M, (3399.99, 54.99, 899.99, 1578.27)}
{R, (699.09, 1777.77, 3528.99)}
{S, (35.99, 120.00)}
{T, (874.99)}
```

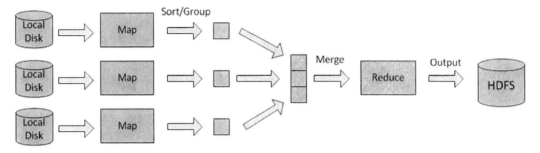

***Figure 17-3.*** *MapReduce job with a single reduce task*

Now you have something you can work with because the key-value pairs are sorted and grouped by key, but remember that this was done by the map step running map tasks on *separate* nodes. It's possible that you could have the same key with different values on every server that executed a map task. The keys need to be brought together in the reduce step, so the MapReduce framework takes care of this by sending them to a common node so they can be processed together, as shown in Figure 17-3.

The reduce step takes this data as input and iterates through it. When it receives a key-value pair, it is up to the developer to process the data accordingly. To satisfy your requirements, the developer would need to iterate through each Sale Amount value and aggregate it. Simply speaking, the reduce step allows you to sum sales for a key and return the key with the aggregated total. When the reduce step finishes, the job is complete, and the output is written to HDFS. Clients must read the output data from HDFS to make it visible to the end user. For this example, the reduce output is a small file with four rows of data, total sales by Product Line.

```
var reduce = function (key, values, context) {
    var sumsales = 0.0;
        var productLine = key;

    while (values.hasNext()) {
        sumsales += parseFloat(values.next());
        }
    context.write(productLine, sumsales);
};
```

### Reduce Output

```
{M, 5933.24}
{R, 6005.85}
{S, 155.99}
{T, 874.99}
```

MapReduce is the most important part of this chapter, so let's take the example a step further to emphasize how much we made Hadoop do with a small amount of code. In a real-world scenario, this simple job could be executed on hundreds of computers at the same time, if the data is distributed across that number of data nodes, each of them taking on their own share of the load. While our code snippets have a big role to play in how the data is processed, a lot happens that isn't visible to us. With so many servers involved, you're probably thinking that there has to be a substantial amount of coordination, organization, and management going on—and you would be correct.

The MapReduce framework takes care of this, starting MapReduce jobs on the data nodes that contain the data you need, monitoring the jobs for success or failure, and bringing the data together after it is processed independently. If a job fails, the framework can reexecute it, and this is good because you could be potentially running jobs on hundreds of servers at the same time and you wouldn't want a failure on a single machine to stop you from your pursuit. A data node can fail for any number of reasons (such as a hardware problem, memory pressure, low disk space, etc.), yet the MapReduce framework can restart the job on another server that has the same set of data to keep things running.

Figure 17-4 depicts how values that reside on separate data nodes are brought together using their associated keys by MapReduce.

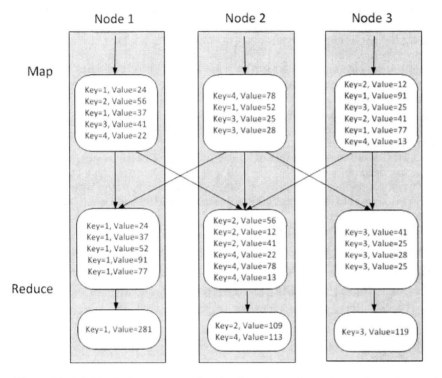

***Figure 17-4.*** *A MapReduce process showing how key-value pairs are brought together in the reduce step*

Even if you never write a line of MapReduce code, it's important to know how it works because there are numerous tools available to DBAs for importing, exporting, and manipulating Hadoop data. These tools implement MapReduce to do their work, but hide the details from the user, while the JavaScript code allows you to customize the MapReduce function to suit your needs. In SQL Server terms, the JavaScript code would be T-SQL, while the Hadoop tools would be BCP and SSIS. The Hadoop tools you'll use in the sample scripts later in the chapter will allow you to set some parameters that affect how they employ MapReduce to do their work, so understanding MapReduce at the code level is important for knowing how to use the tools effectively.

For in-depth coverage on setting up Hadoop, writing MapReduce code, and tuning and testing MapReduce jobs, see *Pro Hadoop* written by Jason Venner (Apress, 2009). Venner's book covers MapReduce in much more detail and also discusses debugging, testing, and tuning MapReduce.

Another important factor in how MapReduce works is the hardware configuration. Even though we've been talking about a cloud configuration with Hadoop on Azure, it's important to have some knowledge about the hardware that drives Hadoop.

# Hardware

You might have heard that Hadoop can use commodity hardware, suggesting second-rate or low-quality machines, but don't assume we're talking about the old servers that have been sitting under your desk for years. The majority of your servers will be Slave Nodes with lots of local disk storage and moderate amounts of CPU and RAM. Some of the machines will be Master Nodes that might have a slightly different configuration with more RAM and CPU, but less local storage. These machines might be cheaper than the machines you normally use for SQL Server, but not necessarily. Many SQL Server DBAs are running their databases on this type of commodity hardware, so the term *commodity* might be misleading, allowing them to think that they can use even lower-end hardware for Big Data. In addition, for Big Data you'll need a lot more servers that will still need a minimum level of storage and memory to perform in a satisfactory manner. In this context, commodity hardware refers to a collection of servers that can be purchased off the shelf, not high-end computers that are custom designed and built for super-high performance.

A generic minimum configuration for Hadoop should include two machines with two multicore CPUs, four directly attached local hard disks with at least 1 TB of storage each, and 24 GB of RAM. You would need two of these data nodes, giving you 8 TB of storage. If you are expecting to quickly ramp up a production Hadoop cluster to a larger scale, you could put together eight multicore servers, each with 32 GB of RAM and 12 2-TB disks, totaling 24 TB of storage. This would give you 192 TB of total storage, but since the data is stored three times for redundancy, it means you actually have 64 TB to work with. What happens if usage takes off and you need more storage? You simply add more data nodes. One of Hadoop's strengths is the ability to add more data nodes to a cluster seamlessly, so whether you start with the smaller or larger configuration, you can always grow to a very large size. Consider that it would take approximately 130 24-TB data nodes to scale up to 3 PB (petabytes) of redundant data, while the framework has been designed to handle 10,000 data nodes!

---

▓ **Caution**    Notice that we didn't talk about the storage being handled by a SAN. There's a good reason for this. Hadoop was designed for locally attached direct storage so that each node controls its own data storage. A SAN could become a bottleneck when multiple data nodes access it simultaneously (or if used by other applications in an enterprise setting), and it's a more expensive way to store data than commodity disk drives. Disk access is often the bottleneck when you process large amounts of data, and not sharing the storage reduces this bottleneck. Using separate storage dedicated to each data node allows the disk to be used in parallel more effectively.

---

While this high degree of distribution and parallelism provides an ability to store an almost infinite amount of data, an important thing to understand is that HDFS is limited in ways we're not accustomed to as RDBMS-focused data architects. It supports forward-only parsing, so you are either reading ahead or appending to the end of a file. There is no concept of update or insert, and files can only be written to once. This is what makes HDFS very different from SQL Server, and will even seem crude at times compared to the tables, columns, views, and other database objects you're familiar with.

---

▓ **Caution**    With such a highly distributed infrastructure running on so many servers, you think it's going to be really fast, don't you? Actually, it's not fast when run on a small amount of data. The overhead of starting up the various MapReduce jobs, getting the data, and assembling the output together is very high, so it makes sense to crunch through a large amount of data when you do this. However, the process is excessive when working with a small dataset, since spinning up MapReduce jobs each time a data request occurs is so expensive. The code examples later in this chapter will seem to be slow on the small sets of data you'll use. However, it will be much faster than traditional means when you get to the point where you're processing data that is terabytes in size, but unlike SQL Server you'll still get used to measuring query response times from a Big Data system in minutes and hours instead of milliseconds and seconds.

# DBA As Data Architect

Previously, we looked at how an online retailer with a large set of sales data could aggregate it by product line with MapReduce. We'll continue working with product data to work through more business problems and their solutions.

In this setting, you are a SQL Server DBA at the fast-growing online retailer and the company is looking to track more of what is happening with its product data. One uneventful morning, a developer you work with stops by your desk and starts talking about the new requirements he's been handed. He wants a large amount of disk space allocated on the database server because he has been tasked with keeping a record of every change made to the Product table. In particular, because of dynamic pricing, the list price of a product changes frequently, an average of 20 times per day. Based on current activity and a total of 500,000 active products, this adds up to 10 million rows per day. Yikes!

Trying to clear your head from the initial shock, you ask the developer how the data is going to be used. He claims that part is a bit unclear because the finance department wants him to capture it just in case they need it later for an audit. Immediately, thoughts race through your head about disk space, memory, and impact to existing databases. Do you create a new database for this data, install a new SQL Server instance, or fire up a new server? How will you manage it if it starts getting used heavily? It's a scenario an experienced DBA is all too familiar with.

With Hadoop added to your DBA toolset, you make a wise decision by implementing a solution that makes the best use of the many features of SQL Server, while using Hadoop for what it does best. To get this done, your main challenge as DBA will be to define, regulate, and manage the flow of data among the various places it can reside. An example of the many ways the data can flow is shown in Figure 17-5.

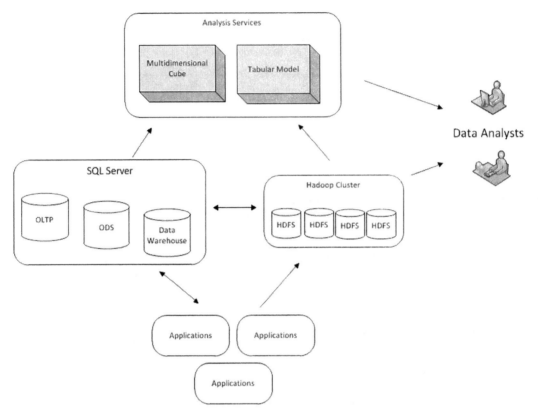

***Figure 17-5.*** *Complicated data flow makes data architecture decisions more varied and complex.*

# Big Data for Analytics

Many of the demonstrations, webinars, papers, and other presentations you might have seen for using Big Data in a Microsoft environment are targeted at using it for analytics or to enhance a Business Intelligence framework. Microsoft has good reason for this; it's an opportunity to show off tools such as PowerView and Excel, which shine in those situations, giving them practically unlimited power as the amount of data an analyst can work with approaches infinity. It isn't just Microsoft pushing this, as using it for analytics is also the most common reason for building a Big Data infrastructure.

The usual technique for analyzing data with these tools is a three-step process of selecting the data to work with from within the HDFS data store, extracting a portion of it to a place the analyst can access it, and then analyzing it using Excel or a statistical analysis tool. Based on any findings or discoveries, the analyst repeats the process in an iterative fashion until a conclusion is reached. All of this, other than the analysis itself, is done in a noninteractive way. Getting the data to a point where an analyst can work with it could take hours because the extract runs as a batch process in the background.

As an example of this, suppose an analyst wants to look at web logs for the past three months to determine which web page a potential customer goes to after viewing the About Us page on the web site. The web logs have been stored in HDFS for the past year and the storage has gotten large compared to the size of data this company is accustomed to, growing to over 100 TB in size. The analyst starts by setting some boundaries for this work, such as the dates of interest and the URL of the web page being targeted, which would be something like `www.mywebsite.com\aboutus.aspx`.

This criterion set by the analyst becomes the filters that allow MapReduce to extract just the data the analyst wants. A MapReduce job is fired off to access the web log that has been distributed over 75 servers, potentially grabbing data from all of them and outputting the results to a place and in a form the analyst can access. The data is now trimmed down to a size the analyst can work with instead of the initial 100-TB dataset. The analyst is ready to do her job using tools she's familiar with. She creates graphs to better visualize trends and patterns, runs the data through a statistical model for better understanding, and asks what-if questions that provoke more questions that require data the analyst doesn't yet have. The analyst goes back to Hadoop to get more data and is ready to do it again. This iterative process continues until the analyst is satisfied with the results she is getting. This type of data access and analysis is the main reason for Hadoop's existence and the primary use-case DBAs will need to support in a SQL Server + Hadoop environment.

# Using SQL Server with Hadoop

The best reason for adding a Hadoop data store to work side by side with SQL Server is to let Hadoop be responsible for handling data that isn't transactional in nature, isn't required to be ACID compliant, and grows in size quickly. As a DBA, your job in this new era of data management will be to make the right choices for where your data resides.

## The DBA's Role

Some DBAs are data architects and modelers, but many are not. Most DBAs have as their first priority data protection, including backup/restore, disaster recover, and high availability and security. Others work on improving performance and reducing contention. The roles are muddled and the responsibilities are often unclear, and with Big Data, things are going to get murkier.

In newer software and database environments, such as those seen in technology startups or companies that don't perform intentional data architecture, the role of the DBA as data architect is often nonexistent. Developers decide how and where to store data and the DBA's involvement is that of an order taker, if any at all. In some enterprise environments where the data architect is king, every data-modeling decision is made or approved by his majesty. If the architect is simply another subject, the choices for storing data are made by the DBA in union with the development team. Often though, there is no data architect to play the role of gatekeeper on the data model and it's developed in an ad-hoc manner. In any case, the DBA has a significant role in storing and maintaining the data to ensure its integrity and availability, and should be prepared to take on the management, safety, and reliability of the Big Data framework.

The lack of control and stewardship will be a challenge to a DBA adding Big Data to their sphere of responsibility. Consider what it will do to your current environment when you introduce the following characteristics of Big Data environments:

- You have unrelated mounds of data without foreign keys that comes in all shapes and sizes.

- Most data is processed in batch processes.

- The data model is programmer driven.

- The server hardware can be built out to a practically endless size.

- The life cycle of data is undefined and unbounded.

- Data cleansing is a question mark.

- Tools for managing Big Data are in their infancy.

- Bringing together disparate datasets will take expertise, effort, and money.

# Big Data in Practice

Let's explore a few patterns that show how to make use of Hadoop, and take a look at some examples that illustrate some ways that you might implement Big Data. One of the first decisions you'll have to make, after deciding what data to store using Hadoop, is how you will use it and how it will interact with your SQL Server databases. There are numerous architectural choices, and numerous techniques for moving data back and forth. We'll start by using Sqoop, a tool that will allow you to transfer data in bulk into and out of SQL Server.

## Importing and Exporting

The first example you'll work through is simply moving data into and out of HDFS. Assume that you need to solve a problem for your marketing department. The AdventureWorks Company is implementing a new sophisticated dynamic pricing system and marketing wants to know the price of a product for any day throughout the product's history. Today, the AdventureWorks database has a ProductListPriceHistory table, but because product prices changed infrequently in the past, it tracked price changes by wide date ranges, so you'll want to replace it so you can store a higher volume of data. You also know that, in the future, you'll want to track everything about a product, including inventory levels, cost, marketing description, and more. To make sure you don't miss anything, you store every product in HDFS at midnight every night using your new Hadoop infrastructure. Using the AdventureWorks for SQL Azure database, the Product table has the following definition, using two user-defined data types:

```
CREATE TYPE dbo.Name FROM nvarchar(50) NULL
CREATE TYPE dbo.Flag FROM bit NOT NULL

CREATE TABLE Production.Product(
    ProductID int IDENTITY(1,1) NOT NULL,
    Name dbo.Name NOT NULL,
    ProductNumber nvarchar(25) NOT NULL,
    MakeFlag dbo.Flag NOT NULL,
    FinishedGoodsFlag dbo.Flag NOT NULL,
    Color nvarchar(15) NULL,
    SafetyStockLevel smallint NOT NULL,
    ReorderPoint smallint NOT NULL,
    StandardCost money NOT NULL,
    ListPrice money NOT NULL,
    Size nvarchar(5) NULL,
    SizeUnitMeasureCode nchar(3) NULL,
    WeightUnitMeasureCode nchar(3) NULL,
    Weight decimal(8, 2) NULL,
    DaysToManufacture int NOT NULL,
    ProductLine nchar(2) NULL,
    Class nchar(2) NULL,
    Style nchar(2) NULL,
    ProductSubcategoryID int NULL,
    ProductModelID int NULL,
```

```
    SellStartDate datetime NOT NULL,
    SellEndDate datetime NULL,
    DiscontinuedDate datetime NULL,
    rowguid uniqueidentifier NOT NULL,
    ModifiedDate datetime NOT NULL,
 CONSTRAINT PK_Product_ProductID PRIMARY KEY CLUSTERED
(
    ProductID ASC
)WITH (PAD_INDEX = OFF, STATISTICS_NORECOMPUTE = OFF, IGNORE_DUP_KEY = OFF,
ALLOW_ROW_LOCKS = ON, ALLOW_PAGE_LOCKS = ON)
)
```

The tool you'll use to do this bulk data load work is Sqoop, a component of the Hadoop ecosystem (Hadoop on Azure includes Sqoop as part of its offering, so you don't have to install it separately). Sqoop is important for DBAs because it's the best way to perform bulk data transfers between Hadoop and SQL Server. The first thing to know about Sqoop is that an import moves data into HDFS and an export moves data out of HDFS (and into SQL Server, in this example). This example will show the movement of this data where both the SQL Server AdventureWorks database and the HDFS data store are in the cloud. Later, you'll work through an example where both data stores are inside your organization's network, although any of the code can be made to work with either SQL Server or HDFS inside your network or in the cloud.

---

■ **Note**   Apache Sqoop is a tool designed for efficiently transferring bulk data between Apache Hadoop and structured data stores, such as relational databases.

---

To start, you'll need a SQL Azure account. The first thing to do is add the AdventureWorks database to SQL Azure, which you can download from http://msftdbprodsamples.codeplex.com/releases/view/37304. Follow the instructions to get the database uploaded.

Then, you're going to need access to a Hadoop cluster. For these examples, I allocated a Hadoop cluster in Windows Azure using the Community Technology Preview (CTP) edition at https://www.hadooponazure.com. After it's allocated, you're ready to go with a Hadoop cluster in the cloud, as shown in Figure 17-6. Note that because, as of this writing, Microsoft has released only the CTP edition of Hadoop, the figure shows that the cluster will expire soon, but it also displays a set of tiles that will let me use the cluster. You'll spend most of your time running jobs from the command line that import and export data, so click Remote Desktop to directly log in to the cluster.

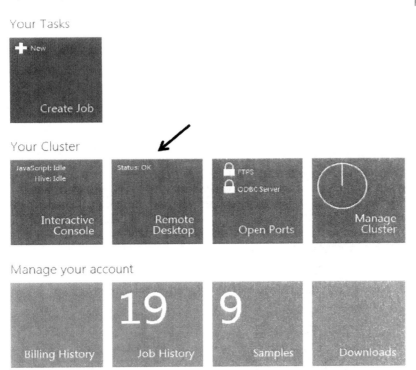

*Figure 17-6. Hadoop on Azure CTP main menu*

Now you can put this cluster to use by putting some data in there. After you RDP and log in to the cluster, go to the desktop and launch the Hadoop Command Shell. Once at the command line, you'll be at the root path for Hadoop and you'll see the c:\apps\dist> prompt. Before you do anything else, set the Hadoop home environment variable by executing the following line:

```
SET HADOOP_HOME=c:\Apps\dist
```

The next step is to change the command-line path to c:\Apps\dist\sqoop\bin, which is where you'll run Sqoop jobs to get data from AdventureWorks in SQL Azure into Hadoop and back.

```
cd sqoop\bin
```

Then, you need to log in to your AdventureWorks database and add a synonym. It's required because Sqoop puts brackets around table names, so it will need them when it accesses SQL Server. Go to SQL Azure and execute this SQL command:

```
CREATE SYNONYM [Production.Product] FOR Production.Product
```

The setup is done and you're ready to get some work done! The first Sqoop job will copy the Product table from SQL Server to HDFS. This is akin to using the BCP utility for SQL Server, a tool you're probably more familiar with. You aren't specifying any filters, columns, or an explicit query, so the whole table will be copied.

Go back to the Hadoop Command Shell and enter the following script, replacing myserver in the connect argument with the name of your database server, and use an actual username and password that can log in to SQL Server. The --connect argument looks like a familiar connection string, and the import command tells Sqoop to copy data from the database to HDFS. The --target-dir argument is the folder path where the data will be stored in HDFS, and -m tells Sqoop the number of map tasks to run in parallel for the import. A partial list of Sqoop arguments and descriptions is shown in Table 17-4. Execute the script to get Sqoop running.

```
sqoop import --connect "jdbc:sqlserver://myserver.database.windows.net;
username=mysqluser@myserver;password=mypwd;database=AdventureWorks2012" --table
Production.Product --target-dir /data/ProductTable -m 1
```

**Table 17-4.** *Partial Descriptive List of Sqoop Arguments*

| Argument | Description |
| --- | --- |
| --connect <jdbc-uri> | Specify JDBC connect string |
| --username <username> | Set authentication username |
| --password <password> | Set authentication password |
| --append | Append data to an existing dataset in HDFS |
| --columns <col,col,col…> | Columns to import from table |
| -m,--num-mappers <n> | Use *n* map tasks to import in parallel |
| -e,--query <statement> | Import the results of statement |
| --split-by <column-name> | Column of the table used to split work units |
| --table <table-name> | Table to read |
| --target-dir | This is the folder where the output data is stored |
| --where <where clause> | where clause to use during import |

You'll see a lot of logging messages and then, hopefully, success. At the end of the logging, you should see a couple of messages that tell you the time it took to run this job, the number of bytes transferred, and that all 504 rows from the Product table were imported into HDFS. It should look something like the following:

```
12/07/18 02:14:58 INFO mapreduce.ImportJobBase: Transferred 102.9434 KB in 43.5506 seconds
(2.3638 KB/sec)
12/07/18 02:14:58 INFO mapreduce.ImportJobBase: Retrieved 504 records.
```

If you're like me, the first thing you asked is "Where did the data go and how can I look at it?" Go back to the desktop and launch the HadoopNameNode. The screen will show you a link labeled "Browse the filesystem" (see Figure 17-7). Click it and a web browser will open with a list of directories, one of them being the data folder. Click this folder and you should see another folder called ProductTable, which is what you specified would be the HDFS location of the data in your Sqoop script. Click this folder and you'll see a file with the name part-m-00000. Sqoop creates files with a file name format of part-m-*xxxxx*, where *xxxxx* is a sequential number starting at 0. This is where your data should be.

Now open the file by clicking it and you'll see what looks like a comma-delimited file of the Product table. I know, not too exciting, but that's it. This is the way Sqoop loaded the table into HDFS and the way it lives there. Don't worry too much, though, it's very functional this way.

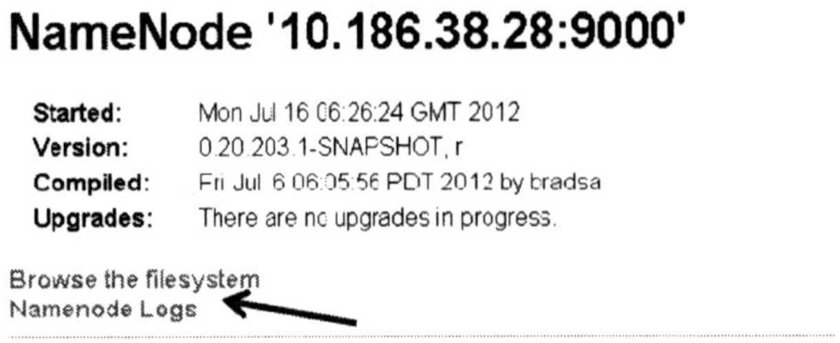

NameNode '10.186.38.28:9000'
Started: Mon Jul 16 06:26:24 GMT 2012
Version: 0.20.203.1-SNAPSHOT, r
Compiled: Fri Jul 6 06:05:56 PDT 2012 by bradsa
Upgrades: There are no upgrades in progress.
Browse the filesystem
Namenode Logs

***Figure 17-7.** Click the "Browse the filesystem" link to browse the datasets you're storing in HDFS.*

There are a few things to note about this initial data load. First, it didn't make the best use of Hadoop. It was a small amount of data, and you'll get more bang for the buck from your cluster with a larger dataset. Also, we asked Sqoop to do a vanilla load of the table into HDFS, so it loaded the whole table without using parallelism. To force parallelism, you could change the `-m` operator to a number greater than 1, and you would have to tell it the primary key of the table so it could split the data into multiple import jobs. If you don't tell Sqoop what the primary key of the table is, then the operator `-m` must have a value of 1 or else it will fail. Take a look at Figure 17-8 to see a diagram of Sqoop importing data in parallel by breaking the work up into multiple map tasks.

Sqoop Import
MapReduce Job
Data Node 1
Map Task
HDFS
Data Node 2
Map Task
HDFS
Data Node 3
Map Task
HDFS
Data Node 4
Map Task
HDFS
SQL Server
Database
Hadoop Cluster

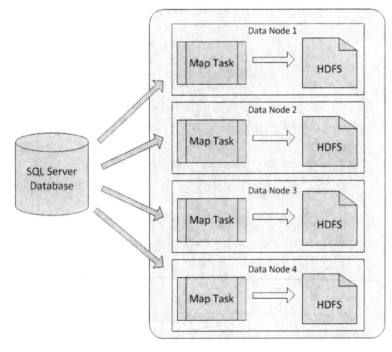

***Figure 17-8.** The Sqoop import data flow using MapReduce*

What if you executed the same job again? It would fail because the file part-m-00000 already exists in the ProductTable folder. To succeed, you would have to add the -append operator, which would import the complete Product table again into the same folder, except this time put it in a file called part-m-00001. If you did this on a daily basis, you would store a complete snapshot of the Product table in HDFS with one file per day.

There are many more options for importing data with Sqoop. This example showed a general use of Hadoop, but often you'll want to run a more targeted import, so next you'll do one that gets data based on using a filter.

## Extract Using a Date Filter

Imagine that your AdventureWorks SQL Server database contains 500,000 unique products, as you're a huge online retailer. You're still trying to build a data store that captures the history for product changes, especially pricing. As you saw in the previous section on import and exporting, you can take a complete snapshot of the Product table and capture it in HDFS every day. Instead, you choose to capture all changes to products, so you decide to run a job at the end of the day that grabs only product rows that have changed during the day. You can use Sqoop to do this by adding a few parameters.

First, you'll issue a SQL UPDATE statement to increase the price of every product in your database by $1 if the price is between $45 and $100, which should be 42 rows in AdventureWorks. This will also update the ModifiedDate column to the time of the update using getdate().

```
UPDATE  Production.Product
SET     ListPrice = ListPrice + 1,
        ModifiedDate = getdate()
WHERE   ListPrice between 45 and 100
```

## Sqoop Import from Azure

Because we're still using SQL Azure, you'll next get the changes from there and put them in the same HDFS folder you've been using, but you'll embellish the Sqoop import first. You'll notice we added a where clause to the import, so this pulls only the five rows that changed on the date 2012-07-19 (note that the date depends on when you execute the sample Update statement). We changed the –m parameter to 4, so four MapReduce tasks can run in parallel (I know, overkill for 42 rows, but it's an example).

Next, because you are using an –m setting of greater than 1, you need to identify the key that the MapReduce jobs can use to split the data up among themselves, so they aren't overlapping each other when grabbing data. This way every row belongs to one and only one job. To indicate the split key, you use -split-by and tell it that the key column is ProductID. Finally, you decide not to get every column from the Product table, so you use the -columns operator and list only the columns that you're interested in.

```
sqoop import --connect
"jdbc:sqlserver://myserver.database.windows.net;username=mysqluser@myserver;password=mypwd;
database=AdventureWorks2012" --table Production.Product --where "ModifiedDate
between '2012-07-19' and '2012-07-20'" --target-dir /data/ProductTable -m 4 -append
--columns "ProductID,ProductNumber,ListPrice,ModifiedDate" --split-by ProductID
```

After executing the job, go back to the ProductTable folder in HDFS. What you see might surprise you. There are four new files, one for each MapReduce task. Each file has a different number of rows because Sqoop doesn't balance the load among the four MapReduce tasks, but simply divides the work by getting the min and max values of the primary key and arithmetically splitting it into four groups. This way, each row that changed on 2012-07-19 ends up in one, and only one, of the four files. Notice too that each file has only the four columns you requested in the Sqoop job.

Just to show that there's more than one way to accomplish anything, the following script gets the same results. What is interesting about this technique is that you can write SQL queries using Sqoop. Notice the use of the $CONDITIONS token in the where clause. Sqoop replaces this token with a unique condition expression so the job can be run in parallel and each task get a different range of data.

```
sqoop import --connect  "jdbc:sqlserver://myserver.domain.com; username=mysqluser;
password=mypwd; database=AdventureWorks"
--query "SELECT ProductID,ProductNumber,ListPrice,ModifiedDate FROM Production.Product
where $CONDITIONS and ModifiedDate between '2012-07-19' and '2012-07-20'"
--target-dir /data/ProductTable -m 4 --split-by ProductID -append
```

This Sqoop job executes several queries in SQL Server. One of the queries gets the minimum and maximum ProductID. Sqoop uses the results of this query to divide the ProductID into four equal parts so it can execute four separate queries in parallel that access a different set of rows in the table (but not necessarily an equal number of rows).

```
SELECT MIN(ProductID), MAX(ProductID) FROM
(SELECT ProductID,ProductNumber,ListPrice,ModifiedDate FROM Production.Product where  (1 = 1)
and ModifiedDate between '2012-07-19' and '2012-07-20') AS t1
```

Sqoop then executes the following four queries in SQL Server. The $CONDITIONS expression is replaced in each query by the clause where ProductID between MIN and MAX. See how the MIN and MAX values for each query are determined by the results of the calculation performed in the previous query that split the data being read into four parts.

```
SELECT ProductID,ProductNumber,ListPrice,ModifiedDate FROM Production.Product where
( ProductID >= 1 ) AND ( ProductID < 251 ) and ModifiedDate between '2012-07-19' and '2012-07-20

SELECT ProductID,ProductNumber,ListPrice,ModifiedDate FROM Production.Product where
( ProductID >= 251 ) AND ( ProductID < 501 ) and ModifiedDate
between '2012-07-19' and '2012-07-20

SELECT ProductID,ProductNumber,ListPrice,ModifiedDate FROM Production.Product where
( ProductID >= 501 ) AND ( ProductID < 750 ) and ModifiedDate
between '2012-07-19' and '2012-07-20

SELECT ProductID,ProductNumber,ListPrice,ModifiedDate FROM Production.Product where
( ProductID >= 750 ) AND ( ProductID <= 999 ) and ModifiedDate between '2012-07-19'
and '2012-07-20
```

The result is no different from the prior Sqoop job you executed and the data is again split into four files.

As mentioned previously, Table 17-4 shows a list of the Sqoop arguments we've used with their descriptions. To see a full list of Sqoop parameters, go to http://sqoop.apache.org/. You've done some good work, but when you show the marketing people, you learn that the requirements have changed. They really want a complete audit trail of every change made to a product. The data load script you've developed with Sqoop gets the last version of a product for the date range you used in the query. If you run the  script once per day, changing the date range each time, you'll get the latest row for every product that was changed during that day. You're losing all of the information in between, so you would lose the change detail if a product changed five times in between your jobs running. You want all of the changes made to a product, so when a price is lowered by 50 percent for five minutes, you would know about it because you will capture the change.

Also, your dynamic pricing system has gone crazy. It is now changing prices on products 20 times per day, and since you have 500,000 active products, that's 10 million rows each day you'll capture in HDFS. Good thing you've got Hadoop ready to go, because now you're really getting some Big Data! For the future, marketing is already saying they want to see more than just price changes. They also want to know the inventory levels, cost, and other important data about a product every time it changes.

Let's see how you can make better use of SQL Server to get this work done. SQL Server can identify every change to the Product table with Change Data Capture (CDC). CDC will store an image of every insert, a before and after image of every update, and a before image of every delete. To enable CDC for the AdventureWorks database and the Product table, execute the following:

```
Use AdventureWorks
Go
exec sp_cdc_enable_db
Go
exec sp_enable table @source_schema='Production', @source_name='Product', @capture_instance
Go
```

Next, change some data so you have data in the CDC tables. To do this, execute the following T-SQL commands for the AdventureWorks database. These inserts, updates, and deletes will generate change rows that are stored in the cdc.dbo_Product_CT table.

```
INSERT INTO Production.Product(Name, ProductNumber, MakeFlag, FinishedGoodsFlag,
SafetyStockLevel, ReorderPoint, StandardCost, ListPrice, DaysToManufacture, SellStartDate)
VALUES '29 Inch Wheel','WH-8232',0,0,125,80,85.9500,126.9500,1,'2012-08-01 00:00:00'

INSERT INTO Production.Product(Name, ProductNumber, MakeFlag, FinishedGoodsFlag,
SafetyStockLevel, ReorderPoint, StandardCost, ListPrice, DaysToManufacture, SellStartDate)
VALUES 'MH Hybrid','HY-2452',0,0,210,100,865.0000,1295.0000,1,'2012-08-15 00:00:00'

UPDATE Production.Product SET StandardCost = 1799.00 where ProductID = 776
UPDATE Production.Product SET ListPrice = 2195.99 where ProductID = 771
UPDATE Production.Product SET ReorderPoint = 400 where ProductID = 936
UPDATE Production.Product SET SafetyStockLevel = 120 where ProductID = 961

DELETE FROM Production.Product where ProductID = 712
```

Go back to Sqoop and run the following script. It will read data from the CDC tables and put it in HDFS, this time capturing every single change made to the Product table with CDC helping you out. Make sure you put the correct start and end dates for when you executed the changes so the import actually retrieves data.

```
sqoop import --connect  "jdbc:sqlserver://myserver.domain.com;username=mysqluser;
password=mypwd;database=AdventureWorks" --query "SELECT * FROM cdc.Production_Product_CT
where $CONDITIONS and ModifiedDate between '2004-03-11 08:00:00' and '2004-03-11 09:00:00'"
--target-dir /data/ProductAudit -m 1
```

## Exporting from HDFS

You're successfully putting every change made to the Product table into HDFS, but what do you do with it? I'm glad you asked, and next we'll develop two different ways to work with it. One approach you can take is to export a subset of the data and put it back into SQL Server. The advantage of this is that your applications, developers, and analysts can use it in ways they are used to, in particular employing tools that they're familiar with, such as T-SQL. An alternative method to using the data is to query and analyze it as it is in HDFS. I'll display the former technique and once again use Sqoop to export it from HDFS into SQL Server. To drop it in SQL Server, I have to have a database and table to target. The latter technique will use Hive to work with the data directly in HDFS.

Now that you've collected billion and trillions of rows, and are able to track changes to your products, the time has come for you to use the audit trail. Your financial team wants to know how a certain product was priced throughout the year and the exact amount of time any price was in effect. You can extract that data from HDFS and put it in a familiar SQL Server table by using Sqoop.

The financial people aren't asking you to retrieve every single piece of data about the product for this report and they say that all that will be needed is `ProductName`, `ProductNumber`, `ListPrice`, and `ModifiedDate`. However, since you also imported `ProductID` and `ProductNumber` into HDFS, then you also have to export it, because Sqoop doesn't allow you to export select columns, and it doesn't give you a chance to filter the data you export. As you can see, it's all or nothing, so you need to create a table in SQL Server to hold all of the data in HDFS.

```
CREATE TABLE dbo.Product_Changes(
    ProductID int NULL,
    Name nvarchar(50) NULL,
    ProductNumber nvarchar(25) NULL,
    ListPrice money NULL,
    ModifiedDate datetime NULL
)
```

After you create this table, you are ready to go back to the command line and execute the following job from the `c:\Apps\dist\sqoop\bin` directory:

```
sqoop export --connect
"jdbc:sqlserver://myserver.domain.com;username=mysqluser;password=mypwd;database=AdventureWorks"
--table [Product_Changes] --export-dir /data/ProductAudit -m 4
```

After this job successfully executes, you now have the product data in a familiar place, SQL Server, and can do whatever you want with it. This puts you (and your users) in a comfortable situation, and you can use familiar and powerful tools like Excel, SSRS, and PowerView to analyze the data and create reports. There are good reasons for moving data from Hadoop into SQL Server, including joining Hadoop data to existing SQL Server entities in star schemas, cubes, and other reporting structures. The location of data storage is a decision DBAs will have to make, but in organizations where analysis is already happening in a SQL Server environment, it will be a normal practice to move some data from Hadoop to SQL Server. This doesn't mean that you will move every petabyte of data from Hadoop to SQL Server, but if were to happen, it would be in a filtered and/or aggregated manner.

Take note, however, that this is just one use-case of many, and that bringing data back into SQL Server is not necessary to use visualization tools such as Excel. You'll see in the next section how you can directly access data stored in HDFS using Excel, and how Hadoop provides you with a tool like Hive that lets you do this.

# Hive

What if you don't want to put the data in SQL Server? Can you use it where it resides? Yes you can, and Hive is a tool you can use to work with it in HDFS. Hive provides you with HiveQL, a SQL-like language that you can use to query data in HDFS. Apache states that Hive is a data warehouse system for Hadoop that facilitates easy data summarization, ad-hoc queries, and the analysis of large datasets stored in Hadoop-compatible file systems. Hive provides a mechanism to project structure onto this data and query the data using a SQL-like language called HiveQL.

---

■ **Caution** For people experienced with SQL Server and data warehousing, take the statement that Hive is a data warehouse system loosely. It doesn't use a recognized data warehouse model or any data structures that you might be familiar with in data warehousing, but it is useful as a SQL-like query language on top of HDFS.

---

You'll need to have some data in HDFS, so if you haven't done this yet or have wiped out previous data load we've worked with, use Sqoop to populate HDFS so you have something to work with.

```
sqoop import --connect "jdbc:sqlserver://myserver.database.windows.net;
username=mysqluser@myserver; password=mypwd; database=AdventureWorks2012"
-table Production.Product --where "ModifiedDate between '2012-07-19' and '2012-07-20'"
--target-dir /data/ProductAudit -m 4 -append
--columns "ProductID,ProductNumber,ListPrice,ModifiedDate" --split-by ProductID
```

To start using the data, you need to define a Hive table. Use CREATE EXTERNAL TABLE to do so, which provides you with an interface to HDFS. This is good since you already have data there. If you didn't tell Hive the location, it would create the table in its own default location. In effect, what you are doing is defining a table in the Hive metabase and telling it where the data that it represents resides. For SQL Server people, this might sound backward, since you usually create the table first, then add data. In this case, Hive is simply a front-end to your HDFS data. Hive also allows you to create new tables that you populate with data when you create them, so it can be more than just an interface to existing data.

To run a Hive command, use the user interface provided by Hadoop on the Azure web site (refer back to Figure 17-6). After logging in to your cluster, go to the main screen and click the Interactive Console tile. Then click the Hive button at the top right to change the console to Hive mode. At the bottom, you'll be able to enter a Hive command, so create the table using this command:

```
CREATE EXTERNAL TABLE price_audit (
ProductID INT,
Name STRING,
ListPrice DOUBLE,
ModifiedDate STRING
)
COMMENT 'This is my output'
ROW FORMAT DELIMITED FIELDS TERMINATED by ','
STORED AS TEXTFILE
LOCATION '/data/PriceAudit/';
```

Notice that Hive requires you to specify the name and data type of each column. These should look familiar to you, as I have named the columns with the same names that are used in the SQL Server table. However, you may name the columns whatever you like; they don't have to have the same name as the SQL Server table that was the source of the data.

Hive allows you to specify a number of arguments when you create a table, some of which are listed in Table 17-5. Using the arguments ROW FORMAT DELIMITED FIELDS TERMINATED by ',' and STORED AS TEXTFILE define the Hive table as a comma-delimited text file. The LOCATION keyword lets you specify the HDFS folder where the Hive table data is stored. For a complete description of Hive syntax, see the documentation at http://hive.apache.org.

***Table 17-5.*** *Partial Descriptive List of Hive Commands*

| Command | Description |
|---|---|
| CREATE [EXTERNAL] TABLE *table_name* | This command creates a new HIVE table. The EXTERNAL keyword lets you provide the table's LOCATION. Use EXTERNAL when you already have data in HDFS that you are pointing to. If you don't include it, HIVE creates the table in a default location. |
| COMMENT | This gives the description of the table. You can also add comments to columns. |
| ROW FORMAT *row_format* | Use this command to specify a column delimiter. It also lets you specify a line terminator, among other settings. |
| STORED AS *file_format* | Use TEXTFILE as the file format to store the data as plain text. Specifying SEQUENCEFILE will compress the data. |
| LOCATION *hdfs_path* | Use this command to give the file path of the data in HDFS. |

The column delimiter we used in our example was a comma, which we did with ROW FORMAT DELIMITED FIELDS TERMINATED by ','. We made sure that the LOCATION path was set to the folder where we've been putting data into HDFS. You're now all set to query this data using HiveQL.

Once this is executed, you can execute a HiveQL query. Use this select statement to get the data. Thankfully, the syntax looks just like the SQL language we're so familiar with.

```
select * from price_audit
```

You'll see a result set of the data that you previously stored in HDFS:

```
218 LJ-0192-S 50.99 2012-07-19 03:35:12.0
219 LJ-0192-M 50.99 2012-07-19 03:35:12.0
220 LJ-0192-L 50.99 2012-07-19 03:35:12.0
221 LJ-0192-X 50.99 2012-07-19 03:35:12.0
314 HB-M763 62.92 2012-07-19 04:18:38.12
317 HB-R720 62.92 2012-07-19 04:18:38.12
320 FW-M423 61.745 2012-07-19 04:18:38.12
. . .
```

If you want to limit the size of the results because you've run the sample code using much bigger datasets than I did, then you can use the LIMIT operator, like so:

```
select * from price_audit limit 5
```

```
218 LJ-0192-S 50.99 2012-07-19 03:35:12.0
219 LJ-0192-M 50.99 2012-07-19 03:35:12.0
220 LJ-0192-L 50.99 2012-07-19 03:35:12.0
221 LJ-0192-X 50.99 2012-07-19 03:35:12.0
314 HB-M763 62.92 2012-07-19 04:18:38.12
```

What happened in the background of these queries? Again, these are MapReduce jobs, and Hive is simply acting as a layer for MapReduce that is more familiar to SQL users. If you go look at the job log for Hadoop on Azure, you'll see the jobs that are executed for each of these queries. You can click on the Job History tile of the main screen.

Of course, we don't just want to extract detail data. We could do that with Sqoop. While Hive doesn't provide all of the functionality we're used to with T-SQL, it does give us the ability to group and aggregate, filter and sort, and it also has some join capabilities. For example, you can issue the following command to group, sum, and join. Once again, notice how much these queries look like the SQL were so familiar with.

```
SELECT Name, ListPrice, ModifiedDate
FROM price_audit
where Name = 'LJ-0192-X'
order by ListPrice

221 LJ-0192-X 50.99 2012-07-19 03:35:12.0
221 LJ-0192-X 54.99 2012-07-20 09:24:51.0
221 LJ-0192-X 52.99 2012-07-20 14:32:18.0

SELECT Name, COUNT(*)
FROM price_audit
GROUP by Name

LJ-0192-X 4
HB-M763 1
HB-R720 1
FW-M423 1
```

Getting data using HiveQL is an important part of the complete solution, one that allows you to make Hadoop data accessible to your end users and analysts via Excel. We're going to walk through an example of how to use Excel together with Hive to close the loop and make the most of this data.

## Hive and Excel

An ODBC driver is provided by Microsoft for Hive so that HiveQL queries can be issued from analysis tools and other applications. Excel can use the Hive ODBC driver, and an add-in is available so data can be pulled in for analysis. To work with Hive and Excel, do the following:

1. Click on the Open Ports tile in the Hadoop on Azure main menu.

2. Open the Hive ODBC port by clicking the toggle button so it slides to the right and the status changes to Open.

3. Back on the main menu, click the Download tile.

4. Download and install the Hive ODBC driver and Hive Add-in for Excel. Follow the instructions to make sure you install the right versions (32-bit or 64-bit).

5. Launch Excel and go to the Data menu. Click the Hive Pane and Enter Cluster Details. If it all works, you'll see the list of Hive tables you've created in the table drop-down list.

6. Now you're ready to start working in Excel with the product data you put in HDFS. Simply select a table and some columns, add criteria and groupings, and execute the query.

7. In addition, you can go to Data Sources (ODBC) in Windows and add the Hive ODBC DSN, as shown in Figure 17-9, so you can use it from other applications.

*Figure 17-9. ODBC Hive setup using Data Sources (ODBC) in Windows*

While the primary user of Hive via Excel won't be a DBA, it's good to understand how the data they administer will be used by others. For example, most DBAs won't be doing analysis of Hive data using Excel, but it will likely be used by data analysts because it is a software tool they are familiar with. To develop a strong architecture with Big Data, it's important to know how data will be used and how the tools that use the data work. This helps you make better architectural decisions for managing data.

# JavaScript

Remember the JavaScript that you used to work through the MapReduce example earlier in the chapter? Now that you have data in HDFS, you can put that code to work. The JavaScript will read the product data you imported with Sqoop into HDFS, and stored within the directory /data/ProductTable with the first job you executed.

The product data you're using isn't the same as the sample data you worked with, so you'll change the JavaScript to make use of what you have. The business problem you'll solve is to calculate the average list price of products by product line. You also must consider that the data is comma-delimited, and that some of the product names have a comma in the text.

```
var map = function (key, value, context) {
    var aryValues = value.split(",");
    var pattern = /[A-Za-z]/;
    var productLine;
    var listPrice;

    if (aryValues.length == 25)
    {
        productLine = aryValues[15];
        listPrice = aryValues[9];
    }
    else
    {
        productLine = aryValues[16];
        listPrice = aryValues[10];
    }

    if (pattern.test(productLine) && productLine.toString() != "null")
    {
        context.write(productLine.toUpperCase(), listPrice);
    }
};
```

This map function doesn't use the key passed into it, as you don't care about the offset of the row within the file (and normally won't). The product data you're interested in is passed into the function in the value parameter, which is split into an array using a comma delimiter. Since it's possible there's a comma in the product name, you then check the length of the array to see whether there are more cells than expected. If the length of the array is 25, then there isn't a comma in the product name, so product line is in cell 15 of the array and list price is in cell 9. If there is a comma in the product name, then the product line and list price are in cells 16 and 10, respectively. Because nulls are allowed in the product line in the Production.Product table that we used as a source for this data, you must check the data to make sure it is an alpha character and that it isn't null. This will filter out about half of the rows and is exactly the type of cleansing that belongs in a map function. It also saves resources by making sure you do not pass this data on to the reduce function.

```
var reduce = function (key, values, context) {
    var sumListPrice = 0.0;
    var productLine = key;
    var cnt = 0.0;

    while (values.hasNext()) {
        sumListPrice += parseFloat(values.next());
        cnt++;
    }

    var avgListPrice = sumListPrice / cnt;
    context.write(productLine, avgListPrice);
};
```

The product line is passed in to the reduce function as the key, which is the way you defined it in the map function, and all of the list prices for each product line are passed in as the values collection. The main thing you do in the reduce function is to iterate through the values to sum all of the list prices and count the number of values so you can calculate the average. When finished, you return the product line and average list price, and it's these values that are written to HDFS. The resulting data will look like this:

```
M       827.0639560439561
R       965.3488000000007
S       50.39885714285715
T       840.7621153846153
```

To run this code, copy both the map function and the reduce function into a file called AverageListPrice.js. You can do this using Notepad, then save it to your local machine. After this is done, upload the file using the Hadoop on Azure web site. Go to the main menu and click the Interactive Console tile. When the console displays, make sure that the JavaScript button is clicked on the top right, and that the js> prompt is visible.

To upload the JS file you just created, type fs.put() in the prompt. A pop-up window will ask you to find the JS file you want to upload, so browse to AverageListPrice.js and select it. Leave the destination box empty and click Upload. This will put the file in your user's default file location in Hadoop, which is / user/username.

After the JavaScript file is uploaded, you're ready to run it. To do so, key in the following at the prompt:

```
runJs("AverageListPrice.js", "/data/ProductTable", "AverageListPrice")
```

The runJs function will execute the map and reduce functions you wrote in JavaScript. There are three parameters you pass in to runJs: the name of the JavaScript file you uploaded, the name of the directory that contains the input data, and the name of the directory for the output data. In this example, we're using /data/ProductTable as the input data because we stored the product data there earlier, and the output data will be saved in your /user/username folder in HDFS. Execute runJs and you will see some system messages scroll by as the job runs. When it's finished, the screen will look like it does in Figure 17-10. Now you can look at the output data.

*Figure 17-10. Interactive JavaScript screen in Hadoop on Azure*

Using remote desktop again, go to the desktop and launch the HadoopNameNode, like you did in the section on Sqoop (refer back to Figure 17-7). Click the link labeled Browse the filesystem and a web browser will open with a list of directories, one of them being the user folder. Open it and you'll see another directory named the same as your user name. Click it to see the files and directories under your user name and find the directory named AverageListPrice. This is where your output data is. Open the directory to see a file named part-r-00000 and take a look at the file by clicking it. The file should have four rows that look just like the output we saw earlier in this section.

# Pig

Pig is a platform for analyzing large datasets. It consists of a high-level language for expressing data analysis programs, and allows for a high degree of parallelization. Pig includes Pig Latin, which is a procedural scripting language that allows you to manipulate data in more powerful ways than you can with Sqoop. While Sqoop is analogous to BCP in SQL Server, you can consider Pig the ETL tool of Hadoop, so naturally it is highly parallel when extracting, transforming, and loading data.

Pig has a good set of built-in functions for string manipulation, mathematical operations, and for groupings, aggregations, and comparisons. It also has relational operators for joins, unions, and more functionality for controlling the flow of the script and the processing of data. In more sophisticated scripts, Pig developers can use nested data structures, streaming operators, and user-defined functions. The strength of Pig is that it can load data in parallel, apply analytical functions to the data, and then write the results of the analytic process.

---

■ **Note** Pig will be an option for your environment when you want to do more than simply move data back and forth between SQL Server. It allows you to inspect, crunch, and convert data as you're moving it from one place to another.

---

In today's version of Hadoop on Azure, the primary use of Pig will be to read data from HDFS, process it procedurally, and write the results back to HDFS. It won't involve the SQL Server database engine; although in the future, it seems that it would be sensible to have a way to store the results in SQL Server. The following is a simple Pig script that mirrors T-SQL for grouping by ProductID, counting the number of rows, and sorting by the row count:

```
product_audit = LOAD '/data/ProductAudit/part-m-00001' USING PigStorage(',')
        AS (
ProductID:int,
Name:chararray,
ProductNumber:chararray,
ListPrice:float,
ModifiedData:chararray
);

product_group = GROUP product_audit by (ProductID);
product_count = FOREACH product_group GENERATE group, COUNT($1) as num_products;
product_sorted = ORDER product_count by num_products desc;

STORE product_sorted INTO '/data/ProductAudit/aggregate_products2' USING PigStorage(',');
```

This script defines the structure of the data, groups the data by product ID, gets a count of the number of times a product appears in the dataset, sorts that in descending order, and saves the data back to HDFS in a file called aggregate_products. This isn't very different from what we can do with SQL, so it's a good example to start with to understand the structure of a Pig script and how to execute it. Table 17-6 describes the Pig commands we're using; go to http://pig.apache.org for a full reference.

*Table 17-6. Partial Descriptive List of Hive Commands*

| Command | Description |
|---|---|
| LOAD 'data' [USING function] [AS schema]; | 'data' is the name of the HDFS file or directory you're using. PigStorage is the default load function, unless you write your own load function. The columns and data types are defined in the schema. |
| GROUP...BY group key | This command groups the data in one or more relations using a group key. It works very much like the GROUP BY clause in T-SQL. |
| FOREACH...GENERATE | Use this operation to work with columns of data to generate data transformations. |
| STORE...INTO 'directory' [USING function] | This stores results to the file system. 'directory' is the location in HDFS where the output files are saved. PigStorage is the default store function, unless you write your own store function. |

To run the Pig script, go to Remote Desktop again in Hadoop on Azure and launch the Hadoop Command Shell from the desktop. Enter cd pig at the command prompt to go to the pig directory. Launch Notepad from the Start menu, copy and paste the sample Pig script, and save it as product.pig in the c:\ Apps\dist\pig folder. Execute it from the command line by typing pig product.pig and pressing Enter. If it completes successfully, you'll now see a new file in HDFS in the ProductExtract folder with the output of the script.

Let's do something that will highlight some more features of Pig. Assume the finance department now wants to know what the inventory level of a product is, every time you capture a price change. To get some data that you can use, load the Product table and the ProductInventory tables to HDFS by running the following two Sqoop imports into HDFS. Recall that for Sqoop to work, you created a synonym for the Product table. Now do the same for the ProductInventory table, like so:

```
CREATE SYNONYM [Production.ProductInventory] FOR Production.ProductInventory

sqoop import --connect "jdbc:sqlserver://myserver.database.windows.net;
username=mysqluser@myserver; password=mypwd; database=AdventureWorks2012"
--table Production.Product --target-dir /data/Product -m 1

sqoop import --connect "jdbc:sqlserver://myserver.database.windows.net;
username=mysqluser@myserver; password=mypwd; database=AdventureWorks2012"
--table Production.ProductInventory --target-dir /data/ProductInventory -m 1
```

When this completes, you'll have one file in the /data/Product and /data/ProductInventory folders to work with. Now you can join this data together with Pig, as follows:

```
product = LOAD '/data/Product/*' USING PigStorage(',')
        AS (
ProductID:int,
Name:chararray,
ProductNumber:chararray
);

product_inventory = LOAD '/data/ProductInventory/*' USING PigStorage(',')
        AS (
ProductID:int,
LocationID:int,
Shelf:chararray,
```

```
Bin:int,
Quantity:int
);

product_group = GROUP product_inventory by ProductID;
inventory_sum = FOREACH product_group GENERATE group as ProductID,
COUNT(product_inventory.LocationID) as num_locations, SUM(product_inventory.Quantity)
as total_inventory, AVG(product_inventory.Quantity) as avg_inventory;
inventory_filter = FILTER inventory_sum BY total_inventory<1000;
product_join = JOIN product BY ProductID, inventory_filter BY ProductID;
product_sorted = ORDER product_join by total_inventory desc;
STORE product_sorted INTO '/data/ProductOutput/inventory_list3' USING PigStorage(',');
```

Pig allows for manipulation of HDFS data via its procedural language, Pig Latin, providing a more advanced tool for transforming data and letting you solve more complicated problems. In this example, you used Pig to get data from HDFS and to transform and store it in another HDFS data store, and you did so without impacting the SQL Server. This is why Pig is important to the SQL Server DBA. Not everything has to go through SQL Server and a DBA needs to know when it's more effective to use HDFS as both the input and output data store. Knowing the best ways to take advantage of Pig and its features will reduce the stress you put on your SQL Server databases.

# Big Data for the Rest of Us

The analysis scenarios, while certainly the most popular reason for Big Data's existence, are not the only use-case. Before we let the data analysts take over everything, let's look at how Big Data can impact the rest of the world. We'll also look at scenarios where the work the data analyst is doing can impact the DBA's architecture, and how the DBA can deal with both RDBMS and Big Data working in conjunction.

## Business Intelligence

While Big Data is often used for analytics, it's not necessarily synonymous with Business Intelligence and what it has come to be. Some experts will even tell you that Big Data means the end of BI, but that's not likely. A comprehensive BI framework should encompass Big Data and, at the very least, use it as a data source. BI includes a type of analysis and visualization that allows for rapid-fire what-if analysis with a high degree of user interaction. It can also convey the state of the business, relative to key performance indicators, by taking a snapshot of the business at strategic points in time. Under the BI umbrella, we would also include online analytical processing, data mining, predictive modeling, performance management, and more. For planning purposes, you should expect that data you collect in a Hadoop framework will become part of the data used by the BI framework.

## Big Data Sources

Where is all of this data coming from at such a high *velocity*, in such large *volume*, and of so much *variety*? Sensors, logs, web content, text, map, media, social computing, and click-stream data are being collected at higher rates than ever, and the ability to capture this data has grown enormously over the past several years. This data can be produced at a high rate of speed, or velocity in Big Data terms.

The most common data sources for Big Data analytical applications are web data in the form of web logs, sensors that continuously capture data (such as movement and location), unstructured content (including video and images), and social networking data. Web logs are analyzed to optimize site navigation and to understand the behavior of online customers. Sensors are driving the collection of large amounts of data, since near real-time analytics can be performed on data streams being produced by sensors. If a problem is spotted, swift action can be taken to correct the situation. Data from sensors can also be stored for future analysis to discover patterns that indicate persistent problems.

There is no minimum volume of data to be considered Big Data, but typically the volume starts in the terabytes and could grow to petabytes in size. The same is true for variety. While Big Data has made a name for itself by being good at handling unstructured data, it can also handle more well-structured data, and there's no yardstick as to how much unstructured data qualifies it as Big Data.

## Big Data Business Cases

Let's look at what types of datasets are a good fit for your Big Data framework. Building on the use-case of how web log data can be used for analytics and discovery, there are other types of datasets that can also be handled better by Hadoop than with an RDBMS. As you read on, you'll start to see how they can work in conjunction with SQL Server.

### The Nonrelational Dataset

How many times have you stored data in a flat, nonrelational table because you needed a place to put it? Much of the data we work with is nonrelational, or better said it is pseudo-relational. We treat it nonrelationally because it's unclear what it's related to, it can't be related to anything we have, or relating it to something is unnecessary. Extracts, staging data, logs, and data that originates from external sources can all be put in this category.

### Streaming Data from Sensors

Do you capture a stream of data and only keep a small window (e.g., a rolling two weeks) because it accumulates too fast and makes your database very large quickly? Or do you retain only a random sample because its size overwhelms you? If you're already capturing data from sensors and it's akin to "drinking from a fire hose," then you already know that a sensor has the ability to produce an overwhelming amount of data.

### Archives

Do you constantly delete or archive data either manually or using regular jobs because it clutters your transactional database? This data often gets archived within SQL Server, whether it's another table within the same database, or another database whose main purpose it is to hold archived data. By keeping it in a SQL Server database, it's still accessible when needed by the business, but it can add up fast and grow to an unmanageable size that impacts everything else you're doing with SQL Server.

### Unstructured Data

Many uses of Big Data mention it as a good way to handle unstructured data. Unstructured data is inconsistent and undefined data, with no rules about how the data is arranged, and often with no length limit. This is something that you might often store in SQL Server as a BLOB, and consider it a burden on your database.

## Data Discovery

Sometimes, you don't know what you need until you need it. Unfortunately, when the time comes, you often find out that the data you need to move forward isn't available. Other times, you just want to go look. For example, if you've noticed a change in your customer's buying habits and want know why, you might think it would be helpful to scour through web logs, historical transactions, customer comments, and more. This work might lead you to the answer you're looking for, but it also could help you learn something else about your customers, something you weren't initially looking for.

## Business Rules Driven by Analytic Outcomes

There are times when your OLTP database needs to perform operational analytic functions that require the output of Big Data calculations. For example, assume a marketing department wants to highlight one of three new movies on their home page: a Brad Pitt drama, an Adam Sandler comedy, or a Bruce Willis action movie. The decision of which movie to show is made programmatically, with many inputs that include customer demographic, location, past purchase history, and more. One of the more important factors in making this decision is whether the actor is trending positively on Twitter. You can capture the relevant Twitter stream using a Big Data infrastructure, and in as near to real-time as possible, you can feed the aggregated sentiment back to your OLTP database, so it can be applied by the algorithm that determines what to show on the home page. The key to this process is to change the home page as soon as possible, after the trend changes.

# Big Data in the Microsoft Future

The benefit to Microsoft embracing Hadoop and Big Data is that in the future we should see full integration between Hadoop and the many Microsoft tools that provide and support analytic capabilities, including reporting, dashboards, predictive modeling, and ETL (extract, transform, and load). The types of enhancements I would expect to see include the following:

- You've seen how HDFS data can be used in Excel through Hive. I would expect tighter integration of HDFS with Excel, PowerView, SQL Server Reporting Services, and PerformancePoint.

- I expect better SSIS data flow tasks that allow for data to be input and output from HDFS, and transformation tasks that provide transformation techniques better suited for HDFS.

- I anticipate tighter coupling between SSAS tabular modules using HDFS as a data source.

- I also would expect the ability to create an HDFS table within SQL Server that implements MapReduce seamlessly.

There's much more to come in this area, and I expect that much of it we'll see in the on-premise solution of Hadoop on Windows.

# Conclusion

The implementation of a Hadoop framework in a SQL Server database environment gives the informed database administrator a more effective and powerful data architecture to design and implement. It provides the ability to scale out to a level where the physical size of data is no longer a constraint. This puts the responsibility on DBAs for determining how to build out a data infrastructure, and forces them to make the right decision for a particular dataset; should it reside in SQL Server or HDFS? To make these decisions, DBAs will have to know how the business will use the data, how developers will access it, and how much of it there will be. No longer will the default location be a traditional SQL Server table.

Another important decision DBAs will have to make is whether to store the data on premise or use the cloud. We were able to move data between Hadoop and SQL Server where both were in the cloud. We also moved data to and from a SQL Server instance inside our network and Hadoop in the cloud, and showed how we could use one of the many features of SQL Server, Change Data Capture, to help us do this.

An important process that DBAs will have to support is the movement of data between SQL Server and HDFS. We showed how to do this with Sqoop, which does this in a rudimentary manner but is easy to use. Hive provides a familiar SQL-like interface to get data out of HDFS. Using the ODBC connector, this gives users and applications a way to get data from HDFS. We saw how this works in Excel, and DBAs should expect this type of access in many other ways, including reporting tools, analysis software, .NET application, and web sites. Pig let us access HDFS and manipulate the data procedurally. It requires programming skills and expertise but is worth learning well to make the most of its data transformation capabilities. The key capability of Sqoop, Pig, and Hive is that they all execute MapReduce jobs and can fully take advantage of the Hadoop framework. It's important for DBAs to know how to use these tools and to know the right application of their functions.

We showed in the section on exporting data from HDFS how we can impact SQL Server by moving data there from HDFS, so DBAs should account for this. An example of a business case that could be an impetus for this is when trending statistics are being captured on data coming into HDFS, and the outputs of the trends are sent to SQL Server to drive application behaviors. We didn't show how unstructured data would be stored in HDFS, or how it might be used, but this would require more work with analytic software and algorithms than it does with SQL Server, so we'll defer that demonstration to the analytics books. To see an example of how Hadoop works with semistructured text data, Microsoft provides a word count example under the Samples gallery on the Hadoop on Azure web site.

The scripts we executed didn't run at hyper speed like you might have expected. They were slow, often much slower than the queries and bulk load processes we're used to when using SQL Server. The samples we developed worked with a small amount of data, but don't forget that this chapter is about Big Data and the Hadoop framework shines when processing very large datasets. Firing up 128 servers to execute MapReduce jobs to acquire and assemble the data properly is too much system overhead for small data than the benefit it provides through massive parallelization. Even using two servers was too much overhead for the amount of data we had. However, you'll see the benefit when you scale up to billions and trillions of data elements because the resources used to start and execute MapReduce jobs is small stuff compared to the gain from massive parallelization.

# CHAPTER 18

■ ■ ■

# Tuning for Peak Load

## By Ben DeBow

Today is historically the busiest day of the year for your online shopping business. At 11 AM, the system is starting to show signs of strain and load that exceeds that of the previous year. Customers are having problems completing their orders. Some fail, others are just slow. The operations center calls you in to see what's going on with SQL Server, and you observe that processes are starting to queue up because of large blocking chains, which ultimately affects the checkout process. You didn't code the application, but your job as a database administrator (DBA) is to fix the problem. As this event is unfolding, upper management is concerned and the Chief Information Officer (CIO) is standing over your shoulder watching you try to resolve the issue—no pressure there. Things eventually calm down later in the day, but it is unknown how many sales or potential customers were lost because of the slowdown or failed checkouts. In addition to the orders being affected, replication to the reporting environment now has 12 hours of latency affecting the reports to internal consumers of the raw sales data. Can you prevent this scenario from happening? In many cases, you can.

Every organization has mission-critical applications that run the business. These applications must scale and perform to handle load when the system is at its busiest—otherwise known as its *peak load*. Peak loads might occur daily or at varying intervals, often during the peak season; it's not necessarily just a once-a-year occurrence such as the holiday season (which could be considered a peak season) described in the preceding example. To address these challenges, organizations must plan for these events well in advance so that they can have peace of mind that their systems will meet the increased traffic demands. Failure or downtime is often not an option because most businesses either depend on a large percentage of revenue from these peak times or have mission-critical business events, such as an accounting department's year-end close.

The way your solution looks the day it is put in place is not the way it will look 10, 100, or 1,000 days later. More users are added and traffic increases. You need to anticipate the change not only in daily usage (which might represent your peak time), but also for those special times when system performance is crucial. This chapter will show you how to plan for the times when your servers will need to scale and perform to handle this additional traffic.

## Define the Peak Load

Do you know how many transactions you expect during the peak hour of your peak day? If so, how accurate is that number? Are there documented performance requirements for the core transactions to meet the service level agreements (SLA)? Have you measured how many transactions the current system can handle day to day? These and many other questions are important to answer before the business can feel comfortable about going into the peak season.

Every application and environment is different. However, there is one thing that is constant: no single action will make the system scale. A combination of different things must happen to achieve the desired result. For example, the business cannot assume that purchasing newer, bigger hardware will solve its performance woes and make the application scale. Think about your critical application and how a large blocking chain during the core business hours might affect the application and, ultimately, the business itself. Hardware will not account for, nor fix, blocked internal resources in SQL Server. Blocked resources is an application issue, even if it winds up being as simple as fixing an index or something as complex as rewriting application logic. The process to prepare the application for the peak load is a repetitive one that often must be repeated several times before the environment is ready to scale to meet the additional load.

Before you can do any analysis to possibly remediate the application to handle your peak load, you need to put a multifunctional project team in place. The project team should consist of various groups from across the enterprise, including the technical and nontechnical sides of the business.

Here is the makeup of a typical project team, listed by function:

- Project manager
- Several application representatives
- DBA lead
- Storage resource
- Network resource
- Server resource
- Business representative

The project team's major responsibility is to clearly define the goals that must be met during the peak usage time (whether it's an event, day-to-day use, seasonal use, and so forth) and to implement the changes necessary to enable the systems to meet or exceed these goals. These goals must be formally documented and agreed upon so that everyone is on the same page when it comes to expectations. If this is not done, you might wind up in the scenario that started the chapter.

Start by defining what is expected during the peak window. Depending on the environment and the company, this exercise might be easier for you than others. The expectation should always start as a nontechnical requirement from the business. Discussions to get to that expectation often involve looking at the current market conditions and reviewing a lot of data, both current and historical. The goal is to define how many business transactions the company expects to process within a certain period of time. The transactions represent the core processes the consumer or end user will use or initiate during the peak season. For example, if your company is an online retailer, the core transactions might be product searches, adding products to the shopping cart, the checkout process, processing payments, and reviewing orders. What you're really trying to understand is this: when will the transactions occur, and what is the expected peak volume? How many orders does the company anticipate confirming within an hour or day? Is it 1,000 per hour or 500,000 per day? Does that volume change at certain times of the day, month, or year? Planning for 1,000 transactions per hour is very different than planning for a workload of 500,000 transactions. You need to design solutions to meet the maximum number of transactions during the peak time frame.

Applications are the key, so mapping something like X sales per hour to the number of transactions in the system to how many transactions need to occur in SQL Server is important. This gives the technical side of the team an idea of where to start and what to look for and architect to.

The number of business processes that are expected during the peak season or peak hours is not the only measurement you need to determine. How long can the average response time be? The response time should meet the expectations of end users regarding how long the end-to-end transaction should take. Most of us can design a system to process a high number of transactions, but it is another task entirely to guarantee the transactions are completed within a specific time frame. This is often specified in the performance-based SLA you will be measured against. Even if it hasn't been formally documented, the SLA often has already been defined for the core business processes. The performance SLA is one of the most important factors to the business and the customer because if you do not fulfill the terms of the contract, there are different ramifications, including financial penalties. For example, the credit card industry often specifies in an SLA a response time of two seconds to perform a balance check. If the response does not come back in a certain amount of time, the company on the other side of the transaction might have to stand in for the transaction. For each stand-in, there is a cost and these costs can add up fast. If the system is not available for 10 minutes on a big retail shopping day like Black Friday in the United States, it could cost a company several hundred thousand dollars.

Defining what is transactional volume during the peak load is often one of the most crucial and challenging tasks for the business to do. If the business misses the mark with regard to implementing appropriate response times, it might not have enough resources to process all of the transactions or might even end up seeing its systems fail because there is not enough capacity. Having excess capacity can be a good thing to account for unforeseen growth, and a good rule of thumb is to add 20 percent to the peak numbers. What you want to avoid is having too much capacity, which means that the business might have spent money unnecessarily. At the end of the day, there is a balance that must be achieved.

Once you have the formalized requirements, the technical team has to take the business requirements and map them to technical requirements, which is a vastly different exercise.

# Determine Where You Are Today

Preparing a system for the peak load is like training for a marathon and not getting winded by running a sprint. Once the team sets the formal expectations, you have to analyze whether you can handle your peak load. This is not a straightforward process. To begin, you must put together a list of the applications, servers, instances, databases, and so forth that are affected by the peak-load requirement. For example, in a larger organization, the peak season might involve or touch numerous individual servers, with each one being impacted by the additional load in different ways. For smaller organizations, it might involve a handful of web servers and a single server running SQL Server. Just because there are fewer servers does not necessarily mean it is easier to plan for your peak usage. It depends on what is being asked for when it comes to performance.

You must assess each application and its associated back end to see where you are today versus where you need to be to meet the peak load. An important part of this effort is to discover the environmental constraints, including items that cannot be changed or addressed in the short (or long) term. These environmental constraints need to be identified early on so that a workaround can be planned if necessary, because additional lead time is often needed to address them. Some of the most common limitations are application editions or versions; infrastructure like storage area network (SAN) capacity or performance; and server hardware, such as a motherboard that cannot support additional memory. These constraints are important to know up front because they need to be in the back of your head when you are assessing the environment.

If the environment you support is large and includes many systems that make up the core business, you should prioritize the applications and their associated servers into Tier 1 and Tier 2. The Tier 1 applications initiate and support the core business processes. To determine if an application is Tier 1, ask yourself this question: If the application or its servers are not up, can a transaction be completed? If the answer is no, it is a Tier 1 application. Tier 2 applications provide auxiliary functions and are not required to be up and performing to complete a core transaction. Reporting servers are often classified as Tier 2 because processing the sales transaction is more important than providing a report on how many products were sold. By classifying each application in this way, you will have a smaller list of applications to perform the initial assessment on, which is important if the timeline is tight.

---

▪ **Note**  Because this book is focused on SQL Server, I'll concentrate on assessing each application from the viewpoint of using SQL Server. Your assessment should also take into account other aspects such as infrastructure, the underlying server hardware, and Windows. Everything matters.

---

For the purposes of this chapter, the following scenario will be used:

- The application is an online tax application that allows users to enter their federal tax information online with a workflow to assist them, save the tax return, file the forms online with the federal government, and process the payment.

- Historically, the application has had performance issues during the tax season, specifically with reporting and with some of the payment processes.

- A dedicated environment does not exist for performance testing. All performance and system testing is done in the Quality Assurance (QA) department, which is half the size of the production environment but shares the same type of disk subsystem.

- The growth rate for the number of returns processed online and the number of payments processed is shown in Table 18-1.

*Table 18-1. These figures represent the last three years of historical returns and processed payments as well as the projected filings for 2013.*

| Year | Total Returns Filed | Total Payments Processed | % Change from Prior Year (Return Filed) | % Change from Prior Year (Return Filed) |
|------|--------------------|-------------------------|----------------------------------------|----------------------------------------|
| 2010 | 2,500,000 | 1,800,000 | 28% | 25% |
| 2011 | 3,800,000 | 2,500,000 | 35% | 28% |
| 2012 | 5,400,000 | 4,200,000 | 29% | 22% |
| 2013 | 8,154,000 | 6,300,000 | 51% | 50% |

---

▪ **Note**  Assume that new functionality is being released in the program, which is being heavily marketed. Because of these factors, it is estimated the application will see a 22 percent increase in filings in 2012.

---

As shown in Figure 18-1, this physical environment consists of three web servers running Internet Information Services (IIS), two middle-tier servers, and a single SQL Server cluster running SQL Server Standard Edition 2012, which hosts three databases that consume 900 GB. The application is a .NET application and leverages the middle tier for all data access, connection management, transaction management, and session state. The database has the basic maintenance processes in place and is supported by a part-time DBA.

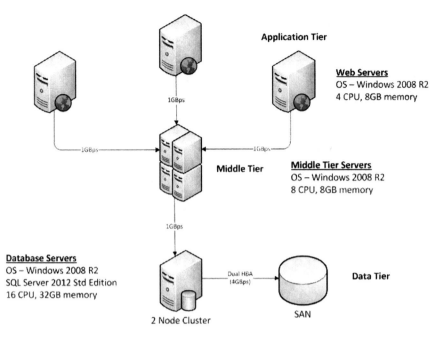

*Figure 18-1. A high-level topology diagram for the tax application.*

## Perform the Assessment

Where do you start to figure out what is going on—especially in a large environment? You need a road map, and creating one is facilitated by identifying existing sources of data within your environment. Check to see if a topology diagram or configuration management database (CMDB) repository exists. The topology diagram will provide the 50,000-foot view of the application. Depending on the level of information maintained in the CMDB, you might be able to see the server details, application owners, as well as application relationships—all of which are important when working with a system you might not be familiar with. The goal is to identify any other applications the primary application might interface with because it might impact the scalability.

If a CMDB does not exist in your environment, work with the server, operating system (OS), and storage teams to gather the basic configuration information about the application environment. Table 18-2 contains a high-level list of important attributes to collect from each server. What if you do not know what a lot of the information in Table 18-2 means? This is why you put together a multidisciplined project team with members from all areas of technology that will be responsible not only for gathering this data, but for working with you to analyze the data. The goal of the project team is to bring together all of the data, analyze it, and determine what needs to be addressed based on the goals the business has defined.

*Table 18-2. Configuration data to collect from the network, server, application, and SQL Server.*

| Team | Attributes to Gather |
|------|----------------------|
| Infrastructure | Network speed (for the LAN)<br>Number of hops between the core application servers and the database servers<br>Uplink speeds and utilization for the switches the application and database servers are using |
| Server | Server manufacturer<br>Server model<br>Windows version, Service Pack level and edition (32 bit or 64 bit)<br>Domain<br>Driver versions for the network interface card (NIC), host bus adapter (HBA), and firmware version for the BIOS<br>Third-party applications that are installed<br>Virus protection: What are the file or directory exclusions?<br>SQL Server products, like reporting services (RS), analysis services (AS), and integration services (IS)<br>Number of sockets and number of cores, along with the speed<br>Indication of whether server is a cluster or standalone server<br>Is hyperthreading enabled?<br>Is Non-Uniformed Memory Access (NUMA) enabled? How many NUMA nodes?<br>Total amount of memory and speed<br>Size of the page file and its location<br>Number of NIC cards<br>Are the NIC cards teamed? Are they Active\Active or Active\Passive?<br>Configuration of NIC cards if iSCSI is used<br>Number of HBA cards and size<br>Are the HBA cards teamed? Are they Active\Active or Active\Passive?<br>What is the queue depth?<br>What local policies are set for the SQL Server service account?<br>Lock page in memory.<br>Perform volume maintenance tasks.<br>Capture the system and application logs.<br>MSTDC – Status and Security<br>Driver versions |
| Storage | Disk subsystem make and model<br>Is this a storage area network (SAN) or direct attach storage (DAS)?<br>What is the total amount of cache? Is it measured by storage processor or is it a single pool of cache?<br>Speed of drives in each storage pool?<br>Which tier of storage do the SQL Server files reside on? (For example: *Tier 1 (SSD), Tier 2 (15K)*)<br>Which LUNs are allocated to the SQL Server hosts?<br>If the storage is a SAN, are the physical paths from the host to the storage multipathed?<br>Estimated MAX I/Ops for the disk subsystem<br>If I/O stress tests were performed, collect output of the tests. |

| SQL Server | SQL Server version, SP level and edition |
| --- | --- |
| | SQL Service accounts |
| | sp_configure |
| | Authentication |
| | Features installed |
| | Cluster or standalone |
| | Virtual name |
| | Port number |
| | Filestream enabled |
| | Database properties |
| | Database file properties |
| | Index utilization statistics |
| | Index usage statistics |
| | Potential index data |
| | Data buffer statistics |
| | Procedural cache statistics |
| | Reviews of system activity. Eyeball the activity |
| | Top 100 query stats (by count, I/O) |
| | IMPLICIT conversions |
| | Number of virtual log files (VLF) per database |
| | Nontrusted constraints per database |
| | Job list |
| | Inventory of jobs and purpose |
| | Schedule with frequency, duration. |
| | Database maintenance processes |
| | Capture the code that performs the maintenance. |
| | Most recent error logs |
| | If error logs are large, capture the last 30days of activity. |
| | Schema from critical databases |
| | Virtual I/O filestats (sys.dm_io_virtual_file_stats)file stat data |
| | Summary of waitstats (Cumulative and peak windows) |
| Application | Application names and server names |
| | Average number of users per day or hour |
| | Ad-hoc or stored procedure calls |
| | Application user for SQL and privileges |
| | Average roundtrips per page |
| | Connection pooling |
| | Error-handling approach |
| | Transaction management |
| | Session state |
| | Auditing |
| | Current state transaction levels |
| | Average number of business transactions by type and by day for the last 30 days |
| | Average response time for the business transactions by type and by day for the last 30 days |

Configuration data by itself is useful, but often it needs to be paired with performance-based runtime information to create the full picture. The configuration data in Table 18-2 will be used later, after you have collected additional application data, additional runtime data, and historical performance data. The data gathered often leads to other questions, other data that will be captured, and ultimately, other conclusions.

# Define the Data to Capture

After you have the base information about the environment, you can collect performance data. Depending on your environment, some or all of the performance data might already exist in some format that you and your team members can access without a lot of extra effort. Most environments have some level of monitoring in place already, which generates alerts based on certain conditions and also stores the performance metrics for a period of time. Historical performance information is a treasure trove of information if it is available because the data can be analyzed to establish trends over time. The farther back you can go, the more trends you can see. If you are lucky, you might have captured the performance data from the last peak time frame. If any of this type of data does exist, be sure to use it, back it up, and save it for future analysis. This type of information is valuable because most products archive or aggregate older data, which results in a loss of data fidelity.

## Collecting System Performance Data

Whether or not you already have performance data for the application and database servers, SAN, and network, you still need to have current information. More importantly, you need to have the right items captured. Capturing information for the sake of capturing information is a pointless exercise. This effort does not need to cost a lot of money or take a lot of work to put in place. Several tools are available that capture performance data. If you do not have money in the budget to purchase them, you can leverage native tools that Microsoft provides for free. You can use Performance Monitor (often referred to as just Perfmon), which is built into Windows, to collect hundreds of performance metrics with very little overhead. Perfmon allows users to create a data collector, which is a saved profile that contains a list of the objects to capture, the file location for the data, the format of the file, the start and end times, and the interval, which can be measured down to the second. Remember, though, that just because it can capture data every second does not mean you should—or could—do it. (For example, collecting data this frequently might add unnecessary overhead, depending on how much data you are capturing.) You need to think about the goal of your data collector and how frequently you need the data to be collected to meet that goal.

What to capture will depend on the application as well as what technologies your application is using. For SQL Server and the related server-level data, the goal of the collection process is to capture information related to the processor, the network, the disk, memory, and SQL Server itself. The goal of the data capture is to identify if there is any pressure within a certain layer. If there is, you should capture additional information to understand why that is happening. The secondary goal of the data capture is to be able to use this data as a performance baseline.

Now that you understand the goals, I'll apply the data-capture principles just described to an example scenario. Before you can start a process like this, you need to answer some questions that will drive the data-collector configuration. An example of what types of questions you need to answer is shown in Table 18-3. Without having answers to these questions, the data collector might not collect data for the core business hours or the right features. If the peak window times are not captured, you will end up with misleading data to analyze.

*Table 18-3. Key questions to ask before a data collector is created.*

| Question | Answer |
| --- | --- |
| What is the goal of the data collector? | Baseline the SQL Server |
| When are the peak times for the application? | 8 AM to 8 AM from January through March, and 7 AM to 12 AM from April 1 through April 15 |
| How many days is one full business cycle? | 7 |

| | |
|---|---|
| In what location can the Perfmon file be placed? | D:\perflogs |
| What features are used with SQL Server? | Database Engine |
| What are the instance names used by the core application? | Default |

Using the answers just shown, follow these steps to create a new data collector set in Perfmon:

1. To open Perfmon, click on Start à Administrative Tools and select Performance Monitor.

2. When Perfmon is open, expand Data Collector Sets. Right-click User Defined, and select New from the context menu.

3. The dialog box shown in Figure 18-2 appears. This is where you have a choice to make. If you are new to Perfmon, you might want to choose Create From A Template so that you can use predefined options. After you have worked with Perfmon a few times, choosing Create Manually is the way to go. The manual mode allows you to create a data collector that is customized to the situation. Make your choice, and click Next.

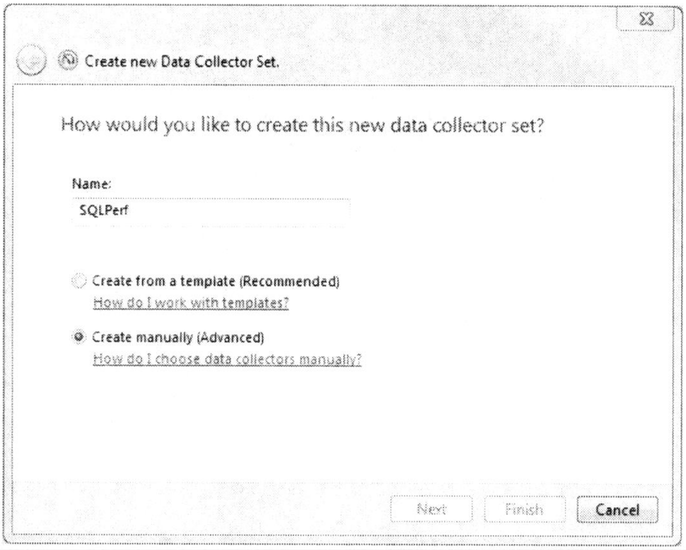

*Figure 18-2. Creating a manual data collector.*

4. The next step is to define what type of data you will collect (as shown in Figure 18-3). Normally, you will choose Performance Counter because you can use this option to collect the performance data from the system. However, as you can see, there are other options in the dialog box you can use to capture more data about a server.

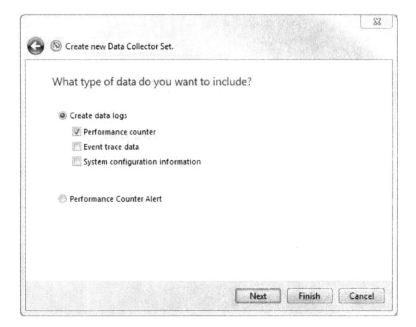

*Figure 18-3. Creating a performance counter data collector.*

5. After you select Performance Counter and click Next, you need to select the objects you want to capture (as shown in Figure 18-4). There are many options, which can be daunting. Before you choose any objects, think back to the core areas of the system: CPU, network, disk, memory, and SQL Server. The goal is to capture high-level data for each of these areas. For the scenario defined earlier, the counters defined in Table 18-4 will be used. You can use this configuration as a starting point for any system where you want to gain high-level insight into how busy the system is, the system's health, and the system's pain points.

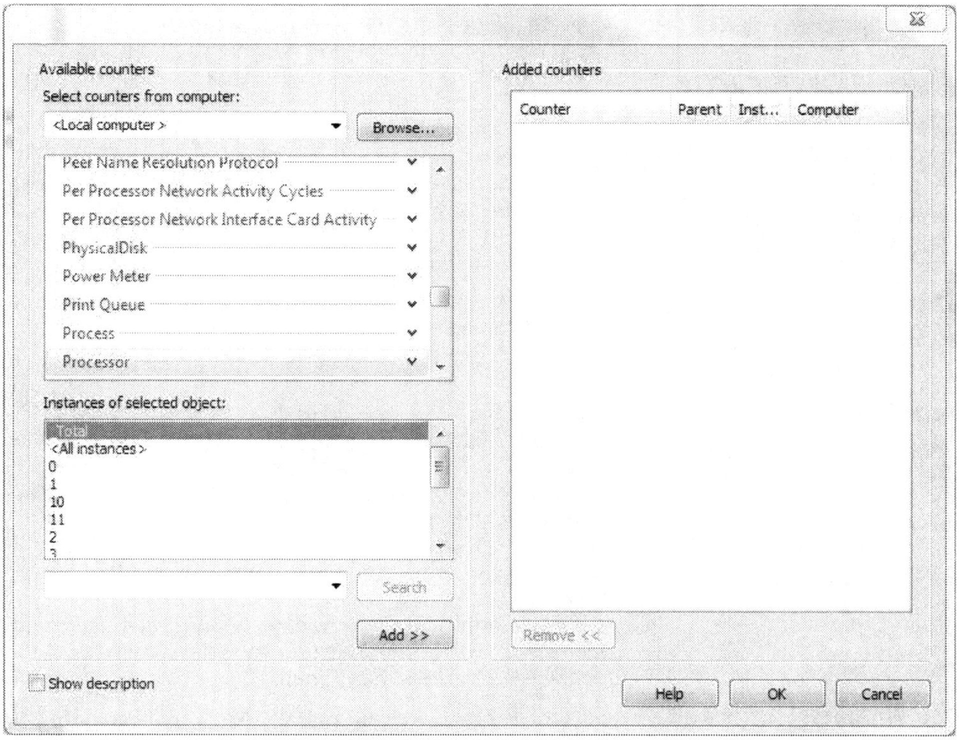

**Figure 18-4.** *Displays the objects that can be selected for monitoring SQL Server, Windows and many other applications*

---

■ **Note**   SQL Server dynamic management views (DMV) can provide additional data for many of the SQL Server–related Performance Monitor counters. If an object counter records a level that is above a certain threshold and additional information is required, consider using DMVs to provide a better picture of the situation.

---

**Table 18-4.** *Displays all of the recommended Perfmon object counters to capture.*

| Category | Counter Group\Counter | Notes |
|---|---|---|
| Memory | Memory\Available Mbytes | Determine the memory health for the OS. If the Pages/sec counter level is higher than X or the amount of Available Mbytes is low, review the memory usage for all running processes on the OS. Check the Max Server Memory within SQL Server, and validate that it is not set too high compared with the total amount of memory in the server. The following article will help guide you on how much memory should be allocated to SQL Server versus the OS: *http://sqlskills.com/blogs/jonathan/post/How-much-memory-does-my-SQL-Server-actually-need.aspx* |
| Memory | Memory\Pages/sec | |
| Memory | Paging File(\??\C:\pagefile.sys)\% Usage | |

| | | |
|---|---|---|
| Networking | Network Interface(*)\Bytes Total/ sec | Validate the network interfaces are set to the correct speed based upon the NIC type and network segment speeds. |
| Networking | Network Interface(*)\Current Bandwidth | Ensure the Output Queue Length remains close to zero over a 24-hour period, because queuing indicates that processes are waiting on the network interface. If a queue |
| Networking | Network Interface(*)\Offloaded Connections | length does exist, review the network interface configuration to ensure it is configured correctly and the total number of bytes per second does not exceed the total |
| Networking | Network Interface(*)\Output Queue Length | NIC capacity. A 1-GBps NIC has the potential to send and receive about 120 Mbytes/sec. |
| Processor | Processor(*)\% Privileged Time | These object counters measure the utilization for each core and can be used for capacity planning. |
| Processor | Processor(*)\% Processor Time | |
| Processor | Processor(*)\% User Time | |
| Processor | System\Context Switches/sec | These counters can be used to determine if the server |
| Processor | System\Processor Queue Length | might need additional cores or faster cores. If the number of context switches is more than approximately 3,000 times the number of cores, a higher number of threads are being switched to other processors. If processor queue lengths are greater than 2 per core, threads are being queued to run, which indicates there is scheduler pressure. Always determine if the server has hyperthreading turned on, because this is an important consideration when reviewing the values mentioned. |
| SQL Server | SQLServer:Access Methods\Full Scans/sec | How many Full scans versus Index searches are occurring in the application? This data can provide insight into how |
| SQL Server | SQLServer:Access Methods\Index Searches/sec | solid the indexing strategy is. Minimize page splits because their activity is costly and leads to higher levels of fragmentation. Ideally, the page splits should be less than |
| SQL Server | SQLServer:Access Methods\Page Splits/sec | 20 percent of your Batch Requests/sec. |
| SQL Server | SQLServer:Buffer Manager\Buffer cache hit ratio | The Buffer cache hit ratio should be 99 percent or more the majority of the time. The additional Buffer Manager object counters provide additional metrics on how healthy |
| SQL Server | SQLServer:Buffer Manager\ Checkpoint pages/sec | the buffer is. The page life expectancy (PLE) reflects the number of seconds a data page will live in memory on |
| SQL Server | SQLServer:Buffer Manager\Free list stalls/sec | average. The challenge with this counter is there are a lot of misconceptions about 300 and 600 being the threshold, which indicates the SQL data cache is not healthy. When |
| SQL Server | SQLServer:Buffer Manager\Lazy writes/sec | the PLE is reviewed, take into account the other object counters because these will help you determine if the PLE |
| SQL Server | SQLServer:Buffer Manager\Page life expectancy | is too low or high. It really depends on your application, the size of the data, the system configuration, and the size of the server. Note that if your system is Non-Uniformed Memory Access (NUMA) enabled, review the Memory Node object counters because they are NUMA node specific. |

| | | |
|---|---|---|
| SQL Server | SQLServer:Databases(*)\Log Flush Wait Time | The ability to write to the transaction log needs to be one of the fastest operations in SQL Server. If the write |
| SQL Server | SQLServer:Databases(*)\Log Flush Waits/sec | performance is impacted, there will be Log Flush wait events. If the number of Log Flush Waits/sec is higher |
| SQL Server | SQLServer:Databases(*)\Log Flushes/sec | (relative), review the LogicalDisk(*)\Avg. Disk sec/Write times and ensure they are averaging less than 10 ms. |
| SQL Server | SQLServer:Databases(*)\Transactions/sec | This is an important object counter to review in the initial server baseline. This measures the total number of INSERT, UPDATE, and DELETE operations per second within a database. Review the total number transactions/sec at the server level and database level. An important item to note is that you should review the total number of transactions/sec that are occurring within TEMPDB. This is a great gauge of the total number of operations occurring inside TEMPDB. |
| SQL Server | SQLServer:General Statistics\Processes blocked | One of the first items to troubleshoot within any system, and especially a system that needs to scale, is database blocking chains. If this object counter is greater than zero, the server has blocking chains that need to be documented and resolved prior to the peak event. |
| SQL Server | SQLServer:General Statistics\User Connections | Measures the total number of user connections, both active and inactive that are connected to SQL Server. Each connection takes space and resources to maintain, so analyze the configuration data collected on user connections to determine if all of the connection pools are defined correctly and the number of old connections are low. Old connections are connections that have not been used for 24 hours or more. Review the sys.sys_dm_connections.last_request_time time to determine whether connections are old. |
| SQL Server | SQLServer:Latches\Average Latch Wait Time (ms) | Latches are lightweight internal structures used to protect physical structures. If the number of latch waits/sec is higher (relative) and the amount of time per latch |
| SQL Server | SQLServer:Latches\Latch Waits/sec | increases, it might indicate a bottleneck. For additional data, review the DMV sys.dm_os_latch_stats, sys.dm_os_waits_stats and sys.dm_db_index_operational_stats. |
| SQL Server | SQLServer:Locks(*)\Lock Requests/sec | Locks are expected, but how many Lock Request/sec operations are occurring in the application today? Compare the Lock Request/sec to the initial capture as the load increases. |
| SQL Server | SQLServer:Locks(*)\Lock Wait Time (ms) | Lock waits occur naturally as processes wait for locks to be released. To determine if there are database concurrency |
| SQL Server | SQLServer:Locks(*)\Lock Waits/sec | issues, review the number of Lock Waits/sec and the amount of Lock Wait Time(ms) together. As the Lock Wait Time(ms) increases, the databases concurrency could be affected if the lock waits are on the same objects. |
| SQL Server | SQLServer:Locks(*)\Number of Deadlocks/sec | If the number of deadlocks is greater than 1, enable trace flags 1222 or leverage extended events to capture additional deadlock data. |

| | | |
|---|---|---|
| SQL Server | SQLServer:Memory Manager\ Memory Grants Outstanding | Every query is allocated a certain amount of workspace memory for the query execution. In a highly transactional environment, all of the workspace memory quickly adds up. Depending on the server configuration and the cumulative amount of memory for all executing queries, there is a point at which SQL Server has used all available memory. The net effect is that future requests will be waiting on workspace memory to execute, which yields Memory Grants Pending. If Memory Grants Pending is greater than 10, document this finding because it will feed into the overall tuning strategy. |
| SQL Server | SQLServer:Memory Manager\ Memory Grants Pending | |
| SQL Server | SQLServer:Plan Cache(*)\* | The plan cache captures the number and size of objects in memory for different types of objects that include ad-hoc plans. For example, this information can be used to determine if enabling the sp_configure setting "Optimize for ad-hoc workloads" would benefit your system. If the number of single-use plans is high relative to the total number of ad-hoc plans in cache, this sp_configure option is recommended. |
| SQL Server | SQLServer:SQL Statistics\Batch Requests/sec | Provides an indication of how busy SQL Server is. Also, review Databases: Transaction /sec. |
| SQL Server | SQLServer:SQL Statistics\SQL Compilations/sec | Compilations consume resources. Monitor how many compiles per second are occurring. |
| SQL Server | SQLServer:SQL Statistics\SQL Re-Compilations/sec | If recompilations are higher than 10 percent of your compilations, research and see if recompiles can be reduced by changing the type of calls the application is making. |
| SQL Server | SQLServer:Wait Statistics(Average wait time (ms))\* | Wait types in SQL Server tell you what resource SQL Server is waiting for, excluding CPU resources. If a SQL Server process is scheduled to run, the total time is the wait time plus the execution time. |
| SQL Server | SQLServer:Wait Statistics(Waits in progress)\* | |
| Storage | LogicalDisk(*)\% Idle Time | By reviewing % Idle Time, you can determine how busy a disk is. A busy disk does not mean it is slow. You need to take into consideration the Avg. Disk sec/Read and Avg. Disk sec/Write performance as well. A busy SQL Server instance requires the average read and write times to be below 20 ms. The transaction log should be placed on the fast disk, with write times below 10 ms on average. |
| Storage | LogicalDisk(*)\Avg. Disk sec/Read | |
| Storage | LogicalDisk(*)\Avg. Disk sec/Write | |
| Storage | LogicalDisk(*)\Disk Bytes/sec | |
| Storage | LogicalDisk(*)\Disk Reads/sec | |
| Storage | LogicalDisk(*)\Disk Writes/sec | |

6. The last step is to schedule the data collector. Click on the Schedule tab, as shown in Figure 18-5. This tab provides several options for scheduling, such as Beginning Date and Expiration Date, along with options for specifying the time and days. You can use the options on this tab to schedule the data collector over a weekend or during off-peak hours. To add a schedule, Click on the Add button and select the beginning date and Expiration Date.

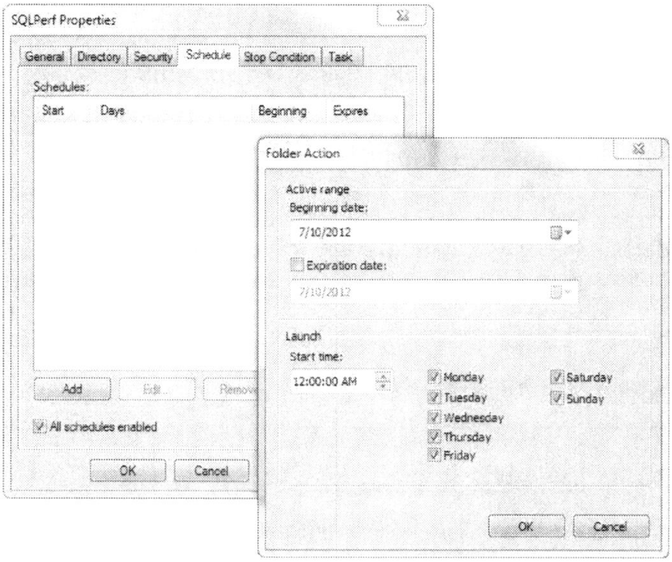

*Figure 18-5. The Folder Action dialog box, which was accessed from the Schedule tab, for a data collector.*

7. Another tab that is commonly used is Stop Condition, which is shown in Figure 18-6. You can use this tab to define stop conditions for the data collector. This is important because you can use it to ensure that the data collector does not run for an extended period of time and eventually cause additional issues on the system. A common rule to follow is to always define a stop condition based on time or file size. This minimizes the risk that the data collector will fill up the system partition and cause an outage.

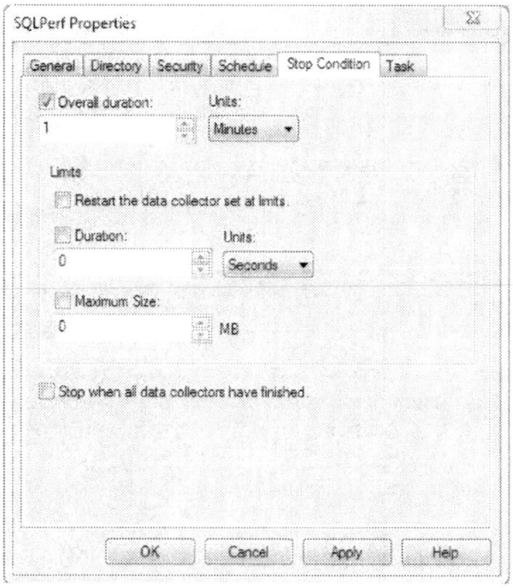

*Figure 18-6. The Stop Condition tab for a data collector.*

## Collecting Application Performance Data

The Perfmon data collected to date provides a view into how the servers themselves are performing, but it is only one view of what is going on. This information does not tell you what type of code SQL Server is running, what type of calls are being executed from the various application servers, and whether the performance is optimal. Capturing this type of data is called *application profiling*. Application profiling involves capturing all of the application calls generated by performing a single action from a process or an end-user request. Profiling an application gives you important data related to performance tuning an application. This information helps you understand what operations the application is performing for a specific request. Following are several questions to get answers to when you are reviewing the application profile data.

---

⬛ **Note**   These application-profile questions are focused on the database tier.

---

- How many database statements were executed for each request?

- Were the database statements part of a single batch, or is each one a separate database call?

- Is the application using connection pooling? If not, how many login\logouts occurred for each application request?

- Are the database calls ad-hoc or stored procedures?

- Are there statements that consume a high number of physical resources—such as CPU or I/O—or are there long-running statements?

To profile an application, you can use SQL Server Extended Events to define custom traces to capture the application requests and other pertinent data. Just like the Perfmon data, this data can be used as a baseline for the application or the database server.

---

⬛ **Note**   SQL Server Profiler was deprecated as of SQL Server 2012, so it is recommended you start learning how to use the Extended Events feature.

---

Before you can start, you need to define the different types of data you want to capture. Typically, there are four types of traces that are run to capture different types of data, as shown in Table 18-5, with some sample guidelines.

*Table 18-5. The four types of transactional activity to capture from SQL Server.*

| Name | Goal |
| --- | --- |
| Error messages and connection issues | By capturing User Error Messages and Attention events you can see many of the errors occurring on the server that are usually not known to the application developers or DBAs. The finding from this trace typically get added to the findings list for you to prioritize and address. |

| | |
|---|---|
| All application activity | As the title states, this trace captures 100 percent of the calls for several short durations during different time windows. This trace data provides insight into the mix of calls from the various applications and parameters you specify. |
| Greater than X duration | Depending on the SLAs for the core transactions, this trace captures every statement that runs for 1 second or more. This trace is run for 48 hours or more, depending on the environment. Once the application has been tuned, run this trace again and compare the number of statements captured before and after the performance-tuning event. The net result should be a reduction in the number of long-running statements. |
| Application Profile | Use this trace to monitor the core business processes and capture all of the database calls for each process. You can use this data to see how many calls are generated to complete one business transaction. Some applications are chattier than others, but this information is good to know because sometimes the number of calls can be reduced if your company owns the code base and has time to devote to this effort. You also can use this data to analyze the statements and start to tune them, if they support one of the core business processes in the application. Saving 100 ms or 2000 CPU cycles here might have a huge impact on the core business transactions. Remember, a positive byproduct of tuning the transactions is faster transactions and a happier end user. |

When using Profiler to capture system activity, make sure to create a server-side trace and log the information to a file locally. If possible, save the file to a faster drive (especially one that does not contain the data and log files for the database being analyzed) to improve the performance. Table 18-6 is a list of recommend columns to capture when you use Profiler or Extended Events.

*Table 18-6. The SQL Server Profiler and Extended Event attributes to collect when capturing the activities defined in Table 18-5.*

| SQL Server Profiler Attributes | Extended Event Attributes |
|---|---|
| Application Name | client_app_name |
| SPID | session_id |
| Database Name | database_name |
| Start Time | N/A |
| Text Data | statement |
| Login Name | server_principal_name |
| CPU | cpu_time |
| Duration | Duration |
| Reads | logical_reads, physical_reads |
| Writes | writes |

# Analyze the Data

By now, you have collected a large amount of data, which might include topology diagrams, configuration information about the servers and applications, runtime data from SQL Server, and performance data from the network, servers, and applications. This information represents the current state of the environment, and you need to analyze it from the top down to fully understand the application and identify potential areas to address related to the business goals.

## Analyzing Application-Usage Data

One of the important questions you asked the business to provide was related to the usage and performance metrics for the core business transactions that need to scale. This usage data, when coupled with the system metrics, provides you with valuable insight into what state the system is currently in. This is important because if you don't know what state the system is in (and what state it has been in recently), it is impossible to plan for the future. When it comes right down to it, this is a capacity-planning exercise. The goal of this specific capacity-planning exercise is to create a mental picture about the application to fully understand the why, when, what, and where of the configuration options, processes, and timing of events. You need to know this to determine how many business transactions the application can support for a specific configuration.

Figure 18-7 shows an example of performance data collected from a third-party monitoring tool. It shows the cumulative number of requests and the response time by day for a two-month period. The Latency (measured in ms) is on the left axis, and the total number of requests are shown on the right axis, while the shaded areas show the total latency or response time for the host, network, Secure Sockets Layer (SSL), idle, and requests. The dotted line represents the total number of requests for that day. Along the top of the graph, you can switch the display to show the X percentile. This data does not have the usage and performance data for each of the core business transactions, but it gives you an overall picture of the roundtrip times for virtual IP (VIP)-to-VIP for the application calls.

If you do not have access to a more advanced and costly monitoring tool that checks all of the application calls, there are alternatives. Most alternatives usually require you to be creative and use native tools (and possibly open-source utilities) that you already own. As mentioned previously, Extended Events can create an application profile, but it can also be used to capture long-term performance data. You can use the raw performance data captured to create charts in Microsoft Excel (or another tool that can process data), as demonstrated in Figure 18-7. The challenge is to capture additional data at the application layer so that you can see the full picture. If you have only the performance numbers for the database, you might not be aware that the application has issues until you get a call from an end user complaining about performance.

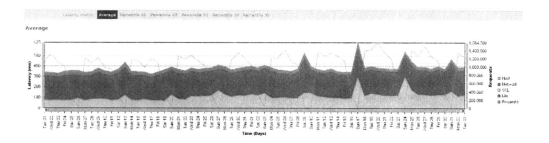

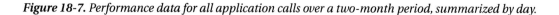

*Figure 18-7. Performance data for all application calls over a two-month period, summarized by day.*

The observations in Table 18-7 represent the high-level analysis of Figure 18-7. From these observations, you can determine the rate of the monthly transaction growth, see the large increase in response time, and identify potential performance issues that might occur on the weekend.

*Table 18-7. Observations related to the data shown in Figure 18-7.*

| Observations | Comments |
|---|---|
| Overall latency averaged 76 ms in the first month and increased to an average of 125 ms in the latest month. | Month over month, there was a 40 percent increase in the average response time. Review additional historical data to determine the long-term change in response time, especially because a 40 percent change is dramatic. |
| The total number of requests peaked at 1.3 million requests per day in the first month, and hit almost 1.6 million requests per day in the second month. | A 300,000 increase in the total number of transactions by day is a 19 percent increase over two months. You can overlay the total number of filed returns and processed payments for the first and second months to get a more comprehensive picture of the environment. |
| The overall performance profile for response time is relatively flat, with spikes on Saturday and Sunday. | As you can see by this graph, which provides data at a day level, Saturdays and Sundays have a higher response time with a lower transactional volume. Add this finding as a research item. |
| The busiest day of the week is Wednesday. | What day of the week do the peak tax days fall on this year? In 2012, April 16 fell on Monday. This is an important consideration because what is executed on different days of the week can vary by 50 percent from one system to another. |

Figure 18-8 shows the cumulative number of requests and the response time by week for a three-month period. The week view provides a different view of the data, which is more helpful when you are looking for trends and anomalies.

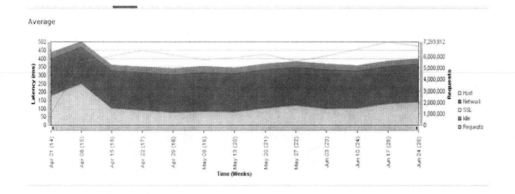

*Figure 18-8. Performance data for all application calls over a three-month period, which is summarized by week.*

The observations in Table 18-8 represent the high-level analysis of Figure 18-8. From these observations, you can determine the monthly transaction growth and observe a decrease, and then an increase, in response time over the three-month period.

*Table 18-8. Observations related to the data shown in Figure 18-8.*

| Observations | Comments |
| --- | --- |
| Overall latency averaged 246 ms for the week of April 8 and decreased to an average of 139 ms in the latest month. | Looking at three months of data allows you to see the trend. In this chart, the average response time decreased over this time, but it still increased from May to June by 40 percent. |
| The total number of requests peaked at 6.6 million requests per week in April and hit almost 7.3 million requests per week in June. | A 700,000 increase in the total number of transactions by week is a 10 percent increase over two months. |
| The overall performance profile for response time is harder to see in the weekly chart. | When analyzing the performance data, always view the data at the most granular level first and then summarize from that level up. If you do not, you might miss important trends. |
| The busiest day of the week is Wednesday. | You cannot determine this fact from this data. |

The chart in Figure 18-9 displays the total number of requests by day and by response time. The categories can be customized to represent the SLAs, which provides another important view of the data. Following are the three categories representing the current SLA:

- **Satisfied**   Less than 2 seconds

- **Tolerating**   2 seconds to 5 seconds

- **Frustrated**   Greater than 5 seconds

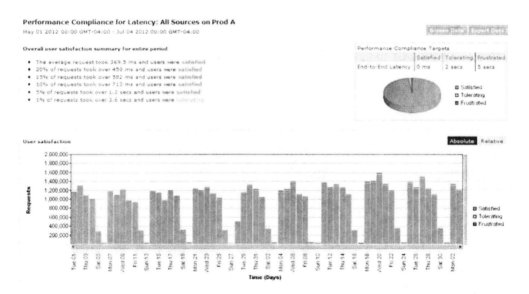

*Figure 18-9. SLA compliance for all application requests by day for the last two months.*

The observations in Table 18-9 represent the high-level analysis of Figure 18-9. From these observations, you can determine that the number of "tolerating" and "frustrated" requests have gone up and are higher on the weekends.

*Table 18-9. SLA compliance observations based on Figure 18-9.*

| Observations | Comments |
| --- | --- |
| The average number of requests in the Satisfied category has decreased from an average of 98 percent to 96.5 percent over two months. | While the total number of requests has gone up by 10 percent, the number of transactions meeting the SLA has decreased by 1.5 percent, or 49,500 transactions per day. You need to do research to determine which transactions are not meeting the SLAs and what events are causing the transactions to miss the SLAs. |
| It is hard to see in this view, but Saturdays and Sundays have the highest percentages for the Tolerating (3.3 percent) and Frustrated (1.1 percent) categories. | You need to find out what events are occurring on Saturday and Sunday to increase the response times even though there are a smaller number of transactions. |
| Overall, a high percentage of requests (96 percent) take less than two seconds to complete. | This figure might sound good, but every percent increase equates to 33,000 transactions per day. Take into account that the total transactional volume is expected to increase by 51 percent in 2013 and 1 percent is 49,500 transactions per day. |

Now you have a better understanding of the usage profile for the application, but what were the utilization levels on the application and database servers? Are the database servers 25 percent or 75 percent utilized to handle 1.6 million daily requests? This is where the performance data you collected earlier becomes important.

## Analyzing Perfmon Data

You might see a statement such as "The SQL Server's CPU is averaging 25%, it is healthy and there is excess capacity." Today's systems and applications are very complex and cannot be measured by only a single metric like processor utilization. The % Processor Time counter is one of the many object counters you collected data from as part of this effort. Each object counter is important and tells a different part of the story. A system averaging 25 percent might be having a problem elsewhere, such as scheduler pressure, and you might overlook it by just looking at the % Processor Time data.

There are several important rules to follow when you are reviewing the performance data and working through the findings:

- When analyzing data, refer only to facts, not hypotheticals. Hypotheticals often lead people down the wrong road.

- Perform proper root-cause analysis. Many times the cause of an issue is identified without the person analyzing the data trying to understand what the real problem was. Instead, the analyst bases her opinion on circumstantial evidence that can be misleading. It would be like saying, "Johnny was in the back yard when the window was broken, so he must have done it."

- Some object counters can be reviewed in isolation, but most object counters need to be reviewed with other related object counters. A periodic increase in I/O on the disk that contains the transaction logs is most likely the result of database checkpoints. If you review both counters together, you can correlate these events.

Analyzing performance data can be a frustrating experience for some DBAs because SQL Server performance metrics represent a small percentage of the overall object counters available and/or captured. As noted earlier, this is where the other members of the team come into play, because each one will analyze his or her respective area of the system. This enables everyone to correlate data points. A specific data point analyzed in isolation might look bad, but when you put it together with all the other information, it might be better or worse than you originally thought.

An example of this is when the Max Server Memory data for a given SQL Server instance is set to a large fixed amount that is actually starving Windows from the memory it needs. It might not be evident in SQL Server, but the OS-level counters show that there is excessive paging in the OS. When the server administrator reviews the server object counters, he might know that SQL Server is on the system but not that the internal memory setting for SQL Server is so high that it can cause such a problem. Only when the two administrator talks to another team member does he figure out that there is a mismatch. That is why communication is key within the team, especially when you are reviewing the performance data. The reality is that many non-DBAs do not understand how SQL Server works. Ensure you fully explain what you are seeing within SQL Server, and this will help others on the team make connections they otherwise wouldn't.

If you are a DBA who likes to learn, use peak load as the perfect opportunity to learn how to analyze Perfmon data. There is a huge amount of information about Perfmon on the web that talks about the object counters and all of the recommended thresholds. There are also several great tools that can help you analyze the collected data, and templates are available that are specific to SQL Server. One of them is Performance Analysis of Logs (PAL), which you can find at http://pal.codeplex.com/. You can use this tool to analyze the Perfmon files with SQL Server–specific thresholds. After you answer some questions about the server, PAL analyzes the Perfmon file, produces a report, and outlines all of the object counters that need to be reviewed. Figure 18-10 shows sample output contained in a PAL report.

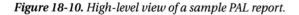

| Time Range | Condition | Counter | Min | Avg | Max | Hourly Trend |
|---|---|---|---|---|---|---|
| 6/11/2012 7:04:16 AM - 6/11/2012 11:54:16 AM | SQL Server is using more than 20% privileged (kernel) mode CPU usage | \\ECCSQLPD01A01\Process(sqlservr)\% Privileged Time | 2 | 8 | 26 | 0 |
| | A ratio of more than 1 freespace scan for every 10 batch requests | \\ECCSQLPD01A01\PAL Generated()\FreeSpace Scans to Batch Requests Ratio Percentage | 0 | 15.826 | 23 | 0 |
| | A ratio of more than 1 page split for every 20 batch requests | \\ECCSQLPD01A01\PAL Generated()\Page Splits to Batch Requests Ratio Percentage | 0 | 7.933 | 43 | 0 |
| | A ratio of more than 1 workfile created for every 20 batch requests | \\ECCSQLPD01A01\PAL Generated()\Workfiles Created to Batch Requests Ratio Percentage | 0 | 15.224 | 23 | 0 |
| | Greater than 20 lazy writes per second | \\ECCSQLPD01A01\SQLServer:Buffer Manager\Lazy writes/sec | 0 | 19 | | 0 |
| | Page life expectancy is less than 5 minutes | \\ECCSQLPD01A01\SQLServer:Buffer Manager\Page life expectancy | | 2,314 | 4,574 | 0 |
| | Greater than 1000 batch requests per second | \\ECCSQLPD01A01\SQLServer:SQL Statistics\Batch Requests/sec | 1,046 | 1,495 | 2,926 | 0 |

***Figure 18-10.*** *High-level view of a sample PAL report.*

PAL breaks down a larger Perfmon data capture into smaller time slices so that numbers better reflect the performance during that specific time window. For example, if the average for PLE is calculated over 48 hours, it might include times when the buffers are under more pressure due to reindexing processes. For each time slice, the minimum, maximum, and average values for each object counter are evaluated to determine if they are within an acceptable range. If the counter is outside of this range, PAL will highlight the finding in yellow for a warning and in red for critical. The condition is shown as a hyperlink to supporting detail, as shown in Figure 18-11. Above the graph is a detailed description for the respective object counter, which is very informative, especially for DBAs who are not familiar with Perfmon data.

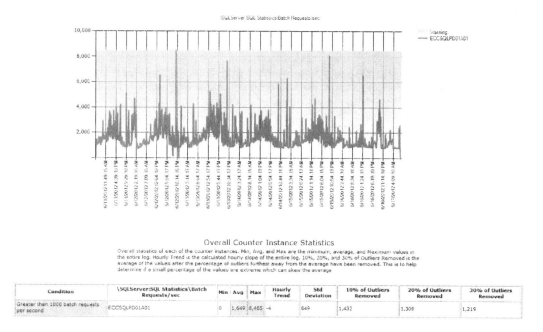

Overall Counter Instance Statistics

Overall statistics of each of the counter instances. Min, Avg, and Max are the minimum, average, and Maximum values in the entire log. Hourly Trend is the calculated hourly slope of the entire log. 10%, 20%, and 30% of Outliers Removed is the average of the values after the percentage of outliers furthest away from the average have been removed. This is to help determine if a small percentage of the values are extreme which can skew the average

| Condition | \SQLServer:SQL Statistics\Batch Requests/sec | Min | Avg | Max | Hourly Trend | Std Deviation | 10% of Outliers Removed | 20% of Outliers Removed | 30% of Outliers Removed |
|---|---|---|---|---|---|---|---|---|---|
| Greater than 1000 batch requests per second | EOCSQLPD01A01 | 0 | 1,649 | 8,485 | -4 | 649 | 1,432 | 1,309 | 1,219 |

*Figure 18-11. Supporting detail for Batch Requests/sec.*

As you can see in Figure 18-11, additional analysis is provided if you remove the outliers for the top 30 percent and calculate the standard deviation. The data points in Figure 18-10 reflect the average over a specific time, but you cannot see the trends of the data. Reviewing the chart in Figure 18-11 provides you with a better view of the data. It is easier to see trends in the chart view than in the report view, as you will see when you analyze the Perfmon files in Performance Monitor.

PAL is a great tool for reviewing a large Perfmon file quickly, but it does not correlate the separate object counters, which as established above, is an important part of this process when analyzing the performance of complex systems. This is where utilizing the Perfmon file in binary (BLG) format comes into play. You can view the BLG file in Performance Monitor in several different formats, but the two formats I'll walk you through are the line view and the report view. The line view displays the data in a graphical format, where it is easier to correlate the data and see trends in the data. The report view lists the values only, which makes it easier to see the values and compare them to the thresholds. You will walk through both types of formats as you analyze performance data for the example tax application.

Figure 18-12 shows the report view from a system that was run for seven days. By default, Perfmon displays the average of all values. In this view, it's easy to see that the values for the F drive Avg. Disk sec/Read is an average of .043 over seven days.

| LogicalDisk | _Total | C: | D: | F: | G: | I: |
|---|---|---|---|---|---|---|
| % Idle Time | 92.254 | 95.724 | 99.680 | 97.802 | 99.935 | 76.370 |
| Avg. Disk sec/Read | 0.023 | 0.010 | 0.008 | 0.043 | 0.000 | 0.021 |
| Avg. Disk sec/Write | 0.008 | 0.004 | 0.005 | 0.004 | 0.002 | 0.008 |
| Disk Reads/sec | 483.135 | 2.679 | 0.304 | 0.057 | 0.000 | 132.411 |
| Disk Writes/sec | 215.387 | 8.637 | 0.493 | 14.880 | 0.355 | 26.058 |

*Figure 18-12. Report view in Performance Monitor for a seven-day capture of the logical disk counters.*

The problem here is that the average over seven days skews the data. Realistically, you need to filter this down to, say, the core business hours. You know Wednesdays are the busiest day of the week based on data you reviewed earlier. Figure 18-13 shows how the data from the BLG can be filtered to show only data from Wednesday between 7 AM and 8 PM. To modify the Time Range setting, slide the left or right time indicator to the appropriate time.

| LogicalDisk | _Total | C: | D: | F: | G: | I: |
|---|---|---|---|---|---|---|
| % Idle Time | 91.843 | 98.191 | 99.863 | 98.050 | 99.955 | 77.882 |
| Avg. Disk sec/Read | 0.017 | 0.007 | 0.007 | 0.027 | 0.000 | 0.014 |
| Avg. Disk sec/Write | 0.005 | 0.003 | 0.003 | 0.002 | 0.002 | 0.004 |
| Disk Reads/sec | 319.270 | 0.246 | 0.105 | 0.041 | 0.000 | 92.549 |
| Disk Writes/sec | 240.576 | 8.431 | 0.483 | 15.950 | 0.348 | 26.068 |

*Figure 18-13. Report view in Performance Monitor for a one-day capture of the logical disk counters.*

As you can see in Figure 18-13, when the F drive is viewed for the core business hours, it is .025 ms healthier than before. If you reviewed only the seven-day capture, you might believe the performance for the F drive is a lot worse than it is. You still want to understand what is causing the latency to increase to .043 ms over the seven days. To do this, you review all of the values in Figure 18-12 to determine if there are any areas of concern. Based on the numbers shown, you need to monitor the F drive's performance over time because it is on the borderline of the threshold for acceptable performance for a transaction application.

The other view in Performance Monitor is the line view. In Figure 18-14, you can observe the Avg. Disk sec/Read performance over time. Notice the frequent spikes every 15 minutes; these are caused by transaction-log backups. One of the most important goals when analyzing the configuration or performance data is to create a mental image of the environment and be able to explain what you are seeing. Here you are looking at the disk performance, and you can see a pattern in the data. By explaining what is creating the load, you can then address the cause if necessary.

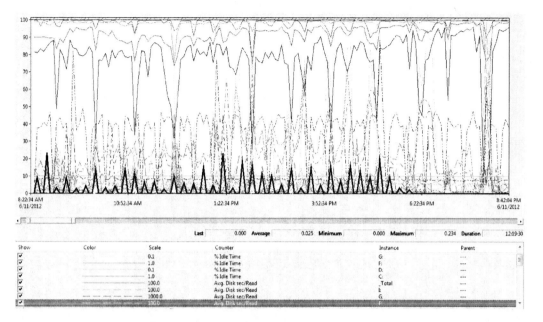

***Figure 18-14.*** *Line view in Performance Monitor for a one-day capture of the logical disk counters. The values have been scaled so that the lines are easier to read.*

The other important data points in Figure 18-14 are the average, minimum, and maximum values. Because scales for the lines in the graphs are frequently different, it is often easier to review the average below the line graph. Remember, when reviewing performance data, the averages are what matter most of the time. You focus on the average of a value because that is the typical load that needs to be sustained for a period of time. If the server's % Processor Time spikes to 80 percent once in a while, it might not indicate a problem—but it takes more information to know if that is true or not.

## Reviewing the Perfmon Data File with PAL

**Objective:** Quickly review a large Perfmon data file, and apply the predefined SQL Server best-practice thresholds.

1.  Generate the report by selecting the SQL Server profile and answering all of the required questions.

2.  Review all warnings and critical events.

3.  Document any unexpected findings or critical alerts. The critical alerts might indicate potential bottlenecks, depending on the time of the day and frequency.

## Review the Perfmon Data File with Performance Monitor – Report View

**Objective:** Review custom time windows, and see additional object counter values that are not included in PAL's analysis.

1. If the data capture is a multiday capture, filter the timeline down to the peak window.

2. Review the report view first because this provides a high-level overview of the object counters.

3. Add all object counters.

   a. The easiest way is to open the BLG file, which will add all the object counters in addition to the ones with instances.

   b. For items like Logical Disk and Databases, add these manually.

3. Start from the top of the report, and go down while documenting all the findings.

4. While you are reviewing the object counters, document your observations so that you can review them later.

5. As you review the object counters, you can remove the objects that are healthy from the report view. The result is a high-level report with only the object counters you are interested in, whether they are usage based or out of compliance with best practices.

6. If you want to save the images of the report, you can right-click and save the image as a GIF.

## Review the Perfmon Data File with Performance Monitor – Line View

**Objective:** Find trends in the data over different time windows, and correlate the data from the related object counters.

1. If the data capture is a multiday capture, filter the timeline down to the peak window. The non-peak window is also important to review, but concentrate on the peak window first.

2. Reviewing the line view is done differently than reviewing the report view. When adding the objects to the line view, add groups of related objects together. There are a couple of important reasons for this, and the most obvious one is space. If you add 75 objects to the line view, the graph will be hard to analyze because of the large number of lines graphed. The goal of the line view is to find trends and correlate values. By adding subsets of object counters, it is easier to find trends in the data. Once the object counters are added to the graph, highlight all of the counters on the bottom and scale the lines. This increases the readability of the graph.

3. For each counter on the bottom, review the line and values over time.

---

▨ **Note**   CTRL+H highlights the line so that it is easier to see, and multiple lines can be selected and viewed at the same time.

---

      a.   Review the line over time, and identify when the counter is under pressure and for what duration.

      b.   Review the average value. Is the counter within an acceptable range?

      c.   How frequently is the maximum or minimum value hit and is the peak value sustained?

      d.   Review related counters during this time to see if their values can be correlated to the event. If the value average is as expected or the counter is immaterial, delete the object counter from the line view.

      e.   Again, remove the normal values so that the more important counters are the ones that remain.

6.   Once you are done reviewing a group of related object counters, you can save the image or add additional ones. Remember, the line view only has the object counters of interest. Reviewing the counters with issues along with the new counters provides you more opportunity to discover different trends in the data.

After reviewing all of the object counters, you should have a clear understanding of the peak usage times when SQL Server is under the most pressure and know what areas of SQL Server are potential bottlenecks. The other important data to incorporate into this review is the number of business transactions that were completed during the corresponding time window. With that data, you can fill in the information for statements such as the following: "My system is only 30 percent utilized when processing X number of payments."

## Analyzing Configuration Data

Typically, when a new server configuration that will run SQL Server is built, it is often done with a standard build approved by the IT organization and it's not necessarily optimized for SQL Server. Most companies like to maintain as few server configurations as possible and make them work everywhere if possible. The build process most likely will be automated to a certain extent, with some items manually configured. The result is expected to be a server that looks, acts, and feels like all other servers within the company for a specific platform and version. Based on my experience, the standard build will usually be 98 percent correct with a 2 percent variation from the norm. The deviations are what cause problems, some of which will not be evident immediately.

Incorrect infrastructure and server configurations often contribute to performance issues. If they are caught in time, such as right after the server is handed off to the DBAs, they are easy to fix. If they are not caught in time, but are caught at some point after a server is in production, this can lead to the need to schedule downtime for the fix—even if it is easy. Some common examples of poor configurations include misconfigured memory settings, local policies, and page-file settings.

A perfect example that seemingly has nothing to do with SQL Server but, in fact, has everything to do with it are the power-management settings in Windows. A base configuration of Windows Server 2008 (or later) has a default power management plan of Balanced. The Balanced power profile turns off cores and reduces the clock speed of cores to conserve power. This throttling can impact the server's performance. If SQL Server is installed on that server, performance could go from blazingly fast to extremely slow because of that one setting. Changing the setting is easy and might improve performance immensely. Similarly, the EFI or BIOS settings related to power might override the Windows settings, so they also need to be checked. This is another case where you need to draw all of the logical dots to come up with a single, correct conclusion.

A large part of the assessment is to collect configuration data from application servers, servers hosting instances of SQL Server, and the infrastructure. While the goal is to review the configuration of the servers and determine if they are configured correctly, what exactly *is* correct? Before you review the configuration data, work with the appropriate team members and get a copy of the standard build documents. The standard build should be the baseline because most companies spend a large amount of time engineering and testing the base builds. Because the standard builds might not be optimized for SQL Server, you might identify places for improvement for future builds in this process.

When you are reviewing the configurations for the various servers, keep in mind the findings from the review of the performance data. Using the example from earlier, if you see a large amount of paging in the OS and review the Max Server Memory in SQL Server, is the memory dynamic or static? Is the memory configured too high or too low? How will it need to be readjusted, or do you need more physical memory in the server? Reviewing the performance data before looking at, and possibly changing, the configuration settings provides you with valuable information you can use when you are analyzing the server's configuration. Now you have some context for determining what the potential bottlenecks are and what areas of the system are healthy.

Because we are focusing on SQL Server, I'll review some of the recommended configuration settings to capture, as shown in Table 18-10.

*Table 18-10. A sample list of SQL Server configurations to validate.*

| SQL Server Configuration | Analysis Required |
|---|---|
| SQL Server version, SP level, and edition | Is SQL Server up to date? What is supported by the application? |
| SQL Service accounts | Are the SQL Server service accounts using dedicated security credentials? Are the security credentials a member of the local Administrator group? |
| sp_configure | What configuration options are enabled? Here are the key ones to review:<br>Backup compression default (TRUE)<br>Cost threshold for parallelism<br>Fill factor (%). Is the default setting being used?<br>Max degree of parallelism. If the system is NUMA enabled, set this to the Number of cores within the NUMA node<br>Max server memory (MB). This setting depends on several factors, but you can find a good reference at the following site: http://sqlskills.com/blogs/jonathan/post/How-much-memory-does-my-SQL-Server-actually-need.aspx.<br>Min server memory (MB). What is the value set to? If there are multiple instances, set this value to a minimum amount of memory that a particular instance requires.<br>Optimize for ad hoc workloads |
| Authentication | Is SQL Server setup to use mixed or Windows Authentication |
| Features installed | Database Engine, Analysis Services, Reporting Services, Integration Services, Filestream |

| | |
|---|---|
| Cluster or standalone | Review the cluster configuration, and ensure the failover process has been tested. |
| Port number | Is the default value being used? |
| Database properties | Here are the key properties to review:<br>Auto Close and Auto Shrink (FALSE)<br>Auto Create and Auto Update Statistics (TRUE)<br>Compatibility Level. Validate that this property is set to the highest level.<br>Page Verify. Set this property to CHECKSUM.<br>Parameterization (FALSE)<br>Transparent Data Encryption (TDE). Is this property enabled?<br>Recovery model. Ensure this property is set to allow the recovery point objective (RPO) to be met. |
| Database file properties | Here are the key properties to review:<br>File location. For the highly transactional databases, do the files reside on the fastest disk?<br>File size. How large is the file, and how much free space exists?<br>Number of files per database. How many files exist? How much free space is there in each?<br>Are there multiple transaction log files? You need only one. What is the growth method and size for each file? Set these properties to a specific size, such as 512 MB. If the transaction log had an autogrow event, the average time on a typical disk subsystem would take about two to five seconds to grow the file. |
| Number of virtual log files (VLF) per database | How many VLFs exist for each database? Are there more than 100? If so, you will want reduce the number of VLFs and better manage the transaction-log growth events. |
| Nontrusted constraints per database | Foreign keys in a nontrusted state can trigger extra scans. Switch the constraints to a trusted state. |
| Job List – Inventory and Schedule | What is scheduled on the server? When do the processes run and for how long? Most people, including me, schedule processes to occur on the hour, half hour, or quarter hour, such as at:15 and :30 after the hour. Stagger the jobs, and minimize the overlapping schedules. |
| Database maintenance processes | What maintenance is being performed on the server? Is it being done the most efficient way? Are only the fragmented indexes being rebuilt? When was the last CHECKDB run? |
| Most recent error logs | What errors are occurring in SQL Server? Are there deadlocks or severe errors? |

Depending on the SQL Server configuration and when the last time an assessment was performed on the server, there might be a lot of changes and tasks that result as part of the configuration assessment. For all changes, always test in a similar environment to ensure the application does not have an unexpected behavior. Production should never be the first place changes are applied. If you do not test in a similar environment first and problems are encountered, you might make things worse rather than better. Some configurations might appear to be only cosmetic, but the majority of the changes you make will change either the behavior of SQL Server or how the application will perform.

The initial Perfmon data is your performance baseline, or what the system performance was before any changes were made to the system. After changes are implemented, a new baseline will need to be created so that you can measure the percent change in the system. You can use the existing data collector to create the new baseline—just change the destination to a new file. Over time, you can start to see the impact of all the changes in the application and the system—good or bad—and adjust the configuration accordingly.

# Analyzing SQL Performance Data

Tuning indexes or queries is what most people probably think about when you mention tuning a SQL Server instance for peak load. However, as you have seen in this chapter, there is a lot more to tuning for that time frame than just adding some indexes and rewriting statements. If the disk subsystem is misconfigured and you are able to perform only 10 I/O per second, all statements will suffer—even with optimized code. You might think, "How could this happen? My SAN guys told me that you had the optimal configuration."

Here is an example from one of my past customers. This particular client was able to achieve only 10 I/Ops on its disk subsystem with reasonable performance. The server with SQL Server was configured using iSCSI to connect to the SAN. Because the disk I/O was slow, this was showing up as a performance issue to end users. It took some time, but we were able to track down the issue by working with the SAN as well as the network teams. As it turns out, the network switch that the iSCSI interfaces were plugged into was misconfigured. Because iSCSI is based on TCP/IP, the lack of performance makes sense if a key component is not configured properly. That is why it is so important to validate the underlying configuration before reviewing any part of the application. Tuning is much like peeling back the layers of an onion—you find one thing, and another gets uncovered.

So where do you start when looking at all of the SQL Server performance data if you have captured a lot of it? It can be daunting. You have data from the Dynamic Memory Views (DMV) that shows the most frequently running code, which will correlate to the largest I/O consumers. You have different data sets from Profiler or Extended Events for long-running statements or all traffic over a specific time. And what about the data set with all of the transactions that are involved in the core business transactions? As you can see, there is a lot of data—and this does not even include any of the metadata from SQL Server about object use or execution plans.

Prior to reviewing the configuration data, you reviewed the Perfmon data to provide more information about what the performance on the SQL Server instance is like. Before you review any of the information from the traces or DMVs, you need to review the current activity. The current activity of the instance that was captured earlier provides you with insight into what type of statements are executed, the common wait stats, the resource usage, and many other factors. After you do this on several of your systems, you will start to recognize patterns in the data and see when the system has an issue. Figure 18-15 is an example of the output from a script that shows details for all active process on a SQL Server instance.

| Session ID | Run Time | Status | Host Name | Login Name | Wait Type | Wait Resource | Wait Time | Start Time | Logical Reads | Writes | CPU | Write in TempDB | Parallel | Blocking SPID |
|---|---|---|---|---|---|---|---|---|---|---|---|---|---|---|
| 2311 | 0:running | SERVER02 | sa | NULL | | · | 11/1/11 2:41 PM | 21 | · | · | · | 1 | · |
| 167 | 4:runnable | SERVER02 | User1 | NULL | | · | 11/1/11 2:37 PM | 59,799,249 | · | 173,594 | · | 1 | · |
| 1887 | 0:runnable | SERVER02 | sa | NULL | | · | 11/1/11 2:41 PM | · | · | · | · | 1 | · |
| 176 | 2541:running | SERVER01 | sa | NULL | | · | 10/30/11 8:20 PM | 4,834,878,236 | 3,407,166 | 149,204,109 | 401,049 | 1 | · |
| 1079 | 2:suspended | SERVER03 | sa | LCK_M_S | KEY: 20:335107163815936 (c500f32fa1a2) | 132,649 | 11/1/11 2:39 PM | 5 | · | · | · | 1 | 2,308 |
| 1807 | 4:suspended | SERVER06 | sa | LCK_M_S | KEY: 20:335107163815936 (300052eae90e) | 220,949 | 11/1/11 2:37 PM | 5 | · | · | · | 1 | 2,618 |
| 2173 | 1:suspended | SERVER06 | sa | LCK_M_S | KEY: 20:335107163815936 (b200d0708da6) | 58,607 | 11/1/11 2:40 PM | 5 | · | · | · | 1 | 1,786 |
| 2508 | 3:suspended | SERVER01 | sa | LCK_M_S | KEY: 20:335107163815936 (c500f32fa1a2) | 162,080 | 11/1/11 2:38 PM | 5 | · | · | · | 1 | 1,286 |
| 1811 | 1:suspended | SERVER03 | sa | LCK_M_S | KEY: 20:287328103563264 (28015355ac5d) | 44,933 | 11/1/11 2:40 PM | 6 | · | · | · | 1 | 1,786 |
| 1170 | 9504:suspended | SERVER03 | User1 | TRACEWRITE | | 1,951 | 10/26/11 12:17 AM | 3 | · | 125 | · | 1 | · |
| 910 | 3:suspended | | User1 | LCK_M_S | KEY: 5:282661119655936 (0c008d258d60) | 160,975 | 11/1/11 2:38 PM | 6 | · | · | · | 1 | 1,557 |
| 943 | 0:suspended | | User1 | LCK_M_S | KEY: 5:72057594039107584 (780043887a7d) | 9,625 | 11/1/11 2:38 PM | 6 | · | · | · | 1 | 1,539 |
| 414 | 3:suspended | SERVER03 | User1 | LCK_M_S | PAGE: 20:1:10855835 | 206,005 | 11/1/11 2:38 PM | 2,399 | · | 15 | · | 1 | 2,618 |
| 1684 | 0:running | SERVER03 | User1 | NULL | | · | 11/1/11 2:41 PM | · | · | · | · | 1 | · |
| 2618 | 4:suspended | SERVER04 | sa | LCK_M_IX | PAGE: 20:1:15950346 | 227,145 | 11/1/11 2:37 PM | 41 | 6 | · | · | 1 | 167 |
| 1786 | 2:suspended | SERVER04 | sa | LCK_M_IX | PAGE: 20:4:15770464 | 105,403 | 11/1/11 2:39 PM | 34 | 3 | · | · | 1 | 414 |
| 1286 | 3:suspended | SERVER04 | sa | LCK_M_IX | PAGE: 20:4:16969876 | 166,816 | 11/1/11 2:38 PM | 34 | 4 | · | · | 1 | 414 |
| 436 | 561:suspended | SERVER03 | User1 | WAITFOR | | 14,180 | 11/1/11 5:20 AM | 129,144,533 | 1,169,270 | 2,210,640 | 1,445,386 | 1 | · |
| 1110 | 0:running | SERVER02 | sa | NULL | | · | 11/1/11 2:41 PM | 1,202,164 | 1 | 12,719 | 489 | 1 | · |
| 2421 | 0:runnable | SERVER02 | sa | NULL | | · | 11/1/11 2:41 PM | 1,447,813 | 2 | 16,468 | 649 | 1 | · |
| 2545 | 0:running | SERVER03 | sa | NULL | | · | 11/1/11 2:41 PM | 1,377,891 | 2 | 15,219 | 617 | 1 | · |
| 1929 | 0:running | SERVER02 | sa | NULL | | · | 11/1/11 2:41 PM | 1,275,396 | 1 | 15,188 | 553 | 1 | · |
| 1986 | 0:running | SERVER02 | sa | NULL | | · | 11/1/11 2:41 PM | 532,736 | 1 | 6,969 | 253 | 1 | · |
| 2053 | 0:running | SERVER02 | sa | NULL | | · | 11/1/11 2:41 PM | 322,920 | 2 | 3,578 | 138 | 1 | · |
| 1864 | 1:suspended | SERVER04 | sa | LCK_M_X | APPLICATION: 20:0:[Sync_SEF_DPcECiBuiBEQFgg2kf~]:(409 196e9) | 45,461 | 11/1/11 2:40 PM | 2 | · | · | · | 1 | 524 |

*Figure 18-15. Current activity of a SQL Server instance gathered from a SQL script.*

If you ran a script that generated this data several times over the course of the day, you could see patterns in the data. Following are observations from analyzing the data shown in Figure 18-15:

- There are several blocked processes, with the longest process being blocked for almost four minutes.

- Session ID is a long-running process that has consumed over 4 billion logical reads and a large number of other resources.

- Session ID 1864 is trying to acquire an application lock.

- Even though the code is not in the view shown in Figure 18-5, the sessions on the bottom of Figure 18-15 are all running the same code with a nonoptimal execution plan.

- A client-side trace is running a deadlock capture.

- There is a WAITFOR process that captures performance metrics for the custom application.

As you can see, from this one execution of the current activity data, you can identify several behaviors about this SQL Server instance. These behaviors will help you start to build the mental image in your mind about what you can expect to see as you monitor the system over time. Some of the behaviors you can expect to see are the following:

- There are large blocking chains.

- There are queries that consume a number of large resources.

- The application is using application locks in the database (sp_getapplock).

- There are nonoptimal plans for some frequently executed procedures.

There are several critical items in the preceding list that need to be addressed before the peak season. For example, at the beginning of the chapter we talked about large blocking chains that are impacting the application. The blocking chain in Figure 18-15 was impacting users for a minimum of 4 minutes, and this potentially could cost the business thousands of dollars in potential orders.

Additional information needs to be captured for all of these items. You need to identify the unique blocking chains, when they occur, and what objects and processes are involved. Another source of blocking information is the `sys.dm_db_index_operational_stats` DMV, which you can use to see which objects are frequently waiting on locks or have lock contention. Frequently executed statements need to be tuned and potentially rewritten to minimize the chance of receiving a nonoptimal execution plan. The goal for the core business transactions is for them to be predictable so that they can meet the performance requirements in the SLAs. If several stored procedures involved in a core business transactions have a large runtime variance, the risk of not meeting the requirements of the SLAs increases. The next step addresses the large resource consumers because we'll review the runtime data that we captured from SQL Server and the application.

Begin by reviewing the index utilization statistics that were captured during the data-collecting stage. Index changes are usually low-risk and high-reward changes to make. If you adjust the indexing strategy on the core tables, you can have a positive effect on a large number of SQL statements. If you start by tuning SQL statements, the risk is higher. Tuning SQL statements requires more effort and a significant amount of testing. After you adjust the indexing strategy and affect many of the execution plans, you will be in a better position to review the runtime performance for the SQL statements.

Figure 18-16 represents a sample data set you will review. It is a subset of the result set for index usage data. Additional columns included in the view are server name, database name, source, object name, object_id, index name, last user scan, last user seek, and run time.

| indexname | index_id | rowcnt | total_pages | is_unique | count | user_seeks | user_scans | user_lookups | user_updates | total_usage |
|---|---|---|---|---|---|---|---|---|---|---|
| idx_p_sites_features_siteid_feature_active_enabled | 3 | 218,061 | 1,218 | - | 7 | 5,874,890,219 | 3,405,830 | - | 1,727,922 | 5,880,023,971 |
| idx_p_features_feature_active_name_enabled | 12 | 454 | 5 | - | 3 | 3,401,268,598 | 917,332 | | 14 | 3,402,185,944 |
| PK_p_sites | 1 | 14,373 | 683 | 1 | 12 | 2,204,524,800 | 4,983,575 | 177,629,212 | 10,298 | 2,387,147,885 |
| PK_p_sites_features | 1 | 218,061 | 2,335 | 1 | 7 | 3,282,688 | 10,772 | 2,074,061,947 | 1,878,521 | 2,079,233,928 |
| idx_jobid_item_siteid_active_val_link | 13 | 32,304,943 | 127,084 | - | 4 | 1,796,453,469 | 5,794 | - | 191,606,634 | 1,988,065,897 |

**Figure 18-16.** *Usage statistics for all indexes.*

Figure 18-16 shows index usage statistics and some other metadata about the indexes on particular objects. This data includes many attributes that are essential for the analysis, such as is_unique, rowcnt, total pages, and the total number of indexes on a table. From this data, you can determine the following scenarios:

- **Unused indexes**  Indexes that have not been used.

- **Costly indexes**  Indexes that require more resources to maintain than is warranted by how much the index is used.

- **High number of indexes**  Review all tables with a large number of indexes. What is considered to be a large number of indexes? The answer to this depends on which of the following types of applications SQL Server is supporting:

  - **Transactional Database**  For this type of database a large number would be about three to five indexes per table, but what qualifies as "a large number" really depends on the amount of system activity.

  - **Reporting Database**  For this type of database , a higher number is acceptable, but a large number might affect the extraction, transformation, and load (ETL) performance.

- **Mix – Transactional and Reporting Database**  If both of the preceding types of databases are used, about five to seven indexes per table is considered to be a large number. However, it really depends on the amount of system activity.

- **Missing indexes**  Larger objects with high scan counts are candidates for additional indexes.

- **High number of lookups**  Review the most frequent statements against the object to see if adding a couple of columns might help offset the need for a lookup. Remember, leverage INCLUDE columns but consider the index width.

- **Non-Optimal Clustered Key**  Notice the nonclustered index in Figure 18-17 with a lower number of seeks and a high number of lookups on the clustered index. This indicates the common access path into this table is on PK_Table1 than on CDX_Table1. Consider changing the columns that are clustered in this example.

| objectname | indexname | index_id | rowcnt | is_unique | count | user_seeks | user_scans | user_lookups |
|---|---|---|---|---|---|---|---|---|
| Table 1 | PK_Table1 | 2 | 176,515 | 1 | 10 | 16,026,799 | 140 | - |
| Table 1 | CDX_Table1 | 1 | 176,515 | - | 10 | 1,048,243 | 4,063 | 11,299,957 |

*Figure 18-17. Usage statistics for a table that needs the clustered key switched to another column(s).*

---

■ **Note**  After the new index changes have been implemented, you need to collect updated DMV performance data as shown in Figure 18-16 and trace data, as shown in Table 18-5 because the index statistics and performance profiles will have changed.

---

After you have performance-tuned a system several times or even tuned the same system over time, you will start to notice that tuning indexes gets you most of the way to where you need to be. Adjusting configurations, the timing of events, and code will get you the rest of the way.

There are several approaches you can use when identifying which SQL statements to performance tune. Following are different sources, in order of preference:

- **Top 100 Query Stats by Execution Count**  These frequently called statements represent the majority of the total resource consumption. If 75 percent of these statements are tuned with indexes or code modifications, you will reduce total resource consumption by a large percentage. Remember, people and time are usually limited, so spend your time tuning processes that will have a large impact on the system. Do not tune the one query that uses 500 million I/O because this is not an effective use of time and the net savings you'll see in terms of system resources is not as great.

- **ALL statements from the core business transaction**  Evaluate these because they have a direct impact on the user experience. If you make these statements faster, the user experience will most likely be better.

- **SQL statements that frequently receive nonoptimal plans and are frequently called**  Based on my experiences, nonoptimal plans are usually magnitudes worse and could cause additional issues on the server.

By adjusting the indexing strategy and performance tuning of the most frequently called procedures, you can reduce the total resource consumption of the server. There is often a single large query that consumes a lot of resources, but tuning that should be secondary to one that is executed 1,000,000 times per day. Once the changes are implemented, measure the new resource levels as talked about earlier to see if things are better or worse. This is an iterative process, so make sure to collect updated metadata and runtime statistics.

At the end of this exercise, if you determine that the current environment will not be able to handle the peak load, start to think about other environmental or process-related changes. Not every change needs to be a code or configuration change. If reporting is going against the transactional environment and the total resource consumption is 25 percent, can you shift this to another server running SQL Server? If you only need 5 percent to 10 percent more resources, what can be delayed or turned off during the peak load? Can you run the maintenance processes two days before? What about disabling nonessential processes? When you are tuning for peak usage, every option should be on the table. Sometimes you need to think outside of the box because certain environments have some unique challenges.

# Devise a Plan

So how do you translate all the analysis and findings into an actionable plan? As you have done up until now, you need to take your time and review all of the findings to come up with the right solutions. The challenge now is determining what change you implement first, and what the expected impact and potential risks are of applying that change. Are there any system limitations that you identified earlier that might impact the potential changes—including figuring out whether the change can even be implemented? These questions are complex and the potential impact of your decision is often not fully understood until the change is fully deployed into a test or production environment.

The same way that you started to analyze the data, you will implement the proposed changes. Always start with the configuration changes. These will correct misconfigurations in the environment or change the behavior of the respective technology. For example, if you choose Optimize For Ad-Hoc Workloads option in SQL Server, this will change the behavior of SQL Server and reduce the amount of memory consumed by the procedure cache at the instance level. After you make a change, make sure you document the actual result of the change if possible. This way, you can have a record of the action and result just in case there is an issue later on and the change needs to be rolled back.

Table 18-11 is the sample order of proposed changes for the tax application. In addition to the server-specific changes shown in Table 18-11, there can also be application, infrastructure, and process-related changes.

*Table 18-11. A sample plan for tuning the tax application.*

| Technology | Proposed changes for tax application |
| --- | --- |
| Firmware and drivers | Update the HBA and NIC drivers. |
| Network changes | Move the application servers to the same switch as the database server. Switch the NICs to an Active\Active configuration. |
| SAN changes | Change the HBA queue depth to 64. Perform a LUN migration for the critical LUN to a faster tier of storage. |
| OS configurations | Change the location and size of the pagefile. Change the power profile to High Performance. Add the SQL Server service accounts to the following local policies: Lock Page in Memory Perform Volume Maintenance Tasks Add file exclusions for SQL Server and Cluster resources. |
| SQL Server – Server properties | Choose the Optimize For Ad-Hoc Workloads option Enable trace flags 1118 and 834. Reduce the Max Server Memory setting from 120,000 to 108,000. |

| SQL Server database configurations | Change the growth method and size for all databases to 512 MB. Pre-grow several database files, and synchronize the file size. Add files to TempDB, from 1 to 8. Reduce VLFs for three databases. Move the primary database data files to the new LUN. |
|---|---|
| Index changes | DROP, ADD, and ALTER indexes. Change the FILLFACTOR from 50 (*existing setting*) to 100. Reduce the FILLFACTOR for several highly transactional objects from 100 to –80. Implement ROW-level compression for all objects. |
| SQL statement changes | Change the nontrusted constraints to trusted. Implement the updated version of the SQL statements. |
| Maintenance changes | Change the index rebuild to rebuild only objects with fragmentation greater than 20 percent, and set this to be done nightly. Cycle the error log nightly at 12 AM. |
| Job timing changes | Disable old jobs. Change the maintenance jobs to start at :12 and :18 past the hour rather than at :00 and :15. Change the schedules for several of the jobs to minimize the number of jobs running concurrently. |
| Monitoring | Add additional alerts in the Enterprise Monitoring tool. Add data-collection processes for capacity planning. Ensure alerts are responded to within five minutes. |

Something that cannot be overemphasized is ensuring there is sufficient support from the developers and all levels of operations during the peak load. If issues occur during this time, people need to be able to respond in a timely manner. Depending on the SLAs, the response time might be minutes rather than an hour. Processes and procedures need to be defined and clearly communicated to the staff.

# Conclusion

Every DBA has servers running SQL Server that must perform and scale day after day, year after year. Over time, things change. The data grows, the load and usage patterns might increase, and the functionality often evolves. So what will you do this peak season to ensure your organization is able to process this year's peak load? What lessons did you learn from last year's peak load so that you don't have the same problems?

By creating an ongoing team that is capable of analyzing the environment and implementing necessary changes, you will have a head start toward making sure the environment can scale to meet increased demands, whether it is the Black Friday sales day or just a busy Wednesday. Things will change in the environment and with the application, but these changes might bring more opportunity, such as long-term recommendations being folded into the application design or the architecture of the entire solution being changed. The key to being successful is to be curious and look under all of the rocks and behind all of the doors for opportunities for improvement.

# Index

## ▓ E

CPSIA information can be obtained at www.ICGtesting.com
Printed in the USA
LVOW111449011112

305452LV00004B/1/P